CUA
10453386
657.046071 ASS
D1343568

ACCA

ADVANCED PERFORMANCE MANAGEMENT (APM)

PRACTICE & REVISION KIT

BPP Learning Media is an **ACCA Approved Content Provider** for the ACCA qualification. This means we work closely with ACCA to ensure our products fully prepare you for your ACCA exams.

In this Practice & Revision Kit, which has been reviewed by the **ACCA examining team,** we:

- Discuss the **best strategies** for revising and taking your ACCA exams
- Ensure you are well **prepared** for your exam
- Provide you with **lots of great guidance** on tackling questions
- Provide you with **three** mock exams
- Provide **ACCA exam answers** as well as our own for selected questions

Our **Passcards** also support the Advanced Performance Management syllabus.

FOR EXAMS IN SEPTEMBER 2018, DECEMBER 2018, MARCH 2019 AND JUNE 2019

BPP
LEARNING MEDIA

First edition 2007
Twelth edition February 2018

ISBN 9781 5097 1672 2
(previous ISBN 9781 5097 0865 9)
e-ISBN 9781 5097 1702 6

Cataloguing-in-Publication Data
A catalogue record for this book
is available from the British Library

Published by

BPP Learning Media Ltd
BPP House, Aldine Place
London W12 8AA

www.bpp.com/learningmedia

Printed and bound by CPI Group (UK) Ltd
Croydon
CR0 4YY

Your learning materials, published by BPP Learning Media Ltd, are printed on paper obtained from traceable, sustainable sources.

All rights reserved. No part of this publication may be reproduced, stored in a retrieval system or transmitted, in any form or by any means, electronic, mechanical, photocopying, recording or otherwise, without the prior written permission of BPP Learning Media Ltd.

The contents of this book are intended as a guide and not professional advice. Although every effort has been made to ensure that the contents of this book are correct at the time of going to press, BPP Learning Media makes no warranty that the information in this book is accurate or complete and accept no liability for any loss or damage suffered by any person acting or refraining from acting as a result of the material in this book.

We are grateful to the Association of Chartered Certified Accountants for permission to reproduce past examination questions. The suggested solutions in the practice answer bank have been prepared by BPP Learning Media Ltd, unless otherwise stated.

©
BPP Learning Media Ltd
2018

A note about copyright

Dear Customer

What does the little © mean and why does it matter?

Your market-leading BPP books, course materials and e-learning materials do not write and update themselves. People write them on their own behalf or as employees of an organisation that invests in this activity. Copyright law protects their livelihoods. It does so by creating rights over the use of the content.

Breach of copyright is a form of theft – as well as being a criminal offence in some jurisdictions, it is potentially a serious breach of professional ethics.

With current technology, things might seem a bit hazy but, basically, without the express permission of BPP Learning Media:

- Photocopying our materials is a breach of copyright
- Scanning, ripcasting or conversion of our digital materials into different file formats, uploading them to facebook or e-mailing them to your friends is a breach of copyright

You can, of course, sell your books, in the form in which you have bought them – once you have finished with them. (Is this fair to your fellow students? We update for a reason.) Please note the e-products are sold on a single user licence basis: we do not supply 'unlock' codes to people who have bought them second-hand.

And what about outside the UK? BPP Learning Media strives to make our materials available at prices students can afford by local printing arrangements, pricing policies and partnerships which are clearly listed on our website. A tiny minority ignore this and indulge in criminal activity by illegally photocopying our material or supporting organisations that do. If they act illegally and unethically in one area, can you really trust them?

Contents

***Note:** Questions 1 and 3 in Mock Exam 3 are taken from the September/December 2017 Sample questions. The other sample questions that ACCA released from the September/December 2017 exams are included in the main body of the Kit.

Question index

The headings in this checklist/index indicate the main topics of questions, but questions often cover several different topics.

Past exam questions are designated with the date of the exam in which they featured, although some have been amended to reflect subsequent changes to the syllabus or in the format of the exam.

Since September 2015 there have been four exam sittings per year, but ACCA only publish two exams' worth of questions per year. These releases are compiled from questions selected from the preceding sessions. These compilation exams are denoted as 'Mar/Jun' and 'Sept/Dec' in the index below.

* **Note: Questions 1 and 3 in Mock Exam 3** are taken from the **September/December 2017 Sample questions**. The other sample questions that ACCA released from the September/December 2017 exams are included in the main body of the Kit.

Topic index

Listed below are the key APM syllabus topics and the numbers of the questions in this Kit covering those topics.

If you need to concentrate your practice and revision on certain topics or if you want to attempt all available questions that refer to a particular subject, you will find this index useful.

Syllabus topic	Question numbers
Accountability and responsibility accounting	19, 29(b)(ii), 32
Activity-based costing	25, 39, 42(a), Mock 1 Qn 3
Activity-based management	40, 41, 42
Appraisals and performance management	6(c)
Balanced scorecard	34, 35, 36, 53, 55(d), Mock 1 Qn 1(i)
Benchmarking	1, 16, 55(b)
BCG matrix	32
Big Data	15
Branding	24(c)
Budgeting and types of budget	3, 4, 5, Mock 1 Qn 2
Building Blocks model (Fitzgerald and Moon)	38, 53, 57(iv)
Business process re-engineering (BPR)	6, 31(a)
Business structure (and performance measurement)	45
Corporate failure	46, 47, 48, Mock 2 Qn 2
Costs of quality	25, 26, Mock 1 Qn 1, Mock 3 Qn 1
Critical success factors (CSFs)	2, 18(a), 39(b), 49, Mock 2 Qn 1
Divisional performance measures	19
Economic value added (EVA™)	19, 20, 33, 41, 54(iii), Mock 2 Qn 1
Environmental management accounting	7, Mock 1 Qn 3
Enterprise resource planning systems (ERPS)	11, Mock 2 Qn 1(iv)
External environment (and impact on organisations)	8, 9, 49
Financial performance	16, 51, Mock 1 Qn 1
Five forces (Porter)	47, Mock 2 Qn 3
Information systems and IT systems	50, 51(v), Mock 2 Qn 1
Integrated Reporting	14, Mock 3 Qn 1(ii)
JIT	26, 55(c), Mock 2 Qn 1(iii; iv)
Joint ventures	44
Kaizen costing	26, 27, 40(c), Mock 2 Qn 1(iii; iv)
Key performance indicators (KPIs)	2, 18(a), 39(b), 49, 57, Mock 2 Qn 1, Mock 3 Qn 2
League tables	1, 21, 23(b)
Lean information systems	10, 12, 13, Mock 1 Qn 1
Management accounting and information systems	50, 52(v), Mock 2 Qn 1
Management and control styles	30(b), 33(c), Mock 3 Qn 3(c)
Mission statements	2, 53(v), Mock 3 Qn 2(a)
Non-financial performance indicators	2, 22, 28(a), Mock 3 Qn 3(a)

Syllabus topic	Question numbers
Objectives	39(b)
Performance management in complex business structures	44, 45
Performance management information systems	10
Performance measures	16(a), 52(ii–iv)
Performance pyramid (Lynch & Cross)	37, 43, Mock 3 Qn 2
Performance reports	51, 52(i), 54(i), Mock 3 Qn 1(i)
Problems of performance measurement	37
Public sector organisations	14(a), 21, 22, 23
Quality	25(b), 28, 29
Responsibility and controllability	12(c), 19, 30
Reward and remuneration schemes	19, 30, 31(b), 32(c), 35(c), 53(v), 57(v)
RFID technology	12
Risk and uncertainty	9, 44, 50, 56(iii)
Role of management accountants	24
Service organisations	38, 53
Short vs long-term decision making	51(d)
Six Sigma	28, 29
Social obligations	8
Stakeholders	20, 34(b), 50, 55
SWOT analysis	56
Target costing	27, 40, Mock 3 Qn 1(iii)
Total quality management (TQM)	26(d), Mock 2 Qn 1(iii; iv), Mock 3 Qn 1(iii)
Transfer pricing	17, 18
Value-based management	41, 54(iv)
Value chain	56(v)
Value for money	22(b), 23, Mock 3 Qn 2
Virtual organisations	45

Helping you with your revision

BPP Learning Media – Approved Content Provider

As an ACCA **Approved Content Provider**, BPP Learning Media gives you the **opportunity** to use revision materials reviewed by the ACCA examining team. By incorporating the ACCA examining team's comments and suggestions regarding the depth and breadth of syllabus coverage, the BPP Learning Media Practice & Revision Kit provides excellent, **ACCA-approved** support for your revision.

Tackling revision and the exam

You can significantly improve your chances of passing by tackling revision and the exam in the right ways. Using feedback obtained from the ACCA examining team:

- We look at the dos and don'ts of revising for, and taking, ACCA exams
- We focus on APM; we discuss revising the syllabus, what to do (and what not to do) in the exam, how to approach different types of question and ways of obtaining easy marks

Selecting questions

We provide signposts to help you plan your revision.

- A full **question index**
- A **topic index** listing all the questions that cover key topics, so that you can locate the questions that provide practice on these topics, and see the different ways in which they might be examined

Making the most of question practice

At BPP Learning Media we realise that you need more than just questions and model answers to get the most from your question practice.

- Our **Top tips** included for certain questions provide essential advice on tackling questions, presenting answers and the key points that answers need to include
- We include **marking guides** to show you what the examining team rewards
- We include **comments from the examining team** to show you where students struggled or performed well in the actual exam
- We refer to the **BPP Study Text** for exams in September 2018, December 2018, March 2019 and June 2019 for detailed coverage of the topics covered in questions

Attempting mock exams

There are three mock exams that provide practice at coping with the pressures of the exam day. We strongly recommend that you attempt them under exam conditions.

Mock exam 2 is ACCA's Specimen exam paper for APM.

Mock exam 1 is compiled from questions selected by ACCA's examining team from the September 2016 and December 2016 exams. **Mock exam 3** contains questions selected from the September 2017 and December 2017 exams. The compilations are not the entire exams, but contain the questions that ACCA's examining team have selected as the most appropriate for students to practice.

Revising APM

Topics to revise

ACCA's Study Guide for APM highlights that 'candidates should expect to see Section A of the exam focus on a range of issues from across syllabus sections A, C and D'. The Study Guide also notes that 'one of the Section B questions will come mainly from syllabus section E' while 'the other Section B question can come from any other syllabus section'.

Taken together though, these points mean that the questions in your exam could cover any area of the syllabus. Moreover, because **all the questions in the APM exam are compulsory**, it is essential to learn the **entire syllabus** to maximise your chances of passing. There are no shortcuts – trying to spot topics to be examined is dangerous and will significantly reduce the likelihood of success. As this is an advanced ('Strategic Professional') level paper, it also assumes knowledge of topics covered in *Performance Management* at Applied Skills level.

That said, the **main capabilities** in the syllabus (which is shown on ACCA's website) take you through what the examination team expects you to be able to do when you have completed your studies:

- Use strategic planning and control models to plan and monitor organisational performance
- Assess the impact of risk and uncertainty on organisational performance
- Identify and evaluate the design features of effective performance management information and monitoring systems
- Apply appropriate strategic performance measurement techniques in evaluating and improving organisational performance
- Advise clients and senior management on strategic business performance evaluation and on recognising vulnerability to corporate failure

These five areas are the syllabus areas covered in the BPP Study Text for *Advanced Performance Management.*

However, whilst it is important that you work through your way through the Study Text and cover all the different syllabus areas, it is also important to try and think how the areas might relate to each other, and how they could be used to help managers in an organisation control and improve the performance of that organisation. Remember, this paper is about performance **management**, as well as performance **measurement**; and you should treat both of these aspects (measurement and management) with equal importance as you are studying for your APM exam.

Remember to come out of the detail once you have finished a chapter and practised some questions. Take some time to reflect on how the chapter has covered the syllabus and how it feeds back into the capabilities which you will need to display in order to pass this paper.

Question practice

You should use the Passcards and any brief notes you have to revise the syllabus, but you mustn't spend all your revision time simply reading or making notes. **Question practice is vital.** Doing as many questions as you can, in full, will help develop your ability to analyse scenarios and produce relevant discussion and recommendations.

Make sure you leave enough time in your revision schedule to practise 50-mark Section A questions. The scenarios and requirements of Section A questions are more extensive than Section B questions, and are likely to integrate several parts of the syllabus. Therefore, practice is essential, so that you become more comfortable with tackling these questions.

Also ensure that you attempt all three mock exams, under exam conditions.

Passing the APM exam

Displaying the right qualities

The technical articles section on ACCA's website include one called the 'Examiner's approach to Paper P5.' (P5 was the former name for APM, prior to September 2018.) This article outlines the way the syllabus will be tested, and the qualities candidates should demonstrate when answering APM questions. The article also addresses the five main syllabus areas for APM in turn, and identifies what qualities candidates should demonstrate under each. We reproduce the main points here.

(1) **The application of strategic planning and control models in performance management.** The models stress the need to take a holistic view of the factors that affect a business and to consider them when giving strategic advice on performance. Good candidates often distinguish themselves by being able to synthesise disparate detailed points into an overall, strategic approach for an organisation.

(2) **Factors external to the business, and the impact of risk and uncertainty on organisational performance.** Candidates need to move beyond the internal factors associated with traditional management accounting to consider the information needs of the strategic level of management as well as the operational and tactical levels.

(3) **The information that management require and the systems that are needed for its delivery.** Candidates are expected to be aware of the effect of information technologies on performance management decision making rather than the detail of these technologies. Candidates will not be required to have detailed technical knowledge of hardware and software, but they should be conversant with the broad hardware and software trends and issues, and how these interact with the provision of performance information throughout the organisation. In particular, candidates need to recognise the impact that technology can have on performance management and decision-making in an organisation.

(4) and (5) **The fourth capability** is the **application** of the techniques and assumed knowledge to specific scenarios. You shouldn't simply discuss theories and models in general terms; you need to apply them specifically to the scenario identified in the question, in order to evaluate an organisation's performance and identify potential ways to improve organisational performance. **The fifth capability**, which builds directly on the fourth, is being able to take performance measurement information and turn it into **advice which is commercially valuable for strategic decision makers.** This capability also requires the candidate to be able to recognise and advise on situations where the organisation is in danger of failing.

Candidates also need to present their answers in a professional manner. There will be four **professional marks** available in the Section A question, and it should be possible for a well-prepared student to score most of these. For example, the effective use of appropriate introductions and conclusions, and helpfully breaking the document into properly headed sub-sections, will help to demonstrate a professional approach to writing a report. However, it should be stressed that the approach taken will vary from question to question and the exam tests the candidates' ability to apply their knowledge of professional presentation. In order to score full professional marks, the answer will have to be tailored to the specifics of the scenario in the question recognising the needs of the readers of the document.

Presentation points. First: on rounding. At this final level, candidates should use their own judgment about the level of detail to which they round figures – the basic rule is that there should be enough detail to make a useful conclusion without obscuring it with insignificant figures. However, it is also very important that you round correctly (ie up or down) according to the underlying figures.

Second, short paragraphs are usually clear but single sentence paragraphs are often insufficient and unable to get to the depth required at Strategic Professional level, where APM sits. Bullet points are useful for lists, but are not sufficient if an analysis or evaluation is required.

Finally, reading model solutions is not a substitute for actually writing out your own answers.

Summarising the advice ACCA's examining team gives for APM:

Candidates should do the following:

- Understand the objectives of the exam as explained in the syllabus and prepare the detailed topics in the Study Guide.
- Be very comfortable with the areas tested in *Performance Management* (at Applied Skills level) which constitute brought forward knowledge for APM.
- Ensure that their preparation for the exam has been based on a programme of study set for the required syllabus and exam structure.
- Use an ACCA-approved textbook for APM. They are structured around the syllabus and ACCA's examining team reviews them so that they give an effective coverage of what is examinable.
- Practise questions under exam conditions in order to improve speed and presentation skills, ensuring these test discursive, computational and analytic abilities.
- Study all the technical articles relevant to APM that are published on ACCA's website.
- Be able to clearly communicate understanding and application of knowledge in the context of a business scenario.

The questions tend to be wide-ranging, as the examining team wants to link topics and mix ideas up. So you are better knowing something about every part of the syllabus than a lot of detail about a few areas only.

Avoiding weaknesses

Our experience of other higher level exams, along with feedback from the examining teams, enables us to predict a number of weaknesses that are likely to occur in many candidates' answers. You will enhance your chances significantly if you ensure you avoid these mistakes:

- **Failing to provide what the question verbs require** (discussion, evaluation, recommendation) or to write about the topics specified in the question requirements
- **Repeating the same material** in different parts of answers
- **Stating theories and concepts** rather than applying them
- **Quoting chunks of detail** from the question that don't add any value. Whilst it is important that you relate your answer to this scenario, this means using issues highlighted in the scenario to help answer the question – not simply re-writing the question.
- **Forcing irrelevancies into answers**, for example irrelevant definitions or theories, or examples that don't relate to the scenario
- **Failing to make the most of the information** given in the question. Remember, you need to apply your knowledge specifically to the scenario given in the question.
- **Giving long lists or writing down all that you know about a subject area**, without considering whether it is relevant to the question or not
- **Failing to set out workings clearly and separately**
- **Not planning and preparing the answer properly,** taking into account mark allocation. Candidates often leave part-questions out – either because of poor time management, or because they have failed to read the requirement properly.
- **Unrealistic, vague or impractical recommendations**
- **Not refreshing brought-forward knowledge** (for example, from *Performance Management*)
- **Failing to answer sufficient questions**, or all parts of a question, because of poor time management.

Choosing which question to answer first

The questions in the APM exam are all compulsory.

We recommend that you spend time at the beginning of your exam carefully reading through all of the questions in the paper, and each of their requirements. Once you feel familiar with your exam paper, we then recommend that you attempt the Section A question first, ensuring that you spend adequate time reading and planning before you begin to write up your answer. As the Section A question accounts for 50% of the total marks, it is very unlikely that you will pass the exam without scoring reasonably well on it. Comments from examining teams across syllabuses that have similar exam formats suggest that candidates appear less time-pressured if they do the big case study question first.

During the second half of the exam, you can put Section A aside and concentrate on the two smaller Section B questions.

However, our recommendations are not inflexible. If you really think the Section A question looks a lot harder than the Section B questions, then do one of those first, but **DON'T run over time on it.** You must leave half of the exam time (one hour and 38 minutes) to tackle the Section A question. If you do one of the Section B questions first, and then come back to the Section A question, you may be able to generate more ideas and find the question is not as bad as it looks.

However, please remember that small overruns of time during the first half of the exam can add up to you being very short of time towards the end.

Tackling questions

You'll improve your chances by following a step-by-step approach along the following lines.

Step 1 **Read the background**

Usually the first couple of paragraphs will give some background on the organisation and what it is aiming to achieve (its mission and objectives). By reading this carefully you will be better equipped to relate your answers to the organisation as much as possible – for example, how effective are the methods which the organisation uses to control, manage and measure performance in helping it to achieve its objectives?

Step 2 **Read the requirements**

There is no point reading the detailed information in the question until you know what it is going to be used for. Don't panic if some of the requirements look challenging – identify the elements you are able to do and look for links between requirements, as well as possible indications of the syllabus areas the question is covering.

Step 3 **Identify the action verbs that are used in each requirement**

These convey the level of skill you need to exhibit and also the structure your answer should have. A lower level verb such as define will require a more descriptive answer; a higher level verb such as evaluate will require a more applied, critical answer.

ACCA's examining team has indicated that **higher level requirements and verbs** will be most significant in this paper, for example critically evaluating a statement and arguing for or against a given idea or position.

Action verbs that are likely to be frequently used in this exam are listed below, together with their intellectual levels and guidance on their meaning.

Level		
1	**Define**	Give the meaning of
1	**Explain**	Make clear
1	**Identify**	Recognise or select
1	**Describe**	Give the key features
2	**Analyse**	Give reasons for the current situation or what has happened
2	**Compare and contrast**	Explain the similarities and differences between two terms, viewpoints or concepts
3	**Assess**	Determine the strengths/weaknesses/importance/ significance/ability to contribute
3	**Discuss**	Examine in detail by using arguments for and against
3	**Advise**	Inform the recipient of an appropriate course of action; or inform the recipient about a fact or situation
3	**Recommend**	Advise the appropriate actions to pursue in terms the recipient will understand
3	**Evaluate**	Determine the value of, in the light of the arguments for and against
3	**Examine**	Critically review in detail

Step 4 **Identify what each part of the question requires**

Think about what frameworks of theories you could choose to support your answer (if the question doesn't indicate a specific one you need to use).

When planning, look at how the different parts of a question fit together, and make sure you don't end up repeating the same points in more than one part of the question.

Also, you're likely to come across part questions with two requirements; for example a requirement may ask you to evaluate some different approaches to budgeting and then recommend one which is appropriate for an organisation. You must ensure that you **fulfil both requirements**, and at the appropriate level indicated by the question verbs.

Step 5 **Check the mark allocation to each part**

This shows you the depth anticipated and helps allocate time. The APM exam is 3 hours 15 minutes (195 minutes), which means you should allocate time on the basis of 1.95 minutes per mark.

Step 6 **Read the whole scenario carefully, highlighting key data**

Put points under headings related to requirements (eg by noting in the margin to what part of the question the scenario detail relates).

It is also important to identify any instructions in the scenario which reinforce the question requirements. For example, a scenario could identify that you (as a management accountant) have been asked for information by the CEO. The requirement could then instruct you to act '... as requested by the CEO.' In this context, it is very important that you pay attention to the original request when preparing your answer, and make sure that your answer addresses any issues which had been highlighted in that original request.

Step 7 **Consider the consequences of the points you've identified**

You will often have to provide recommendations based on the information you've been given. Be prepared to criticise the framework or model that you've been told to use, if required. You may have also to bring in wider issues or viewpoints, for example the views of different stakeholders.

Step 8 **Write a brief plan**

Your plans should be produced within your answer book.

Make sure you identify all the requirements of the question in your plan – each requirement may have sub-requirements that must also be addressed. If there are professional marks available, highlight in your plan where these may be gained; for example, preparing a report.

Step 9 **Write your answer**

Make every effort to present your answer clearly. Feedback from past exams indicates that the examining team will be looking for you to make a number of clear points. The best way to demonstrate what you're doing is to put points into separate paragraphs with clear headers.

Discussion questions

Remember that **depth of discussion** will be important. Always bear in mind how many marks are available for the discussion as this will give you an indication of the depth that is required. Ask yourself the following questions as you are tackling a discussion question:

- **Have I made a point in a coherent sentence?**
- **Have I explained the point?** (to answer the 'so what' or 'why' queries; and to demonstrate which the point is important)
- **Have I related the point to the company in the scenario?** (with material or analysis from the scenario, or perhaps even an example from real life)

In the APM exam a number of requirement verbs will expect you to express a viewpoint or opinion, for example construct an argument, criticise, evaluate. When expressing an opinion, you need to provide:

- **What the question wants**. For instance, if you are asked to criticise something, don't spend time discussing its advantages. In addition if a scenario provides a lot of information about a situation, and you are (say) asked to assess that situation in the light of good practice, your assessment is unlikely to be favourable.
- **Evidence** from theory or the scenario – again we stress that the majority of marks in most questions will be given for applying your knowledge to the scenario.

Gaining the easy marks

Your technical knowledge (including knowledge brought forward from *Performance Management*) should enable you to score a small number of relatively easy marks. There are likely to be some marks available in certain requirements for **definitions** or **explanations** that don't have to be related to the scenario. However don't assume that you can ignore all the scenarios and still pass! The level of marks available in APM for knowledge alone (without application) is nowhere near enough to pass the exam.

There are **professional marks** available in the Section A question, and some of these should be easy to obtain. For example, there are likely to be marks available for presenting your answer in the format, style and tone, requested (eg a report).

Reports should always have an appropriate title. They should be **formally written**, with an **introductory paragraph** setting out the aims of the report. You should use **short paragraphs** and **appropriate headings**, with a brief summary of findings as a conclusion.

Exam formulae

Present Value Table

Present value of 1 i.e. $(1 + r)^{-n}$

Where r = discount rate
n = number of periods until payment

Discount rate (r)

Periods (n)	1%	2%	3%	4%	5%	6%	7%	8%	9%	10%	
1	0.990	0.980	0.971	0.962	0.952	0.943	0.935	0.926	0.917	0.909	1
2	0.980	0.961	0.943	0.925	0.907	0.890	0.873	0.857	0.842	0.826	2
3	0.971	0.942	0.915	0.889	0.864	0.840	0.816	0.794	0.772	0.751	3
4	0.961	0.924	0.888	0.855	0.823	0.792	0.763	0.735	0.708	0.683	4
5	0.951	0.906	0.863	0.822	0.784	0.747	0.713	0.681	0.650	0.621	5
6	0.942	0.888	0.837	0.790	0.746	0.705	0.666	0.630	0.596	0.564	6
7	0.933	0.871	0.813	0.760	0.711	0.665	0.623	0.583	0.547	0.513	7
8	0.923	0.853	0.789	0.731	0.677	0.627	0.582	0.540	0.502	0.467	8
9	0.914	0.837	0.766	0.703	0.645	0.592	0.544	0.500	0.460	0.424	9
10	0.905	0.820	0.744	0.676	0.614	0.558	0.508	0.463	0.422	0.386	10
11	0.896	0.804	0.722	0.650	0.585	0.527	0.475	0.429	0.388	0.350	11
12	0.887	0.788	0.701	0.625	0.557	0.497	0.444	0.397	0.356	0.319	12
13	0.879	0.773	0.681	0.601	0.530	0.469	0.415	0.368	0.326	0.290	13
14	0.870	0.758	0.661	0.577	0.505	0.442	0.388	0.340	0.299	0.263	14
15	0.861	0.743	0.642	0.555	0.481	0.417	0.362	0.315	0.275	0.239	15

(n)	11%	12%	13%	14%	15%	16%	17%	18%	19%	20%	
1	0.901	0.893	0.885	0.877	0.870	0.862	0.855	0.847	0.840	0.833	1
2	0.812	0.797	0.783	0.769	0.756	0.743	0.731	0.718	0.706	0.694	2
3	0.731	0.712	0.693	0.675	0.658	0.641	0.624	0.609	0.593	0.579	3
4	0.659	0.636	0.613	0.592	0.572	0.552	0.534	0.516	0.499	0.482	4
5	0.593	0.567	0.543	0.519	0.497	0.476	0.456	0.437	0.419	0.402	5
6	0.535	0.507	0.480	0.456	0.432	0.410	0.390	0.370	0.352	0.335	6
7	0.482	0.452	0.425	0.400	0.376	0.354	0.333	0.314	0.296	0.279	7
8	0.434	0.404	0.376	0.351	0.327	0.305	0.285	0.266	0.249	0.233	8
9	0.391	0.361	0.333	0.308	0.284	0.263	0.243	0.225	0.209	0.194	9
10	0.352	0.322	0.295	0.270	0.247	0.227	0.208	0.191	0.176	0.162	10
11	0.317	0.287	0.261	0.237	0.215	0.195	0.178	0.162	0.148	0.135	11
12	0.286	0.257	0.231	0.208	0.187	0.168	0.152	0.137	0.124	0.112	12
13	0.258	0.229	0.204	0.182	0.163	0.145	0.130	0.116	0.104	0.093	13
14	0.232	0.205	0.181	0.160	0.141	0.125	0.111	0.099	0.088	0.078	14
15	0.209	0.183	0.160	0.140	0.123	0.108	0.095	0.084	0.079	0.065	15

Annuity Table

Present value of an annuity of 1 i.e. $\frac{1-(1+r)^{-n}}{r}$

Where r = discount rate
n = number of periods

Discount rate (r)

Periods (n)	1%	2%	3%	4%	5%	6%	7%	8%	9%	10%	
1	0.990	0.980	0.971	0.962	0.952	0.943	0.935	0.926	0.917	0.909	1
2	1.970	1.942	1.913	1.886	1.859	1.833	1.808	1.783	1.759	1.736	2
3	2.941	2.884	2.829	2.775	2.723	2.673	2.624	2.577	2.531	2.487	3
4	3.902	3.808	3.717	3.630	3.546	3.465	3.387	3.312	3.240	3.170	4
5	4.853	4.713	4.580	4.452	4.329	4.212	4.100	3.993	3.890	3.791	5
6	5.795	5.601	5.417	5.242	5.076	4.917	4.767	4.623	4.486	4.355	6
7	6.728	6.472	6.230	6.002	5.786	5.582	5.389	5.206	5.033	4.868	7
8	7.652	7.325	7.020	6.733	6.463	6.210	5.971	5.747	5.535	5.335	8
9	8.566	8.162	7.786	7.435	7.108	6.802	6.515	6.247	5.995	5.759	9
10	9.471	8.983	8.530	8.111	7.722	7.360	7.024	6.710	6.418	6.145	10
11	10.368	9.787	9.253	8.760	8.306	7.887	7.499	7.139	6.805	6.495	11
12	11.255	10.575	9.954	9.385	8.863	8.384	7.943	7.536	7.161	6.814	12
13	12.134	11.348	10.635	9.986	9.394	8.853	8.358	7.904	7.487	7.103	13
14	13.004	12.106	11.296	10.563	9.899	9.295	8.745	8.244	7.786	7.367	14
15	13.865	12.849	11.938	11.118	10.380	9.712	9.108	8.559	8.061	7.606	15

(n)	11%	12%	13%	14%	15%	16%	17%	18%	19%	20%	
1	0.901	0.893	0.885	0.877	0.870	0.862	0.855	0.847	0.840	0.833	1
2	1.713	1.690	1.668	1.647	1.626	1.605	1.585	1.566	1.547	1.528	2
3	2.444	2.402	2.361	2.322	2.283	2.246	2.210	2.174	2.140	2.106	3
4	3.102	3.037	2.974	2.914	2.855	2.798	2.743	2.690	2.639	2.589	4
5	3.696	3.605	3.517	3.433	3.352	3.274	3.199	3.127	3.058	2.991	5
6	4.231	4.111	3.998	3.889	3.784	3.685	3.589	3.498	3.410	3.326	6
7	4.712	4.564	4.423	4.288	4.160	4.039	3.922	3.812	3.706	3.605	7
8	5.146	4.968	4.799	4.639	4.487	4.344	4.207	4.078	3.954	3.837	8
9	5.537	5.328	5.132	4.946	4.772	4.607	4.451	4.303	4.163	4.031	9
10	5.889	5.650	5.426	5.216	5.019	4.833	4.659	4.494	4.339	4.192	10
11	6.207	5.938	5.687	5.453	5.234	5.029	4.836	4.656	4.486	4.327	11
12	6.492	6.194	5.918	5.660	5.421	5.197	4.988	4.793	4.611	4.439	12
13	6.750	6.424	6.122	5.842	5.583	5.342	5.118	4.910	4.715	4.533	13
14	6.982	6.628	6.302	6.002	5.724	5.468	5.229	5.008	4.802	4.611	14
15	7.191	6.811	6.462	6.142	5.847	5.575	5.324	5.092	4.876	4.675	15

Exam information

Format of the exam

From September 2018, **all the questions** in the APM exam are **compulsory**.

The format of the exam is:

		Number of marks
Section A:	One 50 mark case study question	50
Section B:	Two questions worth 25 marks each	50
		100

Time: 3 hours and 15 minutes

Section A will contain **one case study question** worth **50 marks in total**, but comprising four or five requirements relating to the same scenario information.

The case study scenario will be based on an organisation in a particular business context, and will include the organisation's mission and strategic objectives. Candidates will be expected to assess the methods by which the organisation is controlling, managing and measuring performance in order to achieve its objectives. This assessment could include an evaluation of the organisation's performance report, its information systems, new strategies or projects, and its performance management and measurement systems. Candidates could be expected to undertake calculations, draw comparisons against relevant information where appropriate, and be prepared to offer recommendations as needed.

Candidates should expect to see Section A of the exam focus on a **range of issues from across syllabus sections A, C and D**, although the issues will vary depending on the business context of the organisation in the scenario.

Professional marks will be available in Section A for the candidate's approach to the format requested for the answer (eg a report to the Board of Directors).

Section B will comprise a further two 25-mark questions.

These questions are more likely to assess a range of discrete subject areas from the main syllabus section headings. However, they will still require evaluation and synthesis of information contained within a scenario, and the application of this information to the question requirements.

Although one subject area is likely to be emphasised in each Section B question, candidates should not assume that questions will be solely about content from that area.

One of the Section B questions will come mainly from **syllabus section E**. The other question can come from **any other syllabus section**.

The **pass mark** for the APM exam is 50%.

Exams prior to 2013

The current format of the questions changed in June 2013, at which point 50-mark Section A and 25-mark Section B questions were introduced. However, much of the underlying syllabus content and the way topics are examined has not changed, so earlier questions can provide useful practice – provided you remember the mark allocations (and therefore the time available for each question) may be different to that in your APM exam.

Questions and answers for past exams are available on ACCA's website:

www.accaglobal.com/gb/en/student/acca-qual-student-journey/qual-resource/acca-qualification/p5/past-exam-papers.html

Please note, these questions reflect of the format of the exam at the time it was sat. In the main body of this Kit, where we have used past exam questions, we have adapted them to fit the current format of the exam (ie with all questions being either 25- or 50-mark questions).

Analysis of past exams

The table below provides details of when each element of the syllabus has been examined and whether it was examined as part of a Section A or Section B question.

Since September 2015, ACCA have been issuing two sample exams each year, one after the December exam session, the other after the June sitting. These exams will be compiled from questions selected from the two preceding sessions, eg in December 2017 the sample questions were compiled from the September 2017 and December 2017 exams.

Covered in Text chapter		Sept/ Dec 2017	Mar/ June 2017	Sept/ Dec 2016	Mar/ June 2016	Sept/ Dec 2015	June 2015	Dec 2014	June 2014	Dec 2013	June 2013
	STRATEGIC PLANNING AND CONTROL										
1	Introduction to strategic management accounting	B					A	A			
2	Performance hierarchy		A	A, B		A	A			A	
3	Performance management and control of the organisation		B	B	B	B			B		B
4a	Business structure, IT developments and other environmental and ethical issues			B	B		A	A	B		A
4b	Environmental and ethical issues							B			
	IMPACT OF RISK AND UNCERTAINTY ON ORGANISATIONAL PERFORMANCE										
5	Changing business environment and external factors	B					A		B	A	B
	PERFORMANCE MEASUREMENT SYSTEMS AND DESIGN										
6a	Performance management information systems		B	A	A	A, B	B			B	
6b	Management information, recording and processing and management reports	A	A		A	B	A		A	B	
	STRATEGIC PERFORMANCE MEASUREMENT										
7	Scope of strategic performance measures in the private sector	B	A, B	A	A		B		A		
8	Divisional performance and transfer pricing issues			B			B				B
9a	Scope of strategic performance measures in not-for-profit organisations	B			B			B		B	
9b	Non-financial performance indicators							B			
10	The role of quality in management information and performance measurement systems	A	B	A		A, B		A			B
11	Performance measurement: strategy, reward and behaviour	B	A		B		B, B		B	B	
	PERFORMANCE EVALUATION AND CORPORATE FAILURE										
12	Alternative views of performance measurement and management		A	A, B	B	B	B	A	A	A	A, B
13	Strategic performance issues in complex business structures								B		B
14	Predicting and preventing corporate failure							B			

IMPORTANT!

The table on the previous page gives a broad idea of how frequently major topics in the syllabus are examined. It should **not be used to question spot** and predict for example that a certain topic will not be examined because it has been examined in the last two sittings. The examining team are well aware that some students try to question spot, and so they try to avoid predictable patterns. Consequently, a topic could well be examined in a number of consecutive sittings. Equally, just because a topic has not been examined for a long time, does not necessarily mean it will be examined in the next exam!

Additional information

The study guide provides more detailed guidance on the syllabus and can be found by visiting the exam resource finder on the ACCA website: www.accaglobal.com/uk/en/student/exam-support-resources.html

Useful websites

The websites below provide additional sources of information of relevance to your studies for *Advanced Performance Management.*

- www.accaglobal.com

  ACCA's website. The students' section of the website is invaluable for detailed information about the qualification, past exams, and technical articles. The website also includes a free downloadable Student Planner App.

- www.bpp.com

  Our website provides information about BPP products and services, with a link to the ACCA website.

- www.ft.com

  This website provides information about current international business. You can search for information and articles on specific industry groups as well as individual companies.

- www.economist.com

  Here you can search for business information on a week-by-week basis, search articles by business subject and use the resources of the Economist Intelligence Unit to research sectors, companies or countries.

- www.cfo.com

  This site provides useful news and insights for financial executives.

- www.investmentweek.co.uk

  This site carries business news and articles on markets from Investment Week and International Investment.

Questions

STRATEGIC PLANNING AND CONTROL

Questions 1 to 9 cover strategic planning and control, and the impact of risk and uncertainty on organisational performance, the subjects of Parts A and B of the BPP Study Text for *Advanced Performance Management* (APM).

1 Ganymede (6/12, amended) 49 mins

Organisation and sector background

Ganymede University (GU) is one of the three largest universities in Teeland, which has eight universities in total. All of the universities are in the public sector. GU obtains the vast majority of its revenue through government contracts for academic research and payments per head for teaching students. The economy of Teeland has been in recession in the last year and this has caused the Government to cut funding for all the universities in the country.

In order to try to improve efficiency, the chancellor of the university, who leads its executive board, has asked the head administrator to undertake an exercise to benchmark GU's administration departments against the other two large universities in the country, AU and BU. The Government Education Ministry has supported this initiative and has required all three universities to co-operate by supplying information.

Administrative costs

The following information has been collected regarding administrative costs for the most recent academic year:

		GU	*AU*	*BU*
		$'000	$'000	$'000
Research				
Contract management		14,430	14,574	14,719
Laboratory management		41,810	42,897	42,646
Teaching facilities management		26,993	27,263	26,723
Student support services		2,002	2,022	2,132
Teachers' support services		4,005	4,100	4,441
Accounting		1,614	1,571	1,611
Human resources		1,236	1,203	1,559
IT management		6,471	6,187	6,013
General services		17,049	16,095	18,644
Total		115,610	115,912	118,488
Drivers				
Student numbers		28,394	22,783	29,061
Staff numbers		7,920	7,709	8,157
Research contract value	($m)	185	167	152

The key drivers of costs and revenues have been assumed to be research contract values supported, student numbers and total staff numbers. The head administrator wants you to complete the benchmarking and make some preliminary comment on your results.

League tables

The Education Ministry in Teeland is also keen that potential students should have as much information as possible to help them choose which university to apply to.

To this end, the Ministry has proposed that summary league tables are published showing:

- The value of research funding secured by each university
- The proportion of students gaining first class and upper second (2:1) class degrees
- The proportion of students completing their courses
- The proportion of graduates who have secured full-time employment within one year of graduating

However, the chancellors of a number of universities in Teeland have written to the minister for education expressing their concern at the proposal to introduce the league tables.

Required

(a) Assess the progress of the benchmarking exercise to date, explaining the actions that have been undertaken and those that are still required. **(7 marks)**

(b) Evaluate, as far as possible, Ganymede University's benchmarked position. **(10 marks)**

(c) Evaluate the usefulness of the proposed league tables for students choosing where to study in Teeland. **(8 marks)**

(Total = 25 marks)

2 CFD (12/09, amended) 49 mins

The Care For Dogs Company (CFD) is a very profitable organisation which was established in 1998. CFD offers accommodation, care and supervision for pet dogs owned by inhabitants of Barkland.

CFD provides temporary accommodation for dogs whose owners are unable to care for them due to holidays, work commitments, illness etc. As part of the service offered to dog owners, CFD collects and returns dogs at the beginning and end of all dog stays.

When CFD was formed, the directors created a mission statement which was 'to provide very high value for money to all of our clients'.

The directors have always attempted to manage CFD in a socially responsible manner. Indeed, they are now considering the creation of a 'Dog Sanctuary' for homeless dogs which would involve an allocation of 20% of the total accommodation available for dogs to the Dog Sanctuary. The Dog Sanctuary would accommodate homeless dogs until a new owner was found for them. CFD would not receive any revenue whatsoever in respect of any homeless dog.

Required

(a) (i) Discuss the purpose, potential benefits and potential problems of mission statements. **(8 marks)**
(ii) Advise the directors of CFD regarding the appropriateness of its mission statement. **(4 marks)**

(b) (i) Explain what 'critical success factors' are, and explain the relationship between critical success factors and key performance indicators. **(4 marks)**

(ii) Discuss **THREE** critical success factors for CFD, and highlight a key performance indicator for each critical success factor. **(6 marks)**

(c) Excluding the number of complaints by clients, identify and briefly explain **THREE** quantitative non-financial performance measures that could be used to assess the 'quality of service' provided by CFD. **(3 marks)**

(Total = 25 marks)

3 Drinks Group (12/12, amended) 49 mins

Company background

The Drinks Group (DG) has been created over the last three years by merging three medium-sized family businesses. These businesses are all involved in making fruit drinks. Fizzy (F) makes and bottles healthy, fruit-based sparkling drinks. Still (S) makes and bottles fruit-flavoured non-sparkling drinks and Healthy (H) buys fruit and squeezes it to make basic fruit juices. The three companies have been divisionalised within the group structure. A fourth division called Marketing (M) exists to market the products of the other divisions to various large retail chains. Marketing has only recently been set up in order to help the business expand. All of the operations and sales of DG occur in Nordland, which is an economically well-developed country with a strong market for healthy non-alcoholic drinks.

The group has recruited a new Finance Director (FD), who was asked by the board to perform a review of the efficiency and effectiveness of the Finance Department as her first task on taking office. The FD has just presented her report to the board regarding some problems at DG.

Extract from FD's report to the board:

'The main area for improvement, which was discussed at the last board meeting, is the need to improve profit margins throughout the business. There is no strong evidence that new products or markets are required but that the most promising area for improvement lies in better internal control practices.

Control

As DG was formed from an integration of the original businesses (F, S, H), there was little immediate effort put into optimising the control systems of these businesses. They have each evolved over time in their own way. Currently, the main method of central control that can be used to drive profit margin improvement is the budget system in each business. The budgeting method used is to take the previous year's figures and simply increment them by estimates of growth in the market that will occur over the next year. These growth estimates are obtained through a discussion between the financial managers at group level and the relevant divisional managers. The management at each division are then given these budgets by head office and their personal targets are set around achieving the relevant budget numbers.

Divisions

H and S Divisions are in stable markets where the levels of demand and competition mean that sales growth is unlikely, unless by acquisition of another brand. The main engine for prospective profit growth in these divisions is through margin improvements. The managers at these divisions have been successful in previous years and generally keep to the agreed budgets. As a result, they are usually not comfortable with changing existing practices.

F is faster growing and seen as the star of the Group. However, the Group has been receiving complaints from customers about late deliveries and poor quality control of the F products. The F managers have explained that they are working hard within the budget and capital constraints imposed by the board and have expressed a desire to be less controlled.

The Marketing Division has only recently been set up and the intention is to run each marketing campaign as an individual project which would be charged to the division whose products are benefiting from the campaign. The managers of the manufacturing divisions are very doubtful of the value of M, as each believes that they have an existing strong reputation with their customers that does not require much additional spending on marketing. However, the board decided at the last meeting that there was scope to create and use a marketing budget effectively at DG, if its costs were carefully controlled. Similar to the other divisions, the Marketing Division budgets are set by taking the previous year's actual spend and adding a percentage increase. For M, the increase corresponds to the previous year's growth in group turnover.'

End of extract

Budgeting methods

At present, the FD is harassed by the introduction of a new information system within the Finance Department which is straining the resources of the department. However, she needs to respond to the issues raised above at the board meeting and so is considering using different budgeting methods at DG. She has asked you, the Management Accountant at the Group, to do some preliminary work to help her decide whether and how to change the budget methods. The first task that she believes would be useful is to consider the use of rolling budgets. She thinks that fast-growing F may prove the easiest division in which to introduce new ideas.

F's incremental budget for the current year is given below. You can assume that cost of sales and distribution costs are variable and administrative costs are fixed.

	Q1	Q2	Q3	Q4	Total
	$'000	$'000	$'000	$'000	$'000
Revenue	17,520	17,958	18,407	18,867	72,752
Cost of sales	9,636	9,877	10,124	10,377	40,014
Gross profit	7,884	8,081	8,283	8,490	32,738
Distribution costs	1,577	1,616	1,657	1,698	6,548
Administration costs	4,214	4,214	4,214	4,214	16,856
Operating profit	2,093	2,251	2,412	2,578	9,334

The actual figures for Quarter 1 (which has just completed) are:

	$'000
Revenue	17,932
Cost of sales	9,863
Gross profit	8,069
Distribution costs	1,614
Administration costs	4,214
Operating profit	2,241

On the basis of the Q1 results, sales volume growth of 3% per quarter is now expected.

The FD has also heard you talking about bottom-up budgeting and wants you to evaluate its use at DG.

Required

(a) Evaluate the suitability of incremental budgeting at each division. **(8 marks)**

(b) Recalculate the budget for Fizzy Division (F) using rolling budgeting and assess the use of rolling budgeting at F. **(8 marks)**

(c) Recommend, with reasons, a suitable budgeting method which could be used at the Marketing Division (M). **(3 marks)**

(d) Analyse and recommend the appropriate level of participation in budgeting at Drinks Group (DG). **(6 marks)**

(Total = 25 marks)

4 Godel (6/14, amended) 49 mins

Company background and strategy

Godel Goodies (Godel) manufactures a variety of own-label sweets for the two largest supermarket chains in Seeland. The business makes several different flavours of the same basic product. The strategy of the business has been to be a cost leader in order to win the supermarkets' business. The sales of Godel vary up and down from quarter to quarter depending on the state of the general economy and competitive forces. Most of the sweet manufacturers have been in business for decades and so the business is mature with little scope to be innovative in new product development. The supermarkets prefer to sign suppliers to long-term contracts and so it is difficult for new entrants to gain a foothold in this market. The management style at Godel is very much command and control which fits with the strategy and type of business. Indeed, most employees have been at Godel for many years and have expressed their liking for the straightforward nature of their work.

Variance analysis

The Chief Executive Officer (CEO) of Godel has asked your firm of accountants to advise him as his Finance Director (FD) will be absent for several months due to a recently diagnosed illness. As the CEO is preparing for the next board meeting, he has obtained the operating statement and detailed variance analysis from one of the junior accountants (Appendix 1).

The CEO is happy with the operating statement but wants to understand the detailed operational and planning variances, given in Appendix 1, for the board meeting. He needs to know what action should be taken as a result of these specific variances.

Budgeting process

The FD had been looking at the budgeting process before she fell ill. The CEO has decided that you should help him by answering some questions on budgeting at Godel.

Currently, the budget at Godel is set at the start of the year and performance is measured against this. The company uses standard costs for each product and attributes overheads using absorption costing based on machine hours. No variations are allowed to the standard costs during the year. The standard costs and all budget assumptions are discussed with the relevant operational manager before being set. However, these managers grumble that the budget process is very time consuming and that the results are ultimately of limited value from their perspective. Some of them also complain that they must frequently explain that the variances are not their fault. The CEO wants to know your views on whether this way of budgeting is appropriate and whether the managers' complaints are justified. He is satisfied that there is no dysfunctional behaviour at Godel which may lead to budget slack or excessive spending and that all managers are working in the best interests of the company.

Shortly before she fell ill, the FD had suggested that in order to stop managers complaining about having to explain variances that were not their fault, the managers should produce their own draft budgets, which would then be reviewed and consolidated centrally. The CEO is not sure what impact this change could have, and wants you to evaluate it before he makes any changes to Godel's current budgeting system.

Required

(a) Advise the CEO on the implications for performance management at Godel of analysing variances into the planning and operational elements as shown in Appendix 1. **(6 marks)**

(b) Evaluate the budgeting system at Godel. **(12 marks)**

(c) Evaluate the FD's proposal to introduce a bottom-up approach to budgeting. **(7 marks)**

(Total = 25 marks)

Appendix 1 is shown on the next page.

Appendix 1

(**Note.** You may assume that all figures in this appendix are correct.)

Operating statement for Godel

Period: May 20X4 (last month)

				$	$	
Budgeted profit					214,200	
Budget fixed production costs					264,180	
Budgeted contribution					478,380	
Sales variances	volume			20,100		Adverse
	price			8,960		Adverse
					29,060	Adverse
Actual sales minus standard cost of sales					449,320	
		Favourable	*Adverse*			
		$	$			
Variable cost variance						
Material	price		4,200			
	usage	3,500				
Labour	rate	1,100				
	efficiency	24,480				
	idle time		5,600			
Variable overhead	expenditure		1,080			
	efficiency	3,060				
		32,140	10,880			
					21,260	Favourable
Actual contribution					470,580	
Budgeted fixed production overhead				271,728		
Expenditure variance				18,696		Adverse
Actual fixed production overhead					290,424	
Actual profit					180,156	

Detailed variances

Total variable cost variances		$	
	Planning	20,680	Favourable
	Operational	580	Favourable
Sales price variances			
	Planning	15,600	Adverse
	Operational	6,640	Favourable

5 Perkin (Sep/Dec 15, amended) — 49 mins

Company background and objectives

Perkin manufactures electronic components for export worldwide, from factories in Ceeland, for use in smartphones and handheld gaming devices. These two markets are supplied with similar components by two divisions, Phones Division (P) and Gaming Division (G). Each division has its own selling, purchasing, IT and research and development (R&D) functions, but separate IT systems. Some manufacturing facilities, however, are shared between the two divisions.

Perkin's corporate objective is to maximise shareholder wealth through innovation and continuous technological improvement in its products. The manufacturers of smartphones and gaming devices, who use Perkin's components, update their products frequently and constantly compete with each other to launch models which are technically superior.

Budgeting process

Perkin has a well-established incremental budgeting process. Divisional managers forecast sales volumes and costs months in advance of the budget year. These divisional budgets are then scrutinised by the main board, and revised significantly by them in line with targets they have set for the business. The finalised budgets are often approved after the start of the accounting year. Under pressure to deliver consistent returns to institutional shareholders, the board does not tolerate failure by either division to achieve the planned net profit for the year once the budget is approved. Last year's results were poor compared to the annual budget. Divisional managers, who are appraised on the financial performance of their own division, have complained about the length of time that the budgeting process takes and that the performance of their divisions could have been better but was constrained by the budgets which were set for them.

In P Division, managers had failed to anticipate the high popularity of a new smartphone model incorporating a large screen designed for playing games, and had not made the necessary technical modifications to the division's own components. This was due to the high costs of doing so, which had not been budgeted for. Based on the original sales forecast, P Division had already committed to manufacturing large quantities of the existing version of the component and so had to heavily discount these in order to achieve the planned sales volumes.

A critical material in the manufacture of Perkin's products is silver, which is a commodity which changes materially in price according to worldwide supply and demand. During the year supplies of silver were reduced significantly for a short period of time and G Division paid high prices to ensure continued supply. Managers of G Division were unaware that P Division held large inventories of silver which they had purchased when the price was much lower.

Initially, G Division accurately forecasted demand for its components based on the previous years' sales volumes plus the historic annual growth rate of 5%. However, overall sales volumes were much lower than budgeted. This was due to a fire at the factory of their main customer, which was then closed for part of the year. Reacting to this news, managers at G Division took action to reduce costs, including closing one of the three R&D facilities in the division.

However, when the customer's factory reopened, G Division was unwilling to recruit extra staff to cope with increased demand; nor would P Division reallocate shared manufacturing facilities to them, in case demand increased for its own products later in the year. As a result, Perkin lost the prestigious preferred supplier status from its main customer who was unhappy with G Division's failure to effectively respond to the additional demand. The customer had been forced to purchase a more expensive, though technically superior, component from an alternative manufacturer.

The institutional shareholders' representative, recently appointed to the board, has asked you as a performance management expert for your advice. 'We need to know whether Perkin's budgeting process is appropriate for the business, and how this contributed to last year's poor performance.'

However, the shareholder representative did also acknowledge that external factors had contributed to Perkin's poor performance in the last year, and suggested that it would be useful if Perkin's performance reports distinguished between variances which had resulted from its own operational performance as opposed to external circumstances which could not have been anticipated when the budgets were produced. You noted that many organisations address this issue by analysing variances into planning and operational elements.

Required

(a) Evaluate the weaknesses in Perkin's current budgeting system and whether it is suitable for the environment in which Perkin operates. **(14 marks)**

(b) Evaluate the extent to which Perkin's poor performance for the last year can be attributed to external factors. **(6 marks)**

(c) Discuss the potential benefits to Perkin of analysing variances into planning and operational elements. **(5 marks)**

(Total = 25 marks)

6 Booxe (6/14) 49 mins

Company background

Booxe is a furniture manufacturing company based in the large, developed country of Teeland. Booxe is the largest furniture manufacturer in Teeland supplying many of the major retail chains with their own-brand furniture and also making furniture under its own brand (Meson). In a highly competitive market such as Teeland, Booxe has chosen a strategy of cost leadership.

Booxe has been in business for more than 70 years and there is a strong sense of tradition and appreciation of craft skills in the workforce. The average time which an employee has worked for the firm is 18 years. This has led to a bureaucratic culture; for example, the company's information systems are heavily paper based. In addition, and in line with this traditional culture, the organisation is divided into a set of functional departments, such as production, warehousing, human resources and finance.

Business process re-engineering project

In order to drive down costs, the Chief Executive Officer (CEO) decided to re-engineer the processes at Booxe. She decided that there should be a small pilot project to demonstrate the potential of business process re-engineering (BPR) to benefit Booxe and she selected the goods receiving activity in the company's warehousing operations for this.

The CEO has asked you as a performance management expert to complete the post-implementation review of the pilot project by assessing what it has delivered in financial terms. The project identified that ten of the warehouse staff spend about half their time matching goods delivered documents to purchase orders and dealing with subsequent problems. It was noted that 25% of all such matches failed and the staff then had to identify the issue and liaise with the Purchasing Department in order to get the goods returned to the supplier and a suitable credit note issued. The project introduced a new information system to replace the existing paper-based system. The new system allowed purchase orders to be entered by the Purchasing Department and then checked online to the goods delivered as they arrived at the warehouse. This allowed warehouse staff to reject incorrect deliveries immediately.

The following are further details provided in relation to the project:

Notes relating to old system:

1 Average staff wage in warehouse $25,000 p.a.
2 Purchasing staff time in handling delivery queries 8.5 days per week
3 Average staff wage in purchasing is $32,000 p.a. for working a 5-day week

Notes relating to new system:

New IT system costs:

		$
4	Hardware for warehouse and purchasing depts	220,000
5	Software total cost	275,000
6	Ongoing servicing cost (p.a.)	22,500
7	It is expected that the new system will last for eight years.	

The CEO now plans to apply BPR across Booxe and, as well as completing the post-implementation review, she needs to know how BPR will change the accounting information systems and the culture at Booxe. Booxe's current accounting system is a traditional one of overhead absorption based on labour hours with variances to budget used as control indicators. She has heard that an activity-based approach using enterprise resource planning (ERP) systems is fairly common and wants to know how these ideas might link to BPR at Booxe.

The CEO is concerned that middle management unrest may be a problem at Booxe. For example, the warehouse manager was uncomfortable with the cultural change required in the BPR project and decided to take early retirement before the project began. As a result, a temporary manager was put in place to run the warehouse during the project.

Appraisal process

The CEO has also begun to reconsider the human resources system at Booxe and she wants your advice on how the staff appraisal process can improve performance in the company. The existing system of manager appraisal is for the staff member to have an annual meeting with their line superior to review the previous year's work and discuss generally how to improve their efforts. Over the years, it has become common for these meetings to be informal and held over lunch at the company's expense. The CEO wants to understand the purpose of a staff appraisal system and how the process can improve the performance of the company. She also wants comments on the appropriate balance between control and staff development as this impacts on staff appraisal at Booxe.

Required

(a) Assess the financial impact of the pilot BPR project in the warehousing operations. **(6 marks)**

(b) Assess the impact of BPR on the culture and management information systems at Booxe. **(11 marks)**

(c) Advise on the appraisal process at Booxe as instructed by the CEO. **(8 marks)**

(Total = 25 marks)

7 PLX Refinery (2013 Pilot Paper, amended) 49 mins

Company background

PLX Refinery Co is a large oil refinery business in Kayland. Kayland is a developing country with a large and growing oil exploration and production business which supplies PLX with crude oil. Currently, the refinery has the capacity to process 200,000 barrels of crude oil per day and makes profits of $146m per year. It employs about 2,000 staff and contractors. The staff are paid $60,000 each per year on average (about twice the national average pay in Kayland).

The government of Kayland has been focused on delivering rapid economic growth over the last 15 years. However, there are increasing signs that the environment is paying a large price for this growth, with public health suffering. There is now a growing environmental pressure group, Green Kayland (GK), which is organising protests against the companies that they see as being the major polluters.

Environmental concerns

Kayland's Government wishes to react to the concerns of the public and the pressure groups. It has requested that companies involved in heavy industry contribute to a general improvement in the treatment of the environment in Kayland. The Government has identified a national goal to reduce carbon dioxide (CO_2) emissions by 20% in the next 5 years, and is currently debating a proposal to raise a tax on CO_2 emissions in order to encourage reductions.

As a major participant in the oil industry with ties to the nationalised oil exploration company (Kayex), PLX believes it will be strategically important to be at the forefront of environmental developments. It is working with other companies in the oil industry to improve environmental reporting since there is a belief that this will lead to improved public perception and economic efficiency of the industry. PLX has had a fairly good compliance record in Kayland, with only two major fines (of $1m each) being levied in the last eight years for safety breaches and river pollution. However, the main focus of PLX's performance measures remains on financial performance.

Information systems

The existing information systems within PLX also focus on financial performance. They support financial reporting obligations and allow monitoring of key performance metrics such as earnings per share and operating margins. Recent publications on environmental accounting have suggested that activity-based costing (ABC) and a life cycle view may be relevant in implementing improvements to these systems.

Capital expenditure and new product development

PLX is considering a major capital expenditure programme to enhance capacity, safety and efficiency at the refinery. This will involve demolishing certain older sections of the refinery and building on newly acquired land adjacent to the site. Overall, the refinery will increase its land area by 20%.

Part of the refinery extension will also manufacture a new plastic, Kayplas. Kayplas is expected to have a limited market life of 5 years after which it will be replaced by Kayplas2. The refinery accounting team have forecast the following data associated with this product and calculated PLX's traditional performance measure of product profit for the new product:

All figures are in $m

	20X2	*20X3*	*20X4*	*20X5*	*20X6*
Revenue	25.0	27.5	30.1	33.2	33.6
Costs					
Production costs	13.8	15.1	16.6	18.3	18.5
Marketing costs	5.0	4.0	3.0	3.0	2.0
Development costs	5.6	3.0	0.0	0.0	0.0
Product profit	0.6	5.4	10.5	11.9	13.1

Subsequently, the following environmental costs have been identified from PLX's general overheads as associated with the production of Kayplas.

	20X2	*20X3*	*20X4*	*20X5*	*20X6*
Waste filtration	1.2	1.4	1.5	1.9	2.1
Carbon dioxide exhaust extraction	0.8	0.9	0.9	1.2	1.5

Additionally, other costs associated with closing down and recycling the equipment in Kayplas production are estimated at $18m in 20X6.

The board wishes to consider how it can contribute to the oil industry's performance in environmental accounting, how it can implement the changes that this might require, and how these changes will benefit the company.

Required

(a) Discuss and illustrate four different cost categories that would aid transparency in environmental reporting both internally and externally at PLX. **(6 marks)**

(b) Explain, and evaluate, how the two environmental accounting techniques mentioned – ABC and life cycle costing – can assist in managing the environmental and strategic performance of PLX. **(6 marks)**

(c) Assess how the increasing focus on environmental accounting will affect PLX's performance metrics and its information systems. **(6 marks)**

(d) Evaluate the costing approach used for Kayplas's performance compared to a life cycle costing approach, performing appropriate calculations. **(7 marks)**

(Total = 25 marks)

8 FGH Telecom (12/10, amended) 49 mins

FGH Telecom (FGH) is one of the largest providers of mobile and fixed line telecommunications in Ostland. The company has recently been reviewing its corporate objectives in the light of its changed business environment. The major new addition to the strategic objectives is under the heading: 'Building a more environmentally friendly business for the future'. It has been recognised that the company needs to make a contribution to ensuring sustainable development in Ostland and reducing its environmental footprint. Consequently, it adopted a goal that, by 20Y7, it would have reduced its environmental impact by 60% (compared to year 20X1).

The reasons for the board's concern are that the telecommunications sector is competitive and the economic environment is increasingly harsh, with the markets for debt and equities being particularly poor. On environmental issues, the Government and public are calling for change from the business community. It appears that increased regulation and legislation will appear to encourage business towards better performance. The board has recognised that there are threats and opportunities from these trends. It wants to ensure that it is monitoring these factors and has asked for an analysis of the business environment with suggestions for performance measurement.

Additionally, the company has a large number of employees working across its network. Therefore, there are large demands for business travel. FGH runs a large fleet of commercial vehicles in order to service its network along with a company car scheme for its managers. The manager in charge of the company's travel budget is reviewing data on carbon dioxide emissions to assess FGH's recent performance.

Recent initiatives within the company to reduce emissions have included:

(a) The introduction in 20Y0 of a home-working scheme for employees in order to reduce the amount of commuting to and from their offices

(b) A drive to increase the use of teleconferencing facilities by employees

BPP LEARNING MEDIA

Data on FGH Telecom:

Carbon dioxide emissions Measured in millions of kg	*20X1 Base year*	*20X9*	*20Y0*
Commercial fleet diesel	105.4	77.7	70.1
Commercial fleet petrol	11.6	0.4	0.0
Company car diesel	15.1	14.5	12.0
Company car petrol	10.3	3.8	2.2
Other road travel (diesel)	0.5	1.6	1.1
Other road travel (petrol)	3.1	0.5	0.3
Rail travel	9.2	9.6	3.4
Air travel (short haul)	5.0	4.4	3.1
Air travel (long haul)	5.1	7.1	5.4
Hire cars (diesel)	0.6	1.8	2.9
Hire cars (petrol)	6.7	6.1	6.1
Total	172.6	127.5	106.6

Required

(a) Briefly evaluate how well FGH's environmental strategy is aligned to the interests of **THREE** different stakeholder groups. **(5 marks)**

(b) Perform an analysis of FGH's business environment to identify factors which will affect its environmental strategy. For each of these factors, suggest performance indicators which will allow FGH to monitor its progress. **(8 marks)**

(c) Evaluate the data given on carbon dioxide emissions using suitable indicators. Identify trends from within the data and comment on whether the company's behaviour is consistent with meeting its targets. **(9 marks)**

(d) Suggest further data that the company could collect in order to improve its analysis and explain how this data could be used to measure the effectiveness of the reduction initiatives mentioned. **(3 marks)**

(Total = 25 marks)

9 Sweet Cicely (Sept/Dec 17) 49 mins

Company background

Sweet Cicely (SC) manufactures sweets and confectionery and has delivered stable but modest increases to the shareholder wealth for many years. Following a change in ownership, the new shareholders are keen to increase the long-term performance of the business and are prepared to accept a high level of risk to achieve this.

New chocolate factory

SC is considering setting up a factory to manufacture chocolate bars. There are three options (1, 2 and 3) for the size and output capacity of the new chocolate factory. SC must choose a size most suited to the expected demand for its products. As well as the impact of the quality, branding and pricing of its products, demand for SC chocolate bars will be influenced by external factors such as consumer tastes for chocolate over other sweets, and even the suggested health benefits of certain types of chocolate.

A high-cost ingredient in chocolate bars is cocoa, a commodity traded on international markets. The market price of cocoa fluctuates with worldwide demand. Due to economic growth, chocolate consumption is rising in many countries, where it was once considered a luxury. In some countries, however, governments are considering introducing additional taxes on products containing sugar in order to reduce the consumption of chocolate and confectionery products. Being derived from an agricultural crop, the availability and price of cocoa is also influenced by climatic conditions, soil erosion, and disease. Conflicts and political instability in cocoa growing regions can also restrict its availability. Recent technological advances in the production of cocoa, such as the use of genetically modified crops, promise higher yields from cocoa plants in the near future.

Planning and decision-making

You have been asked to help SC choose one of the three options for the new chocolate factory. One board member told you: 'The board proposed expanding into cake manufacturing several years ago. With hindsight, our planning on that proposal was poor. We sold only slightly fewer cakes than expected, but hadn't realised how sensitive our operating profit would be to a small change in demand. The previous shareholders thought problems in the cake business would put their dividends at risk, so SC stopped manufacturing cakes, barely a year after it started. The board does not want to repeat these mistakes. We want to minimise the opportunity cost of making the wrong decision about the size of the new chocolate factory.'

Appendix 1 shows the net present values for the three options discounted at SC's current cost of capital. Appendix 2 shows the expected operating profit generated by the three options in the first year of the project, according to the market price of cocoa, and assuming an annual demand of 70 million chocolate bars.

Required

(a) Advise SC why decisions, such as what size of chocolate factory to build, must include consideration of risk and uncertainty, and evaluate the use of PEST analysis in managing the risk and uncertainty surrounding the project. **(14 marks)**

(b) Using the data in Appendix 1, explain which of the three options for the new chocolate factory would be preferred by the board and the new shareholders according to their respective risk appetites. **(6 marks)**

(c) Using the data in Appendix 2, recommend which of the three options for the new chocolate factory a risk neutral investor would choose, and explain any problems with the approach used to make the choice. **(5 marks)**

(Total = 25 marks)

Appendix 1

Net present values for the three options discounted at SC's current cost of capital

Annual demand for chocolate bars	*Option 1*	*Option 2*	*Option 3*
	$m	$m	$m
50 million	4.0	(8.0)	(32.0)
60 million	6.0	16.0	(24.0)
70 million	6.0	16.0	17.0

Appendix 2

Expected operating profit generated by the three options in the first year of the project, assuming an annual demand of 70 million chocolate bars

Probability	*Market price of cocoa*	*Option 1*	*Option 2*	*Option 3*
	$ per ton	$m	$m	$m
0.3	2,500	3.0	5.0	7.0
0.4	3,000	0.5	2.0	1.5
0.3	3,500	(2.0)	(1.0)	(2.0)

PERFORMANCE MEASUREMENT SYSTEMS AND DESIGN

Questions 10 to 15 cover performance measurement systems and design, the subject of Part C of the BPP Study Text for APM.

10 TREN engine components — 49 mins

TREN manufactures standard engine components. It operates a costing system based on absorption costing and standard costs, and the management control system is based on monthly variance analysis reports.

TREN has recently appointed a new Chief Executive Officer (CEO), who has begun to introduce changes to the manufacturing systems. He believes in lean manufacturing principles, and has begun to establish a just-in-time manufacturing system, with a focus on reducing inventories and production cycle times, and eliminating waste. Discussions are in progress with major suppliers to introduce just-in-time purchasing arrangements.

The CEO has informed the Management Accountant that changes will be needed to the company's internal accounting systems, and has indicated that TREN will need a lean management accounting system to support its lean manufacturing system. The CEO is dissatisfied with many of the features of the current management accounting system. There are many errors in data capture for the cost accounting system, and monthly variance reports are not produced until two weeks after the end of each month. He also considers that the wrong information is being reported.

Required

(a) Explain the main principles of a lean information system and discuss why an organisation may not experience the improvements in productivity and profitability they expect if they implement a lean information system. **(11 marks)**

(b) Discuss the reasons why TREN's current cost and management accounting systems do not fulfil the requirements of lean information systems. **(6 marks)**

(c) Identify the changes that should be made to TREN's management accounting system in order to turn it into a lean information system. **(8 marks)**

(Total = 25 marks)

11 Forion Electronics (6/15) — 49 mins

Company background

Forion Electronics (Forion) manufactures a range of electronic goods. Its business has grown rapidly over the last ten years and is now complex and international. Forion manufactures over 100 different products, selling into 25 different countries. There is a supplier base of over 200 companies from which Forion sources. As the business has become more complex, the board has found it difficult to pull together all the information that it requires in order to make decisions.

Information systems

The current information systems are developed in-house and are based in the functional departments (such as purchasing, manufacturing, warehousing and delivery, selling and marketing). The organisation uses the financial system as a means of bringing together information for an overview of corporate performance.

There have been a number of examples of problems encountered with information in Forion:

- There are inefficiencies arising from ordering the wrong amount of subcomponents.
- There are often stock-outs or obsolescence of unsold goods in the warehouses, although the Marketing Department prepares good sales forecasts.
- Sometimes, there are insufficient delivery vehicles available to meet customer deadlines.

The board of Forion believes the problems arise from poor information sharing within the company. It is considering the purchase of an enterprise resource planning system (ERPS) to be the single information system for the whole organisation.

Potential strategic alliance

Also, Forion is planning to launch a smartphone. However, in order to make it competitive they need to have high-visibility, durable screens. As the cost of screen development is considerable, it has been decided to form a strategic alliance with a well-known screen manufacturer to provide this key component for the new smartphone. Bon Accord Screens (BAS) has been chosen as the strategic ally, as it has a strong reputation for its quality of manufacturing and new product development. BAS has been trying to break into the smartphone market for several years.

The alliance agreement has stipulated three critical areas of performance for BAS's supply to Forion:

(1) Quality of manufacturing, measured by fault rates of screens supplied being within agreed tolerances (so that they fit Forion's phone bodies)

(2) Time of delivery, measured by the number of times a shipment is more than one day overdue

(3) The ability to provide technical upgrades to the screens as the market demands

The service level agreement will be based on these three points and there will be financial penalties built into the agreement if BAS fails to meet these.

Required

(a) Discuss the integration of information systems in an ERPS and how the ERPS may impact on performance management issues at Forion. **(10 marks)**

(b) Evaluate, from Forion's viewpoint, the usefulness of the three critical areas in the alliance agreement for measuring the performance of BAS. **(8 marks)**

(c) Evaluate the relative reliability of financial and non-financial data from internal and external sources in the context of the alliance between Forion and BAS. **(7 marks)**

(Total = 25 marks)

12 Quark Healthcare (12/13) — 49 mins

Organisational background

Quark Healthcare (Quark) runs a number of large hospitals which provide general medical care for the people of Veeland. Veeland is an advanced economy and healthcare is considered to be a high skill, high technology and high status industry. It is compulsory for the people of Veeland to purchase health insurance and then the insurance companies reimburse the healthcare providers for services delivered. The insurance companies audit the healthcare providers and grade them for value for money. As there are a number of hospital chains (such as Quark), the insurers will encourage their insured customers to use those which are most efficient. The ultimate sanction for a healthcare provider is for an insurance company to remove them from the list of acceptable providers.

Quark has large amounts of capital tied up in expensive medical equipment and a drug inventory. The existing systems for accounting for these items are traditional ones aimed at avoiding theft and obsolescence. Quark has an inventory system which requires regular (weekly) physical checks of the drugs in inventory in order to update it. It is important that the right drugs must be in easily accessible stores (located throughout the hospital) in order to act quickly in case of a medical emergency. Also, the accounting staff at Quark maintain a non-current asset register (NCAR) which logs the location of all major assets including medical equipment. The problem with the NCAR is that it is often out of date as doctors will take equipment in time of emergency and not properly log its new location. This often leads to equipment lying unused in one area of the hospital while being searched for in another area, to the detriment of patient care.

Radio-frequency identification devices (RFID)

Quark has recently instituted a tagging project where radio-frequency identification devices (RFID) will be attached to the most valuable pieces of equipment used in treatment and also to batches of high-value drugs. The hospitals are fitted with WiFi networks which can pick up the RFID signal so that the RFID tags will be detectable throughout a hospital. The tags will identify the object which they are attached to by a unique identification number and will give its location. The identifier number will link to the inventory system which will identify the product, the quantity initially delivered in that batch and the date of delivery. The RFID information will be accessible through the computer terminals throughout the hospitals.

The Chief Financial Officer (CFO) of Quark has asked you to advise him on the impact of this new system on performance management at Quark. He has suggested that you look at the costs and benefits which will be associated with producing the information from the RFID system, the impact of the nature of the information supplied, the changes to performance management reporting and how the new information could be used for improved control at the hospital. He is keen to be seen to be at the forefront of accounting and management developments and has been reading about cost control techniques. Recently, he has heard about 'lean' systems, so wants to know how the RFID system and its impact on the hospital fit with this concept. Given the importance of the medical staff in running the hospital, he also wants to know how their behaviour will be affected by the control information from the RFID system. There is a very strict social order among these staff (in increasing order of skills: nurses, general doctors and specialist doctors) which regularly causes friction when one group feels it is not given its due status. For example, recently, the general doctors agreed to a new method for nurses to record drugs administered to patients but this new system has not been fully implemented due to complaints by the nurses and specialist doctors who were not consulted on the change.

Required

(a) Assess the impact of the RFID system on the performance management at Quark as suggested by the CFO. **(12 marks)**

(b) Evaluate whether the overall management of the hospital can be considered to be 'leaner' as a result of the RFID information system. **(7 marks)**

(c) Evaluate how the medical staff's attitudes will influence the design and implementation of the RFID system and how it might be used to promote responsibility and accountability at the hospital. **(6 marks)**

(Total = 25 marks)

13 Nelson, Jody & Nigel (Mar/Jun 17) — 49 mins

Nelson, Jody and Nigel (NJN) operates a warehouse and distribution centre, storing and distributing 5,000 product lines on behalf of its client, an overseas sports equipment manufacturer.

Warehouse information system

NJN receives goods in shipping containers, which should include a packing list of the items they contain. Sometimes, packing lists are lost in transit and the manufacturer is asked for duplicates. Packing lists are manually input into NJN's warehouse information system (WIS) in batches, usually within 48 hours of the goods being received. Goods are first unpacked into a sorting area, and later moved to wherever there is available warehouse space once the packing list has been input. The WIS records the location within the warehouse where each item is located. The client's customers, who are retail stores, place orders by email, and do not currently have access to real-time inventory levels in NJN's warehouse.

Each morning picking lists are printed in the warehouse office. These lists show the quantities of items to be picked and the items' 12-digit product codes. Staff use these codes to retrieve items from the warehouse locations for despatch to retailers. In 8% of picking lists, at least one item is not in the location or does not have the quantity specified by the WIS. As a result, the item is not despatched, or the wrong item is picked. A small team investigates these discrepancies, using special reports which the Warehouse Manager extracts from the WIS. The team manually reconciles quantities of missing items in the warehouse to the sports equipment manufacturer's own records of the items which should be in inventory. If missing items cannot be found, the customer is informed via an email that they are unavailable.

Recent issues

The sports equipment manufacturer has a service level agreement with NJN, covering the accuracy of picking and the proportion of customers' orders successfully fulfilled. NJN's performance on these has deteriorated, especially when there is increased seasonal demand for certain products. At these times staff are under increased pressure to pick items quickly, and so picking accuracy deteriorates and absenteeism increases. There have also been accidents where goods have not been safely placed or safely picked from warehouse locations at busy times. These accidents have resulted in minor injuries to some employees.

The sports equipment manufacturer has threatened to end NJN's contract if performance does not improve. In response, NJN has recruited more staff to investigate discrepancies between items physically in warehouse locations, and those shown on the WIS at busy periods. It has also begun a series of cyclical inventory counts where every product line is counted every month to correct the quantities and locations shown on the WIS. NJN has rented an additional nearby warehouse in which to sort incoming items before they are put away.

Lean principles

NJN has hired a Management Consultant who is an expert in 'lean' principles and the application of these to management information systems. She believes that the WIS is wasteful, not adding value to the business or to its customers, and has suggested that NJN would benefit from the application of lean principles to this system.

She has suggested three proposals – that NJN:

- Reorganise the warehouse by storing high volume items close to the despatch area
- Shut down the additional warehouse, and;
- Discontinue the cyclical inventory counts.

To help with the adoption of lean principles in the warehouse reorganisation, the Management Consultant recommends NJN apply the '5Ss'* of lean principles, and she has suggested performance metrics which can be used to evaluate NJN's progress towards adopting these (Appendix 1).

*: Structurise, Systemise, Sanitise, Standardise, Self-discipline.

Required

(a) Assess whether NJN's existing warehouse information system (WIS) is effective in reducing waste and adding value in NJN's workflow. **(10 marks)**

(b) Advise whether the three proposals suggested by the Management Consultant will help to eliminate the different types of waste identified under lean principles. **(6 marks)**

(c) Evaluate whether the application of each of the 5Ss following the warehouse reorganisation at NJN is adequately measured by the performance metrics in Appendix 1. **(9 marks)**

(Total = 25 marks)

Appendix 1 – Performance measures for 5Ss relating to warehouse reorganisation

(1) Warehouse Manager's daily assessment of the tidiness of the warehouse on a scale of 1–10.

(2) The proportion of inventory not stored in order of its alphabetical description with products with names beginning with 'A' nearest the despatch area and 'Z' furthest away.

(3) The number of accidents caused by goods being incorrectly stored or picked.

14 Great National Trains **49 mins**

In contrast to many other countries, the railway system in Pecoland remains nationalised, and services are operated by Great National Trains (GNT). The Chairman of the GNT Railways Board reports to senior civil servants in the Ministry of Transport. However, Pecoland also has a rail regulator who has the power to make recommendations directly to the Minister of Transport in relation to all issues relating to the operation and performance of GNT.

The Rail Regulator's role is to ensure that the rail service in Pecoland is delivered in a safe and efficient manner, and in a way which provides high levels of satisfaction to all rail users. GNT's overall strategic objective is to deliver reliable, punctual and safe rail services to customers efficiently and cost effectively, while continuing to reduce its level of carbon emissions.

The Government views cost effectiveness as the key aspect of all public sector services in Pecoland, and it has also imposed the overriding financial objective that GNT should at least cover its operating costs from the revenue it earns.

Over the last ten years, GNT has made a significant investment in its rail network and its trains. Diesel trains are being replaced by electric trains following the electrification of the network.

There are three subsidiary companies within GNT:

(1) Passenger Co runs passenger rail services, which include express services between the major towns and cities, as well as slower services to more remote locations. (The number of services on some rural routes has been reduced significantly in recent years, due to the relatively low number of passengers using them.

However, these cutbacks provoked strong opposition from groups of local residents who relied on the railways for their transport.)

(2) Freight Co runs freight services, transporting bulk goods such as coal and oil, and industrial products such as steel and cars, and a range of retail products for supermarkets and other retailers. Across the majority of the rail network, freight trains run on the same tracks as passenger trains, although there are a few lines (for example, to power stations) which are used exclusively by freight trains.

(3) Track Co is responsible for managing, and upgrading, the track, signalling and property; for example, station buildings.

The majority of Passenger Co's locomotives are now electric as the lines between all the major cities in Pecoland have already been electrified. Most of Freight Co's trains are hauled by diesel locomotives, but it has recently invested in a number of electric engines which are less harmful to the environment. Passenger Co contributes about 50% of GNT's total revenue.

Freight Co contributes about 40% of GNT's total revenue. Its share of the freight haulage market in Pecoland is approximately 10%, and the majority of freight is transported by road. However, the amount of freight carried by rail has begun to increase in recent years due to worsening congestion on Pecoland's roads.

A number of retailers in Pecoland are currently considering the impact of their supply chains on the environment and looking for ways to reduce the impacts of their supply chain. They are currently evaluating the environmental benefits of switching more of their deliveries from road to rail freight. However, the retailers, like many companies in Pecoland, also value the convenience of road freight, which allows goods to be delivered directly to their premises.

Key performance indicators (KPIs)

Each of the three subsidiary companies measures their performance against a range of KPIs, based upon meeting GNT's overall strategic objectives. Examples of the KPIs include:

Passenger Co

- The number of customer complaints received
- The percentage of trains arriving at their destination on time
- The number of signals passed at danger

Freight Co

- Train capacity utilisation (the actual load capacity as a proportion of the total available load capacity for a journey)
- The percentage of trains arriving at their destination on time
- Carbon emissions generated (per tonne transported per kilometre travelled)
- The number of signals passed at danger

Track Co

- The number of delays to services per month due to signalling failure
- The number of complaints per month relating to station cleanliness

In recent years, there have been suggestions that GNT is not providing a value for money service for rail users, and that the rail services in Pecoland should be privatised. The Minister of Transport and the Rail Regulator both oppose privatisation, however, and believe that retaining GNT under national control provides the best way of creating value from Pecoland's rail system over the medium and long term.

GNT produces an annual report, which summarises its financial and operating performance for the year, including statistics showing actual performance against target for the KPIs. The Group Management Accountant collates all these figures for the annual report. The annual report also describes the governance structures within the organisation.

However, the Rail Regulator has recently recommended that GNT should produce an integrated report, because this would help to focus attention on the organisation's ability to create value in the medium and long term, as well as on its short-term performance. GNT's board is sceptical of the idea, feeling that the costs involved in producing the amount of non-financial information required for an integrated report will outweigh the benefits of doing so.

Required

(a) Discuss the difficulties faced by GNT, as a public sector organisation, in setting and measuring strategic objectives. **(10 marks)**

(b) Discuss the additional information which GNT would provide to its stakeholders in an integrated report, compared to its current annual report. **(6 marks)**

(c) Evaluate the potential impact on the amount and type of information prepared by the Group Management Accountant if GNT starts to produce integrated reports, and the issues the Management Accountant could face in preparing that information. **(9 marks)**

(Total = 25 marks)

15 Amal (6/12, amended) 49 mins

Company background and objectives

Amal Airline (Amal) is the national airline of Jayland. The airline's objective is to be the best premium global airline.

Recent events

Amal provides long- and short-haul services all over the world and is based at its hub at Jaycity airport. Amal has been hit by a worldwide reduction in air travel due to poor economic conditions. The most recent financial results show a loss and this has caused the board to reconsider its position and take action to address the changed environment.

Amal has cut its dividend in order to conserve cash and it is trying to rebuild profitability by reducing costs by 14%. The airline is capital intensive as it needs to maintain a large fleet of modern aircraft. The two major costs for the airline are staff and fuel. In trying to renegotiate working conditions and pay, the management have angered the unionised workforce. There has already been some strike action by the unions representing the aircraft crew and ground staff and more is threatened.

Additionally, the board is pushing forward a large project to improve the design of the company website in order to increase the number of passengers who check in online and so would not require as much assistance at the airport. The new design is also aiming to increase the number of passengers who book their tickets through the company's website rather than other resellers' websites or at booking agents.

The board has also been considering taking advantage of new technology in aircraft engines by making a large investment ($450m) in new low-noise, fuel-efficient aircraft in an effort to reduce the environmental complaints surrounding air travel and also cut costs.

Performance analysis

The Chief Executive Officer (CEO) has provided the data for Amal and two of its main competitors (shown in Appendix 1). Kayland Air is a government-owned and run airline in the neighbouring country of Kayland. It has a similar mix of business to Amal and targets a similar market. Cheapo Air is currently one of the most successful of the new privately owned airlines that have gained significant market share over the last 15 years by offering a cheap but basic short-haul service to customers in and around Jayland. Cheapo Air subcontracts many of its activities in order to remain flexible. The CEO wants you to calculate some suitable performance measures and explain the results.

Big Data

The CEO believes that Amal could be making more use of Big Data. He has recently returned from a conference about 'Big Data in the Airline Industry' where one of the speakers talked about the benefits of Big Data in relation to four key areas:

- Identifying trends in passenger demand and using this to set prices
- Understanding and influencing the customer's selection process (in particular reducing the number of potential customers who start booking a flight online but do not go on to complete the transaction)
- Boosting revenue from in-flight sales by optimising the on-board store for individual flights
- Understanding customer sentiment and improving customer satisfaction

Amal currently offers the same selection of in-flight products on all its flights.

The CEO has asked you to explain how using Big Data in these four areas could help Amal improve its performance. However, he also wants to understand the potential implications that using Big Data could have for Amal's management information systems, given that a number of Amal's IT staff are already working on the website upgrade project.

Required

(a) Using the data provided, analyse the three airlines using appropriate performance indicators and comment on your results. **(12 marks)**

(b) Explain how Big Data could be used to help Amal's performance, in relation to the four key areas identified at the conference. **(8 marks)**

(c) Discuss the potential implications of Big Data for Amal's management information systems. **(5 marks)**

(Total = 25 marks)

Appendix 1

Data provided by the CEO:

Data for the most recent calendar year

		Amal	*Kayland Air*	*Cheapo Air*
Passengers ('000)		23,649	38,272	35,624
Passenger kilometres (millions)		79,618	82,554	40,973
Revenue	$m	5,430	7,350	2,170
Costs				
Fuel	$m	1,480	1,823	535
Staff	$m	1,560	2,998	238
Staff numbers		32,501	56,065	5,372
Operating profit	$m	630	54	127
Number of aircraft		182	361	143
Average aircraft size (seats)		195	163	125
Seat kilometres (millions)		100,654	105,974	46,934

Note. A seat kilometre is generated for every one kilometre flown by an **available** seat on the company's aircraft.

STRATEGIC PERFORMANCE MEASUREMENT

Questions 16 to 33 cover strategic performance measurement, the subject of Part D of the BPP Study Text for APM.

16 Chicory (Sept/Dec '17) — 49 mins

Assume it is now December 20X7.

Company background

Chicory operates a chain of depots in Deeland, supplying and fitting tyres and other vehicle parts to lorries, buses and agricultural vehicles. Chicory's objective is to maximise shareholder wealth. Due to a slowdown in the Deeland economy, Chicory's recent performance has been weak. An unsuccessful acquisition has also caused cash flow problems and a write-off of goodwill of $24.7m in the year to 30 June 20X7.

Benchmarking exercise

The board has commissioned a benchmarking exercise to help improve Chicory's performance. This exercise will involve comparison of a range of financial and other operational performance indicators against Fennel, a similar business in Veeland. Fennel has agreed to share some recently available performance data with Chicory as they operate in different countries. The reason Fennel was chosen as a benchmark is that as well as supplying and fitting tyres and parts to heavy vehicles, a large part of Fennel's business involves supplying electricity to charging points to recharge electric cars. Fennel installs and operates the charging points in public places, and users pay Fennel for the electricity they use. The board of Chicory intends to follow a similar business model as the use of electric cars is increasing in Deeland.

The Veeland economy is growing strongly. Electric car use there has increased rapidly in the last two years, encouraged by tax incentives for businesses, like Fennel, to install and operate charging points. The Veeland government has also underwritten loans taken out by businesses to finance this technology, which has enabled Fennel to borrow funds for the significant capital investment required. The cost of components used in the charging points is falling rapidly. Capitalisation of development costs related to this technology is permitted in Veeland, but not in Deeland. In 20X5, Fennel invested heavily in IT systems which significantly improved performance by increasing the availability of parts in its depots, and reducing inventories.

Chicory uses return on average capital employed (ROCE) as its main financial performance indicator, and this is to be benchmarked against Fennel. One board member suggested that, though it may have some disadvantages, EBITDA (earnings before interest, tax, depreciation and amortisation) could have advantages as a performance measure over the existing measure, and should also be included in the benchmarking exercise.

You have been given the most recently available financial data for both businesses in Appendix 1, with the data for Fennel being converted into dollars ($) from its home currency.

Required

(a) Evaluate the relative financial performance of Chicory against Fennel using the two financial performance measures identified in the benchmarking exercise and evaluate their use as performance measures in this situation.

(i) ROCE **(6 marks)**

(ii) EBITDA **(10 marks)**

(b) Advise Chicory on the problems of using the benchmarking exercise with Fennel as a way to improve performance. **(9 marks)**

(Total = 25 marks)

BPP LEARNING MEDIA

Appendix 1

Benchmark data

Extract from statement of financial position

	30 June 20X7	*31 December 20X5*
	Chicory	*Fennel*[1]
	$m	$m
End of year		
Total assets	140.0	296.0
Current liabilities	(81.0)	(120.0)
Beginning of year[1]		
Total assets	138.0	290.0
Current liabilities	(60.0)	(120.0)

Income statement

	30 June 20X7	*31 December 20X5*
	Chicory	*Fennel*
	$m	$m
Revenue	175.1	350.0
Cost of sales	(130.1)	(299.0)
Gross profit	45.0	51.0
Administrative expenses	(11.0)	(25.0)
Write off of goodwill	(24.7)	–
Operating profit[2]	9.3	26.0
Interest payable	(1.8)	(8.0)
Profit before tax	7.5	18.0
Tax	(3.0)	(1.0)
Net profit	4.5	17.0

Notes

1 $6m of new capital was introduced into Fennel on 31 March 20X5. Normally, new net investment is spread evenly over the year.

2 Operating profit is after charging depreciation of non-current assets of $18m in Chicory, and $25m in Fennel.

17 Landual Lamps (6/13) 49 mins

Company background and organisational structure

Landual Lamps (Landual) manufactures and delivers floor and table lamps for homes and offices in Beeland. The company sells through its website and uses commercial logistics firms to deliver its products. The markets for its products are highly competitive. The company has traditionally relied on the high quality of its designs to drive demand for its products.

The company is divided into two divisions (components and assembly), plus a head office that provides design, administrative and marketing support. The manufacturing process involves:

(1) The Components Division making the housing components and electrical components for the lamp. This is an intricate process as it depends on the specific design of the lamp and so serves as a significant source of competitive advantage for Landual.

(2) The Assembly Division assembling the various components into a finished lamp ready for shipment. This is a simple process.

The Finance Director (FD) of Landual is currently overloaded with work due to changes in financial accounting policies that are being considered at board level. As a result, she has been unable to look at certain management accounting aspects of the business and has asked you to do a review of the transfer pricing policy between the Components and Assembly Divisions.

Transfer pricing policy

The current transfer pricing policy at Landual is as follows:

- Market prices for electrical components are used as these are generic components for which there is a competitive external market.
- Prices for housing components based on total actual production costs to the Components Division are used as there is no external market for these components since they are specially designed for Landual's products.

Currently, the Components Division produces only for the Assembly Division in order to meet overall demand without the use of external suppliers for housing and electrical components. If the Components Division were to sell its electrical components externally, then additional costs of $269,000 would arise for transport, marketing and bad debts.

Potential changes

The FD is considering two separate changes within Landual: one to the transfer pricing policy, and a second one to the divisional structure.

First, the transfer pricing policy for housing components would change to use variable cost to the Components Division. The FD wants to know the impact of the change in transfer pricing policy on the existing results of the two divisions and the company. (No change is proposed to the transfer price of the electrical components.)

Second, as can be seen from the divisional performance report below, the two divisions are currently treated as profit centres. The FD is considering splitting the Components Division into two further separate divisions: an Electrical Components Division and a Housing Components Division. If the board agrees to this proposal, then the Housing Components Division will be treated as a cost centre only, charging its total production cost to the Assembly Division. The Electrical Components and Assembly Divisions will remain as profit centres.

The FD needs to understand the impact of this proposed new divisional structure on divisional performance assessment and on the company as a whole. She has asked that, in order to keep the discussion on the new divisional structure simple, you use the existing transfer pricing policy to do illustrative calculations. She stated that she would reallocate head office costs to the two new components divisions in proportion to their cost of sales.

You are provided with the following financial and other information for Landual.

ACTUAL DATA FOR LANDUAL FOR THE YEAR ENDED 31 MARCH 20X3

	Components Division	*Assembly Division*	*Landual*
	$'000	$'000	$'000
Sales:			
Electrical	1,557		
Housing	8,204		
Sub-total	9,761	15,794	15,794
Cost of sales:			
Electrical	804	1,557	
Housing	6,902	8,204	
Sub-total	7,706	9,761	7,706
Fixed production costs:			
Electrical	370		
Housing	1,302		
Sub-total	1,672	1,268	2,940
Allocated head office costs	461	2,046	2,507
Profit	(78)	2,719	2,641

Note. The Components Division has had problems meeting budgets recently, with an adverse variance of $575,000 in the last year. This variance arises in relation to the cost of sales for housing component production.

Required

(a) Evaluate the current system of transfer pricing at Landual, using illustrative calculations as appropriate. **(10 marks)**

(b) Advise the FD on the impact of changing the transfer pricing policy for housing components as suggested by the FD and comment on your results, using illustrative calculations as appropriate. **(6 marks)**

(c) Evaluate the impact of the change in proposed divisional structure on the profit in the divisions and the company as directed by the FD. **(9 marks)**

(Total = 25 marks)

18 Laudan Advertising Agency (Sep/Dec 16) — 49 mins

Company background, and objectives

Laudan Advertising Agency (LAA) is based in Geeland and has three autonomous subsidiaries: A, B and C. All three subsidiaries are profit centres and LAA seeks to maximise the long-term wealth of its shareholders. A is based in Geeland, while both B and C are located in other parts of the world. LAA is a highly respected advertising agency, which in the last 5 years has created advertising campaigns for 25 of the world's top 100 most recognised brands.

LAA's four key objectives published on its website are to:

- Delight our clients by the quality of our work
- Provide excellent value for money to our clients
- Give our clients access to specialist and local knowledge
- Ensure our clients return to us time after time

There are three main functions within LAA:

(1) Campaign management, which involves researching and understanding clients' requirements and budgets and designing a suitable advertising campaign for them

(2) Creative design, which is where the visual appearance of the advert and graphics are created

(3) Media buying, which negotiates prices with, and buys advertising time and space from, magazine and newspaper publishers, internet search engines and TV companies

Each subsidiary has its own department for campaign management and for media buying. Only A, however, has a creative design department.

The directors at LAA believe that without visually appealing design, any advertising campaign is unlikely to be successful and meet the expectations of the client. They identified the importance of being able to produce high quality creative design as a critical success factor for the business. Two years ago, they decided to concentrate all of LAA's creative design at a 'centre of design excellence' within A. The intention was to improve the quality of creative design within the business by giving staff access to the latest design technology, and by attracting the most talented designers to work there.

Additional key performance indicator

To encourage the three subsidiaries to use the internal creative design department within A, instead of external third-party design agencies, the directors created a new additional key performance indicator on which to appraise the performance of all subsidiaries and of subsidiary managers:

- All subsidiaries, including A, must purchase at least 90% of creative design work internally from A.

Prior to the introduction of this performance indicator, 40% of creative design work in each of the three subsidiaries was purchased from external design agencies.

The directors of LAA have become concerned that the introduction of the new key performance indicator may be causing managers to operate in ways which are not helping to meet LAA's stated objectives. They have asked for comments from subsidiary managers (Appendix 1) about whether they have met the 90% target in the most recent period and, if not, to explain why this is.

Appendix 1

Subsidiary managers' comments on achievement of KPI for 90% creative design work purchased internally

Subsidiary A

'A purchased 86% of design work from our internal design department in the period. It would have been almost 100%, but we won a large order for a new client who operates in a specialised industry of which we have no experience. As a result, we had to use the services of a specialised external design agency, which was much more expensive than using our in-house team.'

Subsidiary B

'B purchased 62% of design work internally in the period. Though the quality of the designs is very good, they were more appealing to consumers in Geeland than here in Veeland, where B operates. The internal design department did not seem to understand consumer preferences in Veeland, and many of their designs were rejected by a key client of ours. As a result, an important advertising campaign missed key deadlines, by which time the internal design department had insufficient capacity to finish the work and we had to use an external agency.

'As there is no formal transfer pricing policy in place at LAA, the basis of the transfer price charged by the internal design department is also unclear to us. It appears to be based on full cost of the design work, including apportioned overheads and an allowance for bad debts and marketing expenses, plus a very substantial mark-up. We have spent a long time trying to negotiate this price with A, which is much more expensive than external designers. Furthermore, we are currently being investigated by the tax authorities here in Veeland who have indicated that the prices charged by A for design do seem well in excess of market rates.'

Subsidiary C

'C purchased 91% of design work from the internal design department in the period, as well as achieving all our other performance targets. A key client of ours ran a major advertising campaign during the period. We used the internal design department for the first time for this campaign, instead of the usual external agency that we have used in the past for work for this client. The client was very unhappy with the extra cost that this incurred, as the number of design hours and the hourly rate was much higher than for previous campaigns. The internal design department refused to reduce the price after long negotiations and we had to give a large discount to the client before they would settle our invoice. As a result, our gross profit margin for the period was significantly reduced.

'It would be much fairer if the transfer price charged by A was based on the market price of the services provided.'

Required

(a) Evaluate how the following help LAA to manage performance in order to achieve its stated objectives:

(i) Identifying the critical success factor of producing high quality creative design; and
(ii) Setting the key performance indicator for the requirement to purchase 90% of design work internally.

(8 marks)

(b) Assess the need for a formal transfer pricing policy at LAA. **(9 marks)**

(c) Advise the directors whether LAA should use a market value transfer price as suggested by the manager of Subsidiary C. **(8 marks)**

(Total = 25 marks)

19 Jenson, Lewis and Webb (Mar/Jun 17) — 49 mins

Company background and objectives

Jenson, Lewis and Webb (JLW) manufactures tubes of acrylic paint for sale to artists and craft shops in Kayland and Seeland. JLW has two divisions, Domestic Division and Export Division, both based in Kayland. All costs are incurred in Kayland dollars ($KL). Domestic Division is an investment centre and sells only to customers in Kayland. Export Division is a profit centre and exports all its products to Seeland, where customers are invoiced in Seeland pounds (£SL), at prices fixed at the start of the year. The objective of JLW is to maximise shareholder wealth.

Capital expenditure

At the beginning of the year ended 31 December 20X6, the head office at JLW purchased new production machinery for Export Division for $KL2.5m, which significantly increased the production efficiency of the division. Managers at Domestic Division were considering purchasing a similar machine, but decided to delay the purchase until the beginning of the following financial year. On 30 June 20X6 the $KL weakened by 15% against the £SL, after which the exchange rate between the two currencies has remained unchanged.

Performance appraisal

The managers of the two divisions are currently appraised on the performance of their own divisions, and are awarded a large bonus if the net profit margin of their division exceeds 8% for the year. Extracts from the management accounts for the year ended 31 December 20X6 for both divisions are given in Appendix 1. On being told that she would not be receiving a bonus for the financial year, the manager of Export division has commented that she has had difficulty in understanding the bonus calculations for her division as it is not based on traceable profit, which would consider only items which relate directly to the division. She also does not believe it is appropriate that the net profit margin used to appraise her performance is the same as 'that which is used to evaluate the performance of Export division itself'. She has asked for a meeting with the directors to discuss this further.

JLW's directors intend to award divisional managers' bonuses on the basis of net profit margin achieved in 20X6 as planned, but have asked you as a Performance Management Consultant for your advice on the comments of the Export Division Manager in advance of their meeting with her. One director has also suggested that, in future, economic value added (EVA™) may be a good way to evaluate and compare the performance of the two divisions. You are asked for your advice on this too, but you have been specifically asked not to attempt a calculation of EVA™.

Required

(a) Evaluate the comments of the Export Division Manager that the net profit margin used to appraise her own performance should be different from that used to appraise the performance of the Export Division itself. **(7 marks)**

(b) Recommend, using appropriate calculations, whether the manager of the Export Division should receive her bonus for the year. **(8 marks)**

(c) Advise whether the use of economic value added (EVA™) is an appropriate measure of performance of the divisions. You are not required to perform an EVA™ calculation. **(10 marks)**

(Total = 25 marks)

Appendix 1 – Extracts from management accounts for year ended 31 December 20X6

	Export Division	*Domestic Division*
	$KL'000	$KL'000
Revenue[1]	8,000	12,000
Cost of sales	(4,800)	(7,800)
Gross profit	3,200	4,200
Depreciation	(395)	(45)
Allocated head office costs	(360)	(540)
Other overheads[2]	(1,900)	(2,300)
Net profit	545	1,315
Net profit margin on revenue	6.8%	11.0%
Capital employed[3]	6,500	8,500

Notes

1 Revenue accrues evenly over the financial year.

2 Other overheads for Domestic Division include the creation of a bad debt provision equivalent to $KL75,000 for a wholesale customer who had financial difficulties during the year, and $KL90,000 for advertising a new range of paints launched at the end of the year.

3 JLW is financed in equal proportions by debt and equity. The cost of equity is 8% and the after tax cost of debt is 5%.

20 Stillwater Services (12/12, amended) — 49 mins

Company background

Stillwater Services (SS) is a listed water utility company providing water and sewage services to the public and businesses of a region of Teeland. The company was formed when the government-owned Public Water Company of Teeland was broken up into regional utility companies (one of which was SS) and sold into private ownership over four years ago.

Industry regulator

As a vital utility for the economy of Teeland, water services are a government-regulated industry. The regulator is principally concerned that SS does not abuse its monopoly position in the regional market to unjustifiably increase prices. The majority of services (80%) are controlled by the regulator who sets an acceptable return on capital employed (ROCE) level and ensures that the pricing of SS within these areas does not breach this level. The remaining services, such as a bottled water operation and a contract repairs service, are unregulated and SS can charge a market rate for these. The regulator calculates its ROCE figure based on its own valuation of the capital assets being used in regulated services and the operating profit from those regulated services.

The target pre-tax ROCE set by the regulator is 6%. If SS were to breach this figure, then the regulator could fine the company. In the past, other such companies have seen fines amounting to millions of dollars.

Economic value added (EVA™)

The board of SS is trying to drive the performance for the benefit of the shareholders. This is a new experience for many at SS, having been in the public sector until four years ago. In order to try to better communicate the objective of maximising shareholder wealth, the board has decided to introduce economic value added (EVA™) as the key performance indicator.

The Finance Director has asked you to calculate EVA™ for the company, based on the following financial information for the year ending 30 September 20X2:

Stillwater Services

	Regulated	*Non-regulated*	*20X2 total*
	$m	$m	$m
Revenue	276.0	69.0	345.0
Operating costs	230.0	47.0	277.0
Operating profit	46.0	22.0	68.0
Finance charges			23.0
Profit before tax			45.0
Tax at 25%			9.5
Profit after tax			35.5

Capital employed:	*20X2*	*20X1*
	$m	$m
Measured from published accounts	657.0	637.0
Measured by regulator (for regulated services only)	779.0	761.0

Notes

1 Total operating costs include:

	20X2	*20X1*
	$m	$m
Depreciation	59	57
Provision for doubtful debts	2	0.5
Research and development	12	–
Other non-cash items	7	6

2 Economic depreciation is assessed to be $83m in 20X2.

Economic depreciation includes any appropriate amortisation adjustments.

In previous years, it can be assumed that economic and accounting depreciation were the same.

3 Tax is the cash paid in the current year ($9m) and an adjustment of $0.5m for deferred tax provisions. There was no deferred tax balance prior to 20X2.

4 The provision for doubtful debts was $4.5m on the 20X2 statement of financial position.

5 Research and development is not capitalised in the accounts.

It relates to a new project that will be developed over five years and is expected to be of long-term benefit to the company. 20X2 is the first year of this project.

6 Cost of capital of SS

Equity	16%
Debt (pre-tax)	5%

7 Gearing of SS

40% equity
60% debt

Required

(a) Evaluate the performance of SS using EVA™. **(13 marks)**

(b) With reference to the issues involved in managing different stakeholder groups, analyse the potential influence of the regulator, the directors, and the shareholders on performance management at SS. **(5 marks)**

(c) Assess whether SS meets its regulatory ROCE target and comment on the impact of such a constraint on performance management at SS. **(7 marks)**

(Total = 25 marks)

21 Essland Police Forces (12/13) 49 mins

You are a performance management expert brought in by the Chief Executive Officer (CEO) of the Department of the Interior for the country of Essland. The department is a branch of the Essland Government which handles security, policing, immigration and border control. The CEO is a civil servant and he reports to the Minister for the Interior. The Minister for the Interior is an elected politician selected by the Prime Minister of Essland, who leads its government.

League tables

The newly elected Minister for the Interior has instructed the CEO to implement his policy for improving the regional police forces' performance by copying the method used for schools. In a recent initiative by the School's Ministry, a league table for the hundreds of schools in Essland was created, showing the best and worst in terms of examination performance only, in order to motivate senior school managers to improve. The league table was used to create targets for assessing the schools' and their managers' performance. Additionally, parents in Essland have the right to choose which school their children attend and so often base their selection on league table performance. Therefore, the Minister has had a policy review body draw up a method of creating a league table for the police forces.

The CEO has requested your help to clarify his own thinking on this new policy for the four regional police forces in Essland (Cashire (C), Dashire (D), Eshire (E) and Fashire (F)). The CEO needs you to assess the use of the league table using the policy review body's suggested method and has collected the data and calculation of the league table given in Appendix 1 to assist you. He also wants to assess whether the table will help in meeting the Department's aim and goals for the police.

Aim and goals

The overall aim of the Department (and its police forces) is 'to provide a value-for-money service to ensure that the community can live in safety with confidence in their physical and legal security'. The detailed goals of the Department are to:

- Tackle the underlying causes of crime and achieve long-term sustainable solutions
- Bring perpetrators to justice
- Provide protection and support for individuals and communities at risk of harm
- Respond to community needs by being accessible and engaging with their concerns

The CEO warned you, 'I'm not interested in the performance of the forces. I'm interested in the method of assessment, so don't waste time with your ideas on how to improve actual policing.'

The CEO also wishes to understand the strengths and weaknesses of the use of a league table, its link to targets and the likely reaction of employees to this system of performance management, especially as there is a strong union representing the police. He is worried about the employees' attitude to the introduction of the system and its effects on their behaviour and their sense of accountability. He is also concerned about importing the use of a league table from the schools sector, as it might not be appropriate here.

Required

(a) Evaluate the method of calculating and measuring the force scores for use in the league table in achieving the Department of the Interior's aims and goals. **(14 marks)**

(b) Discuss the merits of league tables in performance management and address the CEO's concerns over their use in managing the performance of Essland's police forces. **(11 marks)**

(Total = 25 marks)

Appendix 1

The appendix defines the policy review body's method for scoring each force, provides the basic data for each force and then calculates the current force score placing the forces into a league table:

Force score = Rank 1 × 0.25 + Rank 2 × 0.25 + Rank 3 × 0.25 + Rank 4 × 0.25

Where each rank is the ranking from 4 to 1 which each force gets for each of the following variables (4 is best, 1 is worst):

- Rank 1 is based on the number of crimes per 10,000 of population.
- Rank 2 is based on the solution rate for crimes reported in the year.
- Rank 3 is based on the user satisfaction score (based on a survey of the population).
- Rank 4 is based on the percentage of calls to police answered within ten seconds.

For example, a force which was top ranked in each of the ranks would get a force score of 4 (= 4 × 0.25 + 4 × 0.25 + 4 × 0.25 + 4 × 0.25).

Data by region:
For the calendar year 20X2

	C	*D*	*E*	*F*
Population	1,250,000	900,000	1,700,000	1,500,000
Number of crimes reported in year	62,500	47,250	83,300	63,000
Number of crimes solved in year	31,250	22,680	45,815	33,390
User satisfaction score	71%	80%	73%	68%
Percentage of calls to police answered within ten seconds	92%	93%	91%	94%
Number of police force employees	6,200	4,400	8,500	7,900
Cost of police force for year ($m)	404	298	572	510

Calculation of force score:

	C	*D*	*E*	*F*
Number of reported crimes per 10,000 of population	500	525	490	420
Rank 1	2	1	3	4
Solution rate for crimes reported in year	50%	48%	55%	53%
Rank 2	2	1	4	3
Rank 3 (user satisfaction)	2	4	3	1
Rank 4 (call handling)	2	3	1	4
Force score	2	2.25	2.75	3

BPP LEARNING MEDIA

The league table for 20X2 is:

	Force	*Score*
1.	F	3.00
2.	E	2.75
3.	D	2.25
4.	C	2.00

Note. You should assume that the calculations in Appendix 1 are accurate.

22 Beeshire Local Authority (12/14) 49 mins

Waste collection in Beeshire

Beeshire Local Authority (BLA) is a local government body which provides a range of services for the area of Beeshire within the country of Seeland. Beeshire is a wealthy area within the country with many tourist attractions. One of BLA's tasks is to ensure that waste is collected from the homes and businesses in Beeshire. The goal for BLA's Waste Management Department is 'to maintain Beeshire as a safe, clean and environmentally friendly place where people and businesses want to both stay in and return to'. The need for waste collection is linked to public health concerns, the desire to keep the streets clean and attractive and the desire to increase the amount of rubbish which is recycled. BLA is funded through a single local tax and does not charge its residents or businesses separately for most of its services, including waste collection. There is no public or political appetite for outsourcing services such as waste management.

Waste collection is performed by the workforce using a fleet of vehicles. The waste is either taken to recycling plants or else to landfill sites for burying. BLA obtains revenues from all the recycled waste but this only just covers the cost of running the recycling facilities.

Against a background estimate that waste will increase by 1% p.a. in the future, the national Government has ordered local authorities, such as BLA, to promote the recycling of waste and has set a target of 40% of all waste to be recycled by 2015. In order to discourage the creation of non-recyclable waste, the Government has imposed a levy per tonne of waste buried in landfill sites and has stated that this levy will rise over the next five years in order to encourage continuing improvement in the amount of recycled waste.

Performance measures

Currently, Seeland is in a long recession and so local authority revenues have fallen as tax revenues reflect the poor state of the economy. Along with other local authorities, BLA has tried to cut costs and so has focused on financial measures of performance. In a recent, private meeting, the Chief Executive of BLA was heard to say 'keep costs under control and we will worry about quality of service only when complaint levels build to an unacceptable level'. As one of the area's largest employers, cutting staff numbers has been very difficult for BLA due to the impact on the local economy and the reaction of the residents.

The current performance indicators used at BLA are drawn from the existing information systems with national figures given for comparison. Those relating to waste collection for the year ending 31 March 20X4 are:

			BLA	*National total*
Total cost	($m)		250	2,850
Volume of waste				
	landfilled	(tonnes)	1,250,000	13,750,000
	recycled	(tonnes)	950,000	9,500,000
	total	(tonnes)	2,200,000	23,250,000
No. of staff			3,500	39,900
Staff cost	($m)		110	1,190
No. of households			2,380,952	26,190,476
No. of complaints about waste uncollected			18,250	200,750

	BLA	*National average*
Frequency of waste collections (days)	14	12

Notes on BLA data

1 Cost data and number of households comes from BLA's financial systems.
2 Waste data comes from weighing lorries at the landfill sites and recycling facilities.
3 Staff data is collected from BLA's HR system.
4 Complaints data is based on numbers of letters and phone calls to the Waste Management Department.
5 Frequency of collection data is obtained from the department's vehicle schedules.

Required

(a) Explain why non-financial indicators are particularly useful for public sector organisations, illustrating your answer with brief examples relevant to BLA. **(6 marks)**

(b) Explain how the value for money provision of waste services by BLA should be assessed by suggesting and calculating justified performance indicators using the information in the scenario. **(12 marks)**

(c) Discuss the difficulties of measuring qualitative factors of performance, suggesting appropriate solutions for BLA. **(7 marks)**

(Total = 25 marks)

23 Teeland Universities (Mar/Jun 16) 49 mins

Objectives

Universities in Teeland have three stated objectives:

(1) To improve the overall standard of education of citizens in Teeland
(2) To engage in high quality academic research
(3) To produce well-qualified university graduates to meet the needs of the graduate jobs market in Teeland

Government funding

Each university is funded by a fixed sum of money from the Teeland Government according to the number of students studying there. In addition, universities receive extra funds from the Government and also from other organisations, such as large businesses and charities. These funds are used to support academic research.

Following the onset of an economic recession, the Teeland Government has stated its intention to reduce spending on publicly funded services such as the universities.

Proposal to introduce league tables

One senior politician, following his recent visit to neighbouring Veeland, was controversially quoted as saying:

'The universities in Veeland offer much better value for money for the citizens there compared to our universities here in Teeland. There are 25 students for each member of academic staff in Veeland, whereas in Teeland, the average number is 16, and yet, the standard of education of citizens is much higher in Veeland. The Veeland Government sets targets for many aspects of the services delivered by all the universities in Veeland. Furthermore, league tables of the performance of individual universities are published on the internet, and university leaders are given bonuses if their university falls within the top quarter of the league table. In Veeland, the system of performance measurement of the universities is considered so important that there is a special government department of 150 staff just to measure it.'

He went on to add, 'I want to see a similar system of league tables, targets and bonuses for university leaders being introduced here in Teeland. To appear near the top of the league tables, I think we should expect each university to increase the number of graduates entering graduate jobs by at least 5% each year. I would also like to see other steps taken to increase value for money, such as reducing the number of academic staff in each university and reducing the salary of newly recruited academic staff.'

You have been asked to advise the Teeland Government on the measurement of value for money of the universities and the proposed introduction of league tables for comparing their performance.

Appendix A contains details and existing performance data relating to four of the best known universities in Teeland.

Northcity University is famous for its high teaching standards and outstanding academic research in all subjects. As such, it attracts the most able students from all parts of the world to study there.

Southcity University is a large university in the capital city of Teeland and offers courses in a wide range of subjects, though most of the funding it receives for academic research is for science and technology, in which it is particularly successful.

Eastcity University is a small university specialising in the teaching of arts and humanities subjects such as history and geography.

Westcity University currently offers less strict entry standards to attract students from more diverse backgrounds, who may not normally have the opportunity of a university education.

Appendix A

Existing university performance data

	North	*South*	*East*	*West*
Number of students	17,600	30,400	5,200	11,200
Number of academic staff	1,750	2,400	485	625
Entry requirements[1]	100	77	72	48
Total annual payroll cost of academic staff	$109m	$149m	$20m	$37m
Graduate jobs filled each year[2]	4,180	6,555	1,154	1,750
Funds received for academic research	$491m	$474m	$26m	$14m
TSOR survey rating[3]	84%	76%	73%	90%
Position in league table[4]	1	11	14	21

Key to performance data

1 Entry requirements represent students' average attainment in examinations prior to entering university. The entry requirement of the highest ranking university is scored as 100, with the score of all other universities being in proportion to that score.

2 The number of graduates each year who go on to further study or who begin jobs normally undertaken by university graduates. In Teeland, students attend university for an average of 3.2 years.

3 The Teeland students overall satisfaction rating (TSOR) survey is undertaken by the Teeland Government to assess students' overall satisfaction with the standard of teaching, the social and support aspects of university life and their optimism for their own future job prospects.

4 The Education Department of the Teeland Government has produced a provisional league table ranking the overall performance of each of the 45 universities in Teeland, with 1 being the highest ranking university. This has been compiled using a number of performance measures, weighted according to what the Government believes are the most important of these measures.

Required

(a) Advise the Teeland Government how it could assess the value for money of the universities in Teeland, using the performance data in Appendix A. **(12 marks)**

(b) Assess the potential benefits of league tables for improving the performance of universities in Teeland and discuss the problems of implementing the proposal to introduce league tables. **(13 marks)**

(Total = 25 marks)

24 Herman Swan & Co (12/12, amended) 49 mins

Company and industry background

Herman Swan & Co (HS) is a family-owned company that has made fashionable clothes and leather goods for men for over 100 years. The company has been successful in building a strong reputation for quality by sourcing from local textile and leather producers. It sells its goods across the world through a chain of owned shops and also from franchised stalls inside large, well-known stores. The company is still owned and run by the family with no other shareholders. The main goal of the company is to organically grow the business for the next generation of the Swan family.

Customers are attracted to HS products due to the history and the family story that goes behind the products. Customers are willing to pay the high prices demanded as they identify with the values of the firm, especially the high quality of manufacturing.

The competition for HS has been increasing for more than ten years. It is made up of other global luxury brands and also the rising national champions in some of the rapidly expanding developing countries. The competitors often try to leverage their brands into many different product types. However, the Swan family have stated their desire to focus on the menswear market after an unsuccessful purchase of a handbag manufacturer five years ago.

The company is divided into a number of strategic business units (SBU). Each production site is an SBU, while the whole retail operation is one SBU. The head office previously functioned as a centre for procurement, finance and other support activities. The company has recently invested in a new management information system (MIS) that has increased the data available to all managers in the business. This has led to much of the procurement shifting to the production SBUs and the SBU managers taking more responsibility for budgeting. The SBU managers are delighted with their increased responsibilities and with the results from the new information system but feel there is still room for improvement in its use. The system has assisted in a project of flattening the organisation hierarchy by cutting out several layers of head office management.

Management accountant's role

You are the management accountant at HS and have been trying to persuade your boss, the Finance Director, that your role should change. You have read about Burns and Scapens' report 'Accounting Change Project' and think that it suggests an interesting change from your current roles of preparing and reviewing budgets and overseeing the production of management and financial accounts. Your boss is sceptical but is willing to listen to your arguments.

He has asked you to submit an explanation of the change that you propose and why it is necessary at HS.

Also, your boss has asked you for an example of how your role as an 'internal consultant' would be valuable at HS by looking at the ideas of brand loyalty and awareness. You should consider their impact on performance management at HS from both the customer and the internal business process perspectives and how to measure them.

Required

(a) With reference to HS, briefly explain the increasing importance of non-financial performance measures for organisations. **(5 marks)**

(b) Describe the changes in the role of the management accountant based on Burns and Scapens' work. Explain what is driving these changes and justify why they are appropriate to HS. **(12 marks)**

(c) Using HS as an example, discuss the impact of brand loyalty and awareness on the business from both the customer and the internal business process perspectives and evaluate suitable measures for brand loyalty and awareness. **(8 marks)**

(Total = 25 marks)

25 Navier Aerials (6/13) — 49 mins

Company background

Navier Aerials Co (Navier) manufactures satellite dishes for receiving satellite television signals. Navier supplies the major satellite TV companies which install standard satellite dishes for their customers. The company also manufactures and installs a small number of specialised satellite dishes to individuals or businesses with specific needs resulting from poor reception in their locations.

Cost reduction programme

The Chief Executive Officer (CEO) wants to initiate a programme of cost reduction at Navier. His plan is to use activity-based management (ABM) to allocate costs more accurately and to identify non value adding activities. The first department to be analysed is the Customer Care Department, as it has been believed for some time that the current method of cost allocation is giving unrealistic results for the two product types.

At present, the Finance Director (FD) absorbs the cost of customer care into the product cost on a per unit basis using the data in Table 1. He then tries to correct the problem of unrealistic costing, by making rough estimates of the costs to be allocated to each product based on the Operations Director's impression of the amount of work of the department. In fact, he simply adds $100 above the standard absorbed cost to the cost of a specialised dish to cover the assumed extra work involved at customer care.

BPP LEARNING MEDIA

The cost accountant has gathered information for the Customer Care Department in Table 2 from interviews with the finance and customer care staff. She has used this information to correctly calculate the total costs of each activity using activity-based costing in Table 3. The CEO wants you, as a senior management accountant, to complete the work required for a comparison of the results of the current standard absorption costing to activity-based costing for the standard and specialised dishes.

Once this is done, the CEO wants you to consider the implications for management of the customer care process of the costs of each activity in that department. The CEO is especially interested in how this information may impact on the identification of non value added activities and quality management at Navier.

Navier Dishes (information for the year ending 31 March 20X3)

Customer care (CC) Department

Table 1: Existing costing data

	$'000
Salaries	400
Computer time	165
Telephone	79
Stationery and sundries	27
Depreciation of equipment	36
	707

Note. CC cost is currently allocated to each dish based on 16,000 orders a year, where each order contains an average of 5.5 dishes.

Table 2: Activity-costing data

Activities of CC dept	Staff time	Comments
Handling enquiries and preparing quotes for potential orders	40%	Relates to 35,000 enquiries/quotes per year
Receiving actual orders	10%	Relates to 16,000 orders in the year
Customer credit checks	10%	Done once an order is received
Supervision of orders through manufacture to delivery	15%	
Complaints handling	25%	Relates to 3,200 complaints per year

Notes

1 Total department cost is allocated using staff time as this drives all of the other costs in the department.

2 90% of both enquiries and orders are for standard dishes. The remainder are for specialised dishes.

3 Handling enquiries and preparing quotes for specialised dishes takes 20% of staff time allocated to this activity.

4 The process for receiving an order, checking customer credit and supervision of the order is the same for both a specialised dish order and a standard dish order.

5 50% of the complaints received are for specialised dish orders.

6 Each standard dish order contains an average of six dishes.

7 Each specialised dish order contains an average of one dish.

Table 3: Activity-based costs

	Total $	*Standard* $	*Specialised* $
Handling enquiries and preparing quotes	282,800	226,240	56,560
Receiving actual orders	70,700	63,630	7,070
Customer credit checks	70,700	63,630	7,070
Supervision of order through manufacture to delivery	106,050	95,445	10,605
Complaints handling	176,750	88,375	88,375
Total	707,000	537,320	169,680

Required

(a) Evaluate the impact of using activity-based costing, compared to the existing costing system for customer care, on the cost of both types of product. **(13 marks)**

(b) Assess how the information on each activity can be used and improved upon at Navier in assisting cost reduction and quality management in the Customer Care Department.

Note. There is no need to make comments on the different product types here. **(12 marks)**

(Total = 25 marks)

26 Tench (12/11, amended) 49 mins

Company and industry background

Tench Cars (Tench) is a large national car manufacturing business. It is based in Essland, a country that has recently turned from state communism to democratic capitalism. The car industry had been heavily supported and controlled by the bureaucracy of the old regime. The Government had stipulated production and employment targets for the business but had ignored profit as a performance measure. Tench is now run by a new generation of capitalist businesspeople intent on rejuvenating the company's fortunes.

The company has a strong position within Essland, which has a population of 200 million and forms the majority of Tench's market. However, the company has also traditionally achieved a good market share in six neighbouring countries due to historic links and shared culture between them and Essland. All of these markets are experiencing growing car ownership as political and market reforms lead to greater wealth in a large proportion of the population. Additionally, the new Government in Essland is deregulating markets and opening the country to imports of foreign vehicles.

Current plans

Tench's management recognises that it needs to make fundamental changes to its production approach in order to combat increased competition from foreign manufacturers. Tench's cars are now being seen as ugly and pollutive and having poor safety features in comparison to the foreign competition. Management plans to address this by improving the quality of its cars through the use of quality management techniques. It plans to improve financial performance through the use of Kaizen costing and just-in-time purchasing and production. Tench's existing performance reporting system uses standard costing and budgetary variance analysis in order to monitor and control production activities.

The Chief Financial Officer (CFO) of Tench has commented that he is confused by the terminology associated with quality management and needs a clearer understanding of the different costs associated with quality management. The CFO also wants to know the impact of including quality costs and using the Kaizen costing approach on the traditional standard costing approach at Tench.

Required

In response to the CFO's comments:

(a) Discuss the impact of the collection and use of quality costs on the current costing systems at Tench. **(6 marks)**

(b) Discuss and evaluate the impact of the Kaizen costing approach on the costing systems and employee management at Tench. **(8 marks)**

(c) Briefly evaluate the effect of moving to just-in-time purchasing and production, noting the impact on performance measures at Tench. **(6 marks)**

(d) Explain why the adoption of total quality management (TQM) is particularly important within a just-in-time (JIT) production environment. **(5 marks)**

(Total = 25 marks)

BPP LEARNING MEDIA

27 Pitlane (Mar/Jun 17) **49 mins**

Company background

Pitlane Electronic Components (Pitlane) manufactures components for use in the electricity distribution network in Deeland. Demand from Pitlane's biggest customer, to replace identical but worn out components, has been constant for many years. Pitlane has recently renewed an exclusive long-term supply agreement with this customer, who has always agreed to buy the components for their total standard cost plus a fixed profit margin of 15%. Variances between standard and actual costs of the components are negligible. Pitlane runs several production lines in two factories located in different areas of Deeland. The factories' layout is poorly designed and the production process requires components to be transported around and between the factories.

Government incentives

The Deeland Government wants to encourage renewable electricity generation. It is offering a three-year subsidy scheme, beginning in 20X8, for consumers to have solar panels installed on the roofs of their homes. As an added incentive, businesses will be exempt from tax on profits made on the sale of solar panels and related components.

New product development

To take advantage of this scheme, Pitlane has built a prototype of a new electrical component, known as the 'Booster', which increases the output from domestic solar panels. The Booster will be sold to installers of solar panels and not directly to consumers. Pitlane's marketing department has estimated market data for the duration of the scheme based on a similar scheme in Veeland (Appendix 1). As a result of its products being unchanged for many years, Pitlane has little recent experience of developing new products and estimating costs and potential revenues from them. It is expected that many competitor products will be launched during the scheme, at the end of which demand is expected to fall greatly, and production of the Booster will discontinue.

Pitlane's shareholders insist that for the Booster project to go ahead, it must meet the financial performance objective of achieving a 15% net profit margin, after all costs, for the duration of the scheme.

The Booster's total fixed costs during the scheme are estimated to be $10m, including $2.8m upfront development costs to enable the Booster to communicate the amount of solar energy generated directly to consumers' smartphones via an app. The product development team at Pitlane believes this feature, and the use of highest quality packaging, will allow it to charge 10% more that the average price of its competitors. The marketing team, however, has questioned the overall value of these two features and whether customers would be prepared to pay extra for them, as most of the Deeland population do not yet own smartphones.

Pitlane has estimated the direct costs for the Booster (Appendix 2). The largest direct cost is for the four main sub-components. These are bought in bulk from six different suppliers in Deeland, though all are readily available from suppliers worldwide. The sub-components are fragile. During production of the Booster prototype, many sub-components were found to be damaged during the production process by workers incorrectly assembling them. This resulted in the completed prototype Boosters being scrapped after testing by the Quality Control Department. The Manufacturing Director is concerned that the incorrect assembly of sub-components by workers may mean that it may not be profitable for Pitlane to start full scale production of Boosters. To counteract these quality problems, Pitlane will employ more highly skilled workers, who are paid around 30% more than most other workers in the business which is accounted for in the cost estimate given in Appendix 2. Pitlane staff have never been encouraged to suggest any ways to improve the manufacturing process.

Pitlane's directors are concerned that the Booster project will not meet the shareholders' financial performance objective. They have asked you, as a consultant experienced in target costing, Kaizen costing and other Japanese business practices, for your advice.

Required

(a) Calculate the cost gap per unit in each of the three years of the Booster's life, taking into account all estimated costs. **(6 marks)**

(b) Advise on the extent to which target costing would help Pitlane to achieve the financial performance objective set by the shareholders. **(12 marks)**

(c) Advise Pitland how Kaizen costing may be used to help the Booster project achieve the financial performance objective set by the shareholders. **(7 marks)**

(Total = 25 marks)

Appendix 1 – Estimated market data for Booster

	20X8	*20X9*	*20Y0*
Total market size (units)	600,000	500,000	460,000
Average price of competitors products ($/unit)	180	170	160
Booster market share of total market	10%	15%	20%

Appendix 2 – Estimated unit direct cost of Booster

	$
Sub-components	94
Assembly labour	21
Packaging	10
Distribution	2
Internal transport and handling	7
Total	134

28 Thebe (6/12, amended) 49 mins

Company background

Thebe Telecom (Thebe) is a large national telephone business in Fayland. Thebe provides telephone services to more than 11 million customers through its fixed line and mobile services. Thebe has three strategic business units: mobile; fixed line telephone (incorporating broadband); and corporate services (serving other businesses' telephone needs). It has become the largest mobile operator in Fayland through a series of acquisitions of competitors and operating licences.

Thebe's Chief Executive Officer (CEO) has won many awards for being an innovative businessman who recognises the rapid changes in technology, regulation and competitor action that occur in the sector. Thebe's major competitor in Fayland is the original nationalised telephone company, FayTel, which was privatised 20 years ago but which retains many of the features of a monopoly supplier including a massive infrastructure. As a result, Thebe's CEO realised long ago that competition on the basis of price and volume would not work against such a large competitor and so he has focused on customer service as the key to growing the business.

Improving service quality

In order to improve the company's competitive position, the CEO decided that the company should consider a Six Sigma initiative to give an immediate step change improvement to the service quality at Thebe. The initiative involved a number of projects, including one to improve the quality of customers' bills. FayTel was publicly criticised by the Government's consumer advocate who pointed to occasional misallocations of call minutes to the wrong numbers and also, more frequently, the application of incorrect tariffs in calculating the costs of calls. Thebe's CEO is aware that all telephone businesses (including Thebe) have these problems but this is an area in which Thebe can gain a competitive advantage and has taken a special interest in this project by championing it himself.

The project is focused on improving the accuracy of customers' bills and the handling of complaints. Within the Billing Department, the company divided activities into normal money collection, credit control on overdue payments and managing complaints. Process diagrams were created for each of these areas and then data was sourced from customer feedback at the various points of interaction with Thebe employees (such as complaint handling) and internal measurables created. The project team was formed from line managers from all three strategic business units and the Billing Department.

The CEO's involvement in the projects to improve service quality at Thebe made him realise that the performance summary prepared for the monthly board papers does not include any non-financial aspects of performance, and Thebe's key performance indicators also focus solely on financial performance.

Required

(a) Evaluate the benefits of Thebe's board monitoring non-financial aspects of performance as well as financial ones. **(8 marks)**

(b) Explain how the general way in which Six Sigma is implemented helps improve the quality of performance, illustrating your answer with reference to Thebe. **(8 marks)**

BPP LEARNING MEDIA

(c) Explain and illustrate how the DMAIC method for the implementation of Six Sigma could be applied at Thebe. **(9 marks)**

(Total = 25 marks)

29 Posie (Sep/Dec 15) 49 mins

Company background and structure

Posie is a large business which manufactures furniture. It is made up of two autonomous divisions in Deeland.

The Manufacturing Division purchases raw materials from external suppliers, and performs all manufacturing and packaging operations. All sales are made through the Retail Division which has 95 retail stores in Deeland, as well as through Posie's own well-developed website. Posie has retail operations in eight other countries as well as in Deeland. These overseas businesses operate as independent subsidiaries within the Retail Division, each with their own IT and accounting functions.

The furniture is sold in boxes for customers to assemble themselves. About 10% of the products sold by Posie are purchased already packaged from other manufacturers. All deliveries are outsourced through a third-party distribution company.

Customer returns and complaints

Posie's corporate objective is to maximise shareholder wealth by producing 'attractive, functional furniture at low prices'. This is how customers generally perceive the Posie brand. The Chief Executive Officer (CEO) of Posie is concerned about increasing levels of returns made by customers and increasing numbers of consumers complaining on online forums about products purchased from Posie.

Concerned about the impact on the Posie brand and the cost-leadership strategy, the CEO has asked you, as a performance management expert, to help Posie implement the Six Sigma technique to reduce the number of products returned and in particular to define customers' requirements and measure Posie's existing performance. The Production Director has been appointed to sponsor the project and you will be supported by a small team of managers who have recently received training in Six Sigma. The board member responsible for manufacturing quality recently resigned because she thought it was unfair that the Manufacturing Division was being held responsible for the increased level of customer returns.

You have been given access to some information concerning the reasons why customers return goods to help you measure existing performance in this area (Appendix 1). This is an extract from the management reporting pack presented to the board at their monthly meetings. The returns data, however, are only compiled every six months due to the lengthy analysis required of data from Posie's overseas retail operations. It is included twice a year in the board report along with the key performance indicators (KPIs) for customer satisfaction. The last time this information was produced 93% of customers indicated they were satisfied with the quality of the manufacture of Posie's products.

Information requirements

The CEO has heard that Six Sigma requires 'large amounts of facts and data'. He suggested that the returns data contain insufficient detail and that as part of your project you may need to do more analysis; for example, on why customers are not satisfied with the manufacturing quality.

He also added, 'I'm not sure that our current IT systems are capable of generating the data we need to identify which responsibility centres within the Manufacturing Division are the root causes of the problem of customer returns. We are planning to change the designation of the overseas retail businesses from profit centres to revenue centres, but again we need to know first how this will affect the information requirements of the business and any potential problems with doing so.'

Appendix 1

Reasons given by customers for returning goods

Category	*Reason for return of goods*	*% responses*
1	Difficult to assemble or pieces missing	48
2	Goods arrived damaged	14
3	Goods were not as described or were defective	25
4	Goods were of poor quality or no longer wanted	11
5	Arrived late	2
Total		100

Required

(a) Advise the board how the Six Sigma project at Posie to reduce returns from customers could be implemented using DMAIC methodology. **(15 marks)**

(b) Evaluate the impact on Posie's information requirements arising from:

(i) The need to identify and improve on the level of customer returns **(6 marks)**

(ii) The proposed re-designation of the overseas subsidiaries from profit centres to revenue centres **(4 marks)**

(Total = 25 marks)

30 Albacore (2013 Pilot Paper) 49 mins

Company background

Albacore Chess Stores (Albacore) is a chain of 12 shops specialising in selling items associated with the game of chess: boards, pieces, clocks, software and books. Three years ago, the company was the subject of a venture capital buyout from a larger group. A new senior management team was put in place after the buyout. They have the aim of running the business in order to maximise profits.

Budgeting process

The Chief Financial Officer (CFO), along with the other members of senior management, sets the annual budget and uses a standard costing approach with variance analysis in order to control individual shop performance. The head office handles all capital purchases and brand marketing. All inventory purchasing is done centrally and the shop opening times are set as standard across the company. As an illustration of senior management attitude, the CFO had set the budget for staff costs for 20X1 at $7 per hour for part-time staff, and this was rigorously observed in the period.

Each shop is run by a manager who reports their financial results to head office. The shop managers recruit and manage the staffing of their shop. They have some autonomy in setting prices locally and have been given authority to vary prices by up to 10% from a master list produced by the CFO. They also have a local marketing budget agreed each year by the shop's manager and the Marketing Director as part of the annual appraisal process.

Performance appraisal and reward systems

The shop managers have approached the Chairman of Albacore to complain about the way that they are managed and their remuneration. They feel that their efforts are unrecognised by senior management. One manager commented, 'I have had a successful year in hard economic circumstances. I have run a number of promotions in the shop that have been well received by the customers. However, the budgets that are set are impossible to achieve and as a result I have not been paid any bonus although I feel that I have done everything in my power to bring in good profits.'

The shop managers at Albacore are paid a basic salary of $27,000 with bonuses of up to 30% of basic salary dependent on two factors: performance above budget and the Operational Director's performance assessment. The budget for the next year is prepared by the CFO and presented at the shop manager's annual appraisal.

The Chairman has come to you to ask if you can consider the system of performance assessment for the shop managers and give an independent perspective on the reward systems at Albacore. She has heard of variance analysis but is unsure about what would be relevant in this situation. She has provided the following illustrative information from the previous year for one shop:

ALBACORE CHESS STORES

TUNNY BRANCH YEAR TO SEPTEMBER 20X1

		Budget	*Actual*	*Variance*
		$	$	$
Sales		266,000	237,100	–28,900
Cost of sales		106,400	94,840	11,560
Gross profit		159,600	142,260	–17,340
Marketing		12,000	11,500	500
Staff costs:	manager	27,000	27,000	0
	part-time staff	38,000	34,000	4,000
Property costs		26,600	26,600	0
Shop profit		56,000	43,160	–12,840

Notes

1 Property costs includes heating, lighting and rental.
2 Positive variances are favourable.

The manager of this shop commented at the appraisal meeting that she felt that the assessment was unfair since her failure to make budget was due to general economic conditions. The industry as a whole saw a 12% fall in revenues during the period and the budget for the period was set to be the same as the previous period. She was not paid a bonus for the period.

Required

(a) Evaluate the suitability of the existing branch information given as a means of assessing the shop manager's performance and draft an improved branch report with justifications for changes. **(13 marks)**

(b) Analyse the performance management style and evaluate the performance appraisal system at Albacore. Suggest suitable improvements to its reward system for the shop managers. **(12 marks)**

(Total = 25 marks)

31 Cuthbert (Mar/Jun 16) 49 mins

Company background

Cuthbert is based in Ceeland and manufactures jackets for use in very cold environments by mountaineers and skiers. It also supplies the armed forces in several countries with variants of existing products, customised by the use of different coloured fabrics, labels and special fastenings for carrying equipment. Cuthbert incurs high costs on design and advertising in order to maintain the reputation of the brand.

Each jacket is made up of different shaped pieces of fabric called 'components'. These components are purchased by Cuthbert from an external supplier. The external supplier is responsible for ensuring the quality of the components and the number of purchased components found to be defective is negligible. The cost of the components forms 80% of the direct cost of each jacket, and the prices charged by Cuthbert's supplier for the components are the lowest in the industry.

Production process

There are three stages to the production process of each jacket, which are each located in different parts of the factory:

Stage 1 – Sewing

The fabric components are sewn together by a machinist. Any manufacturing defects occurring after sewing has begun cannot be rectified, and finished garments found to be defective are heavily discounted or, in the case of bespoke variants, destroyed.

Stage 2 – Assembly

The garments are filled with insulating material and sewn together for the final time.

Stage 3 – Finishing

Labels, fastenings and zips are sewn to the finished garments. Though the process for attaching each of these is similar, machinists prefer to work only on labels, fastenings or zips to maximise the quantity which they can sew each hour.

Jackets are produced in batches of a particular style in a range of sizes. Throughout production, the components required for each batch of jackets are accompanied by a paper batch card which records the production processes which each batch has undergone. The batch cards are input into a production spreadsheet so that the stage of completion of each batch can be monitored and the position of each batch in the factory is recorded.

There are 60 machinists working in the Sewing Department, and 40 in each of the Assembly and Finishing Departments. All the machinists are managed by 10 supervisors whose duties include updating the batch cards for work done and inputting this into a spreadsheet, as well as checking the quality of work done by machinists. The supervisors report to the factory manager, who has overall responsibility for the production process.

Machinists are paid an hourly wage and a bonus according to how many items they sew each week, which usually comprises 60% of their total weekly wages.

Supervisors receive an hourly wage and a bonus according to how many items their team sews each week. The Factory Manager receives the same monthly salary regardless of production output. All employees are awarded a 5% annual bonus if Cuthbert achieves its budgeted net profit for the year.

Recent problems and issues

Recently, a large emergency order of jackets for the Ceeland army was cancelled by the customer as it was not delivered on time due to the following quality problems and other issues in the production process:

- A supervisor had forgotten to input several batch cards and as a result batches of fabric components were lost in the factory and replacements had to be purchased.
- There were machinists available to sew buttons onto the jackets, but there was only one machinist available who had been trained to sew zips. This caused further delay to production of the batch.
- When the quality of the jackets was checked prior to despatch, many of them were found to be sewn incorrectly as the work had been rushed. By this time the agreed delivery date had already passed, and it was too late to produce a replacement batch.

This was the latest in a series of problems in production at Cuthbert, and the directors have decided to use business process re-engineering (BPR) in order to radically change the production process.

BPR and changes to the production process

The proposal being considered as an application of BPR is the adoption of 'team working' in the factory, the three main elements of which are as follows:

(1) Production lines would reorganise into teams, where all operations on a particular product type are performed in one place by a dedicated team of machinists.

(2) Each team of machinists would be responsible for the quality of the finished jacket and, for the first time, machinists would be encouraged to bring about improvements in the production process. There would no longer be the need to employ supervisors and the existing supervisors would join the teams of machinists.

(3) The number of batches in production would be automatically tracked by the use of radio frequency identification (RFID) tags attached to each jacket. This would eliminate the need for paper batch cards, which are currently input into a spreadsheet by the supervisors.

You have been asked as a performance management consultant to advise the board on whether BPR could help Cuthbert overcome the problems in its production process.

Required

(a) Advise how the proposed use of BPR would influence the operational performance of Cuthbert. **(14 marks)**

(b) Evaluate the effectiveness of the current reward systems at Cuthbert, and recommend and justify how these systems would need to change if the BPR project goes ahead. **(11 marks)**

(Total = 25 marks)

32 ENT Entertainments (6/11, amended) **49 mins**

Company background and objectives

ENT Entertainment Co (ENT) is a large, diversified entertainment business based in Teeland. The company's objective is the maximisation of shareholder wealth for its family owners. It has four divisions:

(1) Restaurants
(2) Cafés
(3) Bars
(4) Dance clubs

Recently, ENT's board has identified that there are problems in managing such a diversified company. They have employed consultants who have recommended that they should perform a Boston Consulting Group (BCG) analysis to understand whether they have the right mix of businesses. The Chief Executive Officer (CEO) has questioned whether using this analysis is helpful in managing the group's performance.

Revenue information for each division

A business analyst has prepared information on each division in the table below.

Revenue	*Actual 20X0* $m	*Actual 20X1* $m	*Forecast 20X2* $m	*Forecast 20X3* $m
Restaurants				
ENT	54	56	59	62
Market sector	10,752	10,860	10,968	10,968
Cafés				
ENT	31	34	41	47
Market sector	3,072	3,348	3,717	4,051
Bars				
ENT	349	342	336	336
Market sector	9,984	9,784	9,491	9,206
Dance clubs				
ENT	197	209	219	241
Market sector	1,792	1,900	2,013	2,195

Economic context

In Teeland, the economy is generally growing at about 2% per annum. The restaurant, café and bar sectors are all highly fragmented with many small operators. Consequently, a market share of more than 3.0% is considered large as that is comparable to the share of the largest operators in each sector. There are fewer small late night dance club operators and the market leader currently holds a 15.0% market share. There have not been many new developments within the divisions except for a new wine bar format launched by the Bars Division which has surprised the board by its success.

Divisional performance

Each division's performance is measured by economic value added (EVA™). The divisional managers have a remuneration package that is made up in two equal parts by a salary set according to industry norms and a bonus element which is based on achieving the cost budget numbers set by the company board. The Chairman of the board has been examining the consistency of the overall objective of the business, the divisional performance measure and the remuneration packages at divisional level. He has expressed the worry that these are not properly aligned and that this might lead to dysfunctional behaviour by the divisional management.

Required

(a) Perform a BCG analysis of ENT's business and use this to evaluate the company's performance. **(7 marks)**

(b) Critically evaluate this BCG analysis as a performance management system at ENT. **(7 marks)**

(c) (i) Evaluate the divisional managers' remuneration packages in the light of the divisional performance systems and your BCG analysis. **(6 marks)**

(ii) Explain the implications of the BCG analysis and divisional performance systems on the management styles which might be appropriate at ENT. **(5 marks)**

(Total = 25 marks)

33 Beach Foods (6/15) 49 mins

Company background and structure

Beach Foods (Beach) is a family-owned business which has grown strongly over its 100-year history. The objective of the business is to maximise the family's wealth through their shareholdings. Beach has three divisions. It manufactures a variety of foods in two of the divisions: Beach Baby Foods (Baby) and Beach Chocolate Foods (Chocolate). Each of these divisions knows its own market and sets prices accordingly. The third division (R&D) researches new products on the instructions of the other divisions and is considered to be vital to the survival and growth of Beach. The board of Beach has been considering the impact of using a divisional structure and has come to you as a performance management consultant to ask for your advice.

Divisional performance measures

There is disagreement at board level about the correct choice of divisional performance measure to be used in the two manufacturing divisions. Currently, the business uses EVA™ but two directors have been questioning its value, complaining that it is complicated to understand. These directors have been promoting the use of either residual income (RI) or return on investment (ROI) as alternatives. The board wants to use the same measure for each division. As well as qualitatively evaluating these different measures, the board needs an assessment of the impact of a change in performance measure on their perception of these divisions' performance. Therefore, as an example, they require you to calculate and discuss the use of ROI and RI at Baby Division, given the data in Appendix 1.

Divisional control and management style

The Chief Executive Officer (CEO) of Beach has engaged a business analyst to perform a study of the portfolio of manufacturing businesses which make up Beach. This has been completed in Appendix 2. The CEO wants your comments (based on the categorisation given in Appendix 2) on how this work will impact on the performance management of the divisions. Specifically, the CEO has asked for your recommendations on how to control each division; that is, whether each division should be treated as a cost/profit/investment centre and also the appropriate management style to use for handling staff in each division. The CEO commented to you:

'I have heard of different approaches to the use of budget information in assessing performance: budget-constrained, profit-conscious and also a non-accounting style. I need to know how these approaches might apply to each division given your other comments.'

Managers' concerns

All of this work has been partly prompted by complaints from the divisional managers. The Chocolate divisional managers complain that they had to wait for a year to get approval to upgrade their main production line. This production line upgrade has reduced wastage and boosted Chocolate's profit margin by 10 percentage points. The Baby Division has been very successful in using the ideas of the Research and Development (R&D) Division, although Baby's managers do complain about the recharging of R&D costs to their division. Head office managers are worried about Chocolate as it has seemed to be drifting recently with a lack of strategic direction. Chocolate's managers are considered to be good but possibly not sufficiently focused on what benefits Beach as a whole.

Required

(a) Assess the use of EVA™ as a divisional performance measure for the manufacturing divisions at Beach. **(8 marks)**

(b) Using Appendix 1, calculate the ROI and RI for Baby and assess the impact of the assumptions made when calculating these metrics on the evaluation of the performance of this division and its management. **(7 marks)**

(c) Provide justified recommendations for each division's control and management style as requested by the CEO. **(10 marks)**

(Total = 25 marks)

BPP LEARNING MEDIA

Appendix 1

Figures from Beach management accounts for year ended 31 March:

Baby Division	*20X5*
	$m
Revenue	220
Costs	
Divisional operating costs	121
R&D costs recharged	11
Allocated head office management fees	28
Profit before tax	60
Capital employed	424

Notes

1 Baby launched a new product with a large publicity campaign during the year.

2 The notional cost of capital for Baby is estimated by the Chief Financial Officer at 11%. Weighted average cost of capital (WACC) for Beach is 7.5%.

3 ROI for similar entities is 20%.

4 EVA™ for Baby is calculated as $35m.

Appendix 2

Star Baby: Market growth 18% Relative market share 105%	**Problem child**
Cash cow Chocolate: Market growth 3% Relative market share 120%	**Dog**

Relative market share is the market share of the division compared to that of the market leader. If an organisation is a market leader, then its market share is compared to the next largest competitor.

Note. You may assume that the calculations and this categorisation are accurate.

PERFORMANCE EVALUATION AND CORPORATE FAILURE

Questions 34 to 48 cover performance evaluation and corporate failure, the subject of Part E of the BPP Study Text for APM.

34 Pharmaceutical Technologies (2013 Pilot Paper) 49 mins

Company background

Pharmaceutical Technologies Co (PT) is a developer and manufacturer of medical drugs in Beeland. It is one of the 100 largest listed companies on the national stock exchange. The company focuses on buying prospective drugs (which have shown initial promise in testing) from small bio-engineering companies. PT then leads these drugs through three regulatory stages to launch in the general medical market.

The three stages are:

(1) To confirm the safety of the drug (does it harm humans?), in small-scale trials;
(2) To test the efficacy of the product (does it help cure?), again in small-scale trials; and
(3) Finally, large-scale trials to definitively decide on the safety and efficacy of the product.

The drugs are then marketed through the company's large sales force to healthcare providers and end users (patients). The healthcare providers are paid by either health insurance companies or the national Government dependent on the financial status of the patient.

Industry regulator

The Beeland Drug Regulator (BDR) oversees this testing process and makes the final judgement about whether a product can be sold in the country.

Its objectives are to protect, promote and improve public health by ensuring that:

- Medicines have an acceptable balance of benefit and risk;
- The users of these medicines understand this risk-benefit profile; and
- New beneficial product development is encouraged.

The regulator is governed by a board of trustees appointed by the Government. It is funded directly by the government and also through fees charged to drug companies when granting licences to sell their products in Beeland.

Balanced scorecard

PT has used share price and earnings per share as its principal measures of performance to date. However, the share price has underperformed the market, and the health sector, in the last two years. The Chief Executive Officer (CEO) has identified that these measures are too narrow and is considering implementing a balanced scorecard approach to address this problem.

A working group has drawn up a suggested balanced scorecard. It began by identifying the objectives from the board's medium-term strategy:

- Create shareholder value by bringing commercially viable drugs to market.
- Improve the efficiency of drug development.
- Increase shareholder value by innovation in the drug approval process.

The working group then considered the stakeholder perspectives:

- Shareholders want a competitive return on their investment.
- Payers/purchasers (governments, insurers and patients) want to pay a reasonable price for the drugs.
- Regulators want an efficient process for the validation of drugs.
- Doctors want safe and effective drug products.
- Patients want to be cured.

Finally, this leads to the proposed scorecard of performance measures:

- Financial – share price and earnings per share
- Customer – number of patients using PT products

- Internal business process – exceed industry standard on design and testing; time to regulatory approval of a product
- Learning and growth – training days undertaken by staff; time to market of new product; percentage of drugs bought by PT that gain final approval

The balanced scorecard now needs to be reviewed to ensure that it will address the company's objectives and the issues that it faces in its business environment.

Required

(a) Evaluate the performance measures proposed for PT's balanced scorecard. **(10 marks)**

(b) Briefly describe a method of analysing stakeholder influence and analyse the influence of four different external stakeholders on the regulator (BDR). **(8 marks)**

(c) Using your answer from part (b), describe how the application of the balanced scorecard approach at BDR would differ from the approach within PT. **(7 marks)**

(Total = 25 marks)

35 Victoria-Yeeland Logistics (6/15) 49 mins

Company background and objectives

Victoria-Yeeland Logistics (Victoria) is a logistics support business, which operates a fleet of lorries to deliver packages of goods on behalf of its customers within the country of Yeeland. Victoria collects packages from its customers' manufacturing sites or from the customers' port of importation and delivers to the final user of the goods. The lorries are run and maintained from a set of depots spread throughout Yeeland.

The overall objective of Victoria is to maximise shareholder wealth. The delivery business in Yeeland is dominated by two international companies and one other domestic business and profit margins are extremely tight. The market is saturated by these large operators and a number of smaller operators. The cost base of Victoria is dominated by staff and fuel, with fuel prices being highly volatile in the last few years.

Balanced scorecard

In order to improve performance measurement and management at Victoria, the Chief Financial Officer (CFO) plans to use the balanced scorecard (BSC). However, she has been pulled away from this project in order to deal with an issue with refinancing the business's principal lending facility. The CFO has already identified some suitable metrics but needs you, as her assistant, to complete her work and address any potential questions which might arise when she makes her presentation on the BSC to the board. The CFO has completed the identification of metrics for three of the perspectives (Appendix 1) but has yet to complete the work on the metrics for the customer perspective. This should be done using the data given in Appendix 2.

Reward management issues

Additionally, two issues have arisen in the reward management system at Victoria, one in relation to senior management and the other for operational managers. Currently, senior management gets a fixed salary supplemented by an annual bonus awarded by the board. Shareholders have been complaining that these bonuses are not suitable. The operational managers also get bonuses based on their performance as assessed by their management superiors. The operational managers are unhappy with the system. In order to address this, it has been suggested that they should be involved in bonus target setting as otherwise there is a sense of demotivation from such a system. The CFO wants an evaluation of this system of rewards in light of the introduction of the BSC and best practice.

Required

(a) Discuss how Victoria's success in the customer perspective may impact on the metrics given in the financial perspective. **(5 marks)**

(b) Recommend, with justification, and calculate a suitable performance metric for each customer perspective success factor. Comment on the problems of using customer complaints to measure whether packages are delivered safely and on time. **(11 marks)**

(c) Advise Victoria on the reward management issues outlined by the CFO. **(9 marks)**

(Total = 25 marks)

Appendix 1

Financial perspective

(How do we appear to our shareholders?)
Return on capital employed
Profit margin
Revenue growth

Customer perspective

(How do we appear to our customers?)
Success factors:
Ability to meet customers' transport needs
Ability to deliver packages quickly
Ability to deliver packages on time
Ability to deliver packages safely

Internal process perspective

(What business processes must excel?)
Time taken to load and unload
Lorry capacity utilisation

Learning and growth perspective

(How do we sustain and improve our ability to grow?)
Leadership competence (qualitative judgement)
Training days per employee

Appendix 2

The process: A customer makes a transport request for a package to be collected and delivered to a given destination. The customer is supplied with a time window in which the delivery will occur. Packages are then loaded onto lorries and delivered according to a route specified by the depot's routing manager.

Total number of customer transport requests	610,000
Total number of packages transported	548,000
Total number of lorry journeys	73,000
Total package kilometres	65,760,000
Total package minutes	131,520,000
Number of delivery complaints from customers:	
from damaged packages	8,220
from late delivery (outside agreed time window)	21,920

Notes

1 All figures are for the last financial year.
2 A package kilometre is defined as a kilometre travelled by one package.
3 A package minute is defined as a minute spent in transit by one package.

36 Soup (Sep/Dec 15) — 49 mins

Company background

Soup operates passenger rail services in Deeland, a technologically advanced country, with high demand for fast, reliable rail travel from business and leisure passengers. Many passengers choose train travel because they see it as less harmful to the environment than other forms of transport.

Operating license and government warning

Soup's main objective is to maximise shareholder wealth. Since becoming licensed to operate routes in Regions A and B by the Deeland Government five years ago, Soup has consistently delivered increased dividends and share prices for investors. In its initial appraisal of the licensing opportunity, Soup expected to operate the routes for at least 15 years; however, its licence may not be renewed when it expires in 3 years' time. The Government has

BPP LEARNING MEDIA

warned Soup it 'is unhappy about high returns to shareholders while there are many reports of poor passenger service, overcrowded trains and unreliable services on certain routes and at busy times'.

Soup owns its fleet of diesel powered trains. Each train in Region A has 7 coaches with 70 passenger seats available per coach. In the less busy Region B, each train has 6 coaches, each with 70 seats. As a condition of the licence, Soup runs a set number of services at both busy and quieter times in both regions. Soup has two larger rivals, both operating electric trains, which cause less harm to the environment than diesel powered trains. They run on the same routes in both regions.

The Government regulates fares charged to passengers, which are the same per distance travelled for every operator in that region. The railway track, stations and other infrastructure are managed by the Government which charges the operators a fee. There are several stations along the route which are only used by Soup trains and others where Soup trains do not stop at all.

Soup's trains are 25 years old, originally purchased cheaply from an operator whose licence was withdrawn by the Government. Soup believes the low price it paid is a key competitive advantage enabling it to steadily increase its return on capital employed, the company's main performance measure, to a level well in excess of its rivals. The shareholders are pleased with the growth in passenger numbers over the last five years, which is the other performance measure Soup uses.

Soup's ageing trains spend increasing time undergoing preventative maintenance, safety checks or repairs. A recent television documentary also showed apparently poor conditions on board, such as defective heating and washroom facilities and dirty, torn seating. Passengers complained in the programme of difficulties finding a seat, the unreliability of accessing wireless internet services and even that the menu in the on-board café had not changed for five years.

Soup's Chief Executive Officer (CEO) responded that unreliable internet access arose from the rapid growth in passengers expecting to access the internet on trains. She said Soup had never received any formal complaints about the lack of choice in the on-board café, nor had she heard of a recent press report that Soup's trains were badly maintained, so causing harm to the environment.

Performance measures

The CEO has asked you, as Chief Management Accountant, for your advice. 'In view of the Government's warning, we must develop performance measures balancing the needs of passengers with the requirements of the shareholders,' she has said. 'I don't want to know how to improve the actual performance of the business – that is the job of the operational managers – nor do I just want a list of suggested performance measures. Instead I need to know why these performance measures will help to improve the performance of Soup.'

The following data applies to Soup:

	Region A	*Region B*
Number of services per day		
Peak times	4	4
Other times	6	8
Number of passengers per day		
Peak times	2,500	1,400
Other times	2,450	1,850

Required

(a) Advise the CEO on how the use of the balanced scorecard could improve the performance management system of Soup. **(10 marks)**

(b) Using the performance data given, evaluate the comments of the Deeland Government that Soup's trains are overcrowded. **(7 marks)**

(c) Assess the problems Soup may encounter in selecting and interpreting performance measures when applying the balanced scorecard to its performance management system. **(8 marks)**

(Total = 25 marks)

37 Graviton (12/13) **49 mins**

Company background

Graviton Clothing (Graviton) is a listed manufacturer of clothing with a strong reputation for producing desirable, fashionable products which can attract high selling prices. The company's objective is to maximise shareholder wealth. Graviton's products are sold through its own chain of stores. Graviton's markets demand designs which are in tune with current fashion trends which can alter every few weeks. Therefore, the business's stated aim is to focus production on these changing market trends by maintaining flexibility to adapt to that market demand through close control of all stages of the supply chain (design, manufacture and distribution).

Performance measurement system

The Chief Executive Officer (CEO) is unhappy with the current performance measurement system at Graviton. The system was created about five years ago by the finance director who has subsequently retired. The aim of the system was to provide the company with a list of measures which would cover performance at the strategic, tactical and operational levels of management. An example of the most recent performance report is given in Table 1.

Table 1

GRAVITON PERFORMANCE DASHBOARD
REPORT FOR THE YEAR TO SEPTEMBER 20X3

	20X3	*20X2*	*20X1*	*Change 20X3/20X2*
Financial				
Revenue ($m)	1,723	1,570	1,413	9.7%
Operating profit ($m)	320	314	308	1.9%
ROCE	15.8%	15.9%	15.9%	
Design				
Design awards won	3	2	3	50.0%
Manufacture				
Average time to market (days)	22.2	22.3	22.1	–0.4%
Distribution				
Deliveries on time	87.0%	86.8%	87.3%	0.2%

Commentary:

- The revenue growth of the business remains strong in a difficult market.
- Return on capital employed matches the industry average of about 16%.
- Time to market for new designs has been maintained at 22 days by paying overtime to designers in order to meet production schedules.

Recent events

Recent press reports about Graviton have been mixed, with positive comments about the innovative new designs and much admiration over the growth of sales which the business has achieved. However, there has been some criticism from customers of the durability of Graviton's clothes and from institutional investors that the dividend growth is not strong.

The CEO believes that there are major gaps in the current list of key metrics used by Graviton. She wants an evaluation of the current system and suggestions for improvements. However, she has warned you that the board wants a reasoned argument for each measure to be included in the list in order to avoid overloading each level of management with too much data.

Although rapidly growing, Graviton has had some problems in the last few years which have appeared on recent internal audit reports. It was found that a senior manager at factory site 1 has been delaying invoicing for completed orders in order to ensure that profit targets are met in both the current and the next accounting period. At factory site 2, there has been excellent return on a low capital employed figure although there is a significant adverse variance in the equipment repairs account.

Problems with performance measures

The board is dominated by long-serving executives who are sceptical of change, given Graviton's growth over the past three years. At a recent board meeting, they have shared the CEO's concern about data overload and also have pointed out a variety of problems with the use of performance measures. They presented the CEO with a list of three common problems (myopia, gaming, ossification) and argued that the current good performance of the business did not justify changing the performance measurement system. The CEO needs to know if these problems apply to Graviton and if they do, then what can be done to manage them.

Required

(a) Evaluate the current performance measurement system using the performance pyramid of Lynch and Cross. **(15 marks)**

(b) Assess whether the three problems listed by the board apply to Graviton and suggest appropriate performance management solutions to them. **(10 marks)**

(Total = 25 marks)

38 APX Accountancy (6/11, amended) 49 mins

Company background

APX Accountancy (APX) is an accountancy partnership with 12 branches covering each of the main cities of Emland. The business is well established, having organically grown over the last 40 years to become the second largest non-international practice in Emland. The accountancy market is mature and expands and contracts along with the general economic performance of Emland.

APX offers accountancy, audit, tax and business advisory services. The current business environment in Emland is dominated by a recession and the associated insolvency work is covered within the business advisory area of APX.

Performance management

At present, the practice collects the following information for strategic performance evaluation:

	Audit	*Tax*	*Business advisory*	*Total*
Revenue ($m)				
APX	69.1	89.2	64.7	223.0
Accounting industry	557.0	573.0	462.0	1,592.0
Change in revenue on previous year				
APX	3.0%	8.0%	22.0%	10.0%
Accounting industry	2.5%	4.5%	16.0%	6.8%
Profit margin at APX	6.4%	7.8%	10.5%	8.1%
Customer service score (1 to 5, with 5 being excellent)				
APX	3.4	3.9	4.1	

The above figures are for the most recent financial year and illustrate the metrics used by APX. Equivalent monthly figures are produced for each of the monthly partner meetings which review practice performance.

The staff are remunerated based on their grade, with non-partners obtaining a bonus of up to 10% of basic salary based on their line managers' annual review. The partners receive a fixed salary with a share of profit which depends on their contractual responsibilities within the partnership.

The Managing Partner of APX is dissatisfied with the existing performance management system, as she is not convinced that it is helping to achieve the long-term goal of expanding and ultimately floating the business on the national stock exchange. Therefore, she has asked you to consider the impact of applying Fitzgerald and Moon's building block approach to performance management in the practice.

In addition, the Marketing Manager at APX believes that the firm as a whole doesn't pay enough attention to customer service. At the last management meeting he said that, in his opinion, the customer service score(*) was the most important figure out of the performance metrics currently used by APX, and he said he felt it was no coincidence that the area of the business with the highest customer service score had also performed best financially.

* Customer service scores reflect ratings given by customers in relation to the level of service they feel they have received from APX.

Required

(a) Briefly describe Fitzgerald and Moon's building block model of performance management. **(4 marks)**

(b) Evaluate the existing performance management system at APX by applying the building block model. **(8 marks)**

(c) Explain the main improvements the introduction of a building block approach to performance management could provide, and suggest specific improvements to the existing system of performance measures at APX in light of the introduction of the building block model. **(8 marks)**

(d) Briefly evaluate the marketing manager's statement about the customer service score. **(5 marks)**

(Total = 25 marks)

39 Robust Laptops (12/10, amended) — 49 mins

Company background

Robust Laptops Co (RL) makes laptop computers for use in dangerous environments. The company's main customers are organisations like oil companies and the military that require a laptop that can survive rough handling in transport to a site and can be made to their unique requirements.

The company started as a basic laptop manufacturer but its competitors grew much larger and RL had to find a niche market where its small size would not hinder its ability to compete. It is now considered one of the best quality producers in this sector.

RL had the same Finance Director for many years who preferred to develop its systems organically. However, due to a fall in profitability, a new Chief Executive Officer (CEO) and a new Chief Financial Officer (CFO) have been appointed. The CEO wishes to review RL's financial control systems in order to get better information with which to tackle the profit issue.

Costing systems and pricing

The CEO wants to begin by thinking about the pricing of the laptops to ensure that selling expensive products at the wrong price is not compromising profit margins. The laptops are individually specified by customers for each order and pricing has been on a production cost plus basis with a mark-up of 45%. The company uses an absorption costing system based on labour hours in order to calculate the production cost per unit.

The main control system used within the company is the annual budget. It is set before the start of the financial year and variances are monitored and acted upon by line managers.

Performance measurement system and performance indicators

More generally, the CEO is concerned about the performance information which is provided in the monthly board papers. The board papers contain a high level summary of financial information, comparing performance against budget for revenue, costs and profit. They also report RL's key performance indicators (KPIs) which are: profit, profit margin, free cash flow and return on capital employed.

Although the CEO acknowledges that the fall in profitability is a concern for RL, he believes that the company's performance measurement systems should not focus solely on financial information. Instead, he wants RL to identify its objectives and its critical success factors, and then link its KPIs to them.

Financial and other information for Robust Laptops

Data for the year ended 30 September 20X1

Volume (units)	23,800	
		Total
		$'000
Direct variable costs		
Material		40,650
Labour		3,879
Packaging and transport		2,118
Subtotal		46,647
Overhead costs		
Customer service		7,735
Purchasing and receiving		2,451
Inventory management		1,467
Administration of production		2,537
Subtotal		14,190
Total		60,837

Labour time per unit	3 hours
Data collected for the year	
No. of minutes on call to customer	899,600
No. of purchase orders raised	21,400
No. of components used in production	618,800

Order 11784

Units ordered	16	
Direct costs for this order:		$
Material		27,328
Labour		2,608
Packaging and transport		1,424
Other activities relating to this order:		
No. of minutes on call to customer	1,104	
No. of purchase orders raised	64	
No. of components used in production	512	
Administration of production (absorbed as general overhead)	3 labour hours per unit	

Required

(a) Evaluate the current method of costing against an activity-based costing (ABC) system. You should provide illustrative calculations using the information provided on the costs for 20X1 and for Order 11784. Briefly state what action management might take in the light of your results with respect to this order. **(16 marks)**

(b) With reference to RL, explain the link between objectives, critical success factors and KPIs, and why it is important to consider non-financial performance information as well as financial information. **(9 marks)**

(Total = 25 marks)

40 SFS (6/10, amended) — 49 mins

The Spare for Ships Company (SFS) has a specialist machining facility which serves the shipbuilding components market. The current job-costing system has two categories of direct cost (direct materials and direct manufacturing labour) and a single indirect cost pool (manufacturing overhead which is allocated on the basis of direct labour hours). The indirect cost allocation rate of the existing job-costing system is $120 per direct manufacturing labour hour.

Recently, the Visibility Consultancy Partnership (VCP) proposed the use of an activity-based approach to redefine the job-costing system of SFS. VCP made a recommendation to retain the two direct cost categories. However, VCP further recommended the replacement of the single indirect cost pool with five indirect-cost pools.

Each of the five indirect cost pools represents an activity area at the manufacturing premises of SFS. Each activity area has its own supervisor who is responsible for their operating budget.

Relevant data are as follows:

Activity area	*Cost driver used as allocation base*	*Cost allocation rate*
		$
Materials handling	Number of components	0.50
Lathe work	Number of cuts	0.70
Milling	Number of machine hours	24.00
Grinding	Number of components	1.50
Inspection	Number of units inspected	20.00

SFS has recently invested in 'state of the art' IT systems which have the capability to automatically collate all of the data necessary for budgeting in each of the five activity areas.

The Management Accountant of SFS calculated the manufacturing cost per unit of two representative jobs under the two costing systems as follows:

	Job order 973	*Job order 974*
	$	$
Current costing system	1,172.00	620.00
Activity-based costing system	1,612.00	588.89

Required

(a) Compare the cost figures per unit for Job order 973 and Job order 974 calculated by the Management Accountant and explain the reasons for, and potential consequences of, the differences in the job cost estimates produced under the two costing systems. **(8 marks)**

(b) 'The application of activity-based management (ABM) requires that the management of SFS focus on each of the following:

(i) Operational ABM
(ii) Strategic ABM
(iii) The implicit value of an activity'

Required

Critically appraise the above statement and explain the risks attaching to the use of ABM. **(8 marks)**

SFS manufactures and sells a range of products. It is not dominant in the market in which it operates and, as a result, it has to accept the market price for each of its products. The company is keen to ensure that it continues to compete and earn satisfactory profit at each stage throughout a product's life cycle.

Required

(c) Explain how SFS could use target costing and Kaizen costing to improve its future performance.

Your answer should include an explanation of the differences between target costing and Kaizen costing. **(9 marks)**

(Total = 25 marks)

BPP LEARNING MEDIA

41 LOL cards (12/10, amended) **49 mins**

LOL Co (LOL) is a chain of shops selling cards and gifts throughout its country. It has been listed on the stock exchange for ten years and enjoys a fairly high profile in the retail sector of the national economy. You have been asked by the Chief Executive Officer (CEO) to advise the company on value-based management (VBM) as a different approach to performance management. The CEO has read about this method as a way of focusing on shareholder interests and in the current tough economic climate, she thinks that it may be a useful development for LOL.

The company has traditionally used earnings per share (EPS) growth and share price in order to assess performance. The changes being proposed are considered significant and the CEO wants to be briefed on the implications of the new analysis and also how to convince both the board and the major investors of the benefits.

Financial data for LOL

	20X9	*20Y0*
	$m	$m
Profit before interest and tax	50.7	43.5
Interest paid	4.0	7.8
Profit after interest and tax	35.0	26.8
Average number of shares in issue (millions)	160	160

Capital employed at the end of the year was	$m
20X8	99.2
20X9	104.1
20Y0	97.8

LOL aims for a capital structure of 50:50 debt to equity.

Costs of capital were

	20X9	*20Y0*
Equity	12.70%	15.30%
Debt (post-tax cost)	4.20%	3.90%

Corporation tax is at the rate of 25%.

Stock market information

	20X9	*20Y0*
Stock market all-share index	2,225.4	1,448.9
Retailing sector index	1,225.6	907.1
LOL (average share price) ($)	12.20	10.70

The fall in profits can, in part at least, be attributed to an increase in costs. The CFO has advised that LOL needs to focus on cost reduction rather than cost containment. She proposes to achieve this through the introduction of activity-based management.

Required

(a) Explain to the CEO what VBM involves and how it can be used to focus the company on shareholder interests. **(4 marks)**

(b) Perform an assessment of the financial performance of LOL using economic value added (EVA™) and evaluate your results compared with those of EPS growth and share price performance. You should state any assumptions made. **(12 marks)**

(c) Evaluate VBM measures against traditional profit-based measures of performance. **(3 marks)**

(d) Discuss how activity-based management (ABM) differs from traditional cost allocation systems, and how ABM seeks to achieve cost reduction. **(6 marks)**

(Total = 25 marks)

42 Dibble (Mar/Jun 16) 49 mins

Dibble is formed of two autonomous divisions, Timber and Steel, and manufactures components for use in the construction industry. Dibble has always absorbed production overheads to the cost of each product on the basis of machine hours.

Timber Division

Timber Division manufactures timber frames used to support the roofs of new houses. The timber, which is purchased pre-cut to the correct length, is assembled into the finished frame by a factory worker who fastens the components together. Timber Division manufactures six standard sizes of frame which is sufficient for use in most newly built houses.

Steel Division

Steel Division manufactures steel frames and roof supports for use in small commercial buildings such as shops and restaurants. There is a large range of products, and many customers also specify bespoke designs for short production runs or one-off building projects. Steel is cut and drilled using the division's own programmable computer aided manufacturing machinery (CAM), and is bolted together or welded by hand.

Steel Division's strategy is to produce novel bespoke products at a price comparable to the simpler and more conventional products offered by its competitors. For example, many of Steel Division's customers choose to have steel covered in one of a wide variety of coloured paints and other protective coatings at the end of the production process. This is performed off-site by a subcontractor, after which the product is returned to Steel Division for despatch to the customer. Customers are charged the subcontractor's cost plus a 10% mark-up for choosing this option. The board of Steel Division has admitted that this pricing structure may be too simplistic, and that it is unsure of the overall profitability of sales of some groups of products or sectors of the market.

Recently, several customers have complained that incorrectly applied paint has flaked off the steel after only a few months' use. More seriously, a fast food restaurant has commenced litigation with Dibble after it had to close for a week while steel roof frames supplied by Steel Division were repainted. Following this, the Production Manager has proposed increasing the number of staff inspecting the quality of coating on the frames, and purchasing expensive imaging machinery to make inspection more efficient.

Activity-based costing and activity-based management

The Chief Executive Officer (CEO) at Dibble has approached you as a performance management expert for your advice. 'At a conference recently,' he told you, 'I watched a presentation by a CEO at a similar business to ours talking about the advantages and disadvantages of using activity-based costing (ABC) and how over several years the adoption of activity-based management (ABM) had helped them to improve both strategic and operational performance.'

'I don't want you to do any detailed calculations at this stage, but I'd like to know more about ABC and ABM, and know whether they would be useful for Dibble,' he said.

You are provided with extracts of the most recent management accounts for Timber and Steel Divisions:

Division	*Timber*	*Steel*
	$'000	$'000
Revenue	25,815	20,605
Materials	12,000	10,100
Direct labour	4,500	850
Subcontract costs	75	650
Analysis of production overheads		
Set-up time for CAM machinery	–	575
Machining time	–	2,777
Storage of goods awaiting or returned from subcontractors	120	395
Transfer of goods to and from subcontractors	50	300
Inspection and testing	35	425
Total production overheads	205	4,472
Gross profit	9,035	4,533

Required

(a) (i) Advise the CEO how ABC could be implemented. **(4 marks)**

(ii) Assess whether it may be more appropriate to use ABC in Timber and Steel Divisions than the costing basis currently used. **(8 marks)**

(b) Advise the CEO how ABM could be used to improve business performance in Dibble. **(13 marks)**

(Total = 25 marks)

43 BEG (6/10, amended) 49 mins

Company background

The Better Electricals Group (BEG) which commenced trading ten years ago manufactures a range of high quality electrical appliances such as kettles, toasters and steam irons for domestic use which it sells to electrical stores in Voltland.

The directors consider that the existing product range could be extended to include industrial sized products such as high volume water boilers, high volume toasters and large steam irons for the hotel and catering industry. They recently commissioned a highly reputable market research organisation to undertake a market analysis which identified a number of significant competitors within the hotel and catering industry.

Quality certification

At a recent meeting of the board of directors, the Marketing Director proposed that BEG should make an application to gain 'platinum status' quality certification in respect of its industrial products from the Hotel and Catering Institute of Voltland in order to gain a strong competitive position. He then stressed the need to focus on increasing the effectiveness of all operations from product design to the provision of after-sales services.

An analysis of financial and non-financial data relating to the application for 'platinum status' for each of the years 20X1, 20X2 and 20X3 is contained in the appendix.

The Managing Director of BEG recently returned from a seminar, the subject of which was 'The Use of Cost Targets'. She then requested the Management Accountant of BEG to prepare a statement of total costs for the application for platinum status for each of years 20X1, 20X2 and 20X3. She further asked that the statement detailed manufacturing cost targets and the costs of quality.

The Management Accountant produced the following statement of manufacturing cost targets and the costs of quality:

	20X1 Forecast	*20X2 Forecast*	*20X3 Forecast*
	$'000	$'000	$'000
Variable manufacturing costs	8,400	10,500	12,600
Fixed manufacturing costs	3,000	3,400	3,400
Prevention costs	4,200	2,100	1,320
Appraisal costs	800	700	700
Internal failure costs	2,500	1,800	1,200
External failure costs	3,100	2,000	980
Total costs	22,000	20,500	20,200

Required

(a) Explain how the use of cost targets could be of assistance to BEG with regard to their application for platinum status. Your answer must include commentary on the items contained in the statement of manufacturing cost targets and the costs of quality prepared by the Management Accountant. **(8 marks)**

(b) Assess the forecasted performance of BEG for the period 20X1 to 20X3 with reference to the application for 'platinum status' quality certification under the following headings:

(i) Financial performance and marketing
(ii) External effectiveness
(iii) Internal efficiency **(12 marks)**

(c) Briefly explain how the performance pyramid (Lynch and Cross) could help BEG gain its 'platinum status' quality certification. **(5 marks)**

(Total = 25 marks)

Appendix

'Platinum status' quality certification application – Relevant statistics

	20X1 forecast	*20X2 forecast*	*20X3 forecast*
Total market size ($m)	300	320	340
BEG – sales ($m)	24	30	36
BEG – total costs ($m)	22	20.5	20.2
BEG – sundry statistics			
% of products achieving design quality standards and accepted without further rectification	92	95	99
Rectification claims from customers ($m)	0.96	0.75	0.1
Cost of after-sales rectification service ($m)	1.8	1.05	0.8
% of sales meeting planned delivery dates	88.5	95.5	99.5
Average cycle time			
customer enquiry to product delivery (days)	49	45	40
Product enquiries not taken up by customers (% of enquiries)	10.5	6	3
Idle capacity of manufacturing staff (%)	12	6	1.5

44 Turing (6/14) — 49 mins

Joint venture: TandR

Turing Aerodynamics (Turing) has formed a joint venture (JV) with Riemann Generators (Riemann) in order to design and manufacture high-performance wind turbines which generate electricity. The JV is called TandR with each party owning 50%. Turing will design and build the pylons, housing and turbine blades while Riemann will supply the generators to be fitted inside the housing.

Turing

Turing is a medium-sized firm known for its blade design skills. It is owned by three venture capital firms (VCs) (each holding 30% of the shares), with the remaining 10% being given to management to motivate them. The VCs each have a large portfolio of business investments and accept that some of these investments may fail provided that some of their investments show large gains. Management is an ambitious group who enjoys the business and technical challenges of introducing new products.

Riemann

On the other hand, Riemann is a large, family-owned company working in the highly competitive electricity generator sector. The shareholders of Riemann see the business as mature and want it to offer a stable, long-term return on capital. However, recently, Riemann had to seek emergency refinancing (debt and equity) due to its thin profit margins and tough competition, both of which are forecast to continue. As a result, Riemann's shareholders and management are concerned for the survival of the business and see TandR as a way to generate some additional cash flow. Unlike at Turing, the management of Riemann does not own significant shareholdings in the company which has preferred to pay fixed salaries.

Choice of design for the turbines

TandR is run by a group of managers made up from each of the JV partners. They are currently faced with a decision about the design of the product. There are three design choices depending on the power which the wind turbines can generate (measured in megawatts (MW)):

Design	*Description*
8 MV	A large 8 MW unit
3 MW	A 3 MW unit
1 MW	A basic 1 MW unit

The engineering for the 1 MW and 3 MW units is well understood and so design is much simpler than for the 8 MW unit which would be world leading if completed.

The demand for the different types of units will depend on government subsidies of the electricity price charged by the electricity generating companies which will buy the wind turbines and the planning regulations for building such large structures. It is believed that there will be orders for either 1,000, 1,500 or 2,000 units but there is no clear picture yet of which demand level is more likely than the others.

The estimated costs and prices for the units are:

Type	*Variable cost per unit*	*Fixed costs*	*Price per unit*
	$m	$m	$m
8 MW	10.4	7,500.0	20.8
3 MW	4.8	820.0	9.6
1 MW	1.15	360.0	4.6

Notes

1 The fixed costs cover the initial design, development and testing of the units.

2 The costs and prices are in real terms with the 8 MW unit likely to take more years to develop than the others.

Required

(a) Assess the risk appetites of the two firms in the JV and provide a justified recommendation for each firm of an appropriate method of decision making under uncertainty to assess the different types of wind turbines. **(9 marks)**

(b) Evaluate the choice of turbine design types using your recommended methods from part (a) above. **(8 marks)**

(c) Discuss the problems encountered in managing performance in a JV such as TandR. **(8 marks)**

(Total = 25 marks)

45 Callisto (6/12, amended) 49 mins

Company background

Callisto Retail (Callisto) is an online reseller of local craft products related to the historic culture of the country of Callistan. The business started ten years ago as a hobby of two brothers, Jeff and George. The brothers produced humorous, short video clips about Callistan which were posted on its website and became highly popular. They decided to use the website to try to sell Callistan merchandise and good initial sales made them believe that they had a viable business idea.

Callisto has gone from strength to strength and now boasts sales of $120m per annum, selling anything related to Callistan. Callisto is still very much the brothers' family business. They have gathered around themselves a number of strategic partners into what Jeff describes as a virtual company. Callisto has the core functions of video clip production, finance and supplier relationship management. The rest of the functions of the organisation (warehousing, delivery and website development) are outsourced to strategic partners.

The brothers work from their family home in the rural North of Callistan while other Callisto employees work from their homes in the surrounding villages and towns. These employees are involved in video editing, system maintenance, handling customer complaints and communication with suppliers and outsourcers regarding inventory. The employees log in to Callisto's systems via the national internet infrastructure. The outsourced functions are handled by multinational companies of good reputation which are based around the world. The brothers have always been fascinated by information technology and so they depend on email and electronic data interchange to communicate with their product suppliers and outsourcing partners.

Recent issues

Recently, there have been emails from regular customers of the Callisto website complaining about slow or non-delivery of orders that they have placed. George has commented that this represents a major threat to Callisto as the company operates on small profit margins, relying on volume to drive the business. He believes that sales growth will drive the profitability of the business due to its cost structure.

Contracts and service level agreements

Jeff handles the management of outsourcing and has been reviewing the contracts that exist between Callisto and its strategic partner for warehousing and delivery, RLR Logistics. The current contract for warehousing and delivery is due for renewal in two months and currently has the following service level agreements (SLAs):

(1) RLR agrees to receive and hold inventory from Callisto's product suppliers.

(2) RLR agrees to hold 14 days' inventory of Callisto's products.

(3) RLR agrees to despatch from its warehouse any order passed from Callisto within three working days, inventory allowing.

(4) RLR agrees to deliver to customers anywhere in Callistan within two days of despatch.

Breaches in these SLAs incur financial penalties on a sliding scale depending on the number and severity of the problems. Each party to the contract collects their own data on performance and this has led to disagreements in the past over whether service levels have been achieved, although no penalties have been triggered to date. The most common disagreement arises over inventory levels held by RLR, with RLR claiming that it cannot be expected to deliver products that are late in arriving to inventory due to the product suppliers' production and delivery issues.

Required

(a) Assess the difficulties of performance measurement and performance management in complex business structures such as Callisto, especially in respect of the performance of their employees and strategic partners. **(17 marks)**

George has also been increasingly concerned about the length of time it is taking for customer complaints to be addressed, and the damage which delays in replying to customer complaints could have on Callisto's reputation. In this respect, he is also worried that Callisto's employees are not working as productively as they could be.

Consequently, he has designed a daily report which lists all the employees in alphabetical order, and then shows four columns of data for each employee:

(1) How long they have been logged on to Callisto's system
(2) How many videos they have edited
(3) How many complaints they have handled
(4) How many suppliers or outsourcers they have contacted

Required

(b) Evaluate the usefulness of George's proposed report, and suggest ways the output report could be improved. **(8 marks)**

(Total = 25 marks)

46 Coal Creek (12/12, amended) 49 mins

Company background

Coal Creek Nursing Homes (CCNH) is a company operating residential care homes for the elderly in Geeland.

The residents at CCNH are those elderly people who can no longer care for themselves at home and whose family are unable to look after them. There are 784 homes with about 30,000 residents under the care of the company. There are about 42,500 staff, who range from head office staff, through home managers, to the care staff and cleaners and caterers.

The company is a private company which aims to make a suitable return to its shareholders. It had revenues of $938 million in the last year and is one of the largest providers of residential care places in Geeland.

The company is split into two divisions: General Care (GC) which handles ordinary elderly residents and Special Care (SC), which is a newer operation that handles residents who need intensive care and attention due to physical or mental ailments.

CCNH does not own its homes but rents them from a number of large commercial landlords. It has taken on a large number of new homes recently in order to cope with the expansion of SC, which has proved successful with 24% p.a. revenue growth over the last 2 years. GC is a mature business with little growth in a sector that is now

BPP LEARNING MEDIA

fully supplied. GC has seen volumes and margins falling as price pressure comes from its main customers (public sector health organisations which contract out this part of their care provision).

Recent events

A new Chief Executive Officer (CEO) has just taken over at CCNH. She was appointed because the board of CCNH believed that the company was in difficulty. The previous CEO had been forced to leave following a scandal involving a number of the homes where residents' money had gone missing and their families had called in the police. The Finance Director and the Operations Director had also resigned, leaving the company without any experienced senior management.

The board has tasked the new CEO with ascertaining the current position of the business and identifying a strategy to address the issues that arise. The CEO wants to address the strategy, deciding whether to divest or retain elements of the business.

The CEO has come to you, as the most senior member of finance staff, for assistance with this task. The first area that she wants help on is the problem that the business is having with its landlords. The company struggled to meet its most recent rental payment, which the bank eventually agreed to cover through an increase to the overdraft, as CCNH had no ready cash. She is upset that the chosen strategic measures of performance (earnings per share growth and operating profit margin) did not identify the difficulties that the firm is now facing. One of the other directors had mentioned gearing problems but the CEO did not follow what this meant.

Also, the CEO has heard of qualitative models for predicting corporate failure and wants to apply one at CCNH. Obviously, she wants to know if CCNH exhibits any symptoms of failure.

You have been given the outline financial statements to help with this task (see Appendix below the requirements).

Required

(a) Discuss why indicators of liquidity and gearing need to be considered in conjunction with profitability at CCNH. Illustrate your answer with suitable calculations. **(11 marks)**

(b) Explain one qualitative model for predicting corporate failure (such as Argenti) and comment on CCNH's position utilising this model. You are not expected to give scores, only to comment on the areas of weakness at CCNH. **(9 marks)**

(c) Advise the CEO why it is important to consider product portfolios when she determines her strategy for the business. **(5 marks)**

(Total = 25 marks)

Appendix

Outline financial statements for CCNH for the year just ended

Summary income statements

	General care	*Special care*	*Total*
	$m	$m	$m
Revenue	685	253	938
Operating costs			
Homes: payroll	397	139	536
running	86	24	110
Rents	193	64	257
Central costs	27	3	30
Operating profit	(18)	23	5
Interest			5
Profit before tax			0
Tax			0
Profit for the period			0

STATEMENT OF FINANCIAL POSITION

	General care	Special care	Total
	$m	$m	$m
Assets			
Non-current assets	244	87	331
Current assets	17	47	64
Total assets	261	134	395
Equity and liabilities			
Share capital			165
Retained earnings reserve			24
Long-term borrowing			102
Current liabilities	76	28	104
Total equity and liabilities			395

(**Note.** A breakdown of the long-term financing into two divisions has not been possible.)

47 BPC (12/07, amended) — 49 mins

The directors of Blaina Packaging Co (BPC), a well-established manufacturer of cardboard boxes, are currently considering whether to enter the cardboard tube market. Cardboard tubes are purchased by customers whose products are wound around tubes of various sizes, ranging from large tubes around which carpets are wound to small tubes around which films and paper products are wound. The cardboard tubes are usually purchased in very large quantities by customers. On average, the cardboard tubes comprise between 1% and 2% of the total cost of the customers' finished product.

The directors have gathered the following information:

(1) The cardboard tubes are manufactured on machines which vary in size and speed. The lowest cost machine is priced at $30,000 and requires only one operative for its operation. A one-day training course is required in order that an unskilled person can then operate such a machine in an efficient and effective manner.

(2) The cardboard tubes are made from specially formulated paper which, at times during recent years, has been in short supply.

(3) At present, four major manufacturers of cardboard tubes have an aggregate market share of 80%. The current market leader has a 26% market share. The market shares of the other three major manufacturers, one of which is JOL Co, are equal in size. The product ranges offered by the four major manufacturers are similar in terms of size and quality. The market has grown by 2% per annum during recent years.

(4) A recent report on the activities of a foreign-based multinational company revealed that consideration was being given to expanding operations in their Packaging Division overseas. The division possesses large-scale automated machinery for the manufacture of cardboard tubes of any size.

(5) Another company, Plastic Tubes Co (PTC), produces a narrow, but increasing, range of plastic tubes which are capable of housing small products such as film and paper-based products. At present, these tubes are on average 30% more expensive than the equivalent sized cardboard tubes sold in the marketplace.

Required

(a) Using Porter's five forces model, assess the attractiveness of the option to enter the market for cardboard tubes as a performance improvement strategy for BPC. **(10 marks)**

(b) Discuss the limitations of Porter's five forces model as a technique for assessing how attractive an industry is to enter. **(5 marks)**

JOL Co was the market leader with a share of 30% three years ago. The Managing Director of JOL Co stated at a recent meeting of the board of directors that: 'our loss of market share during the last three years might lead to the end of JOL Co as an organisation and therefore we must address this issue immediately'.

BPP LEARNING MEDIA

Required

(c) Discuss the statement of the Managing Director of JOL Co and discuss six performance indicators, other than decreasing market share, which might indicate that JOL Co might fail as a corporate entity. **(10 marks)**

(Total = 25 marks)

48 RM Batteries (12/10, amended) — 49 mins

RM Batteries Co (RMB) is a manufacturer of battery packs. It has expanded rapidly in the last few years under the leadership of its autocratic Chairman and Chief Executive Officer, John Smith. Smith is relentlessly optimistic. He likes to get his own way and demands absolute loyalty from all his colleagues.

The company has developed a major new product over the last three years which has necessitated a large investment in new equipment. Smith has stated that this more efficient battery is critical to the future of the business as the company operates in a sector where customers expect constant innovation from their suppliers.

However, the recent share price performance has caused concern at board level and there has been comment in the financial press about the increased gearing and the strain that this expansion is putting on the company. The average share price has been $1.56 (20X8), $1.67 (20X9) and $1.34 (20Y0). There are 450 million shares in issue.

A relevant Z-score model for the industry sector is:

$Z = 1.2X_1 + 1.4X_2 + 3.3X_3 + 0.6X_4 + X_5$

Where:

X_1 is working capital/total assets (WC/TA)

X_2 is retained earnings reserve/total assets (RE/TA)

X_3 is profit before interest and tax/total assets (PBIT/TA)

X_4 is market value of equity/total long-term debt (MVE/total long-term debt)

X_5 is revenue/total assets (Revenue/TA)

A score of more than 3 is considered safe and at below 1.8, the company is at risk of failure in the next 2 years.

The company's recent financial performance is summarised below:

Summary Income Statements

	20X8	*20X9*	*20Y0*
	$m	$m	$m
Revenue	1,460	1,560	1,915
Operating costs	1,153	1,279	1,724
Operating profit	307	281	191
Interest	35	74	95
Profit before tax	272	207	96
Tax	87	66	31
Profit for the period	185	141	65

STATEMENTS OF FINANCIAL POSITION

	20X8 $m	20X9 $m	20Y0 $m
Assets			
Non-current assets	1,120	1,778	2,115
Current assets	235	285	341
Total assets	1,355	2,063	2,456
Equity and liabilities			
Share capital	230	230	230
Retained earnings reserve	204	344	410
Long-term borrowings	465	991	1,261
Current liabilities	456	498	555
Total equity and liabilities	1,355	2,063	2,456

A junior analyst in the company has correctly prepared a spreadsheet calculating the Z-scores as follows:

		20X8	20X9	20Y0
Share price ($)		1.56	1.67	1.34
No. of shares (millions)		450	450	450
Market value of equity ($m)		702	752	603
X_1	WC/TA	–0.163	–0.103	–0.087
X_2	RE/TA	0.151	0.167	0.167
X_3	PBIT/TA	0.227	0.136	0.078
X_4	MVE/Total long-term debt	1.510	0.758	0.478
X_5	Revenue/TA	1.077	0.756	0.780
	Z	2.746	1.770	1.452
Gearing [debt/equity]		107%	173%	197%

Required

(a) Discuss the strengths and weaknesses of quantitative and qualitative models for predicting corporate failure. **(6 marks)**

(b) Comment on the results in the junior analyst's spreadsheet. **(5 marks)**

(c) Identify the qualitative problems that are apparent in the company's structure and performance and explain why these are relevant to possible failure. **(5 marks)**

(d) Critically assess the results of your analysis in parts (b) and (c) alongside details of RMB's recent financial performance and suggest additional data that should be acquired and how it could be used to assess RMB's financial health. **(4 marks)**

RMB used a market skimming pricing strategy for its new product at the introduction stage in its life cycle. However, John Smith now believes that the new product has moved into its growth phase, and he is concerned about how long it will be until the product becomes mature.

(e) Explain the changes that are likely to occur at the maturity and decline stages of the product's life cycle in relation to its selling price and production costs. **(5 marks)**

(Total = 25 marks)

SECTION A QUESTIONS

Questions 49 to 57 are 50-mark questions, covering a range of topic areas, as will be the case in your APM exam. In the exam, you should expect Section A questions to focus on a range of issues from across **syllabus sections A, C and D**.

PEST analysis (in Qn 49), and decision-making under risk and uncertainty (in Qns 50 and 56) are included in section B of the syllabus, while value-based management (in Qn 54) is included in section E. Therefore, while these topics can still be examined in APM exams, you should expect to see them in the 25-mark Section B questions in future, rather than in the 50-mark Section A questions.

49 Lopten (12/13, amended) 98 mins

Company information

Lopten Industries (Lopten) is one of the largest listed consumer durables manufacturers in the world, making washing machines, tumble dryers and dishwashers. It has recently expanded into Beeland which is a developing country where incomes have risen to the point where demand is increasing for Lopten's goods among the growing middle-class population.

Lopten believes in the economies of scale of large manufacturing sites with dispersed selling branches in the markets in which it operates. Therefore, it has entered the Beeland market by setting up a local sales force and supporting them with a national marketing campaign. The company is currently selling only two products in Beeland (both are types of washing machines):

- A basic product (called Cheerful) with functions which are comparable with the existing local competitors' output
- A premium product (called Posh) which has functions and features similar to Lopten's products in other developed countries

Both products are manufactured and imported from its regional manufacturing hub, which is in the neighbouring country of Kayland.

Competitive environment

The competitive environment in Beeland is changing rapidly. The washing machine market used to be dominated by two large local manufacturers which make simple, cheap and reliable machines. There are two other major international manufacturers apart from Lopten. One of these has already opened a factory in Beeland and is producing machines similar to Cheerful to compete directly with the existing local producers. The Government of Beeland has supported this new entrant with grants, as it is keen to encourage inward investment by foreign companies and the resulting expertise and employment which they provide. The other international competitor is now considering entering the Beeland market with more highly specified machines similar to Lopten's Posh brand.

Mission, critical success factors and performance metrics

Lopten's stated mission is to be the 'most successful manufacturer of its type of products in the world'. The board has set the following critical success factors (CSFs) for Lopten's Beeland operations:

(1) To obtain a dominant market presence
(2) To maximise profits within acceptable risk
(3) To maintain the brand image of Lopten for above average quality products

The board is considering using the following key performance indicators (KPIs) for each product: total profit, average sales price per unit, contribution per unit, market share, margin of safety, return on capital employed (ROCE), total quality costs and consumer awards won.

(**Note.** Margin of safety has been defined as [actual sales units – breakeven sales units]/actual sales units.)

The board has asked you as a consultant to assess its current performance measurement systems. It wants a report which calculates the various indicators suggested above and then assesses how the KPIs address issues in the external environment. The report should assess the balance between planning and controlling represented by the KPIs as they want to ensure that these match what they should be doing at the strategic level in Lopten. Also, it should evaluate how the KPIs fit with the CSFs which have been selected. The data given in Appendix 1 has been collated for your use.

Marketing strategies

Finally, the board is considering two new marketing strategies going forward:

Plan A is to continue operations as at present allowing for 4% growth p.a. in volumes of both Cheerful and Posh.

Plan B is to dramatically reduce the marketing spend on Cheerful and to reallocate resources to focus the marketing on Posh. This is expected to lead to an anticipated growth in volume of 15% p.a. for Posh and flat sales for Cheerful.

The target operating profit for the Beeland operation in 2 years' time is set at $135m and the board wants an evaluation of these strategies in meeting that target.

Appendix 1

Beeland operation's information for the most recent financial year

	Cheerful	*Posh*	*Total*
Variable costs	$ per unit	$ per unit	
Materials	90	120	
Labour	60	80	
Overheads	40	50	
Distribution costs	45	45	
Quality costs	20	30	
Fixed costs	$m	$m	$m
Administration costs	18	18	36
Distribution costs	16	16	32
Quality costs	6	6	12
Marketing costs	80	80	160
Other data	$m	$m	$m
Revenue	448	308	756
Capital employed	326	250	576
	Units	Units	Units
Total market size (millions)	9.33	1.33	10.66
Beeland operation's sales (millions)	1.12	0.44	1.56

Notes

1 Cheerful has won one best buy award from the Beeland Consumer Association.

2 Posh has won four best buy awards from the Beeland Consumer Association.

3 The allocations of fixed costs are based on a recent activity-based costing exercise and are considered to be valid.

Required

Write a report to the board of Lopten which:

(i) Calculates the KPIs suggested by the board for the assessment of performance of the Beeland operations **(11 marks)**

(ii) Uses PEST analysis to identify issues in the company's external environment and then evaluates the effectiveness of the suggested KPIs in addressing these issues **(11 marks)**

(iii) Takes each CSF in turn and evaluates how the suggested KPIs fit to the CSF given **(10 marks)**

(iv) Assess the extent to which the suggested KPIs would be suitable for use in planning rather than controlling **(5 marks)**

BPP LEARNING MEDIA

(v) Evaluates whether the two proposed marketing strategies will enable Lopten to achieve its operating profit target **(9 marks)**

Professional marks will be awarded for the format, style and structure of the discussion of your answer. **(4 marks)**

Note. All figures are real for the purpose of this scenario so that inflation can be ignored. Also, round to the nearest $m as appropriate.

(Total = 50 marks)

50 Mackerel (2013 Pilot Paper) 98 mins

Company information and mission

Mackerel Contracting (Mackerel) is a listed defence contractor working mainly for its domestic government in Zedland.

Mackerel's overall mission – and goal – is 'to maximise shareholder wealth' and, currently, the board uses total shareholder return (TSR) as an overall corporate measure of performance. However, a number of shareholders have begun to express concerns about Mackerel's performance.

You are a performance management consultant. Mackerel's Chief Executive Officer (CEO) has brought you in to advise the board on a number of issues facing the company. The CEO has asked for a report from you:

- Outlining the external factors affecting the profitability of a potential new contract and how these factors can be built into the choice of the design budget which is ultimately set;
- Advising on a proposed change to the company's information systems; and
- Advising on suitable performance measures for Mackerel.

Potential new government contract

Mackerel is currently considering tendering for a contract to design and develop a new armoured personnel vehicle (APV) for the army to protect its soldiers during transport around a battlefield. The invitation to tender from the Government specifies that the APV should take two years to develop and test, and be delivered for a full cost to Mackerel of no more than $70,000 per unit at current prices. Normally, government contracts are approximately priced on a cost plus basis with Mackerel aiming to make a 19% mark-up.

At the last briefing meeting, the institutional shareholders of Mackerel expressed worry about the volatility of the company's earnings (currently a $20.4m operating profit p.a.) especially during the economic downturn which is affecting Zedland at present. They are also concerned by cuts in government expenditure resulting from this recession. The Zedland Minister for Procurement has declared 'In the current difficult economic conditions, we are preparing a wide ranging review of all defence contracts with a view to deciding on what is desirable within the overall priorities for Zedland and what is possible within our budget.' The government procurement manager has indicated that the Government would be willing to commit to purchasing 500 APVs within the price limit set but with the possibility of increasing this to 750 or 1,000 depending on defence commitments. In the invitation to tender document, the Government has stated it will pay a fixed sum of $7.5m towards development and then a 19% mark-up on budgeted variable costs.

Mackerel's risk management committee (RMC) is considering how much to spend on design and development. It has three proposals from the engineering team: a basic package at $7.5m (which will satisfy the original contract specifications) and two other improved design packages. The design packages will have different total fixed costs but are structured to give the same variable cost per unit. It is believed that the improved design packages will increase the chances of gaining a larger government order but it has been very difficult to ascertain the relevant probabilities of different order volumes. The RMC needs a full appraisal of the situation using all suitable methods.

The Risk Manager has gathered information on the APV contract, and you have been given a copy of this (Appendix A). She has identified that a major uncertainty in pricing the vehicle is the price of steel, as each APV requires 9.4 tonnes of steel. However, she has been successful in negotiating a fixed price contract for all the steel that might be required at $1,214 per tonne. The Risk Manager has tried to estimate the effect of choosing different design packages but is unsure of how to proceed to evaluate the different options.

Mackerel's information systems

The board is also considering a change to the information systems at Mackerel. The existing systems are based in the individual functions (production, sales, service, finance and human resources). Currently, reports are submitted by each function and then integrated at head office into the board papers which form the main strategic information system of the company. The board is considering the implementation of a new system based on an integrated, single database that would be accessible at any of the company's five sites. The company network would be upgraded to allow real-time input and update of the database. The database would support a detailed management information system and a high-level executive information system.

Performance measures

The CEO believes that the new information system will provide the opportunity for a change in how performance is evaluated within the company.

The CEO has asked you to consider the general impact of the new information system, and also, how profit-based measures such as return on capital employed (ROCE) compare to newer measures such as economic value added (EVA^{TM}) with regard to meeting Mackerel's overall goals and its external measure of performance.

Required

Write a report to the board of Mackerel to:

(i) Analyse the risks facing the management of Mackerel and discuss how the management team's attitude to risk might affect their response **(9 marks)**

(ii) Evaluate the APV project using metrics and methods for decision making under risk and uncertainty, and assess the suitability of the different methods used **(19 marks)**

(iii) Recommend an appropriate choice of method of assessing the project and, therefore, a course of action for the APV contract **(3 marks)**

(iv) Evaluate the potential impact of the introduction of the new executive information system on operational information gathering and strategic decision making at Mackerel **(8 marks)**

(v) Assess how profit-based measures such as ROCE compare to newer measures such as EVA^{TM} given Mackerel's overall goals **(7 marks)**

Professional marks will be awarded for the format, style and structure of the discussion of your answer. **(4 marks)**

(Total = 50 marks)

Appendix A

Budgeted cost for APV

Variable cost per unit

	$
Steel	11,412 (9.4 tonnes at contracted prices)
Engine/transmission	9,500
Electronics	8,450
Other	4,810
Labour	13,800

Design and development (fixed total)

	$
Package	
Type 1	7,500,000
Type 2	8,750,000
Type 3	10,000,000

Risk manager's assessment of likely government order:

		Probability	
Demand	*Type 1*	*Type 2*	*Type 3*
500	85%	25%	20%
750	10%	50%	50%
1,000	5%	25%	30%

51 Metis (6/12, amended) **98 mins**

You should assume it is now June 20X2.

Company information and business model

Metis is a restaurant business in the city of Urbanton. Metis was started three years ago by three friends who met at university while doing courses in business and catering management. Initially, their aim was simply to 'make money' although they had talked about building a chain of restaurants if the first site was successful.

The three friends pooled their own capital and took out a loan from the Grand Bank in order to fit out a rented site in the city. They designed the restaurant to be light and open with a menu that reflected the most popular dishes in Urbanton regardless of any particular culinary style. The dishes were designed to be priced in the middle of the range that was common for restaurants in the city. The choice of food and drinks to offer to customers is still a group decision amongst the owners.

Other elements of the business were allocated according to each owner's qualifications and preferences. Bert Fish takes charge of all aspects of the kitchen operations while another, Sheila Plate, manages the activities in the public area such as taking reservations, serving tables and maintaining the appearance of the restaurant. The third founder, John Sum, deals with the overall business issues such as procurement, accounting and legal matters.

Market environment

Competition in the restaurant business is fierce as it is easy to open a restaurant in Urbanton and there are many competitors in the city, both small, single-site operations and large national chains. The current national economic environment is one of steady but unspectacular growth.

Metis' current position

The restaurant has been running for three years and the founders have reached the point where the business seems to be profitable and self-sustaining. The restaurant is now in need of refurbishment in order to maintain its atmosphere, and this has prompted the founders to consider the future of their business. John has come to you as its accountant looking for advice on aspects of performance management in the business. He has supplied you with figures outlining the recent performance of the business and the forecasts for the next year (Appendix 1).

John has explained that the report he has given you (Appendix 1) represents the quantitative data that is available to the founders when they meet each quarter to plan any short-term projects or initiatives and also to consider the longer-term future. Bert and Sheila have often indicated to John that they find the information daunting and difficult to understand fully.

Performance measures

John has come to you to advise him on the performance reporting at Metis and how it could be improved. He feels that the current report is, in some ways, too complex and, in other ways, too simple. He wants to look at different methods of measuring and presenting performance to the ownership group. As a starting point, he has suggested to you that you consider measures such as net present value (NPV), economic value added (EVA™) and modified internal rate of return (MIRR) as well as the more common profit measures.

John is naïve and wants the NPV and MIRR to be appraised as if the business was a three-year project up to 20X2 so he knows the performance of the business to date. He has requested that other calculations in your performance review should be annual based on the 20X2 figures although he is aware that this may be omitting in his words 'some important detail'.

Operational issues

At recent meetings, Sheila has been complaining that her waiters and waitresses are not responding well to her attempts to encourage them to smile at customers, although her recent drive to save electricity by getting staff to turn off unnecessary lights seems to be working. Bert stated that he was not convinced by either of Sheila's initiatives and he wants her to make sure that food is collected from the kitchen swiftly and so delivered at the right temperature to the customer's table. Also, Bert has said that he feels that too much food is becoming rotten and having to be thrown out. However, he is not sure what to do about it, except make the kitchen staff go through lengthy inventory checks where they review the food held in store. John is worried about these complaints as there is now an air of tension in the owners' meetings. He has been reading various books about performance management and has come across the quote, 'What gets measured, gets done.' He believes this is true but wants to know how it might apply in the case of his business.

John is also concerned at the potential impact the tension between his co-owners could have on strategic decisions at Metis.

Building upgrade

At the last meeting, Bert expressed his concern at the impact the proposed building upgrade was forecast to have on the figures for 20X3, and he suggested that Metis should reconsider whether it needs to undertake the upgrade in the next year. However, Sheila retorted that this was a very short-term view and, if Metis didn't upgrade its restaurant, customers were likely to stop eating there. John explained that he could appreciate both Bert and Sheila's perspectives, because it was important that Metis considers its long-term future as well as its short-term position.

Required

Prepare a report to Mr John Sum addressing the following issues:

(a) Critically assess the existing performance report and suggest improvements to its content and presentation. **(12 marks)**

(b) Calculate and briefly evaluate:

 (i) The use of John's suggested performance measures; and

 (ii) Other profit-based measures, using the most recent year's actual figures where appropriate as examples. **(14 marks)**

(c) Assess how the quote 'What gets measured, gets done' could apply to Metis. **(10 marks)**

 Professional marks will be awarded for the format, style, structure and clarity of your report. **(4 marks)**

(d) With reference to the issues arising at the last owners' meeting, discuss the importance of managing both short-term and long-term performance at Metis. **(10 marks)**

(Total = 50 marks)

Appendix 1

METIS PERFORMANCE REPORT
METIS RESTAURANT

	Year to 31 March				*Latest quarter to 31 March*	
	Actual 20X0	*Actual 20X1*	*Actual 20X2*	*Forecast 20X3*	*20X2 (Q4 20X2)*	*Previous quarter (Q3 20X2)*
	$	$	$	$	$	$
Revenue						
Food	617,198	878,220	974,610	1,062,180	185,176	321,621
Wine	127,358	181,220	201,110	219,180	38,211	66,366
Spirits	83,273	118,490	131,495	143,310	24,984	43,394
Beer	117,562	167,280	185,640	202,320	35,272	61,261
Other beverages	24,492	34,850	38,675	42,150	7,348	12,763
Outside catering	9,797	13,940	15,470	16,860	2,939	5,105
Total	979,680	1,394,000	1,547,000	1,686,000	293,930	510,510
Cost of sales						
Food	200,589	285,422	316,748	345,209	60,182	104,527
Wine	58,585	83,361	92,511	100,821	17,577	30,528
Spirits	21,651	30,807	34,189	37,261	6,496	11,283
Beer	44,673	63,566	70,543	76,882	13,403	23,279
Other beverages	3,674	5,228	5,801	6,323	1,102	1,914
Outside catering	3,135	4,461	4,950	5,395	941	1,634
Total	332,307	472,845	524,742	571,891	99,701	173,165
Gross profit	647,373	921,155	1,022,258	1,114,109	194,229	337,345
Staff costs	220,428	313,650	348,075	379,350	66,134	114,865
Other operating costs						
Marketing	25,000	10,000	12,000	20,000	3,000	3,000
Rent/mortgage	150,800	175,800	175,800	193,400	43,950	43,950
Local property tax	37,500	37,500	37,500	37,500	9,375	9,375
Insurance	5,345	5,585	5,837	6,100	1,459	1,459
Utilities	12,600	12,978	13,043	13,173	3,261	3,261
Waste removal	6,000	6,180	6,365	6,556	1,591	1,591
Equipment repairs	3,500	3,658	3,822	3,994	956	956
Depreciation	120,000	120,000	120,000	120,000	30,000	30,000
Building upgrades				150,000		
Total	360,745	371,701	374,367	550,723	93,592	93,592
Manager salary	35,000	36,225	37,494	38,806	9,373	9,373
Net profit/loss before interest and corporate taxes	31,200	199,579	262,322	145,230	25,130	119,515
Net margin	3.2%	14.3%	17.0%	8.6%	8.5%	23.4%

Additional notes

1 The business was founded with $600,000 which comprised $250,000 of equity from the founders and the remainder in a loan from Grand Bank. Under the terms of the loan, all principal is repayable in 10 years' time and interest is charged at a fixed rate of 8.4% per year.

2 John has estimated the overall cost of capital to be 12.5%.

3 The company earns 4.5% on any returns in its deposit account.

4 John wishes you to use the $600,000 original investment as the capital employed figure for analysis purposes as no new capital has been input and the owners have taken out all residual earnings so far as dividends.

5 The corporation tax rate for Metis is 30%, paid in the same year as profits are generated. Accounting depreciation is a tax-allowable cost.

6 Marketing spending is for the short-term promotion of offers only.

52 Flack (Mar/Jun 16) — 98 mins

Company information and mission

Flack Supermarkets (Flack) is a multinational listed business operating in several developing countries. The business is divided into two divisions: Metro, which runs smaller stores in the densely populated centres of cities, and Hyper, which runs the large supermarkets situated on the edges of cities. Flack sells food, clothing and some other household goods.

Competition between supermarkets is intense in all of Flack's markets and so there is a constant need to review and improve their management and operations.

Flack mission is to be: 'the first choice for customers by providing the right balance of quality and service at a competitive price. We will achieve this through acting in the long-term interests of our stakeholders: earning customer loyalty, utilising all our resources and serving our shareholders' interests.'

Performance report and performance measures

The board has asked for a review of their performance report to see if it is fit for the purpose of achieving the company's mission.

This report is used at Flack's board level for the annual review of the company's performance. The divisional boards have their own reports.

Also, there has been criticism of the board of Flack in the financial press that it is 'short-termist' and so the board wants your evaluation of the performance report to include comments on this. A copy of the most recent report is provided as an example in Appendix 1.

The board is considering introducing two new performance measures to address the objective of 'utilising all our resources'. These are revenue and operating profit per square metre. The Chief Executive Officer (CEO) also wants an evaluation of these two measures explaining how they might address this aspect of the mission, what those ratios currently are and how they could be used to manage business performance. There is information in Appendix 1 to assist in this work. There have been disagreements between Flack's divisional management about capital allocation. The divisions have had capital made available to them. Both sets of divisional managers always seem to want more capital in order to open more stores but historically have been reluctant to invest in refurbishing existing stores. The board is unsure of capital spending priorities given that the press comments about Flack included criticism of the 'run-down' look of a number of its stores. The board wants your comments on the effectiveness of the current divisional performance measure of divisional operating profit and the possibility of replacing this with residual income in the light of these problems.

New stores

As the company is opening many new stores, the board also wants an assessment of the use of expected return on capital employed (ROCE) as a tool for deciding on new store openings. You have been given data for a new store proposal (Appendix 2), as an example to use when making your assessment. The Board have stressed, however, that the focus of your comments should be on the use of an expected value, not on the use of ROCE, as this is widely used and understood in the retail industry.

Information system

The CEO has proposed to the board that a new information system be introduced. She wishes to spend $100 million on creating a loyalty card programme with a data warehouse collecting information from customers' cards regarding their purchases. Her plan is to use this information to target advertising, product range choices and price offers more efficiently than at present.

Required

Write a report to the board of Flack to:

(i) Evaluate the performance report of Flack, using the example provided in Appendix 1, as requested by the board **(14 marks)**

(ii) Evaluate the introduction of the two measures of revenue and operating profit per square metre, as requested by the CEO **(8 marks)**

BPP LEARNING MEDIA

(iii) Assess the proposal to change the divisional performance measure

Note. No calculations of the current values are required. **(8 marks)**

(iv) Calculate the expected ROCE for the new store and assess the use of this tool for decision making at Flack **(8 marks)**

(v) Explain how the proposed new information system can help to improve business performance at Flack **(8 marks)**

Professional marks will be awarded for the format, style and structure of the discussion of your answer. **(4 marks)**

(Total = 50 marks)

Appendix 1

Board's performance report

FLACK YEAR TO 31 MARCH

	Metro budget 20X6 $'000	*Metro actual 20X6* $'000	*Hyper budget 20X6* $'000	*Hyper actual 20X6* $'000	*Flack budget 20X6* $'000	*Flack actual 20X6* $'000	*Flack actual 20X5* $'000	*Change on PY*
Revenue								
Food	1,093,521	1,104,567	5,431,277	5,542,119	6,524,798	6,646,686	6,513,752	2.04%
Clothes	765,465	773,197	3,801,894	3,879,483	4,567,359	4,652,680	4,536,363	2.56%
Other goods	328,056	331,370	1,629,383	1,662,636	1,957,439	1,994,006	1,964,096	1.52%
Total	2,187,042	2,209,134	10,862,554	11,084,238	13,049,596	13,293,372	13,014,211	2.15%
Cost of sales	1,994,583	2,014,730	10,199,937	10,408,099	12,194,520	12,422,829	12,186,796	1.94%
Gross profit	192,459	194,404	662,617	676,139	855,076	870,543	827,415	5.21%
Gross margins		8.80%		6.10%		6.55%		
Other operating costs	34,993	35,346	173,801	177,348	208,794	212,694	208,227	
Operating profit	157,466	159,058	488,816	498,791	646,282	657,849	619,188	6.24%
Operating margins		7.20%		4.50%		4.95%		
Finance costs					76,993	79,760	75,482	
Group profit before tax					**569,289**	**578,089**	**543,706**	6.32%
Tax					142,322	144,522	135,926	
Group profit after tax					**426,967**	**433,567**	**407,780**	6.32%
Total shareholder return						3.10%	2.70%	
Return on capital employed	13.2%	13.3%	13.2%	13.5%	13.2%	13.4%	13.2%	
Number of stores		533		208				
Total square metres		161,227		841,967				

Appendix 2

New store

The following data has been forecast by the Marketing Department for the new store based on Flack's existing experience. There are three possible scenarios:

Demand scenarios	Low	Medium	High
Revenue ($m)	12.5	13.0	13.5
Probability (%)	20	50	30
Forecast operating margin (%)	4.1	4.3	4.4

The new store is expected to cost $4.2m to buy, fit out and stock. The target ROCE for Flack has been set at 13%.

53 Kolmog Hotels (6/13) 98 mins

Company information and mission

Kolmog Hotels (Kolmog) is a large listed chain of branded hotels in Ostland. Its stated mission is: 'to become the No. 1 hotel chain in Ostland, building the strength of the Kolmog brand by consistently delighting customers, investing in employees, delivering innovative products/services and continuously improving performance'. The subsidiary aims of the company are to maximise shareholder value, create a culture of pride in the brand and strengthen the brand loyalty of all stakeholders.

The hotels in the Kolmog chain include a diverse range of buildings and locations serving different customer groups: large conference venues, city centre business hotels and country house hotels for holidays. For reporting purposes, the company has divided itself into the four geographical regions of Ostland, as can be seen in a recent example of the strategic performance report for the company used by the board for its annual review (see Appendix 1). At the operational level, each hotel manager is given an individual budget for their hotel, prepared in the Finance Department, and is judged by performance against budgeted profit.

Kolmog is planning a strategic change to its current business model. The board has decided to sell many of the hotels in the chain and then rent them back. This is consistent with many other hotel companies which are focusing on the management of their hotels rather than managing a large property portfolio of hotels.

Balanced scorecard

In order to assist this strategic change, the Chief Executive Officer (CEO) is considering introducing the balanced scorecard (BSC) across Kolmog. He has tasked you, as a management accountant in the head office, with reviewing the preliminary work done on the development of the scorecard in order to ensure that it is consistent with the goal of meeting the strategic objectives of the company by tying operational and strategic performance measurement into a coherent framework.

The CEO is worried that the BSC might be perceived within the organisation as a management accounting technique that has been derived from the manufacturing sector. In order to assess its use at Kolmog, he has asked you to explain the characteristics that differentiate service businesses from manufacturing ones.

Senior executives at the head office of Kolmog have drawn up a preliminary list of perspectives and metrics as an outline of the BSC in Table 1:

Table 1: Performance metrics

Key strategic perspective	Metric
Strategic financial performance	Financial performance benchmarked to Kolmog's main competitors (share price and return on capital employed)
Customer satisfaction	Customer satisfaction survey scores
Hotel performance against budget	Variance analysis for each hotel
Employee satisfaction	Staff turnover

BPP LEARNING MEDIA

Reward systems

The history of rewards at Kolmog has not been good, with only 1% of staff receiving their maximum possible bonus in previous years, and 75% of staff receiving no bonus. This has led to many complaints that targets set for the reward system are too challenging.

Under a new performance reward system, employee targets are to be derived from the above BSC strategic measures depending on the employee's area of responsibility. The new system is for hotel managers to be given challenging targets based on their hotel's performance against budgeted profit, industry-wide staff turnover and the company's average customer satisfaction scores. The hotel managers will then get up to 30% of their basic salary as a bonus, based on their regional manager's assessment of their performance against these targets. The CEO wants you to use Fitzgerald and Moon's building block model to assess the new system. He is happy with the dimensions of performance but wants your comments on the standards and rewards being applied here.

Required

Write a report to the CEO to:

(i) Explain the characteristics that differentiate service businesses from manufacturing ones, using Kolmog to illustrate your points **(5 marks)**

(ii) Evaluate the current strategic performance report and the choice of performance metrics used (Appendix 1) **(8 marks)**

(iii) Evaluate the outline BSC (Table 1) at Kolmog, suggesting suitable improvements **(12 marks)**

(iv) Describe the difficulties in implementing and using the BSC at Kolmog **(7 marks)**

(v) Explain the purpose of setting targets which are challenging, and evaluate the standards and rewards for the hotel managers' performance reward system as requested by the CEO **(14 marks)**

Professional marks will be awarded for the format, style and structure of the discussion of your answer. **(4 marks)**

(Total = 50 marks)

Appendix 1

STRATEGIC PERFORMANCE REPORT FOR REVIEW
KOLMOG HOTELS YEAR TO 31 MARCH 20X3

	East region $m	*West region* $m	*North region* $m	*South region* $m	*Total* $m	*Total 20X2* $m	*As % of revenue for 20X3*
Revenue	235	244	313	193	985	926	
Cost of sales	28	30	37	21	116	110	11.78%
Gross profit	207	214	276	172	869	816	
Staff costs	61	65	78	54	258	245	26.19%
Other operating costs							
hotels	68	70	97	54	289	270	29.34%
head office					158	150	16.04%
Operating profit	78	79	101	64	164	151	16.60%
Financing costs					78	73	7.92%
Profit before tax					86	78	8.73%

	20X3	*20X2*	*Growth year on year*
Capital employed	$1,132m	$1,065m	6.29%
EPS	$1.36	$1.27	7.09%
Share price	$12.34	$11.76	4.93%
ROCE	14.49%	14.18%	

54 Cantor (6/14) 98 mins

Company information and mission

Cantor Group (Cantor) is a listed company with two subsidiaries, both involved in food and drink retailing in the small country of Deeland. Its mission is 'to maximise shareholder value through supplying good value food and drink in appealing environments for our customers'.

Cantor Cafés (Cafés) is the original operating company for the group and is a chain of 115 cafés specialising in different coffee drinks but also serving some simple food dishes. Cafés has been running successfully for 15 years and has reached the limit of its expansion as the café market is now considered to be saturated with competition. Further growth will occur only as the opportunity to obtain profitable, new sites is presented, although such opportunities are not expected to be significant over the next few years.

Cantor Juicey (Juicey) was started by the Cantor Group two years ago. Now, it is made up of 15 juice bars which serve a variety of blended fruit juice drinks and health snacks. The products served by Juicey have benefited from an increased awareness in Deeland of the need to eat and drink healthily. Cantor Group expects to increase the rate of property acquisition in order to feed the rapid growth of this business, intending to open 25 outlets per year for the next 4 years.

Cantor Group organises its two subsidiaries in a similar way, as they are involved in similar areas of business. There is one exception to this, namely in the arrangements over the properties from which the subsidiaries operate. Cafés rent their properties on the open market on standard commercial terms with a five-year lease at a fixed rental payable quarterly in advance. Juicey, on the other hand, has made a single arrangement with a large commercial landlord for all of its properties. Juicey has agreed that the rent for its sites is a percentage of the revenue generated at each site. Juicey believes that it can continue its expansion by obtaining more sites from this landlord under the same terms.

Performance reporting systems

The board of Cantor is reviewing the company's performance reporting systems and would like your evaluation of the current report (Appendix 1). This report contains information for both the subsidiaries and the group and is used by all three boards. The Chief Executive Officer (CEO) has advised you that the board does not require an evaluation of Cantor's performance. However, the CEO does want you to consider the cost structures at Cantor and advise on the implications of the mix of fixed and variable elements in the key cost areas of staff and property for performance management.

Value based management (VBM) and Economic value added (EVA™)

At a recent shareholder meeting of Cantor, one of the large shareholders expressed concern that the group lacks focus and suggested the introduction of value-based management (VBM) using economic value added (EVA™) as the measure of value. Cantor's CEO has asked you, their Strategic Management Accountant, to give the board more information on the implications of this suggestion. She has asked you to do an example calculation of the EVA™ for the Group using the current data (Appendices 1 and 2) and explain how the shareholders might view the result. The board also needs to have the VBM system explained and evaluated, to be able to make a decision about its use at Cantor.

Potential changes to mission statement

Finally, the board is considering amending the mission statement to include more information on the ethical values of the company. The area being considered for inclusion in the overall mission is the treatment of employees as it is felt that they should share in the progress and profitability of Cantor since a happy working environment will help them to better serve the customers.

The proposed new mission statement would read:

'To maximise shareholder value and to provide a fair deal to our employees by supplying good value food and drink in appealing environments for our customers.'

The CEO has asked you to consider how the Group's performance in the area regarding employees could be measured using the current management information at Cantor. You have obtained additional information from the management information system to assist with this task (Appendix 3).

Required

Write a report to the CEO of Cantor to:

(i) Evaluate the current performance report in Appendix 1 **(15 marks)**

(ii) Assess the balance of fixed and variable elements of the CEO's two key costs in each of the two subsidiaries and the impact which this may have on performance management of these costs

Note. Detailed calculations are not required. **(6 marks)**

(iii) Evaluate the EVA™ of Cantor Group, justifying any assumptions made **(9 marks)**

(iv) Explain how VBM could be implemented at Cantor and evaluate its potential impact on the group **(10 marks)**

(v) Using the information in the appendices, provide justified recommendations for suitable performance measures to reflect the proposed change in the company's mission statement **(6 marks)**

Professional marks will be awarded for the format, style and structure of the discussion of your answer. **(4 marks)**

(Total = 50 marks)

Appendix 1

Cantor Group	**Year to 31 March**						Costs and profit as a % of revenue	
	Cafés Budget 20X4	*Cafés Actual 20X4*	*Juicey Budget 20X4*	*Juicey Actual 20X4*	*Group Budget 20X4*	*Group Actual 20X4*	*Group*	*Industry average*
	$	$	$	$	$	$		
Revenue								
Drink	47,437,500	46,521,000	5,130,000	5,398,000	52,567,500	51,919,000		
Food	15,812,500	15,913,000	570,000	582,000	16,382,500	16,495,000		
Total	**63,250,000**	**62,434,000**	**5,700,000**	**5,980,000**	**68,950,000**	**68,414,000**		
Cost of sales								
Drink	12,808,125	12,560,670	1,385,100	1,457,460	14,193,225	14,018,130		
Food	3,478,750	3,500,860	125,400	128,040	3,604,150	3,628,900		
Total	**16,286,875**	**16,061,530**	**1,510,500**	**1,585,500**	**17,797,375**	**17,647,030**	25.8%	
Gross profit	**46,963,125**	**46,372,470**	**4,189,500**	**4,394,500**	**51,152,625**	**50,766,970**	74.2%	72.8%
Staff costs	**16,128,750**	**15,920,670**	**1,453,500**	**1,524,900**	**20,082,250**	**21,345,000**	31.2%	30.9%
Other operating costs								
Rent	2,875,000	2,875,000	342,000	358,800	3,929,000	3,945,800		
Local property tax	920,000	920,000	60,000	60,000	980,000	980,000		
Insurance	276,000	282,000	18,000	18,400	294,000	300,400		
Utilities	874,000	861,000	61,500	62,900	935,500	923,900		
Marketing	6,957,500	6,888,000	627,000	750,000	7,584,500	7,638,000	11.2%	10.0%
Depreciation	4,427,500	4,427,500	353,400	353,400	4,780,900	4,780,900		
Total	**16,330,000**	**16,253,500**	**1,461,900**	**1,603,500**	**18,503,900**	**18,569,000**	27.1%	
Operating profit	**14,504,375**	**14,198,300**	**1,274,100**	**1,266,100**	**12,566,475**	**10,852,970**	15.9%	15.3%
Finance costs					798,000	801,000		
Group profit before tax					**11,768,475**	**10,051,970**	14.7%	
Tax					2,942,119	2,512,993		
Group profit after tax					**8,826,356**	**7,538,977**	11.0%	

Appendix 2

Data about the group for the financial year:

1	Debt/Equity	30.0%
2	Cost of equity	15.7%
3	Tax rate	25.0%
4	Group ROCE	19.0%

5 Group capital employed: $53,400,000 at period start and $58,500,000 at period end.

6 Pre-tax cost of debt 6.5%

7 There has been $2.1m of tax paid in the year.

8 It is estimated that half of the marketing spend of $7.638m is on building the Cantor brand long term.

9 It is further estimated that there has been the same level of annual spending on long-term brand building in the years leading up to 20X4.

Appendix 3

Additional management information

	Cafés	*Juicey*	*Group*
No. of employees			
At year start	1,495	96	1,611
Leavers	146	15	161
Joiners	152	35	187
At year end	1,501	116	1,637

Note. Group numbers include Cafés, Juicey and head office numbers.

55 Boltzman Machines (12/14, amended) 98 mins

Company information and mission

Boltzman Machines (Boltzman) is a listed, multinational engineering business. Its mission is 'to maximise shareholder value through engineering excellence'.

Boltzman has two divisions, one manufacturing aerospace parts and the other automotive parts. The company is known for innovation and it allows its managers much autonomy to run their own divisions and projects. However, there has been recent criticism at a shareholders' meeting of the executive management for not listening to shareholders' concerns and allowing this autonomy to run out of control.

Therefore, the board at Boltzman has been reviewing a number of aspects of the way performance is controlled and managed in the business. However, there are a number of initiatives already running within the company, which the board feels may help to address the shareholders' concerns.

The initiatives which are running at present are:

(1) An analysis of stakeholder influence at Boltzman leading to suitable strategic performance measures

(2) A benchmarking exercise of the performance measures from Initiative 1 with Boltzman's main competitor, General Machines

(3) The introduction of quality initiatives bringing lean production methods to Boltzman

(4) The introduction of a balanced scorecard performance measurement system

The Chief Executive Officer (CEO) has asked for your views on the impact these initiatives could have on performance management within the company.

Analysis of stakeholder influence

A stakeholder analysis has been completed by one of Boltzman's managers (Appendix 1) but she has gone on holiday and has not written up a commentary of her results. Therefore, the CEO wants you to take the information in Appendix 1 and explain the results and evaluate the suggested performance measures. However, the CEO has asked that you do not, at this stage, suggest long lists of additional indicators.

BPP LEARNING MEDIA

Benchmarking exercise

The CEO wants you to use the suggested performance measures from the stakeholder analysis to benchmark the performance of Boltzman against General Machines. The CEO stated, 'Make sure that you calculate the measures given in Appendix 1. You should also add two justified measures of your own using the data provided. However, restrict yourself to these seven measures and don't drown us with detail about individual business units.' A junior analyst has already gathered the data for you to use in the benchmarking exercise (Appendix 2.)

Quality initiatives

Boltzman has stated that one of its strategic aims is to be the highest quality supplier in the marketplace. In order to achieve this, the Head of the Aerospace Division has already started a project to implement just-in-time (JIT) manufacturing. The CEO has sent you an extract of the email proposing this change (Appendix 3). The CEO feels that there are some important elements hinted at but not developed in this email. In particular, the CEO wants you to explain the problems of moving to JIT manufacturing.

Balanced scorecard

Finally, the CEO feels it is important that the company's performance is measured across a range of non-financial areas as well as financial ones. He believes that the balanced scorecard would provide a good choice, but has asked you to evaluate its suitability in the light of the shareholders' criticism, and the other initiatives currently in progress at Boltzman.

Required

Prepare a report to the board of Boltzman to:

(a) Briefly justify appropriate management approaches to each of the stakeholders and, based on this analysis, evaluate the appropriateness of the performance measures suggested in Appendix 1 **(14 marks)**

(b) Benchmark Boltzman against General Machines as suggested by the CEO, evaluating the approach to benchmarking used **(16 marks)**

(c) Explain the problems which will accompany a move towards just-in-time manufacturing at Boltzman **(7 marks)**

(d) Assess the suitability of using the balanced scorecard as a performance measurement system at Boltzman, as requested by the CEO **(9 marks)**

Professional marks will be awarded for the format, style and structure of the discussion of your answer. **(4 marks)**

(Total = 50 marks)

Appendix 1

Key stakeholders	Level of interest	Level of power
Shareholders	Low – institutions have delegated management to the board and are only interested in financial returns	High – ability to vote out existing management
Employees	Medium – in a high skill industry employees are interested in the new opportunities which the market can present	Low – although there is a group of key employees in product development whose skills must not be lost
Customers	Medium – some of the parts supplied by Boltzman are unique and specifically designed for the customer	High – as there are few major players in the aerospace and automotive businesses, the loss of a customer would have a significant impact on Boltzman
Suppliers	Medium – Boltzman is one of the large customers to many of the company's suppliers	Low – the suppliers are generally bulk component producers and there is significant competition for Boltzman's business

Suggested performance measures:

- Return on capital employed
- Economic value added
- Revenue growth
- Average pay per employee
- Net profit margin

Appendix 2

The figures are drawn from the financial statements for the year to September 20X4.

	Boltzman *20X4* $m	*General Machines* *20X4* $m
Revenue	23,943	25,695
Cost of sales	18,078	20,605
Other costs	2,958	3,208
Operating profit	2,907	1,882
Financing costs	291	316
Tax	663	718
Net income	1,953	848

	Boltzman		*General Machines*	
	20X3 $m	*20X4* $m	*20X3* $m	*20X4* $m
Non-current assets	16,335	16,988	17,716	17,893
Current assets	10,618	11,043	11,515	11,630
	26,953	28,031	29,231	29,523
Equity	8,984	9,961	9,744	10,083
Non-current liabilities	9,801	9,739	10,629	10,405
Current liabilities	8,168	8,331	8,858	9,035
	26,953	28,031	29,231	29,523

		Boltzman *20X4*	*General Machines* *20X4*
Notes:			
No. of employees		86,620	93,940
Staff costs	($m)	4,731	4,913
Revenue for 20X3	($m)	22,506	25,438
Product development costs	($m)	2,684	2,630
No. of top 10 biggest potential customers where the business has top tier supplier status			
Aerospace		6	6
Automotive		7	8

A suitable cost of capital for both companies is 11%.

The tax rate is 28%.

Appendix 3

Extract of Head of Aerospace's email on his quality initiative:

In order to improve the quality and profitability of our products, we intend to begin by introducing a lean approach to manufacturing.

The first step in our move to lean manufacturing will be the introduction of JIT manufacturing. Although this will be a difficult process, the financial rewards in reduced working capital required and a decluttering of the workplace should be significant. We will have to consider how this change impacts up and down our supply chain with customers and suppliers.

BPP LEARNING MEDIA

56 Merkland Sportswear (6/15) 98 mins

Company information, mission and business aims

Merkland Sportswear (MS) is the market leader in sportswear in Ceeland, selling a variety of sportswear products under its own well-known brand. It is primarily a product development and marketing business as it contracts out all of its manufacturing to third parties around the world and it mostly sells its products through third-party retailers. It has only one store which is located in the capital city of Ceeland. The purpose of this store is to act as a centre for its marketing activities and to be a tangible representation of the MS brand. However, the main marketing activity for MS is the recruitment and promotion of star sportsmen and women as MS brand ambassadors. MS tries to have the most well-known sports star in each of the ten most popular sports in Ceeland as an ambassador.

You are a performance management adviser to MS, brought into the company by the Chief Executive Officer (CEO) to help the board with a number of issues. The first area in which the board of MS requires your input is in a review of the existing performance dashboard for MS (Appendix 1). The dashboard is deliberately kept focused as it is for board use and the CEO has indicated that the three performance headings of 'financial, design and brand' will be kept at this time. The board has accepted that there may need to be up to two metrics for each of 'brand' and 'design' but they want to keep the number of financial metrics at three.

The mission statement of the business is designed to be broadly appealing. It is 'to inspire Ceelanders to compete'. From a business perspective, the aims are more focused; MS aims to grow as a business and to maximise shareholder wealth. The CEO further clarified the broad strategy to achieve these aims saying, 'We want to inspire competition not just in our customers but also within the company, to seek our greatest competitive advantage. We will achieve this by creating innovative products which provide reduced risk of injury and enhanced sporting performance supported by the best marketing operation in Ceeland.'

Review of competitive position

In order to assist in providing more detailed strategies to achieve the company's aims, the board has instituted a review of the competitive position of MS by commissioning a SWOT analysis (Appendix 2).

The CEO has asked that, after you have reviewed the current dashboard metrics (Appendix 1), you should review the SWOT analysis to suggest changes to the dashboard metrics, within the constraints which the CEO has outlined.

Child labour scandal

You have been given details on a recent new development in the market. Nush Sportswear, one of the major competitors of MS, has recently suffered a scandal which has been widely reported. An investigative reporter discovered that one of the suppliers who manufactured sports shoes for Nush had been using child labour. The country in which the manufacturer worked had rules prohibiting child labour, but enforcement of these rules was very weak. This story has been widely covered in the media and has led to consumer boycotts and a review by the Ceeland business regulator into Nush's sourcing policies. It has been discovered that this is common practice in the sports footwear business where manufacturing is outsourced to such countries.

Potential responses to the child labour scandal

MS's shareholders have reacted with alarm to the potential damage that this could do to MS's brand. They have asked the board to consider changing their policy of outsourcing footwear manufacture. The board is considering two alternative responses:

(1) Review and ensure that all outsourced footwear manufacture complies with appropriate employment terms and conditions (where necessary manufacturing would move to third-party companies in countries with appropriate regulation and enforcement); or

(2) Create a manufacturing operation for MS in order to have full control of operations.

In Response 1, the review of existing third-party manufacturers is being performed by a team from the Procurement Department. They have also considered the impact of moving all footwear sourcing to more strictly regulated environments. The results of this investigation are given in Appendix 3, and the board wants an evaluation of the qualitative and quantitative impact of this response.

In Response 2, the board is considering setting up a factory for the manufacture of all MS footwear. It wants to understand the impact of this on MS's existing performance metrics. First, it needs a forecast of the profit from the factory as there are three distinct economic scenarios under which it might operate (see Appendix 4 for details).

Second, the board wants to know how the new factory will impact on the existing performance dashboard. However, since the probabilities of these economic scenarios are under debate, the board has said that they want this work to be independent of the results of the profit calculation from Appendix 4. Therefore, the board wants you to use an estimate of $103 million profit before interest and tax from the new factory to evaluate the impact of the new factory on the dashboard. (This estimate is before product development and marketing costs as it only represents the manufacturing operation at the factory.)

Value chain

The consultant who did the SWOT analysis has mentioned to the board that if it is thinking of reviewing its existing strategies, then it should consider using the value chain to secure competitive advantage. The CEO thinks that you should assess the implications of using the value chain for the performance management of MS. (An outline of the value chain is given in Appendix 5.)

Required

Write a report to the board of MS to:

(i) Assess the existing five metrics (Appendix 1). Using the SWOT analysis in Appendix 2, make suggestions for improvements within the constraints outlined by the CEO

Note. You should ignore the impact of the Nush scandal in this part of the question. **(16 marks)**

(ii) Using the data in Appendix 3, assess the qualitative and quantitative impact on performance management at MS of Response 1 **(8 marks)**

(iii) Calculate the expected operating profit of the new factory and evaluate the use of this method of decision making under risk **(6 marks)**

(iv) Using 20X5 figures as a base, evaluate the impact of the new factory on the values and choice of metrics in the existing dashboard **(10 marks)**

(v) Explain the implications of using the value chain for performance management at MS **(6 marks)**

Professional marks will be awarded for the format, style and structure of the discussion of your answer. **(4 marks)**

(Total = 50 marks)

Appendix 1

MS performance dashboard

REPORT FOR THE YEAR TO MARCH 20X5

	20X5	*20X4*	*20X3*	*Change 20X5/20X4*
Financial				%
Revenue ($m)	273	238	209	14.7
Operating profit ($m)	71	60	54	18.3
ROCE	41.7%	37.5%	36.0%	11.2
Design				
Design awards won	2	2	1	0.0
Brand				
Awareness	64%	63%	59%	1.6

Note. Design awards are national clothing design awards which address both the look of and technology in a product. Brand awareness is the percentage of those sampled who could identify the company's logo and can name at least one of its products.

BPP LEARNING MEDIA

Appendix 2

SWOT (completed before the Nush scandal was reported)

S:	W:
• High market share • Excellent brand awareness • Strong revenue growth (compared to industry average of 11%) • Supply chain management	• Loss of a key brand ambassador (who was injured when he tripped over the laces of his MS boots) • Weak IT expertise
O:	**T:**
• New products in the market for new sports (such as those being introduced at each World Championships)	• Growth of social media as main marketing channel

Appendix 3

Procurement review of new outsourced footwear manufacturers

Currently, MS buys two million pairs of shoes at an average of $21 per unit (a pair of shoes) and we assume an average selling price of $75. Cost per unit will increase by 10%. Additionally, there will be a need to perform annual audits of these suppliers which will cost $0.5m.

The change of policy will be marketed as sustaining the values of MS. The MS ethics code states 'we will play fair and source our goods responsibly.' This marketing will cost $0.8m p.a. but it is hoped that this will produce a gain in market share. However, the increase in sales cannot be estimated at this time as competitors are making similar moves. The reviewer commented, 'It would be helpful to know how many units we would need to sell in order to cover these increased costs so this can be used as a marketing target.'

Appendix 4

New factory

The data collected on the new factory depends on three possible economic scenarios in response to MS's change in sourcing policy:

	Bad	*Medium*	*Good*
Probability	30%	60%	10%
Units manufactured ('000)	1,800	2,000	2,200
Variable costs per unit ($)	21	22	23
Fixed costs ($'000)	2,500		
Capital required	$'000		
Building and equipping	36,000		
Working capital	11,000		

Notes

1 One unit is one pair of shoes.
2 Assume all units made are sold.
3 Assume an average selling price of $75.
4 The total Ceeland market for this type of shoe is estimated as 6.25m p.a.

Appendix 5

Value chain analysis

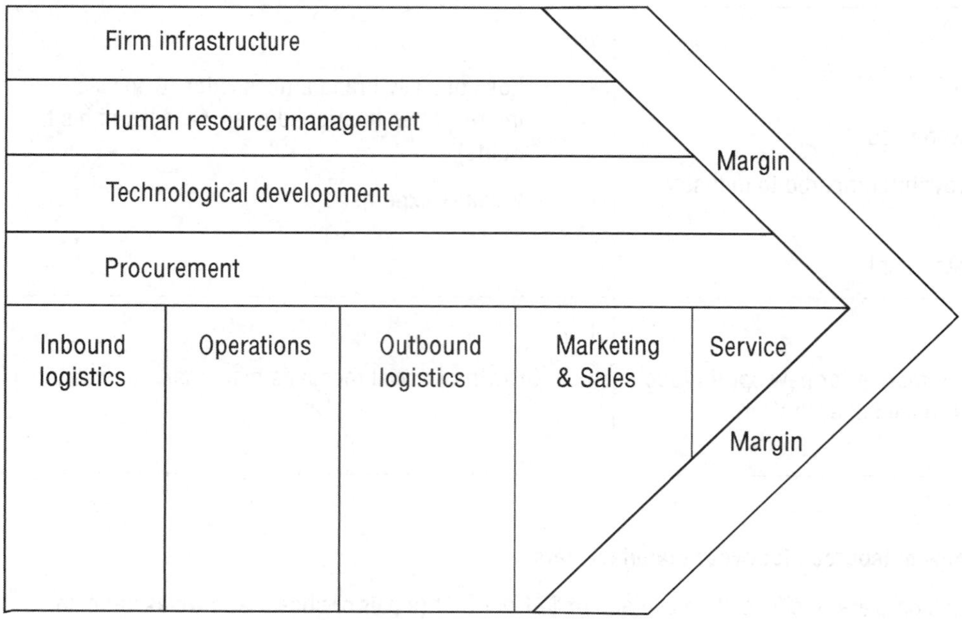

57 Dargeboard Services (Mar/Jun 17) — 98 mins

Company information and mission

Dargeboard Services (DS), a listed company, provides facilities management (FM) services where it manages such activities as cleaning, security, catering and building services on behalf of its clients. Clients can outsource to DS a single activity or often outsource all of these aspects in a full service contract.

The mission of DS is 'to give the shareholders maintainable, profitable growth by developing the best talent to provide world-class services with maximum efficiency.'

Systems review

The board have asked the Chief Executive Officer (CEO) to review the effectiveness of Dargeboard's systems for performance measurement and management. She has turned to you to begin this process by considering the strategic performance dashboard of DS. She has supplied the most recent example in Appendix 1.

She wants a report to the board which will cover three aspects of strategic performance reporting at DS. First, it should address whether the current set of key performance indicators (KPIs) measure the achievement of the mission by showing how each one links to all or part of the mission. She does not want suggestions of new indicators. Second, taking each of the current indicators in turn she wants the assumptions underlying the calculation of the indicators examined. There has been a suggestion made in the press that DS is producing a biased set of results aimed to mislead the markets. This would then artificially boost the share price and so boost the value of the senior management's share holdings. Third, the report should evaluate the other presentational aspects of the dashboard against best practice.

Reward and remuneration schemes

The idea of employee share ownership has always been at the heart of DS's remuneration schemes. Its aim is to support an entrepreneurial culture and is a key differentiator in the market for new employees. The current reward system grants shares based on the appraisal of the individual by the line manager against vague categories such as leadership and entrepreneurship. The results of this scheme have been that only about 5% of staff received their maximum possible bonus in previous years and half of them received no bonus at all. Increasingly, this has led to the staff ignoring the reward scheme and describing it as 'only for the bosses' favourite people'.

In response to this, the board have been discussing methods of analysing and improving the rewards system at DS. One non-executive director suggested using Fitzgerald and Moon's building block model. The CEO was asked to consider this as a project separate from the issues of performance measurement mentioned above. She will select

BPP LEARNING MEDIA

suitable indicators from the dimensions but currently needs you to explain to the board what is meant by results and determinants in this context and how the dimensions link to standards and targets. Finally, she believes that there are two types of reward scheme which might suit DS and wants an evaluation of their relative strengths and weaknesses. The scheme details are given in Appendix 2.

Required

Write a report to the board to:

(i) Evaluate the links between the current key performance indicators at DS in Appendix 1 and its mission **(8 marks)**

(ii) Assess the assumptions and definitions used in the calculation of the current set of key performance indicators in Appendix 1 **(12 marks)**

(iii) Evaluate the other aspects of reporting in the DS performance dashboard given at Appendix 1 **(8 marks)**

(iv) Explain how the building block model works, as required by the CEO **(6 marks)**

(v) Assess the two reward schemes given in Appendix 2 **(12 marks)**

Professional marks will be awarded for the format, style and structure of the discussion of your answer. **(4 marks)**

(Total = 50 marks)

Appendix 1

Dargeboard Services: Strategic performance dashboard

Year to 31 December 20X6

	Cleaning	*Security*	*Catering*	*Building services*	*Full service*	*Total*	*Total 20X5*
Operating profit margin	6.5%	6.4%	6.5%	4.9%	5.9%	5.9%	5.8%
Secured revenue	76%	85%	92%	88%	93%	88%	87%
Management retention	86%	74%	87%	82%	89%	85%	87%
Order book ($m)	1,160	875	357	1,553	3,359	7,304	6,807
Organic revenue growth	7.1%	4.3%	5.0%	8.1%	7.9%	7.2%	4.6%
ROCE						17.2%	16%

KPI definitions and notes

(1) Cleaning, security, catering and building services headings are for single service contracts.

(2) No commentary is provided as the CEO talks the board through the dashboard at each board meeting.

(3) Secured revenue is long-term recurring revenue. This is the percentage of budgeted revenue which is already contracted. The budget is often not completed until well into the year as it is a complex process. In 20X6, the original budget showed revenue of $1,565m with the final budget signed off at the end of Q1 showing $1,460m. The secured (contracted) revenue for the period was $1,285m. The accounts show a year end revenue of $1,542m.

(4) Management retention is the percentage of managers who were still employed throughout the whole year. The figure only includes those employees on full-time contracts (about 65% of all managers).

(5) Order book is the total cash value of future contracted revenue. DS has contracts which run up to 10 years into the future.

(6) Operating profit margin. This excludes exceptional items such as the reorganisation of the catering business which cost $55m in 20X6, where revenue was $245m.

(7) Organic revenue growth is calculated by using the total revenue figure as reported in the accounts. It includes net acquisitions which brought in revenue of $48m in 20X6.

(8) Return on capital employed (ROCE). Capital employed is total assets less current liabilities from the statement of financial position.

Appendix 2

The CEO is considering two schemes, one based on the current scheme and a new scheme.

Scheme 1 (based on the current scheme)

The reward system grants shares in DS based on the appraisal of the individual by the line manager against vague categories (leadership and entrepreneurship). The line managers have been informed that their bonus will in turn be partly dependent on how well they perform this appraisal. The expectation will be that as a result, 20% of staff will receive their maximum possible bonus and 20% will receive no bonus.

Scheme 2 (the new one)

Under scheme 2, employee targets are to be derived from the strategic indicators depending on the employee's area of responsibility. The senior management (with help from line management where appropriate) will cascade down the strategic indicators to the relevant operational or tactical level for that employee.

There will be five targets set by senior and line management in consultation and the employee will then get up to 50% on top of their basic salary as a bonus (10 percentage points for each of the targets achieved).

Answers

1 Ganymede

Text reference. Benchmarking is discussed in Chapter 1 of the BPP Study Text. Public sector league tables are discussed in Chapter 9a.

Top tips.

Part (a). A useful approach to this requirement would be to think through, in order, the stages involved in a benchmarking process. This should help you identify which stages GU has already undertaken and which it still needs to undertake. To answer this question well you need to know the stages involved in a benchmarking process, but don't simply list the stages in general terms. Make sure you consider specifically which stages GU has undertaken, and which are still required.

Part (b). Note that the focus of your evaluation here should be GU's position, not on benchmarking's usefulness for assessing GU's position.

However, the fact that the question requirement says 'as far as possible' should serve as an indicator that some details which would help you evaluate GU's position may be missing from the information provided. In this case, you should highlight the additional information which would help you evaluate GU's position more fully.

Part (c). You are asked to evaluate the usefulness of the league tables from the students' perspective. So, you should consider how they might be useful to students in making a decision about where to study; but, perhaps more importantly, you should also consider the drawbacks or limitations in the league tables, or why they may not be helpful to students in making their decisions about where to study.

Examining team's comments. Part (b) ought to have been a relatively straightforward analysis of the data given in the scenario. However, candidates displayed a disappointing lack of judgement over what constitutes useful advice in this scenario and failed to use the drivers highlighted in the scenario to calculate suitable relative measures.

Marking scheme

			Marks
(a)	For each relevant point on the progress of the benchmarking exercise – 1 mark **Note.** Only 2 marks in total are available for identifying the stages of the benchmarking process in general terms		
	Total for part (a) – Up to 7 marks		7
(b)	Calculation of performance indicators using appropriate drivers – 1 mark each	Up to 6	
	Commenting on the results – 1 mark per relevant point	Up to 6	
	Total for part (b) – Up to 10 marks		10
(c)	Potential benefits of proposed league tables – 1 mark each	Up to 3	
	Limitations of proposed league tables – 1 mark each	Up to 7	
	Total for part (c) – Up to 8 marks		8
		Total =	**25**

(a) Benchmarking exercises can be described using seven stages, and we will use these stages to assess the progress of GU's current benchmarking exercise.

Actions that have been undertaken

(i) Set objectives and determine the area to benchmark.

The underlying objective of the exercise is to improve efficiency, and the area being benchmarked has been identified as the administrative costs incurred in relation to teaching and research.

(ii) Identify key performance drivers and indicators.

It is important that the benchmarking exercise focuses on performance areas which are crucial to GU's success.

Three key drivers of costs have revenues which have been identified (research contract values supported; student numbers; and staff numbers). Key performance indicators can be derived from these; for example, costs per student.

However, although the drivers have already been set, the driver 'staff numbers' could be improved by distinguishing between teaching staff and administrative staff.

(iii) Select organisations to study and benchmark against.

The chancellor has asked the administrator to benchmark GU's performance against the other two large universities in Teeland (AU and BU), and the government has endorsed this proposal.

However, the exercise as it stands will not compare GU's performance against any of the five smaller universities in Teeland, nor against any foreign universities.

This could be a weakness in the proposed exercise, because the universities which are excluded could provide examples of best practice which GU could lead from if they had been included.

(iv) Measure performance for own organisation and the other organisations involved in the exercise.

Information about GU, AU and BU's administrative costs for the most recent academic year has been collected.

The step has been made easier by the Government insisting that all three universities co-operate and supply information to each other.

Actions still required

(v) Compare performance.

This is the stage that the exercise has currently reached. The results of the performance comparison are given in part (b).

(vi) Design and implement improvement programme.

The results of the performance comparison should help identify which areas GU needs to improve in.

For those aspects of performance where GU is lagging behind one (or both) of the other universities it should send a member of staff to the university which is performing best to identify what that university is doing differently to GU which is leading to the difference in performance levels.

In turn, that staff member should devise a programme to introduce improvements at GU and implement the best practices which have been identified at the other universities.

(vii) Monitor improvement.

Whilst implementing the improvement programme should help GU improve its performance, there is no guarantee how successful it will be and how much improvement it will actually deliver. Therefore, management should monitor GU's performance once the programme has been implemented to see if it achieves its goals or if further improvements will still be necessary.

> At the end of the programme, GU's management should also consider a post-project review, to consider any lessons which have been learned from the project and which could be useful for any subsequent projects.

(b) Results from the benchmarking exercise:

	GU	AU	BU
	$	$	$
Research			
(Cost per $'000 of contract value supported)			
Contract management	78	87	97
Laboratory	226	257	281
Teaching facilities management			
(Cost per student)	951	1,197	920
Student support services			
(Cost per student)	71	89	73
Other support services			
(Cost per staff member)			
Teachers' support services	506	532	544
Accounting	204	204	197
Human resources	156	156	191
IT management	817	803	737
General services	2,153	2,088	2,286

Research categories

GU has the lowest costs relative to the value of the research contracts supported, and it has also earned the highest value contracts. This may suggest that the Government monitors factors such as cost control when deciding where to allocate its costs, in which case it is important that GU continues to maintain its good practice in this area, particularly if the other universities will be looking to improve their performance to bring it closer to GU's performance.

Teaching facilities management and student support services

AU spends significantly more per student on its teaching facilities and student support than the other two universities. AU also has significantly fewer students than the other two universities.

We might expect that AU's higher spending on teaching facilities and student support would make it more attractive to students than the other two universities, leading to higher student numbers. At face value, the benchmarked figures would suggest that student enrolment is not significantly influenced by these factors, though. However, the lower student numbers at AU may also reflect that it can accommodate fewer students than the other two universities; or even that it only wants to accommodate a smaller number of students and therefore sets harder entry requirements than the other two.

Therefore, it might also be useful to compare the number of applications each university receives relative to the number of places it has available. Equally, it might also be useful to compare factors such as student drop out rates, pass rates, and students' success rates in gaining employment after they graduate, to assess whether there is a correlation between these and the more expensive teaching environment at AU.

However, these quality measures are not currently reflected in the benchmarking exercise.

Other support services

Human resources – BU's human resource costs per staff member are 22% higher than the other two universities, despite BU having the highest number of staff to spread its HR costs. In this respect, it appears that BU may have more HR staff, or more highly paid HR staff than it needs, whereas GU's model appears more efficient.

Teachers' support services – BU also appears to provide more support services for its staff than the other two universities. The difference between BU and AU is not significant, but GU's costs are around 7% lower per staff member than BU's.

However, it is not clear exactly what costs are included in this category so it is difficult to determine whether the figures suggest that GU is more efficient in the provision of these services, or whether it offers less support services to its teachers than BU.

IT management – In contrast to their respective positions for HR and teachers' support services, GU spends considerably more (around 11%) on IT management than BU. However, this may be due to the subjects being taught. For example, if GU is more oriented to science and technology-based subjects this is likely to mean it will need greater computing resources than if it was more orientated towards arts and humanities.

However, if the difference in IT management costs cannot be explained by variations in the subjects taught, then GU (and to a slightly lesser extent, AU) need to consider how BU appears to have been able to control its IT costs more effectively than them. For example, has BU outsourced any of its IT services rather than managing them all in house?

Accounting services – All three universities' cost control appears broadly the same here. BU has achieved a small advantage (3.5%) over the other two, but there is nothing significant here.

General services – Again, there appears to be relatively little variation between the three universities here, although AU appears to have slightly lower costs than GU, which, in turn, has slightly lower costs than BU.

General point

Although we have identified some variations between GU's performance and that of the other two universities, it is important to exercise a degree of caution when looking at these comparisons. We have no information about the mix of the subjects being taught or researched at the different universities, but this mix could have an impact on their performance statistics. Equally, we do not have any information about the relative locations of the three universities. For example, if one of the universities is in a region which is economically more prosperous than the other two, then that university's staff costs are automatically likely to be higher than the other two's, as a result of the geographical variation in salary weightings rather than any internal factors.

(c) The league tables will provide students with some additional information which could help them compare different universities before deciding which ones to apply to.

Academic and non-academic criteria – The measures chosen seem to recognise the importance of non-academic factors as well as academic ones. For example, if students are strongly dissatisfied with the university facilities this may lead to them not completing their courses, as would the fact that the course content is not what they had hoped it would be.

Equally, the prospects of finding work after graduating is likely to be something which is important to students, so the inclusion of this measure in the league tables could be valuable to them.

However, some of the other measures included in the table may be less important to students when choosing where to study:

Research or tuition – The value of research funding secured by each university may give some indication of the quality of the academic staff it employs, and how highly the university is regarded in the academic and research community. However, a potential student may be more interested in the quality of tuition they will receive than the amount of research the university carries out.

If a university prioritises research above teaching, this would improve its ranking in this element of the league table, but may actually be disadvantageous to the student if the tutors are more concerned with their research than their students.

Choice of measures – In addition, there are a number of other possible measures which the tables do not include, yet which would be valuable for students. For example, information about spending on academic services, and the ratio of students to academic staff might be more useful to students than information about research funding. Equally, information about entry requirements is also likely to be useful to prospective students.

Aggregate measures – However, perhaps the biggest weakness in the league tables is that they look at aggregate figures, rather than figures for particular departments for example.

However, the quality of the particular course they want to study is likely to be a very important factor for a student when choosing where to study. A university which performs relatively poorly overall in the league tables may be a centre of excellence in a particular subject, while conversely a university which performs well overall might have poor departments for certain subjects.

By only considering overall figures, there is a danger that the league tables will obscure variation within them.

Importantly, also, the league tables do not give any indication of the numbers of students taking different courses, but this could also affect the results. For example, if there is a shortage of engineering graduates in Teeland, and a university has a large engineering department, this might lead to the proportion of its graduates in employment being higher than a university with only a small engineering department.

Trends – It is not clear from the scenario how frequently the Ministry envisages the league tables should be produced. However, when looking at any figures in the tables, students should consider whether the figures for a single period are representative, or whether they need to look at an average or a trend over a longer period of time. For example, the numbers of students gaining first class or 2:1 degrees could vary from one year to the next, so looking at one year in isolation may not give an accurate picture of the university's overall performance in this respect.

Unintended consequences – Another potential disadvantage of introducing league tables focusing on only a small number of measures is that they will encourage the universities to focus on their performance in those areas potentially at the detriment of other areas. For example, if there is a focus on ensuring that the proportion of students achieving first class and 2:1 degrees is as high as possible, there could be a danger that a university makes its entry requirements more demanding, with the result that fewer students overall come to the university. The league tables do not show entry requirements, which could be a useful measure for students to consider when choosing which universities to apply to.

Equally, there could be a danger that universities could inflate results (for example, by uplifting marks so that students obtain 2:1 degrees instead of 2:2 degrees) to improve the university's place in the league tables.

2 CFD

Text reference. Mission statements, critical success factors (CSFs) and the relationship between CSFs and performance metrics are discussed in Chapter 2 of the BPP Study Text. The concept of value for money is discussed in Chapter 9a, and non-financial performance indicators are covered in Chapter 9b.

Top tips. Part (a)(i) draws on your knowledge of mission statements and their benefits and drawbacks. Begin with a definition. We use Mintzberg's version which nicely contains the elements of a mission. You aren't asked to refer to the scenario which makes it a bit easier as you are just writing down what you know. We have listed 13 benefits and failings, and ACCA's official answer contained the same number. These are all short one-line points so, in this case, the examining team appears to expect many, but brief, responses. The marking scheme gives six marks in total.

In **part (a)(ii)** think about what value for money (VFM) means. Does CFD provide this for its customers? Will the new initiative require a change in the mission statement?

Part (b)(i) is a test of knowledge; so you should define what CSFs and key performance indicators (KPIs) are, and then explain how they relate to each other. The key point here is that KPIs need to be used to help an organisation measure how well it is performing in relation to its CSFs.

Part (b)(ii) needs to be related back to CSF; so make sure the three critical success factors you discuss are appropriate for CFD. Think about which performance requirements are critical to its success and how these are measured.

Quality of service is important in a service business. In **part (c)** think about what you would want to see in terms of quality if you had a pet and wanted to send it to CFD.

Marking scheme

				Marks
(a)	(i)	Purpose	2	
		Potential benefits	3	
		Failings	3	
				8
	(ii)	Changed circumstances – Up to 2	2	
		Conclusion – Up to 2	2	
				4
(b)	(i)	Definition of CSFs	1	
		Definition of KPIs	1	
		Relationship between CSFs and KPIs	2	
				4
	(ii)	For each CSF discussed – 1 mark	3	
		For KPI highlighted for each CSF – 1 mark	3	
				6
(c)	Performance measures 3 × 1		3	3
			Total =	25

(a) (i) **Purpose, potential benefits and potential problems of mission statements**

Purpose

Mission describes the organisation's **basic** function in society, in terms of the products and services it produces for its clients (Mintzberg). Organisations often write down their mission in a mission statement. A **mission statement** should be **brief, flexible and distinctive**, placing an emphasis on serving the customers. It often **refers to key stakeholder groups** including employees and shareholders. The mission statement should make it clear to employees their **contribution** towards attaining the mission. It should also **remain the same** unless the mission changes.

Potential benefits of mission statements include the following:

- A written, public statement of the reason for the organisation's existence.
- Allied to this, communicate a clear image of what the organisation is to customers and other stakeholders.
- Also help in resolving conflicts between stakeholder groups over what the organisation stands for.
- Identify key cultural values to employees.
- Aid strategy by helping businesses define their nature, services and products and competences.
- Guide policies and standards of behaviour by managers and employees by stating business principles such as social responsibility and anti-discrimination.
- State ways of competing, for instance on price or innovation.

Potential problems of mission statements include:

- Vague statements which don't explain what the business is for, or how it intends to achieve its aims
- Jargon which obscures what the meaning of the statement is
- Failure to be flexible and open ended as the mission will probably change over time as the business changes
- Being unrealistic in its aims
- Not taking account of external factors
- Inconsistency between the elements of the mission

(ii) **Appropriateness of the mission statement for CFD**

Value for money is providing a service in a way which is economical, efficient and effective, and so CFD's mission statement would appear to have accorded with its overall mission (as it has operated on a profit-making basis) and would remain appropriate as long as CFD continued offering its original services. When it decided to open a homeless sanctuary for strays, its mission and services changed and so it needs to recast the mission to include some element capturing the new charitable activity. When CFD decided to undertake this non profit making activity, this meant its new aims would not necessarily be profit making and therefore could not deliver value for money.

(b) (i) **CSFs** are the key factors and processes which enable an organisation to achieve its objectives and thereby achieve future success. In effect, CSFs highlight the areas in which it is crucial for an organisation to perform well in order for it to be successful.

CSFs and KPIs – However, once an organisation has identified its CSFs, it needs to know how well it is performing in relation to them. Simply identifying the areas where an organisation needs to perform well does not guarantee that it will do so. Therefore it needs to measure how well it is performing in these areas. This is done by using KPIs.

KPIs – KPIs are the **measures** which indicate whether or not CSFs are being achieved, and how well the organisation is performing. This idea of measurement is vital for KPIs. KPIs must be measurable, because otherwise an organisation will not be able to measure whether or not its CSFs are being achieved.

(ii) CFD is a service business and so its CSFs are likely to relate to the services it offers, and in particular to the features of those services which are valued by its customers.

(1) Maintaining a high standard of cleanliness of accommodation for the dogs at CFD.

If prospective clients come to visit CFD's kennels and they look dirty and untidy, it is unlikely that the owners will want their pets to stay at CFD.

A performance indicator which could be used to measure cleanliness could be the number of cleans made per day or week of the dog kennels and common areas.

(2) Guaranteed safety of the dogs whilst in CFD's care.

Again, owners are not going to want to use CFD to care for their dogs unless they feel confident their dogs will be well looked after.

This could be measured by the number of accidents over a given period.

(3) An excellent health record.

This means no or minimal breakout of infections which would damage the reputation of the business. This could become particularly important if CSF does start accommodating homeless dogs, because if any of the homeless dogs have got infections or diseases it will need to ensure that none of these get transmitted to the pets in its care.

This could be measured by the number of dogs that fall ill during their time at CFD.

(c) **Three quantitative non-financial performance measures to assess quality of service**

- **Service availability.** This may be measured by the number or percentage of owners able to book their dogs in on preferred dates and times.
- **Care taken of the dogs and the quality of the service experience.** This will be measured in return bookings and possibly word of mouth referral.
- **Prompt and reliable collection and return of dogs to their owners.** This is a key element of the service offered. This could be measured by logs of delivery and return of dogs safely and within the time promised.

3 Drinks Group

Text reference. Different approaches to budgeting are discussed in Chapter 3 of the BPP Study Text.

Top tips.

Part (a). A sensible approach to this question might be to think about the benefits and drawbacks of incremental budgeting in general terms, and then think how these would affect its suitability for each of the different divisions. For example, the scenario identifies that F is growing quite rapidly, so how would this affect the suitability of incremental budgeting in F?

The question specifically asks about its suitability at 'each division' so it is important that you deal with the different divisions in turn, although the similarities between S and H mean you could look at them together.

Part (b). Up to six out of the eight marks available here were for calculations, so this part of the question should have offered you some easy marks. However, it is important you apply the information given in the scenario correctly; for example, noting that administrative costs are fixed, although cost of sales and distribution costs are variable.

Also, remember that because you now have actual figures for Quarter 1 of the current year, the rolling budget should include budgeted figures for Quarter 1 of the next year.

Finally, note that not all the marks in this part of the question are available for calculations; so you still need to comment on the potential benefits (or drawbacks) of using rolling budgets for F.

Part (c). One of the key issues highlighted in the scenario is that the managers of the manufacturing divisions are very doubtful about the value which M adds. Therefore, to try to remove these doubts, the approach to budgeting in M needs to be one which challenges and justifies any proposed expenditure before it is approved. On this basis, zero-based budgeting would seem to be appropriate.

Part (d). The context of this question is the contrast between top-down budgeting (with little participation) and bottom-up budgeting (which involves much greater participation).

However, a useful way to approach this part of the question could be to think how the degree of participation changes in the different types of budget you have considered in parts (a), (b) and (c).

DG's current (incremental) approach appears to be essentially a top-down process with little participation from the divisions. This could provide your analysis of the current level of participation (and if DG decides to retain incremental budgeting in the S and H Divisions, a top-down approach could remain appropriate there).

But could DG successfully introduce rolling budgets or zero-based budgeting (in F and M respectively) without having a greater degree of involvement from divisional managers? Consequently, what level of participation will be appropriate at DG in the future?

Examining team's comments. Candidates are reminded that budgeting is a core topic, and candidates will be expected to know the relative merits of different methods of budgeting, and how to apply them in a scenario.

In part (a), some candidates seemed to assume that because incremental budgeting was being questioned it must be flawed for all the divisions, and they then sought reasons to justify this well. This is a poor approach to any question, however, because it pre-judges the outcome without any consideration of the evidence given in the scenario. In this case, incremental budgeting would actually be appropriate at the stable H and S Divisions.

Candidates generally performed well in part (b) although many did not bother to prepare the new quarter's figures which keep the budget rolling forward. As a result they missed out on some easy marks.

In general, part (c) was answered poorly, and candidates were unable to identify the relevant circumstances at M (such as the project-based nature of marketing activity) which suggest possible budgeting methods.

For part (d) most candidates identified the current level of participation in the budgeting process, although some candidates assumed that the current process was all top-down – ignoring the fact that division managers have input into growth estimates. The best candidates realised that, as different budget methods would be appropriate for the different divisions, the level of participation in each division would also vary, depending on the budget method.

Marking scheme

			Marks
(a)	Evaluation of the advantages and disadvantages of incremental budgeting in general – 1 mark per relevant point	Up to 5	
	Recommendations about the suitability of incremental budgeting in S and H Division – 1 mark per relevant point	Up to 3	
	Discussion about the suitability of incremental budgeting for F – 1 mark per relevant point	Up to 3	
	Discussion about the suitability of incremental budgeting for M – 1 mark per relevant point	Up to 3	
			8
(b)	Explanation of the rolling budget process – 1 mark per relevant point	Up to 2	
	Calculations (up to 6 marks in total for calculations):		
	Actual figures in Q1	1	
	Revenue; Cost of sales; Distribution costs; Administration costs; Operating profit – 1 mark for correct figures for each line in the budget	Up to 4	
	Budgeted figures for Q1 in the next year	1	
	Comments on the use of rolling budgets at F – 1 mark per relevant point	Up to 3	
			8
(c)	Recommendation of an appropriate method (1 mark), plus 1 mark per valid point justifying the choice of method	3	3
(d)	Explanation of top-down vs bottom-up budgeting – 1 mark per relevant point	Up to 2	
	Evaluation of use of bottom-up control at DG, and its impact on current processes	Up to 6	
			6
			Total = 25

(a) **Incremental budgeting**

Advantages

Not too time consuming – DG currently uses incremental budgets. One of the main advantages of incremental budgets is that they are relatively quick and easy to prepare. This is a general advantage at DG given the time constraints which the Finance Department is currently experiencing in relation to the information systems implementation.

Stable environment – Incremental budgets are also appropriate for stable environments, where current or historic figures can provide a reliable basis for projecting future figures, and where only small changes are required to those figures.

Disadvantages

Accepts inefficiencies – A major problem with incremental budgets is that, by their nature, they reinforce existing practices. The fact that the FD has identified that the most promising area for performance improvement lies in better internal control practices suggests that there are inefficiencies in DG's current processes, which are likely to be reflected in its current figures. However, by basing future years' budget on the current figures, these inefficiencies will be perpetuated rather than challenged. Consequently, for example, DG may miss opportunities to make cost savings.

Can encourage spending – Similarly, managers may feel they have to spend the full amount of their current year's budget in order to preserve the same level of budget next year, even though the expenditure may not actually be required at the moment. Once again, such an approach could lead to DG's costs being unnecessarily high.

H and S Divisions

Stable markets – Both H and S Divisions are in stable markets. The fact that sales growth is unlikely suggests that incremental budgeting could be appropriate for them.

Moreover, such an approach would fit with the managers' preference for maintaining existing practices rather than changing them.

Margin improvements – Because H and S have limited opportunities to increase revenues, in order to increase their profitability they will need to improve their margins. However, incremental budgeting will not be suitable to help them do this.

In order to improve their margins, the divisions will need to challenge and reduce their costs. However, by basing future budgets on current figures, an incremental approach will not provide the stimulus for continuous improvement which is required.

F division

Rapid growth – F's rate of growth means an incremental approach is unlikely to be suitable for it. Its rapid growth means that budgets based on current results will quickly become out of date.

The customer complaints and the managers' complaints could both be symptoms of the constraints which incremental budgets have placed on the business. For example, the complaints about late deliveries and poor quality could result from F trying to satisfy rapidly increasing demand whilst also facing budget constraints – which mean it either doesn't have sufficient capacity to keep pace with demand or it has to use poorer quality materials in order to reduce material costs.

The managers' complaints pick up on this point further. If the cost budgets have been set in line with current levels of demand, they are unlikely to be sufficient to cope with the higher levels of demand.

M Division

Justifying costs – The managers of the manufacturing divisions are sceptical of the need for a marketing department and using an incremental budget will not do anything to change their opinion of this.

The current budgetary approach at M (simply adding a percentage to the current year's expenditure) doesn't require M to justify its spending. Until it does this, however, it seems unlikely that M will be able to change the other division's perceptions of it.

Perhaps more importantly, though, simply adding a percentage to the current year's spend could lead to unjustified expenditure. For example, if the Marketing Division commits some expenditure this year on the basis that it is currently within budget (rather than because the expenditure is necessary and will add value for DG) next year's budget will be uplifted from the higher figure. Under such circumstances, the budget will continuously be higher than it needs to be. Again, this would justify the other managers' scepticism about the amount of value that M adds to the company.

(b) Under a rolling budget, another accounting period is added to the budget when the most recent one finishes. The budget is then recalculated using the actual data from the most recent period as a basis.

Because F Division's budget is based on a quarterly basis, the rolling budget will include actual figures for Quarter 1 of the current year, and then forecasts for Quarters 2–4 of the current year, along with Quarter 1 of the following year.

Based on the assumption that cost of sales and distribution costs increase in line with sales, and that administration costs remain fixed as in the original budget, F's rolling budget would be as follows:

	Q1	*Q2*	*Q3*	*Q4*	***Total***	*Q1*
	Actual	*Forecast*	*Forecast*	*Forecast*	***Forecast***	*Forecast*
	$'000	$'000	$'000	$'000	**$'000**	$'000
Revenue	17,932	18,470	19,024	19,595	**75,021**	20,183
Cost of sales	(9,863)	(10,159)	(10,464)	(10,778)	**(41,264)**	(11,101)
Gross profit	8,069	8,311	8,560	8,817	**33,757**	9,082
Distribution costs	(1,614)	(1,662)	(1,712)	(1,764)	**(6,752)**	(1,817)
Administration costs	(4,214)	(4,214)	(4,214)	(4,214)	**(16,856)**	(4,214)
Operating profit	2,241	2,435	2,634	2,840	**10,149**	3,051

As we noted in part (a), F is growing rapidly, and the rolling budget gives F's managers the scope to increase their variable costs to reflect that growth, rather than being constrained by the original budget.

As a result, F should be better able to sustain its growth, and the level of complaints about late deliveries and poor quality (which could otherwise jeopardise its growth) should be reduced.

Moreover, the rolling budget should provide managers with more realistic targets against which to compare actual performance. In this way, the rolling budget provides a more effective control mechanism than an annual budget, which could potentially be disregarded as being out of date.

It is likely that additional resources in the Finance Department will be required to prepare rolling budgets, because updated budgets will need to be prepared each quarter rather than on an annual basis as they currently are. However, the benefits which F's managers would derive from having rolling budgets should outweigh the additional costs incurred to prepare them.

(c) **Justifying expenditure** – The scepticism from the managers of the manufacturing divisions about the need for a marketing department (M), in conjunction with the board's requirement that M's costs should be carefully controlled, suggests that an incremental budget may not provide a robust enough framework for M.

Zero-based budgeting – By contrast, a zero-based budgeting approach may be appropriate, and this is the approach recommended for M.

As each marketing campaign is run as an individual project, it seems more appropriate for M to budget for the campaigns on a project by project basis. A zero-based budget approach would provide a suitable framework for doing this, with the cost of each campaign having to be justified at the start before the campaign is approved.

Under a zero-based budget, M would need to justify every cost which is required for a specific marketing campaign. If a cost element cannot be justified, then no resources will be allocated to it in the budget.

Tighter control – Such an approach should also appease the managers of the manufacturing divisions because it will mean that marketing expenditure is being much more tightly controlled.

(d) **Top-down budgeting**

In a top-down budgeting environment, budget figures are essentially imposed on operational managers and other budget holders by senior management. Operational managers have very little participation in the budgeting process.

Limited participation – The divisional managers at DG do appear to have some input into the budget process because they discuss the market growth estimates with the head office finance managers before the budgets are prepared.

However, the budgeting process still appears essentially top-down, and this appears to be causing resentment about the divisional managers – particularly the F managers who want to be less controlled by constraints 'imposed' by the board.

Bottom-up control

In contrast to top-down budgeting, a bottom-up approach would allow divisional managers **much greater participation** in preparing and setting their own budgets.

This would appear to be the approach which the F managers want, because their greater participation in setting the budgets should mean they feel 'less controlled' by the board.

Improved motivation – If the divisional managers have a greater sense of ownership of the budgets, this should also increase their motivation to achieve the budget targets.

Accountability – Equally, if managers are going to be held accountable for their performance against budget targets, it seems fair that they should have some input into setting those targets; for example, so that they think they are realistic.

Improved decision making – Moreover, the divisional managers at DG should have a more detailed knowledge of their markets than the board. Therefore, by allowing the managers to participate in the budgeting process, the quality of decision making and budgeting may also be improved. In this respect, a bottom-up approach would benefit DG as a whole, not just the divisional managers.

Similarly, if the divisional managers do more of the work to prepare the budgets, this means the budgeting process is less onerous for the senior management team, which allows them more time to spend on other matters.

Levels of participation

Overall control – At DG, the budget system in each business is the main method of central control. Therefore the board needs to ensure that the budgets remain in line with overall corporate objectives, and are not too easily achieved.

Consequently, it appears that an approach which combines aspects of both top-down and bottom-up budgeting would appear to be most appropriate for DG.

It is important that the managers are involved in the budget-setting process, because their own personal targets are set around achieving the relevant budget numbers.

Equally, however, it is important that head office should also be involved, to ensure that the budgets fit with DG's overall strategic objectives and that budget targets remain challenging.

Also, it is debatable how far the managers of H and S Division will voluntarily drive down costs without close monitoring from the head office. In this respect, the board may decide that the control which is imposed by a top-down approach is still required in relation to these two divisions, and therefore the level of participation for these two divisions will be lower than for the other two divisions.

Rolling budgets – If DG introduces rolling budgets for F, the process of preparing these budgets should be delegated to the divisional managers. On the one hand this is due to the resource constraints within the Finance Department, but on the other it is because the divisional managers should be more aware of changes in the market which need to be reflected in the updated figures. However, senior finance staff should still review the budgets, and the underlying assumptions behind them, to ensure they seem reasonable.

Zero-based budgeting – If M adopts zero-based budgeting, divisional managers will have a crucial role to play in the budgeting process, because they will need to assess what activities and expenditure are required to support each campaign.

4 Godel

Text reference. Different approaches to budgeting and different types of budget variance are discussed in Chapter 3 of the BPP Study Text. (The 'PRIME' mnemonic for summarising the purposes of budgets is covered in Chapter 1.)

Top tips.

Part (a). It is important that you focus specifically on the planning and operational variances here rather than discussing the variances shown in the operating statement more generally. As such, the figures you need to be looking at are those shown in the 'Detailed variances' at the bottom of the operating statement.

Part (b). The requirement here is to 'evaluate' the budgeting system. An 'evaluation' should include both the advantages and the disadvantages of the system. As the examining team's comments (below) indicate, if you are asked to evaluate something, it is important that you give a balanced argument – and don't focus only on the advantages or the disadvantages.

One possible way of approaching this requirement would be to use 'PRIME' as a framework for your answer, and to evaluate how well the budget reflects the elements of 'PRIME' – planning, responsibility, motivating, evaluating performance. (This is the approach we have used in our suggested solution.)

Part (c). Note the verb here is also 'evaluate' – so you need to consider what the potential benefits from moving to a bottom-up approach might be, but also what factors may limit those benefits or make it an unsuitable approach.

Importantly, you need to think about not only the context of the scenario here (for example, Godel's command and control management style), but also your evaluation of the current approach to budgeting – in part (b). If Godel is going to change its approach to budgeting, it will only be worth doing so if the new approach helps to address the problems with its current system. But does it?

There is an important general point to note here. Just because the FD has proposed a change in the approach, this doesn't necessarily mean the change is appropriate.

Examining team's comments. In part (a), most candidates appeared not to know the definitions of operating and planning variances, and so those who attempted this question talked about all the other variances in the appendix rather than answering the question.

Part (b) of this question was also inadequately attempted. Too many candidates saw only the negatives of the existing system, and few identified its positives for a traditional company like Godel in a mature market. This meant students failed to grasp that the current budgeting system at Godel was actually well suited to its needs; and therefore (part (c)) that a change in the budgeting process was neither required nor likely to be beneficial for Godel.

Marking scheme

		Marks
(a)	Definitions of planning and operational variances – 1 mark	
	Advice about planning and operational elements of total variable cost variances – up to 3 marks	
	Advice about planning and operational elements of sales price variance – up to 3 marks	
	Total for part (a): up to 6	6
(b)	Benefits of budgeting for Godel – 1 mark per relevant point – up to a maximum of 6	
	Points could include: • Planning and co-ordination – meeting overall strategy • Responsibility • Integration • Motivation • Evaluation of performance	
	Problems with budgeting at Godel – 1 mark per relevant point – up to a maximum of 6	
	Points could include: • Time consuming and unnecessary • Lack of recognition of planning failures • Insufficient planning and operational analysis • Impedes continuous improvement	
	Total for part (b): up to 12	12
(c)	Description of bottom-up budgeting – up to 2 marks	
	Evaluation of appropriateness of bottom-up budgeting for Godel – up to 6 marks	
	Total for part (c): up to 7	7
		Total = 25

(a) **Planning variances** result from the assumptions or standards used in the original budget-setting process not being accurate. For example, if the original budget assumed that sales prices would be increased by 2%, but market conditions have meant that sales prices could only be increased by 1%, the resulting sales price variance should be treated as a planning variance.

In effect, a planning variance is the difference between the original budget and the budget as it would have been revised with the benefit of hindsight.

Operational variances, in effect, are the differences between this 'revised' budget, and actual performance. Operational variances result from the decisions of operational managers, rather than issues with the original budget-setting process.

Variable cost variance

The total variable cost variance considers a number of costs together, and so it is unlikely that any gains or problems highlighted by it can be attributed to one individual. As such, the variable cost variance has little use for Godel, although highlighting the total variance could, in turn, identify the need for more detailed analysis to identify the specific causes of the variance.

BPP LEARNING MEDIA

The $20,680 favourable planning variance suggests that the standard costs have been set too high, and therefore most of the apparent cost improvements are due to this. Compared to the planning variance, the operational variance is very low ($580) which suggests that the operational managers have had little impact in driving down costs in the month.

Sales price variance

The sales price variance indicates the extent to which sales prices were incorrectly estimated in the budget (planning variances) and how effective the sales managers have been in negotiating higher prices with customers (operational variances).

The adverse planning variance ($15,600) suggests that the original budget was too optimistic in the initial price it set for Godel's sweets. However, the favourable operational variance ($6,640) suggests that the sales managers have been quite successful in their price negotiations with customers, although not successful enough to overcome the adverse planning variance.

The initial price-setting process should be examined, to identify why prices were budgeted too high. For example, Godel's market intelligence about the prices being set by competitors, or the commercial situation of its customers (the supermarkets) may have been faulty.

(b) **Cost control** – Godel's competitive strategy is based on it being a cost leader, and therefore it will be very important for the company to control its costs effectively.

The budgeting system provides a mechanism for monitoring costs, and overall it seems that Godel is being successful in controlling its costs – as its total costs show a favourable variance.

Planning – More generally, budgets can be used to help communicate and co-ordinate all the management activities within Godel towards its overall strategic plan – minimising costs, and winning supermarkets' business.

Responsibility – The budget can also help to attribute responsibility for performance, and to identify which managers are responsible for which costs. For example, the favourable material usage variance indicates that fewer raw materials were required than planned, which suggests the Production Manager has been able to reduce waste and/or improve the efficiency of the production process.

Motivation – Although the managers do not appreciate the time taken by the budgeting process, the standard costs and assumptions being used in the budget are nonetheless discussed with them before being included in the budgets. The fact that the managers have the chance to participate in the budget process should help to motivate them to achieve the budget figures set.

In particular, it is important that managers are given the chance to identify any areas of the budget which they think are not realistic or achievable – otherwise the budget will become demotivating to the managers and their teams.

The CEO's feeling that there is no dysfunctional behaviour at Godel, and that all the managers are working in the best interests of the company, suggests that the budgeting system is not damaging motivation, even if it is not necessarily doing anything to enhance it.

Evaluation – Budgets assist performance evaluation by identifying variances which can then be analysed and investigated. This is particularly important for areas where actual performance is adverse to budget, to enable corrective action to be taken to improve future performance.

At Godel, sales are underperforming the budget both in terms of volume and price. However, more favourably, labour costs are considerably under budget – with the favourable labour 'efficiency' variance suggesting that staff are working efficiently.

Problems with Godel's budgeting system

Although the top-down nature of Godel's budgeting system fits with the organisation's strategy and management style, there are nonetheless still several problems with it.

Time consuming – The nature of Godel's business – in a mature market, and with little scope for innovation or new product development – mean that budget setting should not be a complex process. However, the managers' complaints suggest that the current process is very time-consuming.

The managers may be exaggerating here, and their complaints may be more of an indication of the fact that the budgets ultimately have limited value to them (because the operational variances are relatively small), and therefore they do not want to spend much time preparing them.

Nonetheless, there appears to be a danger that Godel's current budgeting system may have become more complicated than it needs to be.

Planning variances – The bulk of the variances at Godel relate to planning variances, rather than operational variances. This reinforces the suggestion that there is little point spending lots of time on the operational aspects of the budget but, instead, more time could be spent analysing the external factors with a view to reducing the level of planning variances.

Responsibility – The fact that the operational managers are frequently asked to explain variances which are not their fault suggests that the distinction between operational and planning variances needs to be more extensive.

Currently, the analysis between operational and planning variance is quite limited in scope. However, for example, instead of only analysing the total cost variance into operational and planning variances, some of the main cost headings in the operating statement could also be analysed in this way, so that managers are only held responsible for the operational variances.

No incentive to reduce cost – Although the CEO does not believe the managers build slack into their budgets, the use of standard costing nevertheless does not provide any incentives for them to try to reduce costs further. Given Godel's strategy as a cost leader, it would be beneficial to it if the budget system encouraged a system of continuous improvements in relation to efficiency gains and cost reductions.

However, given the mature nature of the business, Godel's senior management may feel that it is unlikely there will be a need to update budgeted costs on a regular basis and that a review of them once a year is sufficient.

(c) **Bottom-up budgeting**

The FD's suggestion is a response to managers' complaints that the current variances are not their fault, and so it appears that the FD's intention is to make the managers more accountable for variances, and more motivated to achieve their budgets.

Typically, the arguments in favour of bottom-up budgeting are: that managers should be motivated to achieve their budgets if they have been involved in setting them; and that operational managers should have better knowledge than senior management of the conditions their business units face, meaning that the resulting budgets should be more realistic and achievable.

However, the nature of Godel's business and culture means that bottom-up budgeting may not be appropriate or beneficial.

Fit with culture – The operational managers already discuss the budget assumptions and standard costs, but do so without having the responsibility of producing the budget. Managers are therefore already involved in the budget-setting process, but in a way which fits with the 'command and control' management style at Godel. Moving to a bottom-up approach does not appear to fit with this style.

Resistance to change – The fact that many of Godel's employees have worked for the company for many years could mean that they will be uncomfortable with the change. Equally, if the managers – like most of Godel's employees – like the straightforward nature of their work, they may resent the additional burden of having to prepare their own budgets. Conversely, however, some managers may welcome the change if they feel it will give them more control over their budgets.

Time consuming – If the managers have to produce the budgets themselves, this is likely to increase their complaints about the budget process being time consuming. Similarly, the managers could complain that the increased amounts of time they have to spend preparing budgets is reducing the time they have available for other aspects of their roles.

Dysfunctional behaviour – As the CEO has noted, the current, top-down approach to budgeting means there is no dysfunctional behaviour, as represented by budget slack or excessive spending. However, bottom-up budgeting could increase the risk of dysfunctional behaviour as operational managers will focus on the individual concerns of their business area rather than Godel's overall corporate objectives. Equally, managers may create budgetary slack, and set targets which are too easy to achieve – although any targets which are obviously too easy should be challenged when the draft budgets are reviewed centrally.

Controllability – Most importantly, perhaps, even though the managers have set the budgets, they are still likely to argue, justifiably, that some of the variances they have to explain are not their fault. The proposed changes do not address the weakness in the lack of distinction between operational and planning variances (which we highlighted in part (b)).

Godel's sales are dependent on the state of the general economy and competitive forces – factors which are outside the control of operational managers. Therefore, operational managers cannot be held responsible for variances resulting from unforeseen changes in the level of sales.

Therefore, reiterating the point made in part (b), rather than changing the way the budgets are prepared, a more useful improvement to Godel's performance management systems would be to distinguish the main cost variances into operational and planning variances.

5 Perkin

Text reference. Budgeting and budgeting systems are discussed in Chapter 3 of the BPP Study Text.

Top tips. Although good exam technique is important in all APM questions, it is particularly useful in this one – especially reading all three requirements and identifying how the different parts of the question fit together. The issues being discussed in part (c) highlight one of the weaknesses in Perkin's current budgeting system (the lack of planning and operational variances). However, while it will be important to mention this weakness in part (a), you should not discuss it in detail there – in order to avoid duplicating your answer between parts (a) and (c). Similarly, although perhaps less immediately obviously, the extent to which internal factors have compounded external factors – part (b) – can also be seen as a result of the weaknesses in Perkin's current budgeting system.

Part (a). The scenario highlights a number of problems which Perkin has experienced, so one approach to this requirement could be just to work through the scenario and identify which of these are due to weaknesses in the current budgeting system, or its lack of suitability for the environment in which Perkin operates.

However, a more structured approach for trying to identify the weaknesses might be to use 'PRIME' as a framework for your answer.

Plan – Does the budget process encourage budget holders to plan how to achieve targets which support the company's overall strategic objectives?

Responsibility – Do the budgets help to allocate responsibility, and specify which managers control which costs?

Integration – Does the budget structure help to ensure that the activities of one area support another?

Motivation – Do the budgets help to motivate managers?

Evaluation – Do the budgets allow trends in performance to be identified and investigated?

The scenario identifies a number of issues where Perkin's budgeting system does not help to achieve these 'PRIME' characteristics; and so you can then highlight these as weaknesses of the system.

However, note that you are asked to evaluate the system's suitability for Perkin's environment, as well as the weaknesses in the system. A key point to realise here is that Perkin is operating in a dynamic, fast-moving environment. Therefore, to what extent are incremental budgets, which are produced annually and enforced rigidly, likely to be suitable?

Although the requirement does not ask you to recommend an alternative budgeting system, it could be helpful to think whether the characteristics of alternative budgeting models (eg rolling budgets) would make them more appropriate than Perkin's current system. If another model seems more suitable, briefly mentioning this could help support your evaluation of the suitability (or unsuitability) of the current system.

Part (b). The scenario clearly identifies a number of external factors which have affected Perkin's performance during the year (eg rising silver prices; the fire at the customer), and these factors in themselves are outside Perkin's control.

In effect, however, this requirement is looking at the extent to which factors can fully be classified as controllable or uncontrollable. The key question in Perkin's case is: Although the initial factors were external (uncontrollable), has Perkin's internal response (controllable) also had an impact on its performance?

Part (c). As we noted at the start of these 'Top tips', the link between part (c) and part (a) in this question is important, because the change being suggested in part (c) addresses one of the weaknesses you could have identified in part (a) – the current lack of any analysis between planning and operational variances.

The third paragraph of the scenario is also important here. We are told that the main board significantly revises the budgets, but then divisional managers are appraised on the financial performance of their divisions. Does this seem a fair way of appraising the manager's performance?

Note, however, that the verb in part (c) is 'discuss' rather than evaluate. Therefore you need to focus specifically on the potential benefits of the change – not, for example, the extent to which those benefits could be limited by any difficulties associated with trying to analyse the variances.

Marking scheme

		Marks
(a)	Evaluation of current budgeting system Weaknesses in current system – 1 mark per relevant point – up to 12 marks Suitability of the system for Perkin's environment – 1 mark per point – up to 5 marks Conclusion – 1 mark Total for part (a): up to 14	14
(b)	Discussion of controllable and non-controllable aspects – up to 2 marks Identifying external factors which contributed to Perkin's poor performance – 1 mark Evaluating the extent to which the external factors as opposed to internal weaknesses were responsible for Perkin's poor performance – 1 mark per relevant point; up to a maximum of 4 Total for part (b): up to 6	6
(c)	Definition of planning and operational variances – 1 mark Discussing the benefits of distinguishing between planning and operational variances – 1 mark per relevant point; up to a maximum of 4 Total for part (c): up to 5	5
	Total =	**25**

(a) Perkin uses a traditional approach to budgeting, which has a number of weaknesses.

First of all, the budgeting system does not seem aligned with Perkin's **corporate objective** which focuses on innovation and continuous product improvement. Innovation is a key competitive advantage to both component and device manufacturers in this industry and the products which incorporate Perkin's components are subject to rapid technological change as well as changes in consumer trends. The markets in which the two divisions operate appear to be evolving, as seen by the high popularity of the smartphone model which was designed for playing games. This may mean the distinction between smartphone and gaming devices could be becoming less clear cut. Management time would probably be better spent considering these rapid changes and currently the budgeting process does not facilitate that.

In reality, the budget process at Perkin is **time consuming** and probably therefore a costly exercise. Divisional budgets go through a lengthy process of drafting and then revision by the main board before they are approved. The approval often happens after the start of the period to which they relate, at which point the budgets are already **out of date**. This also means divisional managers are trying to plan activities for the next

BPP LEARNING MEDIA

financial year without a set of finalised targets agreed, which could impact the effectiveness of decisions made.

Another weakness is that the budgets are **only prepared annually**, which is clearly too infrequent for a business such as Perkin. The process is also rigid and inflexible as deviations from the planned targets are not tolerated. Sticking to rigid, annual budgets can lead to problems such as P Division not being able to cope with increasing popularity of a particular product and even other short-term changes in demand like those driven by seasonal factors, or one-off events such as the factory fire. Linked to this problem of budgetary constraints is that to cut costs to achieve the budgeted net profit, managers closed one of the three research and development facilities in G Division. As identified at the outset, a successful research and development function is a key source of long-term competitive advantage to Perkin.

It also appears that Perkin fails to **flex the budgets** and consequently the fixed budgets had discouraged divisional managers from deviating from the original plan. P Division did not make technical modifications to its components due to the cost of doing so, which meant they were unable to supply components for use in the new model of smartphone and had to discount the inventories of the old version. It is unclear why G Division did not take on additional staff to cope with increased demand following the reopening of their customer's factory, but it may be because managers felt constrained by the budget. This then caused long-term detriment to Perkin as it lost the preferred supplier status with its main customer.

Another problem created by annual budgeting is the **management of short-term changes in costs and prices**. A key component of Perkin's products is silver, which fluctuates in price, and though it is not clear how much effect this has on Perkin's costs, any problems in supply could disrupt production even if only a small amount of silver were required. Also Perkin exports goods worldwide and probably also purchases materials, including silver, from overseas. The business is therefore exposed to short-term movements in foreign currency exchange rates which may affect costs and selling prices.

Similarly, there also seems to be **considerable uncertainty** in sales volumes and prices which creates problems in the forecasting process for the two divisions. P Division did not anticipate the high demand for the new component which meant it had to discount products it had already manufactured in order to achieve its forecast sales volumes. G Division did correctly forecast the demand, but based on past growth in the market which may be too simplistic in a rapidly changing industry. Lack of up to date information will hinder decision making and overall performance at Perkin. Perkin would perhaps be better adopting a rolling basis for forecasting.

The two divisions share manufacturing facilities and are likely to compete for other resources during the budgeting process. The current budgeting system does not encourage resource, information or knowledge sharing, for example, expertise in forecasting silver requirements. Divisional managers are **appraised on the financial performance of their own division** and hence are likely to prioritise the interests of their own division above those of Perkin as a whole. P Division would not reallocate its manufacturing facilities to G Division, even though G Division needed this to cope with extra demand following reopening of the customer's factory. The current system is therefore not encouraging goal congruence between the divisions and Perkin as a whole and a budgeting system, if done effectively, should encourage co-ordination and co-operation.

Managers may find the budgeting process **demotivating** because it is **time consuming** for them and then the directors override the forecast which they had made. It is also unfair and demotivating to staff to appraise them on factors which are outside their control. This also identifies another weakness in Perkin's budgeting system related to control, as there does not seem to be any planning and operating variance analysis performed to assess exactly where performance is lacking, and so no appropriate management information is provided. In fact it is not even clear just how often divisional managers receive reports on performance throughout the year. Any budgeting system without regular feedback would be ineffective. It should even be noted that for the industry in which Perkin operates the use of only budgetary targets as a measure of performance is narrow and internal. It should be utilising information from external sources as well to assess performance in a more relevant and contextual way.

Given the rapidly changing external environment and the emphasis on innovation and continuous product development, the current budgeting method does not seem appropriate for Perkin.

(b) As the shareholder representative noted, external factors have adversely affected Perkin's performance over the last year. However, the way Perkin has responded to the external events has also contributed to the problems it has faced. As such, it is important that Perkin doesn't simply use the external factors as an excuse for its poor performance, thereby failing to acknowledge the internal factors and behaviours which have also contributed to it.

The current lack of any detailed analysis into the reasons why Perkin's actual performance varies from budget means it is difficult to hold managers to account for their performance. However, as the three examples we evaluate below demonstrate, the factors that affect performance cannot be categorised entirely as controllable (internal) or as uncontrollable (external). Instead, Perkin's performance reflects a combination of both types of factors.

The **unexpectedly high popularity of the new smartphone** with the large screen was an external factor. However, P Division's inability – or unwillingness – to make the necessary technical modifications to its own components to support the new screen was an internal factor, resulting – as we noted in part (a) – from the fact that Perkin does not flex its budgets.

Similarly, the **global shortage of silver** during the year (and the corresponding increase in silver prices) was an external factor. However, the lack of communication between G Division and P Division which led to G buying silver when P already held large inventories reflected an internal weakness. If the two divisions had liaised more effectively, the impact of the short-term increase in silver prices could have been reduced (or perhaps even avoided) if Perkin was able to wait until prices fell again to top up its inventories.

Again, the **fire which affected G's main customer** was an external factor. However, G's refusal to recruit extra staff to fulfil increased demand when the customer's factory reopened, and P's refusal to allow some of its manufacturing facilities to be used to meet this demand, are both internal decisions. However, it was these responses – rather than the fire itself – which led to Perkin losing its preferred supplier status with the customer.

As we noted in part (a), the response to the silver price increase and the fire both reflect the lack of goal congruence between the divisions and Perkin as a whole. Again, though, this is an internal weakness, reflecting dysfunctional behaviour which has resulted from the way divisional performance is rigidly assessed against budget. Therefore, although external factors have contributed to G's poor performances, internal weaknesses have also played a significant part in G's poor performance.

(c) **Planning variances** result from actual events and circumstances differing from the assumptions used in the original budget. For example, the fire at its main customer meant that the annual growth of 5% anticipated in G's sales forecast was too high (because the budget had not anticipated the fire). The lost sales resulting from the fire should be treated as a planning variance.

In effect, a planning variance is the difference between the original budget and the budget as it would have been revised with the benefit of hindsight.

Operational variances then reflect the differences between this 'revised' budget and actual performance. Operational variances result from the ongoing decisions of divisional managers, rather than issues with the original budget-setting process.

We have already noted – in part (a) – that the lack of planning and operating variance analysis is a weakness, because it means Perkin cannot accurately identify the reasons why actual performance is below budget. Given the dynamic nature of Perkin's markets (and the fact that budgets are only produced annually) it seems likely that there could be significant planning variances.

By isolating these planning variances, Perkin could then get a fairer reflection (through the operational variances) of how well the **divisional managers** are performing. This will also increase the effectiveness of the budgeting system as a **control mechanism** – comparing the manager's actual controllable performance against budgeted targets.

Currently, the divisional managers are appraised on the financial performance of their divisions, so they are being held responsible for planning variances as well as operational variances. However, as the budgets are determined by the main board, the managers should not be held responsible for planning variances over which they have little (or no) control.

Equally, however, by isolating the planning variances, Perkin can get a better insight into the degree to which the original budget was inaccurate. If it becomes clear that the majority of the variances result from changes in circumstance, which couldn't have been known when the annual budget was originally set, this could reinforce the argument for moving away from the current budgeting system – for example, to rolling budgets.

6 Booxe

Text reference. Business process re-engineering is discussed in Chapter 4a of the BPP Study Text. Appraisals and human resource management more generally are discussed in Chapter 11.

Top tips.

Part (a) – Although the requirement here was to 'Assess the financial impact' of the project, the majority of the six marks available were for calculations, and should have proved relatively easy marks to score.

Perhaps the most obvious way to assess the impact of the project is through a cost benefit analysis – and this is the approach we have used in the suggested solution below. However, the marking guide indicated that using other methods – such as payback period or accounting rate of return – would have been equally acceptable.

The crucial point to identify from the calculations is that the benefits significantly outweigh the costs over the life of the project (eight years), but you only need to write a couple of sentences after the calculations to explain this. There are only six marks in total for this part of the question – so there isn't time for a lengthy assessment of the project here.

Part (b) – Whereas part (a) of the question looked at the financial impact of the project, part (b) now looks at two non-financial impacts of it – on culture, and on Booxe's management information systems. And, note, to score well in this part of the question you have to discuss the impact of BPR on both of the areas required by the question: (i) culture and (ii) management information systems.

The scenario is also important in this question because it highlights that Booxe currently operates within a traditional, functional structure. However, BPR focuses on processes and process team rather than functional departments. This change will be central to the impact BPR has on culture at Booxe.

And it will also have important implications for the company's management information systems – for example, will performance reports structured around departments still be relevant in a process-oriented structure? And how might performance measures need to be redesigned to reflect the new approach?

Part (c) – A sensible approach to this part of the question would be to consider the purpose of an appraisal system, and then consider the issues in Booxe's appraisal system in the light of this, before suggesting possible solutions to them.

The reference in the last paragraph of the scenario to 'the appropriate balance between control and staff development' should have given you an indication of the points which needed to be considered here. Obtaining the right balance between control and development is one of the key issues in any appraisal process – but Booxe's current process appears to place very little emphasis on the 'control' aspect of appraisal.

Marking scheme

		Marks
(a)	Calculations: Up to 5 marks Costs: Depreciation – 1 mark; Total cost – 1 mark Savings: Warehousing – 1 mark; Purchasing – 1 mark Net benefit: 1 mark Comments: 1 mark for suitable comments on the calculations Total for part (a): up to 6	6
(b)	Definition of BPR – 1 mark per relevant point – up to a maximum of 2 Analysis of the impact of BPR on culture at Booxe – 1 mark per relevant point – up to a maximum of 5 Analysis of the impact of BPR on management information systems/ accounting systems at Booxe – 1 mark per relevant point, up to a maximum of 5 Total for part (b): up to 11	11
(c)	Definition of appraisal and the appraisal process – 1 mark per relevant point – up to a maximum of 2 For advice on the purpose of appraisal at Booxe – 1 mark per relevant point – up to a maximum of 4 For advice on the balance of control and development in the appraisal process – 1 mark per relevant point – up to a maximum of 4 Total for part (c): up to 8	8
		Total = 25

(a) **Annual cost benefit of the new system**

		$
Benefits of new system (cost savings)		
Warehouse staff	10 × 25,000 × 50%	125,000
Purchasing staff	32,000 × 8.5/5	54,400
Annual costs of new system		
Depreciation – hardware	220,000/8 years	(27,500)
Depreciation – software	275,000/8 years	(34,375)
Ongoing servicing cost		(22,500)
Net benefit		95,025

Tutorial notes

Alternative methods – eg payback period, or accounting rate of return – are equally acceptable. Payback period (as shown below) is 3 years, 2 months; ie well within the 8-year expected life of the new system.

Payback period

	Year 0	*Year 1*	*Year 2*	*Year 3*	*Year 4*	
	$	$	$	$	$	
Hardware	(220,000)					
Software	(275,000)					
Annual savings						
Warehouse staff		125,000	125,000	125,000	125,000	
Purchasing staff		54,400	54,400	54,400	54,400	
Annual costs						
Servicing costs		(22,500)	(22,500)	(22,500)	(22,500)	
	(495,000)	156,900	156,900	156,900	156,900	132,600

Payback: **3 years, 2 months** (24,300/156,900) × 12 = 2 months

The pilot BPR project will yield a benefit of $95,025 per year, meaning it is financially successful.

There are likely to be some other costs which are not included in this analysis, such as redundancy or retraining of the staff whose workload has been reduced, and the training costs for staff on the new system. However, given the figures involved, the project should still be beneficial even when these have been accounted for.

(b) BPR is the fundamental rethinking and radical redesign of business processes to achieve dramatic improvements in critical contemporary measures of performance, such as cost, quality, service and speed.

Culture

Process teams – One of the key consequences of BPR for organisations is a shift from a functional structure to process teams, in order to achieve a more efficient delivery of products and services.

This will have a significant impact on Booxe, since the company has historically been divided into functional departments. The pilot project has shown the effect that BPR could have on the warehousing and purchasing departments.

Skills – The change to a process approach may require employees to retrain in order to gain additional skills. One of the characteristics of BPR is that it leads to multi-skilling; but given Booxe's current (bureaucratic, traditional) culture, it is likely that staff will have specific roles, rather than developing multiple skills.

Organisational hierarchy – BPR also leads to a flattening of organisational structures (from hierarchical to flat). Since processes become the work of the whole team, then similarly the team becomes responsible for managing the process.

Interdepartmental issues become matters the team resolves itself, rather than requiring managerial intervention. As a result, BPR means companies require less managerial input, and managers have less to do.

Although it is not clear which aspect of the cultural change required by the BPR project the Warehouse Manager was uncomfortable with, the risk that BPR would diminish their role could have played a part in the decision to take early retirement.

Change management – Nonetheless, the change required at Booxe – to shift from a well-established functional structure to a process-based structure – is likely to be a major change. Therefore, for it to be implemented successfully will require effective communication and leadership from senior management – for example, explaining the benefits of BPR to the staff, and overcoming any resistance they may have to it.

Management information systems

Performance measures – Performance measures under BPR must be built around processes rather than departments. This again is likely to require a significant change to Booxe's management information systems (assuming that Booxe's current accounting system reflects the functional structure of the organisation).

Focus on value adding – The aim of management information under BPR is to identify where value is being added in processes, so that activities where resources are employed without producing a valuable outcome can be eliminated.

Activity-based costing – As the CEO has suggested, activity-based costing (ABC) is often used to model the business processes as part of BPR. Again, however, the change to ABC from Booxe's traditional overhead absorption based on labour hours could be quite significant for the company's management information.

ABC will provide a more detailed method for allocating overheads and, in turn, should allow Booxe to calculate more accurate product costs, and determine the profitability of each product more accurately.

However, ABC will be more time consuming to administer than Booxe's current basis of overhead absorption.

Performance reports – The change from functional departments to process teams will mean that financial reports also have to be redesigned around process teams.

Also, the variances to budget, used as control indicators, may need to be revised following the introduction of the activity-based approach to overhead allocation.

(c) **Purpose of appraisal**

The overall purpose of appraisal is usually seen as the improvement of employees' performance, but appraisals can also be useful for assessing current performance; determining rewards; selecting people for promotion; and for identifying employees' training and development needs.

Control and staff development

The issue of finding an appropriate balance between control and staff development (which the CEO has identified) highlights one of the inherent problems with appraisals.

Judgement and control – One of the key purposes of appraisals is to assess how well employees have performed (against targets and objectives), with a view to determining pay increases and promotion. This reflects the judgement and control aspect of appraisal.

Development – On the other hand, the development aspect of appraisals focuses on assessing employees' training and development needs; to support them, and to help them perform better in the future.

Booxe's appraisal system

Despite the issue of resolving the balance between control and development aspects, organisations need some kind of performance assessment for their staff.

However, appraisal systems are often criticised as being irrelevant to the organisation's work. And this may well be the case at Booxe.

The current system has become very informal, possibly due to the fact it is not taken very seriously by either the appraiser or the appraisee.

Control aspects – In order for the appraisal process to become relevant to Booxe's work, the control aspects need to be linked to the organisation's overall goals – such as driving down costs, to support the overall strategy of cost leadership.

Development – However, the appraisal system also needs to be linked to the development of appropriate skills and greater motivation among the staff. (This could be particularly important if employees' jobs are redesigned following BPR.)

It is not clear whether Booxe's current appraisal system is linked to the employee rewards, but if the 'control' elements of appraisals are linked to a suitable reward system, this should help to increase performance in the company as staff strive to meet the performance targets set in their appraisals.

However, it is important that the appraisal process still reflects the culture and strategy of the company. Although Booxe has a strategy of cost leadership, there is also an appreciation of craft skills among the workforce. As such, the 'development' aspects of the appraisal process may be important for enabling staff to highlight new skills they want to learn. But equally the 'control' element of the appraisal process may be important for improving efficiency and controlling costs.

It seems likely that the general discussions about how to improve employees' efforts – which currently constitute Booxe's appraisal process – may be focusing more on the 'development' aspects of appraisal, rather than the 'control' elements. However, it seems that the CEO may be looking to change this, by evaluating the balance between control and development in the process.

7 PLX Refinery

Text reference. Environmental management accounting is covered in Chapter 5 of the Study Text.

Top tips. Although **part (a)** is only worth six marks there are still effectively two parts to the requirement. What cost categories could aid transparency in internal reporting? And what cost categories could aid transparency in external reporting? Make sure you address both in your answer, and make sure you give examples, as you are instructed to do.

There are also two stages to answering **part (b)**: 'explain' then 'evaluate'. However, don't just explain the two techniques (ABC; and life cycle costing) in general terms; make sure you link them back to PLX's environmental and strategic performance.

Similarly, in your evaluation, make sure you look specifically at how the techniques could be useful in managing performance at PLX. And because you are 'evaluating' them, try to include some limitations in using them as well as the advantages of using them.

Also, note that requirement (b) asks you how the techniques can assist in managing environmental **and** strategic performance. So, for example, how might a better understanding of environmental costs affect strategic decision making (as well as the more obvious issues of how might an understanding of environmental costs affect environmental performance)?

Part (c). The scenario tells us that PLX's performance measures currently focus mainly on financial performance, and its existing information systems also focus on financial performance. So how will they have to change in order for PLX to monitor its environmental performance? And what issues could this present? The scenario specifically mentions the Government's goal to reduce carbon dioxide emissions, so this could be a useful example to link your answer to – for example, does PLX currently monitor its carbon dioxide emissions?

Part (d). The figures given in the scenario indicate that there are some significant environmental costs associated with the project. Consequently, whether they are included in a project appraisal or not will have a significant impact on the perceived profitability of the project. In effect, then, you could approach by asking: What are the potential problems with Kayplas's current costing approach? And then, how could a life cycle costing approach help address these problems?

Marking scheme

		Marks
(a)	Up to 2 marks for each cost area discussed – Up to a maximum of 6 marks To score 2 marks, the discussion of each cost must include relevant examples, linked to the scenario. Total: up to 6	6
(b)	Up to 2 marks for explaining each technique, and explaining its link to environmental performance – Up to a maximum of 4 marks Up to 2 marks for an evaluation of the techniques. Total: up to 6	6
(c)	For assessing the impact of environmental accounting on performance measurement at PLX – 1 mark per relevant point; up to 3 For assessing the impact of environmental accounting on information systems – 1 mark per relevant point; up to 3 Total: up to 6	6
(d)	Up to 2 marks for calculation of life cycle costs Up to 2 marks for calculating the product profits of the two approaches Up to 4 marks for discussing the potential improvements and issues identified by life cycle costing. Total: up to 7	7
	Total =	25

(a) PLX will need to identify existing and new cost information which is relevant to understanding the environmental impact its operations have.

Operating costs – PLX's current management accounting system is already likely to record conventional costs such as raw material costs and energy costs. However, the costs of waste through inefficiency will not be recorded. If they were, however, this should encourage PLX's management to reduce the amount of waste generated by the company's processes.

Additionally, a number of environment-related costs (such as waste filtration) are currently classified within overheads, meaning that they are not very transparent to management. Similarly, the regulatory fines are also likely to be included within overheads. However, if all these environment-related costs were classified separately they would immediately be more visible to management.

Decommissioning costs – The profit forecast for Kayplas highlights that PLX incurs a number of significant costs at the end of a project, for example the costs of decommissioning equipment, or cleaning industrial sites once they stop being used.

These costs (because they are large) can have a significant impact on the shareholder value generated by a project, and can also make significant demands on PLX's cash resources. However, because they occur at the end of a project there is a danger that they will be given a lower priority if management focuses on short-term financial measures, such as annual profit.

Reporting on costs – As well as making the costs more visible to management, increasing the focus on environmental costs could also be beneficial to PLX from a public relations perspective. If PLX highlights these costs in its financial reports, and also highlights the actions it is taking to reduce to reduce its environmental impact, it can demonstrate to pressure groups and the regulator that it is taking its environmental responsibilities seriously.

BPP LEARNING MEDIA

Reputational costs – By contrast, if PLX is deemed not be taking its environmental responsibilities seriously, this could result in adverse publicity for the group, and ultimately could lead to consumer boycotts and lost revenues.

(b) **ABC**

Traditional ABC allocates costs to cost centres or cost drivers on the basis of the activities that caused the costs.

Environmental ABC looks to distinguish between environment-related costs and environment-driven costs.

Environment-related costs are attributed specifically to an environmental cost centre, for example, waste filtration at PLX.

Environment-driven costs are not allocated to a specific environmental cost centre, but still relate to environmental drivers. For example, PLX may reduce the working life of some of the machinery in its refinery to reduce pollution levels in the later years of its working life. The increased annual depreciation charges that will result from this are environment-driven costs.

Applying ABC in this way will help PLX identify and control environmental costs.

Life cycle view

Life cycle costing looks to record a product's costs and revenues across the whole of its life, rather than for a single year, or for a specific phase of its life (such as the production phase).

This is important because it highlights the importance of costs incurred **prior** to production and those incurred **after** production ceases (for example, in PLX's case, the costs of decommissioning plant and equipment). These costs can often be very large, and so could have a significant impact on the shareholder value generated by a project. As a result they may potentially influence the decision about whether or not to undertake a project.

Given the nature of PLX's business, it is very important that any investment appraisals capture all the costs generated over the whole life cycle of a project – including decommissioning costs, which for the Kayplas project are estimated at $18m.

Evaluation

Costs – One of the major issues PLX would face if it chooses to introduce environmental ABC is that it will need to collect significant additional amounts of information from the management accounting system, and there are likely to be costs involved in upgrading the system to be able to provide this.

Benefits – At the same time, while the techniques can help improve PLX's economic and environmental efficiency, it may be difficult to quantify the benefits which will accrue from using the techniques. Therefore, it may be difficult to justify introducing the techniques on the basis of a financial cost/benefit analysis.

Strategic benefits – However, perhaps the stronger case for using the new techniques is a non-financial one. PLX believes it will be strategically important to be at the forefront of environmental developments, and using the new techniques will demonstrate its commitment to this.

By demonstrating its commitment to environmental issues, PLX could improve its **public image**, appease the **pressure group** (Green Kayland) and reassure the **Government** it is helping to improve its treatment of the environment.

(c) **Performance metrics** – The focus of PLX's current performance measures are predominantly financial, suggesting there are few, if any, environmental performance metrics.

However, the increasing focus on the environmental impact of PLX's activities means that it should also identify some key environmental performance indicators, and measure its performance against them. Carbon dioxide emissions could be a particularly important metric, given the Government's commitment to reducing it, and the threat of a tax on emissions being introduced in the future.

Unlike its current metrics, however, PLX will not be able to see how its environmental performance is directly contributing to its financial performance. For example, it will not be able to put monetary values on its CO_2 emissions figures – although if the Government does introduce the proposed tax then PLX will be specifically able to identify the 'cost' of the emissions.

Information systems – Similarly, given that the focus of PLX's information systems is currently on producing financial performance measures, the addition of environmental performance information could involve significant changes – for example, PLX may need to modify its existing database structure, or add additional records.

However, before it can monitor its CO_2 emissions, PLX will have to start collecting data on the volume of emissions, which can then be recorded in its management information systems. As such, PLX will need to install measuring equipment to capture the relevant data, and then feed it back to the company's management information systems.

The measuring equipment could capture real-time data which is uploaded automatically into the information systems. Having real-time environmental data could be particularly useful in detecting a potential problem in the refinery as early as possible (eg an unexpected increase in the level of CO_2 emissions), and thereby helping to minimise the environmental damage the problem causes.

(d) PLX's traditional performance measure of product profit for Kayplas suggests it will generate a profit of $41.5m over 5 years. However, this ignores the environmental costs (of waste filtration, and carbon dioxide exhaust extraction) as well as the cost of decommissioning at the end of the project.

By contrast, a life cycle analysis would include all of these costs:

Kayplas product profit	$m
Traditional view:	
Revenue:	149.4
Production, marketing & development costs	107.9
Product profit (over 5 years)	41.5
Profit margin	27.8%
Adjusted for environmental costs:	
Revenue	149.4
Production, marketing & development costs	107.9
Waste filtration	8.1
Carbon dioxide exhaust extraction	5.3
Decommissioning costs	18.0
	139.3
Revised product profit	10.1
Profit margin	6.8%

When the environmental costs are all included, the forecast profit margin on the Kayplas project is reduced from 27.8% to 6.8%, which makes it a much less attractive investment. Moreover, if the actual costs of decommissioning in 5 years' time are higher than the forecast ($18.0m) – for example, due to changes in environmental legislation in the next 5 years – then the profit margin will be reduced even further.

Importantly, also, life cycle costing makes the post-production costs visible at the start of the project and in the design stage of the product. This should help PLX appreciate early in the project the need to minimise the costs of decommissioning. So, for example, it could investigate whether it could design any of the equipment to be used to produce Kayplas in such a way that it could also be used to produce Kayplas2.

8 FGH Telecom

Text reference. Stakeholder management is considered in Chapter 4b of the BPP Study Text, where environmental management accounting is also discussed. The impact that external factors can have on an organisation's performance is discussed in Chapter 5.

Top tips. Part (a) asks you to evaluate how well the environmental strategy is aligned to stakeholder interests. So it is important that you link the stakeholders' interests directly to the strategy, and don't just talk about stakeholders in generic terms. Also note that part (a) is only worth five marks, so don't spend too long on this part of the question.

Part (b) asks for an environmental assessment. You could use PEST/PESTEL as these provide a structured analysis. However, you then need to suggest suitable performance indicators for each factor. Remember, performance indicators need to be measurable. To score well, the performance indicators you suggest need to be well explained. So, for example, a vague reference to competitor reviews is not sufficient, and would score few marks.

Part (c) asks for an evaluation of the data in the table. What categories could be used to summarise the data? Remember to refer to the company's stated goal and how it is a long-term goal. The company is part-way though the period covered by the goal so do you think it is on target for reaching a 60% reduction by 20Y7? At this level you need to take an overall view of performance measurement so think about overall performance, not just the detail.

In **part (d)** think of what factors affect the data – for instance, miles travelled using each form of transport.

Marking scheme

		Marks
(a)	Up to 2 marks for the interests of each stakeholder group evaluated in relation to the environmental strategy. Maximum of 5.	5
(b)	1 mark per factor identified as relevant for each section of the broad sections of the analysis (PEST or PESTEL sections are appropriate and competition could be an additional area considered). Up to 1 mark for each performance indicator relevant to the factors identified. Maximum of 8.	8
(c)	Up to 4 marks for analysis of basic data, commenting on overall picture and achievement of target. Up to 2 marks for simplifying data into broad categories and commenting. Up to 4 marks for analysis of mix of methods of travel and commenting (another acceptable categorisation could be related to fuel type: petrol, diesel and aviation – rail is problematic as it is a mix of diesel and electricity but reasonable assumptions will be acceptable) Maximum of 9 marks.	9
(d)	1 mark per relevant point – up to 3 marks.	3
	Total =	**25**

(a) **Shareholders** – The tough economic environment, in conjunction with the competitive nature of the telecommunications sector, is likely to mean shareholders will be particularly concerned about the level of profits which FGH can maintain.

The environmental strategy could be particularly useful for two reasons in this respect:

- It can save costs and increase efficiency through reducing resource usage.
- It could lead to increased sales as a result of improved reputation amongst customers.

Government – Government has been calling for change from the business community in relation to environmental issues, and FGH has taken action which is designed to bring about these changes. If organisations (such as FGH) reduce their environmental footprints voluntarily, this will reduce the need for government to impose regulation and legislation in order to encourage better performance.

Public – Like government, sections of the public have been calling for change from the business community in relation to environmental issues. If it can demonstrate that it has responded to these calls, FGH should be able to benefit from an improved reputation amongst customers and potential customers.

Employees – Although it is not clear from the scenario whether FGH's employees prefer working at home to commuting into an office, it is likely that a number of them will, in which case they will be pleased with the impact of the strategy on their day to day life, regardless of the environmental benefits of the strategy. If other employees prefer working in the office to working at home, they are likely to resent the new initiative. By contrast, the content of some employees' work may mean that they cannot work from home, in which case the home-working initiative is unlikely to affect them, so they may have little interest in it at all.

Similarly, it is not clear whether the employees prefer teleconferences to the travel required to attend regular meetings, but again, it is likely that at least some will be pleased with the reduced amount of travelling they have to do.

(b) **Regulation and legislation** – FGH's environmental strategy will be directly affected by increased regulation and legislation from government. These would include recycling targets for materials, and limits on emissions such as pollution and waste levels. Carbon levies may be an additional tax.

Performance indicators which FGH could use to monitor its progress include the cost of additional recycling, fines for failing to meet regulations and targets, and the cost of a carbon levy.

Economic factors – Economic factors which could affect FGH's strategy include the difficulty in obtaining capital (through the debt or equity markets) as well as general factors such as inflation, interest rates and exchange rates.

The difficulties in raising capital through the debt or equity markets could be monitored through FGH's cost of capital. This could be particularly important if any environmental initiatives it is considering would require significant capital expenditure in order to implement.

The tough economic environment is also likely to mean that firms will find it difficult to maintain their profits, so any cost savings from reductions in energy use could be useful to help offset any fall in profits.

Social factors – The general public has an impact on FGH's environmental strategy as they use its products and are calling for reductions in emissions. So, for example, if FGH is known to be more environmentally friendly than other telecommunications providers, this may improve its brand image and may prompt consumers to switch to FGH in preference to other providers.

A suitable performance indicator could be to measure the perceived image of FGH by means of a customer survey.

Technological factors – Finally technological change will affect FGH's environmental strategy as it can adopt new technologies such as electric and hybrid cars, and new technologies for storing and capturing energy such as recharging solar cells which could be used in production.

Performance indicators would require the measurement of how new technologies affect existing emissions data.

(c) **Progress to date** – The company has set itself a target of reducing emissions by 60% of their 20X1 value by 20Y7 (16 years). In total it has been able to cut emissions by 38% in 9 years from 20X1 to 20Y0 (106.6/172.6).

In just the last year (20X9 to 20Y0) it has cut emissions by 16% (106.6/127.5).

However, this optimistic rate may not necessarily continue as emissions become increasingly hard to cut when the easier targets have been met in the early years of the programme.

Modes of transport – The data used can be usefully summarised into road, rail and air and the individual measures included under each. Detail of the data is included in Appendix 1 below.

In summary, rail travel has seen a decrease of 63%, the largest across the categories, followed by road travel which has seen a reduction of 38%, while the smallest decrease was in air travel which only fell by 16% over the 9 years. Both the first two categories are decreasing at a rate well within the target of 60% as the falls already achieved are at least 38% with 7 years to go. The problem with air transport may reflect increasing globalisation and the need to travel to meet clients and have meetings.

If the composition of the three types of transport are analysed in the base year of 20X1 and compared with 20Y0 it is clear that air travel has increased slightly from 6% to 8% of total travel whilst rail travel has fallen by the same amount which may explain part of its success in reducing emissions. However, the reason for this may be a change in the emissions technology relating to each category travelled rather than the number of miles travelled by each method.

Looking in detail at each category, the largest trend is a move from commercial petrol vehicles to commercial diesel vehicles whereby there are nil emissions in 20Y0 from petrol vehicles. This reduction is easier to achieve with the commercial fleet than the other types of car as there may be an element of choice exercised by employees in the other categories, for instance company cars.

(d) **Total distances travelled** – One key area that could be measured is the number of miles (total distances) travelled by employees so that the impact of the changes on employee behaviour can be monitored. This would allow the assessment of the home-working scheme to see how far employees commute and the effect on this of working from home.

It would also allow FGH to measure how much travel is done by air and the effect of moving from travelling to meetings by air and alternatives such as teleconferencing.

The data could also be used to calculate the effect of switching transport by calculating average emissions per kilometre travelled.

Appendix 1

Measured in millions of kg	*20X1 Base year*	*20X9*	*20Y0*	*Change on base year*
Commercial fleet diesel	105.4	77.7	70.1	–33%
Commercial fleet petrol	11.6	0.4	0.0	–100%
Company car diesel	15.1	14.5	12.0	–21%
Company petrol	10.3	3.8	2.2	–79%
Other road travel (diesel)	0.5	1.6	1.1	120%
Other road travel (petrol)	3.1	0.5	0.3	–90%
Rail travel	9.2	9.6	3.4	–63%
Air travel (short haul)	5.0	4.4	3.1	–38%
Air travel (long haul)	5.1	7.1	5.4	6%
Hire cars (diesel)	0.6	1.8	2.9	383%
Hire cars (petrol)	6.7	6.1	6.1	–9%
Total	172.6	127.5	106.6	

	20X1 Base year	*20X9*	*20Y0*
Index	100%	74%	62%
	Year on year change	–16%	

Simplifying categories

	20X1 Base year	20X9	20Y0	Change on base year
Road travel	153.3	106.4	94.7	–38%
Air travel	10.1	11.5	8.5	–16%
Rail travel	9.2	9.6	3.4	–63%
Total	172.6	127.5	106.6	–38%

Mix of travel methods in each year

	20X1 Base year	20X9	20Y0
Road travel	89%	83%	89%
Air travel	6%	9%	8%
Rail travel	5%	8%	3%

9 Sweet Cicely

Text reference. The impact of external factors on performance management, and the impact of risk and uncertainty – including risk analysis techniques – are covered in Chapter 5 of the BPP Study Text.

Top tips. Although **Part (a)** is presented as a single requirement, there are actually two elements (Advise…; Evaluate...) so make sure you address both of these in your answer.

The second paragraph of the paragraph tells us 'SC must choose a size [of factory] most suited to the expected demand for its products.' It then tells us 'demand for SC chocolate bars will be influenced by external factors' before identifying a number of factors which could affect demand. These external factors are all potential sources of risk and uncertainty, so you should use them to illustrate the advice you are giving.

Note also the requirement refers to both 'risk' and 'uncertainty' so think about the distinction between the two. A useful way to structure your answer could be to consider each issue – risk, and uncertainty – separately; for example, beginning with a brief description of what each is, and then using relevant examples from the scenario to illustrate why it will be important for SC to consider each of them in the decision-making process.

In the second part of the requirement, ('Evalaute the use of PEST'), rather than 'evaluating' in terms of assessing the potential advantages and limitations of using PEST analysis, a more helpful approach will be to think how an awareness of the political, economic, social and technical factors in the environment could help SC manage the risk and uncertainty surrounding the project. A useful way to do this could be to use each of the four factors (P,E,S,T) as a heading in your answer, and then think about the issues in the scenario which relate to that factor.

Importantly, though, note that you are not asked to use PEST analysis to **identify** the potential risks and uncertainties; but rather how SC could use it to help **manage** these risks and uncertainties. For example, political instability in cocoa growing regions is a political risk, but can SC manage that risk, or – if it can't – what are the implications of this risk for the project?

Parts (b) and (c) look the use of at different risk analysis techniques for evaluating projects. In part (b) you need to take account of the different risk appetites of the board and the shareholders, whilst in part (c) the requirement refers to a risk neutral investor. So, in part (b) the potential techniques to consider could be maximax; maximin and minimax regret, while part (c) requires you to use expected values.

Part (b). A key step in answering this question is identifying the risk appetites of the two different stakeholder groups. The scenario tells us, in the penultimate paragraph, that the board wants 'to minimise the opportunity cost of making the wrong decision about the size of the new chocolate factory.' So which of the potential techniques will they use to evaluate the three options? Similarly, in the first paragraph of the scenario, we were told, the new shareholders 'are prepared to accept a high level of risk' in order to increase SC's performance. So which technique will they use?

BPP LEARNING MEDIA

Part (c). As noted above, risk neutral investors will use expected values in order to evaluate potential options, so you need to use the data in Appendix 2 to calculate the expected values of the three options, and then recommend the option with the highest EV.

Note, however, that this requirement doesn't only involve the calculation. There is also a second element: to explain any problems with using expected values to make the choice about which factory to set up.

Marking scheme

		Marks
(a)	Consideration of risk and uncertainty – 1 mark per valid point, up to 8 marks Discussion of use of PEST analysis – 1 mark per point, up to 8 marks	
	Total for part (a): up to 14 marks	14
(b)	Calculation and comments on the board's preference – up to 4 marks Comments on new shareholders' preference – up to 2 marks	
	Total for part (b): up to 6 marks	6
(c)	Calculation of expected value – 1 mark Recommendation, and drawbacks of expected value approach – 1 mark per point	
	Total for part (c): up to 5 marks	5
	Total =	25

(a) **Importance of incorporating risk and uncertainty in making long-term decisions**

Risk relates to the variability of outcomes, the probabilities of which are known, or can be estimated. Uncertainty occurs where the outcomes and their probabilities are unknown. The variability of demand for SC's chocolate bars is a risk, and the probabilities of different levels of demand can be estimated. The outbreak of conflict in a cocoa growing region affecting cocoa prices cannot be assigned a probability, and so is an uncertainty.

The market price of cocoa and the demand for chocolate bars are examples of exogenous variables which significantly affect the performance of SC. Exogenous variables arise from outside the business, and the business doesn't have any control over them. Climatic conditions, soil erosion, for example, all affect the price of cocoa, and therefore the performance of SC.

When investors evaluate businesses, they take into account prospective returns and the level of risk involved. Therefore, managers should consider risk and return when evaluating projects on their behalf. Long-term strategic planning requires forecasts to be made about future events, such as the price of cocoa. These future events are by definition unknown, and subject to risk and uncertainty. Risk and uncertainty must, therefore, be considered when making long-term plans, such as opening the new factory. The further forward plans are projected, the riskier, and more uncertain, events are likely to be, as it is harder to predict what conditions will be. This means that consideration of risk and uncertainty is even more important when making long-term decisions than when making short-term decisions.

Use of PEST analysis

To incorporate risk and uncertainty into long-term strategic planning, SC must identify and monitor the most important exogenous variables, taking action to manage the risks they present. As a traded commodity, the risks of rising cocoa prices could be managed (hedged), for example, by using cocoa futures. The board member's comments suggest planning for the cake business was poor, and did not adequately consider the importance of exogenous variables. Risks in the macro environment could be identified using a PEST analysis.

Political factors

The market price of cocoa is affected by conflicts and political uncertainty, so consideration of these external factors is needed to incorporate risk and uncertainty into long-term planning. By identifying factors such as political instability or conflict, SC can improve its long-term performance by sourcing cocoa from more stable regions. The political situation in a region can change rapidly, which might make it difficult to incorporate these risks into long-term planning, as there is a high degree of uncertainty.

The introduction of increased taxes on products containing sugar is a political factor affecting the long-term demand for SC's products. Once introduced, this factor is likely to operate in the long term and be more predictable. Identifying this, SC could develop products containing less sugar and so reduce the amount of these additional taxes on its products.

Economic factors

Economic factors such as the variation in long-term interest rates can influence SC's performance by affecting exchange rates or overall consumer demand. By identifying these factors, SC could hedge against currency exchange rates. In the longer term, SC could locate its operations in a country where the risks from exchange rate fluctuations are lower, or diversify geographically to spread the risk.

Social factors

Overall demand for chocolate products will be influenced by social factors such as consumer tastes or increased awareness of healthy eating. SC can improve its long-term performance by not investing in a chocolate factory at all, if it believes demand for its products will fall sufficiently to make the venture unprofitable.

Technological factors

The increased cocoa yields from genetically modified crops may reduce long-term cocoa prices and SC could incorporate this into the net present value calculations for the factory. There may be unpredictable consequences which are harder to plan for, such as the acceptance by consumers of genetically modified foods.

(b) **Board**

The board wants to minimise the opportunity cost of making the wrong decision about the size of the new chocolate factory, which means to minimise the regret of making the wrong decision. The minimax regret rule would be the appropriate method to use so they would choose the project with the lowest maximum regret.

The regret table is as follows:

	Option 1	*Option 2*	*Option 3*
Annual demand			
50 million	0	(12.0)	(36.0)
60 million	(10.0)	0	(40.0)
70 million	(11.0)	(1.0)	0.0
Maximum regret	**(11.0)**	**(12.0)**	**(40.0)**

Option 1 is the option with the lowest maximum regret ($11m), and that would be the option preferred by the board according to their risk appetite. A drawback of using the minimax regret rule is that the probabilities of the outcomes are not considered.

New shareholders

The new shareholders are keen to increase the long-term performance of the business and are prepared to accept a high level of risk to achieve this. They will choose the option with the maximum possible outcome, which is option 3, with a maximum possible net present value of $17m. This is known as the **maximax rule**. This also takes no account of the probabilities of the outcomes, and also tends to be over-optimistic. It also ignores the fact that even risk seekers have a risk–return trade off.

(c) **Expected value of each option**

Option 1 – (0.3 × 3.0) + (0.4 × 0.5) + (0.3 × –2.0) = \$0.5m

Option 2 – (0.3 × 5.0) + (0.4 × 2.0) + (0.3 × –1.0) = \$2.0m

Option 3 – (0.3 × 7.0) + (0.4 × 1.5) + (0.5 × –2.0) = \$2.1m

The risk neutral investor's choice, for year 1 only, would be option 3, with an expected value of \$2.1m.

Problems of using an expected value approach

A risk neutral investor would use the expected value approach to choose between the three options. The expected value is a long run average, and is only appropriate where a decision is repeated many times. This does not appear to be the case at SC which has made only one attempt at strategic expansion in the last several years. For the same reason, the expected value will not equal the actual outcome.

Determining the probabilities, of the market price of cocoa for example, is subjective. Even analysis of historical market prices is not necessarily a guide to what will happen in the future. The expected value approach is suitable for a risk neutral investor. This does not apply to the key stakeholders at SC, and hence this approach is inappropriate for use in the decision on the three options. Determining the payoffs is also difficult when demand is subject to uncertainty. SC should not make a decision on the factory based only on the first year's operating profits, and should take a longer term view, for example, based on discounted cash flows.

10 TREN engine components

Text reference. Lean manufacturing and lean information systems are covered in Chapter 6a of the BPP Study Text.

Top tips. This question focuses on one specific part of the APM syllabus: 'Evaluate whether the management information systems are lean and the value of the information that they provide...'

To answer the question, it is necessary to identify the requirements of a lean information system (part (a)) and then to discuss why the existing 'traditional' management accounting system at TREN may fail to do this (part (b)).

Having established the difference between the two types of system, you then need (part (c)) to identify the changes which are needed to convert TREN's 'traditional' systems into 'lean' systems.

Note that there is no requirement to link your answer to part (a) directly to the scenario. However, your answers to parts (b) and (c) do need to be linked directly to the scenario.

(a) A lean information system should provide value to the users of the system. Key principles are the **elimination of waste, speed of information flow,** and **clarity**.

Elimination of waste – A lean system seeks to eliminate all waste. In an information system, waste is created by errors in the information, which means that incorrect information is used and wrong decisions may be taken. Alternatively the information has to be corrected when the error is identified, and this results in a cost of correction. Correcting errors does not add value, because the error should not have occurred, and correcting errors is wasted effort.

Efficiency in the flow of information – A lean manufacturing system is one in which there is an efficient flow of items through the manufacturing process. In a lean information system, there should be an efficient flow of information. Information should be available to individuals when they need it, and there should not be unnecessary delays in providing it or making it available.

While efficiency in the flow of information means that information should be available when it is needed, it should not be provided before it is needed. Information should be available 'just in time' (JIT). This is the concept of **pulling items** through the system rather than pushing them through. If information is provided before individuals are ready to use it, it does not have value.

Clarity is also an element of lean information. Information must be clear to the people who use it and should therefore be presented in a form that they can understand and use. If information is presented in a form that is difficult to understand, it will be difficult to use. Unless it is used for its intended purposes, information has no value.

Together, the elimination of waste, efficiency of information flow, and clarity of information are qualities of an information system that give value to the information that the system produces.

Reasons why lean principles may not lead to improvements in productivity and profitability

In many situations, an organisation supposedly using lean principles has not experienced the improvements in productivity and profitability expected. It is difficult to know whether this is due to shortcomings in the lean philosophy or whether the techniques involved are being **interpreted and applied correctly**.

Change in approach – To be successful, lean techniques should be seen and treated as outward signs of a more **fundamental approach** to operations and quality. However, many organisations seem to treat the techniques as the end itself – they have a mistaken belief that simply putting structures and mechanisms (eg quality circles) in place will improve efficiency and quality. Sustainable differences require a change in thinking and in culture – which are difficult to achieve.

Cost-cutting exercise – Lean production is often viewed as a simple cost-cutting exercise rather than a fundamental commitment to eliminating waste and adding value. Many companies use lean manufacturing to improve quality and reduce costs. But the benefits most businesses realise are only a fraction of what could be achieved if these strategies were applied in conjunction with the aim of creating a workplace with real organisation and order, and with an engaged workforce who take pride in their work.

(b) There are several reasons why TREN's current management accounting system does not fulfil the requirements of a lean information system.

Errors – There are many errors in data capture for the cost accounting system. Errors represent waste in the system, by providing incorrect information about costs, or requiring correction when the errors are found. Errors also reduce the confidence of users in the information that the system provides.

'Push' system – Monthly variance reports are provided but not until two months after the end of the month. There are two weaknesses in this reporting system. The first is the delay in making information available if required. The information about performance is being held by accountants and is not made available to the managers who can use it.

The second problem is that the information is pushed out to management in the form of monthly variance reports, when it would be more appropriate to make the information available when management want to use it for monitoring and control purposes. The information system is dictating how and when the information should be used, whereas management should be doing this.

Not encouraging lean manufacturing – More fundamentally, it can be argued that traditional cost and management accounting methods provide managers with inappropriate information that encourages the wrong sorts of management for an organisation that uses lean manufacturing methods. A key feature of lean manufacturing is the elimination of inventory, because holding inventory is wasteful. Absorption costing, however, encourages manufacturing at full capacity, even if this means manufacturing items that are not yet needed by customers, so that inventory will build up. This is because high volumes of production reduce the unit costs of manufacture by spreading overhead costs over a larger volume of output.

Variance reporting of efficiency also encourages greater volumes of output, because greater efficiency means faster production. When the workforce is paid a fixed wage or salary, attempts to improve efficiency will result in greater production quantities and a build-up of inventory.

The current reporting systems therefore encourage managers to control operations in a way that is inconsistent with lean manufacturing.

(c) **Error reduction** – To create a lean management accounting system, waste must be eliminated and information flow improved. The causes of the data errors in data capture are not known. The problem may be the use of manual documentation for recording costs, or errors in input by inadequately trained staff. Methods of recording costs should be investigated, and the target should be to eliminate input errors entirely.

Flows of information – The flow of information must be improved, so that up to date information is available to management when they want it. The speed of entering data into the accounting system should be reviewed, and the aim should be to minimise the delay between recording data and inputting it into the accounting system. Automated methods of monitoring inventory movement or recording labour times may be considered.

User access to information – The accounting system should also allow managers online access to information about costs, so that they can obtain and use the information they need at a time that they need it. This should apply to senior management as well as to management at the operational level.

Cost allocation – The information provided by the accounting system should be reviewed, and absorption costing should be abandoned. There may be some value in using activity-based management to monitor and control overhead costs, but the most important requirement should be to value inventory at direct materials' cost. This means that there will be no incentive to produce at high capacity volumes or operate at unnecessary levels of efficiency. Favourable capacity and efficiency variances will not affect inventory costs and so will not improve management performance.

Performance measures – Different items of information should be provided for performance measurement purposes. Traditional performance measurement methods for materials – price and usage variances – should be used to control materials costs. For labour, however, non-financial measures of performance may be appropriate, such as production cycle times of throughput times and the ratio of idle time to active time for the workforce. The company is considering JIT purchasing for its main suppliers: if so, a suitable measure of performance may be the order to delivery cycle time for purchase orders.

In a lean information system, information should have a practical use and support the aims of management. The management accounting system should be changed so that it provides value – a practical purpose, with no waste, rapid information flow and clarity of meaning.

11 Forion Electronics

Text reference. ERPS are discussed in Chapter 6b of the BPP Study Text. Non-financial performance indicators are discussed in Chapter 9b.

Top tips.

Part (a). As is the case with a number of APM questions, note that there are two elements to this requirement: first, you need to discuss the integration of information systems in an ERPS; then, second, you need to discuss how the ERPS at Forion may affect performance management issues there.

The first element doesn't specifically require any application to Forion. However, you could use the issues which Forion is facing, and the different departments mentioned in the scenario, to illustrate the way an ERPS could integrate information from different systems.

The marking guide indicates that six out of the ten marks for this requirement are available for the second element – discussing how the ERPS can affect the performance management issues at Forion.

Even if you didn't know much about an ERPS, you should have been able to identify how deficiencies in the information sharing between departments could lead to the problems identified in the scenario. There are six marks available for three problems; so two marks per problem. If, for each problem, you provide a brief discussion of the likely causes of each problem, and then indicate how better information sharing could help to avoid that problem, this should help you earn the majority of the marks available for this part of the requirement.

Part (b). An important factor to consider here is the relationship between Forion and BAS. BAS is a supplier to Forion, and Forion has chosen BAS because of its reputation for quality and new product development. This suggests Forion considers these aspects of performance to be important (and Forion has previously identified it needs to have high-visibility, durable screens in order to be competitive – so visibility and durability could be considered as aspects of 'quality').

A useful way to answer the question would be to consider how well the performance measures chosen allow Forion to assess BAS's performance in the areas which it has identified as important.

In this respect, don't just think about the aspects of performance selected, but also think about the practicalities of measuring the performance. How easy will it be to measure whether or not BAS achieves the desired levels of performance?

Part (c). Note that the question requires you to make two separate comparisons: financial vs non-financial data; and internal vs external data. Also, it is important that you discuss the issues specifically in the context of the SLA between Forion and BAS. For example, will BAS be happy to use internal performance data prepared by Forion given that it (BAS) could be liable for a financial penalty if it fails to achieve the target performance levels?

Examining team's comments (for part (c)) – Evaluating the reliability of data has been a common topic in past exams, yet candidates' answers to this question were unexpectedly poor. Many candidates seemed unaware of what constitutes internal and external sources, and – surprisingly – many considered audited, financial data to be amongst the least reliable sources. In addition, many candidates discussed the type of information that both parties to the alliance would need, without discussing its reliability (which is what the requirement actually asked for).

Marking scheme

		Marks
(a)	For general description of an ERPS and how it integrates information: 1 mark per relevant point – up to 5 marks	
	For specific discussion of the impact an ERPS could have on the problems at Forion: 1 mark per relevant point – up to 6 marks:	
	Total for part (a): up to 10	10
(b)	For relevant points about the usefulness of the three areas for measuring performance – 1 mark per point	
	Note. In order to score a clear pass, all three issues must be addressed.	
	Total for part (b): up to 12	8
(c)	For relevant points about the relative reliability about the different types of data – 1 mark per point	
	Note. In order to score a clear pass, both issues (financial/non-financial; and internal/external must be addressed.	
	Total for part (c): up to 7	7
	Total =	**25**

(a) An ERPS is a software system which supports and automates the business processes in an organisation. An ERPS can assist in identifying and planning the resources needed to perform many different activities in different departments across the whole organisation – including inventory management, manufacturing, distribution, invoicing and accounting. An ERPS can incorporate support functions such as human resource management and marketing.

As such, an ERPS enables the performance information from all departments that are involved in operations or production to be integrated into one system, thereby assisting the flow of information between the departments and across the organisation as a whole. Integrating performance information in this way would seem very useful to Forion, given the problems it has encountered to date.

As well as improving the flow of information between the department in an organisation, ERPSs can help to improve linkages with outside stakeholders – for example, by incorporating customer relationship management (CRM) and supply chain management (SCM) software.

Again, this would seem very useful to Forion, given the high number of customer and supplier relationships it has to manage.

BPP LEARNING MEDIA

The impact of an ERPS on performance management issues at Forion

Information sharing – The board has suggested that a number of the performance management problems at Forion arise from poor communication and information sharing between departments; not least because each of the departments has its own information system rather than having an integrated system across the organisation as a whole.

As such, by providing an integrated system which assists the flow of information between departments, an ERPS could help to solve the three problems identified.

Amount of subcomponents ordered – This reflects a problem with the information being shared between the Purchasing Department (which orders the subcomponents) and the Manufacturing Department (which uses them). If the Purchasing Department has incorrect or out of date information, this will lead to it ordering the wrong amount of subcomponents, which in turn means that Forion's inventory handling and storing costs will be higher than they need to be.

However, if Forion had an ERPS, information from the Manufacturing Department would automatically be shared with the Purchasing Department, meaning the Purchasing Department should be able to identify the quantities of subcomponents to order more accurately.

Stock-outs or obsolescence – Both of these problems arise from the amount of goods being manufactured not reflecting the expected level of orders. Although the Marketing Department may produce good sales forecasts, if these forecasts are not shared with the Manufacturing Department, it will not know what quantities of different goods it needs to make. If it produces too few, this will lead to stock-outs (and a loss of potential revenue); while obsolescence results from producing too many units of a good which cannot then be sold. (The risk of obsolescence could be a particular concern for Forion as a manufacturer of electronic goods.)

If the Marketing Department's forecasts were captured in an ERPS, they would be available to the Manufacturing Department when it was setting its production plans.

Lack of delivery vehicles – The delivery schedule needs to incorporate sales information (customers' orders) and manufacturing information (when goods will be available).

If the Warehouse Department only becomes aware of a customer order after it has scheduled all its delivery vehicles this would help to explain why there seem to be insufficient vehicles to meet customer deadlines. Similarly, if there are delays in manufacturing which the Warehouse Department isn't aware of, this could mean that goods can't be included in their scheduled delivery, and will require an additional delivery and an extra vehicle to fulfil the customer order.

By linking the manufacturing schedule, customer orders, and the delivery schedule, Forion should be able to schedule its deliveries as efficiently as possible, to make best use of its delivery fleet.

Equally, though, by having greater visibility over orders and the manufacturing schedule, the Delivery Department should be able to identify in advance any times when it will not have sufficient vehicles of its own to fulfil all the orders required. Knowing this, it can then make arrangements for a third-party logistics company to deliver the order in time to meet the customer's deadline.

(b) **Usefulness of performance areas**

The three performance areas selected (quality of manufacturing; timeliness of delivery; technical upgrades) all seem appropriate. The 'quality' area derives from underlying logic behind the alliance – Forion's need for high-visibility, durable screens; timeliness of delivery will be important for the smooth operation of the production process; and the ability to make technical upgrades is likely to be critical in a rapidly changing market – such as the market for smartphones.

Quality of manufacturing – BAS's strong reputation suggests the number of faults should be low. Nonetheless, as screen manufacturing is a key part of the assembly process, and having high quality screens is likely to be a critical success factor for the phone overall, it will be important to measure performance in this area.

There could also be significant costs involved in remedying any faults with the screens. If the faults are identified during internal inspection, the time taken to fix them will delay delivery. If the faults are identified by customers, Forion will incur the cost of repairing – or replacing – the faulty phone. Customers' dissatisfaction with faulty items may also mean they are less likely to buy a Forion smartphone again in the future.

Time of delivery – The screen is a key component of the phone so delays to shipments could cause significant disruption to the production process if Forion is trying to use a just-in-time (JIT) production process. Conversely, if Forion holds inventory 'just in case', then concerns about delayed shipments could lead to it holding higher levels of inventory than it might wish to.

If Forion wants to use a JIT production process, then implementing the ERPS and giving BAS access to the system could be very useful. For example, this would give BAS greater visibility around when screens are needed and in what quantity.

Technical upgrades – Whilst upgrades are likely to be important in keeping Forion's phone competitive, it will be difficult to measure BAS's performance against the metric as it is currently defined. For example, there is no timescale in which BAS needs to provide the upgrade, and deciding when the market demands an upgrade could be subjective.

If performance in this area cannot be measured effectively, BAS could pay less attention to it. Although, in theory, building financial penalties into the agreement is appropriate, Forion may not be able to apply them if it cannot measure whether or not BAS has achieved the target levels of performance.

Moreover, as Forion selected BAS as its strategic partner due to its strong reputation for quality of manufacturing and new product development, it is surprising that both of these acknowledged strengths are being measured, rather than any areas of potential weakness.

(c) **Reliability of financial vs non-financial data**

The requirement to produce annual accounts, and to have them audited, means that there should be robust controls in place around the production of financial data. Although non-financial data will be useful to management in controlling the business, it may not be subject to the same scrutiny and controls as financial data.

Similarly, financial data will be quantitative and objective, whereas non-financial data can sometimes be subjective; for example, an issue with a phone screen which some customers may report as a fault, other customers may not report.

Although the subjectivity of non-financial data can sometimes make it difficult to measure, this does not appear to be a problem in this context. The fault rates and the number of shipments overdue should be relatively easy to measure.

Internal vs external sources

Forion is likely to place greater reliance on its own data rather than external data (for example, as provided by BAS in relation to shipments supplied). As such, Forion is likely to use its own warehouse records to determine the number of shipments which are overdue, although this means that Forion will need to have sufficient controls in place to ensure that expected and actual delivery times are recorded accurately.

However, if both parties place greater reliance on their own data than the other party's data, this could be a source of problems for the alliance; for example, if the number of shipments BAS believes to be late differs from the number Forion believes to be late. This could be a particular issue here, given the financial penalties relating to performance.

In this case, it may be useful for both parties to have the right to inspect (audit) each other's data to confirm the reliability of that data.

12 Quark Healthcare

Text reference. RFID tags are discussed in Chapter 6b of the BPP Study Text. Lean systems are discussed in Chapter 6a.

Top tips.

For **part (a)**, it is very important that you think about the impact of the RFID system specifically in the context of the areas highlighted by the CFO: (i) the costs and benefits associated with producing information from the system; (ii) the impact of the system on the nature of the information supplied; (iii) changes to performance management reporting; and (iv) how the new information could be used to improve control at the hospitals.

To this end, it would be sensible to use each of the CFO's suggestions as headings in your answer, to make sure you cover all of them.

The 'control' issues and their impact on performance should be relatively easy to identify from the scenario – for example, staff are unable to find equipment because it hasn't been replaced after being used, and as a result patient care is delayed while staff waste time trying to find the equipment.

However, the marking guide indicates that only 6 out of the 12 marks for this requirement are available for internal control issues. So don't spend too long on this one area at the expense of the other areas.

Nonetheless, the problems staff face in finding equipment and drugs provide a link between parts (a) and (b) of the question. One of the key principles of 'lean' systems is the removal of waste and non value adding activities. Time spent looking for equipment or drugs clearly doesn't provide any value to hospital patients. Similarly, 'lean' systems aim to promote efficiency.

So a sensible way to approach **part (b)** will be to evaluate how far the RFID system can reduce waste and improve efficiency at the hospital.

Part (c). The scenario highlights that an earlier system which the hospital had tried to introduce has not been fully implemented due to complaints from the medical staff. The medical staff are clearly key stakeholders at the hospital and so if they oppose a new system it is unlikely to be successful.

This provides the context to the first part of the requirement: how the medical staff's attitudes will influence the design and implementation of the system.

However, note that there are effectively two parts to the requirement, with the second looking at issues around responsibility and accountability.

One of the key issues here, though, is how the system can promote accountability given the 'strict social order' among the staff. For example, can a nurse be responsible for a piece of equipment being in the wrong place if it has been moved by a doctor?

Marking scheme

		Marks
(a)	Costs and benefits associated with producing the information from the RFID system – 1 mark per relevant point up to a maximum of 3 marks Impact of the RFID system on the nature of the information supplied – 1 mark per relevant point up to a maximum of 3 marks	
	Changes to performance reporting resulting from the implementation of the new system – 1 mark per relevant point up to a maximum of 3 marks	
	Use of information from the new RFID system to improve control at the hospitals – 1 mark per relevant point up to a maximum of 6 marks	
	Total for part (a): up to 12	12

		Marks
(b)	Definition of lean systems – up to a maximum of 2	
	Analysis of the impact of the RFID system on the management of the hospital – 1 mark per relevant point, up to a maximum of 7	
	(Within this 7 marks, up to 2 marks are available for definition of the 5 Ss of lean)	
	Total for part (b): up to 7	7
(c)	Evaluation of how the attitude of medical staff will influence the design of the new system – 1 mark per relevant point, up to a maximum of 4	
	Evaluation of how the system might be used to promote responsibility and accountability – 1 mark per relevant point, up to a maximum of 4	
	Total for part (c): up to 6	6
		Total = 25

(a) **Costs and benefits of the system**

Cost – There is likely to be considerable cost associated with the hardware and software needed to establish the RFID system. A significant amount of time may also be required to tag the equipment and drugs which are to be included in the system.

However, the costs should be compared to the benefits which will accrue from the system:

Efficiency savings – Hospital staff will save time because they will no longer have to search for items once those items have been tagged.

Patient care – Improvements in patient care as a result of hospital staff being able to find equipment or drugs immediately rather than having to search for them.

Impact of the nature of the information supplied

Non-financial information – Although the information being supplied about Quark's equipment and inventory is non-financial (relating to the location and quantity of equipment and drugs in Quark's hospitals), it should already be included in the hospital's information systems.

Timeliness and accuracy – However, the major impact of the new system should come from the improvements it can provide to the timeliness and accuracy of the information being recorded. The RFID tags will update information on a **real-time basis**. Moreover, because movements are **recorded automatically** the problem of the register not correctly reflecting the physical location of an asset will be overcome.

Batches of drugs – However, the quality of the information provided by the RFID tags may be less reliable for the drugs which are delivered in a single packaged batch. If a tag is applied to a batch as a whole when it is delivered to the hospital, then the information provided by the tag will no longer be reliable once the batch is opened and drugs are used from it. Instead, there will still be a need for the hospital to physically count the quantities of these drugs actually held in inventory, rather than relying on the RFID information alone.

Performance management reporting

Weekly physical checks – Under its existing systems, Quark has to make weekly physical checks of the drugs held in inventory in order to update its records on the basis of those checks. However, the information provided by the RFID tags should mean that inventory records can be updated on a real-time basis, rather than being dependent on these weekly checks.

Access to information – The fact that the RFID information will be available on terminals throughout the hospitals should also help the speed with which staff can locate items of inventory or equipment. The ease and speed with which staff can search the information will depend on the number of terminals which are installed. It would also be useful for relevant staff to receive training on how to search for information on the terminals.

Improved control

Control over drugs – Quark's existing accounting systems aim to avoid theft and obsolescence of equipment and drugs. RFID tags should improve controls over security by providing greater transparency about the location of assets. For example, the tags will make it easy for staff to check that all the high-value drugs are stored in secure locations, thereby reducing the risk of them being stolen.

Reduced obsolescence – Additionally, the information available about the date drugs were delivered should help staff identify the order in which different batches of a drug should be used to prevent obsolescence and wastage.

Tagging equipment – We have already noted that tagging items of equipment will allow staff to find them more quickly and thereby provide faster service to patients. However, the RFID tags will also enable the hospitals' management teams to ensure that pieces of equipment are replaced and locked away in secure areas once they have been used. This again should help reduce the risk of theft, but perhaps equally importantly staff should be reminded of the importance of replacing items after they have been used, and of storing them in useful locations. This also links to the ideas of 'lean' systems which the CFO is interested in.

(b) **Lean systems**

Removal of waste – The aim of 'lean' systems is to minimise the amount of resources (including time) which are consumed by the activities of an organisation. A key element of this comes from identifying and eliminating all non value adding activities. In this context, 'lean' also involves the systematic elimination of waste.

In relation to information systems, waste arises from difficulties in accessing and retrieving information, or from having to correct inaccurate information. This kind of 'waste' has clearly been an issue for Quark – for example, where staff have had to waste time looking for equipment or drugs which have not been not stored in the correct place. Such activity is clearly not value adding; rather it detracts from the value (care) which Quark can offer to its patients.

Improved efficiency – In contrast to this, the goal of a 'lean' operating system is to get the right things to the right place at the right time. In the context of Quark, this could mean enabling staff to know where equipment is so that it can be made available in the right place when it is needed by patients. Consequently, introducing the RFID system should help the operations management at the hospitals become leaner.

'Lean' systems can also have wider cultural implications which could be beneficial at the hospitals, in particular in relation to changing attitudes towards 'waste' and 'inefficiency'. The instances of equipment lying unused in one area of the hospital while being searched for in another area (to the detriment of patient care) would seem to be symptomatic of waste and inefficiency in the hospitals.

5 Ss – Lean principles are often characterised through 5 Ss, which could usefully be introduced at Quark:

Structurise – Identify the things which are most important and introduce order where possible. At Quark this could mean identifying the optimal locations for storing equipment, on the basis of where it is used most frequently.

Systemise – Arrange essential items in order so that they can be quickly and easily accessed. The RFID system will make it easier for staff to locate the equipment and drugs they need.

Sanitise – Keep the working environment clean. Be tidy, and avoid clutter. Although the RFID system should help staff to find drugs and equipment more easily, there is a danger that staff may think that this reduces the need for them to replace them after use, or to keep stocks of drugs tidy and in order.

Standardise – Make cleaning and checking a routine. For example, the RFID information could be used by management to check that equipment is replaced after use; and staff could even be monitored on the extent to which they keep their sections of the hospitals tidy.

Self-discipline – Sustain via motivation; for example, by reporting on performance. The system could produce exception reports highlighting pieces of equipment which had not been returned to a secure store once they were no longer being used. Corrective action can then be taken to return the equipment to an appropriate store area.

Impact of the RFID system

In some organisations, 5Ss has become a cleaning and housekeeping exercise only, and the underlying philosophy behind the concept has been lost. If this happens, then RFID's ability to make the management system leaner will be reduced. However, if the RFID information system is seen as an important part of quality management at the hospitals, then its impact should be more beneficial.

(c) **Key stakeholders** – The **medical staff** are likely to be key stakeholders in the hospitals, so their attitude to the new system is likely to be very important. If they resist the system, then its implementation is unlikely to be successful, as appears to have been the case with the new method for recording drugs administered to patients.

In this respect, it will be important to consult the medical staff over the design and implementation of the RFID system. Not only does consulting them recognise their position as key stakeholders, but also it gives them the opportunity to ensure the system is designed in a way which provides them with the information they need.

Improvements to patient care – Crucially, consulting the medical staff about the design of the system should help encourage them to accept it rather than resist it. Equally, it will be important that medical staff realise that the primary purpose of the system is to enable equipment and drugs to be found more easily – thereby improving patient care – rather than as a piece of bureaucracy. If the medical staff realise the benefits of the system, they should be more willing to accept it.

Usability – The user-friendliness and ease of use of the new system will also influence how successfully it will be implemented.

Again, this highlights the importance of consulting the medical staff, to ensure that the system is designed in a way which makes it easy for them to use. Some of the complaints from the nurses and specialist doctors about the new method of drug administration may have been caused by the system proving difficult or time consuming to use.

Responsibility and accountability

The RFID system will provide much greater transparency as to where equipment or drugs are actually being stored, and can provide management with the information to control how well staff are looking after the hospitals' assets. However, in itself, the system cannot promote responsibility or accountability.

Quark will also need to identify who is responsible for ensuring assets are held in the right place at the right time. For example, responsibility schedules could be introduced for each department or ward identifying which assets the nurses are responsible for and which the doctors are responsible for.

Quark's management should only hold people accountable for assets being in the right place if those people have control over how and where those assets are used. For example, can a nurse be held accountable for equipment being in the wrong place if a doctor has moved it? Crucially, if nurses start being criticised for items not being stored in the correct place when those items have been moved by a specialist doctor, this is likely to demotivate the nurses, and could also create resentment between the nurses and the doctors.

13 Nelson, Jody & Nigel

Text reference. Performance management information systems, and lean principles, are discussed in Chapter 6a of the BPP Study Text.

Top tips.

Part (a). There are two aspects of the information system you need to assess here: whether it is effective in reducing waste; and whether it adds value to NJN's workflow.

A sensible approach to this requirement is to work through the scenario and identify features in the current system which relate to waste or adding value. Do these features reduce waste? Or are they actually creating waste?

For example, (in paragraph 2) we are told 'Packing lists are manually input...' and in the third paragraph we are told that in 8% of packing lists, at least one item is not available in the location or the quantity specified by the WIS, and these discrepancies have to be investigated. Do features like these suggest the system is effective in reducing waste?

Similarly, in the second paragraph of the scenario we are told the retail stores 'do not currently have access to real-time inventory levels'. As such, is the system adding any value – compared, for example, to a system in which the retail stores could see the inventory levels, and therefore didn't try to order an item which was unavailable?

The scenario provides a number of hints towards points to include in your answer, so if you use these efficiently you should be able to score well on this part of the question.

Part (b). Before we can identify whether the three proposals will help to eliminate the different types of waste we first need to identify what these types of waste are. The sixth paragraph of the scenario suggests one: activities which do not add value to the customer; but waste can also result from over-production or holding excess inventory.

Having identified the causes of waste, we then need to ask will the proposals help to address then (or, are there problems with the proposals which will limit their effectiveness. One way to consider this might be to ask what changes NJN will have to make as a result of the proposals (and whether these will be beneficial)? For example, shutting down the additional means NJN will be able to hold less inventory (which is one of the types of waste).

Part (c). Since the question asks whether 'each of the 5Ss' is adequately measured by the performance metrics a sensible way to structure your answer would be to use each 'S' as a sub-heading, and then to ask:

- What does that 'S' involve?
- Do any of the measures (in Appendix 1) relate to those aspects of performance?

For example, 'Sanitise' involves being tidy and avoiding clutter, so assessing the tidiness of the warehouse would help to measure this.

Note the verb is 'evaluate' so – where possible – you should try to present a balanced argument: identifying areas where 'S's are adequately measured, as well as areas where they are not.

Examining team's comments

Part (a). This was generally well done, with candidates able to identify and discuss the problems from the scenario. The better candidates then tied these problems to the operation of the information system and often made good suggestions for improvements.

Part (b). Although candidates were asked to view the reduction of waste as an application or lean principles, few structured their answers using lean ideas about waste. Nonetheless, by keeping their answers focused on the specifics of the scenario and the proposals, candidates still scored well in this requirement.

Part (c). Candidates' performance on this part of the question was mixed, as many did not appear to know the meaning of the lean principles (5Ss) given. However, candidates did offer some useful evaluation of the indicators from first principles (about reducing waste or increasing efficiency).

Marking scheme

		Marks
(a)	Assessing whether the existing WIS is effective in reducing waste and adding value – 1 mark per relevant, valid point	
	Total for part (a): up to 10 marks	10
(b)	Advising whether the three proposals will help to eliminate waste – 1 mark per relevant, valid point	
	Total for part (b): up to 6 marks	6
(c)	Evaluating whether performance metrics adequately measure the 5Ss. 1 mark per relevant point, up to a maximum of 3 for each 'S'	
	Total for part (c): up to 9 marks	9
	Total =	**25**

(a) **Manual input**

At NJN, at least some of the inputs to the WIS are manual, and that means they are prone to error. This is time consuming and costly.

The packing lists which are received in the shipping containers are input manually. If incorrectly input, the quantities of items in the locations in the WIS will also be incorrect. Incorrect information in the WIS wastes time by needing teams to investigate the discrepancies, reconcile inventory records with those held by the manufacturer, and correct the information held on the WIS.

Furthermore, customers will not receive the items they have ordered, as in 8% of picking notes, items are not in the location they should be, or are in insufficient quantities. This is a high proportion of errors. Staff will waste time looking for items stored in the wrong locations. This will cause customer dissatisfaction and mean that larger quantities of inventory will need to be held, which is a wasteful use of storage space. Fewer complete orders can be fulfilled per unit of warehouse space, than would otherwise be the case. Both of these are sources of waste.

In the longer term, this means NJN staff must undertake a series of cyclical inventory counts in order to correct the information held in the WIS. This is wasteful activity which does not add value to customers, and should be eliminated.

The provision of accurate inventory information will also be of value to the retailers who can place orders only for items which are available, rather than only finding out about unavailable items by receiving an email from NJN. This would lead to increased customer satisfaction by avoiding having stock outs of particular items by ordering alternatives.

NJN should consider the use of barcodes or radio frequency identifiers (RFIDs) on products, to ensure that accurate data is input into the WIS. Using these devices, the product numbers and quantities of goods entering and leaving the warehouse could be automatically read into the WIS, without any intervention from warehouse staff. This would reduce the time taken to manually input the data and improve its accuracy.

An effective information system may interface directly with the manufacturers' and retail customers' information systems through electronic data interchange (EDI). This would increase service levels by ensuring that all parts of the value chain had access to accurate and timely information.

Time delays

The packing list batches are not available until up to 48 hours after receipt of the goods. The information held in the WIS will therefore be out of date. Items which are required for sales orders may be unavailable for picking. The use of automated input, where possible, will increase the timeliness of the information input into the WIS. This will reduce the labour cost of correcting the system and improve the number, accuracy, and completeness of orders despatched to customers.

Currently, all picking notes are printed in the warehouse office, which may be some distance from the area where items are picked. This also implies the existence of a bottleneck in the provision of information to the staff picking the items and wastes staff time moving to and from the warehouse office to pick up the reports. An improvement would be to ensure that information is available when and where it is needed, using terminals in the warehouse, or portable devices such as tablets. This would reduce time spent collecting picking information.

Similarly, in order to investigate discrepancies, staff have to obtain special reports which the Warehouse Manager extracts from the WIS. Again, this is a bottleneck which could delay staff getting the correct information, and may mean that the reports are inconsistent depending on the parameters set to run them. An effective system would eliminate these problems by providing standardised reports when requested, and in an optimal location.

Complex presentation of information

Effective systems add value to information when they organise and present the information in a clear way, without excessive detail. This allows the users to easily and quickly identify the information they need. It prevents wasting time obtaining the information in the first place, and correcting errors caused by interpreting it incorrectly.

BPP LEARNING MEDIA

The picking sheets show the 12-digit product codes which can easily be misread, increasing the likelihood of errors. A better system would present the information in a more accessible way and prevent information overload; for example, showing product descriptions or product codes only for the items to be picked.

(b) **Eliminating waste**

There are two main types of waste at NJN which can be identified using lean principles: waste which does not add value to the customer, and waste which occurs due to variations in demand and demands on staff.

Reorganising the warehouse to place high volume items near to the despatch area will help reduce the type of waste where the movement of staff to pick goods is more than should be required. Less movement, which means less staff time and cost, will be required by staff to pick these items and bring them to where they are to be despatched. It may be, however, that large and bulky items should be placed nearer to the despatch area instead, to save on the time spent transporting them to the despatch area. This may also address the increased seasonal demand for certain types of product, as products which are popular for that specific period could be stored more closely to the despatch area.

The cost of absenteeism is a waste caused by demanding too much of staff at busy times to compensate for inefficient organisation in the warehouse and errors in the WIS. The cost of searching for items which have been put in the wrong physical location at busy times is a waste due to variation in activity levels.

Another type of waste which does not add value to the customer is holding excessive inventory, for example, the additional warehouse space which NJN has rented. By not making efficient use of the warehouse space it has, NJN is reducing its level of output, and revenue, relative to the resources available to it. In addition, the extra warehouse space means more time spent by staff moving through the warehouses trying to locate goods.

The cyclical inventory counts which the Management Consultant has suggested do not add value to the customer and are also more demanding for staff. This is a wasteful activity, correcting the errors which have occurred in the WIS. NJN should instead concentrate on ensuring that errors do not occur in the first place, which will cost less than correcting them.

(c) **Lean principles (5Ss)**

The 5Ss in the adoption of lean principles during the warehouse reorganisation are Structurise, Systemise, Sanitise, Standardise and Self-discipline.

Structurise

This involves introducing order where possible, for example, by ensuring that items in the warehouse are arranged so that they are easy to find. This would also include segregating damaged or obsolete inventory, or discarding it from the warehouse.

The Management Consultant has suggested the measure of the proportion of inventory not stored in order of its alphabetical description, with 'A' nearest the despatch area and 'Z' furthest away. This may measure how easy to find each product is, but would not necessarily make best use of all available space or make the picking process more efficient. It may also be subjective and prone to errors caused by the interpretation of the product description, for example, in deciding if cricket balls should be measured under 'C' or 'B'.

Systemise

This principle involves organising items so that they are easy to use. At NJN, this means being able to accurately pick the correct items in the shortest possible time. It could also cover access to other resources, such as having computer terminals close to where they are needed.

The measure relating to the storing of goods alphabetically seems to conflict with the Consultant's recommendation to place the high volume lines close to the despatch area. Whereas storing goods alphabetically may make items easy to find, it does not necessarily make them easy to use (pick). By storing the high volume items near to the despatch area, the average time taken to pick orders would be reduced.

Sanitise

This principle means to be tidy and avoid clutter. This helps make things easy to find, allows easy access of staff around the warehouse, and helps make a safe working environment. The Warehouse Manager's daily assessment of tidiness is a suitable measure of this principle, which is a subjective assessment.

There is the possibility that the assessment will be biased, especially if the Warehouse Manager who is undertaking the assessment is also having his performance evaluated on the tidiness of the warehouse. The characteristics of what constitutes a tidy warehouse, compared to an untidy one, will need to be defined. There is the possibility of inconsistent measurement if someone other the Warehouse Manager does the assessment, or the assessment is done at different times of the day.

Standardise

This principle involves finding the best way of undertaking a process or task, and applying it consistently. The suggestion of the number of accidents caused by goods which have not been stored or picked in the correct way would measure this. As NJN should aim to have no accidents, this should be a performance measure with a target level of zero.

Self-discipline

This principle relates to sustaining the other Ss by motivating employees. Motivation is subjective, and hard to measure. None of the performance measures the Management Consultant has suggested directly measure this principle. The consistency in which specific tasks or processes are performed could be a measure of how well they are being sustained.

14 Great National Trains

Text reference. Performance management in not for profit organisations is discussed in Chapter 9b of the BPP Study Text. Integrated reporting, and the management accountant's role in providing information for integrated reports, are discussed in Chapter 6b.

Top tips.

Part (a): Although the context of this question is the issues faced when setting and measuring objectives in a public sector organisation as opposed to a commercial organisation, the requirement is to discuss the difficulties faced specifically by GNT, rather than the difficulties faced by public sector organisations in general.

The difficulties GNT faces may be the same as those faced by public sector organisations in general (for example, multiple stakeholders, with conflicting objectives; the prevalence of qualitative objectives); to score well in this question you need to relate the difficulties specifically to the problem of setting and measuring objectives in GNT.

Also, note that you have to consider the difficulties in two different contexts: the difficulties of **setting** objectives; and then the difficulties of **measuring** performance against those objectives.

The reference to measuring performance against objectives could have highlighted the idea of 'SMART' objectives. For example, are GNT's (qualitative) objectives specific enough to measure; are they time-bound ... and consequently, how effectively can they be measured?

Part (b): In effect, this requirement is asking you about the elements which should be included in an integrated report. The scenario tells you that GNT's current report focuses largely on financial and operational performance for the last year only, meaning that there is little information about GNT's wider strategy or future outlook. However, these are key elements of an integrated report.

Part (c): The focus of this question isn't the integrated report as such, but the role of the management accountant in producing information for the report. What additional information (if any) would be required to produce an integrated report, and what potential difficulties could the management accountant face in providing that information?

Tutorial note. The suggested solutions provided here are designed to show the range of points you could have made in answer to this question, and are consequently much more comprehensive than an answer you would be expected to produce under exam conditions.

(a) **Setting objectives**

Range of stakeholders – As a public sector organisation, GNT has a wide range of stakeholders, including: government, passengers, freight companies, the rail regulator, and society as a whole (for example in relation to carbon emissions). The three subsidiary companies (Passenger, Freight, Track) could also be viewed as stakeholders of GNT.

However, the different stakeholder groups have different expectations of GNT, which in turn means that GNT has multiple objectives to achieve.

Prioritising objectives – Unlike commercial organisations, which have an underlying objective to be profitable and to deliver value for their shareholders, as a public sector organisation, GNT does not have a single defining objective of this kind.

The number of elements in GNT's current strategic objectives highlights the potential difficulties of identifying which elements of performance are most important: reliability, punctuality, safety, cost effectiveness, or environmental impact.

Conflicting interests – Moreover, the nature of these objectives means that GNT may inevitably not be able to achieve all of them, because some of them could be mutually exclusive. For example, GNT might be able to improve reliability and safety, and possibly also to reduce its environmental impact, by investing in new trains, but such a major investment would have significant cost implications, and therefore may not be viewed as being cost effective.

This again highlights the difficulty GNT faces in trying to satisfy the needs of different stakeholder groups. For example, the decision to reduce the number of passenger services on (less profitable) rural routes appears to be driven by a need for cost effectiveness, but reducing the level of services has a detrimental impact on local residents for whom the rail service provided a vital means of transport.

To complicate matters further for GNT, in some cases single stakeholder groups may have multiple interests in the railway. This increases the difficulty GNT has in prioritising its objectives. For example, while supermarkets are clearly concerned by the environmental impact of their supply chains, the reliability and punctuality of freight deliveries are likely to be equally, if not more, important to them. If GNT's key stakeholders have different interests in this way, then its own goals and objectives have to address these different aspects of performance.

Subsidiary company objectives – The interests of the different groups of external stakeholders also create difficulties for GNT in managing the performance of its subsidiary companies. Reliability and punctuality are clearly issues for both passenger and freight trains and so need to be reflected in the objectives and KPIs for both subsidiaries.

However, as passenger services generate more revenue than freight services (50% vs 40% of total revenue) this suggests that greater focus will be given to ensuring passenger services run on time than freight services. Equally, though, the suitability of a KPI measuring punctuality of freight services could be reduced if freight trains are delayed as a result of having to wait for passenger trains to use a section of track in preference to them.

Tutorial note. *Additional point about conflicting interests and objectives*

If GNT focuses primarily on its passenger services, and ensuring that these are on time, there is a danger that freight services get overlooked within its portfolio. However, given that demand for freight services has been increasing in recent years – due to congestion on the roads – freight services could be a source of growth for GNT. Therefore, it could face a dilemma around how to achieve growth in its freight services alongside maintaining punctuality levels for its passenger services.

Measuring objectives

SMART objectives – Effective objectives should be 'SMART' – specific, measurable, attainable, relevant and time-bound.

GNT's overall strategic objective does not exhibit a number of these characteristics. For example, instead of 'continuing to reduce' its level of carbon emissions, GNT's objective would be more specific and measurable if it sought to 'reduce carbon emissions by 5% each year'.

Selecting performance measures – For GNT's performance measurement system to be effective, the aspects of performance which are measured (the KPIs) should be linked directly to GNT's critical success factors and, in turn, to its overall strategic and financial objectives.

However, the difficulties we have identified in relation to setting objectives could also create difficulties in terms of performance measurement.

In particular, if GNT is struggling to decide what its performance priorities are, it may end up measuring performance in too many areas (rather than concentrating only on the **key** performance indicators). If GNT's managers and the board become overloaded with information, this could actually reduce their ability to assess GNT's performance and make strategic decisions effectively.

Objectives and controllability – It appears that there is only a single strategic objective for GNT as a whole, rather than there being strategic objectives for the three subsidiary companies as well. However, each of the individual companies has its own KPIs.

This situation could create problems in relation to controllability. For example, one of Freight's KPIs is the proportion of trains arriving at their destination on time. However, if there is a signal failure (Track's responsibility), Freight's punctuality performance will suffer, even though the cause of any delays is outside its control. Equally, as we have already mentioned, freight trains could be delayed by passenger trains, if they are given priority on the rail network.

Stakeholder influence – There could also be a danger that the aspects of its performance which GNT chooses to prioritise will be influenced disproportionately by interests of the stakeholders which hold the greatest power. For example, if GNT considers the Government to be its most important stakeholder, it could focus on the objectives and performance measures which are most important to the Government, potentially at the expense of the interests of other stakeholders such as customers, or its staff.

This kind of prioritisation of objectives could create problems for GNT, though. For example, a focus on cost effectiveness (to please the Government) may lead to under-investment in new trains. But as GNT's trains (particularly its diesel engines) become increasingly old and unreliable, customers may feel their objectives are not being met. In turn this could lead to them seeking alternative modes of transport and GNT losing customers as a result.

This situation again reflects the problems associated with identifying GNT's key strategic objectives. GNT's performance measures need to be selected to help ensure it meets its key performance objectives. However, if GNT has a number of (potentially conflicting) performance objectives, then the process of selecting performance measures also becomes much more difficult.

Measurement vs management – Whilst GNT can measure factors such as punctuality or safety, these measures by themselves provide relatively little insight into the factors determining performance levels. For example, Freight's punctuality figures could be affected by a number of different factors. Similarly, assessing the safety of the rail network in GNT is likely to be far more complex than simply measuring the number of signals passed at danger.

Therefore, while individual aspects of performance can be measured, a range of factors all need to be considered before any actions are taken to improve individual aspects of performance.

(b) **Context of performance reporting** – In an integrated report, GNT will still report on its financial and operational performance, as it currently does, but the report should make clear to readers the extent to which GNT has achieved its strategic objectives. For example, as well as reporting its KPIs for punctuality, the report should highlight the extent to which GNT has achieved its objectives in relation to the reliability and punctuality of its services.

Importantly, in an integrated report, GNT will also report on social and environmental aspects of its performance. Currently, there appears to be little emphasis in GNT's performance management and reporting on the way it manages and develops its 'human capital' (staff). However, as human capital is one of the six categories of capital identified within the integrated reporting framework, this should encourage GNT to evaluate the contribution of its people to its performance.

Impacts on different categories of capital – More generally, performance reporting within an integrated report should explain the outcomes of an organisation's performance in terms of six categories of capital: financial; manufactured; intellectual; human; social and relationship; and natural. Using these six categories could provide GNT with a framework for analysing its performance; for example, 'manufactured' capital could relate to track work and station upgrades, while 'social and relationship' capital could relate to improving customer satisfaction or customer loyalty.

However, the 'integrated' nature of the reporting also means that in its report GNT should highlight the interrelatedness and dependencies between different factors which affect its ability to create value over time. For example, investing in new engines (manufactured capital) should help to improve performance reliability and reduce pollution (natural capital), but these benefits will come at the financial cost of acquiring the new engines.

Importantly though, one of the key aims of integrated reporting is to reflect the longer-term consequences of the decisions organisations make, in order that they make more sustainable decisions. So, in its integrated report, GNT would be able to highlight the longer-term benefits of investing in the new engines.

Future strategy and outlook – The current annual report appears to focus on GNT's financial and operational performance in the last year. In this respect, it is a backward-looking report. However, an integrated report would provide greater focus on future strategy and outlook.

In an integrated report, GNT would provide not only a summary of past performance but also a summary of how the organisation's strategy, governance and performance can lead to the creation of value in the future – in both the short and the long term; for example, how the investment in new trains or new tracks can help GNT provide an improved service to its customers.

Opportunities and risk – By focusing on its own financial and operational performance, there is a danger that GNT's current report may become inward-looking. However, in an integrated report it would also highlight the opportunities and risks which affect its ability to create value, and how it is dealing with them. Although GNT has a monopoly over rail services in Pecoland, it competes directly against road transport for both passenger and freight services. So, for example, GNT should use its integrated report to explain how it plans to use increasing road congestion as an opportunity to promote rail travel as a substitute for road travel.

Equally, however, GNT needs to consider the risks and threats to its business model. Even though the current Minister of Transport and the Rail Regulator oppose privatisation, this could change if a new government was elected in Pecoland. However, one way to increase GNT's resilience to any threat of privatisation is to demonstrate the value it currently creates, and thereby to highlight to any future governments that keeping the rail network under national control remains the best way to create value from it.

(c) **Amount of information** – The board's scepticism towards integrated reporting appears, at least in part, to come from its concerns about the extra cost and effort involved in producing an integrated report.

However, integrated reporting does not necessarily entail producing **more** information, and one of the potential benefits of integrated reporting is that it encourages organisations to produce shorter, more streamlined communications, rather than longer reports.

Instead of focusing on the quantity of information provided, the focus in integrated reporting is more about changing the way information is presented.

For example, instead of presenting information about GNT's commercial, social and environmental performance in distinct 'siloes', integrated reporting would seek to highlight the connections between these different elements. In this way integrated reporting aims to provide stakeholders with a more holistic understanding of an organisation and its performance.

Therefore, rather than requiring the Management Accountant to prepare lots more information, the change to integrated reporting may be more likely to require the Management Accountant (and members of GNT's senior management) to consider how different performance measures and indicators relate to each other.

Stakeholder interests – However, integrated reporting also seeks to respond to stakeholder interests by providing them with the information they want about the performance and direction of an organisation. As we have seen in part (a), there are a number of stakeholders with an interest in GNT and, if each of them want information about different aspects of performance, there is a danger that this could end up creating information overload in the report.

As part of its preparations for producing an integrated report, GNT could introduce a stakeholder engagement process with key stakeholders to identify what they want to know about the performance and direction of the organisation.

Additionally, the Management Accountant (in conjunction with the management team at GNT) will need to decide what data is most appropriate to collect, as well as what data it is possible to collect given the management information systems currently in operation at GNT.

Type of information

Reporting or focusing on strategy – An important theme in successfully applying integrated reporting is that it is not simply about reporting for its own sake, but that the information being reported needs to focus on an organisation's core strategy.

From the examples given in the scenario, it seems that the KPIs which GNT already monitors are linked to its key objectives. If this is the case, then again integrated reporting should not require the Group Management Accountant to produce additional performance measures. However, rather than simply preparing the figures the Management Accountant would be expected to highlight the significance of the figures, and how they are affecting GNT's ability to create value.

Non-financial KPIs – Another important benefit of integrated reporting is that it helps organisations to make clearer links between financial and non-financial performance.

By focusing on value generation in its broadest sense (rather than, for example, narrower goals of revenue generation) integrated reporting will also encourage organisations to review the set of performance measures they use. One of the main consequences of integrated reporting is likely to be the increased use of non-financial data to gain a clearer picture of an organisation and its performance.

In this case, however, it seems that a number of GNT's KPIs are already non-financial, suggesting that GNT already appreciates the link between non-financial and financial performance. This again suggests that introducing integrated reporting may not require the introduction of many additional KPIs, although some may be required in relation to 'human capital' if this is not already covered by any of the existing KPIs.

Issues

Nonetheless, the increased importance on non-financial information could produce a number of issues for the Group Management Accountant:

- Can GNT's current management information systems supply the full range of non-financial data which stakeholders would wish to see in an integrated report?
- If the data cannot be obtained from GNT's current systems, how can the Management Accountant obtain the information?
- More generally, can non-financial information be gathered and verified within financial reporting timelines?
- How can the accountant ensure the information is reliable and, more generally, what assurance is there over non-financial data in the report? (Non-financial data is typically not audited in the same way that financial data is; but if stakeholders are going to rely on this data, then GNT should consider obtaining some kind of 'assurance' over the data.)

Tutorial note. *Additional potential issues facing the Management Accountant*

Integrated reporting is not yet mandatory, and there are currently no standard formats for producing integrated reports. Therefore a significant practical issue the accountant will face when producing GNT's first integrated report will be to decide what information to include in the report and how to present it.

If the management accountant has to develop and produce the integrated report in addition to their existing work, this means the accountant will have less time available for that existing work. As a result, there is a danger management reports could be delayed, or the quality of them could be reduced – particularly in the short term, following the introduction of integrated reporting.

15 Amal

Text reference. Big Data is discussed in Chapter 6b of the BPP Study Text.

Top tips.

Part (a). Note that there are effectively two parts to this requirement: (i) choosing and calculating appropriate performance indicators, and then (ii) commenting on the indicators you have calculated.

The context of the scenario could also be important here. Amal and Kayland Air both appear to be pursuing differentiation strategies, whereas Cheapo Air is a budget airline.

The requirement doesn't specify how many performance indicators you should analyse. The key point here is perhaps not the quantity of indicators you calculate, but making sure they are relevant.

We have chosen four in our answer below. However, this is not an exhaustive selection. If you have made other relevant calculations, and then commented on them, you would have got credit for this.

A sensible approach here is to select indicators which relate to Amal's key business issues (eg fuel costs), identify the key drivers behind them (eg fuel cost per seat kilometre) and then provide a short commentary showing how the indicator links to the companies' strategies and the issues mentioned in the scenario.

Part (b). There are four areas for you to explain here, and eight marks available, so two marks per area. This means you are not expected to write in depth about any of the areas. However, make sure you explain how the areas could be used to help Amal's performance, rather than explaining what the benefits of Big Data are.

In effect, the key areas from the conference already identify the benefits of Big Data, so you need to think practically here, and assess how Amal could use them.

Part (c). Although the question doesn't ask you to discuss the characteristics of Big Data – and so you can't pass the requirement just by doing this – thinking about the characteristics should nonetheless help you identify the potential implications Big Data could have for an organisation's information systems. For example, what implication could the 'volume' characteristic have for the capacity of an organisation's information systems?

Examining team's comments for part (a). The overall quality of the commentary which candidates provide in relation to numerical results they have calculated remains a concern. Simply putting the numbers which have been calculated into a sentence isn't an analysis of the figures. For example, saying 'Amal has a higher profit margin than either Kayland or Cheapo' doesn't add any value to a reader (who has already seen the calculations which show this). Consequently, such a statement will not score any marks.

However, good answers used the numerical work as an opportunity to show they have understood the scenario; for example, by commenting that Amal's higher profit was not surprising given that Amal is a 'premium airline'.

Marking scheme

		Marks
(a)	Calculations – up to 6 marks 1 mark for each meaningful indicator selected 2 marks for load factor or similar measure of capacity utilisation Commentary – 1 mark per relevant point, up to 7 marks Total – up to 12 marks	12
(b)	For explaining how Big Data could improve performance in each of the four key areas identified – up to 2 marks per area Total – up to 8 marks	8
(c)	For identifying potential implications of Big Data on Amal's management information systems – 1 mark per relevant point Total – up to 5 marks	5
		Total = 25

(a) The following performance indicators could be used to analyse the three airlines:

	Amal	Kayland	Cheapo
Operating profit margin	630/5,430	54/7,350	127/2,170
	11.6%	0.7%	5.9%
Capacity utilisation (load factor)	79,619/100,654	82,554/105,974	40,973/46,934
	79.1%	77.9%	87.3%
Revenue/staff member ($'000)	5,430m/32,501	7,350m/56,065	2,170m/5,372
	167	131	404
Fuel cost/seat kilometre ($)	1,480m/100,654m	1,823m/105,974m	535m/46,934m
	0.015	0.017	0.011

Operating margin – Amal has the highest operating margin of the three airlines (11.6%), which suggests it is being run efficiently overall. We might expect Amal to achieve a relatively high margin because it appears to be pursuing a **differentiation strategy**. However, Kayland, which appears to be pursuing a similar strategy, generates an operating profit margin of less than 1%.

Capacity utilisation – By showing, on average, how full each airline's aircraft are this indicator shows how well the airlines are using their asset base (ie their aircraft). Amal and Kayland's performance is similar in this respect, but Cheapo's is significantly better. This is likely to be because Cheapo (a low cost airline) is pursuing a **cost leadership** strategy. Amal might consider reducing its prices to try to improve capacity utilisation, but it needs to do so in the context of its overall strategy. If it reduces prices too much, it may end up compromising the quality and service it offers to passengers, but these elements are crucial to its strategy as a differentiator.

Revenue per staff member – This is an important measure in the context of the recent disputes over working conditions and pay. Amal's staff appear to be performing better than Kayland's, which in turn might strengthen their claims for a pay rise.

The comparison between Amal and Cheapo's performance for this measure may be less meaningful. Cheapo **outsources** many of its activities, meaning its staff numbers will be significantly lower than Amal which carries out the corresponding activities **in house**.

Fuel costs – The board's interest in new fuel-efficient aircraft indicates that reducing fuel costs is an important concern for Amal. Again, Cheapo appears to be controlling its fuel costs better than Amal or Kayland. This might be because it has more **fuel-efficient planes**, which would support the board's argument for Amal investing in new aircraft. However, Cheapo may have negotiated more favourable fuel contracts with its suppliers, or be using lower grade fuel.

> **Tutorial note.** It is important to use fuel cost per **seat** kilometre as the performance indicator here rather than fuel cost per **passenger** kilometre, because we are looking to monitor the fuel efficiency of the aircraft, rather than the airline's ability to fill their aircraft with passengers.

(b) Amal's business strategy as a premium airline, coupled with the difficult trading conditions, mean that it is increasingly important for the company to provide its customers with the best services and experiences possible, so that they choose to fly with Amal in preference to another carrier. Increasing the data it holds about customers, and potential customers, should help Amal's management make better decisions, and thereby should help the company achieve this.

Detecting key trends – Analysing conversations on social media could help Amal identify potential trends in customer demand; for example, if there are major events taking place in a particular place, or if certain resorts are increasing (or decreasing) in popularity as holiday destinations. Being able to forecast demand more accurately – and almost in 'real time' – could help Amal boost revenue, through applying **dynamic pricing**. For example, Amal could keep prices high on flights which are going to be popular, but could reduce prices on flights which look like they are going to have a lower capacity utilisation in order to try to boost demand for those flights.

Customer selection process – One of the key issues here is for airlines to understand the reason why potential customers have not completed their transaction – for example, this could be due to price, seat availability, difficulties in the booking process itself. In this respect, if Amal was able to capture data about the stage in the booking process which causes potential customers to abandon their booking, it could then look at ways to tackle the problem – for example, if there was a confusing user interface on the Amal website this could be amended to make booking easier. Equally, applying the 'velocity' aspect of Big Data, if a customer abandons a transaction, and Amal already has their contact details, the customer could immediately be sent an incentive to try to encourage them to complete the purchase.

In-flight sales – Amal currently offers a standard selection of in-flight products across all its flights. However, the amount of products Amal sells (and therefore the amount of in-flight revenue ancillary revenue Amal generates) is likely to depend on how well the products offered meet customer needs. By analysing the purchasing patterns of different passengers (or different types of passengers) on different routes, Amal could customise the range of products it offers on different flights, to focus on the products which are most likely to appeal to the passengers on a particular flight.

Customer satisfaction – In the same way that conversations on social media could help to identify trends in demand, they could also help to indicate how satisfied customers are (or aren't) with their flights and the service they receive from Amal. However, although knowing whether customers are satisfied or not is useful, perhaps the greater value will come from identifying any factors which are reducing satisfaction levels so that Amal can then address the causes of any problems and take steps to improve its performance in those areas.

(c) Big Data is typically characterised by a range of 'V' characteristics – volume, variety, velocity and veracity.

Capacity – The potential benefits to Amal of Big Data will come from the useful information it can extract from large amounts of data. However, the 'volume' and the 'variety' of the data could also require increased information systems capacity in order to capture and store the data correctly. If the data is not stored correctly, this will undermine its veracity – its integrity and reliability as a basis for making decisions.

The fact that a number of IT staff are already working on the website upgrade project could be a problem here, if it means that there aren't sufficient staff available to increase the information system capacity to the degree required for Big Data.

Analytical tools – As well as having the capacity to store Big Data, Amal will need the right analytical tools and technologies to be able to analyse it, because it is too large and unstructured to be analysed through traditional means. Again, the lack of available IT staff could present problems here.

Data overload – A more general concern to beware of is the difference between data and information. Management decisions need to be based on relevant information, not raw data. Therefore, by itself, increasing the volume of data available to Amal would not necessarily provide managers with better information for decision making. Here again, Amal would need analysts with the experience and expertise to be able to extract meaning from the captured data, but it seems unlikely that Amal has any such staff currently available.

Similarly, if the volume and variety of the data means that Amal's current information systems are not able to process it, the 'velocity' aspect of Big Data will be undermined. If IT teams or business analysts become burdened with increasing requests for ad hoc analysis and one-off reports (because the systems cannot process the data automatically), the information and analysis from Big Data will not be available for decision makers as quickly as they might want.

16 Chicory

Text reference. Financial performance measures, including ROCE and EBITDA, are discussed in Chapter 7 of the BPP Study Text. Benchmarking is covered in Chapter 1.

Top tips.

Part (a). The marking guide for part (a) of this question is very instructive here:

For part (a)(i), up to 3 marks (out of the total of 6) are available for evaluating how useful ROCE is as a performance measure in this situation.

For part (a)(ii), up to 6 marks (out of the total of 10) are available for evaluating how useful EBITDA is as a performance measure.

As such, more marks are available in part (a) as a whole for the evaluation of the **measures**, than for evaluating the **performance** of the two organisations. The examining team have said many times that, at Strategic Professional level, candidates will not simply be asked to perform calculations, and this question provides a good illustration of that point. Although it is important you calculate the ROCE and EBITDA for both companies correctly, you then need to comment on the figures you have calculated ('Evaluate the relative financial performance...') before moving on to think about the advantages and disadvantages of the measures themselves.

Another point that the examining team make regularly is that theoretical knowledge alone is not sufficient to pass the APM exam. This is also pertinent here, because, to score well in this question, you mustn't just evaluate the usefulness of ROCE and EBITDA in general terms, but specifically in the context of the scenario. For example, in the first paragraph you are told: 'Chicory's objective is to maximise shareholder wealth' – but will using ROCE as a performance measure encourage that?

Part (b). The same point about making use of the scenario also applies to part (b). To score well here, you mustn't simply talk about the problems of benchmarking in general terms, but instead you should focus specifically on the problems of benchmarking Chicory's performance against Fennel's, using the data which Fennel has agreed to share.

The scenario should provide you with a number of clues you could use here. For example, Fennel is based in Veeland (whose economy is growing rapidly), while Chicory operates in Deeland (which is experiencing an economic slowdown) so how might this affect the comparability of the two companies' performance?

Also, don't concentrate purely on the written scenario, and forget about Appendix 1. For example – look at the dates for the data being proposed for the potential comparison. Fennel's data (31 December 20X5) is 18 months older than Chicory's (30 June 20X7). What implications does that have on its usefulness in the benchmarking exercise?

BPP LEARNING MEDIA

Examining team's comments.

Part (a). Many candidates scored poorly on the calculations, with few being able to calculate these correctly for both ration. This is disappointing, because ROCE and EBITDA are ratios which a professional accountant should be fully able to calculate. The evlaution of the methods was generally performed well though.

Part (b). Candidates generally scored well here and demonstrated good knowledge. However, as we have said before, it will be unusual for a question at APM level to ask for purely generic theory. Instead, questions will require theories or models to be applied to a particular situation. Unfortunately, some candidates lost the opportunity to score more marks here by not relating their knowledge to the companies described in the scenario. Also, some candidates wasted time discussing how benchmarking can be used to evaluate performance, or explaining the benchmarking process itself, despite the requirement asking specifically about the **problems** of the benchmarking exercise proposed in the scenario.

Marking scheme

		Marks
(a)(i)	Calculation of Chicory's and Fennel's average capital employed – up to 2 marks Calculation of both companies' ROCE – 1 mark Comment on the results of the ROCE calculation – 1 mark Evaluation of ROCE as a performance measure – up to 3 marks Total for (a)(i) – up to 6 marks	
		6
(a)(ii)	Adjustments to operating profit to get EBITDA – up to 2 marks Calculation of both companies' EBITDA – 1 mark Comment on the results of the EBITDA calculation – 1 mark Evaluation of EBITDA as a performance measure – up to 6 marks Total – up to 10 marks	10
(b)	Advising on relevant problems of the benchmarking exercise – up to 2 marks per point Total – up to 9 marks	9
	Total =	**25**

(a) (i) **ROCE**

As can be seen in the Working, Chicory's ROCE is 13.6% and Fennel's ROCE is 14.9%. Fennel has apparently performed better than Chicory. One benefit of using ROCE as a performance measure in this benchmarking exercise is that it gives a percentage figure and can compare businesses of different sizes. ROCE does not, however, give the absolute level of return. In this case, Fennel has both a higher capital employed and a higher percentage return.

ROCE is easy to calculate and will be familiar to Chicory's management as it is currently one of Chicory's main financial performance indicators. The figures required to calculate ROCE are readily available from published data, which makes this a good financial performance measure for benchmarking.

ROCE shows a weak correlation with Chicory's objective to maximise shareholder wealth, which may limit ROCE's usefulness as a performance measure in this benchmarking exercise. ROCE may be distorted by accounting policies or where different businesses have different levels of intangible assets. This may lead to drawing incorrect conclusions from the exercise. A big disadvantage of using ROCE in this benchmarking exercise is that it may encourage managers not to invest in new non-current assets, which contradicts Chicory's strategy of investing in charging points.

Working: ROCE calculations

Chicory:

Opening capital employed (Total assets – current liabilities)	\$78.0m	(138.0 – 60.0)
Closing capital employed	\$59.0m	(140.0 – 81.0)
Average capital employed	\$68.5m	((78.0 + 59.0)/2)
ROCE (Operating profit / average capital employed)	13.6%	(9.3/68.5)

Fennel:

Average capital employed: (170 × 0.25) + (176 × 0.75)	\$174.5	
ROCE	14.9%	(26.0/174.5)

(ii) **EBITDA**

Using Chicory's main financial performance indicators of ROCE, Fennel has performed better than Chicory. When depreciation of non-current assets and the write-off of goodwill in Chicory are added back to operating profit to calculate EBITDA, Chicory's performance, with an EBITDA of \$52.0m, is slightly better than that of Fennel, which has an EBITDA of \$51.0m.

EBITDA as a proxy for cash flow

EBITDA is easy to calculate from published data, and easy to understand. It is a measure of underlying performance, as it is a proxy for cash flow generated from operating profit. As Chicory is having cash flow difficulties following the unsuccessful acquisition, EBITDA would be a relevant measure for this benchmarking exercise. EBITDA does not, however, take into account the cash flow effect of working capital changes, for example, by Chicory negotiating longer payment terms with its suppliers.

Excludes items which are not relevant to underlying performance of the business

Tax and interest are distributions from profits, unrelated to the underlying performance of the business. Excluding them from measures of performance, therefore, gives a better understanding of the underlying performance of Chicory and Fennel. This is important for the benchmarking exercise since Fennel appears to suffer much lower rates of tax, probably due to the tax incentives given by the Veeland government. Loans underwritten by the Veeland government may be at artificially reduced rates of interest and should also be excluded when measuring performance.

Similarly, depreciation, amortisation and write-offs such as goodwill are not relevant to the current year's underlying performance and may relate to previous years. For example, adding back the write-off of goodwill in Chicory means the two businesses have identical EBITDAs, albeit that Fennel has much greater capital employed.

EBITDA affects comparability of the benchmarking data

Using EBITDA as a performance measure in the benchmarking exercise makes the data for the two businesses more comparable and removes one element of subjectivity, such as in determining useful economic lives of non-current assets. EBITDA does, however, ignore the replacement costs of these assets. This might limit the usefulness of comparisons between Chicory and Fennel if one were to lease non-current assets and the other to purchase them. The introduction of a new accounting standard on the treatment of leases may, however, remove this limitation.

Unlike Chicory's existing measure of ROCE, which is a percentage measure, EBITDA is an absolute measure and so makes it difficult to compare businesses of different sizes. As a profit based measure, its usefulness is also limited by subjective assumptions made in the calculation of profit, or by inconsistent accounting policies. Development costs may be capitalised in Veeland, but not in Deeland, which may make a comparison against the benchmark difficult.

Working: EDITDA calculations

EBITDA	*Chicory* $m	*Fennel* $m
Operating profit	9.3	26.0
Add back:		
Depreciation on non-current assets	18.0	25.0
Write off of goodwill	24.7	–
EBITDA	52.0	51.0

(b) **Benchmarking**

Benchmarking the performance of Chicory against a similar business implies that there is a best way to operate. Though Fennel may be similar to Chicory, there is no indication that it is best in class and benchmarking against it may be inappropriate.

For example, Fennel has taken advantages of tax incentives and loan guarantees to finance new investments. These do not exist in Deeland, so Chicory may be unable to fund investment in this way. It may have to consider leasing assets instead, or accept a slower rate of growth if it wishes to set up charging points in Deeland.

Benchmarking is essentially a catching up exercise. The financial data for Fennel is 18 months older than that for Chicory and may already be out of date. In 20X5, Fennel improved operational performance by investment in IT. The effect of this is not reflected in the financial data given. Benchmarking performance against historical data may not be relevant for current or future performance. The electric car market in Veeland has grown rapidly in the last two years. This growth is not reflected in the financial performance data given for Fennel, nor is the falling price of components for the charging points.

Although Fennel has agreed to share data, this data may be inaccurate or misleading. Though initially the benchmarking exercise is only against Fennel, it may be difficult to find other comparable businesses to benchmark against in the future. The data required for calculation of the three financial performance indicators used in the benchmarking exercise is likely to be readily available and audited, however, which means it is reliable.

A large part of Fennel's business relates to providing charging points for charging electric cars. Though this is a business model Chicory intends to follow in the future, it is very different to its existing business, and so benchmarking against Fennel may be misleading unless more detailed data relating to the two activities can be obtained.

Similarly, Fennel operates in a different country, where the economy is much stronger. Performance targets set following the benchmarking exercise may be unachievable for Chicory. Fennel's financial data has been converted into $ from its home currency. Movements in exchange rates may make the benchmarking data less comparable, especially if the economies in Deeland and Veeland are growing at different rates.

17 Landual Lamps

Text reference. Transfer pricing is covered in Chapter 8 of the BPP Study Text.

Top tips.

Part (a). As the requirement asks you to 'evaluate' the current system of transfer pricing, it might be useful to start by considering what the aims of transfer pricing are. Then, having identified the aims, you can then evaluate how well Landual's current transfer pricing system fits with those aims.

Does the current system promote goal congruence between the individual divisions and the company as a whole?

Does the current system enable the performance of the individual divisions to be measured fairly?

The distinction between the markets available for the two types of component is important: there is a readily available external market for electrical components, while there is no external market for housing components. Therefore a market-based transfer price could be appropriate for the electrical components and a cost-based transfer price could be appropriate for the housing components.

But is it fair to include transport, marketing and bad debt cost in the transfer price for electrical components?

And is it fair that the price of housing components should be at cost only, with no mark-up? On the other hand, should the transfer price for housing components be based on actual production costs or budgeted production costs?

An important part of your 'evaluation' should be what impact these possible changes to the current transfer pricing systems could have on divisional performance. You should demonstrate this through the 'illustrative calculations' the requirement asks for.

Part (b). The change being proposed is to include variable production costs only (rather than total production costs) in the transfer price for housing components. The illustrative calculations here should be relatively simple, but a key issue is what impact the changes have on the profitability of the two divisions. Does the revised position accurately reflect the value added to Landual as a company by the different divisions?

Part (c). The requirement here asks you to evaluate the impact of the changes on the profit in the divisions as well as on the company as a whole. So you need to look at the impact of the changes on four different elements: the new Housing Components Division; the new Electrical Components Division, the Assembly Division, and Landual overall.

Again, you need to calculate the divisional profits under the new structure, and then consider what benefits (or drawbacks) the changes might yield for the divisions, and for Landual overall.

The biggest change will see the Housing Components Division change from a profit centre to a cost centre. Although the 'profit' in the Housing Division will fall significantly because it no longer has any revenue, what might be the benefits of making this change? Remember, the housing components are only sold internally anyway.

Examining team's comments. This question was generally poorly answered with weak (often no) efforts at handling the quantification issues – recalculating the current transfer price; and calculating the impact of the two proposed changes on the various entities in the scenario. As a result, this meant candidates often had very little to say in evaluating or giving advice in the narrative parts of their answers.

For example, in part (b) if the (simple) quantification work was not done, candidates could not see that the proposed change will lead to lower profits in the division which provides the key competitive advantage of the company.

As a general point, during their revision candidates would be advised to consider the impacts that strategic changes – such as designation of cost, profit and investment centres – would have on the performance management of divisions or departments within a company.

Marking scheme

Marks

(a) *Electrical components*

Evaluation of the basic policy to use market-based transfer price – Up to 2 marks

For comments on adjusting market price to exclude additional costs (of transport, marketing and bad debts) – 1 mark

For calculating the impact on divisional profits of adjusting market price – 1 mark

Housing components

Evaluation of the basic policy to use cost-based transfer price – Up to 2 marks

		Marks
	For comments about including a mark-up on cost in the transfer price – Up to 2 marks	
	For comments about the merit of using actual or budgeted costs as the basis of the transfer price – Up to 2 marks	
	For calculating the impact on divisional profits of including a mark-up, and of using budgeted costs – Up to 2 marks	
	Total: Up to 10	10
(b)	For calculating the new revenue figure for the Components Division – 1 mark	
	For calculating the revised profit figures for each entity – 1 mark each	
	For comments on the impact of the changes – 1 mark per valid point; Up to 4 marks	
	Total: up to 6	6
(c)	For calculating new profit figures for each entity (Housing, Electrical, Assembly, Landual) – 1 mark per entity – Up to 4 marks	
	For evaluating the impact of the changes on the profit in the divisions and for Landual overall – 1 mark per valid point – Up to 7 marks	
	Total: up to 9	9
	Total =	**25**

(a) **Aim of transfer pricing** – The aim of transfer pricing is to ensure goal congruence between the divisions of an organisation and the organisation as a whole, by ensuring that the performance of the divisions is measured fairly and is not distorted by any internal transfers.

A good transfer pricing system will also maintain a level of managerial autonomy for the managers of the different divisions in an organisation.

Electrical components

Market-based transfer price – As there is already an external market for electrical components, it seems appropriate to use a market-based transfer price for electrical components. The Assembly Division can choose either to buy components from an external supplier or to source them internally from the Components Division, depending on the respective prices charged by the two sources.

Under the current system, the Components Division generates a contribution of $383k to head office costs from the sale of electrical components: $1,557k – $804k – $370k. Given the generic nature of the components, we would not expect the contribution to profit to be very high, so this figure seems reasonable.

Adjustments to market price – However, the Assembly Division could legitimately argue that the transfer price charged by the Electrical Components Division should be lower than the open market price, because transferring the components internally doesn't incur transport or marketing costs in the way that an external sale would. Also, there is no risk of bad debt. Therefore, the $269,000 in respect of these costs should be deducted in order to get an adjusted market price.

If these adjustments are made, then the contribution to head office costs from electrical components within the Components Division falls to $114k ($383k – $269k).

Housing components

Actual production costs – The transfer prices for housing components are based on actual production costs. Again, this seems appropriate because these components are designed specifically for Landual's products, so there is no external market for them.

However, because the price set for the housing components only covers the actual **production** costs, the proceeds from the sales of the housing components will not make any contribution towards the allocated head office costs.

As a result, since the housing components account for 84% of the division's total sales by revenue ($8,204/$9,761) it will be very difficult for the Components Division ever to earn a significant profit.

Since the housing components make a significant contribution to Landual's competitive advantage, it would seem fair if they are rewarded with greater divisional profit than they currently get. Therefore, rather than selling the components at cost, Landual could consider a transfer price which includes a mark-up on actual production costs. This would also redistribute the divisional profit between the Assembly and Components Divisions.

If a mark-up of 25% (for example) were applied to the total actual production costs of the housing components ($8,204k) this would generate additional profit of $2,051k for the Components Division. If this mark-up were applied, the Components Division would then show a profit of $1,973k, while the Assembly Division would only show a profit of $668k.

Actual vs budget costs – Because the Components Division uses actual production costs rather than budgeted costs as the basis for its transfer price, there is no incentive for the Components Division to control or reduce its costs, because it knows it will recover any additional costs through the price charged to the Assembly Division. By contrast, if budgeted productions were used as the basis for the transfer price, the cost of any adverse variance would continue to be borne by the Components Division.

The current system, based on actual production costs, may be part of the reason behind the $575,000 adverse cost of sales variance in the Components Division for the last year.

Revised divisional reports

The divisional reports could be adjusted to reflect these points:

- Costs relating to transport, marketing and bad debts are no longer included in the transfer price of electrical components: $1,557k – $269k = $1,288k
- Transfer price for housing is now based on budgeted cost, with a mark-up for 25%:

  ($6,902k – $575k) + $1,302k = 7,629k + 25% mark-up = $9,536k

		Components	*Assembly*
Sales	Electrical	1,288	
	Housing	9,536	
	Sub-total	10,824	15,794
Cost of sales	Electrical	804	1,288
	Housing	6,902	9,536
	Sub-total	7,706	10,824
Fixed production costs			
	Electrical	370	
	Housing	1,302	
	Sub-total	1,672	1,268
Allocated head office costs		461	2,046
Profit		985	1,656

(b) **Variable costs basis**

The proposal will reduce the revenue of the Components Division (and correspondingly the cost of sales of the Assembly Division) by the fixed production costs relating to housing components: $1,302k. There will be no change to the company's overall profit as a result of the change.

This change further tilts the balance in the relative profitability of the two divisions towards the Assembly Division.

Given that the housing components are specifically designed for Landual's products, and therefore could be a source of significant competitive advantage, the proposed change doesn't seem particularly appropriate. The Components Division adds significant value to Landual's overall product, but the change seems to be emphasising the importance of the Assembly Division to the company.

If the results are balanced too heavily in favour of the Assembly Division, this will understate the importance of the work done by the Components Division, and could demotivate its staff. This would be a mistake given the intricate nature of the work.

Despite these concerns, the decision to use variable costs as a basis for transfer pricing (rather than total costs) is not necessarily a bad one. The clarity gained by using only variable costs may help Landual to set the optimal prices and profits for its products.

Note. The following solution shows the full data for the two divisions under the revised basis. However, you did not need to show these figures in full to earn the marks available here (for the new revenue figure for the Components Division, and for the revised profits figures for both divisions).

		Components	*Assembly*
Sales	Electrical	1,557	
	Housing	6,902	
	Sub-total	8,459	15,794
Cost of sales	Electrical	804	1,557
	Housing	6,902	6,902
	Sub-total	7,706	8,459
Fixed production costs			
	(No changes)	1,672	1,268
Allocated head office costs		461	2,046
Profit/(loss)		**(1,380)**	**4,021**

(c) **Housing Division**

Cost centre – Under the proposed changes, the Housing Division will be a cost centre only.

Given that the Housing Division only sells its (bespoke) products to the Assembly Division, and therefore the difficulty of determining a fair revenue figure for its work, it seems more appropriate to treat the Housing Division as a cost centre rather than a profit centre. Treating the division as a cost centre is better aligned with the ideas of responsibility accounting.

Moreover, because the focus of the division will now be on cost control, this should help avoid adverse cost of sales variances like the one incurred in the last year. The performance measures and reward packages in the division will also need to be redesigned to reinforce the focus on costs.

In addition, the change in status could enable a greater focus on the quality of the division's output, which will be important given the key role which the housing components play in Landual's overall manufacturing process.

In this respect, it is important that the change from being a profit centre to becoming a cost centre is not seen as downgrading the status of the division. If it is, such a perception will demotivate the divisional managers, and any fall in morale is also likely to filter through the staff.

Electrical Division

Under the proposed new divisional structure, the Electrical Division will make a profit of $335k (see Working at the end of the answer).

As the electrical components are generic and could easily be obtained externally, it is appropriate to continue treating the Electrical Division as a profit centre. Under this basis, Landual has the information it needs to decide whether to 'make or buy' the electrical components for its lamps.

The current figures, showing that the Electrical Division is making a contribution to head office costs, suggest that the Electrical Division should continue to supply components to the Assembly Division.

Assembly Division

The changes do not directly affect the Assembly Division. However, being able to see the Electrical Division's results more clearly will allow the managers of the Assembly Division to ensure that the Electrical Division remains competitive (compared to any external suppliers which could provide the components instead).

Landual

The changes have no direct effect on the company's reported profit. However, if the changes help to improve cost control (in the Housing Division) and reinforce the need for competitiveness (in the Electrical Division), they should help to improve the company's profits in the future.

Working: Revised profits for each of the divisions, and for the company as a whole

Allocated head office costs for the Components Division have been reallocated between the Housing and Electrical Components Divisions in proportion to their cost of sales.

		Housing	*Electrical*	*Assembly*	*Landual*
		$'000	$'000	$'000	$'000
Sales				15,794	15,794
	Electrical		1,557		
	Housing				
Cost of sales					
	Electrical		804	1,557	804
	Housing	6,902		8,204	6,902
Fixed production costs				1,268	1,268
	Electrical		370		370
	Housing	1,302			1,302
Allocated head office costs (apportioned in line with cost of sales)		413	48	2,046	2,507
Profit/(Loss)		(8,617)	335	2,719	2,641

18 Laudan Advertising Agency

Text reference. Objectives, critical success factors (CSFs) and key performance indicators (KPIs) – and the relationship between them – are discussed in Chapter 2 of the BPP Study Text. Transfer pricing is discussed in Chapter 8.

Top tips.

Part (a)

(i) The scenario identifies that LAA has published four objectives on its website:

- To delight our clients by the quality of our work
- Provide excellent value for money to our clients
- Give our clients access to specialist and local knowledge
- Ensure our clients return to us time after time

As the requirement asks how identifying the CSF will help LAA to manage performance 'in order to achieve its stated objectives' it is important to consider how the CSF could relate to each of the objectives in turn. The question verb is 'evaluate' – so if the CSF is more relevant to some objectives than others, highlighting this would be a relevant part of your evaluation.

Similarly, for **part (ii)**, you need to evaluate how the KPI helps (or doesn't help) to achieve each of the four objectives. The comments in Appendix 1 of the scenario relate to the KPI in question, so these comments should have provided you with some useful clues to help answer this part of the requirement.

Importantly, note that the question is asking about the extent to which the CSF and the KPI might help LAA achieve its objectives. It is not asking whether the CSF or the KPI are appropriate measures, so you shouldn't waste time evaluating the measures themselves.

Part (b).

A sensible approach to a requirement like this – to assess the need for a transfer pricing policy – is to start by thinking what the main aims of the transfer pricing policy would be: for example, to enable performance evaluation of divisions; to maintain divisional autonomy; and to promote goal congruence.

Then think how well – or not – these aims are achieved under LAA's current arrangements (in the absence of a transfer pricing policy). The scenario provides a lot of information about how the current practices for transferring goods between the different divisions are causing problems, in terms of performance management, autonomy and goal congruence. These are the same areas which the transfer pricing policy would address. So, what does this suggest about the need for a transfer pricing policy at LAA?

Although ACCA's suggested solution (below) isn't specifically structured around the aims of a transfer pricing system, the examining team have stated that such an approach would have been acceptable for this question.

Part (c).

In order to advise whether an organisation should use a particular approach to something, you need to consider what the potential advantages or disadvantages of that approach are. And, to score well in this requirement, that is what you need to do here.

The scenario tells us that LAA's current transfer pricing arrangements appear 'to be based on full cost' plus a substantial mark-up. So, in effect, you need to consider what the potential benefits, or problems, with using a market value transfer price would be, compared to the current 'cost plus' approach.

Marking scheme

		Marks
(a)	Discussion of the CSF in relation to achieving the stated objectives – up to 6 marks Discussion of the KPI in relation to achieving the stated objectives – up to 6 marks Total for part (a): up to 8 marks	8
(b)	For each relevant point about the need for a formal transfer policy – 1 mark each Total for part (b): up to 9 marks	9
(c)	Benefits of a market value approach – up to 6 marks Problems with a market value approach – up to 6 marks Total for part (c): up to 8 marks	8
		Total = 25

(a) (i) **CSF of high quality design**

Delight clients with quality of work – The directors of LAA have identified the importance of producing high quality creative designs as a CSF to ensure successful advertising campaigns, and therefore client satisfaction. It is likely that having this as a CSF will help LAA achieve its objective to 'delight clients with the quality of work', as creative design is an important part of the service which LAA provides.

Value for money – It is not clear, however, whether this CSF will help achieve the second of LAA's objectives to provide excellent value for money. It may be that other agencies produce a similar quality of work, but charge a lower price. Alternatively, the quality of LAA's design work may exceed that required by the client, who will be unlikely, therefore, to perceive it as good value for money.

Specialist and local knowledge – Identifying this CSF will not directly help achieve the stated objective of providing clients with access to local and specialist knowledge. External suppliers may have more specialist knowledge than LAA can realistically replicate in its own design department.

Client retention – The relationship between the quality of the creative design and the clients' perception of its value for money will determine whether the fourth objective, to have returning clients, will be achieved or not. All other things being equal, high quality design work will probably make clients more likely to return. Other aspects of LAA's service, though, such as designing effective advertising campaigns and negotiating competitive rates for media buying, may be at least as important to the client.

(ii) **KPI to buy 90% internally**

Setting a KPI should lead managers to try to achieve this target, as they are appraised (and presumably rewarded) according to their performance against the target.

Delight clients with quality of work – Having this target will only help achieve the objective of delighting clients if the quality of the design done internally exceeds that done by third-party external designers. Though LAA has set up the 'centre for design excellence', this does not automatically mean the quality of work is any better than external agencies.

Value for money – Encouraging managers to buy creative services internally does not necessarily help achieve the objective of giving value for money for clients. Managers at both B and C have indicated that the prices charged by the in-house design department are significantly higher than other agencies in the market. The use of the internal design department may not be best value for the client.

BPP LEARNING MEDIA

Specialist and local knowledge – Encouraging the use of internal services may not help achieve LAA's third objective to offer specialist and local knowledge to clients. The design department is based entirely in Geeland and may not meet the needs of clients in other countries. The manager of B has already commented that the department did not understand the requirements of consumers in Veeland. This is also inconsistent with the objectives to delight clients and to have them return to LAA.

Client retention – Similarly, managers in A have also commented that the internal department did not have specialist knowledge to meet the needs of a new client. Again, encouraging managers to use the internal department seems contrary to the objectives of providing clients with specialist knowledge in order to delight them and to have them as return customers.

(b) **Transfer pricing policy**

Autonomy of the subsidiaries

The purposes of a transfer pricing policy are to encourage subsidiaries' autonomy, facilitate performance evaluation and promote overall goal congruence with the aim of LAA to maximise shareholder wealth.

As the three subsidiaries are profit centres, they will tend to make decisions which maximise their own profit. This may be at the expense of the other subsidiaries. By charging a higher transfer price to B and C for design services, A will increase its own revenue and also the costs for B and C. This may also be at the expense of LAA as a whole, for example, as C's client was unhappy with the high charges levied by A.

A transfer pricing policy helps to prevent subsidiaries from acting in an entirely self-interested way where this may not be in the best interests of LAA as a whole. Though a transfer pricing policy should promote autonomy of the subsidiaries, LAA's head office should have the power to impose a transfer price to maintain goal congruence across the organisation. This is not currently happening, and the high transfer prices charged for design services are causing dissatisfaction.

Both B and C have commented that they have spent large amounts of time trying to negotiate transfer prices with A. This is a waste of managers' time. The ability of head office to impose a transfer price, or the existence of a clear transfer pricing policy, would allow managers more time to deal with other key aspects of the business, such as ensuring client satisfaction.

Performance measurement in the three subsidiaries

A transfer pricing policy will enable the performance of the individual subsidiaries to be fairly measured. If the policy is unfair, for example, the gross margin at subsidiary C was reduced by the seemingly excessive transfer prices charged by A, managers' motivation will be reduced, especially if this reduces the subsidiaries' managers' rewards.

Setting clear, transparent and understandable transfer prices

Managers at B have complained that the basis for setting the transfer price from A is unclear. A transfer pricing policy should ensure that the basis for setting the prices is transparent, straightforward and well understood by managers so that they do not see prices as being set unfairly and thus become demotivated.

The basis for the prices set between subsidiaries in different countries should also be clear about how exchange rate movements are reflected in the transfer price, so that managers' performance is not appraised on factors which are outside their control.

Also, the transfer pricing policy for transfers between different countries should ensure that the prices are likely to be acceptable to the local tax authorities. The tax authorities in Veeland, where B is located, are already investigating the transfer prices charged by A. This is presumably because the authorities suspect that the transfer price may be set at an artificially high level in order to reduce tax paid on profits earned in Veeland. Having a clear transfer pricing policy may help to demonstrate that B is operating within relevant taxation laws and is acting ethically in setting a fair transfer price. As the internal design department has no external customers, then it may be preferable to operate it as a separate cost centre and make all transfers at marginal cost.

(c) **Market value transfer prices**

Advantages of setting transfer prices on the basis of market value

Transfer prices on the basis of market value reflect the prices of purchasing creative design services on the open market. Both buying and selling subsidiaries will know what the market price is and be able to compare this to the price they are paying or charging internally.

Where subsidiaries have autonomy to negotiate their own transfer prices, in order to maximise the performance of the individual subsidiaries, the transfer price agreed is likely to reflect market price. The buyer will be unwilling to pay more than the price it can pay on the open market. The seller will be unwilling to charge less to sell internally than can be obtained on the open market. This encourages efficiency in A, which has to compete with external suppliers of creative design services.

Where a market value transfer price is used, it will usually be beneficial for buyer and seller, as well as for LAA as a whole, to transfer internally. This is because selling and administration costs overall for both parties are reduced, and the buyer should get better customer service and reliability of supply by buying internally.

The transfer price charged by A currently includes an allowance for marketing costs and bad debts. These are unlikely to be incurred where internal transfers are made. The cost savings may be shared by both parties and the transfer price reduced to a level below the market value. This lower transfer price is known as the adjusted market price.

If the transfer price charged by A is calculated on a different basis from market value, which appears to be the case as A's prices are higher than the market rates, the subsidiaries will waste time arguing over the transfer price. This current approach may improve the subsidiaries' own performance, but this is not in the best interests of LAA overall.

Disadvantages of using market price

The use of external market price will only be the optimal transfer price when a perfectly competitive external market exists. For example, though creative services can be purchased on the open market, those services may not be identical with those provided internally. Subsidiary A had to use a third-party design agency for its new client as it did not have the industry knowledge to do the work itself. In this case, there may not be an equivalent service available internally to those available externally, and vice versa. There may therefore be no realistic option to buy on the open market in this situation and the use of an external market price as a transfer price would be inappropriate.

The market price may be temporary, changing according to capacity of the service providers or changes in economic circumstances or, in the case of LAA, short-term variations in the exchange rate. In this case, the transfer price would need to be frequently changed if it were to continue to reflect market conditions. This would be time consuming and probably confusing to the subsidiaries' managers.

Where allowance is made in the transfer price for the reduced costs, for example, of marketing and bad debts, it may be difficult to agree an adjusted market price which is acceptable to both A and the subsidiary purchasing design services from A.

19 Jenson, Lewis & Webb

Text reference. The concepts of controllability and accountability are discussed in Chapter 3 of the BPP Study Text. EVA™ is discussed in Chapter 7.

Top tips.

Part (a). The context for this question is the issue of controllability, and the fact a manager's performance is not necessarily the same as a division's performance. This is the point which the Export Division Manager appears to be making when she suggests it is not appropriate to use the division's net profit margin to appraise here performance.

BPP LEARNING MEDIA

To score well in this question it is important that you relate your answer specifically to the scenario and the context, rather than talking about controllability and accountability in general terms. For example, Appendix 1 shows that the division's net profit is shown after deducting apportioned head office costs – but is it appropriate to include them in an assessment of the divisional manager's performance?

Part (b). The importance of looking, in part (a), at specific issues from the scenario is reinforced in part (b).

In effect, part (b) involves recalculating controllable profit – but the evaluation in part (a) should have helped to identify the items which need to be excluded from the original net profit figure in order to generate the controllable profit.

As so often in Advanced Performance Management questions, it is important to pick out all the clues from the scenario. For example:

- In the first paragraph, you are told the Export Division is a profit centre (whereas the Domestic Division is an investment centre). In terms of controllable profit, what is the significance of the Export Division being a profit centre rather than an investment centre?
- Similarly, in the second paragraph you are told that the $KL weakened by 15% against the £SL half way through the year. What is the significance of this?

Note, that although the majority of the marks in part (b) are for 'appropriate calculations', you also need to make a recommendation (based on your calculations) as to whether or not the manager should receive her bonus.

Part (c). A useful way of approaching this requirement could have been to consider the advantages and disadvantages of using EVA™ as a measure of performance compared to net profit margin, and weighing up the relative advantages and disadvantages to advise whether or not EVA™ is appropriate.

For example, JLW's objective is 'to maximise shareholder wealth'; so is EVA™ more appropriate than net profit margin for measuring how well an organisation is generating wealth for its shareholders?

Importantly, as always in Advanced Performance Management, make sure you consider the appropriateness of EVA™ specifically in the context of the scenario, rather than giving a generic discussion of its potential advantages and disadvantages. For example, since the EVA™ calculation is influenced by WACC, is it appropriate for a profit centre (like the Export Division)? Or, since Appendix 1 suggests that the Domestic Division is significantly larger than the Export Division, how useful will EVA™ be in comparing the relative performance of the divisions (since it generates an absolute value, rather than a percentage)?

Examining team's comments.

Part (a). To score well in this part of the question, it was important to pick up on the issues mentioned in the scenario and examine their impact on the question. Those candidates who did this, scored well in this part.

Part (b), which required a calculation of the relevant profit to judge the manager's performance in order to assess their suitability for a bonus payment, was generally done well.

Part (c), which required an evaluation of the suitability of economic value added as a divisional performance measured was answered surprisingly poorly. This was often due to candidates believing that the question required a lengthy description of the method of calculation of the indicator, rather than focussing on its suitability for use in the scenario.

Marking scheme

		Marks
(a)	Evaluation of manager's comments – 1 mark per relevant point Traceable net profit calculation – 2 marks Total for part (a): up to 7	7
(b)	Depreciation and allocated head office costs – 2 marks Currency gain – 2 marks Controllable revenue – 2 marks Controllable profit margin – 1 mark Conclusion/recommendation – 1 mark Total for part (b): up to 8	8
(c)	Evaluation of EVA™ – 1 mark per relevant point Total for part (c): up to 10	10
	Total =	25

(a) **Assessing managerial vs divisional performance**

A key characteristic of divisional performance measurement is that divisional managers, and the divisions themselves, should only be appraised on performance that they control. For example, costs which are not controlled by divisional managers, such as JLW's apportioned head office costs, should be added back to profit when appraising manager's performance.

Similarly, as Export Division is a profit centre, divisional managers are not able to make capital investment decisions and so depreciation is out of their control and should be added back to profit for their appraisals. Domestic Division is an investment centre, so managers there can make investment decisions, and depreciation is a cost which they can control.

On 30 June 20X6, the $KL weakened by 15% against the £SL. This meant Export Division benefited from an increase in revenue which was not under the control of the divisional manager. This amount must be deducted from revenue when calculating the controllable net profit for Export Division.

The net profit arrived at after items which are not under managers' control are added back is known as the 'controllable profit'. This is what divisional managers should be appraised on. This is because it is unfair to appraise them on factors outside their control, and may mean they become demotivated or give up trying to improve performance, which is not in the interests of JLW as a whole.

Divisional performance should be evaluated on all the items which relate directly to the division which is its 'traceable profit'. Allocated head office costs do not directly reflect the activity of the division and should be excluded when calculating the traceable profit.

The traceable net profit for Export Division, after adjusting for allocated head office costs, was $KL905,000 (Working), and the traceable net profit margin was 11%.

A difficulty with calculating controllable and traceable profits in this way may be that it is difficult to determine which items are controllable or not. For example, though the new machine purchased for Export Division by head office did lead to improvements in productivity, the extent of this increase must be attributed to good management, or otherwise, by the divisional managers. This increase in productivity is therefore due partly to controllable factors, and partly to uncontrollable.

Working: Traceable net profit

	$KL'000
Reported net profit	545
Add back: Allocated head office costs	360
Traceable net profit	905
Traceable net profit margin (905/8,000)	11.3%

(b) **Export Division Manager's bonus**

The controllable net profit is arrived at after items which are not under the manager's control are added back. The net profit margin controllable by the manager of Export Division is 10%. Given that it is difficult to assess the effect of the increased productivity on controllable net profit, the manager should be awarded her bonus for the year. This is because the controllable net profit margin of 10% exceeds the target of 8%.

Workings

1 *Controllable net profit margin for Export Division; year ended 31 December 20X6*

Controllable net profit	$KL'000
Reported net profit	545
Non-controllable items	
Add back:	
Depreciation	395
Allocated head office costs	360
Deduct:	
Currency gain	(522)
Controllable net profit	778
Controllable revenue	
Reported revenue	8,000
Deduct currency gain	(522)
Controllable revenue	7,478
Controllable net profit margin (778/7,478)	10.4%

2 *Currency gain*

Six months revenue from 1 July 20X6 was increased by 15% due to currency gain.

Six months revenue before currency gain 4,000/1.15 = 3,478

Therefore non-controllable currency gain is 4,000 – 3,478 = 522

As the exact increase in productivity resulting for the new machinery on Export Division is unclear, it is difficult to accurately adjust the controllable net profit margin to reflect this. It would seem the Divisional Manager is benefitting from productivity improvements which are not entirely under her control. To reduce the controllable net profit margin to 8%, the threshold at which the manager is awarded her bonus, the net profit would have to fall by approximately $KL179,760 (778,000 – (7,478,000 × 8%)). This is equivalent to 3.7% of cost of sales (179,760k/4,800,000). It is difficult to conclude, therefore, whether the 'significant' improvement in productivity would make the difference between the manager of Export Division receiving her bonus or not.

(c) **EVA™ as a performance measure for Export and Domestic Divisions**

EVA™ makes adjustments to the financial profit to calculate the economic value generated by each division, and then makes a deduction for the cost of the capital invested in the division. A positive EVA™ indicates a division is creating value above that required by those who finance the business. It is therefore consistent with JLW's objective to maximise shareholder wealth. Appraisal of divisional performance on this basis would therefore align the interests of managers with those of JLW's shareholders.

EVA™ involves making many adjustments to operating profit and capital employed. These may be time consuming, and be poorly understood by managers. The manager of Export Division has already commented that she finds the bonus calculations difficult to understand. Failure of managers to understand the EVA™ calculations would make it difficult for them to work towards targets set for the division.

EVA™ avoids distortion from estimates and financial policies

EVA™ avoids the financial results from being distorted by accounting policies and estimates made by divisional managers, for example, the $KL75,000 bad debt provision made in Domestic Division, as increases in provisions are added back to operating profit in the EVA™ calculation. Whilst this provides a consistent basis to evaluate performance of divisions within JLW, EVA™ is not suitable for comparing divisional performance as it is an absolute measure and does not make allowance for their relative sizes.

EVA™ encourages managers to take a long-term view

The advertising costs for the new range of paints would be capitalised as these generate future value. The use of EVA™ would encourage managers to incur costs, such as these, which will benefit the business in the long term.

However, the calculation of EVA™ is backwards looking, and based on historical financial information, whereas shareholders need information about future performance on which to base their decisions.

EVA™ takes into account the cost of capital

The current performance measure of net profit margin is a poor measure as it takes into account neither the absolute net profit achieved, the capital employed in the division, nor the cost of capital. By making a deduction for the cost of capital employed in the division, the EVA™ calculation makes managers consider both the capital employed and the cost of capital in their divisions.

Export division is a profit centre and managers do not have control of investment decisions. Therefore, it is not a suitable measure for the evaluation of the performance on Export Division because there is no controllable capital employed. Domestic Division is able to control investment decisions, and does have controllable capital employed, so EVA™ would be a suitable measure for evaluating Domestic Division's performance.

However, to use the weighted average cost of capital (WACC) in the EVA™ calculation requires a number of assumptions and estimates to be made, for example, in calculating the cost of equity or market value of debt. The WACC is normally based on historic data, which may not reflect circumstances in the future, and may not be accurate.

20 Stillwater Services

Text reference. EVA™ is discussed in Chapter 7 of the BPP Study Text. Stakeholder management and the potential impact of stakeholders on performance are discussed in Chapter 4b.

Top tips.

Part (a). Up to ten of the marks available in part (a) are for calculations. There should be some relatively easy marks here (for example, for identifying the adjustments to operating profit), even if you don't get all of the figures correct.

A few months before the exam which included this question, a technical article was published on ACCA's website – 'Economic value added versus profit-based measures of performance'. This article explained the adjustments to operation profit which are required in EVA™, as well as the logic behind them. Candidates who had read (and understood) this article should have been well placed to tackle this question. This highlights the importance of reading relevant technical articles on ACCA's website as part of your preparation for your exams.

One particular point to note in relation to the EVA™ calculation itself: Remember that your calculations for the capital employed figure need to be based on the published accounts figure at the start of 20X2, not at the end of it.

However, also note that the question requirement isn't simply to calculate EVA™; you should also have used the EVA™ figure you have calculated to evaluate SS's performance. In other words, how well is it creating value for its shareholders?

Part (b). The reference in the requirement to 'analysing the potential influence' of different stakeholder groups should have suggested that Mendelow's ideas of power and interest could be relevant here. However, perhaps more importantly, the reference to 'managing different stakeholder groups' should have also alerted you to the potential conflict of interests between different groups. In particular, how are the regulator's interests likely to differ from shareholders' interests, and how do these differences affect SS's directors?

Part (c). As in part (a), this part of the question combines calculations with a discussion related to the figures you have calculated. Crucially, though, you must make sure your ROCE calculations relate solely to the regulated parts of SS's business.

Also it is vitally important that you recognised that the ROCE target of 6% is the **upper** limit that SS can achieve on its regulated business, not a minimum target it is trying to achieve.

This is very important because the presence of this target means that SS has very little scope to increase its profits from regulated business. So, in terms of performance management for SS as a whole, what implications does this have for the role of unregulated business in increasing the company's profits?

Examining team's comments. The calculation of EVA™ was discussed in a technical article on ACCA's website, and had clearly been well prepared for by many candidates who scored most of the calculation marks available in part (a). The calculations of net operating profit after tax (NOPAT) could be done by starting from PAT, or from Operating Profit, and both approaches gained credit. The weakest area of the calculations was the adjustments to capital employed.

Most candidates realised the need to comment on the figures they had calculated and gave a summary sentence. However, many candidates did not offer any broader comment on the key assumptions in the EVA™ method, or the limitations of the method. This could be seen as a failure to appreciate the need to 'evaluate' performance using EVA™, rather than simply to 'calculate' performance.

Part (c) was generally poorly answered, with many candidates not appearing to realise that the ROCE target was an upper limit on the company. Few candidates spotted that the constraints on the regulated side of the business would mean that the unregulated side would be the engine of growth for SS, while the regulated side could act as a cash cow.

Marking scheme

			Marks
(a)	Adjustments to operating profit:		
	Non-cash items	0.5	
	Accounting depreciation	1	
	Doubtful debts	1	
	Research and development	1	
	Interest	0.5	
	Tax (cash amount paid; tax on interest)	Up to 2	
	Capital employed figure:		
	Capital employed (per accounts) at start of year	0.5	
	Provision for doubtful debts	1	
	Other non-cash items	1	
	WACC	1	
	EVA™	1	
	Note. Maximum 10 marks available for calculations	10	
	Comments about SS's performance, consistent with EVA™ calculation – 1 mark per relevant point	Up to 3	
			13
(b)	Analysis of different interest and power of each stakeholder group – up to 2 marks each	Up to 6	
	Identifying potential conflicts between interests of regulator and shareholders	1	
			5

		Marks
(c)	*Calculations:*	
	ROCE (on regulated business only)	1
	Maximum regulated operating profit allowed	1
	Operating margins (regulated vs non-regulated business)	1
	Other relevant calculations	1
	Commentary:	
	On calculations – 1 mark per relevant point	Up to 2
	On performance management of regulated areas of SS – 1 mark per relevant point	Up to 2
	On performance management of unregulated areas of SS – 1 mark per relevant point	Up to 2
		7
	Total =	**25**

(a)

	$m	$m	Comments
Operating profit		68.00	
Add back: Depreciation	59.00		
Doubtful debts	2.00		
Research and development	12.00		
Other non-cash items	7.00		
		80.00	
Less: Economic depreciation		–83.00	
Tax		–9.00	Cash amount only
Tax adjustment on finance charges		–5.75	$23m × 25%
NOPAT		**50.25**	

		$m	Notes
Capital employed		637.00	Based on figure b/f at start of 20X2
Add back: Provision for doubtful debts	2.50		(see Working)
Other non-cash items	6.00		Non-cash items in 20X1
		8.50	
		645.50	

		$m	Notes
WACC:			
Equity: 40% × 16%	6.4%		
Debt: 60% × 5% × (1 – 25%)	2.3%		
	8.7%		

EVA™:

NOPAT – (Capital employed × WACC)

50.25 – (645.5 × 0.087) **–5.91**

No adjustment for depreciation required at the start of 20X2.

Working	$m
Provision for doubtful debts at end of 20X2	4.5
Movement in year	–2
Provision at start of year	2.5

BPP LEARNING MEDIA

Negative EVA™ – SS's negative EVA™ figure for 20X2 suggests that, instead of creating wealth for its shareholders, it is actually destroying value. More specifically, the value which SS is generating (NOPAT) is not sufficient to cover the economic cost of the capital it has employed to generate that value.

Such a position is not sustainable in the long run, and will lead to dissatisfaction amongst SS's shareholders. SS could look to address this issue either by increasing its net operating profit or by reducing its cost of capital; or through a combination of both.

NOPAT – SS's current NOPAT of $50.25m leaves it with a negative EVA™ of $5.91m. At the current cost of capital, SS would need to increase its NOPAT to $56.16m to break even on EVA™.

Cost of capital – Alternatively, SS would break even on EVA™, with its current level of NOPAT, if its WACC was 7.8% ($645.5m × 7.8% = $50.3m). In this respect, SS's current cost of equity (16%) appears high, particularly given the highly regulated nature of the industry. Moreover, given that 80% of SS's sales (for water and sewage services) are for services which are necessities for everyday life, there is relatively little risk that demand will fall. Again, this suggests that SS's cost of equity should be lower than it currently is.

Asset base – SS could also look to reduce its asset base by selling under-utilised assets. If it could reduce the amount of capital employed without any significant reduction in its NOPAT, this could help its EVA™ break even or become positive.

(b) **Regulator**

Interest – The regulator is likely to have a high interest in SS. Although the regulator will only be interested in SS's regulated services, these still constitute 80% of its total revenue. The regulator's interest is in controlling the prices SS charges, and the returns it generates.

Power – The regulator also has a high level of power to influence SS's performance. Not only does the regulator set the level of pre-tax ROCE which SS is allowed to generate, but it also has the power to impose significant fines if SS exceeds this figure.

Shareholders

Interest – Although the shareholders will be interested in the wealth which SS creates for them, they will be less interested in the day to day business of the company and the operational decisions taken within it. (They have delegated authority for these to SS's management.) Therefore, shareholders' interest in performance management at SS is likely to be lower than that of both the regulator and SS's management.

However, shareholders' interests are likely to differ from those of the regulator. Whereas the regulator is interested in controlling profits, the shareholders are likely to want SS to maximise the profits and earnings it generates.

Power – It is not clear how SS's shares are distributed, but this could determine the level of power the shareholders have. If SS's shares are owned primarily by institutional investors they are likely to have more power than if the shares are held by a large number of private investors. For example, institutional investors will have more voting power than individuals, and so could look to replace SS's management if they felt the company was underperforming.

It seems that SS's shareholders have at least a moderate level of power since the board is trying to drive performance for the shareholders' benefit.

Management

Interest – SS's management have a high level of interest in the company's performance, because if the company is unsuccessful their jobs will come under threat. However, SS's management also have to ensure that the conflicting interests of the regulator and the company's shareholders are managed successfully.

Power – The management team also have a relatively high level of power because they dictate the strategies which the company will pursue. However, the presence of a strong regulator means that the management team's power is less than it would be in an unregulated market because, for example, performance levels in SS's regulated services have to comply with the parameters imposed by the regulator.

(c) Target ROCE: 6%

Operating profit from regulated business: $46.0m

Average capital employed: (779.0m + 761.0m)/2 = $770.0m

ROCE: 5.97%

> **Alternative calculation:**
>
> The examining team's answer uses capital employed at the end of 20X2, rather than average capital employed during the year.
>
> Under this basis ROCE is: 46.0m/779.0m = 5.90%.

Return within prescribed limit – The return which SS generates from its regulated business (5.97%) is within the limit set by the regulator (6.0%).

However, because SS's current return is so close to the limit there is very little scope for it to increase the profitability of the regulated aspect of the business. The maximum operating profit that SS could generate in its regulated business is $46.2m ($770m × 6%).

Non-regulated activities – The constraints on the regulated business increase the importance of the non-regulated activities as a potential source of profit growth for the business.

Additionally, the operating profit margins which SS earns from non-regulated business are significantly higher than those from regulated business.

Regulated services: $46m/$276m = 16.7%

Non-regulated services: $22m/$69m = 31.9%

Consequently, SS should be looking to expand its non-regulated business, as a source of profitable growth.

In effect, SS's regulated business could be seen as a 'cash cow'. SS should look to invest cash generated by its regulated business to help support the expansion of its non-regulated business (either through organic growth or through acquisition).

Cost control – The regulator's primary concern appears to be that SS doesn't increase its prices unjustifiably. If SS has little scope to increase prices, then in order to maintain its profits it needs to ensure that its costs do not increase significantly either.

Therefore, controlling costs will be a key element of performance management within the regulated part of the business. On the one hand this highlights the importance of variance analysis (comparing actual costs to budget), but on the other hand it also suggests the importance of identifying potential cost savings (for example, through efficiency improvements).

> **Lack of investment** – The target level of 6% is lower than SS's WACC (of 8.47%; see part (a)). If SS uses WACC as a discount rate for decision making, then it would be reluctant to invest in the regulated part of the business at all.
>
> The infrastructure in the regulated side of the business is likely to suffer as a result. This could have an adverse effect on other aspects of SS's performance. For example, if SS has increasing problems with burst water mains due to lack of investment in its infrastructure, this could lead to an increase in repair costs, and also a decline in customer service if customers' water supplies are disrupted.

Growth – By contrast, the focus of performance measures for the non-regulated services should be on revenue and profit growth. For example, SS should look to set targets for revenue growth or market share growth. However, it is equally important for SS to set targets for profit margins, to ensure that it doesn't sacrifice profitability in search of revenue growth.

21 Essland Police Forces

Text reference. The use of league tables in relation to measuring public sector performance is discussed in Chapter 9a of the BPP Study Text.

Top tips.

Part (a). It is vital that you read the requirement very carefully before starting to answer this requirement.

In particular, note the following:

- You are asked to evaluate the **method** of calculating and measuring the force scores, not to evaluate the performance of the different forces based on their force scores.
- You need to evaluate how useful the league tables are in improving the performance of the police forces in the context of achieving the Department of the Interior's aims and goals.

The scenario reiterates this first point, with the reference to the CEO's comment: 'I'm not interested in the performance ... I'm interested in the method of assessment.'

Nonetheless, the statistics provided in Appendix 1 are very important to the question; for example, for indicating other measures which could potentially be included eg number of police force employees per head of population.

In relation to this second point (about the usefulness of the tables) a key question is: how well do the variables included in the tables relate to the Department's overall aim (achieving value for money) rather than being linked to the Department's goals?

Part (b). Although the majority of requirements in APM require you to apply your knowledge specifically to a scenario, the first part of this requirement asks you to discuss the merits of league tables in general terms.

However, the second part of the requirement then links directly back to the scenario. The CEO has raised concerns about how staff will respond to the introduction of the league tables, and has also raised concerns about how appropriate it will be to transfer league tables from the schools sector into the police forces. Are these concerns valid? For example, will the league tables lead to police forces focusing only on the measures of performance included in the league tables at the expense of other aspects of performance?

In terms of structuring your answer, it could be useful to use the main points of the CEO's concerns as headings for your answer and then address them in turn.

Marking scheme

		Marks
(a)	Evaluating the appropriateness of variables used in the context of achieving the overall aim of the Department of the Interior – 1 mark per relevant point – up to a maximum of 3 marks	
	Evaluating the appropriateness of variables used in the context of achieving the detailed goals of the Department of the Interior – 1 mark per relevant point – up to a maximum of 5 marks	
	For relevant comments on other indicators which could be included in the tables – up to a maximum of 2 marks	
	Evaluating the allocation of the weightings across the different forces – 1 mark per relevant point – up to a maximum of 4 marks	
	Up to 2 marks for other relevant points	
	Total for part (a): up to 14	14

		Marks
(b)	General evaluation of league tables – 1 mark per relevant point – up to a maximum of 4 marks	
	Comments on employees' attitude to the introduction of the system – up to a maximum of 2 marks	
	Impact of the league tables on employee behaviour and their sense of accountability – 1 mark per relevant point – up to a maximum of 5 marks	
	Appropriateness of using league tables from schools in relation to the police forces – 1 mark per relevant point – up to a maximum of 2 marks	
	Total for part (b): up to 11	11
		Total = 25

(a) **Choice of variables selected**

The variables used to measure the force score should be aligned to the aims and goals of the police forces. At the highest level, the two main aims of the police forces are: to provide a **value for money** service, and to ensure the **security** of the community.

Detailed goals – However, the detailed goals of the Department focus primarily on crime, justice and community support without providing any more detail about the economy, efficiency or effectiveness (value for money) of the policing service.

Choice of 'ranks' – In turn, the four 'ranks' used to calculate the force score appear to be derived from the detailed goals, rather than the overall aims.

Goal	'Rank' indicator used
Tackling the underlying causes of crime	Rank 1 – number of reported crimes
Bringing perpetrators to justice	Rank 2 – proportion of reported crimes solved
Providing protection and support for individuals and communities	Rank 3 – user satisfaction score (for service offered by police forces)
Responsiveness, accessibility and community engagement	Rank 4 – responsiveness (to calls) Rank 3 – user satisfaction will also reflect responsiveness, accessibility and engagement more generally

The indicators selected don't measure all aspects of the goals exactly, but they provide a reasonable coverage of them. For example, one way to reduce the number of reported crimes would be to tackle the underlying causes of crime so that fewer crimes are committed.

Nonetheless, the 'ranks' could still be improved. For example, the number of public meetings between the police and the local community could be used to measure the level of community engagement.

Value for money

More importantly, however, because the goals focus on tackling crime and promoting community safety, the ranks also focus on these aspects of performance rather than the degree of value for money achieved by the police services. For example, whereas the current Rank 2 is based on the solution rate for crimes, it might also be useful to measure the number of crimes solved per police force employee in order to assess the efficiency of the police service.

The data which the police forces already keep (Appendix 1 in the scenario) would be suitable for calculating some value for money performance measures. For example, using the data already available, the following additional 'rank' scores could be calculated:

	C	*D*	*E*	*F*
Number of police per 10,000 population	49.6	48.9	50.0	52.7
Cost of police force per head of population ($)	323.2	331.1	336.5	340.0
Number of crimes solved per police force employee	5.0	5.2	5.4	4.2

BPP LEARNING MEDIA

Weightings used

Another potential issue with the current system is that it assigns the same weighting to each of the four ranks. This approach has the benefit of simplicity, but it also presumes that each aspect of performance is equally important to the performance of the force. In practice, this may not be the case, but no explanation is given to justify the weightings used.

Importantly, however, the weightings used could affect the overall ranking of the forces in the league table. Currently, Force F is top ranked, while Force C is bottom ranked. However, if, for example, user satisfaction was given greater weighting than the other factors, this would be likely to mean that Force E became top ranked.

Equally, as we noted earlier, if value for money measures were included, the rankings would also change – particularly because Force F performs worst in relation to this area.

Therefore the Department faces a trade-off between preserving the simplicity of the calculations and including additional factors and prescribing different weightings to different factors.

> **Additional point:**
>
> **Impact of using ranks** – The difference between the best and worst performing forces in relation to call handling is only 3 percentage points (94% vs 91%), whereas the equivalent difference for user satisfaction is 12 percentage points (80% vs 68%). However, both of these performance spreads generate a difference of 0.75 in the forces' scores. In this way, the ranking system currently being applied doesn't take into account the degree of variation in performance between the different forces for any of the measures.

(b) **Merits of league tables in performance management**

Benchmarks – By providing a single performance summary, league tables can provide a useful way of benchmarking performance between not for profit organisations. Moreover, because they are not directly competing with each other, not for profit organisations should be more willing to exchange data than commercial organisations, thereby making it easier to carry out a benchmarking exercise.

Benchmarking performance in this way could help identify areas of best practice among the police forces, and could help to motivate poorer performers to improve their performance levels to bring them closer to the best performers.

Limited comparisons – In effect, benchmarking and league tables are both relative measures of performance – comparing the performance of an organisation against other similar organisations. However, there could still be other organisations (not included in the benchmarking exercise) which are performing better.

In this case, although Force F performs best at call handling (with 94% of calls answered within 10 seconds) this figure may still be relatively low compared to the performance of the other emergency services (fire, ambulance) in Essland or compared to police forces in other countries.

To overcome this issue, the league tables could try to include figures for comparable organisations (in particular, foreign police forces). However, it could be difficult to find the comparable data necessary to calculate a force score for a foreign police force (as opposed to benchmarking individual elements of performance).

Factors affecting performance – One of the main issues with league tables is that while they can highlight variations in performance, they do not take account of any factors leading to those variations in performance. For example, the number of reported crimes per 10,000 of population could reflect the social and economic conditions of a region.

Controllability and motivation – Perhaps even more importantly, the police forces do not have the power to affect the external environment, such as economic conditions. Therefore, if the police forces feel their performance is being judged on factors they cannot control, introducing the league tables could serve to demotivate, rather than motivate, the forces.

As the CEO has pointed out, the police forces have strong union representation. Therefore if the forces resist or resent the introduction of the league tables, with the backing of their unions, the forces could potentially discredit the league tables, and possibly even the way the Department of the Interior manages the forces.

Measure fixation – Another potential issue with league tables is that they could lead to the police forces concentrating on those aspects of performance which are included in the tables at the expense of others. The notion that 'what gets measured, gets done' would seem to be appropriate here.

In particular, the league tables do not currently include any measures linked to the value for money provided by the forces. Therefore, the league tables could lead the police forces to overlook this aspect of the Department's aims, because they are focusing solely on the aspects of safety and security being measured in the league tables. So, for example, the police forces could recruit additional staff to answer phone calls (and improve their call handling score) but it is debatable how much value for money this would provide overall.

Use of league tables from the schools sector – Although the introduction of school league tables may have been successfully applied in Essland's schools, there are some significant differences between schools and police forces which may make the use of league tables less appropriate for the police forces.

Users of the league tables – In particular, parents in Essland have a choice about which school their children attend, so they can use information about the relative performance of different schools to help them make that choice. However, residents cannot choose which police force is responsible for their safety and security – unless they relocate to a different area of the country. Therefore, whereas the school league tables can help users (parents) in their decision-making, the police force league tables do not have an equivalent benefit for the residents of their regions.

Number of measures included – Additionally, the school league tables are entirely based on a single measure of performance (exam results) whereas the force score tries to include a wider range of factors. However, as we have already noted, this then raises questions about which factors should be included in the tables, and whether all the factors being considered are equally important.

22 Beeshire Local Authority

Text reference. The issues surrounding performance measurement in public sector organisations are discussed in Chapter 9a of the BPP Study Text. Non-financial performance indicators are discussed in Chapter 9b.

Top tips.

Part (a). A useful starting point for understanding the importance of non-financial indicators in public sector organisations will be to think about the goals and objectives of those organisations, and how they differ from commercial organisations.

The first paragraph of the scenario provides some very useful pointers here. We are told the goal for BLA's Waste Management Department is 'to maintain Beeshire as a safe, clean and environmentally friendly place', and also that the department does not charge residents or businesses for most of its services.

If it doesn't charge for its services it can't possibly make a profit, which therefore rules out any profit-based performance measures. Nonetheless, the scenario tells us, BLA has so far 'focused on financial measures of performance' rather than, for example, quality of service. Does such an approach seem consistent with the department's goals, or might looking at non-financial performance indicators be more constructive?

Part (b). There are several different elements in the requirement, so it is important that you cover all of them to score the marks available in this part of the question.

In effect, the requirement can be broken down into three parts: (i) explain how value for money provision should be assessed; (ii) by suggesting (and justifying) suitable performance indicators; and then (iii) calculating performance in relation to those indicators.

BPP LEARNING MEDIA

Value for money is typically measured in terms of the three Es: economy, efficiency and effectiveness. So a useful approach to this requirement would be to explain the Es first, and look at each one in turn to suggest suitable performance indicators for it. The requirement to 'calculate justified performance indicators using the information in the scenario' should have been a reminder that the indicators you suggest need to be specifically relevant to the scenario, rather than being generic measures of economy, efficiency or effectiveness.

Part (c). In the same way that a useful approach to part (a) was to think how public sector organisations differ from commercial ones, a useful starting point for this requirement would be to think how qualitative factors of performance differ from quantitative ones. What are the key characteristics of qualitative data?

The key characteristic of qualitative data is that it is subjective (based on people's opinions). Once you identify this point, the difficulties of measuring it should become easier to identify.

However, note you aren't only asked to discuss the difficulties of measuring qualitative performance; you also need to suggest appropriate solutions to help BLA overcome the difficulties associated with measuring qualitative performance.

Marking scheme

		Marks
(a)	General discussion of the usefulness of non-financial indicators in public sector organisations – up to 4 marks	
	For identifying examples relevant to BLA – up to 4 marks:	
	Total for part (a): up to 6	6
(b)	General description of VFM (economy, efficiency, effectiveness) – up to 3 marks	
	For discussing each heading (economy, efficiency, effectiveness) in relation to BLA – 1 mark per relevant point – up to 12 marks	
	Total for part (b): up to 12	12
(c)	For identifying difficulties of measuring qualitative factors of performance – 1 mark per valid difficulty identified	
	For suggesting appropriate solutions for BLA – 1 mark per relevant point	
	Total for part (c): up to 7	7
	Total =	**25**

(a) Unlike commercial organisations which have an underlying objective to maximise the profits they generate for their shareholders, it is often much harder to define the objectives of public sector organisations.

Multiple objectives – The Waste Department's goal identifies three potential objectives: cleanliness, safety, and environmental friendliness. As such, its performance indicators will need to measure how well it is performing in these three areas. However, as none of the areas are financial, non-financial performance indicators – such as survey scores for how clean residents or tourists feel the area is – are likely to be more relevant than financial ones.

Lack of profit measure – The goal also highlights that generating a profit is not a priority for the department in the way it is for commercial organisations. The Chief Executive's desire to keep costs under control suggests that financial performance measures (focusing on costs) will still be important. However, if BLA focuses too much on cutting costs (for example, by reducing the frequency of waste collections), this could be detrimental to the primary goal of maintaining cleanliness and safety. As such, BLA needs a range of performance indicators, linked to how clean, safe and environmentally friendly the area is.

Difficulty in selecting financial measures – As with many public sector organisations, the results (output) from the Waste Department's services are non-financial: for example, clean streets, a safe environment.

Therefore it will be difficult to find any financial indicators which measure the outputs of the department's services in any meaningful way.

Consequently, in any assessment of the department's services it will be difficult to introduce any direct comparison between cost (financial) and benefits (non-financial). In addition, it could be difficult to define the cost unit against which to measure the department's performance. For example, should BLA be measuring the cost per tonne of waste collected, or the cost per household?

(b) **Value for money**

The extent to which BLA provides value for money services should be assessed in relation to:

Economy – the extent to which services of an acceptable quality are provided at the cheapest cost possible

Efficiency – the way BLA's services are organised, to ensure that the department maximises the benefits and outputs it obtains from its resources

Effectiveness – the extent to which the Waste Services Department's activities achieve its goals

Possible performance indicators at BLA

Economy

BLA's staff costs account for 44% of its total costs, and so the extent to which BLA controls its staff costs will have a significant impact on the economy of its services.

The average salary for BLA's waste collection staff is $31,429 compared to the national average of $29,825. The fact that BLA's average salary exceeds the national average suggests its services are not being provided as economically as they could be. However, this may reflect the fact that Beeshire is a wealthy area, so wage levels in general may be higher there than in other parts of the country. Equally, though, by paying above the national average for staff, BLA may be able to recruit more experienced or higher quality staff. As a result, this could improve its efficiency.

Another significant cost driver for BLA is likely to be its fleet of vehicles. Therefore, it could also measure economy in relation to the costs it pays for its vehicles, their fuel and their maintenance.

Efficiency

Benchmarking the performance of BLA's waste collections against the national figures indicates that BLA is relatively efficient:

	BLA	*Nationally*
Tonnes of waste collected per member of staff	629	583
Cost per tonne of waste collected ($)	114	123
Staff cost per tonne of waste collected ($)	50	51

This supports the point we made earlier: that although BLA's average salary is above the national average, BLA benefits from the greater efficiency of its staff.

Effectiveness

Effectiveness needs to be measured against a variety of aspects, linked to the need for waste collection:

Public health concerns – The fact that waste is only collected every 14 days (compared to the national average of 12 days) could suggest that BLA is less effective in maintaining public health. However, the level of public health concerns could also be measured by the number of complaints about vermin or other problems related to waste. If the level of complaints BLA receives is in line with national average (or below it) there would seem to be little reason to increase the frequency of the collections it carries out.

Clean and attractive streets – Finding a way to measure the cleanliness of BLA's streets could be difficult, because 'cleanliness' is inherently subjective, and therefore difficult to quantify. However, BLA could use the number of complaints it receives from residents or businesses as an indirect measure. If the number of complaints is relatively low, this would suggest that the cleanliness of the streets is being maintained at an acceptable level.

Increased recycling – The Government has set a target of 40% of all waste to be recycled, therefore BLA needs to measure the percentage of its total waste it recycles. It currently recycles 43% of all waste collected (950,000/2.2m). As such, BLA has already achieved the target level, and the proportion of waste it recycles is above the national average (41%).

Nonetheless, as the Government is planning to increase the levy charged on landfill, it will be important for BLA to ensure the proportion of waste that it recycles is as high as possible. As such, this remains an important indicator to monitor.

(c) **Difficulties of measuring qualitative performance**

Subjectivity – One of the main problems in measuring qualitative performance is that it is based on people's opinions and judgements and therefore is subjective. For example, people's assessment about what constitutes an acceptable level of cleanliness in BLA's streets may differ, and this in turn could affect the degree to which the area's streets are perceived to be 'clean'.

Equally, as Seeland is currently in a long recession, some people may prefer that waste be collected less frequently to allow the local Government to save money, instead of, for example, increasing local taxes to pay for more frequent collections. In this case, people's priorities could dictate their willingness to complain about uncollected waste or the frequency of collections.

The fact that the underlying data is qualitative rather than quantitative can, in itself, create problems for measurement. For example, if the Waste Management Department receives a phone call from a resident complaining that some uncollected waste is 'disgusting', it will be difficult for the department to gauge whether this is a more serious or less serious problem than the uncollected waste described by another resident as 'foul'.

Currently, BLA records the number of complaints it receives, but there is no indication of the seriousness of these complaints – possibly due to the subjective nature of the data involved.

Scoring – One way of addressing the problem of subjectivity could be to try to make the data quantitative. For example, the Waste Management Department could introduce a scoring system to judge how satisfied residents are with the cleanliness of their streets. The scoring system could ask residents to rate cleanliness on a scale from 1 to 5, with '1' signifying 'Very satisfied' and '5' signifying 'Very dissatisfied'.

However, scoring systems are still subjective, because the level of cleanliness which one person grades as 'Very satisfactory' may only be deemed 'Satisfactory' by another person. In general, there is also a tendency to score towards the middle in this type of scoring system: people feel more comfortable selecting scores in the range '2' to '4', rather than using the extreme scores of '1' or '5'.

Trends – One way to reduce the subjectivity in non-financial performance measures is by looking at trends over time rather than one-off metrics – for example, monitoring trends in the average scores for cleanliness.

Although individual scores will still be subjective, looking at average scores over time can help to overcome this subjectivity and highlight changes in quality or satisfaction. For example, if the residents are surveyed about the cleanliness of BLA annually, and the average score declines from one year to the next, this should provide a good indication that the quality of the waste collection services is declining.

23 Teeland Universities

Chapter references. Not for profit organisations and the concept of 'value for money' are discussed in Chapter 9b of the BPP Study Text.

Top tips.

Part (a). Teeland's Government wants to assess the value for money provided by universities in the country, and a senior politician has asked for advice on how to do this. The reference to 'value for money' should have prompted you to think about the three Es – economy, efficiency and effectiveness – and these would have provided a useful framework for structuring your answer. (ACCA's marking guide also indicates that there were up to three marks available for a general description of the three Es approach in the context of assessing value for money in public sector organisations.)

Since the requirement refers specifically to the performance data in Appendix A, a sensible way to approach this question would be to think what the data in the appendix can tell us about the universities' performance – in relation to economy, efficiency and effectiveness.

Remember that 'effectiveness' relates to the extent to which an organisation is achieving its objectives. The three objectives for universities in Teeland are clearly identified at the start of the scenario, so the universities' effectiveness should be judged in relation to these three points.

In this respect, as well as thinking about the relative performance of the four universities described in the scenario, it would be relevant to consider how useful the data in Appendix A is for assessing value for money. For example, one of the universities' objectives is 'to engage in high quality research' but would the data in Appendix A help the Government to assess the quality of the universities' research?

More generally, when thinking about value for money and the three Es, it is important to think about the linkages between the different Es. This point is relevant here as well. For example, if a university looks to reduce its costs (to improve economy) what impact might this have on the standard of education or the quality of its research (effectiveness)?

Part (b). Although the requirement asks candidates for benefits and problems, it is important to note that it asks about the problems of 'implementing the proposal to introduce league tables', and not simply 'the problems of league tables'. So think about the practical implications of implementing the tables, not just the potential disadvantages of league tables more generally.

As is often the case, the scenario provides some useful clues here – in particular by highlighting the level of resources which will be needed to compile the league tables. (In Veeland, there is a special government department of 150 staff who administer a similar system of performance measurement.)

To score well in this question, you need to address both the benefits and the problems associated with the league tables, although on balance there are actually more problems than benefits (and the relative marks available in the marking guide reflect this).

The short descriptions in the scenario of each of the four universities should also have been useful for identifying some of the problems with the proposal – for example, by raising concerns about how comparable the universities actually are. However, the more general problems of league tables (for example, in terms of motivation or behaviour – what gets measured, gets done) would also be relevant here.

Note that the solution below is, deliberately, longer than an answer that a student would be expected to write under exam conditions, in order to show the range of valid points that could have been made in response to this question.

Examining team's comments. In part (a), many candidates made good use of the three Es to structure their answers. Good answers also used the data in the scenario to illustrate the points being made.

Part (b) was answered fairly well in general, with candidates splitting their answers into two sections (benefits and problems) and illustrating their answers with specific issues relating to the universities in the scenario.

Marking scheme

		Marks
(a)	General description of three Es approach (economy, efficiency, effectiveness) in public sector organisations – up to 3 marks	
	Applications of the three Es to assess the performance of the three universities – 1 mark per relevant point – up to 12 marks	
	Total for part (a): up to 12	12

		Marks
(b)	Potential benefits from the league tables (linked to improving the universities' performance) – 1 mark per relevant point – up to 6 marks	
	Potential problems associated with the league tables – 1 mark per relevant point – up to 10 marks	
	Total for part (b): up to 13	13
	Total =	**25**

Tutorial note. The solution given below is very detailed, and is intended to give an idea of the range of relevant points which could have been made. However, candidates would not be expected to provide an answer of this length in the exam.

(a) Public sector organisations such as the Teeland universities receive all their funding from central government and do not have the generation of profit as an objective. Furthermore, their objectives such as 'improving the standard of education of the citizens of Teeland' cannot be measured in financial terms. The value for money of the universities can be assessed using the three Es framework of economy, efficiency and effectiveness.

Economy

This involves obtaining the inputs to the service at the lowest possible cost, while still maintaining the quality of the inputs. In practice, this may be difficult to do, and a reduction in cost may lead to a reduction in quality.

From the performance data given, the average annual payroll cost per member of academic staff is highest in Northcity University at $62,286 ($109m/1,750). This is 51% higher than Eastcity University, which has the lowest cost at $41,237 of the 4 universities given. The high costs in Northcity University may reflect the fact that staff there may be more highly qualified or that highly skilled, trained staff are attracted to work there because of the high standards of teaching and academic research.

A higher payroll cost per member of academic staff may not necessarily mean a particular university is not giving good value for money. The relatively high salary costs in Southcity University of $62,083 may simply reflect the higher costs of living in the capital city and so comparison between the regions may be inappropriate.

As such, there may be a conflict between this performance measure and the ability of the universities to achieve their objectives, such as to improve educational standards in Teeland. The politician's proposal to reduce salary levels for new recruits may reduce the number of appropriately qualified and skilled staff who wish to work there. This may reduce the standard of teaching and academic research and, as a result, the universities' performance against their stated objectives.

This means that focusing solely on economy would not ensure the universities achieve value for money.

Efficiency

Efficiency measures the amount of outputs relative to the amount of inputs. The number of academic staff per student may be a suitable measure, but there may be differences between universities which would make it hard to compare results.

For example, there are 10.1 (17,600/1,750) students per member of academic staff in Northcity University, which is ranked number one in the Teeland Government's provisional league table. There are 17.9 in Westcity University which is ranked much lower at 21. It would seem, therefore, that increasing the number of students relative to the number of academic staff as per the politician's proposal may reduce the performance of the universities against their stated objectives and as such will not increase value for money.

The politician's comparison with the number of students per academic staff in neighbouring Veeland may not be appropriate. Whilst the politician's assertion that educational standards are higher in Veeland may be correct, the undertaking of high quality academic research may not be a key objective of the universities there, or the quality of research may be lower than in Teeland.

Effectiveness

Effectiveness measures whether the objectives of the organisation are being met. The stated objectives of the Teeland universities are to improve the overall standard of education of citizens in Teeland, to engage in high quality academic research and to produce well-qualified university graduates to meet the needs of the graduate jobs market in Teeland.

Objective to improve the overall standard of education in Teeland

Currently, there is no direct measure of the performance of the universities' stated objectives to increase the level of education of the citizens of Teeland. The number of graduates entering graduate jobs and the results of the TSOR survey may indirectly measure the effectiveness of the universities in achieving this aim. More direct measures such as the number of students completing their studies or obtaining good results in university exams may be more appropriate.

The effectiveness of the universities in improving the standard of education should really be related to the entry requirements of each university. Westcity University is the lowest ranking of the four universities in the provisional league table and has the lowest proportion of graduates entering graduate jobs at 50% (1,750/(11,200/3.2)). It also receives the lowest amount of research funding per student at around $1,250 ($14m/11,200), but it has the lowest entry requirements, which have been relaxed to encourage students from a more diverse range of backgrounds to study there. Therefore, the improvement in educational standards relative to students' attainment on entry may be higher than the position in the league table may suggest.

Objective to engage in high quality academic research

The stated aim of the universities to engage in high quality academic research is also not currently measured. The amount of research funding received from government and other organisations by each university may indirectly reflect the quality of the research there as providers of funds for research would probably look to fund high quality research.

This measure may, however, equally reflect that some types of research are more expensive than others. Southcity University, which is successful in science and technology subjects, receives $15,592 per student compared to $5,000 in Eastcity, which specialises in arts and humanities subjects. The funding received may be more indicative of the past quality of academic research rather than future quality, or may not even reflect the quality of the research and may be high due to wastage or inefficiency. The definition of 'quality' of research is unclear.

Objective to meet the needs of the graduate jobs market

The number of graduates from each university obtaining graduate jobs each year is an indirect measure of how well each university is achieving this objective. However, the number of graduate jobs filled may simply reflect the number of students at each university and demand for graduate jobs in the economy.

Many graduates, including the most talented of them, may take graduate jobs overseas, in which case the measure of graduate jobs filled may not be a clear measure of the objective to meet the needs of the graduate jobs market in Teeland. A more precise measure of graduates entering graduate jobs in Teeland may be more appropriate. Even this may be misleading, if graduates later return from overseas to enter graduate jobs in Teeland.

The definition of what is a 'graduate' job is subjective and likely to change over time, for example, as a result of changes in the economy. This again limits the usefulness of this measure in determining whether universities have met this objective.

The TSOR survey is a measure of effectiveness reflecting a basket of measures, one of which is students' own perceptions of their future job prospects. The measures in the TSOR survey are, however, highly subjective according to individuals' personal perceptions, for example, about students' job prospects and the quality of teaching at the university. Furthermore, the survey covers a wider range of factors such as their overall satisfaction with university life. As such, this may not reflect the stated aims of the universities in Teeland. The TSOR score for Westcity University is considerably higher than for all the other universities, despite it having the lowest overall ranking.

(b) **Effect of league tables on the quality of the Teeland universities**

League tables encourage competition between universities

The publishing of league tables of the performance of the universities in Teeland should stimulate competition for high ranking between them. This should encourage them to find better ways to improve the quality of the service, achieve their performance objectives, and deliver greater value for money.

Sharing of resources may be discouraged

However, this may discourage knowledge or even resource sharing between the universities if they see themselves in competition for the best students and limited research funding. This could particularly be a problem if the university leaders were given performance targets and rewards based on their university's position in the league table. They may be encouraged to undertake 'gaming' and focus solely on their position within the league table to the detriment of other aspects of performance. This may mean the objectives for the universities overall in Teeland may not be achieved.

University leaders may focus on a narrow range of objectives

Students' overall experience of university life may be influenced by access to social, pastoral and sporting facilities.

Management time and resources may be diverted away from these important areas by focusing on a narrow range of performance objectives such as improving educational standards and high quality research in order to boost the position in the league table.

Use of league table to ensure accountability of the universities

If the performance league tables are made publicly available, for example, on the internet as they are in Veeland, this should ensure the performance of the universities is transparent. This will mean that they are held accountable by the public for the quality of service and value for money which they provide.

League tables give choices to students and staff

To be really effective, league tables should provide users of the performance data, such as the public, with the ability to make choices based on the data given. Prospective students and staff will be able to make choices about which university to study or work at according to their position in the league tables. In addition, providers of funding such as the Government will be able to identify where corrective action or additional funding may be required.

This could also be a disadvantage of using league tables, as the best students are likely to be attracted to the best universities, which are in turn likely to attract the most funding for academic research. This may cause a reduction in the overall performance of lower ranking universities, and therefore a failure of the universities as a whole to achieve the stated aim of improving educational standards in Teeland.

League tables may not reflect variation of standards at each university

There may also be considerable variation of the standards within one university, which a ranking in a league table will not address. For example, Southcity University offers courses in a variety of subjects and is particularly successful at science and technology subjects. This may mean that it achieves a high overall ranking in a league table, whereas its performance in other subjects may be weaker. For all of these reasons, the provision of league tables or performance data at a lower level, such as by subject area, may therefore be a better way to make the universities accountable to the public.

Regions may not be directly comparable

There may be inherent differences between universities which make comparison using league tables misleading or of limited value. For example, Eastcity University specialises in teaching arts and humanities. It may be inappropriate to compare it to universities offering a wide range of courses or specialising in science and technology subjects. Similarly, it may be misleading to compare universities of different sizes or in locations in different parts of Teeland. Universities which also attract students from outside Teeland, for example, those in capital or major cities, are likely to have more access to the most able students.

Due to its capital city location, Southcity University may incur additional costs of providing facilities and have to pay staff more to reflect the higher cost of living there. It may be more appropriate to produce league tables at a lower level, like within individual cities, to make the comparisons more meaningful and eliminate the effect of regional variations such as this.

There may be differences in the way different universities collect and report performance data. These problems can be reduced by the use of consistent and enforced policies for compiling performance data.

Resources required to produce league tables

Other problems relate to the targets chosen, external influences on results and cost of collating and measuring performance for the league table.

In Veeland, there is a sizeable government department dedicated to measuring performance. The cost of collecting performance data and compiling the league tables may therefore outweigh the benefits to be gained from doing so. It will use up resources which could be used, for example, in providing additional funding to the universities themselves.

Performance measures used to create league tables may be confusing and conflicting

By having a large number of targets such as in Veeland, this may cause confusion to managers, who may not know which to focus on. Similarly, it may be difficult to decide which performance measures are the most important.

Many performance measures chosen are likely to conflict. Reducing the salaries paid to academic staff may make it harder to recruit and retain experienced and well-qualified staff, which may lead to failing to meet the universities' key objectives.

Similarly, increasing the number of students per member of academic staff is unlikely to help achieve any of the universities' objectives as staff will have less time available for teaching and for engaging in high quality research.

League tables may demotivate staff and students

The Teeland politician's proposed target of a 5% annual increase in the number of students entering graduate jobs sounds very challenging and may be unrealistic. This will be especially so if accompanied by a reduction in the number of academic staff and a reduction of the salaries of new recruits. If the targets are felt to be unachievable by the university leaders, they may become demotivated, and give up on trying to achieve them altogether. This will especially be the case if this is an 'all or nothing' target. A more realistic target may at least ensure that some progress is made.

Students may also become demotivated if their university ranks poorly in league tables, even if the students themselves are satisfied with the standard of education they are receiving.

Similarly some performance measures, such as the number of students entering graduate jobs, which may be highly dependent on the economic conditions in Teeland, are not entirely under the control of the university leaders. The economic conditions in Teeland will be a key factor in determining the number of graduate jobs available there. University leaders may become demotivated by this measure as well and stop trying to improve.

The relative importance of different performance measures is subjective

The weighting of the different performance measures used by the Teeland Government in arriving at the provisional ranking of the universities is subjective. It is difficult to determine which measures are the most important, and hence how each should be weighted. The opinions of different stakeholders on which are the most important measures will also vary. Academic staff and students may view different measures as important compared to the providers of finance (the Teeland Government) and organisations which recruit university graduates.

Determining the relative importance of different performance measures in order to publish a league table is therefore difficult. Furthermore, the measures chosen, and their relative weightings, could differ from those in other countries. This would make it difficult to benchmark performance against universities in other countries, such as Veeland.

24 Herman Swan & Co

Text reference. The changing role of the management accountant, as outlined by Burns and Scapens, is covered in Chapter 1 of the BPP Study Text. Issues around branding, and brand loyalty, are discussed in Chapter 9b.

Top tips.

Part (a). In effect, the requirement for part (c) should have given you some useful context for part (a). If brand loyalty (and presumably, therefore, also customer retention) are important issues for HS, then HS needs to measure how well it is performing in these areas.

Similarly, the scenario also highlights that quality is a critical success factor (CSF) for HS. And in this respect, the link between CSFs and key performance indicators (KPIs) is a very important aspect of this requirement. HS needs to have performance measures to gauge how well it is achieving its CSFs. But can it do this by measuring financial performance alone?

Part (b). Although part (b) is presented as a single requirement (for 12 marks) there are, in effect, three components to it:

(i) Describe the changes in the role of the management accountant
(ii) Explain what is driving these changes at HS
(iii) Justify why the changes are appropriate to HS

However, a sensible way to tackle this question would be to deal with the first two components together. In other words: take each of the changes identified by Burns and Scapens, describe the changes in general terms, and then consider whether the conditions which promote the changes are present at HS. You can then give a short justification of whether the changes as a whole are appropriate after you have looked at each of the changes in turn.

Crucially, though, to score well in this question you must link the factors driving the changes specifically to HS, rather than simply discussing Burns and Scapens' factors in general terms.

Part (c). Here again, it is vital to break down the components of the requirement very carefully. You are asked to discuss the impact of both brand loyalty **and** brand awareness on the business, and you are asked to do so from the customer perspective **and** the internal business process perspective. Finally, you are asked to evaluate suitable measures for brand loyalty and awareness.

Given that there are only eight marks available for part (c) in total, though, it should be clear that you shouldn't spend too long on any single aspect of the requirement. However, it is important that you distinguish between brand loyalty and brand awareness. Brand awareness is primarily relevant to attracting **new** customers, while the main benefits of brand loyalty relate to the retention of **existing** customers.

Examining team's comments. This question was based on a company which makes fashionable clothes and leather goods. Although this question was the least popular of the Section B questions, those candidates who tackled it clearly grasped the nature of the business featured in the scenario and typically did well in the scenario-related comments and illustrations.

In part (b), most candidates demonstrated a broad grasp of the issues addressed by Burns and Scapens, and candidates did well trying to weave these into the specific circumstances at HS. However, few candidates appeared to be able to remember the detail of Burns and Scapens' report, and so their analysis often missed out on one of the three factors mentioned in the report (technology, management structure and competition).

In part (c), most candidates were able to discuss brand loyalty from a customer perspective and suggest suitable measures, but fewer were able to distinguish the internal process perspective, even though they had realised that quality was a key part of the product offering. Similarly, only the better candidates successfully differentiated between customer loyalty and awareness. However, by doing so, these candidates distinguished themselves from the rest.

Marking scheme

		Marks
(a)	Identifying the need for performance measures to support CSFs, and the non-financial aspect of CSFs – up to 3 marks For illustrating CSFs and performance measures specifically in the context of HS – up to 3 marks Total for part (a): Up to 5 marks	5
(b)	Describing Burns and Scapens' view of the overall change – up to 2 marks Up to 3 marks for identifying each of the three factors driving change (technology, management structure, competition) and illustrating them in the context of HS – up to 9 marks across the three factors For justifying why the changes are appropriate at HS, and what the benefits of them are for HS – up to 3 marks Total for part (b): Up to 12 marks	12
(c)	Describing brand loyalty and brand awareness – up to 2 marks Discussing the impact of brand loyalty and brand awareness on the business – up to 6 marks (**Note.** To score well in this part of the question, your discussion needs to include both the customer perspective and the internal business perspective.) Evaluating measures of brand loyalty and brand awareness – up to 4 marks Total for part (c): Up to 8 marks	8
	Total =	**25**

(a) **CSFs** – Historically, performance measures have tended to focus mainly on aspects of an organisation's financial performance. This may appear sensible as financial performance indicators play an important role in allowing organisations to **measure** success.

However, organisations also need to monitor the aspects of performance which **ensure** success. These aspects which ensure success are an organisation's CSFs.

Crucially, CSFs are often **non-financial in nature**:

Quality – For example, it appears that HS's continuing success is dependent on it continuing to produce high quality clothes. The company has built a strong reputation for quality, and the high quality of its clothes enables HS to charge high prices for them.

Brand loyalty – The competition HS faces has been intensifying for more than ten years, and therefore issues of brand loyalty and brand awareness are likely to become increasingly important for it. The strength of HS's brand is likely to play an important role in the company's ability to maintain (or even grow) its market share.

BPP LEARNING MEDIA

In this respect, ensuring it produces high quality clothes, and ensuring that it develops brand loyalty and brand awareness are likely to be CSFs for HS.

Performance measures – Once HS has identified its CSFs, it then has to develop KPIs to measure how well it is actually performing in these key areas of the business. If HS's performance is below target in relation to key areas, then performance will need to be improved in order for HS to remain competitive in an increasingly competitive environment.

Because the CSFs are non-financial, it follows that the KPIs used to measure them are also non-financial. For example, HS could use indicators such as the number of garments returned to help measure the quality of its clothes.

Longer-term objectives – Another reason why non-financial aspects of performance are becoming increasingly important is that they tend to have less of a short-term focus than financial performance measures.

Financial performance measurement systems often focus on annual, or short-term, performance against financial targets. However, these may not be directly linked to an organisation's longer-term objectives. For example, financial performance measures do not assess how well an organisation is meeting customer-related objectives.

However, non-financial objectives (such as achieving customer loyalty or brand loyalty) may be vital in sustaining profitability, competitiveness and other longer-term strategic goals.

(b) **Financial control role** – The traditional view of accounting is as a mechanism for control, and therefore the focus of the management accountant's role has traditionally been on financial control within an organisation.

In this traditional model, it was felt that management accountants needed to remain independent from operational managers, in order for accountants to be able to judge performance objectively and then report on it to senior management.

Business support role – However, Burns and Scapens' studies found that the primary purpose of management accounting has now changed from financial control to business support. The management accountant's role has also had to change accordingly.

In particular, instead of remaining detached from operating divisions, management accountants now need an understanding of these divisions and the commercial issues they are facing, so that, in effect, accountants can provide an internal consultancy service to the divisions.

Hybrid accountant – Burns and Scapens characterise the management accountant's new role as being that of a hybrid accountant. As such, an accountant is no longer simply a financial or numbers specialist, but also needs an understanding of the operating functions and commercial processes of their organisation. The accountant acts as a source of **business support and advice** for operational managers.

Accordingly, management accountants have become increasingly involved with the operations of their business, rather than working in a separate 'accounting department'.

Burns and Scapens state that there are three main forces for change in the role of the management accountant: changes in technology, management structure and competition.

Technology

In recent decades there have been major changes in the quality and quantity of information technology (IT) resources available in organisations.

Historically, the management accountant was one of the few people in an organisation who had access to the IT system and the information generated, because the outputs from the IT system were usually used to prepare financial reports to management. Data input was strictly controlled, and only a few people were allowed to enter data onto the IT system.

Impact of management information systems (MIS) – Now, however, MIS allow users across an organisation to run reports, providing them with the type of analysis once only provided by the management accountant. Therefore, rather than having exclusive access to information, the management accountant is simply another user of the system, in the same way that operational managers are.

This force for change is evident at HS, because the new management information system has increased the data available to all managers throughout the business.

Management structure

Changes in management structure have also affected the role of the management accountant in organisations.

Responsibility for budgeting – One of the main changes in organisations has been a shift in the responsibility for budgeting. Instead of budgets being produced by head office, and imposed on operational managers, operational managers now have greater responsibility for producing their own budgets.

This force for change is also evident at HS. The SBU managers have taken on greater responsibility for budgeting, whereas this had previously been carried out by the finance team at head office.

The increased autonomy given to the operational managers in organisations also means they have increased responsibility for managing the performance of their operations; for example, by monitoring actual performance against key financial and non-financial performance indicators, and producing revised forecasts based on current performance and trading conditions.

Producing reports – Consequently, whereas in the traditional model, the management accountant was the only person who produced performance reports for senior management, now operational managers will also be producing them.

Therefore, the nature of the reports produced by the management accountant will need to change. For example, the accountant's reports may have to try to highlight the financial consequences of the information presented in the operational reports, or may have to illustrate how operational performance is affecting the organisation's progress towards achieving its strategic goals.

Competition

Strategic focus – Burns and Scapens' project found that the management accountant's role had an increasingly commercial orientation. This change reflected organisations' own needs to respond to competition and deploy a more strategic focus to help achieve, and maintain, competitive advantage.

Traditionally, management accountants focused largely on the 'bottom line' profit figure. However, this focus on profit has subsequently been associated with a **short-term approach** to performance management.

A commercial and strategic orientation recognises the importance of an organisation's future earning capacity as well as its profit in the current period. Therefore, management accountants need to look at a wider range of performance measures to try to capture **longer-term trends** in performance and future profitability, as well as reporting on current profits.

This strategic orientation also encourages management accountants to assess an organisation's performance in the context of its wider **external environment**.

Competitive position at HS – Competition and the competitive environment is having a significant impact on the role of the management accountant at HS.

HS sells its goods across the world and its main goal is to grow the business organically for the next generation of the family. This highlights that HS isn't solely interested in short-term performance, but also has longer-term goals.

However, HS is also faced with increasing competition in its markets, and it needs to be aware of the threat from large brands which will try to dominate markets using economies of scale to their competitive advantage. Therefore, HS needs to be flexible and innovative in its response to larger competitors, but will also need to ensure it maintains the high quality of its products which could help it differentiate itself from these competitors.

Appropriateness of the changes at HS

The three main forces for change in the management accountant's role (changes in technology, management structure and competition) are all present at HS.

The changes in organisational structure (leading to SBU managers taking more responsibility for budgeting) would appear to fit particularly well with the concept of the accountant as an internal consultant. For example, the accountant could work with the operational managers to identify ways of improving how the new MIS is used, and tailoring the reports it produces to the managers' particular needs.

Equally, the accountant can play an important role in ensuring that the aspects of operational performance which the SBU managers measure are properly aligned to, and support, HS's overall strategic goals and objectives.

(c) **Brand identity** helps to convey information about the quality or price of a product or service to customers. A strong brand identity can help create customer loyalty to the brand, thereby improving customer retention rates and encouraging repeat purchases, which in turn can be a means of increasing or maintaining sales.

Brand loyalty results in a consumer consistently buying the same brand within a product class, rather than buying a range of different brands. Again, this loyalty helps to maintain sales.

Brand awareness is an indicator of the strength of a product or organisation's position in the marketplace, and in customers' minds. Whereas brand loyalty helps to retain existing customers, brand awareness is important for attracting new customers and thereby generating new revenues.

Customer perspective

Competitive advantage – From the customer perspective, HS's brand is part of its competitive advantage. Customers are attracted to HS by its history and the family story which goes behind its products. In particular, customers are willing to pay high prices because they identify with the company's values, and because HS's brand signifies a high quality of manufacturing. In this respect, branding acts as a form of product differentiation which can make it possible for HS to charge premium prices for a luxury product.

Brand loyalty – In this respect, customers' loyalty to the HS brand can help compensate for the price differential between HS's products and those of its global competitors who benefit from economies of scale.

Equally, since HS's family story is an important part of its brand, the company will need to ensure that this story is maintained, and customers remain aware of it.

Brand awareness – However, because HS is competing against global brands, awareness of HS's brand among the public at large may be lower than awareness of some of the competitor brands. This highlights the importance of marketing expenditure within HS to increase public awareness of its brand.

Marketing and promotion – While HS needs to promote itself in order to maintain brand awareness, it must also ensure that its marketing campaigns are tailored to places and media which fit with its brand story, for example by sponsoring public events attended by stylish or high income people.

However, as well as any regular marketing expenditure (reminder advertising) required to maintain HS's brand in general, it may also need one-off marketing campaigns, for example linked to the launch of specific new products.

Performance measurement – The management accountant could have an important role in monitoring the effectiveness of HS's marketing spend; for example, by trying to identify any relationships between marketing and sales growth. In particular, it could be useful to identify which marketing channels are most effective for different campaigns.

A measure such as return on marketing expenditure could be useful here: looking at the incremental revenues which are generated following different marketing campaigns.

Market segmentation – In this respect, it will also be important for HS to identify the different markets in which it operates, so that these can be segmented appropriately (for example, by age, gender, income or lifestyle), and then marketing campaigns can be specifically targeted, based on the target market, and the products or product ranges being promoted.

Internal business perspective

Quality – In order to sustain the reputation of its brand, HS needs to ensure that it maintains the high quality of both its **manufacturing** and also its **retailing** operations.

Quality in production – Since the HS brand promotes the idea of high quality, customers will be disappointed if the products they buy do not live up to their expectations. In this respect, **quality assurance**

and **quality control** will be very important for HS. Therefore, it could be useful for the management accountant to monitor the expenditure incurred in relation to preventing or detecting faulty goods in the production process. However, it will equally be important to monitor the level of customer complaints about goods which do not meet their quality standards.

Retail quality – The quality of the service customers receive in HS's shops will also shape their perception of the brand. In this respect, the amount of **training** given to staff will need to be high in order to ensure a high quality of service is offered to customers in HS's shops. In addition, there may need to be high **capital costs** in order to fit out the retail premises to the standards expected of a premium brand such as HS.

Brand loyalty – If customers continue to receive high quality goods and high quality service from HS (which meet, or even exceed their expectations), they are more likely to remain loyal to HS than if they receive products and services which do not meet their expectations.

Suitable measures

Tutorial note. The marking guide indicates that there are up to four marks available for evaluating suitable measures for brand loyalty and awareness.

The solution below includes a range of possible measures which you could have referred to in this context, but you would not have needed to include all of them to score the four marks available.

Brand loyalty

Retention rates – Brand loyalty can be measured through customer retention rates and the level of repeat purchases by customers. We would expect there to be a correlation between brand loyalty and the level of repeat purchases: the higher the proportion of HS's customers who make repeat purchases from it, the stronger the loyalty to the HS brand would appear to be.

Price elasticity of demand – Another way of measuring brand loyalty could also be to measure price elasticity of demand. If HS's customers continue to buy its products despite an increase in price, this would suggest they are loyal to the HS brand. A brand's ability to increase prices with only a relatively small reduction in demand is one of the key benefits of brand loyalty.

Profit margins – Another benefit of branding is that it could help HS charge premium prices for its products, thereby enabling it to earn higher profits than if products had to be sold at a lower price. In this respect, it would be useful to measure the profit margins HS can earn, and compare these to other companies which make similar products to HS but which don't have such a strong brand.

Brand awareness

Market share – A relatively crude way of trying to gauge customers' awareness of HS's brand would be to measure the market share that HS enjoys. If HS's market share is increasing, this should suggest that customers' awareness of the brand is also increasing.

Brand awareness surveys – A more detailed way of assessing brand awareness would be through brand awareness surveys; for example, HS could test whether customers can correctly associate the brand associated with its logos or products.

Such an exercise could be particularly useful in assessing the impact that an advertising campaign has had on brand awareness. However, given the segmentation of HS's markets, it will be important for HS to test its brand awareness in different markets.

25 Navier Aerials

Text reference. Activity-based costing in relation to cost reduction is covered in Chapter 12 of the BPP Study Text. Quality management is covered in Chapter 10.

Top tips.

Part (a). In order to evaluate the impact of using activity-based costing (ABC), compared to the existing costing system, we need to know what difference there is between the cost allocations under the two systems. Accordingly, you need to do the calculations before you can begin to evaluate the impact of any change.

Note the cost allocations should be 'per dish', not 'per order'.

Once you have done the calculations, you then need to compare the allocations under the two systems. For example, are the cost allocations similar under the two systems, or are there any significant differences? How accurate is the FD's assumption that the cost of the additional CC for specialised dishes is $100 per dish?

Remember that ABC is likely to be more time consuming than the current method. So are the cost allocations sufficiently different under the two methods to justify the extra work involved in applying the ABC method?

Part (b). Make sure you read the requirement for part (b) very carefully. Although the issues of cost reduction and quality management in the CC Department are important, the key element in the requirement relates to how **information** about the activities can be used and improved.

So, for example, whilst reducing the number of customer complaints could reduce complaint handling costs, Navier needs to know what the main reasons for customer complaints are in order for it to tackle the causes of those complaints. If Navier doesn't have any information about why customers are complaining, how can it decide what changes need to be made to its current processes?

Examining team's comments. This question was generally answered poorly, with weak efforts at handling the quantification of the two costing systems, compounded by lack of knowledge about quality issues.

Part (a) required candidates to use the partially completed calculations in the question to work out cost per dish (using the two methods for allocating overheads), and then to consider the implications of the results. Many candidates seemed perplexed that the calculations were not more difficult; and yet commonly failed to do them accurately.

In an APM question, candidates could easily be presented with data which has already been prepared (by a more junior accountant) and then be asked to complete or to assess/interpret the work done. However, candidates seemed ill-prepared for this kind of task, and for evaluating the impact of ABC on overhead absorption systems.

The scenario presented a situation which candidates could easily come across in real life. The FD has estimated the impact of different product types, and candidates were then required to do the work more accurately and comment on the results. A key question posed here – which few candidates identified – was: is the effort required to generate a more accurate overhead allocation worth the effort?

Candidates should be wary of simply **assuming** that the newer, more complex method (in this case, ABC) is the best solution in practice.

Part (b) moved from the performance measurement aspect of the scenario into the performance management implications. The question required an assessment of the information available about each of the activities, and how that information can be used – or improved – in order to help reduce cost and improve quality.

Unfortunately, most candidates displayed a weak grasp of quality cost issues, and also failed to prioritise their work towards the major cost areas of 'handling enquiries and prepared quotes' and 'complaints handling'.

Marking scheme

		Marks
(a)	Calculating the number of dishes – 1 mark	
	Calculating the standard absorption cost per dish – 1 mark	
	Calculating costs to be allocated to each dish using ABC; 1 mark per type of dish – up to 2 marks	
	For comments on the consequences of using the current costing system – 1 mark per valid point, up to 4 marks	
	For comment on the impact of using ABC – 1 mark per valid point, up to 7 marks	
	Total: up to 13	13

		Marks
(b)	For general comments on costs for each activity – 1 mark per point; up to 2 marks	
	For comments on pre-sales work and related information required – 1 mark per point; up to 2 marks	
	Complaints handling: for comments about complaints handling as a non value adding activity, and information required in relation to complaints handling – 1 mark per point; up to 4 marks	
	For potential benefits of quality management in the CC Department, and information required in relation to quality management – 1 mark per point; up to 4 marks	
	For other relevant points: 1 mark per point, up to a maximum of 2 marks	
	Total: up to 12	12
	Total =	**25**

(a) **Current absorption costing** – Under the current costing system, the total costs of the CC Department are allocated to each dish by dividing total departmental costs by the total number of dishes. Under this basis, the cost of CC per dish is $8.03. This cost is then added to the other costs incurred in the production of the dishes (such as material and labour) to obtain a total cost per dish.

Specialised dishes – The FD adds an additional $100 per specialised dish to cover the cost of CC in relation to these dishes. However, because the total costs of the CC Department have already been absorbed in the $8.03 charge, this additional charge means that CC costs will be over-absorbed. (Assuming that Navier manufactures 1,600 specialised dishes per year, the CC cost over-absorbed will be $160,000.)

ABC costing

As Navier produces two different types of product, which use different amounts of the CC Department's resources, applying ABC will enable overhead costs to be allocated to the different products more accurately.

The activity-based analysis (see Working: Costs per dish) shows that the costs of CC per standard dish should be $6.22, instead of $8.03. As a result, the profit per dish will be higher under the ABC system than under the current system.

Under the activity-based system, the CC costs attributed to each specialised dish are $106.05. It should not be a surprise that the costs attributed to the specialised dishes are so much higher than for the standard dishes because of the disproportionate amount of time spent handling enquiries, preparing quotes and dealing with complaints in relation to specialised dish orders.

Working: Costs per dish

Standard absorption cost per dish

		$
Total cost of CC Department		707,000
Number of dishes (16,000 × 5.5)	88,000	
Standard absorption cost per dish		**8.03**
FD's adjusted cost per specialised dish		**108.03**

Activity-based costs

	All orders	*Standard*	*Specialised*
Total costs ($)	707,000	537,320	169,680
Average dishes per order		6	1
Number of orders	16,000	14,400	1,600
Total number of dishes ($)		86,400	1,600
ABC absorption cost per dish ($)		**6.22**	**106.05**

The difference between the allocated CC costs of specialised and standard dishes under the activity-based system is $99.83 ($106.05 – $6.22). This appears to justify the FD's estimate, under the current system, of adding $100 to the CC costs of a standard dish in order to find the costs of a specialised dish.

However, the fact that the absorption costs of both standard and specialised dishes are lower under the ABC system than under the current system again suggests that costs are being over-absorbed under the current system. (No adjustment is being made to the basic figure of $8.03 to reflect the additional $100 costs being allocated to the specialised dishes.)

Evaluation of ABC analysis

Value-adding activities – ABC analysis enables Navier to identify the activities which are driving the higher costs of the specialised dishes.

Given the CEO's wish to be able to identify non value added activities, further analysis could then be undertaken to determine whether customers value the additional CC work associated with their bespoke dishes (and therefore whether the additional costs of almost $100 per dish add value or not). If there are any processes which do not add value for the customers, these should be removed or redesigned.

Cost benefit analysis – Although the ABC exercise has enabled costs to be allocated to the two types of product more accurately, it is debatable whether the extra effort involved in calculating the activity-based costs is worthwhile. The FD appears to have been able to estimate the costs to be allocated to the products reasonably accurately before any ABC analysis was undertaken.

If the current absorption calculations are adjusted to correct the over-absorption in relation to the specialised dishes, then the costs to be allocated per dish (see Working below) would be very similar to those proposed under the ABC system.

		$
Total cost of CC Department		707,000
Costs attributable to specialised dishes		(160,000)
General costs to apportion		547,000
Number of dishes (16,000 × 5.5)	88,000	
Standard absorption cost per dish		**6.22**
FD's adjusted cost per specialised dish		**106.22**

(b) **Cost activities**

The main cost activities in the CC Department are pre-sales (handling enquiries and preparing quotes: $282,800) and post-sale (handling customer complaints: $176,750). Together, these activities account for 65% of the total cost of the department.

Sales enquiries – The pre-sale work is vital for converting customer enquiries into firm orders. Currently just under 46% of all enquiries are converted into actual orders (16,000/35,000). Given the importance of pre-sale activities for the CC Department, it would be useful to know how effectively the department converts enquiries into orders compared to other similar departments.

In this respect, some kind of benchmarking exercise could be very useful. Navier could try to benchmark its enquiries to orders ratio against its competitors (competitor benchmarking), although its competitors may not publish this information as they may consider it to be commercially sensitive. Alternatively, Navier could monitor the number of enquiries and its own conversion rate of enquiries to orders over time (historical benchmarking).

Complaints handling – Complaints handling should be seen as a non value adding activity. Whilst dealing effectively with customer complaints is important from a relationship management perspective, it doesn't in itself add any value to the product which customers buy from Navier. Instead, complaint handling is only required where the products or services customers receive do not meet the standard they expect.

Quality management – In this respect, reducing complaint handling costs could be linked to quality management. If the quality of Navier's products is improved, this should reduce the number of customer complaints, and in turn the level of customer handling costs.

Currently there are 3,200 complaints per year in respect of 16,000 orders. Although there could be more than one complaint in relation to a single dish, this level of complaints suggests that there is a complaint in relation to approximately 20% of Navier's total orders, which seems quite a high proportion. Moreover, the level of customer complaints (**external failure costs**) suggests that there is scope for Navier to improve its internal controls so that problems can either be prevented or else detected before they reach the customer.

In order to reduce the number of complaints, Navier needs to identify what is causing them. There could be a number of different issues which lead to complaints. Some of the complaints may relate to the CC Department, while others are likely to result from the manufacturing process.

If the CC doesn't understand a customer's order correctly, the instructions it passes on to the manufacturing and installation teams are also likely to be incorrect.

Equally, although the instructions were correct, there could be problems with the work undertaken by the manufacturing and installation teams. It is not clear what level of supervision and inspection is in place, but it is possible that this needs to be increased in order to prevent and detect quality issues. In this respect, it may be beneficial for Navier to increase the level of inspection and detection costs, in order to reduce the level of non-conformance costs which would otherwise result if a dish does not meet the customers' expected standards.

Financial information – The other activities in the CC Department (such as credit checks and order processing) are administrative, and the financial information systems can provide some measures of their quality. The quality of order processing can be measured by reference to the number of invoice disputes or the value of credit notes issued. Equally, the effectiveness of Navier's credit checks can be assessed by measuring the level of bad debts incurred.

26 Tench

Text reference. Quality issues and Japanese business practices and management accounting techniques such as Kaizen costing and JIT are discussed in Chapter 10 of the BPP Study Text.

Top tips.

Part (a). A common theme across a number of areas of performance management is: 'What gets measured, gets done'. And this theme is relevant here too. If Tench starts focusing on quality and quality costs, this should help it increase the quality of its cars.

However, before you start discussing the impact of quality costs in this way, it would be sensible to explain what quality costs are. The analysis of costs into 'prevention', 'appraisal', 'internal failure' and 'external failure' costs could be a useful way of thinking about the range of quality costs which could affect Tench.

Whereas part (a) asks you to discuss aspects of Tench's current costing system, parts (b) and (c) focus on its planned new systems. In effect, then, this question as a whole is highlighting the contrast between traditional views of quality costs (part (a)) and the Japanese approaches based around the ideas of continuous improvement (Kaizen) and JIT.

Part (b) picks up on this point specifically, and a key point to note here is the distinction between cost reduction (in Kaizen costing) and cost control (in traditional approaches). However, note that there are two sub-requirements to this part of the question: the impact of Kaizen costing on: (i) Tench's costing systems, and (ii) employee management.

Part (c) then considers the related issue of moving to a JIT system. Note that you are asked to 'evaluate' the effect, so you need to consider the advantages and disadvantages of doing so. In this respect, it is important you appreciate the context in which Tench currently operates. It is based on a former communist state and still seems to have a very bureaucratic culture; how suitable is such a context for introducing JIT systems?

Part (d) then considers the related issue of TQM. This should have been a straightforward part of the question. However, time management is important here to make sure you get time to gain these easy marks.

Importantly, to score well in all four parts of this question, you need to answer the question set. Answers which simply **describe** quality costs, Kaizen costing, TQM and JIT systems in general terms will earn very few marks.

BPP LEARNING MEDIA

Marking scheme

		Marks
(a)	Impact of quality costs – 1 mark for each relevant point made, up to 4 marks	
	Use of quality costs and explanation of traditional view of quality costs – 1 mark for each relevant point made, up to 3 marks	
	Maximum of 6 marks	6
(b)	Description of Kaizen costing – up to 4 marks	
	Comparison of standard costing with Kaizen costing – 1 mark for each relevant point, up to 3 marks	
	Effect of Kaizen costing on employee management – 1 mark for each relevant point, up to 3 marks	
	Maximum of 8 marks	8
(c)	Description of JIT purchasing and production – up to 2 marks	
	Benefits of JIT for Tench – 1 mark for each relevant point, up to 2 marks	
	Problems of introducing JIT at Tench – 1 mark for each relevant point, up to 3 marks	
	Maximum of 6 marks	6
(d)	Explanation of importance of TQM – up to 2 marks for each relevant and fully explained point, up to 5 marks	5
		Total = 25

(a) **Quality costs hidden** – It is likely that Tench's quality costs are currently hidden within overheads and the standard costing system. Tench's quality costs are likely to relate to: designing and developing quality control equipment; inspection and performance testing; and repairs and reworking. The current costing system will need to be modified to allow Tench to view its quality costs separately.

The quality costs can be categorised into two groups:

Costs of conformance – These are the costs of achieving the desired quality standards.

They will include **prevention costs** (such as staff training and building quality into the design of the cars and Tench's business processes) aimed at preventing cars being rejected on the grounds of poor quality.

They will also include **appraisal costs** such as the costs of inspecting components coming in from suppliers and inspecting the cars while they are being built and once they are completed.

Costs of non-conformance – These are the costs which arise if Tench's cars do not meet the required quality standards. They will include internal failure costs and external failure costs.

Internal failure costs arise if a fault is identified before a car leaves the factory and has to be rectified. **External failure costs** arise if the fault is identified by the customer once they have bought the car. External failure costs could include both the cost of repairing cars returned from customers and the administration costs of maintaining a customer complaints department.

Opportunity costs

There could also be opportunity costs related to quality which are not currently recognised by Tench; for example, the loss of possible future sales resulting from dissatisfied customers, or the impact on the manufacturing process of having to repair faults rather than working on new cars.

Impact of quality on Tench's costing systems

Tench's management appear to have already recognised the need to focus more on the quality of their cars in order to compete with the new (foreign) entrants into the market.

However, identifying and collecting quality costs will reinforce the importance of quality, and will sustain management's focus on quality. In addition, applying the logic that 'What gets measured, gets done', the focus on quality should allow Tench to make the quality improvements it needs to compete more effectively with the new imports.

Traditional view of quality

The discussion of costs of conformance and non-conformance represents the traditional view of quality which suggests that there is an optimal effort that minimises quality faults, although it never entirely eliminates them. This approach recognises that there is a trade-off between the costs of conformance and non-conformance, up to a point where the cost of reducing the error rate any further is greater than the benefit from preventing that additional fault.

(b) **Kaizen costing** – In contrast to traditional costing systems which focus on **cost control**, Kaizen costing systems focus on **cost reduction**.

Kaizen costing involves a process of **continuous improvement** in which the costs of producing a product are constantly reduced over the product's life.

Functional analysis is applied at the design stage of a new product, and a **target cost for each function** is set. The functional target costs are added together and the total becomes the **product target cost**.

Once the product has been in production for a year, the actual cost of the first year becomes the starting point for further cost reduction in the second year, and so on into subsequent years.

Impact of Kaizen approach at Tench

Kaizen costing vs standard costing – Tench currently applies the standard costing system, where the focus is on **cost control** rather than **cost reduction**.

However, because Kaizen focuses on continuous improvement and cost reduction, standard costs have much less value for monitoring performance as they are fixed over the relevant period. However, the nature of Kaizen costing means that the 'standard' costs themselves should be reduced over time.

Therefore, the impact of introducing Kaizen costing at Tench is likely to be significant. Whereas standard costing doesn't provide any motivation to improve performance levels, the whole focus of Kaizen costing is on cost reduction and performance improvement.

Employee management

Attitude to employees – Kaizen costing will also have a significant impact on employee management at Tench, because the **management attitude to employees** will be different under Kaizen compared to a standard costing approach.

In standard costing systems, employees are often viewed as the **cause of problems** in an organisation. Under Kaizen, employees are viewed as the **source of solutions**, and they are **empowered** to find, and implement, these solutions.

Culture change – This idea of employee empowerment indicates the way that changing the costing system will also lead to a major **cultural change** at Tench. Tench appears to have a history of bureaucratic control, but now employee teams will be empowered to make changes themselves rather than having to have them approved by a management hierarchy first.

Implementing Kaizen – In time, the Kaizen system should increase staff motivation through empowerment. However, in the shorter term there could be difficulties in encouraging workers who are used to a command and control structure to change their behaviour and suggest possible improvements themselves.

(c) **Demand–pull system** – The essence of JIT systems is that they are demand–pull systems, rather than supply–push ones. Materials are only purchased (JIT purchasing), and finished products are only produced (JIT production) as needed to meet actual customer demand.

This is in contrast to traditional manufacturing systems in which manufacturers forecast demand for their products in the future and then try to smooth out production to meet that forecast demand.

Effect on Tench

Benefits of JIT systems – However, one of the main characteristics of traditional manufacturing systems is that they lead to high levels of inventory being held. By contrast, by only producing goods as they are needed, JIT systems significantly reduce **inventory levels, factory floor space required** and **reduce working capital requirements**, all of which could be beneficial to Tench.

Moving to a JIT system should also make Tench's **production processes more flexible** and should **reduce** throughput times, leading to faster response times to changes in product specification or customer demands.

Potential drawbacks of JIT systems

Supplier reliability – In order to implement JIT successfully, Tench will need to be able to rely on its supplier. With no inventories to fall back on, any disruption in supplies (in relation to either the quality or timeliness of deliveries) could force production to cease, which is likely to be costly for Tench.

If there is not already a **JIT culture** in Essland, it may be difficult for Tench to find **suppliers** who are capable of meeting the required **quality and delivery standards** needed to run a JIT system.

Performance measures

Quality measures/supplier performance – The increased importance of quality and reliability which are necessary in JIT systems means that Tench's performance measures will need to include quality measures, and will need to monitor supplier performance in delivering the quality required.

Multi-skilled teams – Another feature of JIT production is that teams are multi-skilled. Teams need to be formed to work by component or product rather than by the type of work performed. This means that **functional divisions of cost** become less appropriate. By contrast, performance measures focusing on **spare capacity** or **bottlenecks** in production are likely to become more important. Also, as staff will need training to work in the new teams, measures surrounding the **amount and effectiveness of training** will be required.

(d) **JIT systems incorporate:**

(i) **JIT production**, which is a system driven by demand for finished products so that work in progress is only processed through a stage of production when it is needed by the next stage. The result is **minimal** (or in some cases non-existent) **inventories of work in progress and finished goods**.

(ii) **JIT purchasing**, which seeks to match the usage of materials with the delivery of materials from external suppliers. This means that **material inventories** can be kept at **near-zero levels**.

Production management within a JIT environment therefore needs to **eliminate scrap and defective units** during production and **avoid the need for reworking of units**. **Defects stop** the **production line**, creating **rework** and possibly resulting in a **failure to meet delivery dates** (as **buffer inventories** of work in progress and finished goods are **not held**). **TQM** should ensure that the **correct product** is made to the **appropriate level of quality** on the **first pass through production**.

For JIT purchasing to be successful, the organisation must have confidence that the **supplier** will **deliver on time** and will deliver **materials of 100% quality**, and that there will be no rejects, returns and hence **no consequent production delays**. This confidence can be achieved by **adopting supplier quality assurance schemes** and stringent **procedures for acceptance and inspection of goods inwards**, which are integral parts of TQM.

27 Pitlane

Text reference. Target costing and Kaizen costing are discussed in Chapter 10 of the BPP Study Text.

Top tips.

Part (a). Although we often tell you that the majority of the marks in Advanced Performance Management relate to analysis and evaluation, calculations are still an important part of performance management – and therefore you should still expect there to be some calculations in the exam. All 6 of the marks for part (a) of this question relate to calculation.

The calculations themselves should not be difficult, but you need to work carefully through the scenario and the Appendices to gather relevant information; for example, a 15% net profit margin is required (fourth paragraph of the scenario); and there is a 10% uplift on the basic price (Appendix 1).

Note that you are asked to calculate the gap for each of the three years, so it would be sensible to lay out your answer in a three column format, with one column for each year.

You should then be able to slot in the relevant figures, in a format something like this:

Price	x
Margin required	(x)
Target cost	x
Expected cost	(x)
Cost gap	**x**

Part (b). The process of calculating the cost gap in part (a) should have reminded you how the process of target costing works:

- Set an acceptable price
- Determine the required margin
- Derive the cost

Thinking about these general principles could be a useful starting point for tackling this requirement. But note the requirement asks you to 'Advise on the extent to which target costing could help...' so, as well as the potential benefits of target costing, you also need to identify factors which could reduce the extent to which it could help.

For example, identifying a target cost up front will allow management to Pitlane's managers to assess whether Booster can be produced for that price. If it can't, are there any ways to reduce cost?

However, the target cost ultimately depends on the price set. How does the uncertainty over price (for example, Pitlane's ability to charge 10% more than its competitors) affect the extent to which target costing could help Pitlane achieve the 15% net profit margin required by the shareholders?

Part (c). A useful starting point here might be to think about key features of Kaizen costing – continuous improvement – and then identify how this could be important for the Booster project. For example, Appendix 1 shows that average price is expected to fall over the three years, so Pitlane will also need to reduce costs to maintain the 15% profit margin.

The penultimate paragraph in the scenario also identifies that 'staff have never been encouraged to suggest any ways to improve the manufacturing process.' How would this situation be different under a Kaizen costing approach?

Examining team's comments.

Part (a) required a basic calculation of the cost gap. Many candidates scored well on this part. However, a significant number chose to present their answers using absolute figures rather than 'per unit'. This is not only a failure to answer the question requirement, but it also illustrates a lack of understanding about the application of the method, where per unit calculations are most helpful.

Part (b). Candidates scored reasonably well on this part but often failed to score as many marks as they could because they did not analyse all the problems areas mentioned in the scenario. The scenario will often provide hints of areas to consider in an answer, and good candidates use these to efficiently compile high marks in the longer parts of questions.

Tutorial note. The Examining team's comment about using the hints in the scenarios is a very important piece of advice which applies to many, if not all, of the scenario questions in Advanced Performance Management.

Marking scheme

		Marks
(a)	Calculations:	
	Estimated unit selling price – 1 mark	
	Less: 15% net profit – 1 mark	
	Target total cost per unit – 1 mark	
	Less: Fixed cost per unit – 1 mark	
	Target direct cost per unit – 1 mark	
	Cost gap – 1 mark	
	Total for part (a): up to 6	6
(b)	General description of target costing – up to 2 marks	
	Advice on target costing for Pitlane – 1 mark per relevant point	
	Comments about additional revenue generated from features – up to 2 marks	
	Total for part (b): up to 12	12
(c)	General description of Kaizen costing – up to 2 marks	
	Advice on using Kaizen costing at Pitlane – 1 mark per relevant point	
	Total for part (c): up to 7	7
		Total = 25

(a) **Calculate cost gap for each of the three years of the Booster's life**

	20X8	*20X9*	*20Y0*
	$	$	$
Basic selling price	180.0	170.0	160.0
10% uplift for features/packaging	18.0	17.0	16.0
Estimated selling price	198.0	187.0	176.0
Less: 15% net profit	(29.7)	(28.1)	(26.4)
Target cost per unit	168.3	159.0	149.6
Current expected cost			
Estimated total direct cost per unit	134.0	134.0	134.0
Estimated fixed cost per unit (see Working)	44.1	44.1	44.1
Estimated total cost per unit	178.1	178.1	178.1
Cost gap	**9.8**	**19.2**	**28.5**

Working: Fixed cost per unit

Fixed overhead cost per unit = Total fixed overheads/Number of units sold
= $10,000,000/227,000
= $44.05

(b) **Tutorial note.** The solution for part (b) is a detailed solution showing the range of relevant points which could have been included, for tutorial purposes. Candidates were not expected to produce a solution as detailed as this.

Target costing

Pitlane currently operates a traditional cost plus pricing method, where customers pay a fixed mark up on Pitlane's standard cost. This has been appropriate because the components currently produced have been manufactured in the same way for some time and their cost structure is well understood. Actual costs of production are very close to the standard costs. There is little competition in the market for Pitlane's current products, as a long-term contract was recently renewed with its biggest customer.

In contrast, for the proposed Booster product, the market price is only estimated. To compete with similar products, the Booster will need to sell at a price reflecting that of competitors' products, taking into account the different benefits and quality which each product has.

Target costing begins with taking the price which the market will pay for the product for a given market share. From that, the required profit margin is deducted to arrive at a target cost. The difference between the estimated cost for the product and the target cost is the cost gap. Where the estimated costs exceed the target cost, steps are taken to reduce the cost gap. The product can then be sold at a price which the market will accept, and which generates an acceptable profit margin.

Determining the market price

Pitlane's marketing department has estimated the average market price of competitors' products and the likely market share over the three years of the scheme. The estimates are based on the success of a similar scheme in Veeland, and the assumptions used could be incorrect. Electricity prices may already be higher in Veeland than in Deeland, meaning consumers there would reduce their energy costs more by installing solar panels. Similarly, consumers in Veeland could save more on energy costs if there is more sunshine there than in Deeland, enabling solar panels to generate more energy. Both factors would, in this case, reduce the take up of subsidies by consumers in Deeland and the amount they would be willing to pay for solar panels.

The domestic solar energy market is new in Deeland, and Pitlane has no experience in estimating market share or price for this type of product. Pitlane's belief that consumers would be willing to pay a 10% premium for highest quality packaging, or for the Booster to communicate with consumers' mobile phones, may be incorrect.

Calculating the target cost using the required profit margin

Pitlane charges a 15% profit margin on its existing projects. The shareholders' financial objective indicates that they require the same profit margin to be earned on Booster.

For its existing products, Pitlane can set a selling price based on its own costs, whereas the Booster's price must reflect external market conditions more closely. Target costing will focus Pitlane on the external environment by considering prices and relative benefits of competitors' products.

Estimating the total costs of Booster

The total direct costs of Booster have been estimated at $134.00. The fixed overhead per unit relating to Booster for the three years of the scheme is $44.05, making total estimated costs per unit of $178.05. The cost estimates may be incorrect, especially as Booster is new, and different from Pitlane's existing products. As Booster includes costs which are fixed, estimating sales volumes is also crucial in determining costs per unit.

Pitlane has no recent experience of developing new products or of estimating costs and sales volumes for them. This makes it more likely that the cost estimates for the Booster will be incorrect. Estimating the total costs is needed for the next stage in the target costing process, to identify the cost gap.

Reducing the cost gap

A big advantage for Pitlane of using target costing is that it is often easier to reduce costs of a product at the design stage rather than after it has entered production.

As Boosters are not sold directly to consumers, the buyers of the product, who are professional installers, may not see value in the highest quality packaging. This could be a significant yet unnecessary cost, to be eliminated at the design stage. In deciding what costs to eliminate, Pitlane will have to take into account the effect of these on the quality and perception of the final product.

The features where the Booster can communicate with consumers' smartphones, and the use of highest quality packaging, are believed to enable Pitlane to charge 10% more than competitors' products. The $3.8m (see Working below) of estimated additional total revenue from the packaging and smartphone features may not justify the $2.8m upfront development costs for the smartphone feature alone, especially if the time value of money were to be taken into account. Consumers may not value these two features or be prepared to pay more for them. Eliminating them would therefore have little effect on sales volumes and would enable Pitlane to charge a more competitive price, or obtain higher gross profit margins.

Due to damage of sub-components when assembling the prototype, the estimated assembly labour cost assumes highly skilled labour will be used. This is 30% more expensive than other labour. By providing additional training, lower paid labour could be used to produce the Booster, and hence reduce the cost gap.

Pitlane plans to purchase the four main sub-components in bulk from six different suppliers. Consolidating suppliers, or using suppliers in lower cost countries, could help reduce the cost gap by reducing purchase costs. Moving to a just-in-time (JIT) production system, rather than buying supplies in bulk, would help reduce costs of holding inventory as suppliers would only deliver sub-components when needed. This may increase other costs such as by requiring investment in information technology. It would also take time to develop the close relationship required with suppliers.

Another source of waste is due to internal transport and handling, which forms over 5% of the total direct cost of the Booster. This will also increase production cycle times, and is an unnecessary process which does not add value. It could be eliminated by changing the layout of the factory, or reorganising production into teams and ensuring all production was done at a single factory, rather than in both of Pitlane's factories.

Working: Additional revenue from smartphone feature and highest quality packaging

20X8: 60,000 units × $198 = $11,880,000
20X9: 75,000 units × $187 = $14,025,000
20Y8: 92,000 units × $176 = $16,192,000

Total revenue (over 3 years) = $42,097,000

10% premium = $42,097,000 × 10/110 = $3,827,000

(c) **Kaizen costing**

Unlike target costing, which occurs at the beginning of a product's life, Kaizen costing is a process of long-term continuous improvement by cost reduction throughout the life of the product.

The Booster will be produced only for the three years during which the Deeland Government offers subsidies and tax incentives. Generally, Kaizen costing is used over longer periods, and it is likely the full benefits of this approach will not be achieved in such a short timescale. The target cost is the starting point for Kaizen costing. After production begins, each period's target is based on the previous period's reduced costs.

Target costing can achieve large cost reductions at the design stage of the product, eg by choosing not to develop the smartphone feature. Kaizen costing, however, reduces costs in much smaller, incremental steps.

The need for continuous improvement

Even though Booster's share of the market rises over the three years of the project, the market price falls, as does the size of the market. This means that in order to achieve the shareholders' financial targets, the direct costs of the Booster must fall over the three years. Continual incremental improvements using Kaizen costing, and measuring these improvements against targets from the previous period rather than the original estimated cost, could help to achieve this.

Ways to reduce waste using Kaizen costing

Traditional costing methods often see employees as the cause of high costs, whereas Kaizen costing sees the employees as a source of ideas on how to reduce costs. The Manufacturing Director's comments, that the damage caused by employees to delicate sub-components may mean it may not be possible to produce the Booster, indicates that Pitlane is currently following the traditional approach. Employees are seen as the source of the waste.

To benefit from Kaizen costing, Pitlane must undergo a culture change to encourage employees to suggest ideas, perhaps using quality circles, to reduce costs. That way, improvements could be made in the way sub-components are assembled during production, which would shorten the production cycle and lead to a reduced cost of scrapped items.

28 Thebe

Text reference. Quality issues and Six Sigma are considered in Chapter 10 of the BPP Study Text.

Top tips.

Part (a). The scenario highlighted that customer service is likely to be key to helping the business grow. However, the absence of any non-financial information in the performance report presented to the board suggests that the board isn't monitoring customer service levels.

You should have identified that this seems odd, given the importance of customer service to the business's success. But, if the non-financial performance information was included in the performance report alongside financial information, this would help redress the balance.

Parts (b) and (c) of this question provide a good illustration of why it is important to read all the requirements before starting to answer a question.

In **part (b)** of the question you are asked to discuss the general ways in which Six Sigma could help improve quality. You shouldn't spend time discussing **how** Six Sigma is implemented in this part of the question, but rather how the process of implementing Six Sigma (in general terms) improves the quality of performance in an organisation.

The reason why you shouldn't discuss how Six Sigma is implemented in part (b) becomes clear when you look at part (c) of the requirement: to explain and illustrate how the DMAIC method could be applied at Thebe.

Part (c). A sensible approach to this question would be to use 'DMAIC' as the framework of your answer, and then to work through each of the elements (Define, Measure etc) in turn.

However, note that you aren't asked simply to explain DMAIC in general terms, but to illustrate how it could be applied specifically at Thebe, so make sure you include examples of issues from the scenario.

Examining team's comments. Part (b) was poorly answered, with much evidence of candidates trying to use DMAIC as a template for their answer, although the question asked about the Six Sigma method in general rather than a specific implementation method. This was possibly caused by candidates not reading the whole question before starting to plan their answer, and not identifying the links between parts (b) and (c).

Marking scheme

		Marks
(a)	1 mark per relevant point up to 2 marks for each benefit of non-financial performance measures evaluated	
	Up to 8 marks	8
(b)	1 mark per relevant point up to 2 marks for each way Six Sigma can improve performance	
	Up to 8 marks	8
(c)	Up to 3 marks for each stage of the DMAIC process; being 1 mark for a general description and 2 marks for application to the scenario	
	Up to 9 marks	9
	Total =	25

(a) **Importance of non-financial measures** – The CEO has identified that customer service is crucial in growing the business and differentiating it from competitors (such as FayTel) which suggests that providing excellent customer service is a critical success factor for Thebe.

By performing well in this area of the business, Thebe should be better placed to perform well financially than if it offers poor customer service.

In this case, there would seem to be a clear link between non-financial performance and financial performance. However, if the board is not aware of how well Thebe is performing in key operational (non-financial) areas of the business they may not notice performance issues which could subsequently have an impact on Thebe's financial performance.

What gets measured gets done – Thebe's employees and line managers are likely to pay more attention to those areas of the business in which performance is being measured, compared to those areas which are not being measured.

Similarly, there is a danger that what doesn't get measured, might not get done. The focus of the board meetings, on financial performance, suggests that this might be prioritised over non-financial aspects of performance.

However, the fact that the CEO has championed the project to improve billing accuracy suggests that he believes it is important. In turn, however, this suggests Thebe should be measuring its performance in relation to billing accuracy – for example, through measuring the number of complaints it receives from customers who are complaining that they have been billed incorrectly.

Information for decision making and control – The current position suggests that it could be difficult for the board to know how to improve Thebe's performance, if it does not have adequate information about its current performance. Although the CEO is aware that all telephone businesses (including Thebe) have problems in relation to applying incorrect tariffs, it seems unlikely that he will have any actual information about how Thebe is performing in this area of the business.

Again, having this information would have been useful before deciding to undertake the project to improve the quality and accuracy of billing – both to decide whether the project was necessary and to see how much impact the project has on the quality of Thebe's billing.

Linkages – However, directors will need to be careful which non-financial measures they choose to monitor, and in particular how the non-financial measures link to Thebe's financial performance. For example, there will be little value in monitoring aspects of operational performance which add little value to Thebe's financial performance. Indeed, the CEO may find that, ultimately, customers choose their telephone provider based on price rather than the quality of customer service they receive.

In this respect, it is also important that the directors continue to monitor financial performance as well as non-financial performance, because there is no guarantee that favourable performance in customer service or other non-financial areas will necessarily translate into favourable financial performance. For example, even though Thebe may provide its customers with accurate bills, and may provide a very high level of customer service, its revenues may still fall if FayTel introduces new tariffs so that customers can get a cheaper phone service by switching to them.

Despite the increased importance of non-financial performance measures, the ultimate measure of Thebe's performance will be how well it generates financial value for its owners.

(b) **Focus on the customer** – One of the key aspects of Six Sigma methodology is that it requires organisations to have a genuine focus on the customer. Thebe's CEO has clearly identified that customer service is crucial to the success of the business, and so the project to improve customers' bills is an important element of this.

Importance of facts and data – Another important element of Six Sigma is that it highlights that decisions should be taken on the basis of facts and data, rather than intuition, and this in turn highlights the importance of performance measurement.

This is evident at Thebe in the way that data has been sourced from customer feedback. This data could relate, for example, to the number of customer complaints, or to customer satisfaction ratings.

Business process improvement – One of the key themes in Six Sigma is that processes are the key to success. Therefore implementing Six Sigma will encourage Thebe to identify which processes (and which activities within a process) are critical to its success, so that it can then focus on understanding those processes and improving them where necessary.

Involvement of management – When an organisation commits to Six Sigma, it will normally appoint an implementation leader and a steering committee at a senior level, to oversee the implementation. By involving management in this way it highlights a business's commitment to improving quality; as appears to be the case at Thebe where the CEO is championing the project to improve service quality.

Increased profile of quality issues – Six Sigma project teams are made up of staff experienced in the process under review. By involving team members in the project, they will realise the importance of quality issues, and improve their knowledge of quality management.

The nature of Six Sigma **project leadership** means that managers should learn from working with layers of trained experts. For example, line managers who are 'Green Belts' helping to lead a Six Sigma project can learn from 'Master Black Belts'.

Collaboration – Another key theme in Six Sigma projects is the need for collaboration between staff from across different departments or divisions within an organisation. In this way, Six Sigma implementation highlights the importance of the whole organisation focusing on quality, not just individual departments. For example, the project team at Thebe brings together line managers from all three business units, as well as from the billing department.

(c) **Define customer requirements/Define the problem**

Customers' underlying requirement is that they are billed accurately, and if they aren't this could lead either to delayed revenue (while the customers dispute their bills) or lost revenue (if customers switch to an alternative provider).

However, the organisational structure at Thebe highlights that this project also needs to focus on complaint handling as well as billing itself, and in this respect customer requirements may need to be defined further. It is likely that there will be a minimum acceptable level of service (for example, that billing errors are corrected), but Thebe should identify ways which its customers feel would improve its service above that minimum level: for example, in relation to how quickly any complaints are responded to; or by offering some form of compensation as a goodwill gesture.

Measure existing performance

The CEO's customer service project has highlighted two key areas of focus: the accuracy of customers' bills, and the handling of complaints.

BPP LEARNING MEDIA

Accordingly, Thebe needs information to assess how well it is performing in both of these areas; so it needs to measure its performance in both areas. For example, Thebe could measure the number of customer complaints per million bills issued, or the average time it takes to resolve a customer complaint fully. (Measures such as looking at the number of complaints links directly to Six Sigma methodology which identified that there should be less than six defects per million.)

However, when selecting the aspects of performance to measure, it is important that Thebe focuses on those areas where improvement will be valued by the customer, rather than, for example, areas which are easy to measure.

Analyse the existing process

In part (a) we identified that the Six Sigma methodology highlights the importance of facts and data, rather than intuition. This stage of the DMAIC process focuses on collecting the data, which can then be analysed to identify the root causes of problems in Thebe's existing processes.

Thebe can then focus its improvements towards those issues which lead to the most problems (complaints). If a relatively small number of problems give rise to the majority of complaints, then this will highlight the importance of tackling the causes of those problems as the most urgent priority. For example, if a large proportion of customer complaints relate to the length of time it takes Thebe to issue revised bills, then it will be important to analyse what factors are slowing down the process.

Improve the process

Once the causes of problems have been analysed, Thebe should then be able to identify potential changes which could be made to improve performance in these areas of its business. For example, in relation to the time taken to reissue corrected bills, Thebe may need to consider whether it needs more staff to be authorised to make changes to bills.

However, before any specific improvements are recommended it will be important for Thebe to check that they are feasible; for example, that they will not be prohibitively expensive to implement, and that Thebe has the resources necessary to implement them.

Control the process

Once the improvements have been implemented, the line managers (and the board) need to continue to monitor performance to ensure that the benefits from reduced complaints and improved customer satisfaction are maintained.

At an operational level, Thebe can do this by continuing to monitor complaint numbers – perhaps by means of exception reporting, so that managers are only alerted of a potential issue if the number of complaints increases above a specified threshold level.

However, Thebe can also measure its success in relation to customer service levels more generally in relation to customer retention rates or the churn rate (the percentage of existing customers lost each year).

If the company has successfully improved its performance in those areas which customers value as important, then the number of customers who switch to another service provider should be reduced. This in turn will mean that a greater proportion of the new customers which Thebe acquires will contribute to growing the business rather than replacing lapsed existing customers.

29 Posie

Text reference. Quality management and Six Sigma are discussed in Chapter 10 of the BPP Study Text. Information requirements for responsibility centres are discussed in Chapter 6a, while performance reports are discussed in Chapter 6b.

Top tips.

Part (a). Arguably the most important words in the requirement are 'could be implemented'. This is because they indicate that the advice you need to give the board is about how the project could be implemented; not how Six Sigma could help Posie to reduce the level of returns from customers.

The specific reference in the requirement to the 'DMAIC' methodology should help you structure your answer. If you use each of the five elements of 'DMAIC' as headings to provide a framework for your answer, you can then assess the activities which Posie needs to undertake at each phase of the project.

Note, however, that the marking scheme indicates that there were more marks available for advice given in relation to the 'define' and 'measure' phases of DMAIC than for the other three. The CEO's concerns about the quality of Posie's data should have alerted you to the fact that 'measurement' of performance is currently an issue at Posie. This, in turn, is reflected in the marking scheme – where up to six marks are available for advising on the 'measure' phase of DMAIC.

Part (b) (i). The last paragraph of the scenario sets up the context for this requirement – identifying that the data generated by Posie's current IT systems isn't sufficient to identify which responsibility centres are the root cause of the problem of customer returns. This reference should highlight the need to produce performance information at a responsibility centre level.

However, the requirement is not only about responsibility centres; you should also think more generally about the qualities of good performance reports (eg level of detailed provided, timeliness) and whether the current returns data enables Posie's management team to manage returns effectively.

Part (b) (ii). It should be obvious that re-designating the overseas subsidiaries as revenue centres means that their managers will only be held accountable for their revenue (rather than for revenues and costs, as they currently are). Hence, performance data will need to focus on revenues. However, simply stating this one point is only likely to earn you one mark (and there are up to four marks available here). So, you also need to think more widely here: for example, even though the divisional managers' focus will be on revenue, there will still be costs associated with operating the subsidiaries. How will these be recorded and controlled?

Examining team's comments. The standard of candidates' responses to part (a) was mixed, but responses to part (b) were, generally speaking, quite poor.

Part (a) asked how a Six Sigma project could be implemented using DMAIC methodology. The use of DMAIC methodology was central to this requirement but some candidates demonstrated little knowledge about how it worked. These candidates scored very few, if any, marks.

Candidates who explained the DMAIC methodology scored a few marks, but the majority of the marks in this question were earned by applying the methodology to the scenario. One of the main shortcomings in many answers was a failure to recognise properly how to relate the data given to each part of the methodology (ie define, measure, analyse, improve, control) and how this all connected to customer requirements and expectations.

Part (b) (i) was answered poorly overall, as many candidates did not read the requirement properly and offered responses which considered the impact that identifying and improving the level of customer returns could have on the organisation's performance. Such responses scored few marks, because the question asked specifically about the impact on the organisation's information requirements.

The impact of Six Sigma projects and a DMAIC methodology on information requirements can be fundamental – in particular, in relation to the 'measure' and 'analyse' aspects of DMAIC.

More generally, candidates sitting APM need to be aware of the impact that new initiatives or developments could have on the information requirements in an organisation. For example, if a project is introduced, what information will be required to measure its performance? Can the organisation's systems provide the information required? How will the information be captured?

Part (b) (ii) was also answered very poorly. Few candidates attempted this question in a meaningful way, and many failed to differentiate between the two types of responsibility centre.

Marking scheme

			Marks
(a)		Use of DMAIC Define – 1 mark per point – up to 4 marks Measure – 1 mark per point – up to 6 marks Analyse; Improve; Control – 1 mark per point – up to 3 marks for each heading Total for part (a): up to 15	15
(b)	(i)	Definition of responsibility centres – 1 mark Impact on information requirements of the need for greater detail about customer returns – 1 mark per relevant point; up to a maximum of 6 Total for part (b) (i): up to 6	6
	(ii)	Impact on information requirements due to the re-designating overseas subsidiaries as revenue centres – 1 mark per relevant point; up to a maximum of 4 Total for part (b) (ii): up to 4	4
		Total =	**25**

(a) The DMAIC process is a technique used to implement Six Sigma to improve existing processes. It is split into five phases as described below.

Define the problem

The CEO is concerned that the increase in returns from customers is increasing costs and threatens to affect the Posie brand.

Six Sigma focuses closely on the requirements of the customer, and it is important for Posie to be clear exactly what customers' requirements are, and specifically why products are returned.

The objective of the project needs to be clear – in this case to reduce the number of customer returns.

Customers will expect certain minimum requirements from the manufacturing and packaging process, for example, that they can assemble the furniture properly and all the necessary components for them to be able to do this are included in the box. Customers will also expect the goods to be delivered undamaged within a reasonable time, and at the time and date promised when the order was placed. Customers' perceptions of quality should correspond to the price paid, though different customers will have different expectations of this.

Beyond this basic requirement, there may be aspects of the manufacturing product which further enhance the customers' experience of the product, and presumably of the Posie brand. Customers may be particularly pleased with furniture which is delivered early or at a time especially convenient to them, or which is robust, durable and 'well made'. These perceptions are subjective, and may equally relate to design or the quality of raw materials as to the manufacturing process. By identifying where the products exceed customers' expectations, it may be possible to focus more on these aspects in the future. While products which significantly exceed customers' expectations will enhance the Posie brand, it may also indicate a quality of manufacture which is too high and allow Posie to reduce manufacturing costs in accordance with its cost leadership strategy whilst still having mainly satisfied customers.

Measure the existing process

The current returns figures do give some data to as to why products are returned, but their usefulness is limited as it is unclear which of the categories relate to defective manufacture, and which relate to activities of other divisions. The ambiguity of the data and category definitions will need addressing to enable the process to be measured effectively.

Returns in Category 1 could be because the goods were not manufactured or packed properly in the Manufacturing Division, but could also be due to poor design, or customers losing components or simply being unable to assemble furniture.

Damaged goods in Category 2 probably do not arise because of defective manufacturing either, though customers may wrongly categorise defective goods as damaged. For the other categories it is less clear. Though goods may become damaged by the distribution company, it seems that only a small number of returns relate directly to them.

Returns in Categories 3 and 4 could be due to defective manufacture or if the customer had simply changed their minds and no longer wanted the product. In Category 3, the identification of 'defective' items is too broad.

Returns in Category 5 which arrived late are clearly not due to manufacturing defects and, as this causes only 2% of returns, is relatively insignificant.

Currently 10% of Posie's sales are of products from other manufacturers. There is no indication from the data given how many of the returns relate to these products, nor of the total number of returns relative to the number of items sold.

Therefore the existing data are insufficient to reliably measure existing performance and take no account of inputs such as raw materials. Only items which customers value should be measured. The CEO has suggested more detailed data are required, for example, on overall customer satisfaction with the manufacturing, but this is at 93% which already seems high and there is little point in incurring costs to measure what customers are already satisfied with. In the context of the Six Sigma project at Posie, there is little that can be done to improve this particular area and such items should not be measured.

Analyse the process

This stage is where the root causes of the problems are identified. Additional information may be needed, for example, to analyse customer returns by type of product, by country of sale or with a clearer definition of what is meant by 'defective'. By doing so, Posie may identify areas of the business where customer returns are particularly high and so be able to focus on these.

Improve the process

At this stage the proposals for improving the process are implemented and availability of resources and likely costs of making the improvements need to be carefully considered. Posie may need to consider which aspects of the production or packaging process could be improved, for example, by better maintenance or calibration of machinery. Additional training of staff may also be required.

Control

This is the ongoing monitoring that the reduction in customer returns due to defective manufacturing is being maintained. Reporting on the number of returns may be done by exception if they reach a particular level. In Posie, it seems likely that the data on customer returns used to manage this process will need to be redesigned to make it clearer in which responsibility centre the problems arise. The ongoing monitoring may indicate that some of the earlier stages in the DMAIC process need to be revisited.

(b) (i) The CEO wants to identify which responsibility centres are the root causes of the problem of customer returns. A responsibility centre is a part of the business where a manager has specific authority and accountability for its performance and so Posie will need information relating to aspects of performance specific to the centre. For example, performance data relating to the reasons for customer returns need to be clearly segregated between responsibility centres. Currently, the information compiled on customer returns does not do this and some categories of return may result from manufacturing defects but some will be from problems outside the Manufacturing Division, or even outside Posie itself, for example, from poor quality raw materials purchased externally, or because of late deliveries or damaged goods caused by the distribution company.

Once information has been analysed and responsibility has been identified, then the managers of those areas will need the information drilled down into even further, as in order to improve they need to know which specific areas they can control. It would be unfair to make managers responsible for

BPP LEARNING MEDIA

aspects of performance which they are unable to control, and the board member responsible for manufacturing quality has recently resigned because of this.

Posie needs to ensure it produces performance data to an appropriate level of detail so as not to overload the users with too much data. For board level reporting, the information in the current board reporting pack may be too detailed and it would be sufficient just to produce summary data on the overall level of returns relative to sales. Responsibility centres would need much more detailed information, perhaps even down to product or production line level.

However, Posie should also consider the costs and resources required to provide more detailed performance data. Given Posie's cost leadership strategy, the costs of data collection may outweigh the benefits of doing so.

Performance data should be provided at an appropriate frequency. For the Posie main board, monthly reporting may be sufficient to alert them to any problems. Responsibility centres will need much more frequent, even daily or weekly, details of the levels of customer returns so that they can react quickly to any problems identified. At the moment, the returns data are compiled every six months, possibly due to the difficulties in obtaining data from the IT systems in the overseas businesses. Even for a board level report, this seems much too infrequent.

(ii) At the moment, the overseas subsidiaries are being designated as profit centres and managers will be held accountable for both revenues and costs. As they do not manufacture, it seems reasonable to designate them as revenue centres. As such, managers would be held accountable for just revenues as they have little or no control over costs as most goods for resale are purchased from the Manufacturing Division.

The performance data produced by Posie's subsidiaries' IT systems will therefore switch to focus more on revenues rather than costs. As revenue centres they may well have some freedom to change selling prices. Posie will need to ensure the subsidiaries have information to monitor the impact of different pricing strategies and will need to provide the management of these subsidiaries with information gleaned from the external environment. It will be important to evaluate competitors' pricing strategies when making pricing decisions.

A potential problem with providing only performance data relating to revenue is that managers could focus too much on achieving revenue targets rather than maintaining or improving profitability. As they are autonomous subsidiaries, there will be aspects of their own costs, such as staffing costs and other overheads, which they will be able to have some control over. It is important that Posie ensures the management still has sight of this information to ensure that such costs are still controlled effectively.

Furthermore, if the overseas managers are only held responsible for sales, this may mean they do not focus sufficiently on addressing reasons why goods are returned, and so levels of returns may increase. This means that once Posie undertakes the exercise to identify the root causes of the returns from customers, this information is shared and monitored.

Posie needs to be aware of these issues when determining information requirements if the reclassification of the subsidiaries goes ahead. It will not be as simple as assuming that they will now only need information on revenues.

30 Albacore

Text reference. Controllability and accountability are discussed in Chapters 3, 6a and 11 of the Study Text. Performance management styles are discussed in Chapter 11.

Top tips.

Part (a). The scenario identifies that the budget in Albacore is imposed by the corporate centre and a number of costs are also controlled centrally. However, in terms of assessing a shop manager's performance, is it fair to assess them on factors they cannot control?

The current branch information measures the shop's performance, rather than the manager's performance. How would the branch information for the Tunny branch be different if it only included factors the manager could control? This should suggest the improvements you could make to the report in relation to the second part of the requirement – drafting an improved report.

Importantly, though, note that part (a) is **not** asking you to assess the performance of the branch manager; it is asking you to assess the **suitability of the information** as a means of appraising the shop manager's performance.

Part (b). In effect, there are three component parts to this requirement: (i) analyse the performance management style; (ii) evaluate the current performance appraisal system; and (iii) suggest suitable improvements to the reward system for the shop managers. To score well here, you need to address all the different parts of the requirement.

Marking scheme

		Marks
(a)	Calculation and discussion of operation and planning variances – 1 mark per point, up to a maximum of 4	
	Discussion of other variances – 1 mark per point, up to 2	
	For highlighting the importance of measuring controllable costs – 1 mark	
	Revised performance report distinguishing controllable and non-controllable costs – 1 mark	
	For highlighting the importance of controllable profit as a measure of the manager's performance – 1 mark	
	Total: up to 8 for suitability of existing report	
	Alternative report – highlighting controllable costs, controllable profit – Up to 3	
	Comments on report – including controllability, realistic budgets – 1 mark per point, up to 3	
	Total: up to 5 for alternative report and justifications for changes	
	Total: up to 13	13
(b)	Analysis of performance management styles – 1 mark per relevant point, up to a maximum of 6	
	Evaluation of performance appraisal system – 1 mark per relevant point, up to a maximum of 6	
	Total: up to 12	12
	Total =	**25**

(a) **Accountability** – The managers should only be held responsible for those aspects of performance they can control. However, the branch information does not appear to distinguish between the factors that the shop managers can control and those they can't, which suggests the information is unsuitable for assessing the managers' performance.

Budgets – If one measure of the manager's performance is comparing actual performance against budget, then it is important that the budgets are realistic and achievable.

The fall of 12% in sales across the industry as a whole suggests that the original shop budget (showing the same figures as the previous year) was unrealistic.

Although the shop shows an overall gross margin variance of $17,340 (adverse) based on the original budget, this can more usefully be split into **planning** and **operational** variances as follows:

Planning variance		$	
Original sales	(1)	266,000	
Revenue variance due to economic conditions (12%)	(2)	31,920	(A)
Gross profit variance (gross margin 60%)		**19,152**	(A)
Operational variance			
Actual sales		237,100	
Revised budgeted sales	(1)–(2)	234,080	
		3,020	(F)
Operational variance (gross margin 60%)		**1,812**	(F)

The operational variance more accurately reflects the shop manager's work in promoting sales, and here we can see that the manager's efforts have actually reduced the fall in gross profit by $1,812. The overall gross profit variance (of $17,340 adverse) comprises an adverse planning variance of $19,152 partially offset by a favourable operational variance of $1,812.

Discounting – One area where the managers have a degree of autonomy is in setting prices; for example, it is possible they could reduce the sales price of particular titles to boost sales of those titles. This is therefore an aspect of the manager's performance which could be measured, for example, by looking at the sales price and volume for individual product lines, and then looking at the impact of any promotions on gross profit.

The figures for the Tunny branch suggest that the manager has not made use of the discounting authority, though. The actual gross margin achieved for the year has remained constant with the budget (60%) but discounting would have led to a reduction in the margin percentage.

Controllable and non-controllable costs – A number of non-controllable costs are currently included in the manager's performance assessment. In particular, the shop manager will have very little scope to control **property costs**, as the shop heating, lighting and rental contracts will all be managed by the Central Purchasing Department. The shop managers may have some control over the amount of heat and light that are used in their shops, but the managers don't have any control over the unit prices paid for them.

Similarly the managers can't control their own wages. However, it is reasonable to classify the **part-time staff costs as controllable**. The managers manage the staffing for their shops, and so they could save on part-time staff costs by working longer hours themselves.

Consequently, a fairer way of assessing the shop managers' performance would be to distinguish costs into two groups: controllable (marketing; part-time staff) and non-controllable (managers' wages; property costs).

Controllable profit – Following on from this, a controllable profit could then be shown as well as the overall shop profit. The shop manager's performance should then be assessed on the controllable profit performance of their shop only.

If we apply this logic to Tunny branch, then instead of the shop manager facing an adverse variance of $12,840, she would have achieved a positive variance of $6,312, and would therefore have been entitled to a bonus, because she has actually been performing well in difficult economic circumstances.

Improved report

The revised report should split costs into two groups as we have suggested above (controllable, and non-controllable) to show the controllable profit as well as the shop's overall profit. In addition, it would be useful to analyse variances into operational (controllable) and planning (non-controllable) variances, because this enables a greater understanding of the causes of the variances.

Revised performance report

TUNNY BRANCH: YEAR TO SEPTEMBER 20X1

		Budget	*Actual*	*Variance*	*Planning variance*	*Operational variance*
		$	$	$	$	$
Sales		266,000	237,100	(28,900)		
Cost of sales		106,400	94,840	11,560		
Gross profit		159,600	142,260	(17,340)	(19,152)	1,812
Controllable costs						
Marketing		12,000	11,500	500		
Staff costs	Part-time staff	38,000	34,000	4,000		
Controllable profit		109,600	96,760	(12,840)	(19,152)	6,312
Non-controllable costs						
Staff costs	Manager	27,000	27,000	–		
Property costs		26,600	26,600	–		
Shop profit		56,000	43,160	(12,840)		

The report now highlights that if the gross profit planning variance ($19,152) is added back to the controllable profit (of –$12,840), the manager would have achieved a positive variance in her controllable profit of $6,312.

(b) **Budget-constrained style**

The performance management style at Albacore seems to be **budget-constrained style**, in which the predominant focus is a short-term one, centred around achieving the budget set.

This style can be seen in the way the shop managers' performance is primarily evaluated on their ability to meet the budgets set, even though the general economic conditions mean that the budgets are no longer realistic or achievable.

Job-related tension – One of the characteristics of the budget-constrained style is that it leads to job-related tensions and poor relations between staff and the managers. This appears to be the case at Albacore, where the shop managers have complained about the way they are managed and their remuneration.

Performance manipulation – The budget-constrained style can often motivate staff to manipulate performance reports to try to make it look as if they have achieved their budget targets. However, given the centralised nature of control at Albacore, it seems unlikely that any such performance manipulation would be possible at shop level.

Alternative performance management styles

Profit-conscious style – In contrast to the short-termist nature of a budget-constrained style, under a profit-conscious style, a manager's performance is evaluated in relation to their ability to increase the general **effectiveness of their business unit** in relation to the organisation's **long-term purposes**.

It is possible that such a style could be suitable for Albacore, given the management team's aim of running the business in order to maximise profits. However, the long-term perspective may be at odds with the venture capitalist's likely requirements.

Non-accounting style – Budget information is relatively unimportant in performance evaluation, and other non-financial factors are deemed to be more important.

Performance appraisal system

Reflects budget-constrained style – The performance appraisal system at Albacore reflects the budget-constrained management style in the business.

Lack of discussion and negotiation – The shop managers appear to have little or no opportunity to influence their shops' budgets; they are simply presented to the managers at their annual appraisals.

BPP LEARNING MEDIA

Despite this, the bonus criteria appear to be rigidly enforced. If the Tunny branch manager's experience is representative of the other managers, it appears that the failure to achieve budget has led to no bonus being paid at all.

This is despite the shop still being profitable (making an operating profit of $43,160), and the manager's **controllable profits actually being higher than budget** (see part (a)).

This total lack of discussion and flexibility in the appraisal system, along with the apparent lack of appreciation of the managers' efforts in difficult economic conditions, is likely to **demotivate them**, and this appears to be the case, with the managers (justifiably) calling the current system unfair.

Improvements to the reward system

Focus on controllable aspects of performance – As we have noted in part (a), the reward system should distinguish between the **manager's performance** and the **shop's performance**.

If the managers feel that they are being judged on aspects of performance they can control, this should help to **motivate them**, and hopefully as a result also improve their performance.

However, given that Albacore's aim is to maximise profits, it is still important to monitor the shop's performance overall as well as the manager's profits. One possible solution might be to base part of the manager's bonus on their own performance (controllable profit) while another part of it could be determined by the shop's performance overall.

Stepped bonuses – Although the current bonus is 'up to 30% of basic salary', it is not clear how this is calculated. The current system seems to have an 'all or nothing' approach under which managers get a bonus if their shop achieves budget, and they don't if it doesn't.

One way this system could be improved is by introducing a graded system. For example, the amount of bonus the managers get will be determined by actual profit as a percentage of budget, with the bonus amount increasing above certain trigger levels. For example, above 90% of budget = 3% bonus; above 95% of budget = 6% bonus; above 100% = 9% etc.

Budgets agreed – Rather than the annual budget being determined centrally and then imposed on the shop managers, the managers should be involved in setting the budgets. The managers could be aware of factors that will affect the performance of their shops that central management are not aware of. Such a process may lead to more realistic budget targets being set for the shop, and in doing so increase the managers' motivation.

Nonetheless, it may still be necessary for the senior management team to adjust the budgets overall, to bring them in line with Albacore's overall financial objectives or any performance expectations the venture capitalist may have.

Non-financial factors – Finally, the reward system could recognise longer-term and non-financial factors in the manager's performance. For example, they could be rewarded for innovative marketing ideas and staff development (eg part-time staff from their branch who progress to become managers in other branches).

31 Cuthbert

Text reference. BPR is discussed in Chapter 3 of the BPP Study Text. Reward systems are discussed in Chapter 11.

Top tips.

Part (a). The scenario highlights that the cancellation of the army's order for jackets was 'the latest in a series of problems in production at Cuthbert' which has prompted the directors to look at using BPR 'to radically change the production process'.

The scenario also specifically identifies the three main elements of the proposed BPR project at Cuthbert:

(1) Reorganising production lines into teams
(2) Making machinists responsible for quality (changing job roles)
(3) Tracking batches with RFID tags (instead of the paper batch cards currently being used)

As such, it is vital to look at how each of these three specific elements could influence performance at Cuthbert, rather than simply considering the potential influence of BPR in general terms. A useful way to structure your answer would be to use each 'element' as a heading, and then assess how the changes arising from that element could affect operational processes at Cuthbert. For example, what are the potential implications of reorganising the production lines into teams?

Note. The 'operational' element is important here. Your answer needs to focus on how the BPR project could influence day to day activities and performance, not the wider impact it could have on Cuthbert's financial performance or its reputation.

Part (b) looks at Cuthbert's reward systems, but there are two distinct parts to the requirement, so make sure you address both of them in your answer:

(1) Evaluating the effectiveness of the current reward system
(2) Recommend – and justify – how the reward systems will need to change if the BPR project goes ahead

One of the key issues when evaluating any reward system is the extent to which it influences staff behaviour, and in turn how this affects their performance. This is an important consideration in evaluating Cuthbert's reward system. For example, the fact that the machinists are rewarded for the **number** of items they sew is likely to encourage the machinists to work quickly, but a focus on speed alone could have a negative impact on quality – and quality problems were a major factor in the army cancelling its order from Cuthbert.

Another important point to note from the scenario is that each machinist's weekly bonus is determined by the number of items that they, individually, sew each week. However, the proposed BPR process will lead to production lines being reorganised into teams. Moreover, machinists will now be responsible for quality (as well as quantity).

These points from the scenario should have helped you answer the second part of the requirement: for example, if machinists are now working in teams, bonuses based on team performance may be more appropriate than ones based on individual performance. Similarly, if machinists are responsible for quality, will bonuses based purely on the number of items produced be appropriate?

The requirement isn't only about the machinists, though, so it is important to consider the reward systems in relation to the different grades of staff identified in the scenario – machinists, supervisor, and factory manager.

Examining team's comments. Part (a) was generally well done, with those candidates who broke their answers down into a detailed discussion of the impact of each part of the BPR project scoring most highly.

Part (b) was also reasonably well done, with the candidates who addressed the specific issues in the scenario relating to each level of employees scoring most highly.

Answers to this question which used the detailed structure of the scenario (in relation to the BPR proposal and the existing employee hierarchy) generally made points that scored easily, since they directly addressed relevant issues for the business that was seeking advice. It is important to remember that, in APM, candidates need to apply their knowledge to the specific scenario, rather than just making generic points that could apply to any business.

Marking scheme

		Marks
(a)	Up to 2 marks for an explanation of BPR For advising how each of the three elements of the BPR proposal could affect operational performance at Cuthbert – up to 4 marks for each of the three elements (up to 12 marks in total) For other practical advice about how BPR could affect operational performance at Cuthbert – 1 mark per relevant point, up to 4 marks	14
(b)	Evaluation of Cuthbert's current reward system – 1 mark per relevant point; up to 8 marks Recommendations for changes to the reward system if the BPR project goes ahead – 1 mark per relevant point; up to 6 marks	11
	Total =	**25**

BPP LEARNING MEDIA

(a) **BPR** involves radical and fundamental changes in the way processes in organisations are designed. A focus on the needs of the customer, and customer satisfaction, are key to BPR. BPR aims to improve key performance measures such as reducing costs, improving quality, service delivery and customer satisfaction.

The proposal is to move away from the existing functional structure where staff are attached to only one stage of the production process, or even to one type of machine within each function, to team working. This is a radical change for Cuthbert and, as such, is an example of BPR.

Reorganising into teams

Currently, there is very little multi-skilling of production staff at Cuthbert. This was seen where there were insufficiently trained zip machinists available for the emergency order for the Ceeland army, even though there were enough machinists to sew buttons. This led to the emergency order failing to meet the customer's requirements as it was not delivered on time.

Furthermore, it seems that machinists also prefer to work on one particular type of machine. This is probably because they are currently rewarded according to the speed of production, rather than the quality of production, and can work faster when using just one machine.

A change to team working would imply job enlargement for machinists, who would need to be trained so that they were multi-skilled in different parts of the production process. They could then perform the roles of other members of their team, to ensure that there were no bottlenecks in production.

The cost of reorganisation and the costs of training the machinists should be outweighed by the resulting improved efficiency and flexibility of production. In this way, there is more focus on the outcome (goods of the correct quality produced on time) and less focus on the individual tasks within the process, which is a key principle of BPR.

Production teams are responsible for quality

Cuthbert's brand has a strong reputation, and the use of its products for protection in harsh environments and by the armed forces means that quality is a key element of customer satisfaction. Cuthbert must be able to manufacture goods which are free of defects, unlike the emergency order for the Ceeland army.

Reorganising the production into teams of machinists, sometimes known as production 'cells', would make machinists responsible for decisions about quality of a particular product type. This should lead to improvements in quality and therefore to meeting the needs of the customer.

Reducing the number of processes for checking is typical of a re-engineered process, and the quality checking currently performed by the supervisors would no longer be necessary. The production teams will be managing themselves in this respect, and the distinction between supervisors and machinists will be removed, which is again typical of organisations which have undergone BPR.

Encouraging machinists in each team to suggest improvements in the production process should bring about improvements in both quality and efficiency, and hence a reduction in costs. It is the machinists who are closest to the production process and may be able to see how it can be improved. Cuthbert could also consider a more formal system of incremental continuous improvements such as Kaizen costing.

Tracking with RFIDs

Typically, organisations with re-engineered processes end up having a flatter hierarchy. It seems that the supervisors' current roles will no longer be required if the proposal is adopted. Quality checks will no longer be undertaken by them, nor will recording of batches, which will become automated using RFID tags. This should save salary costs and improve lines of communication in the business.

The use of RFID tags would capture the information required to manage the production process at source, and there would be no distinction between the gathering of information and processing it. This is in contrast to the current system of inputting batch data into a spreadsheet, and is a feature in organisations which have undergone BPR.

Practical and cultural aspects of the proposal

New performance measures related to quality rather than just quantity produced will have to be developed and processes and systems developed in order to record and report these. New rewards systems will also have to be developed and introduced as a result of the changes proposed.

The proposal, by definition, represents a significant cultural change for Cuthbert, and may meet resistance by staff who may perceive it as a threat and a one-off cost-cutting measure rather than a fundamental long-term change in the business. It will also affect the organisational hierarchy, relationships between employees and the roles within Cuthbert. There will be significant costs with training staff and with the disruption the transition may cause.

(b) **The current reward system**

The machinists are currently paid a basic hourly wage plus an amount depending on how many items they sew. This will encourage them to work quickly, which will reduce product costs. However, as they are not directly rewarded for the quality of the work which they produce, they may not be motivated to produce high quality work. Furthermore, in order to work quickly, machinists prefer to work on only one type of machine. This reduces Cuthbert's overall flexibility to respond to customer needs, as illustrated by the failure to deliver the emergency order for the Ceeland army.

The production supervisors also receive a bonus according to how many items machinists in their team are able to sew. This too does not reward the production of high quality work, and supervisors may also neglect quality in order to increase the speed of production. The machinists in their teams could also see it as unfair that the supervisors obtain a bonus based on what they see as their efforts.

The Production Manager does not receive a bonus for production or quality. It seems that he has currently no direct motivation to improve on either of these two aspects of the process.

At 5% of salary, the bonus related to Cuthbert's overall profits is relatively small and it is unclear whether it is a significant motivator to any of the employees. Furthermore, machinists in particular may perceive their own efforts as too remote from the company's overall profit for them to bother to achieve it. Even if they were to be motivated by this, it is unclear what proportion of the total costs are related to direct labour as Cuthbert incurs many other costs such as advertising to maintain the brand. If the costs of direct labour were relatively low, even a large improvement in production efficiency by the machinists may have little effect on overall profit.

Changes to reward systems under the new proposal

The existing reward systems would likely need to change if the move to team-based production were to be adopted.

It may still be appropriate to reward machinists with volume-related bonuses but, as they worked in teams, a team-based performance bonus would be more appropriate. In that way the rest of the team would ensure that any underperforming machinists would improve their performance.

Rewards based on other factors such as quality, innovation, on-time delivery and the ability to work as part of a team would also be appropriate and consistent with the machinists' enlarged job role. This would be a significant change for Cuthbert, where machinists are now being encouraged for the first time to bring about improvements in the production process. Rewards based on direct costs of production, or for the number of suggestions made by each machinist may be appropriate here.

New performance measures would need to be developed against which to align rewards to ensure that employees work towards the overall objectives of the organisation. New reporting systems will need to be put in place to feed back information regarding quality to each cell. This may incur additional costs in the development of existing or new information technology systems.

The commitment of senior management to these changes would be required, as well as communication and training of employees at all levels. This may again incur additional costs and divert management time away from existing activities.

32 ENT Entertainments

Text reference. The BCG matrix is discussed in Chapter 1 of the Study Text. Management styles are discussed in Chapter 11.

Top tips. In effect, **part (a)** contains two requirements, although it is only worth seven marks. First (i) you need to perform a BCG analysis of ENT's business, and then (ii) you need to use your BCG matrix to evaluate the company's performance. How is the balance of ENT's portfolio affecting its performance?

Note that the 'growth' axis on the matrix refers to the growth of the market sector and not the growth of the division itself (see Examining team's comment below).

Whereas the focus in part (a) is on ENT's performance, the focus in **part (b)** is on the BCG analysis itself. An important part of the APM syllabus is that candidates appreciate the advantages or disadvantages of different models which could be used in performance management. In this requirement you needed to highlight not only how the BCG could be useful for helping ENT to manage its performance, but also the weaknesses of the BCG matrix in this context.

Part (c) (i): You should have drawn on your analysis from part (a) to help you with part (c) (i). The BCG analysis has highlighted that some divisions offer growth or growth prospects for ENT, while the focus in other divisions should be on controlling costs. These different aims require a different style of management; but the bonus scheme (for all the divisions) is linked to performance against the cost budget, so there appears to be a lack of alignment here.

Part (c) (ii) picks up on the idea that some divisions are focusing on growth and some on cost control, because this is likely to mean that different management styles are required in the different divisions.

Examining team's comments. Many candidates did not appear to know that the growth element of the BCG analysis referred to the growth of the market sector and either ignored this element or calculated the growth of the division instead.

(a)

Market growth (%)

Division	*20X1*	*20X2*	*20X3*	*Average of annual growth rates (20X0–X3)*
Restaurants	1.0	1.0	–	0.67
Cafés	9.0	11.0	9.0	9.66
Bars	(2.0)	(3.0)	(3.0)	(2.67)
Dance clubs	6.0	5.9	9.0	7.01

Market share (%)

	ENT market share	*Market leader*	*Relative market share*
Restaurants	0.50	3.00	0.17
Cafés	1.01	3.00	0.34
Bars	3.50	3.00	1.17
Dance clubs	10.99	15.00	0.73

BCG analysis and evaluation of performance

Restaurants Division – This division has a low market share of a market sector with low growth, making it a **dog** in the BCG classification. The Restaurant Division therefore looks a likely candidate for **divestment**, unless it has any links with any of the other divisions in ENT's business.

Cafés Division – The Cafés Division also has a relatively low market share, but it is operating in a market sector with high growth. It should therefore be classified as a **question mark**.

The market sector is already showing good growth, but it currently seems quite fragmented. There could be additional opportunities for ENT to grow by acquiring some rival businesses. Alternatively, if ENT does not want to invest in this way, it might consider selling its Café Division to another business looking to consolidate in the sector.

Bars Division – The Bars Division is the market leader (high market share) in a market which has low (actually, negative) growth. This should be classified as a **cash cow**.

The Bars Division is currently ENT's largest division, and it contributed about 55% of the group's total revenue in 20X0. The current decline in the bars market should therefore be a concern for ENT, given the Bars Division's role as a cash cow in the group. ENT is likely to want to use the Bars Division to generate cash for the other businesses in its portfolio, but if the bars market starts declining in time this may limit the division's ability to generate cash for the rest of the group.

Importance of controlling costs – The fact that the bars sector seems to be in the mature stage of its life cycle also highlights the importance of controlling costs. The degree of profit growth ENT will be able to generate through increasing revenues seems limited, so instead it could look at reducing costs as a means of increasing profitability.

Dance clubs – The Dance Clubs Division has a moderately high market share (although still less than 1) in a market with reasonably high growth. This should currently be classified as a **question mark** as ENT is not yet the market leader in the sector, but it has the potential to become a star if it can achieve market leadership.

Its market share is already relatively close to the market leader's share, so with continued investment the division could grow to become the leader. The performance of this division is likely to be crucial to ENT's longer-term success, particularly if the performance of some of ENT's more mature businesses continues to decline.

(b) **Context for performance** – The BCG provides a useful context in which to assess the performance of the different divisions. For example, it illustrates to management that they shouldn't expect the Bars Division to grow at the same rate as the Clubs Division, due to the underlying differences in the growth rates of the two sectors.

Management approach – Equally, identifying the differences in the growth potential of the different divisions identifies that different styles of management will be appropriate for the different divisions. For example, the Clubs Division may require capital investments to enable it to sustain its rate of growth, but the focus in the Bars Division (in a more mature business sector) should be on cost control.

Help set performance metrics – By helping to set expectations and approach in this way, managers can then also tailor their performance management systems and metrics to reflect the different contexts of each of the divisions. So, the metrics for the high growth divisions (cafés and clubs) should be based on profit or return on investment, while the metrics for the low growth divisions (bars and restaurants) should be focused on maintaining margins, cash control and cash generation.

Limitations of BCG approach

Problems of definition – Although we have identified that the BCG matrix can be useful for providing a context for performance management, its usefulness is limited by its simplicity. For example, a business unit is only considered to have a high market share if its relative market share is greater than 1. By definition, however, this means that only the market leader can have a high market share, and therefore also there can only be one star or cash cow in each market sector.

Overlooks possible synergies – Another issue which arises from the simplicity of the model is that it treats business units in isolation, and in doing so can overlook possible synergies between them. For example, some of ENT's bars and restaurants may be linked to its clubs, such that customers may go for a drink or a meal and then go on to a club afterwards. However, if in time the restaurants and later some of the bars are divested then this link between the business units will be lost.

Defining the market sector – Another potential issue with using the BCG matrix comes from defining market sectors themselves. For example, the Bars Division has launched a new wine bar format which appears to have been successful. This suggests it has been growing, although the rest of the Bars Division has actually

BPP LEARNING MEDIA

had negative growth. However, this raises an issue of whether the wine bar format should be treated as a separate sub-section (and as a problem child which is given the support and investment needed to grow) or whether it should be subject to cost control in the same way that the rest of the Bars Division is.

Portfolio analysis, not performance management – It is also important to remember that the BCG matrix was designed for analysing a product portfolio, not as a performance management system. Therefore, while it can help to determine the appropriate performance management approach for a business, it is not in itself a performance management system.

(c) (i) **Focus on cost budgets** – The bonus element (50%) of the remuneration package is based on divisional performance against cost budget. As a result, divisional managers are likely to focus on controlling costs. Such an approach may be appropriate in the Bars and Restaurants Divisions, but is unlikely to be suitable for the faster-growing divisions (cafés and clubs).

In the Cafés and Clubs Divisions, ENT should be looking to encourage growth, but the current remuneration package is unlikely to do this. As a result, there is likely to be a lack of **goal congruence** between the divisional managers and the ENT overall.

Short-term performance – In a similar way, the focus on controlling costs may also lead to divisional managers taking a short-term view of performance. Again, it may actually be more beneficial for some of the divisions to spend now (for example, on marketing) in order to increase revenues and profits in the future.

Use of EVA™ – There also appears to be an inconsistency between this focus on cost budgets and the use of EVA™ as the measure of divisional performance. The underlying logic behind EVA™ will be to try to **maximise the wealth of ENT's shareholder** – which is the company's objective – but this is not necessarily the same as controlling costs.

Importantly, EVA™ specifically identifies that some costs which are treated as expenses in the financial statements (for example, advertising costs) should actually be considered as investments for the future.

Therefore, rather than basing the bonus element of the managers' reward package on achieving cost budgets, ENT may be better advised to base the bonus element on achieving target EVA™ figures. In this way, the reward system at divisional level will reflect the **company's overall objective**.

(ii) **Context** – The fact that some of ENT's divisions should be focusing on growth (cafés, clubs) while others (bars, restaurants) need to focus on cost control suggests that different management styles may be appropriate for the different divisions.

Budget-constrained style – Under a budget-constrained style, a manager's performance is primarily assessed by their ability to meet the budget on a short-term basis, particularly in relation to ensuring that actual costs do not exceed budgeted costs. 50% of the bonus elements at ENT are based on achieving the cost budget numbers set by the board, which suggests that ENT may be using a budget-constrained style.

A budget-constrained style can be appropriate in a business where it is important to keep costs under control, which suggests that it may be appropriate to use this style in the Bars or Restaurants Divisions. However, it is less likely to be appropriate for the Cafés or Clubs Divisions.

Moreover, the budget-constrained style often leads to poor relationships between managers and subordinates, and also encourages the manipulation and misreporting of information, so ENT needs to be aware of these potential problems.

Profit-conscious style – Under a profit-conscious style, a manager's performance is evaluated more in terms of long-term performance, and the ability to generate future growth, rather than short-term performance and cost control.

This style is likely to be appropriate for the Cafés or Clubs Divisions at ENT. However, the current bonus structure suggests that this style is not being used, which could suggest that not only do ENT's remuneration packages need revising but also that the management styles need reviewing too.

33 Beach Foods

Text reference. Financial performance measures including EVA™, ROI and RI are discussed in Chapters 7 and 8 of the BPP Study Text. Control and management styles are discussed in Chapter 11.

Top tips.

Part (a). Note the requirement here is to 'Assess the use of ...' so you should focus on the potential advantages and disadvantages of using EVA™ as a performance measure, rather than, for example, describing how EVA™ would be calculated, or detailing the different adjustments which might be required to calculate it. In this respect, it is important to note (from the second paragraph of the scenario) that Beach already uses EVA™, so we can assume that Beach's management accountants already know how to calculate it.

Part (b). The need to evaluate management's performance as well as the division's performance should have prompted you to think about issues of controllability. For example, if Baby's managers cannot control the R&D costs which are recharged to the department, is it fair to include them in an assessment of the manager's performance?

The reference to 'the assumptions made' also relates to the profit figure being used to assess performance – again, recognising the difference between divisional and managerial performance. Crucially, though, your 'assumptions' should relate to the level of profit to include, not the cost of capital figure to use. The cost of capital figures used must be that for the division (11%), not the one for Beach as a whole (7.5%).

Part (c). Note the requirement here is that you recommend suitable styles, rather than discussing or evaluating different styles. Also, note that you need to recommend a suitable way to control each division (cost/profit/investment centre) as well as recommending a suitable management style (budget-constrained, profit-conscious and non-accounting). In both cases, the options to choose from were identified in the scenario – control styles in the third paragraph, and management styles in the fourth.

Importantly, the requirement asks for recommendations for **each** division, so you need to cover all three divisions – Baby, Chocolate and R&D – not just the two operating divisions (Baby and Chocolate).

Examining team's comments on part (c). This part was poorly answered as many candidates clearly did not know the criteria for the choice of responsibility centre, even though the centre headings to choose from were given in the scenario. Such a lack of knowledge continues to surprise the examining team.

Lengthy descriptions of the three management styles were not helpful here either, as candidates were expected, instead, to demonstrate their understanding of the styles by applying it to the scenario.

Marking scheme

		Marks
(a)	For relevant points assessing the use of EVA™ as a divisional performance measure – 1 mark per point	
	Total for part (a): up to 8	8
(b)	Calculations:	
	For applying the correct method to calculate RI – 1 mark For applying the correct method to calculate ROI – 1 mark	
	For correct calculation of both RI and ROI based on different profit figures (controllable profit, profit after R&D, divisional profit) – 1 mark per profit figure used; up to a maximum of 4 marks	
	Comments: 1 mark per relevant comment up to a maximum of 4 marks	
	Total for part (b): up to 7	7

BPP LEARNING MEDIA

		Marks
(c)	Up to 4 marks for valid recommendations for any one division	
	All recommendations must be justified within the answer to gain credit High marks within the answer for any divisions can only be scored by discussing both the type of centre and the management style which would be appropriate	
	Total for part (c): up to 10	10
	Total =	**25**

(a) **EVA™ as a divisional performance measure**

Advantages

Maximising wealth – Beach's overall objective is to maximise the family's wealth through their shareholding – in effect, to maximise shareholder wealth.

One of the main benefits of EVA™ as a performance measure (rather than profit-based measures such as ROI) is that it is a value-based approach, and therefore it will be aligned to the overall objective of maximising shareholder wealth.

Goal congruence – Moreover, using EVA™ as a divisional measure will help to ensure that decisions taken at divisional level support the best interests of Beach as a whole, rather than just the individual division.

The **other advantages of EVA™** are:

(i) It gives an absolute measure of performance, and so shows the overall contribution the divisions make to the company.

(ii) The basic test of performance is simple. If a division has a positive EVA™, then it is generating a return above that required by the providers of finance. (ROI requires a target level to be set, usually based on benchmarking to the industry sector.)

(iii) The adjustments required when calculating net operating profit after tax mean that it is closer to cash flows than traditional accounting profits are, and also mean that EVA™ is less subject to choices in accounting policies.

(iv) EVA™ encourages investment in the future (for example, in advertising and development) by adding back these costs to profit in the performance period and treating them like capital expenditure. This will reduce the temptation for dysfunctional, short-termist decision making, which could otherwise be a problem where the capital employed figure from the financial statements is used in ROI and RI. This is likely to be particularly appropriate at Beach where R&D is significant.

Disadvantages

However, EVA™ does also have some disadvantages. Some of these are also disadvantages of ROI and RI, and some are specific to EVA™.

All three measures are dependent on historical data and so have limited use in forecasting future performance.

The directors' complaint that EVA™ is complicated to understand appears reasonable, because of the number of adjustments which need to be made to the information from Beach's financial statements. By contrast, ROI and RI are derived from headline information in the financial statements which would be more familiar to the board. A related issue here would be the time and cost involved for Beach's management accountant in calculating the division's EVA™.

EVA™ (like RI) uses a charge for the capital employed in the division. EVA™ uses the weighted average cost of capital (WACC) for the company as a whole, which may not reflect the risks of the manufacturing divisions. Also, as an unlisted business, WACC may be difficult to estimate. By contrast, RI uses a notional cost of capital based on the risk of the divisions – although this will also be subject to an element of judgement and estimate.

Unlike ROI (which gives a percentage measure, rather than an absolute measure) EVA™ will not help to assess relative divisional managerial performance at Beach if the divisions are of different sizes.

(b) **ROI and RI**

A key consideration when calculating either ROI or RI for Baby is what profit figure to use for the calculations.

The data in Appendix 1 suggests three potential profit figures, which could be used for assessing the performance of Baby as a division, and its manager:

Controllable profit – The only costs included in controllable profit are those under the direct control of the Divisional Manager (ie the divisional operating costs of $121m).

R&D costs recharged – Although the Divisional Manager cannot influence the costs of the R&D Division, Baby's divisional revenue includes the profit which results from new products and ideas generated by the R&D Division. Therefore, in order to match costs with revenues more fairly, a proportion of the R&D Division's costs should be included in Baby's profit figure.

Divisional profit – The division's performance (as distinct from the manager's performance) should take account of all relevant costs, including Baby's share of the head office management fees. As such the divisional profit ($60m) would be an appropriate figure to use in this respect.

Performance analysis

Regardless of which profit figure is chosen, Baby seems to be performing relatively well. Baby's EVA™ is positive ($35m) and its RI is also positive.

In terms of ROI, the return based on divisional profit (14.2%) is lower than the ROI for similar entities (20%), but the return based on controllable profit, or profit after R&D, is higher than the benchmark figure. However, we do not know which profit figures were used in the benchmark figure, which means we cannot tell whether Baby's ROI figure is above or below the average achieved by similar entities.

	Controllable profit	*Profit after R&D*	*Divisional profit*
ROI			
Profit ($m)	99	88	60
Capital employed ($m)	424	424	424
ROI	**23.3%**	**20.8%**	**14.2%**
RI			
Profit ($m)	99	88	60
Cost of capital ($m)			
(424 × 11%)	46.6	46.6	46.6
RI ($m)	**52.4**	**41.4**	**13.4**

(c) **Management styles for the divisions**

Baby Division

Responsibility centre – Baby's position as the star in Beach's portfolio, coupled with the fact it is developing and introducing new products, means that the division's focus should be on growth rather than cost control.

As such, it might seem appropriate for Baby to be treated as an investment centre, giving its managers autonomy to develop their business as they see fit.

However, it is not clear whether the divisional managers have the authority to make capital investment decisions or whether these are taken by head office. (Chocolate had to get approval from head office to upgrade its production line.)

If the authority for investment decisions remains with head office, then Baby should be treated as a **profit centre**, and managed according to its ability to generate profit.

Management style – A profit-conscious style focuses on longer-term performance and objectives (such as growth) whereas a budget-constrained style focuses on short-term performance and cost control.

Therefore, given the nature of Baby's market – and the market's rapid growth – the profit-conscious style would seem more appropriate for Baby.

However, elements of a non-accounting style (such as new product development) may also be appropriate.

Given the costs associated with new products and rapid growth (such as the publicity campaign Baby ran to support its new product launch), we recommend that a **non-accounting style** is applied initially.

However, once the market sector begins to mature, then given Baby's strong market share its focus should shift to optimising its profits – at which point, a profit-conscious management style should be adopted.

Chocolate Division

Responsibility centre – As the Chocolate Division is the cash cow in the portfolio, Beach needs it to generate the profits and cash necessary to support Baby's growth.

However, as a cash cow, and operating in a market with limited growth opportunities, Chocolate is unlikely to receive much investment. As such, it would seem appropriate to treat Chocolate as a profit centre.

Nonetheless, it appears that Chocolate does still makes some capital expenditure (for example, the upgrade to its main production line). As such, it could be appropriate to treat Chocolate as an **investment centre**, so that its managers have the autonomy to take these decisions, rather than having to wait for head office to approve them.

Management style – Because it is operating in a mature market with limited growth opportunities, cost control is likely to be crucial in maintaining Chocolate's profitability. As such, a **budget-constrained style** will be the most appropriate management style for Chocolate.

R&D Division

Responsibility centre – The R&D Division does not generate any revenue in its own right, and therefore should be treated as a cost centre.

Nonetheless, it is important that the contribution the division makes to the group (through the overall profit generated by the products it develops) is not overlooked. The complaints which Baby's managers make about the recharge suggests they are only thinking about the costs rather than the revenue which the new products have generated for them.

As such, whilst Beach should continue to treat the R&D Division as a cost centre for control purposes, it would also be useful to **monitor the profit generated by each new product** over its life cycle, to demonstrate the division's value to the group as a whole.

Management style – As the R&D Division is a cost centre, it might seem appropriate to apply a budget-constrained management style.

However, it is important that potentially profitable developments are not rejected simply to keep the division's costs within a fixed budget – and there is a danger this could be the case under a budget-constrained management style.

Therefore, elements of a non-accounting style might also be appropriate – with a focus on the number of new product ideas being generated, and the market reaction to new products being developed.

As such, it may be necessary to adopt a management style which combines some elements of the **budget-constrained style** with others from the **non-accounting style**.

34 Pharmaceutical Technologies

Text reference. The balanced scorecard is discussed in Chapter 12 of the BPP Study Text.

Top tips.

For part (a), you should be asking 'how well will the proposed measures help PT deliver its objectives and, in turn, its corporate strategy?' The scenario provided you with considerable detail about objectives and measures, and you should have used it to help answer this requirement.

Part (b). Note there are two distinct parts to this requirement. The first is a pure test of knowledge: describing a method for analysing stakeholder influence. Mendelow's matrix seems the obvious choice here.

However, don't spend too long on this part of the requirement (**briefly** describe ...), because the second part of the requirement is more substantial: analyse the influence of four different external stakeholders on the regulator. Note that the question refers to stakeholders who could influence the regulator (not PT). Although some of the stakeholder groups identified by the working group (eg doctors, patients) could also be stakeholders of the regulator, it is important that you analyse their influence in relation to the regulator.

However, as there are only eight marks available for part (b) in total you should only give a relatively brief analysis of each stakeholder's influence on the regulator – highlighting what power they have, and how interested they will be in exerting that power.

In part (c), you need to establish how BDR differs from PT, because this will affect how the scorecard is applied in both organisations. In effect, the requirement is asking how the application of the scorecard would vary in a private sector organisation (PT) compared to a public sector one. To score well here, you need to make a comparison between the two, rather than simply talking about the application of the scorecard at one or other of them.

Marking scheme

		Marks
(a)	1 mark per relevant point – up to a maximum of 10 Relevant points include: Evaluation of whether each of the measures suggested cover the perspective intended Consideration of whether there are other suitable measures Discussion of linkages between the measures and the company objectives Discussion of the difficulty of collection of appropriate data, and ranking the measures Total: up to 10	10
(b)	Description of suitable method of stakeholder analysis – 1 mark per point – up to a maximum of 2 Analysis of the power and interest of each stakeholder – 1 mark for power, and 1 mark for influence of each stakeholder – up to a maximum of 8 Total: up to 8	8
(c)	1 mark per relevant difference between the application of the scorecard at BDR and PT. Differences must be clearly linked to the scenario to score the marks available. Total: up to 7	7
	Total =	25

BPP LEARNING MEDIA

(a) **Financial measures**

Existing indicators – The two financial performance measures proposed for the scorecard (share price and earnings per share) are the same two which are PT's current measures of performance. So in this respect, introducing the scorecard will not change the way strategic performance is measured. However, as well as simply measuring earnings per share (EPS) PT could also consider measuring growth in EPS.

Link to shareholder value – Share price and EPS are both appropriate measures to use, given the overall objective of enhancing shareholder wealth. However, measures such as economic value added (EVA™) or shareholder value added may actually be better long-term measures for enhancing shareholder wealth.

Liquidity – Although it is important to look at earnings and profits, PT should not overlook the importance of cash flow and liquidity, which will be essential to its survival. Therefore it could also include a measure relating to its cash flows in its scorecard.

Customer perspective

Type of customer – PT has two different types of customer: users (healthcare providers and patients) and the people who fund the drug use (insurance companies or government). The measure currently proposed seems to focus mainly on the end users. However, their concerns may not always be same as those who are paying for a course of treatment. For example, the healthcare providers and patients are likely to focus primarily on how effective the product is as a cure. However, the funding bodies will also be interested in the cost of the treatment.

Recognise cost – Therefore, PT should consider a measure looking at the cost of its drugs; for example, comparing the cost of its drugs against similar alternative drugs offered by rival manufacturers.

Internal business processes

Efficiency of drug development – One of the objectives from the medium-term strategy is to improve the efficiency of drug development. Performance measures designed to improve the standard of design and testing, and to reduce the time to gain regulatory approval, should help achieve this objective.

These measures also help support the financial objectives. If PT can reduce the time it takes to get new drugs approved by the regulator, it will also be able to be start selling those drugs more quickly, thereby increasing sales and earnings.

Learning and growth

Innovation – The third of the objectives from the medium-term strategy highlights the importance of innovation in the drug approval process. The measures in the learning and growth perspective of the scorecard should therefore directly help PT to achieve this objective.

Ranking of measures – We are not told anything about the relative importance or ranking of any of the measures in the scorecard, but it is debatable whether the number of training days attended is the main measure of learning and growth. Reducing the time to market of new products, and increasing the percentage of drugs that gain final approval, are likely to be more directly strategically important.

Measurement issues

Although the measures suggested seem largely appropriate in relation to PT's objectives, the management will also need to consider how practical it will be to collect data for some of the non-financial measures. For example, an assessment of whether PT has exceeded industry standard on design and testing is likely to be subjective, unless there are industry-wide quality audits which formally assess companies against a common set of criteria.

Conversely, measures should not be chosen because they are easy to measure. The number of training days undertaken by staff will be easy to measure by staff. However, there may be a danger that staff will simply end up going on training days simply to achieve a target number of days. Training will only be valuable to PT and its staff if it is relevant and appropriate for the people attending.

(b) **Stakeholder influence**

Power and interest – A stakeholder's influence over an organisation can be analysed in relation to the stakeholder's power and interest, using Mendelow's matrix.

Power identifies the extent to which a stakeholder (or group of stakeholders) has the power to influence a decision or situation.

The level of interest reflects the likelihood that a stakeholder will exercise their power in relation to any given decision or situation.

Four key stakeholders of BDR are: the drug companies being tested, the Government, healthcare providers, and patients.

Drug companies

Interest – The drug companies are likely to have a **high interest** in BDR, because it makes the final judgement about whether a product can be sold in the country. Without approval from BDR, the drug companies will not have any products to sell.

Power – However, the drug companies will have **little power** to influence BDR. BDR's responsibility is to the public and to public health, rather than to the drug companies. Therefore, BDR needs to be (and be seen to be) independent from the drug companies.

Government

Power – The Government has **high power** because it appoints the board of trustees and also directly funds BDR.

Interest – The Government will have a keen interest in public health overall, but their direct interest in BDR is likely to be **relatively low**. The Government has appointed the trustees to manage BDR on its behalf so, unless there is a specific financial or medical scandal which requires it to do so, the Government is unlikely to intervene in any decision making at BDR.

Doctors and healthcare providers

Interest – The healthcare providers will have a **high level of interest** in the approval process, because they will want to be confident that any new drugs approved are safe for use. However, they will also have an interest in BDR's role in encouraging the development of beneficial new drugs. These new drugs could help them treat patients and diseases that they would not otherwise be able to treat as effectively.

Power – Nonetheless, the healthcare providers are only likely to have low power over the approval process because BDR is an independent regulator. However, one way doctors and healthcare providers may be able to exert some power is through lobbying the Government.

Patients

Interest – In the same way that healthcare providers will have a **high level of interest in** the process that may lead to the approval of new drugs, so will patients. They will want to be reassured that any drugs approved are safe, but equally they will have an interest in potential new cures being available on the market quickly.

Power – Similarly, in the same way that healthcare providers only have **low power**, so patients also only have low power over any decisions made at BDR.

(c) **Differences in objectives** – BDR's objectives are less explicitly financial than PT's, not least because it does not have any shareholders. Therefore the emphasis the balanced scorecard places on non-financial performance will be relevant for BDR.

Stakeholder structure – BDR is a public sector organisation, while PT is a commercial organisation, which means that the Government is a much more important stakeholder for BDR than for PT. It is likely that this will need to be reflected in BDR's scorecard, with there being a political dimension to measuring performance.

Complexity of the scorecards – BDR's scorecard is likely to be quite complex, because it needs to reflect the diverse nature of its stakeholders and their interests. For example, on the one hand, drug companies will be keen for new drugs to be approved as quickly as possible, while healthcare providers and patients will be most interested in the risk-benefit profile of any potential new drugs. Equally, the Government will want effective drugs and treatments to be available for patients, but in terms of paying healthcare providers the Government may not be willing to pay for drugs it considers to be too expensive.

In this respect, the **customer perspective** of BDR's scorecard is likely to be crucial because, in effect, the drug companies, healthcare providers and patients are all BDR's customers. In PT's scorecard the relative significance of the four perspectives is likely to be more equal. The financial perspective will be very important for satisfying shareholders, while the internal business processes and learning and growth perspectives will be crucial in developing and manufacturing the new drugs effectively. Process and innovation are likely to be less directly important in BDR because it doesn't develop 'products' of its own.

Selecting performance measures – However, the nature of BDR's work means that it will be quite hard to measure how well it is performing against its objectives. For example, determining whether a medicine has an 'acceptable balance of benefit and risk' will involve a degree of judgement and selectivity, and it is likely to be difficult to set a quantifiable performance measure to determine whether this objective is being achieved.

Potential conflicts – Of BDR's three objectives, the easiest to set quantifiable measures for is likely to be 'encouraging new beneficial product development' because a performance measure could be set around the number of new products developed. However, there is a danger that imposing quantifiable measures in this way may have unintended consequences. For example, it may lead to new drugs being introduced even if the new product is not a significant improvement on an existing drug.

35 Victoria-Yeeland Logistics

Text reference. The balanced scorecard (BSC) is discussed in Chapter 12 of the BPP Study Text. Reward systems and reward management are discussed in Chapter 11.

Top tips.

Part (a). One of the key arguments in favour of multi-dimensional performance measurement systems (such as the BSC) is that an organisation's financial performance ultimately reflects its performance in key non-financial areas.

This is the broad context of part (a) of this question, but read the requirement very carefully: it does not ask about the impact that success in the customer perspective will have on Victoria's financial position in general terms. Rather it asks specifically about the impact that success in the customer perspective will have on the three financial metrics identified in Appendix 1. Therefore, your answer must also focus specifically on the impact that achieving the success factors in the customer perspective is likely to have on Victoria's return on capital employed (ROCE), profit margin and revenue growth.

Part (b). As the marking guide indicates, there are two marks available for each metric you recommend: one for calculating a suitable metric; and one for justifying why you have chosen it. Therefore, as is so often the case in APM, the requirement is not simply about calculation. Justifying the metric you have chosen is equally as important as the calculation.

Note, also, that there is a second part to the requirement – a discussion about the problems of using customer complaints as a performance measure. For example, can Victoria be sure that all customer complaints are valid?

Part (c). The requirement asks you to advise on 'the reward management issues outlined by the CFO'. The context for this requirement is provided by the last paragraph in the scenario, but crucially you need to recognise that there are two sets of issues here: one relating to the senior management bonus scheme, and one relating to the operational managers' bonus scheme.

As the marking guide indicates, you can only score up to five marks for advising on the issues with either scheme, so it is vital to analyse both schemes in order to score well on this requirement.

The fact that the shareholders have been complaining about the senior management's bonus should be a clue that agency theory is an issue here – is the scheme designed with shareholders' best interests in mind, or management's?

Similarly, in relation to the operational managers' scheme, the fact that the scenario identifies a change to the way that bonus targets are set should prompt you to question whether these changes are appropriate.

Examining team's comments. Many candidates used the building block model as a template for their answer but failed to go further than a generic response – around the need for standards to be fair, achievable and owned, and for rewards to be clear, motivational and controllable. In order for answers based around the model to score well, candidates needed to show how each aspect could be applied to the specific scenarios at Victoria.

Candidates seemed unwilling to say that employees (either senior management or operational managers) may be unhappy but this need not be an issue for Victoria, as there will usually be a conflict of interest between employees and the company/shareholders. Good answers identified and discussed how to address this issue fairly. However, simply stating that employees should set their own targets is not a practical solution, nor one which is commercially valuable to Victoria.

Marking scheme

		Marks
(a)	For relevant points discussing the linkage between customer perspective and the financial perspective – 1 mark each	
	Note. Answers must discuss all three financial metrics in order to score the full 5 marks.	
	Total for part (a): up to 5	5
(b)	Each suitable performance measurement recommended – up to 2 marks (for each of four perspectives; so up to 8 marks in total) (1 mark for calculating a suitable metric; 1 mark for justifying the choice of metric)	
	For discussing the problems of using customer complaints as a performance measure – up to 4 marks	
	Total for part (b): up to 11	11
(c)	For relevant points relating to issues in the senior management reward system – 1 mark each, up to a maximum of 5 For relevant points relating to the operational managers' bonus scheme – 1 mark per relevant point, up to a maximum of 5	
	Total for part (c): up to 9	9
	Total =	**25**

(a) **Links between customer perspective and financial perspective**

The success factors identified for the customer perspective should help Victoria to increase customer satisfaction. Since the delivery business in Yeeland appears to be very competitive, increasing (or, at least, maintaining) customer satisfaction levels is likely to be crucial to Victoria's financial success.

Revenue growth – Since the market is saturated, in order to increase its revenues Victoria will need to win new customers (from its competitors) whilst retaining its existing customers. Victoria's reputation for delivering packages quickly, safely and on time is likely to be crucial in helping it attract business from competitors.

In addition to increasing its customer numbers, Victoria could consider increasing its selling prices as a means of increasing revenue. In effect, Victoria could look to differentiate itself from its competitors, by virtue of its service quality, and could then charge premium prices for its service. The success factors linked to the customer perspective are ones in which Victoria will need to outperform its competitors in order to pursue a differentiation strategy successfully.

Profit margin – Charging premium prices should provide a direct way of increasing profit margins.

Alternatively, increasing customer numbers should enable Victoria to benefit from economies of scale, which in turn could improve profit margins by reducing unit costs. For example, if Victoria can increase its capacity utilisation (the number of packages on each delivery lorry) the amount of fixed costs apportioned to each package on that lorry will be lower.

Return on capital employed – As the ways of increasing revenue and profit margins will not require any additional capital expenditure, then any increases in operating profit should also increase Victoria's ROCE.

(b) **Ability to meet customers' transport needs**

This success factor can be measured by the proportion of customer requests which Victoria is able to undertake.

$$\frac{\text{Total number of packages transported}}{\text{Total number of customer transport requests}}$$

$$\frac{548{,}000}{610{,}000} = 89.8\%$$

Ability to deliver packages quickly

This measure needs to take account of how far packages have to travel as well as how long it takes them to get to their destinations. Therefore, a suitable measure will be one which measures **time taken per kilometre** (rather than one which measures time taken per journey).

$$\frac{\text{Total package minutes}}{\text{Total package kilometres}}$$

$$\frac{131{,}520{,}000}{65{,}760{,}000} = 2.0$$

Ability to deliver packages on time

This measure needs to reflect the proportion of packages which are delivered within the time window given to the customer.

$$\frac{\text{Deliveries within agreed window}}{\text{Total number of packages transported}}$$

$$\frac{(548{,}000 - 21{,}920)}{548{,}000} = 96\%$$

Ability to deliver packages safely

This measure needs to reflect the number of packages delivered undamaged as a proportion of the total number of packages transported.

$$\frac{\text{Deliveries with no reported damage}}{\text{Total number of packages transported}}$$

$$\frac{(548{,}000 - 8{,}220)}{548{,}000} = 98.5\%$$

Problems of using customer complaints as a basis for performance measurement

Victoria delivers packages to a large number of different customers, and it could respond to problems with their delivery in different ways. This means it will be difficult for Victoria to get an accurate picture of the number of deliveries which were damaged or late.

Problems understated – Some customers may not bother to report that a package has been delivered late or was damaged. However, due to the inconvenience caused by the lateness or damage they will use one of Victoria's competitors to deliver their packages in future.

In such cases, the performance measure gives a misleading impression that Victoria is performing better than it is. And, given the importance of customer retention in Yeeland's competitive market, this could have very significant consequences on Victoria's revenue performance in the longer term.

If Victoria recorded its own delivery performance it could take direct action to try to retain customers who have suffered from late or damaged packages. For example, acknowledging the problem at the point of delivery, it could offer to discount the next order for a customer whose package is delivered late.

Problems overstated – In contrast to customers who do not report valid complaints, others may report unjustified complaints in the hope of obtaining a refund or a credit against future orders. Currently, the measures simply record the number of complaints received, even though some of these may not be valid.

In this respect, it would be better to measure the number of refunds or discounts given (as an indicator of the number of valid complaints) rather than simply recording the total number of complaints.

(c) **Senior managers' reward system**

Assuming that the members of the senior management team are all on the board, the potential problem here is that senior management could be deciding their own bonuses.

Agency issues – As such, there is a danger that the reward system will favour the managers' interests, rather than those of Victoria's shareholders. For example, if the targets used to determine managers' bonuses are easy to achieve, this will maximise the chances of managers receiving bonuses. This would justify the shareholders' complaints that the bonuses are not suitable – because they are not supporting Victoria's objective of maximising shareholder wealth.

The introduction of the BSC should help to align the senior management's objectives with those of the shareholders, particularly in relation to the financial perspective. However, the financial measures suggested for the BSC do not directly address shareholder wealth, because they are essentially still based around profitability rather than value-based management.

Controllability – The fact that the market is saturated, and dominated by two international companies, will constrain management's ability to grow revenue. Similarly, fuel prices – which management cannot control – will be a significant influence on profit margin. This again suggests these may not be the most appropriate measures to use when assessing management's performance.

Operational managers' reward system

Choice of measures – Although the senior managers assess the operational managers' performance, it is not clear what measures are used as the basis of this assessment. The measures of performance against which operational managers are assessed should be aligned to Victoria's overall objectives.

However, the measures should also relate to the aspects of performance that the operational managers can influence (and therefore will typically come from the 'customer' and 'business' perspectives in the scorecard).

Setting own bonus targets – However, the suggestion that the operational managers should be involved in setting their own bonus targets does not seem appropriate. In the same way that senior management shouldn't set their own performance targets, neither should operational managers.

Although it could be beneficial to explain the **target setting process** to the manager, this should not be confused with the idea of letting managers set their own targets. Targets should still be set by a higher level of management, and should be set at a level which is stretching but achievable.

The target set should then be explained to the managers so that they understand what they have to do in order to earn their bonus.

36 Soup

Text reference. The balanced scorecard is discussed in Chapter 12 of the BPP Study Text.

Top tips.

Part (a). The number of times the word 'passenger' is mentioned in the scenario should have been an inherent clue that managing passenger (or 'customer') satisfaction should be a key part of Soup's performance management process.

The last paragraph highlights this point even more clearly, with the reference to the need for performance measures which 'balance the need of passengers with the requirements of the shareholders'. The reason why the scorecard is called the 'balanced scorecard' is because it encourages organisations to develop performance measures which ensure a 'balance' between the four perspectives. As such, it is also important to try to think how performance information in each of the four areas could be useful for Soup – don't just focus, for example, on the benefits of having passenger-focused performance measures.

Also, make sure you take note of the instructions the CEO has given in the last paragraph. She has said, specifically, that she doesn't want a list of suggested performance measures; instead she wants to know **why** those performance measures will help to improve Soup's performance.

Similarly, note that the CEO has specifically said that she doesn't want to know about how to improve Soup's performance, but instead how to improve Soup's performance management systems. Recognising the distinction between 'performance' and 'performance reporting' is absolutely crucial in APM. In a question like this – where the focus is on Soup's performance management system – you will score no marks for suggestions about how to improve the company's underlying performance.

Part (b). Whereas your focus in part (a) should have been on Soup's performance management systems, the focus here is on the underlying performance – in particular, the occupancy rates on Soup's trains.

The third paragraph of the scenario provides details of the capacity of Soup's trains, so you need to use these details in conjunction with the data at the end of the scenario to work out how many seats are available per day compared to the number of passengers.

However, note that you aren't asked simply to calculate occupancy rates, but rather to evaluate the comment that Soup's trains are overcrowded. So, how far do the figures you have calculated support the comment?

Part (c). The focus in this third part of the question returns to the balanced scorecard as a performance management system. However, whereas part (a) looked at the ways the scorecard could improve the performance management system at Soup, part (c) now looks at the problems which Soup could encounter when applying it.

There are two key points to note here, though. First, the requirement is looking specifically at the problems which could be encountered in 'selecting and interpreting performance measures' – not, more generally, about the problems which could be encountered in introducing the balanced scorecard. Second, you are asked to assess the problems 'Soup may encounter ...' rather than to discuss the problems in general terms. To score well in this part of the question, it is vital that you link your answer directly back to Soup.

Examining team's comments. In **part (a)** the majority of candidates clearly knew the structure of the balanced scorecard, but the question did not simply ask for an explanation of the four perspectives of the scorecard. It asked how the scorecard could improve the performance management system at Soup – therefore candidates needed to explain how using the scorecard could be beneficial to Soup.

The calculations for **part (b)** were generally done well. However, few candidates then attempted to discuss the claim of overcrowding in any detail, other than to say whether or not capacity was exceeded. The scenarios in APM are intended to reflect real world examples, and – in this scenario – discussing practical considerations could have been beneficial.

Part (c) was answered well by many candidates, who understood the advantages and disadvantages of the model, and then demonstrated how they related to the scenario.

However, one of the main weaknesses in many responses to this question was a failure to specifically answer the question which focused on 'selecting and interpreting' – so, for example, issues arising from conflicting metrics. Several candidates simply discussed the difficulties in implementing a balanced scorecard approach (such as commitment from management) and a general discussion of target setting (such as measure fixation). We have said this many times before, but candidates must ensure that they specifically answer the question that has been set.

Marking scheme

		Marks
(a)	For relevant points about how using the balanced scorecard could improve Soup's performance management system – 1 mark per point, up to a maximum of 10 marks No marks are to be awarded for a list of new measures without justifying why they would benefit Soup A maximum of 1 mark is to be given for a generic description of the balanced scorecard without clear references to the scenario	
	Total for part (a): up to 10	10
(b)	For relevant calculations – 1 mark each, up to 4 marks – Seats available per train – Seats available per day by region/time – Seat occupancy by region/time – Total seat occupancy Comment on whether the figures are consistent with government's claims about overcrowding – 1 mark Other comments – up to 2 marks Up to 2 additional marks for identifying journey time is an important factor and for attempting to quantify journey times from the data given	
	Total for part (b): up to 7	7
(c)	For each problem Soup may encounter – 1 mark per relevant point, up to 2 marks per problem Problems include: – Selection of appropriate measures – Prioritisation of measures – Difficulties of making measurements – Conflicting measures – Overload of measures A maximum of 3 marks to be given, in total, for general problems of applying the balanced scorecard, but not applied to Soup	
	Total for part (c): up to 8	8
	Total =	25

(a) The balanced scorecard consists of four perspectives: customer, internal, innovation and learning and financial. It requires an organisation to have a number of goals supported by performance measures in each perspective. The customer perspective measures what it is that customers value from the business; internal looks at what processes the organisation needs to be successful; innovation and learning considers how future value can be created; and the financial perspective measures whether performance is acceptable to investors.

It is useful because it uses both internal and external information to assess performance and measures **financial and non-financial aspects** of a business to ensure long-term future success, rather than just focusing on historic results. It can also be used as a mechanism to link key performance indicators (KPIs) into the critical success factors which are vital to deliver strategy.

Financial perspective

Soup currently uses return on capital employed (ROCE) as its key financial performance measure, but this does not correlate directly with the **objective to maximise shareholder wealth** and could encourage short-term decisions to be taken at the expense of long-term success. This is the case at Soup which purchased old trains and subsequently failed to reinvest, meaning that Soup's ROCE is probably higher than its rivals. However, the trains are becoming unreliable and their condition is deteriorating. In the long term this will reduce customer satisfaction and financial performance.

Using the scorecard, Soup should have a **broader range of financial measures** which encourage managers to take decisions, such as investment decisions, consistent with the objective to maximise shareholder wealth in the long term. Economic value added would be a suitable measure to help achieve this, and would be preferable to the current focus on ROCE.

Customer perspective

Soup does measure growth in passenger numbers which could be a measure of customer satisfaction. However, it is a limited, quantitative measure. Though Soup does have rivals and is likely to be required to operate a specified level of service under the terms of the licence from the Government, some passengers may be forced to travel on Soup trains, rather than those of another operator because of where they live or the times they need to travel. The number of operators (competitors) is limited by the capacity of the railway infrastructure as well as by passenger demand. This means that the level of repeat customers may not be appropriate for Soup.

Passenger numbers are also externally focused but again this fails to fully consider the environment in which Soup operates. Within the customer perspective Soup could use a range of performance measures. This will be beneficial as where passengers are able, they are likely to choose to use Soup if they provide a good service. This can be easily measured by surveying or asking passengers' opinions. This will give Soup more qualitative information about their customers and their expectations, which will vary; for example, passengers will have different perceptions of overcrowding, or what is an acceptable delay. Certain groups may be more affected by overcrowding like frequent travellers and the elderly. Passengers who are unable to find a seat will probably be the most dissatisfied, though this will depend on how long their journey is. Other aspects of Soup's service may be less valued than reliability and occupancy, like wireless access and the on-board café, but will be important to certain groups.

Another key element of customer satisfaction will relate to the amount of fare paid. Fares are regulated in Deeland so the interaction between fares and other aspects of the service is unknown. Many customers, while valuing a particular aspect of the service, may be unwilling to pay more for it; some may accept a reduction in the level of service if fares were reduced.

This detailed information about customers will allow Soup to focus performance improvements on key areas using more external data to make decisions.

Internal processes

Measures of the internal processes are likely to be closely linked to customer satisfaction. Soup apparently neglects this area in its performance management system. The scorecard could be used to help to address reliability, overcrowding and environmental factors.

Reliability will be highly valued by customers, especially those who travel frequently and who rely on rail travel to get to work. The number of trains arriving late would be a suitable measure of reliability, as would the number of train services cancelled, though the length of the delay is also critical and should be carefully defined. The scorecard would allow more detailed measures as some of the factors affecting reliability will be within Soup's direct control but others such as failures in the railway infrastructure are controlled by the Government. This is useful information for Soup to effectively assess its controllable performance and feed back as necessary to external parties.

Seat occupancy, the number of passengers on a train compared to the number of available seats on different routes and at different times, is a suitable measure of train overcrowding and is important for passenger safety. To fully utilise its trains and achieve its objective of maximising shareholder wealth, Soup must try to maximise both the seat occupancy and the amount of time its trains are actually running. These internal measures would then help to support financial targets.

Soup's licence to operate rail services in Regions A and B expires in three years' time and, as with the operator from whom Soup purchased the trains, it may not be renewed. Soup must balance the needs of shareholders for short-term increases in dividends and share price with the long-term need to renew to its operator's licence.

Innovation and learning perspective

The creation of long-term future value can be addressed by the innovation and learning perspective. The immediate scope to innovate the service experienced by the passenger is limited, but there are some quick wins available in the choice in the on-board café and improving the reliability of the internet access. Also time spent training staff may improve customer satisfaction and reduce maintenance time. Fundamental innovation like the use of faster or environmentally less harmful trains requires long-term planning and large capital investment. The scorecard will encourage Soup to be forward looking, unlike the present system which is limited to historic performance.

(b) To measure the extent of overcrowding, some measure of occupancy is needed. The number of passengers per available seat can be used as a measure of occupancy.

		Region A		*Region B*	*Total*
Seats available					
Per service (70 per carriage)		490		420	
Seats available per day					
Peak times	4 services	1,960	4 services	1,680	
Other times	6 services	2,940	8 services	3,360	
Total		4,900		5,040	9,940
Passenger demand per day					
Peak times		2,500		1,400	
Other times		2,450		1,850	
Total		4,950		3,250	8,200
Occupancy (demand/availability)					
Peak times		127.6%		83.3%	
Other times		83.3%		55.1%	
Total		101.0%		64.5%	82.5%

Overall occupancy (82.5%) is significantly below 100%, which means on average there are more seats available than passengers. This is not consistent with the Government's claims that the trains are overcrowded. However, these averages may be misleading as trains running on certain days or at certain times may be relatively overcrowded. This may generate customer dissatisfaction even on services which are on average not fully occupied. The total number of passengers without seats would be a better measure.

There are **significant variations between regions and times travelled**, with only the trains in Region A travelling at peak times being over-occupied. This affects only 18% (4/22) of all services.

The people most affected by this will be the 28% of the passengers travelling at peak times in Region A who are unable to obtain a seat. This represents only 9% (28% × 2,500/8,200) of total passengers per day. There is some overcrowding, but the claim that Soup's trains are overcrowded seems exaggerated given

BPP LEARNING MEDIA

the data provided. However, certain routes or specific times or sections of the trains may be more affected and more analysis is needed.

The impact of overcrowding on passengers also depends on the length of journeys passengers are making, with the lack of seating typically causing a greater inconvenience to passengers on long journeys compared to passengers only making a shorter journey. Equally, some passengers may board a service at intermediate stations, rather than travelling the full length of a route. These passengers are relatively more likely to have to stand, but will have to stand for a shorter length of time than passengers who are travelling the full length of the route.

(c) When applying the balanced scorecard in Soup, the measures need to be chosen carefully. A balance needs to be struck, and only measures which help Soup to **achieve its objectives** should be chosen. Currently Soup focuses on short-term financial measures such as ROCE, whereas the balanced scorecard considers more **long-term measures**.

Some measures are more important than others, so **prioritising measures** will be difficult. Customers may value some aspects of the service more than others; for example, the choice available in the on-board café is probably unimportant to most passengers provided they can obtain some food and drink. The punctuality of Soup's trains or whether they even run at all is fundamental to achieving customer satisfaction and needs careful measurement. Soup must have measures for regulatory or safety reasons too.

Some aspects of the business may be **harder to measure** than others. For example, it may be relatively easy to measure seat occupancy as a measure of overcrowding, but passengers' perceptions of overcrowding may differ. Non-financial aspects such as customer satisfaction may be subjective and any surveys done may not reflect the experience of the majority of passengers. Performing and analysing surveys would also be time consuming and resource intensive.

Measures chosen may conflict. Overcrowding may be unwelcome by passengers but making them less crowded conflicts with Soup's presumed objective of fully occupied trains. Time spent maintaining trains to reduce their impact on the environment or ensure reliability will mean they are not operational for periods of time, though safety will be a key factor here.

Care must be taken to **avoid overloading** with too many performance measures. The current objective to maximise shareholder wealth is very broad. Having a clearer strategy would enable Soup to determine suitable performance measures so it is not overloaded with KPIs which do not contribute towards achieving this strategy.

37 Graviton

Text reference. The performance pyramid is discussed in Chapter 12 of the BPP Study Text. Problems of performance measurement are discussed in Chapter 11.

Top tips.

Part (a). The scenario identifies that the CEO is 'unhappy with the current performance measurement system', and that there are 'major gaps in the current list of key metrics used'. Equally, the evidence from the press reports suggests that Graviton is being successful in some areas, whilst performing less well in other areas.

A sensible approach to this question might be to think how far these variations in Graviton's current performance reflect the areas which are monitored by Graviton's current performance measures; and then to think how far the weaknesses in the current system could be addressed by using the performance pyramid.

Crucially, however, note that the requirement asks you to evaluate Graviton's performance measurement **system**, not its current performance. You will not earn any marks for discussing Graviton's performance as such.

Part (b). The issues listed by the board (myopia, gaming, ossification) are three of the problems listed by Berry, Broadbent and Ottley in relation to the use of performance measures.

If you were aware of Berry, Broadbent and Ottley's list, then identifying the problems at Graviton should have been relatively straightforward, because evidence of them is fairly clearly illustrated by the scenario.

A sensible way to approach this part of the requirement would be to take each of the three problems in turn; provide a short definition of the problem; assess whether they apply to Graviton; and then suggest possible solutions for the problem.

There are ten marks available for this part of the question, so if you describe each problem (one mark each) and then make a couple of relevant points applying each problem to Graviton (two marks per problem) this would enable you to score almost all the marks available.

If you weren't familiar with Berry, Broadbent and Ottley's terminologies, you are likely to have struggled with this part of the question. Nonetheless, you should have realised that the issues at Factories 1 and 2 had been included in the scenario for a reason. Therefore, even if you didn't know what myopia, gaming and ossification were, the scenario should have given you a clue that these issues were linked to problems with the company's performance measures, and so you should have been able to suggest appropriate performance management solutions to them.

Marking scheme

		Marks
(a)	General description of performance pyramid (including diagram of the model) – up to 3 marks	
	All the remaining marks must have specific relevance to Graviton:	
	Current issues at Graviton where current performance measurement system leads to tunnel vision and focus on selected aspects of performance only – 1 mark per relevant point, up to maximum of 5 marks	
	Linking performance metrics to the company's vision – 1 mark per relevant point, up to a maximum of 4 marks	
	Using performance pyramid to identify ways Graviton's current performance measures could be improved: Market satisfaction; financial performance; customer satisfaction; flexibility; productivity; quality; delivery; cycle time; waste – 1 mark per relevant point, up to a maximum of 6 marks	
	Total for part (a): up to 15	15
(b)	Clear definition of each term – 1 mark per term, up to a maximum of 3	
	For assessing whether the problems apply at Graviton, and for suggesting appropriate solutions – 1 mark per relevant point, up to a maximum of 3 for each problem	
	Total for part (b): up to 10	10
	Total =	**25**

(a) **Performance pyramid** – The logic of the performance pyramid is that although organisations operate at different levels (for example, strategic and operational) those levels need to support each other in achieving business objectives. The structure of the pyramid seeks to highlight the links between the day to day operational performance and overall strategic performance.

Graviton's current performance measurement system

The aim of Graviton's current performance measurement system (to provide a list of measures at strategic, tactical and operational levels of management) seems to be consistent with the logic of the performance pyramid (to link strategic and operational performance drivers).

However, the CEO's concern that there are gaps in the current list of metrics could also be linked to a concern that the current performance measurement system at Graviton is concentrating attention on certain aspects of performance to the detriment of other aspects of performance.

Tunnel vision – Although this is not one of the problems listed by the board executives, the focus on selected measurements, at the expense of others, characterises the problem of tunnel vision in performance measurement systems.

For example, Graviton's recent results might suggest that the focus of the company's attention has been on revenue growth rather than profitability, which could help to explain why revenue has risen considerably more rapidly than operating profit in the last year. In such a case, the problem could be addressed by including performance metrics relating to operating costs or profit margins.

More generally, one way to prevent tunnel vision being a problem for an organisation is to ensure that the dimensions of performance being measured are comprehensive, and include metrics relating to all the critical success factors in the organisation. Importantly also, this means that performance measures shouldn't focus narrowly on financial indicators, but should also address the range of processes and driving forces which guide an organisation's ability to achieve its strategic objectives.

This recognition of the importance of focusing on the range of processes and activities which shape an organisation's ability to achieve its strategic objectives is one of the key characteristics of the performance pyramid.

Moreover, the pyramid does not focus purely on financial objectives, but includes a range of objectives of **external effectiveness and internal efficiency**. Lynch and Cross propose that these elements of effectiveness and efficiency are the key driving forces on which company objectives are based.

The pyramid diagram highlights the way the performance of operational and business processes underpins an organisation's financial performance:

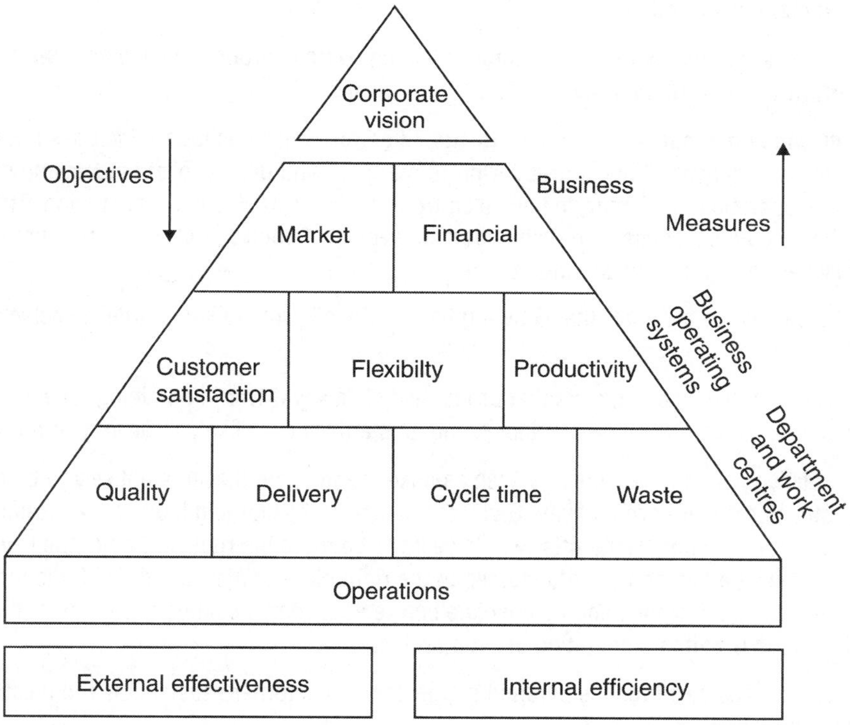

Corporate vision

Shareholder wealth – Graviton's overall objective is to maximise shareholder wealth; and therefore it seems surprising that the performance measures do not include **total shareholder return** (thereby recognising the importance of dividends and share price growth).

It is possible that Graviton is using return on capital employed (ROCE) as an overall measure of productivity and performance, but given the company's objective refers specifically to maximising 'shareholder wealth' then a performance measure focusing specifically on shareholder return would be more appropriate.

Moreover, the absence of any measures linked to the level of dividends may also explain why Graviton's dividend growth has not been strong – leading to criticism from the institutional investors.

Focus on changing market trends – Graviton's business aim is to satisfy changing market trends, and it seeks to do this by maintaining flexibility in production and close control across the supply chain. The elements of 'flexibility' and 'productivity' are included at the business operating system level in the performance pyramid, but it seems that they are higher level objectives at Graviton.

Flexibility – The measure of the average time for bringing new designs to market in Graviton's performance measurement system supports the importance of flexibility in its operations.

However, the current performance system does not measure the company's ability to replenish successful product lines, and therefore to take advantage of consumer demand. Whilst it is important for Graviton to introduce new designs quickly, it is equally important for the product availability of different clothes to reflect levels of demand.

Production control – Equally, however, it is important to maintain the quality of the production process. The criticisms from customers about the durability of Graviton's clothes may suggest there are issues relating to the controls in place in the production process.

The current performance measures do not include any measures around production quality or durability.

The apparent lack of focus on the production process could also help to explain why operating profits are increasingly significantly less than revenue. If Graviton's cost controls in the production process are weak, this would lead to falling operating profit margins.

Market and financial performance

The pyramid suggests that the two key drivers for obtaining overall corporate vision are **satisfying the market** and **performing well financially**.

Financial performance measures – Although Graviton's performance dashboard includes figures for revenues and profits, it doesn't show figures for profit margins. And despite profit increasing slightly from 20X1 to 20X3, the operating profit margin has fallen from 21.8% to 18.6% over this period. This again suggests that there could be issues with rising costs or weak cost control, but the current performance measurement system doesn't draw attention to this.

Alternatively, there could be a danger that Graviton has sacrificed profitability in order to achieve revenue growth.

Productivity – The pyramid also suggests that productivity is a key driver in obtaining financial objectives, and the nature of Graviton's market means that production efficiency is likely to be very important.

The measure of 'deliveries on time' could be seen as linked to this; but it seems unlikely to be the most important indicator to measure productivity. Given the nature of the clothing industry, a measure of waste or obsolescence (such as inventory write-offs) would seem to be more instructive. One of the keys to Graviton's success will be getting the right clothes to the right place at the right time. If it is too slow in producing clothes, and its designs become obsolete before it has had a chance to sell them, this could have a significant impact on Graviton's operating profit margins.

Market satisfaction – The performance pyramid suggests that customer satisfaction and flexibility are crucial in achieving market satisfaction.

We have already noted that Graviton uses 'time to market' as a measure for its ability to introduce new products in response to changing market trends, suggesting that it already considers this aspect of flexibility is important in achieving its corporate objectives.

Customer satisfaction – Although the current performance measures do not directly measure customer satisfaction, revenue growth could be seen, indirectly, as an indicator of customer satisfaction levels. If customers are not satisfied with the products they have bought from Graviton in the past, they are unlikely to make any repeat purchases.

BPP LEARNING MEDIA

Quality – In this respect, customer criticism over the durability of Graviton's clothes should be seen as a concern, because if these concerns remain they could hinder the company's sales and revenue in the future.

Alternatively, though, we could question how much customers value durability in a fast-changing industry. If customers are regularly buying new clothes to keep up with the changes in fashion, how important will durability actually be in their decision about which clothes to buy?

In this respect, it would be useful for Graviton to estabish how important the issue of durability is in customers' decision-making process. If it is significant, then it would be useful for Graviton to include a related metric (such as the number of customer complaints) in its performance measures.

Design awards – Although the current performance measures don't specifically refer to product quality, the number of design awards could also be seen, indirectly, as an indicator of quality – and possibly also of customer satisfaction. Graviton's clothes would be unlikely to be nominated for awards if they are felt to be of poor quality or if customers are critical of them.

Again, however, measuring the number of design awards is not the most obvious way of measuring quality or customer satisfaction (both of which are highlighted in the performance pyramid as drivers of external effectiveness).

(b) **Myopia**

Myopia relates to the problems caused by short-termist decisions leading to the neglect of longer-term objectives.

This currently appears to be an issue at Factory Site 2, where the factory appears reluctant to invest in any new machinery in order to preserve its excellent return on capital employed.

However, the failure to invest in the new machinery has led to a significant adverse variance in the cost of repairs and maintenance. It also seems likely that Site 2's production is less efficient than it would otherwise be if it had invested in some new machinery.

The use of ROCE as one of the metrics in the performance measurement systems (and in particular annual ROCE figures) could be one of the main reasons for myopia within Graviton; and specifically at Factory Site 2. One solution for this specific issue would be to include a performance measure for production efficiency (eg number of breakdowns or repairs required) at each of the factory sites.

More generally, Graviton could address the issue of myopia by measuring performance over a longer time period than a single accounting period.

Gaming

The problem of 'gaming' relates to the deliberate distortion of a performance measure in order to secure some kind of strategic advantage.

There is clear evidence of gaming at Factory Site 1, where the manager is manipulating revenue and profit figures (by delaying invoicing) in order to achieve profit targets.

It is not clear whether Graviton has an internal audit department, but if it does one specific action which could be taken is a review of the invoicing procedures, or a review of period-end cut-offs, to try to prevent such manipulation recurring.

More generally, the problem of gaming also appears to have been driven by the desire to achieve short-term (annual) performance targets. So, as with the proposed solution to myopia, one solution would be to reward performance over a longer time period than a single accounting period. For example, the Factory Manager's profit targets could be set as an average figure over a number of periods, rather than having single targets for individual periods.

Additionally, behaviour such as the Factory Manager's could be addressed by promoting a culture of honesty within the organisation. It is not clear whether Graviton currently has a corporate Code of Ethics, but a Code of this sort could be useful for highlighting the standards of behaviour which are expected in the company.

Ossification

The problem of 'ossification' relates to an unwillingness to change a performance measurement system once it has been set up. Ossification is likely to be a particular problem when the current system appears to be showing adequate results – because this situation could be hiding issues which could be highlighted if different measures were being monitored.

Ossification appears to be a problem at Graviton, where the board is sceptical of change and has argued that the business's good performance means there is no justification for changing the performance measurement system.

The CEO will have to convince the board that Graviton's current good performance has been achieved despite the current performance measurement system rather than because of it. More specifically, the CEO will need to highlight how the gaps in the current list of key metrics will lead to longer-term difficulties in achieving Graviton's overall objective to maximise shareholder wealth.

Once again, recognising the importance of longer-term performance is likely to address this problem. For example, the remuneration and incentive plans for Graviton's executives and board members could be linked to the longer-term, sustainable performance of the company, rather than to its historical results, or to its results in the short term.

38 APX Accountancy

Text reference. The building block model is discussed in Chapter 12 of the Study Text.

Top tips. Part (a) is a pure test of knowledge. You are simply asked to describe Fitzgerald and Moon's model; you do not need to apply it to the scenario.

However, in parts (b) and (c) you do need to apply your knowledge of the model to the scenario.

It is vital that you read the requirement for **part (b)** carefully and answer the question set. You are asked to evaluate APX's performance **management system**, not APX's performance.

Notice also the link between parts (b) and (c). In part (b) you need to evaluate the existing system, and then in **part (c)** you need to explain and suggest improvements. Therefore, you should not have suggested any improvements while you were answering part (b); but should have saved these for part (c) instead.

Part (d) – At one level, the Marketing Manager seems to be highlighting the importance of non-financial performance measures, which seems reasonable. However, he also seems to have overlooked the environmental factors which have contributed to the relative financial performance of the different service areas. Has the Business Advisory Division really performed best financially because it has the highest customer service score, or because the business advisory sector had a growth year across the industry as a whole?

Examining team's comments. It was sad to note how many candidates did not even know the names of the three building blocks. This demonstrated inadequate preparation for the examination.

Better candidates had read the full requirement to the question before beginning their answers, and so held back from offering improvements to the faults recognised in part (b) until their answers to part (c) of the question.

(a) **Performance measurement in service businesses** – Fitzgerald and Moon's building block model aims to provide a framework to improve performance measurement in service businesses.

The model suggests that performance systems should be based on three concepts: dimensions, standards and rewards.

Dimensions – The model identifies six dimensions (competitive performance, financial performance, quality of service, flexibility and resource utilisation and innovation) and suggests that the performance measures companies choose should focus on these six areas.

The model also suggests that the dimensions can be divided into two sets: **results** (competitive performance and financial performance) and **determinants** (the other four). The logic here is that controlling and improving performance in respect of the determinants will then lead to improved results.

Standards – This aspect of the model relates to the targets which are chosen to be measured. Here, the model highlights three key properties which performance measures (standards or targets) should possess: **ownership, achievability** and **fairness**.

Rewards – Finally, the model also highlights the properties which reward schemes need to possess in order to encourage staff to work towards the performance standards set. Again, there are three key properties: **clarity, controllability** and **motivation**. The reward system needs to help motivate staff and, in order to achieve this, staff need to be clear about the goals they are working towards, and feel that the rewards are related to areas of responsibility that they can control.

(b) The current performance management system appears to be based primarily on financial performance, and so does not focus on a number of the determinants highlighted by the building block model.

Dimensions

Results – The current system does allow **financial** and **competitive performance** to be measured. The figures for **revenue growth** and **profit margin** can be used to measure APX's financial performance, while the data on accounting industry revenue can be used to calculate **market share**.

Determinants – However, the management information collected provides less opportunity to measure the determinants of performance. The customer service score could be used as an indicator of the quality of service offered, but there appears to be no information on which to measure flexibility and resource utilisation and innovation.

Standards

Measuring competitive performance – The industry figures will allow APX to monitor its market share, and its revenue growth relative to the industry as a whole, but they only look at revenue rather than profit. Therefore, it does not look as if APX can measure its profit margin against the industry as a whole.

Consequently, any standards for profitability will have to be **set internally**; for example APX could measure the profitability of each of its business streams. However, this could raise issues in relation to **achievability** and **fairness**. Given that Emland is currently in a recession, it is perhaps to be expected that the growth and margins in the audit businesses will be lower than those in the Business Advisory Division, so the fact that this is the case does not necessarily tell us anything about the relative performance of the divisions.

The scenario does not tell us anything about the target scores for customer service or how these are set, so we cannot comment on this aspect of the standards.

Reward system

Clarity – Non-partners receive a bonus based on their line managers' annual review, but the scenario does not indicate what aspects of their performance staff are judged on in this review. If they are not clear what their performance is being judged on, or if the judgement is perceived to be too subjective, this may serve to demotivate staff.

Controllability – APX's performance management system appears to focus predominantly on financial indicators, which may suggest that financial measures are used as the basis for the annual review. Again, though, this could be a cause for concern, because non-partners have relatively limited scope to influence revenue or profit margins.

Divisional or group-wide performance – There may be similar issues of controllability in relation to the partners' reward system. The partners currently receive a share of profit, but it is not clear if this profit share is based on APX's profit as a whole or the profit for their area of the business. If the partners feel their rewards are being based on measures they cannot control, this is likely to adversely affect their motivation. For example, if partners' rewards are based on group profits, then partners in the Audit Division may not maximise their own performance if they know that they will benefit (regardless of their own division's performance) from the favourable performance of the Business Advisory Services Division.

(c) **Cover all dimensions of performance** – One of the key improvements a building block system can make to performance management is ensuring that all the key dimensions of successful performance are measured.

At APX, this will mean considering the importance of flexibility, resource utilisation and innovation to the firm's success and then developing performance measures for these dimensions.

Flexibility – Flexibility is likely to be important for APX in terms of the scheduling of its work (to meet client deadlines) and, in this respect, flexibility is also likely to have an impact on customer satisfaction. Accordingly, APX could introduce a performance measure looking at the percentage of jobs delivered on time.

Resource utilisation – APX's key resource is its staff, so it would seem very important to measure staff utilisation rates. One way of doing this would be to measure the percentage of chargeable hours worked as a percentage of total working hours, and such a measure would provide APX with information about the productivity of its staff. Moreover, if this measure were recorded on a monthly basis it would highlight periods when the business is busy and when it is less busy. The partners could then try to win new clients who need work done in APX's less busy periods.

Innovation – Innovation could be useful for improving APX's internal systems and working practices, but its impact is likely to be greater in relation to the new services APX can develop for its clients. In this case, it may be useful to have a performance measure which looks at the percentage of revenue earned from new customer initiatives.

Standards and rewards

Although the introduction of additional measures which cover the non-financial dimensions of successful performance is perhaps the biggest improvement the building block approach could make to APX, there are also **issues with the way standards are currently set**.

To address this, APX needs to ensure that the measures chosen (and performance targets set) are **achievable** and **fair**. In turn, this should encourage the staff to try to achieve the performance targets.

Similarly, the current rewards system should also be reviewed to ensure that it serves to **motivate partners and staff**. For example, if this is not already the case, an element of the partners' profit share should be based on the profitability of the work from their divisions, rather than it all being based on APX's profitability overall.

Equally, it may also be beneficial to give the non-partners their own targets or objectives for the year, because then the line managers have some more clearly defined objectives to assess their staff against in the annual review process.

(d) **Top tip.** The measure being commented on is customer service, not customer satisfaction. You may have been tempted to discuss the potential trade-off between financial and non-financial performance measures – by suggesting that APX might be able to increase customer satisfaction by reducing its prices, and thereby also reducing its profit margins.

However, we have focused specifically on the customer service score, rather than customer satisfaction more generally, and so we have not included this more general argument in our suggested solution below.

Importance of customer service – Customer service is undoubtedly important for a service firm like APX, because if the service it offers its customers is poor it may look for other advisers.

It is not clear what factors contribute to the customer service scores which customers give, but the quality of the advice which APX gives its clients is likely to be an important factor in its ongoing success, so this aspect of customer service is important to measure.

Reasons for scores – However, the inherent nature of the services provided could also contribute to the customer service scores, and so, in this respect, the Marketing Manager's statement could be misleading.

APX's clients have to have an audit, and they may almost resent this if they perceive the audit brings them little value. So the fact that the audit gets the lowest customer service score may reflect this rather than the quality of APX's audit staff.

External environment – However, perhaps more importantly, the Marketing Manager seems to be attributing the Business Advisory Division's favourable performance to its customer service score alone, without considering the environmental factors which have also affected its performance. The current recession in Emland has led to an increase in demand for business advisory services across the industry as a whole. It seems likely that APX's performance reflects this more than its customer service scores.

Equally, the Marketing Manager's implication that the customer service score is a more important performance metric than financial measures is also misguided. Whilst it is important that APX considers non-financial aspects of performance, it should not do so at the expense of financial performance measures. Instead, APX's performance evaluation needs to consider both financial and non-financial performance measures.

39 Robust Laptops

Text reference. ABC is discussed in Chapter 12 of the BPP Study Text in the context of activity-based management. Critical success factors (CSFs) and KPIs are discussed in Chapter 2, while the importance of non-financial performance measures is discussed in Chapter 9b.

Top tips. In **part (a)** look at the verb requirement here: it asks for an **evaluation** of the existing method and an ABC system. So you need to consider the respective benefits and limitations of the current method and the ABC method, specifically in relation to Robust Laptops. What features of Robust Laptops would make the method suitable or not? The calculations you are also asked to provide should help you identify the issues here.

However, note that as well as evaluating the two methods, you then need to advise management what action they might take. Try to be practical here, though. For example, if the ABC method suggests that the price of the laptops is too low, can Robust simply raise its prices as it wishes?

Part (b). Much of this part of the question is a test of knowledge. Although you need to relate your answer to Robust, a key issue here is the point that CSFs identify the key processes which an organisation needs to perform in order to be successful, and KPIs are the measures which are used to assess whether or not it is achieving this.

As is often the case with the requirements in APM questions, note that there are two elements to this requirement: first, explaining the links between objectives, CSFs and KPIs; second, explaining the importance of non-financial performance information as well as financial. However, answering the first element should help you answer the second element. If most of an organisation's CSFs are non-financial, what implications will this have for the performance information the organisation needs in order to measure whether or not it is achieving its CSFs?

Marking scheme

		Marks
(a)	General discussion of the two methods – 1 mark per point up to 4 marks Discussion of illustrative calculations – 1 mark per point up to 3 marks Further action to undertake – up to 2 marks Conclusion on system of costing – 1 mark Maximum of 9 marks	
	Workings *Absorption cost* Cost per unit – 1 mark Price per unit – 1 mark *ABC cost* Driver rates – 2 marks Cost per unit – 1 mark Price per unit – 1 mark Difference between prices – 1 mark Ignore minor rounding differences provided the candidate has used a reasonable level of detail. Maximum of 7 marks for workings	
	Maximum of 16 marks for part (a)	16

Marks

(b) Explaining what objectives, CSFs and KPIs are – 1 mark each (max: 3)
Explaining the links between them, with reference to Robust – 1 mark per relevant point; up to 4 marks
Explaining the importance of non-financial as well as financial performance information – 1 mark per point; up to 3 marks
Maximum for part (b): 9 marks — 9

Total = 25

(a) **Evaluation of the current method of costing against an ABC system**

The costing system is important at RL because not only is it a method of reporting activities in the business, but it also sets the prices that customers pay, and therefore it affects competitiveness.

The traditional system of absorption costing allocates overhead costs to products based on production activity (labour hours in RL's case). Absorption costing suits traditional production environments with few activities and fairly low overheads.

ABC is an alternative method for allocating overheads, intended to reflect the different activities that lead to costs being incurred. The principal benefit of ABC is that identifying and monitoring cost-generating activities leads to more accurate cost control. As such, ABC may be a more appropriate method of allocating overheads than absorption costing when overheads form a large proportion of an organisation's costs.

At RL, overheads comprise 23% of the total costs, meaning the overheads are a significant proportion of the total, although they are not dominant. ABC is most often used in manufacturing where production is typified by small batches and where there is significant tailoring of products to meet customer specifications. This is the case at RL.

We can use Order 11784 to assess the impact of introducing ABC. Under the current absorption costing system, the cost per unit would be $2,556 and the price would be $3,706 as there is a mark-up of 45%. Under an ABC system, the units would be costed at $3,194 and the mark-up would mean the price is $4,631. This represents an increase of 25% on the current figures. The overhead allocated to the order by the traditional absorption costing method is $596, while ABC allocates $1,234 per unit sold on the order.

Absorption costing cost and price per unit	*Current method standard costing*	*ABC cost and price per unit*	*Difference*	
Costs	$	$	$	%
Direct	1,959.96	1,960.00		
Overhead allocated (14,190,000/(23,800 × 3)	596.22			
Customer service		593.28		
Purchasing and receiving		458.13		
Stock management		75.86		
Administration of production	–	106.60		
Total cost	**2,556.18**	**3,193.87**		
Mark-up (45%)	1,150.28	1,437.24		
Price	**3,706.46**	**4,631.11**	924.65	24.9

	Total of cost activity $'000	*No. of driver units*	*Cost per driver unit* $
No. of minutes on call to customer	7,735	899,600	8.60
No. of purchase orders raised	2,451	21,400	114.53
No. of components used in production	1,467	618,800	2.37
Administration of production (absorbed as general overhead)	2,537	71,400	35.53

BPP LEARNING MEDIA

	Driver units on order	Cost allocated to order	Cost per unit on order (16 orders)
		$	$
No. of minutes on call to customer	1,104	9,492	593.28
No. of purchase orders raised	64	7,330	458.19
No. of components used in production	512	1,214	75.86
Administration of production (absorbed as general overhead)	48	1,706	106.60
			1,233.93

This difference in costs indicates that there is currently a significant underpricing of the order. ABC has identified that the major components of the overhead are the time spent discussing the order, and the number of purchase orders that subsequently have to be raised. RL's management should review these two areas of activity to see if they can be made more efficient. If not, then management need to consider whether orders such as this should be repriced.

However, before increasing the price, RL's management need to assess the impact that any increase in price will have on customers and RL's competitive position. It seems unlikely that customers will accept a 25% increase in price, which is what the calculations are suggesting should be the case.

A change to an ABC system may be warranted as an ABC system would provide valuable extra costing data particularly on product costs and prices that could assist in profitability. However, ABC systems can be time consuming, in terms of collecting the volume of data needed and the systems needed to support this. So a cost-benefit analysis would need to be done between the additional costs of putting in such a system and the extra value of the data produced.

(b) **Objectives** – An organisation's objectives are the operational goals it is trying to achieve. For example, RL could set a financial objective to increase operating profit by 5% in the next year, or it could set an objective of ensuring that its market share remains constant over the next year.

Equally, one of RL's objectives could be to ensure that it keeps pace with technological developments, and incorporates these into its laptops in order to maintain its reputation for quality.

CSFs – Once RL has established its objectives, it needs to identify the key factors and processes which will enable it to achieve them – its CSFs. In effect, the CSFs are the building blocks which will enable RL to be successful in the future.

Although the prices RL charges for its laptops are likely to affect the quantity it sells and the profits it makes, the factors which will determine its future success extend across all aspects of its operations, not simply pricing and costing. For example, innovation in product design could be important in improving the durability of RL's laptops in rough conditions.

This also highlights that performance measures need to reflect what matters to RL's customers, because to be successful RL needs to perform well in those activities which matter most to its customers – for example, meeting the individual specifications required by each customer.

KPIs – Once RL has identified what its CSFs are, it also needs to know whether it is achieving them. This is done by using KPIs, which measure how well it is performing against its CSFs. In effect, RL's CSFs will indicate what it needs to do to be successful, and its KPIs are the means of measuring whether these CSFs are being achieved or not.

For example, RL could select the number of repeat orders it receives as a measure of how well it is meeting customer requirements. If its computers don't survive rough handling, and don't meet the customers' requirements, it is unlikely the customer will make future orders from it.

Importance of non-financial information – Although, ultimately, RL's performance will be measured in terms of its financial results, financial performance indicators typically **measure** success, rather than helping to **ensure** it. By contrast, many of the factors which ensure success (the CSFs) will be non-financial in nature – such as quality, or flexibility in meeting customer specifications. If these variables are important elements in RL achieving its strategy successfully, then it follows that the company should also measure its performance in relation to them.

Although the CEO has not specifically mentioned the idea of introducing a multi-dimensional performance measurement system (such as a balanced scorecard), such a system would highlight the linkages between non-financial and financial performance in the way he is suggesting.

40 SFS

Chapter references. ABM is discussed in Chapter 12 of the BPP Study Text. Japanese business practices and management accounting techniques, including target costing and Kaizen costing, are discussed in Chapter 10.

Top tips. In **part (a)** start by comparing the recharges using the two methods and what the differences are. Think about how the increase or decrease would affect decisions on whether to continue with the jobs, design issues and whether margins could be preserved.

Parts (b) (i) to (iii) are trickier as they want you to relate what you know about ABM and activity-based costing (ABC) to the decisions made at different levels of the organisation. Implicit value refers to the non-financial value of an activity such as reputation.

Part (c). A sensible way to approach this question would be to think what the aims of target costing and Kaizen costing are, and then think how SFS could use them to improve its future performance (in effect, by reducing its costs).

Examining team's comments. Overall answers were mixed. Many candidates seemed unprepared for part (a) despite comparisons between costing methods and performance measurement being fundamental in this paper. Better answers showed how different answers can be arrived at using the two methods and how there were cost implications for instance in the design of products using the two methods.

Part (b) saw a wide spread of marks. Better candidates related the general definitions of operational and strategic ABM to the company.

(a) **Compare cost figures for two jobs**

Under the current costing system, Job 973 is charged $1,172 which implies 9.77 direct labour hours are spent on this job. Job 974 receives a lower charge of $620 or 5.17 direct labour hours. The ABC system building up a recharge based on activity areas results in a higher recharge to Job 973 of $1,612, or a 38% increase but a lower recharge to Job 974 of $588.89, or a 5% decrease. Assuming the data for the activity is accurate, and these are representative jobs, then this shows previous recharges may have considerably over- or underestimated the true activity and therefore costs involved in manufacturing jobs.

Often it is found when ABC is implemented that low-volume products see an increase in reported costs (because it is no longer based on direct labour hours) whilst high-volume products see a decrease. The reasons for the differences arise from the underlying processes or activities that comprise the manufacture. Each job consumes differing amounts of the five activity areas. Clearly direct labour hours may have once been a suitable measure but the five activity areas identified reveal a lot more goes into the manufacture than man hours and this should be a broader measure of actual resources consumed in manufacture.

However, this is only a starting point. The managers responsible for the jobs will have to look at the resources consumed (the activity areas) and decide whether the jobs are worth continuing, whether they may need to negotiate costs with the departments making the recharges or indeed whether they need to increase their own recharges or prices charged to maintain margins. However, this may affect customer demand too.

The manager responsible for Job 973 would probably prefer to retain direct labour hours but this may not be possible as the organisation is going over to ABC recharges. Product design is also a consideration where at the design stage consideration can be given to the processes going into the manufacture, for instance the number of components required or number of cuts needed in the process. The data available from the ABC system is more detailed and credible than just using labour hours for product design purposes.

(b) **Explain the risks attaching to the use of ABM**

ABM sees the business as a set of linked activities which ultimately add value to the customer. The business should be managed based on the activities that make it up.

Operational ABM is using ABC to identify activities which add value to products and those which don't. It takes decisions at the operational level. The latter activities should be reduced. Products and services that take up more activity time than others should be reviewed with the aim of reducing the time required. Operational ABM is about 'doing things right'.

Strategic ABM uses ABC information at a strategic level using it to decide on which products to develop and which activities to use. It looks at profitability analysis deciding on which products or customers are the most profitable. Strategic ABM is about 'doing the right things'.

The implicit value of an activity refers to the value in the product not necessarily captured by financial analysis. It can be quality of service or a particular design feature. If this is reduced as an outcome of an ABC review customers may see a fall in value and stop buying the service.

ABM can lead to bad decisions where it doesn't show the complete context of a decision. For instance, operational ABM will not capture quality issues such as pleasant service. Strategic ABM will not identify intangibles that could be important in making decisions on products and activities.

(c) **Target costing**

Target costing is a costing system that can be used when a company (such as SFS) is unable to dictate a selling price and is forced to accept the prevailing market selling price for a product.

After the specification of the product is completed, SFS will determine the price that the market is prepared to pay for the product (this may be by considering similar products already available or by carrying out market research). SFS then would subtract a target profit from the selling price to determine its cost target. If the expected cost of the product already meets the target cost over its life cycle, including any expected cost reductions, then production can commence. If the expected cost exceeds the target cost then major changes are introduced to reduce costs so that the target cost is achieved. If SFS cannot achieve the target cost then the product will be abandoned.

Kaizen costing

Kaizen costing has been used by some Japanese firms for over 20 years and is now widely used in the electronics and automobile industries. 'Kaizen' translates as continuous improvement.

Functional analysis is applied at the design stage of a new product, and a target cost for each function is set.

The functional target costs are added together and the total becomes the product target cost. Once the product has been in production for a year, the actual cost of the first year becomes the starting point for further cost reduction. It is this process of continuous improvement, encouraging constant reductions by tightening the 'standards', that is known as Kaizen costing.

SFS could apply Kaizen costing as follows. The previous year's actual production cost serves as the cost base for the current year's production cost. A reduction rate and a reduction amount are set. Actual performance is compared to the Kaizen goals throughout the year and variances are monitored. At the end of the current year, the current actual cost becomes the cost base for the next year. New (lower) Kaizen goals are set and the whole process starts again.

Differences

One of the main differences between the two methods is that target costing is applied before production commences, but Kaizen costing is applied after production has started.

Another difference is that target costing requires significant changes to be made, but Kaizen costing involves making a number of small improvements to the whole process as part of continuous improvement.

41 LOL cards

Text reference. VBM is discussed in Chapter 12 of the BPP Study Text.

Top tips. In **part (a)** you need to explain what VBM is and how it focuses on shareholder wealth maximisation. You need to explain what performance measure is used in a VBM approach and how it is set throughout the organisation.

In **part (b)** you need to use the EVA™ calculation to make calculations and critically compare these with other measures of shareholder performance.

Part (c) requires an evaluation so be critical of the merits and drawbacks of EVA™ and the other measures you refer to. Remember to state any assumptions you make as you are using a model.

Part (d). A useful approach to this question might be to compare and contrast traditional approaches to cost containment with ABM and cost reduction. There is no requirement to link this part of the question to the scenario, so it should just be a test of knowledge.

Marking scheme

		Marks
(a)	Up to 2 marks on the explanation of VBM and then up to 2 marks on how it aids focus in the management process (Maximum 4)	4
(b)	Workings: NOPAT 1 Capital employed 1 Cost of capital 1 EVA™ 1 Assumptions 0.5 each up to a maximum of 1.5 EPS 1 Share price 3 × 0.5 Comments: 1 mark per reasonable point up to 2 on EPS and share price and 2 on EVA™. Total 12	12
(c)	1 mark for each relevant point made up to a maximum of 3.	3
(d)	1 mark for each relevant point made up to a maximum of 6.	6
	Total =	25

(a) **What VBM involves and how it can focus the company on shareholder interests**

The VBM approach starts with the primary objective of the business as shareholder wealth maximisation and develops a performance approach based on this. At the strategic level the primary measure of performance is EVA™ because this EVA™ is equivalent to discounted cash flow in the long term which is a widely used method of valuing shares by equity analysts.

EVA™ is used as the sole measure of performance by management and even throughout the organisation (at strategic, tactical and operational levels) thereby avoiding the conflict between multiple objectives and resulting measures. The variables within EVA™ that drive performance such as PBIT can be used by management to achieve value-based targets set down from the strategic value-based goal.

BPP LEARNING MEDIA

(b) **An assessment of the financial performance of LOL using EVA™. Evaluate this against EPS and share price performance**

EPS has fallen by 23.4% (21.88 in 20X9 ($35m/$160m) compared with 16.75% in 20Y0 ($26.8m/$160m)) which suggests the company is not favoured by investors but the average share price has only fallen from $12.20 to $10.70 over the same period which doesn't suggest the company is out of favour as much. Indeed this is against a sector fall of 26% (907.1/1,225.6) over the same period and a main market index decline of 34.9% (1,448.90/2,225.40) thus inferring LOL has actually outperformed its sector and the main market.

The sector comparison is more relevant to LOL's performance as this includes only comparative companies. The view of the market that LOL is outperforming its sector is confirmed by the calculation of EVA™. This remains positive at $22.6m in 20Y0 compared with $29.6m in 20X9. Calculations are in Appendix 1. Thus LOL continues to create value for shareholders even in difficult conditions.

(c) **Evaluate VBM against traditional profit-based measures of performance**

Value measures take into account capital employed and the cost of capital and are therefore considered superior to profit measures which capture these less clearly. They are adjusted to take out accounting adjustments so they arrive at cash flow measures which are less affected by accounting adjustments. In the case of LOL the accounting and economic depreciation are assumed to be the same but may differ if additional information becomes available.

However, EVA™ and other value-based measures are complex and unfamiliar to calculate and so may be off-putting to management used to profit measures. They also contain assumptions on the capital asset pricing model (used to calculate the cost of capital) and data is historic and so may change in the future. For instance, share values are calculated based on dividend flows in the future. However, provided users are aware of the assumptions and become familiar with the process of calculating EVA™ it could be a useful measure.

EVA™ can be manipulated by choosing projects with low set-up costs to massage the initial EVA™ figure which then falls in later years. It also fails to recognise the increase in shareholder wealth over the life of the project better captured by the use of net present value.

(d) **Traditional cost allocation systems**

Traditional costing systems, notably **absorption costing**, assume that all products **consume resources in proportion to their production volumes**. While this may be true for overheads such as power costs, it does not necessarily hold for all overheads, especially those connected with support services.

The amount of **overhead allocated** to individual products by absorption costing therefore bears **very little resemblance** to the **amount of overhead actually incurred** by the products and hence gives management **minimal understanding of the behaviour of overhead costs**. Consequently management also only have a limited ability to control/reduce overhead costs.

ABC/ABM approach

Activity-based costing (ABC) attempts to overcome this problem by identifying the activities or transactions (**cost drivers**) which underlie an organisation's activities and which cause the incidence of the activity, and hence the cost of the activity (overheads) to increase. Costs can then be attributed to products according to the number of cost drivers they cause/consume using cost driver rates.

ABM is the term given to those **management processes that use the information provided by an activity-based cost analysis to improve organisational profitability**.

ABM and cost reduction

Because ABM analyses costs on the basis of what causes them, rather than on the basis of type of expense/cost centre, it provides management with vital information on why costs are being incurred. If management can **reduce the incidence of the cost driver, they can reduce the associated cost**.

ABM involves a variety of **cost reduction techniques**.

- Ensuring activities are performed as efficiently as possible
- Reducing or eliminating the need to perform activities that do not add value for customers
- Improving the design of products
- Developing better relationships with customers and suppliers

In short, it aims to ensure that customer needs are met while fewer demands are made on organisational resources.

Appendix 1

Workings: EVA™ calculation

EVA™ calculations for the periods given are:

	20X9	*20Y0*
	$m	$m
Profit after interest and tax	35.0	26.8
Interest (net of tax at 25%)	3.0	5.9
Net operating profit after tax (NOPAT)	38.0	32.6
Capital employed (at year start)	99.2	104.1

Assumptions:

Economic and accounting depreciation are equivalent.

There are no non-cash expenses to adjust in the profit figure.

There are no additional adjustments to make regarding goodwill.

Cost of capital

WACC = (%e × Ke) + (%d × Kd)

20X9	(50% × 12.7%) + (50% × 4.2%)	=	8.45%
20Y0	(50% × 15.3%) + (50% × 3.9%)	=	9.60%

EVA™ = NOPAT – (Capital employed × WACC)

20X9	38.0 – (99.2 × 8.45%)	=	29.6
20Y0	32.6 – (104.1 × 9.6%)	=	22.6

42 Dibble

Text reference. ABC and ABM are discussed in Chapter 12 of the BPP Study Text.

Top tips. The opening paragraph of the scenario tells us that 'Dibble has always absorbed production overheads to the cost of each product on the basis of machine hours'. In other words, Dibble currently uses a simple absorption method of cost allocation. In effect, the context for part (a) of this question is based around the differences between ABC and overhead allocation based on a simple absorption method.

Part (a) (i) asks how ABC could be implemented. Thinking about the contrast between ABC and Dibble's current method of overhead allocation could help you identify the additional information needed to implement ABC. Dibble currently allocates all of its overheads to the cost of each product on the basis of machine hours. But what would it have to do differently if it was using an ABC approach?

Note, however, that there were only four marks available for this part of the question, so you were only expected to provide a relatively brief overview of the key features of ABC.

Part (a) (ii) asks whether it may be more appropriate to use ABC in the Timber and Steel Divisions instead of the current absorption costing method. In effect, having identified the key features of ABC in part (a) (i), you now need to consider its potential advantages and disadvantages, and the contexts in which it is appropriate, in order to assess whether it would be appropriate for the two divisions in question.

To score well here, it is vital that you appreciate the main characteristics of the Timber and Steel Divisions – and the differences between them. The Timber Division produces a limited range of standardised products. By contrast, the Steel Division produces a wide range of bespoke products. (And, as the fourth paragraph of the scenario tells us, the board of the Steel Division feels the pricing structure may be too simplistic, and it is not sure of the profitability of some groups of products.)

The key point to note here is that it seems likely that the Steel Division will benefit from a more detailed (and accurate) method of allocating overhead costs, and therefore ABC would seem to be appropriate for that division. However, the existing basis seems perfectly adequate for the Timber Division.

Note that, in the scenario, the CEO tells you he doesn't want detailed calculations. So you shouldn't waste time trying to use the figures from the management accounts to assess the impact of introducing ABC.

Note also – as a general point in APM exams – just because a model (or approach) is new, this doesn't necessarily make it better than the existing one. It needs to be appropriate to the context. ABC is more time consuming than absorption costing so, in this case, would the benefits it might generate for the Timber Division justify this extra effort?

Part (b) asks how ABM could be used to improve business performance in the company as a whole.

A useful approach to this requirement could be to think about the key principles of ABM – for example, satisfying customer needs while using the fewest resources possible; eliminating activities which do not add value for customers in order to focus on value-adding activities; improving the design of products – and then assess how Dibble's performance might be improved if it applied these principles.

For example, the scenario tells us that protective coatings are added to Steel products, by subcontractors, at the end of the production process. These are then returned to the Steel Division for dispatch to the customer. But does returning the products to Dibble add any value? Or could they be sent directly from the subcontractors to the customer?

Think also about how part (b) of the question fits with part (a). One aspect of ABM is the way organisations can use ABC information to help manage costs, and to focus on those activities which add value. The scenario has identified that the Steel Division has concerns around the pricing and profitability of its products; but introducing ABC could help to address these concerns. In turn, if Dibble has a better understanding of pricing and product profitability, could this help to improve its (financial) performance?

Examining team's comments. Part (a) (i) required candidates to advise the CEO on how to implement ABC. This should have been a relatively simple question, but it was not answered very well.

Although candidates appeared to know the terminology of ABC, it was often not correctly used. A lack of understanding of the basics of ABC also meant that it was difficult for candidates to score well in the next part of the question.

Part (a) (ii) required candidates to assess the appropriateness of ABC compared to the current costing systems in the Timber and Steel Divisions. This part was answered reasonably well, although the weaknesses in candidates' basic understanding of ABC – shown in part (a) (i) – often led to vague answers. In particular, it was surprising to find that candidates often seem unaware that ABC is specifically an overhead allocation system.

Part (b) asked candidates to advise on the benefits ABM would bring to Dibble. This part of the question was not well answered. Many candidates provided lists of benefits that were not specifically related to an activity-based approach, and again reflected candidates' lack of understanding of the general principles of such an approach – in particular, analysing activities' cost drivers, and cost pooling.

Marking scheme

			Marks
(a)	(i)	Implementation of ABC – 1 mark per relevant point	
		Total for part (a) (i): up to 4	4
	(ii)	Appropriateness of ABC – 1 mark per relevant point – up to a maximum of 6	
		Problems with ABC – 1 mark per relevant point – up to a maximum of 6	
		Total for part (a) (ii): up to 8	8
(b)		Improving performance using ABM – 1 mark per relevant point	
		Differences must be clearly linked to the scenario to score the marks available.	
		Total for part (b): up to 13	13
		Total =	**25**

(a) (i) **Implementation of ABC**

ABC is an alternative to absorption costing, which is the method currently used by Dibble. ABC is a detailed fact gathering and data analysis technique.

In order to implement ABC production, overheads need to be grouped into cost pools as in the analysis of production overheads for Dibble in the management accounts extracts.

Then cost drivers for each cost pool must be identified. Cost drivers are the activities which bring about the costs; for example, the set-up of the CAM machinery in Steel Division will be driven by the number of batches of production.

Once the cost pools and their associated cost drivers have been established, the cost per unit of cost driver can be calculated for each individual activity. The overhead costs are absorbed into each unit based on how much of the activity the unit uses, therefore, for example, units which require more inspection and testing will be allocated more of those costs. The overhead costs are then added to the prime costs in order to calculate the full cost of production.

(ii) **Appropriateness of ABC**

ABC is especially useful where there is a wide range of complex products and where production overheads form a larger proportion of total production costs. In Steel Division, there is a large range of products, many of them bespoke or one-off designs. Production overheads form 28% (4,472/(20,605 – 4,533)) of total production costs, and the use of ABC will be appropriate in this division.

ABC enables a more accurate cost of production to be calculated, which is very useful in setting product prices. This could be especially useful in Steel Division which has a wide range of products subject to a number of manufacturing processes. It will help to ensure that each product is priced high enough in order to produce an acceptable margin, but not so high as to become uncompetitive. This is especially important as Steel Division's strategy is to produce bespoke products at prices comparable to competitors which produce simpler, more conventional products.

ABC enables managers to determine what activities drive the costs, and so focus on reducing those activities to control costs. Not all production overheads, for example, inspection costs of the coatings in Steel Division, are related to production volumes. It is equally possible to apply ABC techniques to overheads other than production overheads.

Problems with ABC

ABC is less useful in businesses such as Timber Division where there is a small range of relatively simple products and where production overheads only comprise around 1% of total production costs. Of the production overheads in Timber Division, storage is by far the biggest and is likely to be driven by production volumes.

It may be difficult to determine what the drivers of production costs are. Storage costs could also be related to the insolvency of a customer. It may be impossible to allocate all overheads to the specific activities which drive them and so management will have to apply judgement.

Calculation of ABC may be time consuming, complex and poorly understood by managers. As such, the time and expense of doing so may not be justified. This appears to be the case in Timber Division where there are only a few, relatively simple products and few production overheads. Whereas in Steel Division, where there is a wide range of more complex products and a high proportion of production overheads, ABC is more appropriate than the traditional absorption costing method currently used at Dibble.

(b) **ABM**

ABM is the use of ABC methods in order to improve organisational performance by meeting the needs of customers using the lowest possible amount of resources or costs. ABM can be applied at the operational level or to help develop strategy.

Product pricing

By accurately determining the cost of each product using ABC, Dibble would be able to ensure that prices are set so as to achieve an acceptable margin and also remain competitive with the prices currently charged in the rest of the market.

Steel Division charges customers a standard mark-up of 10% on top of the $650k subcontractor costs for the coating and painting of the steel. This means that customers are only being charged $65k whereas the costs of storage of goods awaiting subcontract work and of transporting the goods to the subcontractor total $695k.

By identifying the cost pools relating to the subcontract work, Steel Division can determine that it is making a loss on the subcontract work as a whole. It could therefore adjust the price of painted and coated products to ensure that an acceptable contribution margin is achieved. This is an example of operational ABM. At the strategic level, this type of information could help Dibble decide which product types to develop or discontinue.

The same principle may also apply where ABC can be used to identify which types of customers are the most profitable. In that way, resources can be focused on retaining and managing these customer groups. Action can be taken by additional advertising or product development in order to focus on these particular markets. By analysing customer profitability, it may be possible to reduce costs or increase revenue to make certain customer groups or product lines more profitable, in both the short and long term.

By identifying lines of business with poor profitability, Dibble could discontinue selling to particular customers, or selling particular products, if appropriate action could not be taken to improve profitability.

Analysis of activities

By analysing the activities which drive the costs, Steel Division could determine which activities may not be required or could be done in a more efficient way. It may be possible to introduce improvements in the short term, for example, changes in the production process which may improve efficiency. In the longer term, strategic changes could be made to the way in which activities are undertaken, such as by outsourcing other activities in addition to the painting and coating which is currently outsourced.

Identifying the costs of transporting painted finished goods back from the subcontractors to Steel Division could lead them to evaluate ways to reduce this cost, for example, by despatching goods to customers directly from the subcontractors' premises. This is a non value added activity, ie one which consumes resources, such as time and cost to transport goods to and from the subcontractors, but which is of no additional value to the customer. In contrast, ABM may help identify value-adding activities, such as the coating and painting, which customers are prepared to pay for.

Of the five categories of production overheads, only machining time is a value-adding activity, sometimes categorised as a primary activity. Setting up the CAM machinery is a secondary activity, which does not itself add value, but is required in order to perform a value-adding activity (machining).

The other overheads, storage, transfer and inspection, are all non value adding activities which should be eliminated or reduced. By identifying the activities which drive these costs managers can attempt to do this.

However, given the nature of Dibble's products, it is likely that some inspection will still be required for safety or commercial reasons, as shown by the litigation case relating to the faulty product. The Production Manager's proposal to increase the costs of inspection is inappropriate as, having identified inspection as a non value adding activity, it would be better to focus attention on getting the product right first time.

Design improvements

Steel Division has a wide range of relatively complex or even bespoke products. ABM can help managers take decisions at the product design stage, where many of the product's costs are already committed. These can include using fewer or more standardised components, such as a more limited range of paints and coatings.

Where strategic decisions are being taken, for example, about new product lines or lines of business, such as with Steel Division's strategy to develop novel innovative products, ABM can help assess whether such developments are likely to be profitable at an early stage. This would help avoid development costs for products which could turn out to be unprofitable. This could also help allocate resources, such as capital investment, to the most profitable lines of business.

Performance measurement

For ABM to be successful, it will require the commitment of senior management and effective communication and training of employees at all levels in the organisation as to the benefits and methods of ABM. This will incur management time and cost, and divert attention from existing management activities.

New performance measurement systems will need to be developed. Employee rewards will need to be aligned to key performance measures, such as the reduction of non value adding processes like inspection. This will ensure that employees work towards the objectives of the organisation. Additional information gathering systems, or adaptations to existing information systems, will also be required, which will again incur additional cost and may disrupt existing activities.

43 BEG

Chapter references. The performance pyramid is discussed in Chapter 12 of the BPP Study Text.

Top tips. In **part (a)** you are asked to comment on cost targets, relating these to quality (the application for platinum status) and the four categories of quality cost.

Part (b) (i) to (iii) looks at the performance pyramid model which relates strategic management to daily operations. The three headings are taken from the pyramid and data for each can be found in the appendix.

Part (c) then looks at the benefits of the performance pyramid as a performance measurement model. However, don't just discuss the model in theoretical terms; make sure you link it back to the scenario. The references in the scenario are clear signposts to the different aspects of the pyramid, so make use of these in your answer.

Examining team's comments. Some candidates misread the question as being about target costing rather than the use of target costs to achieve the quality standard. Good answers showed that candidates were aware the numbers were forecasts and not historical basing their analyses on future activity. There was little awareness of how the cost categories affected each other, for instance the effect that spending on conformance costs could have on non-conformance costs. In part (b), stronger candidates linked their analyses to the general headings whereas weaker candidates merely provided an analysis of trends without linking these to the headings and business objectives.

(a) **Cost targets and platinum status**

BEG is aiming for platinum status and has been advised to focus on effectiveness in its services. This refers to operations meeting any objectives set. One way of measuring whether objectives have been achieved is through **quantitative measures** such as costs.

The Managing Director has asked for an analysis of **manufacturing cost targets** and **quality costs**. Cost targets have advantages in that they can be compared with competitors using benchmarking which then enables targets to be set based on market leaders. This does require the cost measures to be comparable or else like with like is not being measured. They can also be used as an internal comparative to monitor performance year on year and set stretch targets against which current profitability and hence return on investment is measured. The outcome of the comparison is that a gap may exist and BEG will need to act to close this gap.

The statement shows variable costs increasing 25% ($8.4m to $10.5m) from 20X1 to 20X2 and another 20% to 20X3 ($12.6m). Sales revenues are projected to increase by 50% over the total period from $24m to $36m so variable costs as a percentage of sales have remained stable at 35% and the increase here is down to volume. Fixed manufacturing costs are expected to increase 13% year on year to 20X2 and remain static at $3.4m thereafter.

Costs of quality are made up of **conformance costs (prevention costs and appraisal costs)** and **non-conformance costs (internal and external failure costs)**. Internal and external failure costs are the difference or gap between current expected cost levels and cost targets regarding the application for platinum status for quality. **Internal failure costs** arise before the goods or services pass to the customer and are a failure to meet design quality standards. They include manufacturing flaws and incorrect processing of orders. **External failure costs** arise after sale and include warranty claims and costs of rectification. These can be compared to the manufacturing cost target in each year as a means of setting a projection. Internal failure costs are expected to fall from 21.9% (2,500/(8,400 + 3,000)) of the cost target to 7.5% from 20X1 to 20X3. External failure costs are expected to decline from 27.2% of the cost target to 6.1% from 20X1 to 20X3.

In a traditional manufacturing approach to quality, management spend more on conformance costs to reduce non-conformance costs but, as costs of conformance are high, especially to secure zero defects, there is an acceptable level of defects. However, in a **total quality management (TQM) system**, management would aim for zero defects and spend on conformance costs to reduce total quality costs over time. The emphasis is on getting things right first time and designing in quality.

BEG is projecting a decrease in all categories of quality cost over the three years which suggests a TQM approach is being taken. Prevention costs are the costs of management acting to achieve quality standards before and during manufacture and include the costs of training sales staff taking customer enquiries. These are predicted to fall by 50% in the first year from $4.2m to $1.32m by 20X3. Appraisal costs are incurred when ensuring compliance with quality standards and performance testing. These are projected to decrease by 12% from 20X1 to 20X2 and remain static to 20X3. These projections are quite ambitious and come on top of a reputation established for high quality. It would be useful for BEG to obtain some data on costs of quality from the competition in the hotel and catering industry to get a benchmark for what reasonable costs of quality are.

(b) **Forecast performance of BEG**

The headings come from the performance pyramid, a model that links the overall strategic view of management with day to day operations. The application for platinum status may be measured in financial and marketing terms.

(i) **Financial performance and marketing**

BEG is aiming for an increase in sales of 50% to $36m from 20X1 to 20X3. This is allied to an overall fall in costs from $22m to $20.2m in the same period which can be attributed to the fall in costs of quality seen in the statement produced by the Management Accountant. The net margin has gone up from $2m or 8.33% to $15.8m or 43.89% over the 3 years but this large increase is due to the 2 trends just mentioned and is from a small base of $2m. The sales target is ambitious and may be unrealistic in a market with a number of significant competitors.

A less ambitious target of 8% rising to 11% is predicted for market share although the basis for this calculation is not stated especially as this is a new market for BEG. Presumably the data for the market share calculation and that of growth in the market from $300m to $340m is based on the market research analysis. Nonetheless the market does have a number of significant competitors, although there is no quantification of their market shares such as a BCG analysis would illustrate.

(ii) **External effectiveness**

This is measured through **customer satisfaction** for example. There are four measures that capture how satisfied customers are through measuring the quality of services provided and delivery. The external effectiveness of the business relies on all stages of the business cycle from design through to delivery and involving quality.

The first of the measures is the percentage of products accepted as meeting design **quality standards** without rectification. This appears to refer to the Institute's verification and it is predicted to rise from 92% to 99% over the 3 years to 20X3. This high quality standard aligns with the fall in the costs of quality suggesting a TQM approach to manufacture. Allied to this is a measure showing a fall in rectification claims from $0.96m to $0.1m over the period and another showing the cost of rectifying goods sold after sales decreasing from $1.8m to $0.8m.

These reveal that the business intends to build in quality before sale rather than relying on repairing goods sold (external failure costs).

Finally, a measure of sale service is projected to rise from 88.5% of sales meeting delivery dates to 99.5% doing so over the 3 years.

All of these measures are ambitious, especially the first and last where the percentages are near 100% perfection. It would be useful to have comparatives in the industry if this data is available. Nonetheless these targets suggest a quality-led approach to manufacture which may be achieved by setting stretch targets.

(iii) **Internal efficiency**

This is captured through measures such as **productivity** and **flexibility**.

Productivity is the management of resources whilst flexibility is the responsiveness of the business as a whole. The average time from customer enquiry to product delivery is a measure of flexibility and is projected to fall from 49 days in 20X1 to 40 days in 20X3. This has added cash flow benefits as inventory is being converted to receivables and cash faster. A non-conversion rate of enquiries to sales (%) is planned to fall from 10.5% of all enquiries to 3% over the 3 years. The idle time measure and this measure are both productivity indicators and measures of waste. They also relate to costs of conformance preventing failure before it arises.

The final measure in this part is idle capacity of manufacturing staff which is also projected to fall, from 12% (which seems high) to 1.5%. However, this may mean that if any unanticipated changes in production arise the company may not be flexible enough to absorb these and may have to bring in outworkers. It would be a good idea to obtain comparable data on competitors if possible.

We don't know the precise standards required to obtain platinum status. Nonetheless, BEG is clearly setting ambitious targets for improvements in performance during the three years reviewed.

(c) **Performance pyramid**

The Marketing Director has stressed that BEG needs to focus on increasing the effectiveness of all operations as part of its application for platinum status.

The performance pyramid should encourage it to do this because it focuses on a range of objectives looking at both **external effectiveness** and **internal efficiency**. Of the areas which the director mentions, product design will be addressed through looking at internal efficiency, while after-sales services is likely to be addressed through looking at external effectiveness, specifically in relation to customer satisfaction.

Operational criteria – The statistics which are relevant for the platinum status application correspond to the operational criteria in the pyramid, which are: **quality, product delivery, process time** and **waste**. For example, the cost of rectification claims could be a reflection of quality; the percentage of sales meeting planned delivery dates will reflect the effectiveness of BEG's product delivery; while the idle capacity of staff is an indicator of waste.

Importance of processes – Using the pyramid will also highlight the importance of understanding the processes which drive BEG's costs and financial performance, rather than simply looking at costs and sales figures. However, the pyramid also highlights that BEG's business level strategies and day to day operations need to come together to enable it to achieve its financial objectives, such as increase sales by 50% over 2 years.

Developing strategies – The pyramid also highlights the way that different levels within an organisation support each other and relate to each other. BEG appears to have some fairly ambitious performance targets in relation to its application, and so it will be important that it develops a coherent set of objectives and performance measures across the organisation which will give it the best chance of being able to achieve those targets.

44 Turing

Text reference. Risk appetite and the different methods which can be used for decision making under uncertainty are covered in Chapter 5 of the BPP Study Text. The issues involved in managing performance in JVs are discussed in Chapter 13.

Top tips.

Part (a). For each of the firms, you need to assess the risk appetite and then recommend a method of decision making under uncertainty which is appropriate for that risk appetite.

The reference to 'uncertainty' was very important here, because it indicated that you should use techniques such as maximax and maximin, rather than expected values.

Note also that the requirement is to recommend an appropriate method for each firm. Therefore, you must make a clear recommendation, rather than evaluating the advantages and disadvantages of possible different methods for each firm. You will need to evaluate the appropriateness of different methods in order to decide which method is most suitable for each firm, but the final answer itself needs to be a recommendation.

When evaluating the method more appropriate for Riemann, a key point to note is the business's need to achieve a guaranteed minimum level of return, in order to aid the survival of the business. As such, this means that maximin should be chosen as the appropriate method, rather than minimax regret. However, the examining team indicated that students would be given some credit for suggesting minimax regret, because it is a risk averse solution (and therefore fits Riemann's risk appetite). However, minimax regret is not as clearly focused on obtaining a minimum level of return.

Part (b). Having identified in part (a) which method each firm would use, you now have to apply the methods in order to determine which turbine each one would choose to build.

The calculations in this part of the question should have been relatively straightforward, and the marking guide indicates that you could have scored marks in part (b) for correct calculations of minimax regret, even though it was not one of the methods which should have been recommended in part (a) – which were maximax and maximin.

Part (c). Parts (a) and (b) should have clearly identified one of the major problems facing the joint venture: that the different circumstances and risk appetites of the two venture partners are going to make it difficult for them to agree on strategic decisions. In this case, how do they decide which turbines to build, since Turing will want to build the 8 MW design, and Riemann will want to build the 3 MW design?

More generally, answering part (a) should also have helped you identify that the two firms are likely to have different cultures and management styles – which again could make it difficult for them to work together to manage the JV.

Examining team's comments. Part (a) of the question was generally well answered, and it was pleasing to note that most candidates understood that decision making 'under uncertainty' is different from 'under risk' or else, they realised that the lack of information on probabilities meant that expected values were not appropriate here.

However, candidates should note that their answer needed to contain a single recommendation of the method for each firm to use, not a list of the available ones.

Part (b) was also well answered with many candidates scoring full marks. However, one point for future candidates to note is that the companies cannot choose to produce a certain number of units, as this is the uncertain factor. Therefore, conclusions such as 'Turing should make 2,000 units of the 8 MW in order to gain a profit of $13,300m' are misleading. Given the uncertainty inherent in the scenario, the appropriate conclusion here would be 'Turing should choose to make the 8 MW turbine, because this offers the highest potential maximum profit'.

Marking scheme

		Marks
(a)	Turing	
	Assessment of risk appetite – 1 mark per relevant point up to a maximum of 3 marks	
	Method of decision making – 1 mark for selecting an appropriate method (maximax); 1 mark for describing the method	
	Riemann	
	Assessment of risk appetite – 1 mark per relevant point up to a maximum of 3 marks	
	Method of decision making – 1 mark for selecting an appropriate method (maximin); 1 mark for describing the method	
	Total for part (a): up to 9	9
(b)	Calculations:	
	Variable costs – 2 marks	
	Total costs – 1 mark	
	Revenue – 2 marks	
	Profit – 1 mark	
	Maximax result – 1 mark	
	Maximin result – 1 mark	
	Conclusion – 1 mark	
	Total for part (b): up to 8	8
(c)	For each relevant point (linked to the scenario) about potential problems in managing the JV – 1 mark	
	Potential points include: differences in goals and choice of performance measures between the venture partners; different risk appetites; differing time horizons for achieving results; deadlock in decision making; different management styles, and cultural differences between the venture partners; information sharing; intellectual property.	
	Total for part (c): up to 8	8
		Total = 25

BPP LEARNING MEDIA

(a) **Turing**

Risk appetite

The appetite for risk at Turing will be determined by the three VCs, which collectively own 90% of the company.

Each of the VCs hold a large portfolio of investments, and are prepared for some of these to fail provided that others show large gains. As such, the VCs are **risk seekers**.

The other key stakeholders at Turing are the management team, who own the remaining 10% of the company. The fact the management have been given an equity stake in the business, coupled with their ambition and their enjoyment of the challenges of introducing new products, suggests that they will be comfortable with the high-risk approach taken by the VCs.

Turing's management are also likely to be attracted to projects which are innovative, such as the 8 MW unit. They enjoy the challenges of introducing new products, and are likely to be motivated by the prospect of developing a world-leading unit.

Method of decision making

Maximax – The fact that both of Turing's key stakeholder groups (the VCs and management) are prepared to accept high-risk approaches suggests that Turing will be a risk seeker. As such, the appropriate method of decision making under certainty for it will be maximax.

Using the maximax approach, the design choice selected will be the one which offers the highest maximum profit possible, across any of the three demand scenarios.

Riemann

Risk appetite

The risk appetite at Riemann is likely to be determined largely by its investors – particularly as it has recently had to seek emergency refinancing.

Riemann's shareholders are concerned about the survival of the business, and its debt providers will also be concerned about its survival – and therefore its ability to repay any loans.

Riemann's management are also primarily concerned with the survival of the business. Although they do not own any shares in the company, they will lose their jobs if the company collapses.

The fact that Riemann's shareholders and management both view TandR as a way to generate additional cash flow reinforces the fact that their primary concern is with identifying initiatives which can help secure the survival of the business.

The precarious nature of Riemann's current position suggests that all of its key stakeholders will be **risk averse**.

Equally, they are likely to favour projects which will start generating income soon. As such, the 8 MW unit – which takes two years longer to develop than the others – may be less attractive to Riemann than the two units which can be developed more quickly.

Method of decision making

Maximin – Riemann's focus on the survival of the business means that a maximin approach to decision making under uncertainty will be appropriate for it.

Using the maximin approach, the design selected will be the one which maximises the lowest profit which could be achieved across the three demand scenarios.

(b) **Turbine design types**

Demand		1,000	1,500	2,000		
		$m	$m	$m		
Revenue						
8 MW	$20.8 per unit	20,800	31,200	41,600		
3 MW	$9.6 per unit	9,600	14,400	19,200		
1 MW	$4.6 per unit	4,600	6,900	9,200		
Variable cost						
8 MW	$10.4 per unit	10,400	15,600	20,800		
3 MW	$4.8 per unit	4,800	7,200	9,600		
1 MW	$1.15 per unit	1,150	1,725	2,300		
Fixed cost						
8 MW		7,500	7,500	7,500		
3 MW		820	820	820		
1 MW		360	360	360		
Profit					*Max payoff*	*Min payoff*
					$m	$m
8 MW		2,900	8,100	13,300	**13,300**	2,900
3 MW		3,980	6,380	8,780	8,780	**3,980**
1 MW		3,090	4,815	6,540	6,540	3,090

Maximax = $13,300 earned by the 8 MW units

Maximin = $3,980 earned by the 3 MW units

Due to the differences in their preferred methods of decision making under uncertainty, Turing and Riemann would choose to build different turbine design types. Riemann would choose to build the 8 MW units, while Riemann would choose to build the 3 MW units.

(c) **Problems of managing performance in a JV**

Decision making – As we have seen in part (b), one of the main problems in a JV will be that of reaching a consensus between the venture partners when making strategic decisions.

This could be a particular problem for TandR, given that both partners own 50% of the venture, and so it is difficult to prioritise the interests of one partner over those of the other.

Goals and objectives – As well as their differences in attitude to risk, it appears that the venture partners have different goals and objectives for the venture. In this case, Riemann's primary goal from the venture is to generate additional cash flow in the short term. However, Turing appears to be more interested in the potential long-term returns which can be earned from designing and manufacturing the turbines. As such, it could be difficult for the venture partners to agree what TandR's goals and objectives should be.

Similarly, the venture partners could have different interests in relation to the performance measures they consider to be most important. Although TandR could measure a variety of different indicators – including profit, growth and cash flows – Riemann is likely to prioritise cash flow measures and short-term performance indicators, while Turing is more likely to be interested in the growth and the longer-term prospects of the business, for example.

Management styles – In the same way that Turing and Riemann have different attitudes to risk, it is also likely that they will have different management styles and organisational cultures. This could cause problems at an operational level at TandR, since it is run by a group of managers from each of the JV partners – and therefore who may adopt different management styles.

Sharing capabilities and information – One of the problems, in general, with JVs is that they require the venture partners to share information, capabilities and intellectual property with each other. However, many of these elements may be commercially sensitive, and so the venture partners will be reluctant to share too much information about their own business with each other.

In this respect, establishing a climate of trust between the venture partners is likely to be important for the success of the JV. However, if the venture partners have very different cultures and management styles – as Turing and Riemann seem likely to – this trust could be harder to achieve.

Valuing the contribution of the venture partners – Another issue which arises from sharing information and capabilities relates to how the value of the different partners can be valued. It is likely that Turing's blade design skills will be a significant advantage for the venture, for example. However, it is likely to be difficult to measure the contribution that intangible assets (such as skills and competences) make to the venture in their own right.

Nonetheless, given that both partners hold a 50% stake in the venture, if one of them thinks they are contributing significantly more value to the venture than the other, this could quickly become a source of disagreement between the partners.

45 Callisto

Text reference. Performance management in complex business structures is discussed in Chapter 13 of the BPP Study Text. Management reports and the problem of information overload are discussed in Chapter 6b.

Top tips.

Part (a). Note that the requirement distinguishes between performance **measurement** and performance **management** issues. Accordingly, you need to consider both in your answer.

Note also that the requirement highlights that Callisto deals with two different types of external partner: individual workers (employees working remotely) and strategic partners (which are multinational companies). The issues Callisto faces in managing the performance of a multinational company are likely to be very different to those involved in managing an individual worker.

Part (b). The key problem with George's report appears to be information overload, so in the first part of your answer you need to consider how this will affect the usefulness of the report.

In effect, in the second part you then need to suggest ways to reduce the amount of figures and data being presented on the report. However, note the requirement is asking about the output of the report – essentially its presentation – so make sure you focus on this, rather than suggesting amendments to the underlying aspects of performance being measured, or the frequency of the report. There may be problems with these too, but you are not asked to comment on them, so you should not spend time doing so.

Examining team's comments. Although part (a) was presented as a single requirement, candidates were correct to split it into areas such as the general impact of such a complex structure on the business as a whole, and then the impact on employee management and strategic partner management. However, the key to scoring well was making points which were relevant for Callisto – related to the difficulties of measuring and managing home-working employees and strategic outsourcing partners.

Marking scheme

			Marks
(a)	Up to 2 marks per relevant point relating to performance measurement		
	Relevant points include (but are not limited to): Geographical distance; reliance on IT; difference between employees and strategic partners; technology solutions; use of service level agreements	Up to 9	
	1 mark per relevant point relating to performance management Employees – up to 4 marks Strategic partners – up to 6 marks		
	Maximum marks relating to performance management	Up to 8	17
(b)	Evaluation of proposed report and issues of potential information overload – 1 mark per relevant point – Up to 5 Suggested ways of improving presentation – 1 mark per point – Up to 5 (**Note.** Improvements should only relate to the presentation of the report.)		
	Total for part (b) – Up to 8 marks		8
		Total =	25

(a) **Performance measurement issues**

Data collection – The main difficulties in performance measurement at Callisto are likely to arise from the fact that its employees do not work 'on site', and also a number of key business functions have been outsourced. As a result, before it can begin to measure its performance, Callisto first has to collect the necessary performance data for its remote workers and outsource partners.

IT systems – Callisto needs to rely on information technology for collecting and handling data from its partners and remote workers. As far as possible, this data should be collected and monitored automatically, for example making use of electronic data interchange.

Given the likely number of remote workers and partners that Callisto uses, it is likely that it will need a large database for storing this performance information.

However, in order for the database to be automatically updated (with inputs from remote staff and suppliers), Callisto will need the systems which staff and suppliers use to be compatible with its system.

While Callisto can control the systems its employees use, it seems unlikely that it will be able to exert much, if any, influence over the systems its strategic partners (which are multinational companies) use.

Measuring employees' performance – Callisto's employees log in to its own systems via the internet. In this way, although the employees are not physically in the premises, Callisto is still able to monitor aspects of their performance. For example, monitoring the number of hours employees are logged into the system gives an indication of the number of hours they have worked.

However, it is harder for Callisto to monitor the work the remote employees have actually done; for example, the number of videos they have edited, or the number of customer complaints they have resolved satisfactorily.

In this respect, it is important for Callisto to define its outputs clearly: for example, it should define the various steps which need to be completed for a video edit to be complete. If outputs are not defined in this way, there is scope for disputes between staff and managers about the amount of work they have done; for example, with staff claiming to have completed the editing on more videos than they actually have.

Strategic partners – Whereas Callisto's employees log on to its own systems, the strategic partners, such as RLR, will have their own systems. Therefore they will continue to use their systems rather than using Callisto's systems.

System reconciliations – As a result, there can be **discrepancies** between Callisto's systems and RLR's systems. Therefore, an added complication in the performance measurement process is that, before RLR's performance can be measured against the key SLAs, Callisto will first have to reconcile its inventory records with RLR's.

Lack of control – Without having any agreement over the figures, Callisto will not be able to enforce the SLAs. The disagreements with RLR illustrate this. For example, if an item is despatched late, it will be difficult for Callisto to prove that RLR has broken the SLA, if RLR argues that the item was not actually in stock when an order was placed, so that it couldn't be expected to despatch that item within three working days from when the order was placed.

The difficulty which Callisto faces is establishing whether RLR is responsible for the delay, or whether the product suppliers are responsible.

SLAs as controls – This lack of control over the SLAs is likely to be a significant problem for Callisto, because the SLAs represent its key control over the relationship with its strategic partners.

A potential solution would be for the partners to agree a standard reporting format for all data relating to the SLAs. This would then remove the need for the reconciliations Callisto currently has to carry out.

Performance management issues

Employee management – Because Callisto's employees work from home rather than at company premises, the brothers cannot monitor what the employees are doing in the same way as they could if everyone was working in the same place. For example, Jeff and George cannot monitor what hours their staff are working, or how productive they are being.

Equally, because Jeff and George have no direct contact with their staff, it is difficult for them to judge how motivated the staff are.

Reward schemes – Because the brothers cannot directly monitor or control how productive their employees are being, they need to ensure Callisto's reward scheme is designed such that it encourages productivity and motivation. One way to do this would be to link the reward scheme directly to achieving agreed outputs and targets for each employee.

Managing strategic partners

Reliance on partners – A key issue Callisto faces is that it is reliant on external partners (such as RLR Logistics) for the successful day to day operation of its business. The nature of Callisto's business structure means that some of the functions which have been outsourced are business critical.

For example, if RLR decides not to renew its contract (when it is due for renewal in two months' time) this could create major problems for Callisto. Equally, the reliability of partners such as RLR is vital, because Callisto's customer service reputation will be damaged if products are delivered late.

However, there is a danger that Callisto's reliance on strategic partners in this way strengthens the strategic partners' bargaining power in any negotiations with Callisto (because it is unlikely that Callisto will be able to replace a strategic partner immediately if it stopped working for Callisto).

Relationship management – However, the success of the relationship between Callisto and its strategic partners is likely to depend on establishing an atmosphere of trust between the parties. Currently, it appears the trust between the partners is limited; meaning, for example, that Callisto feels it has to reconcile performance data between RLR's figures and its own. However, such reconciliations do not ultimately add any value for Callisto, so they are a wasteful activity. Therefore, if Callisto was able to trust RLR's figures, this would be beneficial because the detailed reconciliations would no longer be required.

Pricing – Another issue which will have to be managed is how the agreements between Callisto and its strategic partners can be arranged so that they are motivating and profitable for both parties. George has already acknowledged that Callisto operates on small profit margins, so it needs to secure sales growth and high volumes of business in order to be profitable.

However, Callisto is dependent on partners such as RLR to deliver a good quality service to its customers. If the customers don't receive this, then Callisto's reputation is likely to suffer, which in turn will reduce its ability to achieve the sales growth it needs (either by retaining existing customers or acquiring new ones).

So Callisto needs to negotiate contracts which motivate the strategic partners to deliver the high quality it needs, whilst at the same time not being prohibitively expensive for it. Therefore, Callisto needs to ensure that the contracts are motivating and profitable for both parties.

(b) **Content**

Information overload – Whilst having a daily report will mean that George has up to date and timely information, there is a danger that its frequency will actually lead to **information overload**. In practice, George may find he doesn't have time to look through a detailed report each day. We do not know how many employees work for Callisto, but its turnover ($120m per annum) suggests there are likely to be quite a large number of employees. Therefore, George's report is likely to contain a large amount of data for him to look at each day.

There is a also a danger that if George spends too much time looking at detailed, daily reports he may overlook more strategic issues in the business, or higher level trends in performance.

Control – It is not clear from the scenario whether the employees will be told that George is monitoring their productivity. However, if the employees know that George is monitoring their productivity on a daily basis, then this could prompt any who are not currently working as hard as they could to work harder. It seems likely that this is what George hopes will happen.

Usefulness of information – However, it is debatable how useful some of the measures George has chosen will be. For example, simply monitoring the number of complaints employees deal with doesn't reflect how long or complicated each complaint was. Equally, although an employee may have been logged on to the network this doesn't necessarily mean they have been working all the time they have been logged on.

The frequency of the reports could also be a problem in itself. If the reports looked at the average number of complaints employees dealt with in a month, this might be a fairer reflection of their activity than looking at a single day at a time.

Equally, it is not clear whether all the employees are expected to carry out all the tasks being monitored. For example, some may specialise in editing videos, while others concentrate on dealing with customer queries and complaints. However, this could mean that the report shows a large number of zeros in the columns for work the employees do not attend to.

Possible improvements

Sorting – If employees do have separate roles, George may find it more useful to produce separate reports for each role; for example, producing one report for video editors, and a separate one for customer service employees.

However, there are more fundamental ways in which George could improve the reports.

Exception reports – Instead of showing the performance of all employees, the report would only show results which are unusual or require attention; in other words, where an employee's figures are particularly high or particularly low.

Summaries and drill down reports – Alternatively, instead of showing performance for individual employees, the report could show totals in the first instance; for example, totals for the number of customer complaints dealt with, or the number of videos edited.

If George was concerned about any of the summary totals, he could then 'drill down' into the total figure, to find out why it was lower (or higher) than he expected.

Charts and graphs – However, perhaps the most significant change would be showing performance graphically, rather than as columns of figures.

In this way, George could see not only the actual daily figures, but could also place them in context – for example, by comparing them to a rolling average, or to a target.

By using charts or graphs, George would be able to see how performance is changing over time, which is something he would not be able to do from the proposed numerical report.

BPP LEARNING MEDIA

46 Coal Creek

Text reference. The importance of considering indicators of liquidity and gearing as well as profitability is discussed in Chapter 7 of the BPP Study Text. Models for predicting corporate failure are discussed in Chapter 14.

Top tips.

Part (a). It is important you recognise that the main focus of this requirement is on the value of using different **indicators** rather than on CCNH's **performance** as such. In other words, you need to discuss why monitoring liquidity and gearing (in conjunction with profitability) is important rather than simply discussing CCNH's liquidity and gearing positions. For example, why would it be useful for CCNH to monitor its ability to pay its liabilities when they become due (rather than simply: What is CCNH's working capital position?)?

Also, although you are asked to 'illustrate your answer with suitable calculations' this does not mean that your answer should just become, in effect, a sequence of different ratios. The calculations should be used to **support** your answer, rather than **becoming** your answer in their own right.

In relation to gearing – remember that there are two aspects of gearing: financial gearing and operational gearing. The requirement doesn't limit you to dealing with one aspect or the other, and therefore you should have considered both in your answer. In CCNH's case, the question of monitoring the level of fixed costs compared to variable costs (operational gearing) seems to be particularly important.

Part (b). There are two aspects to this part of the requirement: (i) explain a qualitative model; and (ii) apply that model to the scenario in order to comment on CCNH's position.

However, note that 'explaining' the model doesn't simply mean listing the headings in the model; you need to explain why the different elements of the model could be useful for predicting corporate failure.

A sensible approach to part (b) of this question would be to illustrate each aspect of the model (in Argenti's case: defects, mistakes, and symptoms of failure) by referring to weaknesses at CCNH. In this way, you will ensure you address both aspects of the requirement: to explain the model, and to comment on CCNH's position.

The marking guide indicates that there are up to five marks available for describing the qualitative model, but up to six marks for using it to identify weaknesses in CCNH's position. Therefore, as so often in APM, there are potentially more marks available for applying a model to the scenario than for explaining the model itself.

Technical article. In the Technical Articles section of ACCA's website there is an article called 'Business Failure' which discusses different failure prediction models. If you haven't already done so, you are strongly advised to read this article to supplement your knowledge of this area of the syllabus.

Part (c). The scenario identifies that HC's revenue had grown significantly in the last two years. This could give you a clue that HC is in the growth phase of its life cycle. By contrast, GC is a mature business – with little scope for growth, and operating in a sector which is fully supplied. What implications does this have for the CEO's plans? Although the question requirement refers to 'product portfolios' rather than any specific model, the product life cycle model could be a useful framework to apply here, given that CCNH's two divisions appear to be at different stages of their life cycles. The BCG matrix could also be useful, although the scenario does not give any specific details about the relative market shares of SC and GC. (However, we do know that CCNH is one of the largest providers of residential care places in Geeland.)

Examining team's comments. Candidates still appear not to be reading question requirements carefully enough, with the result that they are not answering the requirements actually set. In part (a) of this question, instead of explaining why liquidity and gearing were important alongside profitability, many candidates chose to review the **performance of the company** in the scenario, leaving the reader to draw their own conclusions about the relative importance of liquidity, gearing and profitability.

Moreover, although many candidates successfully dealt with issues around financial gearing, only a few addressed the operational gearing in the business. It appeared that candidates failed to identify the cost structures (fixed/variable) within CCNH although this ought to be a basic point in the financial assessment of a business by a management accountant.

In part (b) few candidates demonstrated a clear understanding of the issues in using a qualitative model, and the Argenti model in particular. Only a minority could explain defects, mistakes made, and symptoms of failure. Although many students could quote the headings from the model, few could explain what they referred to. The wiser candidates tried to cover this shortcoming by illustrating each heading with an example from CCNH, and it was pleasing to see that candidates managed to score reasonably well in this part of the question by identifying the specific issues at CCNH.

Marking scheme

		Marks
(a)	Explaining liquidity, financial gearing and operational gearing – up to a maximum of 4 marks For illustrating the importance of considering liquidity at CCNH – up to 4 marks For illustrating the importance of considering financial gearing at CCNH – up to 2 marks For illustrating the importance of considering operational gearing at CCNH – up to 4 marks Total for part (a): Up to 11 marks	11
(b)	For describing qualitative models (such as Argenti's A score model) and including examples of possible failure indicators – up to 5 marks For identifying weaknesses at CCNH – 1 mark per relevant weakness identified; up to a maximum of 6 marks Possible weaknesses include: culture of fraud in previous management; lack of senior management; poor cash flow planning; over-trading at SC; weak financial ratios; and inability to pay landlords. Total for part (b): Up to 9 marks	9
(c)	For discussing life cycle stage and strategic position of SC and implications of this – up to 2 For discussing life cycle stage and strategic position of GC and implications of this – up to 2 For discussing the implications of CCNH's portfolio on any future strategy – up to 3 marks Total for part (c): Up to 5 marks	5
		Total = 25

(a) **Profit-based measures** – It appears that CCNH's current performance measures (operating profit margin; earnings per share) are primarily focused on the amount of profit the business is generating.

However, these measures have not identified the problems which CCNH is now facing, even though these problems could potentially threaten the overall survival of the business. Profit-based measures can often be insufficient to highlight issues relating to an **organisation's survival**, either in the long term or the short term.

Liquidity

Liquidity – CCNH's liquidity relates to the level of funds it has readily available in order to pay its liabilities as they become due; for example, having sufficient cash to pay its rents, or to pay other suppliers.

CCNH struggled to meet its most recent rental payment, which suggests that it has liquidity problems.

CCNH's liquidity – At the end of the year just ended, CCNH's current assets were $64m, but its current liabilities were $104m. Therefore, its current ratio was 0.62. The fact that this ratio is significantly less than 1 helps explains why CCNH is having trouble making payments (such as its rental payments) when they are due. CCNH's current liabilities are significantly greater than the funds it has available to pay them.

Furthermore, at the end of the year, CCNH has no ready cash.

As CCNH is a service company rather than a manufacturing company, it is unlikely to hold a significant level of inventory. Therefore, given that CCNH has no ready cash, it seems likely that the vast majority of CCNH's current assets are receivables.

Receivable days – The significance of receivables suggests that receivable days should be a key performance measure for CCNH. If it can collect the amounts it is owed from residents as quickly as possible, this should help increase the amount of funds it has available to pay for its liabilities.

Currently, however, it appears that there may be problems collecting the amounts owed to SC. SC's receivable days are 68 [(47/253) × 365], compared to only 9 for GC [(17/685) × 365].

Gearing – Whilst liquidity issues can often be a problem in the short term, looking at gearing can highlight potential issues in the **longer term**. In this respect, monitoring gearing helps an organisation **measure risk**. Gearing indicates the level of an organisation's fixed regular liabilities compared to the cash generators which will enable the organisation to cover its liabilities.

Financial gearing

Financial gearing – Financial gearing is measured by the ratio of debt to equity. Debt is a fixed liability for an organisation (for example, the annual interest payments which are due on loans), and equity is the capital equivalent which needs to generate the funds necessary to cover the liability (for example, to pay the interest due).

If the gearing ratio is high, this indicates that an organisation has to cover large fixed liabilities from only a small equity investment. As a result, the business could be at financial risk.

As well as looking at the gearing ratio itself, a second indicator which could be useful in relation to financial gearing is **interest cover**. Interest cover compares an organisation's profit before interest to the level of interest payable; again indicating whether it is generating sufficient returns to cover its fixed liabilities.

Gearing ratio – CCNH's debt (long-term borrowings of $102m) is currently 54% of its equity (share capital + retained earnings: $189m). A gearing ratio of 54% by itself should not be a particular cause for concern because it is relatively low.

Interest cover – CCNH's interest cover appears to be more of a concern, though. Its operating profit was the same as the interest it had to pay for the year just ended, meaning that if its profit falls in future, CCNH may not be able to cover its interest payments.

CCNH appears still to have a relatively good relationship with its bank, since the bank agreed to increase CCNH's overdraft facility in order to enable it to make its most recent rental payments. However, if CCNH doesn't generate sufficient earnings to cover its interest payments this could be fatal for its relationship with its bank, and will also seriously damage its chances of receiving any further financing.

Operational gearing

Operational gearing – Operational gearing (or leverage) compares the ratio of fixed costs to variable costs in an organisation, by comparing contribution to profit with operating profit (PBIT). Operational gearing helps to identify the level of **business risk** in an organisation.

If an organisation has high operational gearing this suggests it also faces a high level of business risk. High operational gearing means that an organisation's fixed costs as a proportion of its total costs are also high. This is risky because, although variable costs will fall if revenue falls, fixed costs will not. Therefore, an organisation with a high level of operational gearing may find itself unable to cover its fixed costs if its revenue falls.

This inability to cover fixed costs could have been the type of gearing problems which the director was talking about at CCNH; because it seems likely that CCNH has a **high level of fixed costs**.

CCNH's rent payments are a fixed cost, and they alone take up 27% ($257m/$938m) of its revenue. In addition, it seems likely that the central costs and the costs of permanent staff in the care homes will be relatively fixed.

The danger for CCNH of having a high level of operational gearing is that if its revenues drop then it will quickly become loss making, given that it was only just breaking even at the end of the last year. Again, this could have been the problem which the director was referring to.

> **Operational gearing ratio** – If we treat rent costs, payroll costs and central costs as all being fixed (or relatively fixed), then the ratio between CCNH's fixed costs and variable costs (running costs) is 7.5:1 (536 + 257 + 30 = 823:110).
>
> This ratio is very high, and so should also be viewed as a concern for CCNH.
>
> In this respect, it is important for CCNH to see if it can change the nature of any of the costs within its business. In particular, it may be possible to use temporary or contract staff in its homes rather than permanent staff. Such a change would mean that staff costs effectively then become variable costs.
>
> However, using temporary staff might also compromise the **quality of service** CCNH provides to its residents, which would not be acceptable.

(b) **Qualitative models of business failure** – Qualitative models of business failure look at a variety of qualitative and non-accounting factors to help identify the likelihood of corporate failure in organisations. These factors can include: the business environment (as exemplified by 'PEST' factors); the organisation's customer profile (for example, whether it is dependent on a small number of key customers); the level of management experience in the organisation; and whether the organisation has a history of qualified audit opinions.

Argenti's A score model – Argenti's A score model is a qualitative model which can be used to assess the risk of poor management causing corporate failure. The model looks at three different groups of indicators of poor management:

- Defects
- Management mistakes
- Symptoms of failure

These three groups are then further divided into a number of problem areas, and an 'A score' is obtained by assigning a score for each problem area. As such, Argenti's model attempts to quantify the causes of failure (defects, management mistakes) and the symptoms associated with failure.

> **'A scores'** – The 'A score' model sets a maximum acceptable score of 25 overall. An 'A score' of greater than 25 indicates that an organisation is at risk of failing. However, the scores for each group of indicators are also important individually. In particular, if an organisation scores anything at all for 'symptoms' this immediately signifies that the organisation should be considered at risk of failing.

Defects

In Argenti's model, 'defects' are divided into 'management defects' and 'accounting defects'.

Management defects result from deficiencies in the senior management team: for example, a failure to separate the roles of chairman and CEO; having a passive board of directors; having a lack of experience and/or relevant skills among the senior management team; or having a management team with a poor record of responding to change in the business environment.

Lack of senior management – The fact that CCNH does not have any experienced senior management (following the recent departures of the CEO, Finance Director and the Operations Director) can be seen as a management defect for the company.

Accounting defects – Examples of accounting defects could be a lack of budgets or budgetary control, a lack of cash flow planning, and an absence of costing systems.

The fact that CCNH struggled to meet its most recent rent payments may suggest a lack of cash flow planning, particularly as CCNH had no cash available when the rent payments were due.

Management mistakes

If a company's management and accounting systems are weak, this could increase the chances of mistakes being made within the company. Argenti suggests that management mistakes should be analysed under three main headings: **high gearing; overtrading**; and **failure of major projects**.

As we saw in part (a), CCNH's financial gearing of 54% is actually relatively low, and so would not indicate a risk of failure. However, CCNH's high operational gearing should be viewed as more of a concern.

Moreover, SC's rapid growth, coupled with the apparent weaknesses in its credit control and receivables collection, may suggest that there has been some overtrading at SC. In turn, the weaknesses in SC's credit control (and the resulting high level of receivables) are straining the business's working capital.

Symptoms of failure

The logic of Argenti's model suggests that, over time, defects and/or management mistakes will lead to symptoms of failure emerging, at which point the prospect of corporate failure becomes more apparent.

These symptoms can be directly financial, such as poor ratios in the financial statements. However, evidence of creating accounting could also be a symptom of imminent corporate failure.

Equally, there can be non-financial symptoms of failure, such as high staff turnover, or declining market share.

CCNH's most recent financial statements show a number of symptoms of failure: CCNH made no profits in the last year, it has very low interest cover, and it has a very high operational gearing ratio. Moreover, the difficulty which CCNH faced in making its rental payments could be seen as an indication that failure is imminent.

In addition, the recent directors' resignations, coupled with the police investigation into the thefts of residents' money could be seen as symptoms of impending failure.

Overall position

Overall, it appears that CCNH's position is very weak, and it looks in serious danger of failing unless drastic action is taken to improve its performance.

(c) **Portfolio mix** – An organisation needs to plan the range of products (or services) it offers so that it has a mix of products at different stages in their life cycles: for example, products at the growth stage alongside established (mature) products generating cash. Planning ahead in this respect is a vital element of organisational survival.

Special Care (SC) Division – SC appears to be growing rapidly, with revenue growth of 24% p.a. over the last 2 years. Therefore, it seems likely that SC is in the **growth stage** of its life cycle.

However, one of the characteristics of products in the growth stage of their life cycle is that capital investments are required in order to enable the business to expand in order to fulfil levels of demand. Consequently, the cash flows generated by products in the growth stage of their life cycle are lower than their profits.

This reiterates the importance of CCNH monitoring liquidity as well as profitability. However, in terms of the CEO's strategy, it also highlights the need to have a division within CCNH which generates sufficient cash to support SC's growth.

General Care (GC) Division – GC appears to be a mature business, operating in a mature sector.

The lack of opportunities for growth in the sector is characteristic of a mature sector. Usually, however, mature products are able to generate healthy profits. Equally, because they require relatively low levels of investment, mature products are usually cash generators for a business.

Given that CCNH is one of the largest providers of residential care places in Geeland, we could suggest that the GC Division be classified as a **cash cow** using the BCG matrix.

However, the CEO needs to assess how well GC displays the usual characteristics of a cash cow. Rather than being a cash generator and earning good profits, GC made an operating loss for the last year.

Given that GC is coming under increasing price pressure from its main customers (the public sector health organisations), it appears that **cost control** is likely to be very important for GC, in order to preserve its margins.

SBUs in portfolio – The combination of a growing business unit (SC) with a mature one (GC) should be a relatively beneficial one for CCNH, because the company should be able to use the cash generated by GC to support SC's growth.

However, the CEO will need to assess whether GC is actually able to fulfil this cash generating role. In particular, the CEO needs to consider whether GC is in danger of moving from a mature business to a declining business, and therefore whether divestment is an appropriate strategy. Equally, however, the CEO needs to consider what impact divesting of GC would have on CCNH's business portfolio.

47 BPC

Text reference. Chapters 1 and 4a of the BPP Study Text consider Porter's five forces model and how it can be applied in the performance management process. Chapter 14 discusses corporate failure.

Top tips. In **part (a)** BPC is assessing **its option to enter the cardboard tube market** so remember this when you use the five competitive forces to comment on the information in the question. If you have time, it is a good idea to write a little introduction explaining a model and your understanding of how a scenario can be appraised using that model. We have done this in two sentences.

Part (b). In APM, you should be prepared to explain the advantages and disadvantages of using different models, as well as being able to apply them to different scenarios. In this part of the requirement, there is no need to apply your answer to the scenario, but simply to demonstrate you are aware of the potential limitations of Porter's model.

Part (c) draws on your knowledge of predicting corporate failure though there is very little in the scenario to comment on. However, note that JOL Co has already been mentioned in note (3) in the scenario.

Rather than labouring to apply your answer to the scenario, you may have to make general comments. You could use information from one of the writers in Chapter 14 of the Study Text and we have used Slatter's ideas. Argenti's A score could also be useful here, as the variables are a good mix of financial and non-financial indicators.

Marking scheme

					Marks
(a)	Comments (on merit):				
	Each of the five forces	5 × 2	10		
	Conclusion		1	Maximum	10
(b)	Limitations – up to 2 marks for each limitation discussed		Up to 5		5
(c)	Comments (on merit)				
	Fall in market share significant		1		
	(with percentage 18%)		1		
	Indicators	6 × 1.5	9	Maximum	10
				Total =	25

(a) **Porter's five forces and the option to enter the cardboard tube market**

Porter's five forces model assesses **five competitive forces** that affect a firm's positioning in its market and ultimately its profitability.

BPC is considering whether it wants to enter the cardboard tube market. So using the model to assess the option to enter this market:

(i) **Threat of new entrants**. A new entrant such as BPC will bring **more competition** and **extra capacity**. The strength of this threat depends on the barriers to entry to the market such as high fixed costs or expertise in technology. It also depends on the response of the existing competition in the market. New machinery to make the tubes costs from $30,000 per machine, it only needs one operator and the expertise needed to operate it is fairly low as an operator only needs one day's training. This appears to be a high threat. Another threat would be the foreign multinational company which has the machinery to manufacture cardboard tubes.

(ii) **Threat of substitutes**. A substitute product is a good or service produced by another industry which satisfies the same customer needs. PTC has a range of plastic tubes that can be used to **house** small products. This use appears to be different from that of the manufacturers who use the tubing to **wind products around**. It is possible that the uses could be extended to satisfy some of the uses made of cardboard tubes. However, the plastic tubes are at present an average of 30% more expensive than the cardboard tubes on offer.

(iii) **The bargaining power of customers**. Customers, who appear to be manufacturers, use the tubing for a variety of purposes and buy very large quantities. The customers seem to have some bargaining power in their purchasing as they buy in bulk, and may also be price sensitive as the tubing costs a tiny part of the total cost and they may wish it to remain so. The product is not likely to be specialised and so customers could switch suppliers readily. There are four main suppliers with similar ranges, so customers have some choice. This also appears to be a high threat.

(iv) **The bargaining power of suppliers**. Suppliers can drive up prices for goods and services supplied to the industry. Obviously a monopoly supplier with a **differentiated product** will have more influence than a range of small suppliers with a simple product. The tubes are made from a specialist paper that can be in short supply. So suppliers do have some influence. Again this is another high threat.

(v) **Rivalry amongst current industry competitors**. The intensity of competition within an industry will affect overall profitability. The industry has four main manufacturers with 80% share in total and between 18% and 26% share each. So the industry is fairly concentrated. There has been little market growth recently at 2% p.a. and the product is undifferentiated. Therefore the competition is likely to be quite strong for a shrinking market and a homogenous product. This therefore poses yet another high threat.

In summary, there are some good reasons for entering the market, which include **low entry barriers**, as the manufacture of the product is unspecialised (though this could be a threat once BPC has established itself in the market and wishes to keep out other competition). There is also a **small likelihood of substitution**. However, the market is likely to be **very competitive** with a **high concentration of entrenched competitors and customers who have considerable buying power**.

On balance, the option to enter the market for cardboard tubes appears to be unattractive and BPC should consider alternative strategies for improving performance.

(b) **Limitations of the five forces model as a technique for assessing the attractiveness of an industry**

Problem of market definition – The aim of Porter's model is to identify the level of profits which can be sustained in an industry or market. However, it can sometimes be difficult to define exactly what the industry or market in question is – particularly for a large organisation, or one operating in a complex environment. Even in the BPC example, are cardboard tubes and plastic tubes in the same 'tube' market, or should they be distinguished on the basis of the different materials used?

This issue around market definition identifies a potential problem with Porter's model. The model is best used for analysing **simple market structures**, but analysis of the different forces can get very difficult in more complex industries with lots of interrelated segments or product groups.

Environmental change – Moreover, the model **assumes relatively static market structures**. However, this is often not the case in today's markets. For example, technological breakthroughs can change business models in relatively short timescales. Yet while the model can provide some useful analysis of the new market structure once it has emerged, it can only offer limited advice for any preventative measures.

The need for careful analysis is, perhaps, most important in the area of substitute products or services. It takes a particular alertness to discern potential substitutes in the early stages of their development.

Equally, while there may currently be strong barriers to entry into an industry, new technological developments could remove or severely reduce those barriers to entry.

Competition or co-operation? – It is also important to recognise that Porter's model is based on the idea of competition between firms. It assumes that companies try to achieve competitive advantages over other players in the markets as well as over suppliers or customers. With this focus, it does not really reflect the dynamic of approaches such as strategic alliances, electronic linking of information systems of all companies along a value chain, or in a virtual organisation, in which the focus is primarily on collaboration rather than competition.

(c) **JOL Co and corporate failure**

JOL Co had a market-leading share of 30% just 3 years ago. The current market share is 18% (see Working) so there has been a decline of 12% in 3 years. There are several performance indicators that could be used to flag up corporate failure. These are both financial and non-financial indicators and could include:

(i) **Declining profitability.** JOL is losing market share in a slow growing market. It is very likely that profitability will be affected. If JOL starts to make losses it will become unviable to continue operating.

(ii) **Decreasing sales volume.** JOL has lost market share in a near static market and therefore it has lost sales.

(iii) **An increase in gearing.** JOL may well need to borrow if it is not earning sufficient revenue to fund operations and future growth. This is usually achieved through increasing its overdraft limit or long-term debt which can eventually lead to lenders refusing further borrowing. High levels of debt or financial gearing create financial risk affecting the company and its stakeholders.

(iv) **Poor financial controls.** Organisations that lose control over costs and operations can fail spectacularly. Audit committees that do not exercise proper controls can fail to spot fraud or mismanagement.

(v) **Lack of planning.** The remark by the MD suggests that JOL has not done anything to date to stem the decline in market share. This shows a lack of planning by the board having let things drift for three years.

(vi) **Frequent changes in senior executives.** Mobility can be a sign of dissatisfaction with how the company is performing. The challenge of turning around a troubled company is outweighed by whether the company can be saved and the risk of being associated with a failed company.

Working: Market share

From Note (3) in the scenario: The four leading manufacturers have a market share of 80%. The market leader has a market share of 26%, so the other three (including JOL) together have a share of 54%. The three are equal in size, so each company has a share of 54/3 = 18%.

48 RM Batteries

Text reference. Models for predicting corporate failure are discussed in Chapter 14 of the BPP Study Text.

Top tips. Part (a) asks for your knowledge of quantitative and qualitative models. However, note you are not asked to describe the different types of models themselves, but to discuss their strengths and weaknesses. In effect this question could be broken down into four elements: strengths of quantitative models; weaknesses of quantitative models; strengths of qualitative models; and weaknesses of qualitative models.

Part (b) requires you to review the data in the spreadsheet. Remember the analyst has correctly prepared the data so you don't need to evaluate it.

In **part (c)**, you need to use data from the question in conjunction with a suitable model. We use Argenti's A score model which has three categories – and data from the question is available for most of these.

Part (d) asks for a critical assessment. Do the models give a complete picture of RMB's position? Is it safe to conclude from the data you have already considered whether the company is failing? What else would you need to know and do you need to compare the company with its market?

Part (e). This part of the question isn't looking at corporate failure, but looks at the wider issue of product life cycles as a whole. How do pricing and production strategies vary across the life cycle? One of the key issues here is the extent to which RMB may have to switch from a differentiation strategy to a cost leadership strategy as its product approaches maturity.

Easy marks. A good question if you are comfortable with quantitative and qualitative models but if you couldn't think of a suitable qualitative model you would miss out on five marks in part (c). Still there are plenty of marks available across four question parts.

Marking scheme

		Marks
(a)	1 mark for each point made. Up to 3 for each type of model. Maximum of 6 marks	6
(b)	1 mark for each point made. Maximum of 5 marks	5
(c)	0.5 mark for identifying problem and up to 1 mark for explaining how this relates to corporate failure. Maximum of 5 marks	5
(d)	1 mark for each point explained. To score full marks some appreciation of the information not captured by parts (b) and (c) must be demonstrated. Maximum of 4 marks	4
(e)	1 mark for each point made in relation to selling prices – Up to 3 1 mark for each point made in relation to production costs – Up to 3	Up to 5
	Total =	25

(a) **Strengths and weaknesses of quantitative and qualitative models for predicting corporate failure**

Quantitative methods such as the Z-score use publicly available financial data to predict whether a firm is likely to fail in the two-year period. The calculation is easy to make using the model but the calculation is only a probability, not an absolute likelihood, so it may need to be used with other data to make a more rounded assessment. It also only gives guidance below the danger level of 1.8 so other scores are difficult to interpret.

Furthermore, the model is based on historical trading patterns of a specific group of companies so a change in trading patterns or a company that falls outside the industry grouping used may find the model inaccurate. There is also a danger that companies in trouble use creative accounting in calculating figures which means where these go into calculations they are unreliable.

Qualitative models attempt to 'fill in the gaps' that quantitative models leave by using in-depth questionnaires but again these have their flaws. For instance, the Argenti A score uses fairly subjective categories to calculate an overall score. These are wide ranging but can be answered subjectively and be open to bias.

(b) **Comment on the results in the junior analyst's spreadsheet**

The Z-score for RMB in 20Y0 is 1.45 which is below the danger level of 1.8 and so suggests a likelihood of insolvency in the next 2 years. It has fallen over the past 3 years between 2.746 and 1.45. During this period the variables making up the model have been mostly static or declining. Roughly half the decline in the Z-score arises from variable X_4 (market value of equity/total long term debt) which has fallen from 1.510 to 0.478 or 68%. The bulk of the movement arises from a significant increase in long-term borrowings from $465m to $1,261m because of the investment in new equipment. The average share price has fallen from $1.56 in 20X8 to $1.34 in 20Y0 or 14% in the last year, though it would be useful to see if this is a general market trend and so a comparison with competitor share prices is advisable.

The other variable that has seen most decline is variable X3 (PBIT/TA) falling from 0.227 to 0.078 which reflects a sharp fall in profits ($185m to $65m) and an increase in total assets ($1,355m to $2,456m) thus the company has failed to extract profit from available assets. Maybe this will improve in future periods as revenue from the new investments is earned.

(c) **Qualitative problems in the company's structure and performance and why these are relevant to possible failure**

Using the Argenti A score model, the problems a company is experiencing may be broken down into three broad categories: defects, mistakes made and symptoms of failure. Looking at RMB, defects exhibited are a dominant chief executive officer, a failure to split the chief executive and chairman roles and passive senior management.

Mistakes made by RMB include a reliance on one large project to fuel growth, which is risky and relies on the success of the project. Overtrading as revenue rises is another mistake mainly funded by debt thus gearing has risen from 107% to 197% and interest cover has declined from 8.8 times to 2.0 times. This reliance on debt funding leads to a risk of failure to service debt payments.

Finally symptoms of failure. The information available doesn't reveal these yet but they typically include high turnover, low morale and creative accounting.

(d) **Assess the results of analysis in parts (b) and (c) and state what additional data should be obtained to assess the company's financial health**

The company is still profitable, making $65m of profits in 20Y0. Its revenues are still growing (from $1,560m to $1,915m over the past year) but operating costs have increased by 50% from 20X8 to 20Y0 and interest charges have gone up by $60m over that period. Thus margins have suffered (falling from 21% to 10% operating margin over the period). It is likely at the early stage of the project that costs will be high and revenues low. So a longer-term view needs to be taken before concluding the company is definitely failing.

However, the decline in the margin needs further explanation looking at costs in detail and how these are being controlled.

Finally it would be useful to compare the fall in the share price with the movement in the market to assess whether this is a general trend or reflecting sentiment over RMB's prospects.

(e) **Selling price changes**

Maturity – Sales prices are likely to decrease significantly at the maturity stage. Competitors will have flooded the market with alternative products and RMB is likely to have to reduce its sales prices as a means of sustaining demand for its product and maintaining its market share.

Decline – At the decline stage, demand is likely to fall further, as the product becomes superseded by the next generation of 'new' products. Therefore, price will be lowered further in order to try to attract business sales. RMB may attempt to prolong the life of its product by reducing selling prices significantly at this stage, although such a decision may depend on whether RMB has developed a next generation product of its own.

Prices are also likely to be forced down by over-capacity in the industry. If the selling price becomes too low (so that the product becomes loss making) RMB may decide to stop selling it.

Production cost changes

Total production costs are likely to change with unit sales over the course of the product life cycle. However, the more important changes for RMB will be how unit production costs vary over the life cycle.

Maturity – At the maturity stage, the growth in demand for the product will have slowed significantly. As we have already mentioned, price becomes more sensitive as firms compete with one another to try to increase their share of a static market.

In order to maximise profits, while defending market share, RMB will look to reduce its costs; for example, by automating and standardising production processes as far as possible.

Decline stage – RMB will need to continue to control costs at a low level during the decline phase, to try to retain a positive cash flow for as long as possible despite falling prices and falling demand.

However, as there is unlikely to be any investment in the machinery used to make the product, there could be an increase in costs due to machine breakdowns and inefficiencies.

[Answers to the 50-mark Section A questions begin on the next page.]

49 Lopten

Text references. CSFs and KPIs are considered in Chapter 2 of the BPP Study Text. Environmental factors and their impact on performance are discussed in Chapter 5.

Top tips.

Part (i). Note that the requirement here is only to 'calculate' the KPIs. You are not asked to comment on them, nor to comment on the relative performance of the two different products.

The calculations here are not technically difficult, and so should offer some easy marks. Note that the KPIs you need to calculate are specifically listed in the scenario: total profit; average sales price per unit; contribution per unit; market share; margin of safety; return on capital employed (ROCE); total quality costs; and consumer awards won. You would not have earned any marks for calculating additional performance indicators of your own.

Also, it is vital that you look at the figures in Appendix 1 carefully before doing the calculation. The variable cost figures are given per unit, whereas the fixed cost figures are given for Cheerful and Posh in total.

And remember, you have been asked to write a report; so detailed working should be included as an appendix rather than in the main body of the report.

Part (ii). There are two parts to this requirement, and your answer needs to address both of them. The first part is the easier part – applying PEST analysis to identify issues (in effect, opportunities or threats to Lopten's performance) presented by the external environment: for example, what impact could the growth of the middle-class population have on demand for Lopten's products, or what could be the consequences of the Government offering grants to one of its competitors?

Once you have identified the issues, you then need to evaluate how well the KPIs can help Lopten's management address them. A useful way to structure your answer might be to take each environmental factor (political, economic, social and technological) in turn, identify the relevant issues in the environment, and then evaluate how far any of the KPIs will help to identify the impact that the issues are having on Lopten's performance.

Part (iii). The relationship between CSFs and KPIs is a very important one in performance management. CSFs are the key areas of performance in which an organisation has to perform well in order to be successful; and KPIs are the indicators which management use to measure how well an organisation is achieving its CSFs.

However, the key issue in this question is how well Lopten's KPIs will enable management to measure how well the Beeland operations are achieving the CSFs identified in the scenario.

However, the question requirement provides you with a clear direction about how to structure your answer, by asking you to relate to each CSF in turn.

Part (iv). Although this question again relates to the KPIs, a key point is distinguishing between the nature of planning and control activities. For example, planning is often seen as being relatively more 'strategic' and control as being more 'operational'.

Part (v). This final part of the question combines some relatively simple calculations with an analysis based on them. Note, however, that you will need to use your calculations from part (i) to calculate the most recent profits.

The first thing to assess is what impact the two strategies will have on Lopten's profits. The board has set a target operating profit of $135m for 2 years' time, so the key issue is whether or not the strategies will help the operations achieve that target level of profit.

However, in addition to the calculations, you need to question how realistic or achievable the two plans are. For example, will Lopten really be able to achieve a 15% annual growth rate for Posh (as anticipated by Plan B)? And if the plans don't achieve the growth rates which have been assumed, what impact will that have on Lopten's operating profits?

Overall. Once again, remember that you have been asked to write a report, so make sure the style and structure of your answer, as a whole, is appropriate for a report.

Marking scheme

		Marks
(i)	Calculation of variable costs – 2 marks Fixed costs – 1 mark each Calculation of profit for each product – 1 mark Average sales price per unit – 1 mark Calculation of contribution per unit – 1 mark Calculation of market share – 1 mark Calculation of breakeven point – 1 mark Margin of safety – 1 mark ROCE – 1 mark Total quality costs – 1 mark Total for part (i) – Up to 11 marks	11
(ii)	PEST factors For identifying relevant issues (political, economic, social and technological) in the scenario – Up to 2 marks for each issue identified For commenting on the relevance of the suggested KPIs to each issue – Up to 2 marks per issue Total for part (ii) – Up to 11 marks	11
(iii)	For evaluating how well the KPIs fit with the CSF to obtain a dominant market presence – Up to 4 marks For evaluating how well the KPIs fit with the CSF to maximise profits within acceptable risk – Up to 4 marks For evaluating how well the KPIs fit with the CSF to maintain brand image for above average quality products – Up to 4 marks Total for part (iii) – Up to 10 marks	10
(iv)	For each relevant point about the suitability of the KPIs for planning or controlling – 1 mark per point Total for part (iv) – Up to 5 marks	5
(v)	For calculating contribution (1 mark) and profit (1 mark) for Plan A – Up to 2 marks for calculations for Plan A For calculating contribution (2 marks) and profit (1 mark) for Plan B – Up to 3 marks for calculations for Plan B For calculating difference in actual profits vs target profits under the two plans – 1 mark For relevant points evaluating whether the strategies will enable the business to achieve its target profits – Up to 4 marks Total for part (v) – Up to 9 marks	9
	Professional marks – for style and structure of report – Up to 4 marks	4
	Total =	**50**

Report

To: Board of Lopten Industries
From: Consultant
Date: [today's date]
Subject: Strategic performance and performance indicators

Introduction

This report calculates the KPIs suggested by the board for measuring Lopten's performance, and then evaluates the effectiveness of those KPIs in addressing issues in the company's external environment. The report also evaluates how well the KPIs measure performance in relation to Lopten's CSFs. The report concludes by evaluating two marketing strategies which have been proposed, and their impact on Lopten's ability to achieve its target operating profit in two years' time.

(i) **KPIs**

The board has identified a number of KPIs which can be used to assess the performance of the Beeland operations.

These are shown below:

	Cheerful	*Posh*	
Total profit ($m)	42.4	45.0	See Appendix 1
Average sales price per unit ($)	400.0	700.0	
Contribution per unit ($)	145.0	375.0	
Market share (%)	12.0	33.1	
Margin of safety (%)	25.9	27.3	See Appendix 1
ROCE (%)	13.0	18.0	
Total quality costs ($m)	28.4	19.2	
Consumer awards won	1.0	4.0	

(ii) **Issues in Lopten's external environment**

Political factors

Government grants – The Government has given grants to an international manufacturer (one of Lopten's competitors) which has opened a factory in Beeland. Lopten will not be eligible for any similar grants, however, because it manufactures its washing machines at its regional hub in Kayland and then imports them into Beeland – rather than manufacturing them in Beeland.

It will be difficult for the KPIs to measure the impact of the government grants directly. However, monitoring average sales price per unit of Lopten's machines (compared to the competitors' machines) could indicate whether the government grants have enabled the competitor to sell its machines more cheaply than Lopten can. Equally, if the Government imposes any import tariffs on Lopten's machines this could adversely affect their average price compared to the price of the competitors' products.

Similarly, the market share KPI could also help Lopten assess whether the Government's actions are influencing Lopten's market share (as a result of the competitor's washing machines becoming relatively cheaper than Lopten's products).

Economic factors

Market growth – The growth of the middle class, and rising incomes in Beeland, is leading to an increase in demand for Lopten's products.

The KPIs do not directly include any measure of sales growth rates (for example, by measuring annual sales increase compared to the prior year). However, measuring market share does provide an indicator of the rate at which sales of Lopten's washing machines are increasing relative to its competitors' sales.

Foreign exchange risk – Lopten's reported financial performance from its operations in Beeland could also be affected by movements in currency exchange rates between Beeland, Kayland and Lopten's own country. However, the KPIs do not reflect this foreign exchange risk.

Social factors

Customer tastes – As national income in Beeland continues to increase, it is likely that there will be increasing demand for premium products (such as Posh) relative to more basic products (such as Cheerful). This would justify the approach, taken in marketing Plan B, to focus Lopten's marketing resources onto Posh.

Again, a measure of the sales growth rates for the two products would be useful for identifying changes in demand, but the KPIs do not currently provide this. However, the market share KPI could be useful for identifying how successful Lopten is in selling products – particularly Posh.

Technological factors

Developments in technology could affect Lopten in two ways:

New features – Technological developments could mean that Lopten needs to develop new features for its washing machines (for example, if competitors introduce new features into their machines). However, this could be less of an issue in Beeland than developed countries, because Beeland's customers may not yet be as demanding as customers in more developed countries.

Moreover, as Lopten manufactures its products at a regional hub, and only sells them locally, it seems unlikely that the Beeland operation will have any impact on product development for the company as a whole. Therefore, although none of the KPIs address new product development, this seems to be reasonable.

Reduced costs – New technologies could also improve the efficiency of the manufacturing process for Lopten's existing products; for example, by increasing the levels of automation in the manufacturing process.

As such, this should help to reduce the cost of producing Lopten's washing machines. While any such cost reductions will be reflected in the contribution per unit KPI, the contribution figure is also affected by selling price.

Therefore, a more effective indicator to use in order to measure the impact which technological developments have had on the manufacturing process would be 'Manufacturing cost per unit'.

(iii) **Links between CSFs and KPIs**

Dominant market presence

Market share – The market share KPI provides an indication of Lopten's presence in the market but, in order to gauge whether or not it dominates the market, Lopten's market share also needs to be measured relative to its competitors. In this respect, a KPI of 'relative market share' (comparing Lopten's market share to that of the market leader) could be more suitable.

Growth strategies – One way in which Lopten could seek to increase market share is by reducing the price of its products in order to increase demand for them. However, this will also affect KPIs for average price per product.

It is important that Lopten doesn't discount the price of its washing machines too aggressively, to the extent that they no longer generate a contribution to profit. In this respect, the contribution per unit KPI will be valuable in ensuring that a balance is maintained between profitability and increasing market share.

Maximise profits within acceptable risk

Profit for each product – The amount of profit earned for each product is one of Lopten's KPIs, so this should encourage a focus on profits. Although the KPI only shows profit for a single period, monitoring this profit figure over a number of periods will highlight trends in the level of profit being earned.

Contribution per unit – The contribution per unit KPI can also be used to monitor how effectively Lopten is controlling its variable costs relative to the price of its products. A focus on cost control in this way should also help to increase profits.

ROCE – ROCE indicates how efficiently Lopten is using its capital in order to generate profits. As such, this KPI should also encourage profit maximisation, although there could be concerns that using ROCE as a profit measure encourages short-termist behaviour (for example, not investing in new capital projects even though such investment would be beneficial in the future).

Risk – The margin of safety provides an indication of the extent to which sales would have to fall before Lopten reaches a breakeven profit situation. In this way, the margin of safety could provide an indication of the level of risk relating to the marketing and pricing strategies of both types of washing machine.

Maintaining brand image for above average quality

Consumer awards – The number of consumer awards won provides an indicator of the reputation of Lopten's products because consumers are unlikely to nominate a product for an award if they are unsatisfied with the quality of the product.

Quality costs – The 'quality cost' KPI gives an indication of how much Lopten has spent on quality management but, by itself, it doesn't give any insight into whether the quality of Lopten's products is 'above average'. For example, are there customer reviews which could be used to rate the quality of Lopten's products against rival products?

In this respect, the KPIs might be improved by including a more specifically customer-focused indicator (for example, customer satisfaction ratings, or numbers of complaints) which could potentially also be benchmarked against competitors' products.

Finally, the need to 'maintain brand image' suggests a need for marketing activity. However, there are no KPIs which monitor the level of effectiveness of Lopten's marketing activities in Beeland.

(iv) **KPIs and planning**

Forward looking – KPIs which are to be used for planning (rather than control) need to be forward looking.

Control indicators – In general, financial performance measures tend to be backward looking rather than forward looking, in the sense that they are used to compare the actual performance achieved against some kind of budget or target. For example, KPIs for 'Contribution per unit' and 'ROCE' are more likely to be useful for controlling performance.

In order to monitor its control indicators effectively, though, Lopten should look to measure actual performance against budget or forecast. Currently, it appears to monitor actual performance only, with no reference to either a budget or prior years. However, having some kind of benchmark against which to measure actual performance will help the board to identify those areas where corrective action may be required to improve performance.

Planning indicators – By contrast to financial indicators, non-financial indicators can often be more appropriate as planning indicators.

Margin of safety – In Lopten's case, the margin of safety could be useful as a planning indicator. The margin of safety addresses the risk of making a loss going forward; although, at the moment, the size of the margin should reassure the board that it can afford to take a reasonable degree of strategic risk without jeopardising the survival of the Beeland operation. For example, even if sales of both types of washing machines fell by 25%, Lopten would still make a contribution to profit from its operations in Beeland.

Consumer awards – The number of consumer awards won could also be useful as a planning indicator. Customers' perceptions of Lopten's products will shape the company's ability to increase sales in the future. For example, if Lopten can continue to win awards for 'Posh', it could highlight this in any marketing material designed to boost sales of the product. Moreover, if Lopten can use its success in winning awards to illustrate the quality of its products, it could then use this as a factor which differentiates its washing machines from competitors' products. In turn this could be used to justify Lopten's washing machines being sold at a higher price than rival products.

Planning vs control – In general terms, planning activities tend to be high level, strategic activities, whereas control measures tend to be more appropriate at an operational level. In this respect, the mix of Lopten's KPIs seems rather unusual – because, although the KPIs are presented to the board, there appears to be a greater focus on control indicators rather than planning indicators.

However, this issue could be addressed by modifying the indicators to include market share growth, for example, rather than simply market share. In this way, the board could look to use growth trends to help establish financial projections, rather than solely looking at their market share percentage at a given point in time.

(v) **Impact of marketing strategies**

Plan A

	Most recent $m	*Year 1* $m	*Year 2* $m
Contribution			
Cheerful	162.4	168.9	175.7
Posh	165.0	171.6	178.5
Fixed costs	240.0	240.0	240.0
Profit	**87.4**	**100.5**	**114.2**

Plan B

	Most recent $m	*Year 1* $m	*Year 2* $m
Contribution			
Cheerful	162.4	162.4	162.4
Posh	165.0	189.8	218.2
Fixed costs	240.0	240.0	240.0
Profit	**87.4**	**112.2**	**140.6**

The target operating profit in 2 years' time is $135 million. If the board pursues Plan A, Lopten's forecast operating profit will be approximately $21 million below the target at this point.

By contrast, if the board adopts Plan B the target profit figure could be achieved.

However, it would seem likely that there is more uncertainty around the figures used in Plan B than those in Plan A. In particular, Plan B assumes an annual growth rate of 15% in demand for Posh.

It is possible that the level of growth in the economy in Beeland can support this level of growth, because demand for premium products could be sustained by the continuing growth of the middle-class population in the country.

However, the prospects of achieving a growth rate of 15% per year are also likely to depend on the effectiveness of Lopten's marketing expenditure. In this respect, it is important to question how much impact any additional marketing expenditure will have. Lopten already spends $80 million on marketing of Posh, and so it is debatable whether the additional marketing expenditure will generate proportionately more sales, or instead whether the effectiveness of the expenditure will be reduced by decreasing marginal returns.

In addition, the board needs to consider whether it is realistic to assume that sales of 'Cheerful' will remain constant – even if marketing expenditure on the product is reduced, as proposed in Plan B.

Conclusion

Lopten's current KPIs focus primarily on internal aspects of performance, rather than including a balance of internal and external factors. In addition, the link between the KPIs and Lopten's CSFs – particularly the need to obtain a dominant market presence – appears relatively weak.

Currently, the focus of the KPIs appears to be on control, rather than planning, whereas the board's focus should ideally really be more forward looking. The board should consider revising the KPIs used, in order to address these concerns.

The current marketing plan (Plan A) will not enable Lopten to achieve its profit target of $135 million in 2 years' time. Therefore the company could be advised to adopt Plan B, which has the potential to achieve this figure. However, Plan B assumes some fairly ambitious growth figures, so it will be important to assess how realistic these are before starting to implement the new marketing strategy.

Appendix 1

	Cheerful	*Posh*
Units sold (millions)	1.12	0.44
	$m	$m
Revenue	448.0	308.0
Variable costs		
Materials	100.8	52.8
Labour	67.2	35.2
Overheads	44.8	22.0
Distribution costs	50.4	19.8
Quality costs	22.4	13.2
Contribution	162.4	165.0
Fixed costs	18.0	18.0
Distribution costs	16.0	16.0
Quality costs	6.0	6.0
Marketing costs	80.0	80.0
Total fixed costs	120.0	120.0
Total profit	**42.4**	**45.0**

Margin of safety

Contribution per unit ($)	145.0	375.0
Units sold (millions)	1.12	0.44
Breakeven sales (millions)	0.83	0.32
Margin of safety	**25.9%**	**27.3%**

BPP LEARNING MEDIA

50 Mackerel

Text reference. Risk and uncertainty are considered in Chapter 5 of the BPP Study Text. Information systems are discussed in Chapter 6a, while performance measures (including ROCE and EVA™) are discussed in Chapter 7.

Top tips.

Part (i). Note that there are effectively two parts to this requirement: (a) analyse the risks facing the management committee; and (b) discuss how the management team's attitude to risk might affect their response. The scenario identifies a number of risks (eg earnings volatility, economic downturn, uncertainty over the size of the order) so these should help you get started.

The reference to 'attitude to risk' should also have prompted you to discuss different risk appetites: risk averse, risk seeking, and risk neutral. This links parts (i) and (ii) of the question, because the management team will evaluate the project using different approaches depending on their attitudes to risk.

Part (ii) is a combination of calculations and then a critical analysis based around those calculations. As we have just noted, the relevant knowledge base here is the different approaches to decision making which could be used: in this case, maximax, maximin, minimax regret and expected values. Remember, however, that maximax, maximin and minimax regret are calculated on **profits**, not expected values.

Step 1, in effect, is to calculate the profitability of the different packages at the different levels of demand, and then to work out which option Mackerel would choose using the four different approaches to decision making.

Step 2 is to assess the suitability of the different methods for Mackerel: how appropriate are they given the management team's attitude to risk.

Remember, however, that you have been asked to write a report. Therefore any detailed calculations should be presented in an appendix at the end of the report, and referred to, rather than being included in the main body of the report.

Note. For tutorial purposes, our answers below have given full calculations. You may have found some short-cuts to avoid writing out the calculations in full, and ACCA's examining team has indicated that it was not necessary to write out all the calculations in full to obtain a good, correct answer.

Your evaluations in part (ii) then need to form the basis of your answer for **part (iii)**: the recommendation. Again, note, however, that you need to recommend two different things here: an appropriate choice of method, and a course of action.

Part (iv). Remember you are asked to evaluate the impact of the new information system at both an operational level and a strategic level. And note you are asked to 'evaluate' the impact; so as well as considering its potential benefits you should also consider any limitations which would restrict those benefits.

Part (v). The scenario identifies that Mackerel's overall goal is to increase shareholder wealth, so in effect the question is asking how well ROCE or EVA™ will help Mackerel increase shareholder wealth. Note, you are not simply asked to compare ROCE and EVA™ as performance measures in general terms, but specifically in relation to the aim of increasing shareholder wealth.

Also, the question requirement highlights that ROCE and EVA™ are profit-based performance measures; how will this affect their usefulness in relation to increasing shareholder wealth?

Overall. Once again, remember that you have been asked to write a report, so make sure the style and structure of your answer, as a whole, is appropriate for a report.

Marking scheme

		Marks
(i)	Identifying appropriate metrics – 1 mark Identifying risk appetites (averse; seeking; neutral) – ½ mark each Identifying key stakeholders and risks – Up to 2 marks Discussion of risk appetite – Up to 3 marks Demand risk – 1 mark Cost overrun risk – Up to 2 marks Total for part (i) – Up to 9 marks	9
(ii)	Calculation of variable cost per unit – 1 mark Calculation of total cost under each package – Up to 2 marks Calculation of cost per unit for each package, and comparison to target figure – Up to 2 marks Calculation of total profits for each package – Up to 2 marks Description of different methods (maximax; maximin; minimax regret; expected values) – ½ mark each – Up to 2 marks Maximax: 1 mark for calculation; ½ mark for conclusion Maximin: 1 mark for calculation; ½ mark for conclusion Minimax regret: 2 marks for calculation; ½ mark for conclusion Expected values: 1½ marks for calculation; ½ mark for conclusion [**Note.** Workings rounded to thousands are acceptable] Evaluation of different methods – Up to 4 marks Total for part (ii) – Up to 19 marks	19
(iii)	Recommendation of method – Up to 2 marks Final recommendation on contract – 1 mark Any other relevant comments about risk reduction – 1 mark Total for part (iii) – Up to 3 marks	3
(iv)	Impact of new information system on information gathering – Up to 3 marks Benefits of new system for strategic decision making – Up to 4 marks Potential problems of new system for strategic decision making – Up to 3 marks Total for part (iv) – Up to 8 marks	8
(v)	Comments on TSR – Up to 2 marks Comments on usefulness of ROCE (in relation to increasing TSR) – Up to 2 marks Comment on usefulness of EVA™ (in relation to increasing TSR) – Up to 3 marks Total for part (v) – Up to 7 marks	7
	Professional marks – for style and structure of report – Up to 4 marks	4
	Total =	**50**

BPP LEARNING MEDIA

Report

To: Board of Mackerel Consulting

From: Accountant

Date: December 20X1

Subject: APV contract, information systems and performance measurement

Introduction

The report assesses the risks facing Mackerel in relation to the APV contract and the choice of which package to tender. The report also assesses how this decision will be influenced by the management team's attitude to risk.

(i) **Analysis of risks facing the management team**

Profit on contract

Mackerel is a commercial company, and therefore its ultimate objective will be to maximise the wealth it generates for its shareholders. In this context, one of the key performance measures for the APV project is the level of profit it can deliver for Mackerel.

Attitudes to risk

There is currently a significant degree of risk and uncertainty about the government contract; for example, which design to offer, and the number of APVs the government is likely to order. The amount of uncertainty the management team is prepared to accept will affect Mackerel's course of action for the APV project.

Risk seeking – Risk seekers will try to secure the best outcome and try to **maximise the benefit** this would have on their organisation, no matter how small the chance that this outcome will actually occur.

Risk neutral – Risk neutral decision makers are concerned with the **most likely outcome** in any situation.

Risk averse – Risk averse decision makers act on the assumption that the **worse outcome** will occur, and they try to minimise the effect this will have on their organisation.

It would seem sensible for Mackerel to evaluate the contract using different methods and then select the method which fits best with its objectives and risk appetite.

Earnings volatility

The institutional shareholders have expressed concern about the volatility of Mackerel's earnings. In this sense, it appears that the shareholders are **risk averse**. This may influence the management team's attitude to risk, but there are other factors which will also influence it.

Context of the contract

In this respect, it is important to think about the context of the government contract.

Economic conditions – The economic downturn in Zedland means that Mackerel is currently operating under difficult economic conditions. This increases the importance of winning the government contract, as does the fact that the contract is a major one for Mackerel.

Importance of the contract – The expected value of the contract is around $5 million (see Appendix 2), and Mackerel's current operating profit is $20.4 million per year.

Equally, the size of the contract should affect the risks Mackerel is prepared to take in connection with it. If such a large project were to fail, this could put the company's survival at risk.

Follow-on contracts – Mackerel also needs to consider the APV contract in the context of the other work it does for the Government. Winning the bid could lead to additional future work for Mackerel, so it may be more important to secure the bid than to maximise the profit on this single project alone.

Level of demand – Nonetheless there is still significant uncertainty about the project itself. The level of demand is uncertain, and this could have a major impact on the return Mackerel can earn from the project.

Cost overruns – The Government is going to pay a fixed price for the contract, based on budgeted variable costs. If actual costs turn out to be higher than budgeted costs, this will again reduce the actual returns earned from the project.

Forecast price of steel – The price of steel could also have had a major impact on the profitability of the project. However, the Risk Manager appears to have removed this uncertainty by agreeing a fixed price for all the steel that might be required for the contract.

(ii) **Evaluation of the APV project**

As we have identified in part (i) of this report, it seems likely that the profitability of the contract will be an important performance measure in helping Mackerel maximise the value it creates for its shareholders.

Ideally, any decisions about the contract should be based on discounted future cash flows, but there is insufficient data available to calculate the cash flows. Therefore decisions about the project will be taken in relation to the profits it could generate for Mackerel.

Compliance with cost specifications

The first priority is to ensure that the cost to Mackerel of fulfilling the contract fall within the Government's cost requirements (of $70,000 per unit).

The calculations in Appendix 2 indicate that the costs are within this limit:

		Demand	
	500	750	1000
Cost per unit	$	$	$
Package 1	62,972	57,972	55,472
Package 2	65,472	59,639	56,722
Package 3	67,972	61,305	57,972

Profits from design packages

The calculations in Appendix 2 also show that the profits for each package will vary significantly according to the different levels of demand:

		Demand	
	500	750	1000
Profit	$	$	$
Package 1	4,557,340	6,836,010	9,114,680
Package 2	3,307,340	5,586,010	7,864,680
Package 3	2,057,340	4,336,010	6,614,680

Methods for selecting a package

There are four possible approaches which Mackerel could use to select a package.

Three of these (maximax, maximin, and minimax regret) assume that there is insufficient information to estimate the likely level of demand for each package, and so are based on the profits which can be achieved under different demand scenarios. The calculations relating to each of these approaches are included in Appendix 1 of this report.

The fourth (expected values) tries to incorporate the Risk Manager's assessment of the probabilities of the different demand levels into the decision about which package to offer (see Appendix 2).

Maximax

Risk seekers (decision makers who aim to maximise the possible returns from the different scenarios) will use a maximax method to evaluate the different packages. If Mackerel adopts this approach, it would be advised to choose **Package 1**, which will have a maximax profit of $9.1 million (where demand is 1,000).

Maximin

Risk averse decision makers (who seek to maximise the minimum possible returns from the different scenarios) will use a maximin method to evaluate the different packages. If Mackerel adopts this approach, it would still be advised to choose **Package 1**, which will have a maximin profit of $4.6 million (where demand is 500).

Regret

Pessimistic decision makers will focus on the amount of any profit they might lose in any scenario compared to the best choice at the same level of demand. In this way, they aim to minimise the maximum level of regret they could suffer under any demand scenario. If Mackerel adopts this type of **minimax regret** approach, it would still be advised to choose **Package 1**, because this will lead to zero regret at each level of demand.

The fact that all three methods indicate Package 1 as the preferred choice should not come as a surprise. Package 1 has significantly lower fixed costs than the other two packages, while the variable costs per unit are the same for each package and at all levels of demand.

Importantly, though, these three methods used so far do not take account of the probabilities attached to the different levels of demand for each package.

Expected values

A risk neutral manager will choose the option that yields the maximum expected value once the probabilities for each of the outcomes is factored into the decision-making process.

Probabilities – Mackerel's Risk Manager has tried to quantify the probabilities of the different levels of demand for each of the packages offered. These estimated probabilities allow the calculation of an expected profit for each design package (see Appendix 2).

Appendix 2 indicates that the maximum expected profit (of $5.6 million) can be earned if **Package 2** is chosen. This is because the improved design in Package 2 significantly increases the likelihood of securing a higher demand than for Package 1. Although Package 3 also has an improved design, the benefits of this in terms of expected demand do not outweigh the additional $1.25 million design and development costs incurred.

However, it is difficult to ascertain the relevant probabilities of different order volumes and so the management team need to recognise that the Risk Manager's estimates are likely to be subjective. Therefore the team should consider getting some other opinions on the probabilities before using them; for example, by consulting the sales team, or by referring back to any similar government tenders they have worked on in the past.

(iii) **Recommendations**

Method of assessing the project

The method chosen to assess the project needs to reflect the management team's **attitude to risk**. The context of risk averse shareholders, a difficult economic environment, and a major contract for the company suggests that a low risk method will be appropriate here.

The use of expected values appears debatable here because they appear to be based only on one person's estimate. Instead, the **risk averse method of maximin** appears to be most appropriate here, and I recommend Mackerel use this method.

Course of action for the APV contract

Design Package 1 should be chosen, because this carries the least risk for Mackerel and guarantees a profit of at least $4.6 million.

Although the expected values indicate that there could be the potential to earn an additional profit of $573k by choosing Package 2 in preference to Package 1, the level of uncertainty over the probability estimates does not justify such a decision in relation to a major contract such as this.

(iv) **New executive information system**

The new system will improve the availability of data (at operational level) and will help improve Mackerel's decision making (at strategic level), but it will be important that the costs of the new system do not outweigh the potential benefits of the system. However, it will be much harder to quantify the benefits of the system compared to the costs.

Operational level

Immediate update – Once the new system is introduced, users will expect to be able to gather information about operational performance immediately, on a real-time basis. Whilst having this information on a real-time basis could help improve control over performance, there are also likely to be costs associated with gathering the data.

Data entry – It is not clear how data is currently entered onto Mackerel's systems but, if users are going to be able to view data on a real-time basis, all transactions will need to be entered immediately, rather than, for example, on a batch basis. This could generate increased costs in relation to data processing and data entry, unless Mackerel already has a system of automated data input.

If Mackerel doesn't already have a system of automated data input, this would be an opportunity to automate the process, in order to maximise the benefits from real-time data availability.

Strategic decision making

Summary information – The executive information system (EIS) should allow improved decision making by presenting summary information relating to all the performance areas of the company, but with the option for senior managers to **drill down** and get more detailed information about specific aspects of performance if they want to.

Consistency – Whereas summary data used to come from a range of different systems, it will now come from a single database, which should remove any inconsistencies within the data and the way it is structured. This could be a significant aid to decision making, because it will enable managers to focus on analysing the data, rather than having to spend time reconciling different figures or reports prepared by different functions within Mackerel.

External information – However, the system should also be linked to external data sources so that managers do not focus solely on internal information at the expense of what is happening in the wider business environment and, for example, the risk of any cutbacks in government expenditure (which could have an impact on the number of APVs the Government may buy).

However, including external information in the EIS will mean that Mackerel will need to include new data sources which again could increase the cost of the system.

Amount of information available – The new system will increase the amount of information which is available to managers, and the speed with which it is available to them. This will therefore increase the amount of analysis they could perform in relation to any strategic decisions.

However, if the level of information available is not controlled, managers could suffer from **information overload**. Therefore the new system will need to be structured so that managers only receive information which is necessary or appropriate to them.

Training – In order to gain the maximum benefit from the new system, managers will need to be trained how to use it, and this training should occur just before the system becomes available so that managers are able to use it immediately.

(v) **Performance measures**

Shareholder wealth – Mackerel's overall goal is to maximise shareholder wealth, and TSR is used as an overall performance measure to assess how well the company is achieving this.

TSR – TSR is concerned with both the current performance of a business and its future performance. Current performance is likely to dictate current dividend payments, while expected future performance is likely to dictate share price.

ROCE – By contrast, profit-based performance measures focus on historical performance rather than potential future performance.

Whilst ROCE is a simple, commonly used measure of performance, it can be criticised as potentially being detrimental to future performance rather than enhancing it. Using ROCE as a performance measure can discourage investment in net assets, because such an investment will increase the level of capital employed and thereby reduce the ROCE figure (which is calculated as profit before interest and tax divided by capital employed).

Profit rather than cash – In addition, ROCE has the disadvantage of being based on profit rather than cash. Measures such as net present values (NPV) use cash flows, which are less subject to a company's accounting rules and policies, and so are more directly aligned with shareholder interests.

Overall, it is unclear whether ROCE will align with the overall performance measure of TSR, since TSR depends on share price and dividends paid rather than profit. In particular, given that share price is based on a long-term view of dividend prospects and future performance, it seems likely that short-term performance measures, such as profit-based measures, will have limited use in supporting TSR.

EVA™

Calculating EVA™ involves a more complex calculation than calculating ROCE, because a number of adjustments are made to the accounting figures for profit and net assets.

Value-creating expenditure – However, these adjustments are intended to avoid the distortion of results by accounting policies, which we noted was one of the limitations of ROCE. In addition, EVA™ treats value-creating expenditure (such as marketing) as an investment rather than a cost, and so it can encourage appropriate capital expenditure rather than discouraging it in the way that ROCE does.

Shareholders' interests – In this way, EVA™ is more aligned with the shareholders' interests in future performance than ROCE is.

This should not be a surprise, because the logic behind the development of EVA™ was that, if an organisation's primary objective is to maximise the wealth of its shareholders, then performance measures need to evaluate how well the organisation is achieving that objective.

However, EVA™ is still calculated based on historical data while shareholders will be focused on future performance. Therefore, although it is more directly aligned with the objective of increasing shareholder wealth than ROCE is, it still doesn't measure shareholders' expectations which are present in the share price.

Conclusion

Given the current risk appetites of key stakeholders, and the current volatility in the economic environment, it is recommended that Mackerel chooses design Package 1 for the APV, because it carries the least risk.

The EIS provides an opportunity to improve the information for control and decision making, but it is important that the costs of the new system are properly understood before it is finally approved.

EVA™ is more closely aligned to Mackerel's overall goal of increasing shareholder wealth than ROCE is. However, neither measure is a perfect match to the company's main performance measure of TSR, because they are based on historic performance information rather than expectations of future performance.

Appendix 1

Mark-up per unit

Variable cost per APV	$
Steel (9.4 tonnes at $1,214 per tonne)	11,412
Engine/transmission	9,500
Electronics	8,450
Other	4,810
Labour	13,800
Total	47,972

Mark-up @ 19%; $9,114.7

Payoff table

	$	$	$	$	$
Demand	500	750	1000	Max payoff	Min payoff
Design package					
Type 1	4,557,350	6,836,025	9,114,700	9,114,700	4,557,350
Additional fixed costs	1,250,000	1,250,000	1,250,000		
Type 2	3,307,350	5,586,025	7,864,700	7,864,700	3,307,350
Additional fixed costs	1,250,000	1,250,000	1,250,000		
Type 3	2,057,350	4,336,025	6,614,700	6,614,700	2,057,350
Maximum of the maximum payoffs – Package 1				9,114,700	
Maximum of the minimum payoffs – Package 1					4,557,350

Regret table

Design package				Max regret
Type 1	0	0	0	0
Type 2	1,250,000	1,250,000	1,250,000	1,250,000
Type 3	2,500,000	2,500,000	2,500,000	2,500,000
Minimum of max regret – Package 1				0

Appendix 2

Demand	500	750	1000
	$	$	$
Variable cost (@ $47,972 each)	23,986,000	35,979,000	47,972,000
Fixed cost			
Package 1	7,500,000	7,500,000	7,500,000
Package 2	8,750,000	8,750,000	8,750,000
Package 3	10,000,000	10,000,000	10,000,000
Total cost			
Package 1	31,486,000	43,479,000	55,472,000
Package 2	32,736,000	44,729,000	56,722,000
Package 3	33,986,000	45,979,000	57,972,000
Cost per unit			
Package 1	62,972	57,972	55,472
Package 2	65,472	59,639	56,722
Package 3	67,972	61,305	57,972

Revenue				
[$7.5 + (budgeted variable costs × 1.19)]				
	36,043,340	50,315,010	64,586,680	
Profit				
Package 1	4,557,340	6,836,010	9,114,680	
Package 2	3,307,340	5,586,010	7,864,680	
Package 3	2,057,340	4,336,010	6,614,680	
Expected profit				
	500	750	1,000	Total
Package 1				
Probability	85%	10%	5%	
Expected profit ($)	3,873,739	683,601	455,734	5,013,074
Package 2				
Probability	25%	50%	25%	
Expected profit ($)	826,835	2,793,005	1,966,170	5,586,010
Package 3				
Probability	20%	50%	30%	
Expected profit ($)	411,468	2,168,005	1,984,404	4,563,877

51 Metis

Text reference. Management information and reports are discussed in Chapter 8 of the BPP Study Text. EVA™, MIRR and financial performance measures are discussed in Chapter 7.

Top tips.

Part (a). One of the key issues here is that the current report focuses solely on financial performance (and within that, only really profit measures). Therefore, one significant improvement could be for the report to include a range of non-financial performance indicators alongside financial ones.

In this respect, you might have used one of the multi-dimensional frameworks such as the balanced scorecard or the 'building blocks' model to help you plan your answer (although these were not specifically required). In particular the 'Results and Determinants' element of the 'building blocks' model could have been useful here, given that Metis is a service business.

However, if you do decide to use one of these frameworks as a guide you must still make sure your answer is tailored to the scenario. For example, although one of the dimensions in the 'Results and Determinants' block is 'Innovation' the scenario does not provide you with any information about innovation at Metis. Therefore you should not have invented any, or included this dimension in your answer. To this end, the suggested solution below isn't structured around any given model.

However, remember that the question requirement is to critically assess the performance **report**, not Metis's performance itself.

Also, make sure you assess both the content and the presentation of the report. For example, how user-friendly is the layout and presentation of the report?

Part (b). The scenario identifies NPV, EVA™ and MIRR as three methods to use as performance measures, as well as the 'more common profit measures'. You should have identified that ROCE and return on equity were relevant here.

Although the requirement asks you to 'calculate' Metis's performance using the different measures, it also asks you to 'briefly evaluate' the use of the different measures. In other words, once you have done the calculations you also need to consider how useful they are for assessing Metis's performance.

Part (c). The idea that 'What gets measured, gets done' is a key issue in performance management because people tend to focus on performing well in those areas which are being measured (possibly at the expense of other areas). The underlying suggestion is that the things which are measured are those that are important to an organisation, but what implications could this have for the way staff (or managers) treat those aspects of performance which are not measured? For example, is there too much emphasis on financial performance at Metis, rather than non-financial aspects such as customer service?

To score well here, though, it is important you don't just assess the quote in general terms, but apply it specifically to Metis. For example, how far does the choice of what is measured (or not measured) contribute to the performance issues identified in the scenario?

Part (d). In effect, this picks up on the ideas of the quote in part (c). If too much focus is given to short-term performance, will long-term performance suffer, or vice versa?

And again, as in part (c) make sure you don't just discuss the potential conflict between short-term and long-term performance in general terms, but link it specifically to the scenario; for example, in relation to the decision to upgrade the restaurant.

Examining team's comments. In part (a) any candidates used the report given in the scenario to make specific criticisms and suggestions for improvements in a practical way and scored well. However, a number of candidates chose to 'critically assess Metis's performance', rather than the report itself, and consequently these candidates scored few marks for the question. It is vital you read the question requirement carefully and answer the question actually being asked.

Marking scheme

		Marks
(a)	Strengths of current reporting (eg measures overall objective) – 1 mark per point, up to 2 marks	
	Weaknesses of current reporting – 1 mark per point, up to 12 marks Possible weaknesses include: Data overload; use of absolute numbers only; no breakdown into functional areas; timescales used; lack of non-financial performance indicators	
	Total for part (a) – up to 12 marks	12
(b)	NPV calculation Deriving free cash flows – up to 3 marks Calculating NPV – up to 2 marks	
	EVA™ Calculating NOPAT – 1 mark Calculating EVA – 1 mark	
	MIRR Present value of investment – ½ mark Terminal value of returns – 1½ marks Calculating MIRR – 1 mark	
	ROCE – 1 mark	
	Return on equity – up to 2 marks	
	Evaluation of measures used – 1 mark per point; up to 4 marks	14

BPP LEARNING MEDIA

		Marks
(c)	General commentary on the quote – up to 2 marks	
	Specific examples appropriate to Metis – up to 3 marks per example; up to 10 marks	10
	Examples can include illustrations of how management responds to measures, or the problems which arise from the lack of certain measures in the performance report.	
	Professional marks for the format, style and structure of the discussion	4
(d)	General commentary on the potential conflict between short-term and long-term performance measures – up to 2 marks	
	Specific examples appropriate to Metis – up to 2 marks per example; up to 10 marks	10
	Total =	50

REPORT

To: J. Sum
From: Accountant
Date: [Today's date]
Subject: Performance management at Metis

This report assesses the existing performance reporting pack and suggests improvements which could be made to it. It also evaluates different methods of measuring performance, and assesses the extent to which the choice of what gets measured could have an impact on the business's performance.

(a) **Current performance report**

The existing report does provide some useful performance information; however, there are also a number of areas where it could be improved.

Profit information

Highlights profit – The existing report shows clearly how profitable the business is, both in terms of gross profit and net profit. Showing the net profit margin (%) is also useful because, for example, it shows that not only has Metis been able to increase its revenue over the last three years, but also it has been able to control its costs sufficiently well so that the **net margin** (%) has increased.

Absolute figures only – However, although the figures show that revenues and profits have increased over the three years under review, the figures would be more useful if they showed the percentage increases each year, rather than just showing each year's figures.

Product information

Revenue streams – It is also useful that the report shows revenues and costs for different product categories, because this could help identify if the revenues or costs for certain products are increasing more than for other products.

Again, however, this information could be more useful if it showed the percentage increases each year.

Margins by product – Equally, although the report shows revenues and cost of sales for different product categories, it doesn't show the gross profit or gross profit percentage for each product category. However, such information would be useful for decision making. For example, in 20X2, the gross margin Metis earned on food was 68% ($657k/$974k) and the margin on beer was 62% ($115k/$186k) but on wine it was only 54% ($109k/$201k).

Performance comparison

Comparative figures – The report clearly shows how revenues and costs have changed over the last three years, and it also provides a **forecast** for the next year. This could be useful to assess how well Metis's actual performance compares to the forecast.

Budget controls – However, for any year of reported figures, the report only shows the actual results; it doesn't show any budget or forecast figures as a comparison. It would be useful if these were included, in order to gauge whether Metis is performing better or worse than had been anticipated, and therefore whether any corrective action is required to bring actual performance back in line with forecast.

Quantity of information – While it would be useful to have some additional information (percentage changes; performance against budget) it is important to avoid showing too much information in the report.

Given that the report is a quarterly summary, there is a danger that it already contains too much detailed information in the report; for example, instead of showing the detail of all the operating costs, this could be shown as a single line for 'Operating costs'. If this total line showed any unusual results, these could then be investigated separately by drilling down into the total.

Value of historical information – Equally, it is debatable how much value is added by showing three years' worth of historical information. It could be useful to show the current year and the prior year, but any more than this seems to be superfluous. As Metis was only started three years ago, there is likely to be little value in comparing performance in 20X2 with 20X0 as the business will have developed and become much more established over the intervening period. Equally, market conditions could have changed over this period.

Seasonality – The comparison between the latest quarter and the previous quarter also appears to have little value. There is a fall in revenue of 42% between Q4 and Q3, which suggests Metis's business is seasonal. Therefore, it might be more useful to compare performance in the current quarter with the equivalent quarter in the previous year.

Presentation – The overall presentation of the report could also be improved. It might not be clear to a non-accountant what the most important figures are, so the key figures (eg gross profit, net margin) could usefully be highlighted in bold. Similarly, the report might look less crowded if the figures were shown in thousands of dollars rather than to the last dollar.

Other areas for improvement

Cash flows – The focus of the current report appears to be exclusively on how much profit Metis is generating. Although the business's stated aim is to 'make money', this does not mean that profit is the only aspect of financial performance which should be monitored. For example, it would be useful for the report to include some measures relating to Metis's cash flow and liquidity.

Performance objectives – More generally, it might also be useful to define some more specific objectives of the business. These might then highlight which aspects of the business are most important to its success, and which should therefore be monitored in the performance report.

Functional areas – The report does not currently provide any information about how the different functional areas of the business are performing. For example, there are no measures which indicate how well the **service staff** are performing. Again, this issue could be addressed by identifying key objectives and establishing KPIs which will support those objectives. For example, Metis could use a customer survey to find out how satisfied its customers are with the service they have received, and average scores from these surveys could be used as an indicator of the quality of service being offered.

Similarly, there don't currently appear to be any indicators which relate to the performance of the **kitchen operations**. For example, it might be useful to monitor how long it takes for meals to be delivered from the kitchen, or how much food is wasted (for example, if the chef is not happy that a plate of food is up to standard and so it has to be thrown away).

Both of these points also highlight that the current report only looks at financial performance. However, the owners should also be monitoring how well Metis is performing in relation to its **non-financial performance indicators**. These are likely to be crucial in attracting and retaining customers, and hence to the longer-term success of the business.

It is likely that **procurement** is another important functional area, because Metis will need sufficient food to satisfy customer demand, but it will need to avoid over-ordering perishable items. Equally, it will be important that Metis buys food and drink of high enough quality to satisfy its customers, yet secures it for the best price possible. The gross margins obtained for different product categories could be used as an indicator for this area, which again highlights the need for gross margin percentages to be provided rather than just an absolute figure.

External information – The existing report only looks at internal aspects of performance. For example, it does not give any indication of how Metis's margins or product mix compare against those of other similar restaurants. Such comparisons or benchmarking could be useful, although it may be difficult to obtain the necessary data. There may be a local restaurant association, or similar trade association, which Metis could join, which has a database of such information.

(b) **Summary of results for 20X2** (see Appendix for details)

Net profit after tax	$163,045
ROCE	43.7%
Return on equity	65.2%
NPV (20X0–20X2)	$(55,475)
MIRR (20X0–20X2)	6.75%
EVA™ (20X2)	$108,625

Profit and EVA™ – The results show that Metis is generating a healthy post-tax profit for the owners (equivalent to approximately $55k each), and it is generating a positive EVA™ which also suggests that the business is adding value for the owners (shareholders).

NPV – At first sight, the negative NPV figure does not look good, but it is important to remember the business has only been running for three years, and there was a significant initial investment to establish it ($600,000). Although it is not clear what period the owners wanted to appraise their initial investment over, it is likely that it will longer be than three years; for example, the bank loan was taken out for ten years. Moreover, Metis's cash flows suggest that the NPV will be positive by the end of the next year, which presents the initial investment in a more favourable light.

MIRR – Similarly, although the fact that the MIRR is less than the overall cost of capital (12.5%) might normally be a concern, this again is due to the time frame under review. As with NPV, the MIRR figure should increase in subsequent years as the business generates additional cash inflows.

Longer-term performance – In this respect, NPV and MIRR could both be useful in appraising the business's performance over the longer term, but they are less useful in judging the current state of the business.

This issue of longer-term performance and short-term results may also need to be highlighted next year. Profits for the year are forecast to decline as a result of the building upgrade, but the upgrade is necessary to maintain the business. In this context, EVA™ will be an important performance measure because it adds back 'value adding' expenditure, and so may help encourage a long-term (rather than short-term) focus. For example, the net profit margin for 20X3 is forecast to decline to 8.6%. However, the main reason for this is the $150,000 scheduled for building upgrades in 20X3. If this were excluded, the net margin for 20X3 would be 17.5%.

(c) **What gets measured, gets done**

Making money – The logic behind the quote is that staff and managers will pay more attention to those areas for which they know performance is being measured, compared to those areas which are not being measured. For example, Sheila's recent drive to save electricity seems to have been successful; utility costs only rose 0.5% between 20X1 and 20X2, compared to 3% the previous year. Controlling costs in this way will also help Metis 'make money' which is ultimately its aim.

Lack of non-financial measures – By implication, the quote also suggests that there is a danger that what doesn't get measured might not get done. There appears to be a danger at Metis that non-financial aspects of performance are not receiving as much attention as they could.

While Sheila appears to have been successful in her electricity cost-saving campaign, she has not been successful in getting her waiting staff to smile at customers. Perhaps this is not surprising, though. The staff are not currently assessed on how well they interact with customers, and there do not appear to be any customer-driven performance measures (such as customer satisfaction ratings). Therefore, the staff may feel there are no incentives for them to smile at customers.

Equally, it appears that Bert thinks that food could be collected from the kitchen more quickly, and also that the amount of food wasted could be reduced. Again, however, these aspects of performance do not currently appear to be measured, which may explain why performance in them is not as good as it could be.

Lack of management information – More generally, the quote also highlights that it could be difficult for the managers to improve Metis's performance if they do not have adequate information about its current performance. Although Bert 'feels' that too much food is becoming rotten and having to be thrown out, he does not seem to have any information about actual wastage levels to support his feeling. Consequently, he is making the kitchen staff go through lengthy inventory checks, when they could potentially be carrying out more value-adding activities.

Information for decision making – Nonetheless, Bert's checks on inventory could be useful if they help highlight the reason for the wastage. There could be several different reasons why food is becoming rotten: the quantities ordered are too high, creating surpluses of perishable products; Metis could be buying poorer quality goods to save costs; or the temperature and storage facilities in the kitchen, or the way produce is handled, may not be satisfactory.

It is important that Metis highlights the reason for the wastage, because the first two potential reasons are procurement issues, while the third falls under Bert's area of responsibility. Equally, this suggests that rather than simply looking at gross margin, the performance report needs to identify some separate critical success factors for both procurement and the kitchen operations.

Choice of measurements – However, the quote could also highlight that there is a danger that too much focus could be placed on the aspects of performance which are measured. For example, the current performance report seems to place too much emphasis on financial results, rather than encouraging analysis of the underlying operations and activities in the business. Moreover, because the report shows quarterly revenue figures, this might lead to a focus on quarterly growth. However, the seasonal nature of the business means there is little value in such a comparison. In fact it could be counter-productive; a decline in quarterly revenue may prompt managers to try to introduce new strategies to reverse the perceived decline, when such a change is not required. In this respect, a more useful measurement would be to compare revenue against the equivalent quarter in the previous year.

Conflicts between owners – John is rightly worried about the air of tension which now exists in the owners' meetings. Therefore, it is important that the owners choose carefully what aspects of performance to measure. If, for example, there is an increased focus on food wastage but not on customer service this could increase the tension between Bert and Sheila, because it could give the impression that kitchen operations are more important than the public areas. Consequently, the quote could serve as a reminder that Metis needs a balanced set of measures from across all three elements of the business, because ultimately they are all important to its continuing success.

BPP LEARNING MEDIA

Appendix:

Calculation of financial performance measures

		20X0	20X1	20X2	
		$	$	$	
Profit					
PBIT		31,200	199,579	262,322	
Interest ($350,000 @ 8.4%)		29,400	29,400	29,400	
PBT		1,800	170,179	232,922	
Tax (@ 30%)		540	51,054	69,877	
Profit after tax		**1,260**	**119,125**	**163,045**	
Cash flows and NPV					
PBIT		31,200	199,579	262,322	
Tax on operating cash flows (@ 30%)		9,360	59,874	78,697	
Depreciation (added back)		120,000	120,000	120,000	
Free cash flows		141,840	259,705	303,625	
NPV					
Initial investment	–600,000				–600,000
Present value of cash flows		126,080	205,199	213,246	544,525
(Discount factor 12.5%)					
NPV					**–55,475**
MIRR					
Initial outflow	–600,000				**–600,000**
Returns					
Cash flows		141,840	259,705	303,625	
Factor (Deposit account rate 4.5%)		$(1.045)^2$	1.045	1	
		154,893	271,392	303,625	**729,910**
MIRR =	$(-729{,}910/-600{,}000)^{1/(4-1)} - 1$				0.0675
MIRR					**6.75%**

Tutorial note. There were only three marks available for MIRR calculation. The method demonstrated in the suggested solution shows the impact of the reinvestment rate being lower than the cost of capital. However, you could still have scored well here if you had used the standard approach for calculating MIRR, as follows:

MIRR					
Initial outflow	–600,000				**–600,000**
Returns					
Cash flows		141,840	259,705	303,625	
Factor (Discount factor 12.5%)		1.125	$(1.125)^2$	$(1.125)^3$	
		126,080	205,199	213,245	**544,525**
MIRR =	$(-544{,}525/-600{,}000)^{1/3} \times (1.125) - 1$				**8.92%**

		20X2
		$
EVA™		
NOPAT		
Operating profit (PBIT)		262,322
Tax on operating profit		78,697
NOPAT		183,625
Capital employed	600,000	
WACC	12.5%	
		75,000
EVA™		**108,625**
ROCE		
PBIT	262,333	
Capital employed	600,000	
		43.72%
Return on equity		
PAT	163,045	
Equity invested	250,000	
		65.22%

Notes and assumptions re EVA™ and NOPAT:

Economic depreciation has been assumed to be the same as accounting depreciation so no adjustment is required.

Since marketing spending is for short-term promotional offers only it has not been treated as capital and added back to profit in the EVA™ calculation. As it relates to short-term promotions only, it seems more prudent to retain marketing spending as a cost to the period.

(d) **Strategic and operational issues**

The contrast between short-term and long-term performance could be seen as an illustration of the contrast between strategic and operational level performance in an organisation. For example, the focus for the kitchen staff or waiting staff is most likely to be on short-term operational issues which affect the number and quality of the meals they can prepare and serve to customers, and therefore their ability to meet short-term customer demands.

Strategic issues – However, alongside this, the owners should also be considering the more strategic issues which the business is facing. The owners have identified their aim as being to 'make money' but given that competition in the restaurant business in Urbanton is fierce, it would seem sensible for them to have an overall strategy for Metis; for example, to define how Metis might be able to distinguish itself from the competitors in the long term.

At the moment, Metis does not have any particular culinary style (serving popular dishes regardless of style), and it prices its dishes in the middle of the range. So the owners might decide that the quality of service or the ambience within its restaurants is what will distinguish Metis from its competitors. However, this strategic decision will then have an impact on operational decisions because, for example, if customer service becomes a key success factor for the business, it will be vital that the waiting staff provide Metis's customers with excellent service on a day to day basis.

Performance hierarchy – In this way, Metis could establish a performance hierarchy throughout the organisation. For example, if part of its overall mission is to provide excellent customer service, then the individual staff can also be set personal targets and goals which focus on the levels of customer service they provide, including – for example – smiling at customers.

Targets – One of the challenges which Metis will face is linking its strategy to its day to day operations. For example, if the owners decide to refine their aim to simply 'make money' into a more specific target to grow the business by a certain percentage each year, or to open a number of new restaurants over a given period of time, they will need to consider what practical steps need to be taken to generate this growth. Equally, setting targets in this way will provide the owners with a means of measuring how well the business is performing (for example, in relation to the level of profit it is generating, or in relation to the number of customers eating in the restaurant as a percentage of capacity).

Trade-offs between long term and short term

Tension – The tension between Bert and Sheila also highlights the tension and conflict which businesses can face between long- and short-term priorities. Bert's opposition to the proposed building upgrade seems to be driven by a desire to reduce expenditure, or to maximise Metis's profits in the short term.

Short-term cost saving – Metis's net margin is forecast to fall to 8.6% in 20X3. However, if the $150,000 forecast for building upgrades was not spent, the forecast net margin for 20X3 would be 17.5%. This appears to be the logic of Bert's argument against doing the building upgrade work.

Longer-term consequences – However, as Sheila has pointed out, this appears to only look at the short-term rather than the potential longer-term consequences of not doing the upgrade work. The restaurant needs to be refurbished in order to maintain its atmosphere.

Consequently there is a risk that if Metis does not refurbish the restaurant the customer may choose to eat at one of its competitors instead, with a better atmosphere. This issue could be particularly important if the atmosphere and ambience of the restaurant is one of the key factors which Metis currently uses to differentiate itself from its competitors.

In this respect, Bert's suggestion to try to reduce expenditure in the short term could end up being counter-productive in the longer term, as revenues and profits will fall if customers stop eating at Metis. In turn, this would also jeopardise the idea of expanding Metis into a restaurant chain, because this expansion is dependent on the first restaurant being successful.

Choice of performance measures

This relationship between short-term and longer-term objectives also has significant implications for the way Metis should **measure performance** and the performance measures it uses.

What gets measured, gets done – In this respect, the idea that 'What gets measured, gets done' is again important. For example, if return on capital employed (ROCE) is selected as one of Metis's key financial performance measures, the owners are likely to want to maximise its ROCE.

However, one of the disadvantages of measures such as ROCE is that they can lead to too much focus on short-term performance. For example, ROCE can discourage capital investment, because it will increase capital employed and so potentially the ROCE figure generated in the following period, even if the operating profit figure remains unchanged.

Nonetheless, Metis must not overlook short-term aspects of performance. For example, it is important that it continues to have sufficient liquidity to meet its short-term liabilities and obligations as they fall due. However, its forecast performance suggests there shouldn't be any problem in this respect.

52 Flack

Text reference. Performance reports are discussed in Chapter 6b of the BPP Study Text, as are management information systems. Performance measures (including ROCE, RI) are discussed in Chapter 7, while expected values are discussed in Chapter 5.

Top tips.

Part (i). There are two key points to note in this requirement:

- First, you need to evaluate the performance report, not Flack's underlying performance.
- Second, the reference to the board's request means that part of the requirement is embedded in the question scenario itself.

The second paragraph of the scenario identifies that the board wants to know whether the performance report 'is fit for the purpose of achieving the company's mission' (which, in turn, is also quoted in the scenario).

A key part of this requirement is identifying what information the performance report provides the board about the issues identified in the mission (eg earning customer loyalty; resource utilisation; serving shareholders' interests). A useful way to structure your answer could have been to use each of the issues identified in the mission as a sub-heading, and then consider what information – if any – the report provides the board in relation to that issue.

However, as well as evaluating the performance report in the context of Flack's mission, the fourth paragraph of the scenario tells you that the board also wants you to comment on whether the performance report is 'short-termist'. So to score well in part (i), you also need to address this issue: do the aspects of performance being included in the performance report encourage a short-term focus?

Part (ii). As in part (i), the requirement for part (ii) also relates back to an instruction given in the scenario – in this case, in the fifth paragraph. The CEO wants an evaluation of how the two new measures (revenue per square metre; operating profit per square metre) could help Flack assess the aspect of its mission: 'utilising all our resources'.

However, make sure you look at the CEO's request very carefully, because it contains a number of elements:

- Explain how the new measures relate to the aspect of the mission
- What the ratios are (ie **calculate** the ratios themselves, using the figures from Appendix 1)
- Explain how the ratios could be used to manage business performance

To score well here, you need to address all three of the elements. However, note that there are only eight marks available in total for this part of the question, so you only need to cover each element quite briefly.

Part (iii). The board currently uses divisional operating profit as the measure for assessing divisional performance, but is considering replacing this with residual income. You are asked to assess this proposed change.

It is important to recognise the context of this proposed change. Flack has been criticised for its stores looking 'run down' and store managers have been reluctant to invest in refurbishing existing stores, preferring instead to use capital to open new stores. A key issue here is whether the change in performance measures will change managers' behaviour in this respect.

A useful approach to answering requirements like this which require a comparison between current and proposed measures is to identify what the potential problems are with the existing measure and then consider whether the proposed new measure will help to address them.

Importantly, note that the requirement specifically tells you that 'No calculations of the current values are required'. In other words, you need to focus on the measures themselves, not on the performance of the divisions.

Part (iv). There are two elements to this requirement: one a calculation (of the expected ROCE for the new store using the data in Appendix 2); the second an assessment of whether using ROCE based on expected values is an appropriate metric for evaluating new stores.

Once again, the information in the scenario – specifically, the final sentence of the seventh paragraph – provides very clear instructions for the focus of your answer. 'The focus of comments should be on the use of an **expected value**, not on the use of ROCE, as this is widely used and understood in the retail industry.'

Similarly, it was crucial to use expected value operating profit as the basis of the ROCE calculation (ie expected value operating profit/capital cost) not operating profit from any of the individual demand scenarios.

Part (v). The 'proposed new information system' being referred to is a customer loyalty card scheme, supported by a data warehouse – as described in the final paragraph of the scenario. The paragraph also describes three areas where the CEO thinks the scheme can help Flack become more efficient: target advertising, product range choices and price offers. These should provide some useful clues about how the scheme – which is essentially a marketing information system – could help improve Flack's performance.

More generally, it could also be useful to think back to Flack's overall mission, one of whose key elements is 'earning customer loyalty'. By definition, a customer loyalty card scheme should help to achieve that aim.

Overall. Remember that you have been asked to write a report, so make sure the style and structure of your answer, as a whole, is appropriate for a report. For example, a report should have a short introduction explaining the key issues to be discussed in it, and should have headings for each section or part.

Examining team's comments. Part (i) was generally well done. Candidates performed well when they used the signposts given in the scenario to identify specific issues to look for in Flack's performance report.

Part (ii) again required candidates to address specific requirements identified in the scenario. However, this part of the question was not answered well, with many candidates failing to identify how the new measures fit with the specific strategy point they were intended to address. In addition, candidates often didn't pick up the simple calculation marks on offer by failing to recognise that they were working in $'000.

Part (iii) was answered reasonably well, with candidates structuring their comments into criticism of the existing performance measure and then analysis of how the proposed new measure would address the issues with the existing measure. Unfortunately, a number of candidates decided to focus their answer on a different, new performance indicator of their own choice, which cost them a number of marks.

Part (iv) was often well done, with many candidates scoring all the marks for the calculations. However, the commentary on the method often lacked an appreciation of the circumstances in which 'expected values' are appropriate. Also, many candidates ignored the advice to focus their answer on the concept of an 'expected' value for the indicator, rather than offering a general discussion of the indicator itself.

Part (v) was also generally well done, with most candidates showing an understanding of the information that a loyalty card system could provide and how that information could be used to improve the company's performance.

Report format. As we have seen in previous sittings, those candidates who had practised writing professional answers prior to the exam performed admirably in the presentation area (four marks). The markers were looking for:

- Suitable report headings;
- An introduction;
- A logical structure (signposted by good use of sub-headings); and
- A clear, concise style.

Report

To: Board of Flack
From: A. Accountant
Date: [today's date]
Subject: Performance reporting and management issues at Flack

Introduction

This report evaluates the current performance report for Flack and the introduction of two new performance measures. Then, the effect of a proposed change in the divisional performance measure is assessed. Next, the use of expected ROCE for new store proposals is evaluated. Finally, the report explains how the proposed new information system can help to improve business performance at Flack.

(i) **Performance reporting at Flack**

The current report has a number of strengths and weaknesses. These will be discussed according to whether the report:

- Addresses the mission;
- Contains appropriate information for decision making;
- Shows signs of being short term; and
- Is well presented.

The current mission can be broken down into two parts:

- To be the first choice for customers; and
- To provide the right balance of quality, service and price.

There are three strategies for achieving this mission, reflecting stakeholder concerns:

- Earning customer loyalty;
- Utilising all resources; and
- Serving shareholders' interests.

Addressing the mission

Customer loyalty. The report does not address the first part of the mission (earning customer loyalty). This can only be measured using external data but the report is utilising only Flack's internal data. This part of the mission relates to the first strategy to gain customer loyalty. Customer loyalty could be gauged through repeat purchases or market share information but neither is supplied. This is clearly important to a retailer and may be more easily gathered once the data from the new information system are available for inclusion in this report.

The current report provides no measures of the balance of quality, service and price other than through the historic growth in revenue. It would only be through comparison with competitors or customer survey data that a picture of the mix of these qualities could be gained.

Utilising all resources. The second strategy of utilising resources requires that the key resources be identified. Clearly, the stores themselves (and thus the capital invested) are an important resource and the introduction of the revenue and profit per square metre and comparison with competitors will indicate the efficiency of their use. However, there are likely to be other important resources such as staff and no measure of their performance is offered. Staff costs are not shown in the trading account, although a more sophisticated measure such as revenue per employee is a commonly used metric and would address this.

Serving shareholders' interests. The report is much better on the third strategy of serving shareholder interests as it supplies two helpful measures: total shareholder return and return on capital employed. However, most shareholders will want comparison with benchmark returns within the retail sector and the market more widely, since these represent their alternatives.

Short-termism. The criticism of the company's management as being short term is reflected in the performance reporting. The only benchmarks in the report to compare actual performance against are the budget information and the previous year's figures. There are no longer-term forecasts or information on future capital investment. Also, there are few indicators which would be described as determinants of

BPP LEARNING MEDIA

performance. These are often non-financial and focused on the external business environment (behaviour of customers and competitors).

As already noted, there is a significant gap in the information in the report as it contains no external information. Also, although revenue is broken down into broad product categories, no further information about growth within these categories nor the margins being earned is supplied. As a result, it could be questioned whether this breakdown is worthwhile.

Presentation. In terms of presentation, the data is clear and in a form which would be easily recognisable to those used to reading accounts. However, no narrative commentary is provided which would highlight the key features in the report such as major deviations from the budget or performance well outside industry norms. There should be a comment on each of the five areas within the mission and strategies as well as comments about specific, material issues arising in the period covered. The report could be made easier to read by reducing the volume of numbers present both by cutting out unnecessary measures (see earlier discussion of product categories) and also by rounding all figures to millions.

(ii) **New asset utilisation indicators**

Revenue and operating profit per square metre reflect the utilisation of the key capital asset used in their generation (the store). Therefore, they are directly addressing a major part of the aim of utilising all resources; however, they do not address **all** resources which the business uses. There are likely to be significant staff costs and so similar measures of revenue and operating profit per employee could also be introduced in order to reflect these human resources.

	Metro	*Hyper*	*Flack*
Revenue per sq. metre ($)	13,702	13,165	13,251
Operating profit ($'000)	159,058	498,791	657,849
Operating profit per sq. metre ($)	987	592	656

These measures reflect the importance of the use of the store's space which is an area which the business does not give sufficient attention as is reflected in the problems with divisional performance measures. Focus on these measures will require addressing issues of volume of sales and the profitability of those sales. The two types of store at Flack will have different impacts on these measures. For example, the smaller Metro stores may be capable of earning higher margins as they are convenient to customers while selling lower volumes. The Hyper stores may concentrate on selling in volume to customers who come to buy in bulk. However, in terms of the overall performance of the business it is essential that Flack sells in high volumes as it is a low margin business but it must not sacrifice profitability, in effect buying customers' revenue by selling at or near a loss.

(iii) **Divisional performance assessment**

The current measure of divisional operating profit reflects the trading in the period under consideration. Profit will link to the whole business's operating profit which is the correct level to reflect the efforts of the divisional managers. However, this measure only indirectly addresses the capital being used by the divisions (depreciation charged to operating profit). This is distorting the behaviour of the divisional managers.

The managers are not investing in refurbishing their stores which is causing the press (and presumably customers) to notice their run-down appearance. This may reduce the depreciation charge against operating profit. They are prioritising new store capital expenditure over the refurbishment since they are not being charged for the use of that capital (financing charges are deducted after operating profit is calculated). This may not be optimal since small spending on existing capital assets often yields higher returns than new spending (which may be subject to greater risks).

The proposal to change the divisional performance measure addresses the issue of not reflecting the capital used since residual income (RI) deducts an imputed interest charge. Divisions can then be set targets in terms of their RI. The difficulties in calculating RI lie in correctly setting the imputed interest rate and calculating the capital being employed by the division. However, since both divisions are types of stores they will have similar assets and so the same rules can be applied to each to fairly calculate the capital used.

An advantage of RI is that the imputed interest rate can be changed to reflect the different risks of the divisions. The two divisions here do not seem to have significant risk differences unless the geographical locations introduce these (city centres and city edges). However, it is worth noting that using RI can discourage investment. As net book values of assets fall over time, RI automatically increases and 'do not invest' could become an attractive option to the managers.

Overall, the proposed change addresses existing problems and would be considered a normal solution to measuring divisional performance in this industry.

(iv) **Use of expected ROCE in new store appraisal**

The expected ROCE, based on the different demand scenarios, is as follows:

	Low	*Medium*	*High*	
Revenue ($m)	12.5	13.0	13.5	
Forecast operating margin (%)	4.1	4.3	4.4	
Forecasting operating profit ($m)	0.5125	0.559	0.594	
Probability (%)	20	50	30	
Expected operating profit ($m)	0.1025	0.2795	0.1782	**0.5602**

ROCE = Expected operating profit/Capital cost
= $0.5602m/$4.2m = **13.34%**

The expected ROCE is greater than 13% which is Flack's required ROCE, so this should be an acceptable investment.

The use of expected values in the calculation of ROCE is appropriate if the probabilities used can be reasonably estimated and the decision is likely to be one which is made a number of times. Since Flack has opened many stores, it is likely to be able to predict volumes and margins with reasonable accuracy. Since Flack is going to continue to open stores, this decision will occur a number of times which makes using a probabilistic approach viable. In general, ROCE is considered neither as accurate nor as direct a measure of shareholder wealth as, for example, net present value (NPV).

(v) **Loyalty card system**

The proposed new information system will collect data from customers' purchases and store it for data mining purposes in a data warehouse. The capital required will be significant at $100m (the equivalent of about 24 new stores at $4.2m each). There will also be considerable annual running costs. However, the benefits could be significant, although quantifying them will be difficult as they depend on influencing customer behaviour and so are not simply cutting costs.

Improved customer loyalty. The new system will help to address the mission of Flack as it will help the board to understand customers better and so improve their loyalty to the business. By focusing offers on those things which customers enjoy Flack can enhance the brand and also take the opportunity to sell greater volumes alongside the offered products.

The data warehouse will allow data mining for relationships, for example, geographical preferences for products; links between price offers and volumes sold; products which are often bought together; and seasonality of product purchases. These relationships can then be used to address the CEO's three target areas of advertising, product range choices and price offers.

Advertising. Potentially, there will be cost savings by more efficient advertising. The data on each individual customer can be searched to profile customers and identify their individual preferences. Marketing can then be targeted to groups of customers using products which they commonly buy. Data mining will also identify associated products (those often bought together) so that offers can be grouped, for example, with a price reduction on buying a linked pair of products.

Product range. A problem in most retail businesses is the size of the product portfolio which they offer since more products (and potentially more suppliers) require more effort to manage. The new system may allow a Pareto-style analysis where the least profitable non-essential products are identified and can be cut from the product range.

53 Kolmog Hotels

Text reference. The characteristics of service industries are highlighted in Chapter 4a of the BPP Study Text. The BSC and Fitzgerald and Moon's building block model are both discussed in Chapter 12.

Top tips.

Part (i). Although the requirement here asks you to 'explain' the characteristics, there are only five marks available for this part of the question. So you should keep your explanations relatively brief. There are five key characteristics which differentiate service businesses from manufacturing ones (and five marks available), meaning that there is only one mark available per characteristic. However, don't forget that you need to illustrate how the characteristics relate to Kolmog Hotels. Don't just talk about the characteristics of service businesses in generic terms.

Part (ii) asks you to evaluate Kolmog's current strategic performance report. The word 'report' is crucial here. It is vital that you evaluate the **report** and the choice of metrics used in the report, rather than evaluating Kolmog's strategic **performance**.

The key issue to evaluate here is how well the performance report allows Kolmog to assess its performance against its mission. For example, does the report (or the metrics selected in it) help assess Kolmog's performance in relation to it becoming 'the No. 1 hotel chain in Ostland'?

Also think about the 'segmentation' of the report. For example, how useful is it to know how each of the four regions has performed, as opposed to how each type of hotel has performed?

Part (iii). One of the key problems with Kolmog's current performance report (which, hopefully, you identified during your evaluation in part (ii)) is that the report only includes financial metrics, rather than a range of metrics which can be used to measure performance in relation to the different elements of Kolmog's mission.

By contrast, the different perspectives included in the proposed BSC look at key aspects of non-financial performance as well as financial performance. This should be beneficial for Kolmog.

However, while the idea of introducing a BSC may be a good one, note that the question asks you to 'suggest suitable improvements' to the scorecard. So, are there any ways which the proposed metrics could be improved so that the aspects of performance being measured support the mission and objectives more effectively?

Part (iv). The requirement to part (iii) should immediately have highlighted that some of the measures originally proposed for the outline scorecard could be improved. In turn, this should have highlighted one of the main difficulties of implementing the scorecard: choosing what measures to actually include in it.

As Kolmog has not used the scorecard before, selecting appropriate measures and then educating the managers in how to interpret the reported results are likely to be significant challenges in relation to implementing the scorecard.

Part (v). The scenario highlights that 75% of Kolmog's staff have received no bonuses in previous years, and there have been many complaints that the targets are too challenging.

This suggests that the staff don't regard the bonus targets as achievable, and consequently the staff are not motivated to try to achieve them.

Achievability is one of the three key 'standards' identified in the building block model (along with ownership and fairness). Similarly, motivation is one of the three key aspects of 'rewards' identified in the model (along with clarity and controllability).

The key issue in this part of the question is whether the new performance reward system fits with these standards and rewards any better than the old system appeared to. For example, will hotel managers feel they 'own' their performance targets if the budgets are imposed by head office?

Overall. Once again, remember that you have been asked to write a report, so make sure the style and structure of your answer, as a whole, is appropriate for a report. For example, a report should have a short introduction explaining the key issues to be discussed in it.

Examining team's comments. It was pleasing to note in part (ii) that there were fewer examples of candidates evaluating the performance of the company and many more evaluating the performance **report**, which was what was required by the question.

Most candidates handled part (iii) relatively well, but they could have scored more efficiently if they attended to the mission of the company, and how the scorecard would help the company achieve its mission.

However, part (iv) was answered very poorly, with many candidates choosing to discuss improvements required rather than the **difficulties** faced in implementing and using the BSC at Kolmog. It is vital to answer the question set!

In part (v), most candidates demonstrated good understanding of the use of 'stretch' targets and the reward system implications at Kolmog. However, there was weaker understanding of the 'standards' element from Fitzgerald and Moon's building block model.

Marking scheme

		Marks
(i)	Service industry characteristics – 1 mark per characteristic (intangibility; inseparability; variability (or heterogeneity); perishability; and no transfer of ownership) Characteristics must be illustrated in relation to the hotel industry to score the full mark available for each characteristic.	
	Total for part (i) – Up to 5 marks	5
(ii)	For comments on how well the current report enables Kolmog to measure performance against its objectives – 1 mark per point; up to 6 marks For comments on the choice of measures used in the report – 1 mark per point; up to 6 marks	
	Total for part (ii) – Up to 8 marks	8
(iii)	For comments on the outline BSC which has been proposed for Kolmog; evaluating current metrics and suggesting suitable improvements to the scorecard – 1 mark per point, up to 4 marks for each perspective of the scorecard Other relevant comments about the scorecard – 1 mark per point	
	Comments must be linked directly to the scorecard proposed for Kolmog, rather than being a generic description of the scorecard.	
	Total for part (iii) – Up to 12 marks	12
(iv)	For difficulties in implementing and using the scorecard at Kolmog – 1 mark per point	
	Again, to score the full marks available difficulties should be linked directly to implementing the scorecard at Kolmog.	
	Total for part (iv) – Up to 7 marks	7

Marks

(v) Explanation of the purpose of setting challenging targets – 1 mark per point; up to 3 marks. (To score the full 3 marks, the answer must be specifically relevant to Kolmog.)
Standards – for explaining the criteria of ownership, achievability and fairness; 1 mark per standard; up to 3 marks
Rewards – for explaining the criteria of clarity, motivation and controllability; 1 mark per reward; up to 3 marks
For comments on the new reward system which has been proposed at Kolmog – 1 mark per point; up to 7 marks

Total for part (v) – Up to 14 marks — 14

Professional marks – for report headings and introduction, clarity of report, and language used – Up to 4 marks — 4

Total = 50

Report

To: CEO Kolmog Hotels
From: Accountant
Date: June 20X3
Subject: Performance measurement and targets at Kolmog Hotels

Introduction

This report explains the key characteristics which differentiate service businesses from manufacturing ones, and then evaluates the performance reports and measures which are being used to monitor Kolmog's performance. The report then evaluates the balanced scorecard (BSC) which has been proposed for use at Kolmog, and describes the difficulties which could be associated with using the scorecard.

Finally, the report explains the purpose of setting challenging targets, and uses Fitzgerald and Moon's building block model to evaluate the standards and rewards which are applied to the managers' performance reward system at Kolmog.

(i) **Characteristics of service businesses**

There are five key characteristics of services that distinguish services from manufacturing.

(1) **Intangibility** – In contrast to manufactured goods which are tangible, physical products, services do not have any substantial material or physical aspects. When a customer books a room in one of Kolmog's hotels, they are not buying a physical product; rather they are buying their overnight accommodation in the hotel.

The fact that Kolmog isn't producing a physical product also helps to explain why its cost of sales (at around 12% of revenue) is much lower than the equivalent figure would be for a manufacturing business.

(2) **Inseparability (or simultaneity)** – Whereas manufactured goods need to be produced before they can be consumed, services are created at the same time as they are consumed. For example, a guest's experience of one of Kolmog's hotels is formed during their stay in the hotel.

(3) **Variability (or heterogeneity)** – One of the key issues which service businesses face is ensuring consistency in the standard of their service. For example, it could be difficult for Kolmog to control the level of service provided to customers by the different hotels in the group, not least because the behaviour of individual staff working in a hotel on any given day will have a significant impact on the level of service which customers receive.

(4) **Perishability** – Services are innately perishable. If a room is unoccupied (unused) for a day, then the revenue which could have been earned from the room for that day can never be recovered. This explains why room occupancy rates are often used as key performance measures by hotel companies.

(5) **No transfer of ownership** – When a customer purchases a service, this does not result in a transfer of property to the customer. For example, when a customer buys a car, they become the owner of the car. However, when a guest books a stay at a hotel, they are only buying the right to stay at the hotel for a limited period of time; they do not own the hotel.

(ii) **Current strategic performance report**

Financial information only – The strategic performance report should help the board monitor how well Kolmog is performing in the light of its stated mission.

However, despite the mission highlighting non-financial aspects of performance, the performance report currently includes only financial information. As a result, the report does not provide any indicators of how well Kolmog is performing in relation to the non-financial elements of the mission, such as **customer satisfaction, employee development** or **product innovation**.

Shareholder value – The report covers the subsidiary aim of maximising shareholder value by providing figures for earnings per share (EPS), share price performance and return on capital employed (ROCE), although total shareholder return and economic value added might be better measures than ROCE in this respect.

Importantly, however, maximising shareholder value is only a subsidiary aim, rather than a primary aim of the mission.

Key performance indicators – Hotels often have high levels of operational gearing because many of their costs (such as staff costs and property costs) are fixed. Consequently, their profit levels are likely to be sensitive to relatively small changes in revenue. As a result, hotel chains often view measures such as occupancy rates and revenue per available room as key performance indicators. Kolmog's performance report could be improved by including some key performance indicators like this – particularly indicators which are linked to revenue performance.

Market position – Perhaps the most important aspect of Kolmog's mission is the desire to 'become the No. 1 hotel chain in Ostland'. However, the report does not provide any indication as to how well the chain is performing in this respect, for example by measuring Kolmog's market share.

The absence of any external data is significant in this respect. Not only does it prevent the board from measuring overall market share, it also means it cannot benchmark Kolmog's performance in key performance areas against competitor hotels. For example, although the ratios of staff costs and hotel operating costs are useful, it would also be useful to know how these figures compare to the equivalent ratios for competitor hotels.

Segmental analysis – Although it is useful for the board to have information about how different segments of the chain are performing, breaking down the results into **geographical areas** may not be the most valuable basis of segmentation. For example, if the **mix of hotel types** varies significantly between each region, then simply comparing the performance of the four geographical regions may not be very instructive. In this respect, it may be more useful for the operating results to be broken down by hotel type (for example, conference venues, city centre business hotels, and country house hotels).

Budget figures – Although the individual hotel managers are judged by their hotel's performance against budget, the strategic performance report doesn't show any budget figures. This appears to be a significant weakness in the report. Including budget figures and variances in the report would enable the board to identify any significant deviations in actual performance compared to budget, and take corrective action where necessary.

(iii) **The BSC**

In general terms, the BSC is intended to help a company translate its mission into objectives and measures such that the measures are coherent with, and support, the overall mission. A company can also use the measures in its scorecard to inform its employees about the key drivers of success.

BPP LEARNING MEDIA

The BSC also highlights the importance of measuring both non-financial performance and financial performance. This could be particularly valuable to Kolmog, given the importance of the non-financial elements in its mission.

Although it may be easier for Kolmog to measure aspects of financial performance than non-financial performance, the long-term success of the hotel chain is likely to depend on how it performs in key non-financial areas. Nevertheless, it remains important to measure financial performance, and the financial perspective of the scorecard highlights this.

Financial perspective

The financial perspective in the outline BSC focuses on measures of strategic financial performance: **share price** and **ROCE**. This fits with the overall objective of maximising shareholder value, although it would be useful to measure **dividend per share** as well as share price in order to reflect **total shareholder return**.

Operational gearing – Although ROCE is often used as a measure of overall performance, the change in Kolmog's business model may make it less suitable as a measure for the company. Once Kolmog has sold and rented back many of its hotels, the business will have a much lower capital base. However, its fixed costs (notably rental costs) will be much higher. Therefore, it may be more appropriate to include a measure such as **operational gearing** in the scorecard.

Revenue growth – It would also seem appropriate to include **revenue growth** as a measure, given Kolmog's stated intention to 'become the No. 1 hotel chain in Ostland'.

Customer perspective

Customer satisfaction survey scores – This measure seems to be appropriate because it is aligned to the mission and the aim of 'consistently delighting customers'.

Brand loyalty – However, measuring customer satisfaction alone does not provide any indication as to whether loyalty to Kolmog's brand is strengthening. In this respect, it would also be useful to measure the number (or proportion) of customers who are repeat customers, as opposed to customers who are staying in a Kolmog hotel for the first time.

Alternatively, it could be useful to measure the value of the revenues (or the proportion of the revenues) which are generated by returning customers, as distinct from customers who are staying in a Kolmog hotel for the first time.

It is not clear from the scenario whether Kolmog has any kind of loyalty card programme. If it does, then a measure based around the number (or value) of bookings from loyalty card customers could also be a useful measure in relation to brand loyalty.

Internal business perspective

Variance analysis – In the outline scorecard, variance analysis (comparing actual performance to budget) for each hotel has been proposed as a measure to support the internal business perspective.

Occupancy rates – In this respect, it will be important for the budgets to include non-financial performance indicators as well as financial ones. As we have already noted, room occupancy rates are a key factor in shaping a hotel's performance, and so should be monitored here alongside financial variances.

However, as we noted in relation to segmental analysis, it is also important to recognise that different business processes or elements of performance may be important in different types of hotel hotels. For example, city centre business hotels may be able to maintain reasonably consistent occupancy rates throughout the year, whereas occupancy rates in the country house hotels are likely to exhibit greater seasonality. Likewise, operating margins in the country house hotels may vary more during the year, because they will still be incurring fixed costs even in months when occupancy rates are low.

Therefore, it may be necessary to adapt the key scorecard measures being used for different types of hotel.

Internal benchmarking – Nonetheless, the performance of individual Kolmog hotels can be compared against others of the same type. Internal benchmarking in this way should enable Kolmog to identify which hotels are performing best, and in turn whether there are any 'best practices' which can be shared between those hotels and others which are not performing so well.

In this way, knowledge sharing between different hotels may help Kolmog to 'continuously improve performance', which is one of the aims of its mission.

Innovation and learning perspective

The innovation and learning perspective of the scorecard should underpin this drive to continuously improve performance. Equally, the measures chosen in relation to the perspective should be ones which encourage the delivery 'of innovative products/services', which again is an aspect of Kolmog's mission.

New products/services – There are not currently any measures proposed which relate to innovation or new products. A measure which could be appropriate here is a measure of the proportion of revenue which is generated from new products or services; for example, any new packages which might be offered by the country house hotels. However, as the hotel industry in general is now a fairly mature industry the scope to deliver innovative products and services may be relatively limited.

Employee satisfaction – As a service business, Kolmog's employees play a particularly important role in delivering customer satisfaction. If the staff in a hotel are happy and motivated this is likely to lead to guests in that hotel enjoying their stay more than if staff were grumpy and unhelpful. The performance metric of staff turnover could give an indication of how satisfied staff are with their jobs. In general, the higher staff turnover rates are, the less satisfied staff are likely to be with their jobs.

Alternatively, instead of using staff turnover as a surrogate for employee satisfaction, Kolmog could perhaps also introduce staff surveys in which staff satisfaction scores could be measured more directly.

No. 1 hotel chain in Ostland – Whichever measures Kolmog finally chooses for its scorecard, it is important to remember the underlying emphasis of the stated mission is 'to become the No. 1 hotel chain in Ostland'. Therefore, wherever possible, Kolmog should seek to benchmark its performance in all of the scorecard areas against its competitors, in order to identify whether or not it is actually achieving this 'No. 1' status.

(iv) **Implementing and using the BSC**

The BSC has not been used at Kolmog before, and therefore, as with any new framework, the company could face difficulties as it is introduced for the first time.

Selecting measures – In the previous section of this report we have suggested some alternative measures to the preliminary ones proposed by senior managers at head office. This highlights the first potential difficulty in using the scorecard: selecting which measures to include.

When deciding which measures are the most appropriate to include in Kolmog's scorecard, it is important to include measures which are related to key business processes and activities which add value to the company, not simply those that are easy to measure.

It is also important to remember the scorecard's role in translating strategic measures down to the operational level. So, for example, while there might be an overall measure focusing on customer satisfaction levels, at the operational level this may need to be broken down further into customer satisfaction on the service they received at reception, or the cleanliness and comfort of their room.

The innovation and learning perspective can often be the most difficult to measure directly. However, Kolmog appears to have worked round this problem by selecting measures relating to employee satisfaction.

Equally, it is important not to include too many measures. There is a danger that if the scorecard contains too many measures the impact of them will be reduced as a result of information overload.

Conflicting measures – Some measures in the scorecard may naturally conflict. For example, Kolmog may look to improve customer satisfaction scores by recruiting extra staff in some of its hotels. However, the costs of these staff could adversely affect financial performance in those hotels (at least in the short term).

The board may find it difficult to decide what combination of measures is likely to encourage the best results for Kolmog, but when making such decisions it will be important to look at how well each possible measure helps the company achieve its overall mission.

Interpretation – Even if Kolmog selects an appropriate set of measures for its scorecard they will ultimately only prove valuable to the company if managers can interpret the results of the measures adequately, and use them to initiate appropriate actions to improve performance. If managers have difficulty analysing the figures, or interpreting what the figures are demonstrating, then it will be difficult for the managers to know what actions need to be taken in the light of the results being indicated by the scorecard.

Again, this also reinforces the importance of not including too many measures, in order to avoid information overload.

Management commitment – The scorecard is only likely to be effective if senior managers are committed to using it. If they revert to focusing solely on the financial measures they are used to, then the value of introducing additional (non-financial) measures will be reduced.

In this respect, the proposal to derive employees' targets for the performance reward system to the BSC seems sensible, because it encourages managers and staff to focus on all four perspectives of the scorecard.

(v) **Setting targets**

Challenging targets – When setting targets it is important to find a balance between ones which are too easy (and therefore don't require any effort to achieve) and ones which are too difficult (and are therefore demotivating because staff feel they are unachievable.)

In this respect, challenging – or **stretch** – targets provide a middle ground between targets which are too easy and those which are perceived to be unachievable.

This is the balance which Kolmog is trying to find with its new performance reward system.

Unachievable targets – The history of rewards at Kolmog suggests that, in the past, the targets set have been too difficult to achieve. The fact that 75% of staff have received no bonus in previous years suggests that the bonus scheme would not motivate staff because they would never expect to qualify for a bonus.

Standards

In their 'building block' model, Fitzgerald and Moon highlight that in order for performance measures to be effective, employees must view the measures as being **fair** and **achievable**, and the employees must take **ownership** of them.

Achievability – The fact that 75% of the staff have not received a bonus in previous years suggests that Kolmog's reward scheme has historically not been an effective tool for motivating employees. If the staff feel the bonus targets are unachievable, they will only put in the minimum amount of effort they need to keep their jobs, rather than making any extra effort in the hope of receiving some extra reward as a result.

If the new targets are to be more effective in this respect, it is important that they are perceived to be more realistic to achieve.

Ownership – If the performance targets are based on budgets set by the Finance Department, this may also contribute to the sense of staff not accepting the targets and trying to achieve them. In particular, hotel managers' performance should only be judged against factors they can **control**. For example, if there is a downturn in market conditions, there is likely to be a downturn in revenue which managers cannot control.

Fairness – As we noted earlier in relation to segmental analysis, there are likely to be differences in the performance of different types of hotel. The concept of fairness suggests that targets should be adjusted for different types of hotel. For example, targets for city centre hotels should be comparable to each other, but may not be comparable to country house hotels.

Rewards

Rewards are the motivators which encourage employees to work towards the standards set. In order for rewards to be effective, they need to be clear, motivating and controllable.

Clarity – The employees need to be clear about the goals they are working towards.

Motivating – Employees need to be motivated to work towards the targets and in pursuit of the organisation's strategic objectives.

Controllability – Staff should not be held responsible for aspects of performance over which they have no control.

Issues with the proposed system

Ownership – The new system will propose that managers' targets are based on their hotel's performance against budgeted profit. However, if the budgets continue to be set by the head office Finance Department with no input from the managers, then there is likely to be a lack of ownership of the targets. Therefore, hotel managers should be involved in the budget-setting process.

Fairness – Comparing staff turnover against an industry-wide standard may not be fair if managers cannot control staff wages. If wages are set centrally, and are not attractive compared to the wages offered by other hotel chains, staff turnover is likely to be high, and there will be little that managers can do to prevent this. A fairer measure would be to compare the staff turnover for individual hotels against other hotels of the same type within Kolmog.

Aligned to mission – Customer satisfaction is a controllable factor for hotel managers and therefore customer satisfaction scores should be an important element of performance assessment. However, given Kolmog's stated mission 'to become the No. 1 hotel chain' it would be better to compare customer satisfaction scores against the scores achieved by Kolmog's competitors. The current proposal (to measure managers against the internal average) will not directly help Kolmog improve its performance against its competitors.

Clarity – The hotel managers' bonuses will be determined by their regional manager's assessment of their performance against the targets. In order for the reward system to be effective, the regional managers will need to explain the structure of the new scheme (for example, if there are different levels of bonus below the full 30%), and also the factors which will influence their assessment of the hotel managers' performance.

Ultimately, the success of the new scheme will depend on the extent to which it motivates staff and managers to help Kolmog achieve its mission. To do this, the targets will need to be stretching, but also to be perceived as achievable. In this respect, Kolmog should monitor the number of staff receiving bonuses to assess whether more staff are qualifying for some kind of bonus than under the old scheme.

54 Cantor

Text references. Performance reports are discussed in Chapter 6b of the BPP Study Text. EVA™ is discussed in Chapter 7, and VBM is discussed in Chapter 12.

Top tips.

Part (i). A crucial point to note here is that the requirement asks you to evaluate Cantor's performance **report**, not evaluate Cantor's **performance**.

There is a technical article on ACCA's website titled 'Reports for performance management' and this article suggests looking at four key aspects of a report to identify whether it is a good report or not: the purpose of the report; who the report is produced for; what information is needed; and the layout of the report.

A sensible approach to this question would have been to use each of these four aspects as headings in your answer, and then to evaluate how well the report deals with each of them.

Purpose – The examining team noted that candidates seemed reluctant to use the mission/strategy of the business to evaluate the report. A key issue in evaluating the report is whether it helps the board understand how well Cantor is achieving its mission/strategy.

Audience – Has the report addressed the needs of its readers? In this case, a key point is that the report has three groups of readers (the main group board, and the boards of each of the two subsidiaries). This should have prompted you to think whether a single report can satisfy the needs of these different groups. For example, how much detail will the different groups need about different aspects of the business?

Technical article. Part (i) of this question is the subject of a two-part technical article on ACCA's website: 'Improving your [Paper P5] Answers (Parts 1 and 2)'.

[Note: Prior to 2018, APM was known as P5.]

In the article, a member of the examining team highlights some of the errors which students made when answering the requirement to evaluate an organisation's current performance report. The article then goes on to demonstrate the sorts of points which candidates would have been expected to make in order to score well in this part of the question.

You are strongly advised to read this article as part of your preparation for your APM exam.

Part (ii). The scenario has identified that the two key costs for review here are staff and property costs; and it also describes the rental arrangements of the two subsidiaries in detail.

Although this question is essentially about operating gearing, it is also important that you think about the different context of the two subsidiaries. Juicey's business appears more dynamic than Cafés', so what implications could this have for the appropriate balance of fixed and variable costs in each? Also, think about the nature of the costs involved. How can Cantor manage the balance between fixed and variable staff costs?

Part (iii). Make sure you note that the requirement here isn't simply to 'calculate' the EVA™ but to 'evaluate' it.

Equally, importantly, note that you weren't simply asked to state any assumptions you made when calculating EVA™, but to 'justify' them.

Although this question was generally well answered, with most candidates appearing to understand the adjustments to profit and capital employed that are required when calculating EVA™, the examining team highlighted three areas where candidates struggled:

- When calculating WACC, many did not seem to be able to work out the weighting coefficients from the debt/equity.
- Many did not appreciate that the cost of debt needed an adjustment for it to be post-tax.
- The capital employed figure used for working out the cost of capital employed should be based on capital employed at the start of the year, not at the end of the year.

There are two articles about EVA™ in the technical articles section of ACCA's website: 'Economic value added versus profit-based measures of performance – part 1 and part 2'. You are advised to read them as part of your exam preparation if you have not already done so.

Part (iv). There are two parts to this requirement: (i) explain how VBM could be implemented at Cantor and (ii) evaluate VBM's potential impact on the group.

One of the key elements of VBM is identifying the drivers which create value for an organisation, so that the organisation can then focus its performance management efforts on those drivers. This issue is also important in this requirement – because identifying Cantor's value drivers and performance targets linked to them will be a key part of implementing VBM at the organisation.

One follow-on question is then: how different are Cantor's performance metrics likely to be under VBM compared to its current performance measurement system? The degree of difference between them – and differences in the aspects of performance being measured – could be useful in evaluating the potential impact VBM could have.

Examining team's comments. The problem for the majority of candidates in part (iv) was a lack of knowledge, with many talking vaguely about value without an understanding of it, or of VBM, in the context of the scenario. The fact that the question had just considered EVA™ ought to have provided a memory jog, but there is little indication that it did. Some candidates also incorrectly appeared to think that VBM and activity-based management (ABM) are the same thing.

Part (v). It is important that you read the requirement very carefully here.

Firstly, note that the performance measures suggested need to relate to the proposed change in the mission statement ('to provide a fair deal to our employees') rather than to the mission statement as a whole. As such, performance measures looking at shareholder value or customer satisfaction were not relevant here.

Secondly, note that you are asked to use the information in the appendices as the source for the performance measures you recommend. So, for example, although employee satisfaction surveys might, in other circumstances, be a good way of finding out about employee satisfaction levels, they are not appropriate here, because they do not relate to the information in Appendix 3.

Finally, you need to justify why the measures you have recommended are suitable, rather than simply listing the measures.

Overall – As is the case with all of the Section A questions in APM, remember that you have been asked to write a report, so make sure the style and structure of your answer, as a whole, is appropriate for a report. Markers are looking for an introduction, suitable report headings, a logical structure, signposted by the use of sub-headings, and a clear, concise style.

The post-examination report noted that a conclusion was not required for the four professional marks available in this question but, if candidates provided an appropriate one, they were given credit for doing so.

Marking scheme

		Marks
(i)	Each relevant point about Cantor's performance report – 1 mark Points must be based on the scenario information, and must focus on Cantor's performance report, rather than on its performance. Possible relevant points include: Assessment of whether the report supports Cantor's mission Appropriateness of the level of detail provided for the three different boards Use of budgets Use of industry averages Lack of historical/trend information	
	Total for part (i) – Up to 15 marks	15
(ii)	Each relevant point about the balance between fixed and variable costs in each of the subsidiaries, and the impact this may have on managing these costs – 1 mark	
	Total for part (ii) – Up to 6 marks	6
(iii)	EVA™ calculation Add back brand-building expenditure – 1 mark Taxation and tax relief on interest – 2 marks Capital employed – marketing – 1 mark WACC – 1 mark EVA™ result – 1 mark Brief evaluation of the EVA™ result – 1 mark Assumptions made – identified and justified – Up to 3 marks	
	Total for part (iii) – Up to 9 marks	9
(iv)	For general description of VBM – up to 2 marks Description of how VBM could be implemented at Cantor, and of what its potential impact could be – 10 marks	
	Total for part (iv) – Up to 10 marks	10

BPP LEARNING MEDIA

		Marks
(v)	For calculations of suitable measures (eg average salaries; staff turnover rates) – up to 3 marks For each relevant point in justifying performance measures – 1 mark per point	
	Total for part (v) – Up to 6 marks	6
	Professional marks – for style and structure of report: introduction (1 mark); use of headings and suitable sub-headings (1 mark); clarity of report, and of language used – Up to 4 marks	4
	Total =	**50**

Report

To: CEO
From: Strategic Management Accountant
Date: [today's date]
Subject: Performance reporting and VBM at Cantor

Introduction

This report evaluates the current performance reports at Cantor, and the cost structures in the group.

It then calculates Cantor's EVA™ (as an alternative measure of performance to the profit-based measures currently used in the performance reports) before evaluating the potential impact that VBM could have at the group.

Finally, the report recommends some new performance measures to reflect the change in Cantor's mission statement.

(i) **Current performance report**

We can use four basic criteria to evaluate Cantor's current performance report:

Purpose – What the purpose of the report is, and whether it provides information which is relevant to Cantor's performance against its mission

Audience – Whether the report is appropriate for its audience and their requirements

Information – Whether the report provides information which is relevant for decision making and control

Layout – Whether the report's layout is clear for its readers, and identifies the most important information

Purpose

Performance against overall goals and objectives

One of the overall aims of Cantor's performance reports should be to enable the Board to identify how well the company is fulfilling its mission, and achieving its goals and objectives.

Cantor's mission statement identifies three key points:

- Maximising shareholder value
- Supplying good value food and drink
- Providing an appealing environment for customers

Shareholder value – The report currently only focuses on historic profits. It does not include any future cash flows, EVA™, share price or dividends – all of which could provide an indication of shareholder value.

As such, the report does not directly measure shareholder value. This point has also been highlighted by one of Cantor's large shareholders who has suggested the introduction of EVA™ as the company's main measure of value. (We will return to this point later in this report.)

One of the dangers of using annual profit as the main performance measure is that it can lead to a focus on short-term performance. However, shareholders are likely to be interested in longer-term value creation as well as short-term performance.

Nonetheless, the comparison between budget and actual performance in the report is useful – both as a means of control and for giving some insight as to whether Cantor is performing in line with strategic targets.

Good value food and drink – Comparing Cantor's gross profit against the gross profit for the industry as a whole can give some indication of whether Cantor provides good value or not.

Cantor's gross profit margin is slightly higher than the industry average (74.2% vs 72.8%) which might suggest that the prices Cantor charges its customers are slightly higher than the industry average. However, the gross profit margin by itself is not a good indicator of whether Cantor is offering good value, because it doesn't provide any insight into the reasons behind the relative margins (for example, Cantor's costs of sales might be lower than its competitors) or the quality of the food and drink it is offering might be higher, enabling it to charge higher prices.

Another limitation of the report is that it does not provide any historical comparisons, although these could potentially give some insight into how attractive Cantor is to its customers. If Cantor is consistently able to increase its revenues over time, this could be seen as an indicator that its customers feel it is providing them with good value.

Appealing environments for customers – It is difficult to measure the appeal of Cantor's cafés or juice bars from financial data alone (which is all the report provides). However, revenue growth gives some indication of customer satisfaction, because customers are unlikely to continue to use Cantor's premises if they are too unappealing.

Customer loyalty and price elasticity of demand could give a greater indication of the appeal Cantor's premises have for customers, but without surveying customers directly it will be difficult to assess the extent to which the environment has an impact on their purchasing decisions, compared, for example, to the price and quality of the food and drink provided in them.

Audience

The same performance report is used by Cantor's main group board, as well as the boards of the two subsidiaries. However, the information requirements of the subsidiary boards may be different to those of the group board.

Main board – The main board is less likely to be interested in detailed figures, and so a summary of key performance measures for each of the subsidiaries may be more useful to them than, for example, the detailed information about operating costs currently provided.

Subsidiaries' boards – The report seems to treat the subsidiaries in the same way as the group, using profit and comparison to industry average margins and budgets as the main assessment tools. However, the different nature of Cafés' and Juicey's business may make comparison to an overall industry average less meaningful.

Moreover, as the subsidiary boards are likely to be interested in more detailed performance issues than the main group board, it doesn't seem appropriate to only provide the subsidiary boards with the high-level overview which is produced for the group board.

For the subsidiaries, it would be useful to provide a more detailed breakdown of revenues and gross margins by product line, and by geographical region.

Similarly, it would be useful for the subsidiary boards to be provided with more detail about operating costs by geographical region so that they identify the profitability of different regions and, if necessary, they may then need to drill down further to look at the profitability of individual outlets if some appear to be underperforming.

It seems that the measure being used to assess subsidiary performance is operating profit, which is appropriate as it contains the elements of performance controllable by the subsidiaries' managers. However, if the performance reports are only produced annually this would not appear appropriate for the needs of the subsidiary boards. They need more frequent information, to allow them to control their operations effectively.

Appropriate information for decision making

The annual reporting period also reduces the report's usefulness as a basis of decision making for the subsidiaries' boards.

In relation to operational/tactical decision making, the report would be more useful if it provided greater detail for individual products or sites to assist the managers of the subsidiaries in their planning and control activities.

Conversely, at a strategic level, the report is likely to be more useful if it provided some external information – for example, competitor information – rather than focusing on internal financial information. Currently, the only external benchmarks provided are the industry average figures, but these may be less useful than figures for competitors which compete directly with Cantor in the same sectors of the market.

Also, for both boards, it would be useful to provide some historic information to help identify growth and trends. This is likely to be particularly important at Juicey, given the levels of growth it is currently enjoying.

Similarly, it would be useful, for both boards, if the report included some non-financial key performance indicators in relation to the three key areas of Cantor's mission: shareholder value, product value and customer satisfaction with Cantor's sites.

The current focus (on financial performance only) only provides the boards with 'lagging' information on how well Cantor has performed, rather than providing them with any 'leading' indicators – and some insight into how well it will perform in future.

Layout

In terms of presentation, the data is clear and in a form which would be easily recognisable to those used to reading accounts. However, it could be useful to provide a short narrative commentary in conjunction with the report in order to highlight the key points highlighted by the figures – such as major deviations from the budget, or areas where Cantor is performing significantly better or worse than industry norms.

The report could also be made easier to read by rounding all figures to thousands and thus removing unnecessary detail.

(ii) **Cost structures**

The costs in each of the two subsidiaries include a mixture of fixed and variable costs. In general terms, higher fixed costs will constitute a higher level of risk to Cantor than variable costs. If Cantor's revenues fall, but level of fixed costs remains unchanged, then its operating gearing will increase.

In practice, however, it may not be possible to analyse costs simply into 'fixed' and 'variable' costs. Some will be partly fixed and partly variable.

Staff costs

Staff costs are likely to be part-fixed and part-variable. As these represent a significant part of the cost base, it will be necessary to establish what element is fixed (how many staff are the minimum required to run a site?) and what element is variable (how many staff can be used as needed when the sites are busy?).

This cost area will be managed through decisions over the balance of the numbers of permanent and casual staff, with casual staff being used to manage fluctuations in business. As such, this suggests that Juicey may need to use proportionately more casual staff than Cafés.

Property costs

The nature of the property costs is also different in the two subsidiaries:

Cafés – Rent is a fixed cost for Cafés, with fixed rental charges being payable quarterly in advance.

Juicey – Rent is a variable cost, being a percentage of revenue.

This structure appears appropriate to the nature of the different businesses. Cafés is a mature business whose revenues are likely to be relatively stable and predictable – meaning that there should be little risk of it not being able to cover its rental costs each month.

By contrast, Juicey is a relatively new business, but it is also rapidly growing, and therefore agreeing negotiating variable rental costs is more appropriate for it.

However, the percentage demanded will reflect the risk which the landlord is taking on the success of Juicey and so is likely to be higher than a fixed rent, such as that negotiated by Cafés. As Juicey becomes established, it may be worth considering beginning to move to negotiating fixed rental deals for Juicey in order to cut this cost.

This last point illustrates the dilemma which many businesses face in thinking about the balance of fixed and variable costs. Variable costs are more desirable as they do not threaten the survival of the business but they are often higher than a fixed cost deal.

(iii) **Economic value added**

	$	*Notes*
Operating profit	10,852,970	
Add back: Brand building	3,819,000	50% of marketing expenditure
Less: Taxation	(2,100,000)	Tax paid in year
Lost tax relief on interest	(200,250)	Finance costs @ 25%
NOPAT	**12,371,720**	
Capital employed	53,400,000	At start of 20X4
Brand building expenditure capitalised	3,819,000	Spending in previous years
Adjusted capital employed	57,219,000	
Cost of capital employed (@ 13.2%)	**(7,552,908)**	See Working for WACC calculation
EVA™	**4,818,812**	NOPAT – Cost of capital employed

	$	*Notes*
Working		
Equity: 100/130 × 15.7%	12.1	
Debt: (30/130 × 6.5%) × (1-25%)	1.1	Adjusted for tax at 25%
WACC	13.2	

The EVA™ calculation suggests that the group's economic profits for the year (NOPAT) were significantly greater than its cost of capital – such that it was able to add $4.82 million to shareholder value over the year.

However, the EVA™ which has been calculated is only an example, and it has made several simplifying assumptions which would need to be investigated in more detail if we started to use EVA™ as one of our main performance measures.

(1) **Depreciation** – We have not made any adjustments to the depreciation charge, which assumes that economic depreciation is the same as accounting depreciation. However, this may not be the case, in which case the depreciation charge in NOPAT would need to be adjusted to reflect economic depreciation.

(2) **Marketing and brand building** – We have estimated that half of the marketing spend relates to brand building, but this figure may need to be investigated more closely.

More importantly, perhaps, although we have added back the brand-building expenditure in 20X3 to adjust the figure for capital employed at the start of 20X4, we have not made any further adjustments for previous years. However, to calculate EVA™ properly, the total amount of the brand-building expenditure in the years leading up to 20X4 should all be added back to capital employed.

BPP LEARNING MEDIA

Subsidiaries – As with the current profit measures in the performance report, if Cantor decides to use EVA™, it may be useful to calculate EVA™ separately for the two subsidiaries as well as for the group. This will help to identify how much value each subsidiary is generating for the shareholders.

(iv) **VBM**

The premise behind VBM is that the value of a company is measured by its discounted cash flows, and value is only created when the capital which companies invest generates returns which are greater than the cost of that capital.

Therefore, in contrast to Cantor's current approach to performance measurement which focuses on profits, VBM will encourage a focus on future cash flows, and the creation of value.

Importantly, given Cantor's mission, management decision making under VBM focuses on what activities ('drivers') increase the value of a company – and create value for its shareholders.

The VBM approach also aligns strategic, operational and management processes so that they all work together to create value.

Understanding value drivers

Implementing VBM at Cantor will require that management understand the key value drivers which create value for the business.

Equally, VBM will also require management to establish processes which ensure that all business unit managers adopt value-based thinking when making decisions. For VBM to be effective, it will eventually have to involve every decision maker in the company.

Management processes and implementing VBM

There are four underlying management processes which govern the adoption of VBM (be it at group level, subsidiary level or operational level):

Step 1 – A strategy is developed to maximise value

Step 2 – Key value drivers are identified in relation to the strategy, and then performance targets (both short and long term) are defined for those value drivers

Step 3 – Action plans are drawn up to define the steps to be taken to achieve the performance targets

Step 4 – Performance measurement systems and incentive systems are set up to monitor performance against targets and to encourage employees to meet their goals

Strategy development

Corporate level – Using VBM, Cantor's management will need to devise a corporate strategy which focuses specifically on maximising the overall value of the company – including acquiring or disposing of business units if appropriate. Currently, Cantor appears to be growing organically – with the growth of Juicey – but the board should consider whether this growth needs to be reinforced with external growth.

Subsidiary level – Similarly, the subsidiary boards will need to evaluate whether there are any alternative strategies for their businesses which could enable them to achieve competitive advantage and to create value.

Target setting

Once Cantor has agreed its strategies for maximising value, this will need to be translated into specific targets which can be used to manage performance at both strategic and operational levels. The targets should be based on key value drivers, and should include both financial and non-financial aspects of performance – so, for example, customers' rating of the appeal of Cantor's sites could be used as a target if this is a key factor in maintaining customer satisfaction levels.

Impact of VBM at Cantor

Implementing VBM would require Cantor to introduce new performance measures based on the drivers, and the company's reward and incentive systems will need to focus on value creation and performance against value-driven targets.

Performance measures, targets and rewards will need to be developed at the group level, then at the subsidiary level and, finally, at the individual site level in order to ensure full co-ordination of the system across Cantor. In order to align the interests of employees and management with shareholder value – particularly in the longer term – the new reward system may include a share-based payment scheme.

The key benefits of VBM are the focus on value as opposed to profit, so reducing the tendency to make decisions which have positive short-term impact but may be detrimental in the long term. VBM thus will help to make Cantor more forward looking.

However, a danger of the VBM exercise is that it becomes an exercise in valuing everything but changing nothing. It is important that the detailed operational issues of the organisation are addressed through the new measures/targets.

A further difficulty in implementation is that the measurement of the key value drivers can often involve non-financial indicators and these can represent a significant change for accounting-based management information systems.

(v) **Performance measures – fair deal for employees**

The proposed change to the mission statement means that Cantor will need to find a way of measuring whether it provides a 'fair deal' to its employees. This will be inherently difficult to measure, due to the subjective nature of determining how Cantor treats its employees.

Staff turnover

However, the information about staff numbers and staff turnover given in Appendix 3 of Cantor's current performance report can provide some indication of employee satisfaction.

The figures indicate that the staff turnover rate for the group as a whole was 9.9% for the last year, with staff turnover being significantly higher in Juicey (14.2%) than in Cafés (9.7%). Some of this difference may be due to the fact that Juicey is a much newer and more dynamic operation, and that it may have been employing staff on short-term or temporary contracts. However, the variation in rates should still be investigated, and Cantor's staff turnover rates should also be compared against competitors if possible. If Cantor's staff turnover rates are higher than its competitors, this could be an indication that employee satisfaction at Cantor is lower.

Staff turnover rates

	Cafés	*Juicey*	*Group*
Average number of employees in 20X4	1,498	106	1,624
Number of leavers	146	15	161
Staff turnover rate (%)	9.7%	14.2%	9.9%

Tutorial note. We have used the average number of employees across 20X4 to calculate staff turnover rates, but ACCA's marking guidance indicated that it was also acceptable to use year-end figures.

Average pay

The figures in Appendix 3 can also be used in conjunction with the staff from Appendix 1 to calculate the average wages Cantor pays to its staff:

	Cafés	*Juicey*	*Head Office*	*Group*
Average number of employees in 20X4	1,498	106	20	1,624
Staff costs ($'000)	15,921	1,525	3,899	21,345
Average pay per employee	10,628	14,387	194,950	13,143

These figures could again be compared to competitors to indicate whether Cantor is offering its staff fair – or competitive – rates of pay. Benchmark information is not currently provided in the performance reports, although the fact that Cantor's staff costs as a proportion of revenue are slightly higher than the industry average (31.2% vs 30.9%) suggests Cantor offers its employees a reasonably fair deal.

However, the overall Group figures appear to be distorted by the salaries paid to Cantor's head office staff, and the average wages earned by staff in the Cafés subsidiary are significantly lower than the group average of $13,143.

Conclusion

> **Tutorial note.** ACCA's marking guidance indicated that you did not need to provide a conclusion for your report in order to score the professional marks available, although you would have earned additional credit if you did so.

Cantor's current performance report has a number of weaknesses – in particular that it does not provide an indication of how well the group is performing against the three aspects of its current mission. The report focuses on Cantor's profitability rather than shareholder value, but moving to a VBM approach and introducing EVA™ as a performance measure could help to address this issue.

It would also be useful to produce separate reports for the main board and for the subsidiaries' boards, due to the differing information requirements.

55 Boltzman Machines

Text references. Stakeholder management is discussed in Chapter 4b of the BPP Study Text; benchmarking in Chapter 1, JIT is covered in Chapter 10 and the balanced scorecard is discussed in Chapter 12.

Top tips.

Part (a). Although the analysis of the different stakeholder groups in Appendix 1 indicates that Mendelow's matrix is the relevant framework for analysing the different stakeholder groups, you shouldn't spend time describing the matrix itself. Instead you need to use the aspects of the matrix (power; interest) as the basis for identifying how Boltzman should manage the different stakeholder groups; for example, by ensuring that any strategies it introduces are acceptable to key stakeholders.

In order to justify how Boltzman should manage the different stakeholder groups, you need to identify how important the different stakeholder groups are. However, you also need to consider the relative importance of the stakeholder groups in the second part of the requirement – evaluating the appropriateness of Boltzman's performance measures. In effect, the requirement is asking you to evaluate how far the measures relate to those aspects of performance which the stakeholders are most interested in.

Part (b). In APM, you need to be able to evaluate the approaches used to measure performance of an organisation, as well as being able to evaluate the performance of the organisation itself. In part (b) of this question you need to do both.

First you need to benchmark Boltzman's performance against General Machines (ie how well is Boltzman performing) and then you need to evaluate competitive benchmarking as a type of benchmarking (ie how useful is competitive benchmarking as a way of measuring/managing Boltzman's performance? Might other types of benchmarking be more useful?).

When tackling the first part of the requirement, it is vital you do exactly what has been asked. You are asked to use the measures 'suggested by the CEO' (ie the five performance measures given in Appendix 1). However, the instruction from the CEO (in the penultimate paragraph of the scenario) says 'You should also add two justified measures of your own, using the data provided'. So, in total you need to include seven performance measures in the benchmarking exercise.

When choosing your two additional measures, it would be useful to think back to your stakeholder analysis and the assessment of Boltzman's current performance measures in part (a). For example, as far as possible Boltzman should try to benchmark the aspects of performance which are important for its competitive success.

Economic value added (EVA™) and development costs – When calculating EVA™, one of the potential adjustments needed to convert operating profit to net operating profit after tax (NOPAT) is adding back research and development costs which have been charged to the profit or loss account. In the notes for Appendix 2 there is a figure for 'Product development costs', but there is no specific indication whether these had been charged to the profit or loss account, or capitalised.

Given the level of product development costs ($2,684m) compared to the total of 'other costs' in the financial statements ($2,958m), and given the reference to 'development costs' only (rather than 'research and development'), the examining team's original assumption was that these development costs had been capitalised rather than charged to profit or loss. Therefore, no adjustment to operating profit would have been required when calculating NOPAT.

The suggested solution below has been produced on this basis. However, if candidates assumed development costs had been charged to profit and loss, and added it back when calculating NOPAT, they were given credit for doing so.

Part (c). Perhaps the most important word in the requirement for this part of the question is 'problems'. You are not being asked to explain what just in time (JIT) is, or what the advantages of a move towards JIT manufacturing might be, but what the problems which accompany that move will be. Appendix 3 gives you some pointers here by mentioning the impacts on the supply chain with customers and suppliers.

For example, under a JIT system, Boltzman will carry very little inventory. But what problems could this cause if Boltzman can't predict customer demand accurately, or if its suppliers don't deliver components when they are scheduled to?

Part (d). The final paragraph in the scenario provides important context for this requirement: the CEO has asked for you to evaluate the suitability of the scorecard in the light of the shareholders' criticism, and the other initiatives currently in progress.

The link between this requirement and Initiative 1 (part (a) of the question requirements) could be particularly important in this respect. In part (a) you were asked to evaluate the performance measures which have currently been suggested, so one way of assessing the suitability of the balanced scorecard would be to assess the extent to which using it would improve Boltzman's performance measures, compared to the ones currently suggested.

Importantly, though, this question requires an application of the scorecard to the scenario. You will score very few marks – if any – for simply describing the different perspectives of the scorecard.

Overall. Remember that you have been asked to write a report, so make sure the style and structure of your answer, as well as its tone, is appropriate for a report.

Marking scheme

		Marks
(a)	For analysing each of the four stakeholders, and identifying appropriate management approaches for each stakeholder – Up to 2 marks per stakeholder	
	For evaluating the appropriateness of the five performance indicators suggested – 1 mark per relevant point – Up to a maximum of 10 marks	
	Total for part (b) – Up to 14 marks	14
(b)	For calculating ROCE; revenue growth; average pay per employee; net profit margin; and two other appropriate measures – 1 mark each – Up to 6 marks For calculating EVA™ – Up to 3 marks For justifying each of the two new indicators suggested – 1 mark per indicator	
	For evaluating the method of benchmarking – 1 mark per relevant point – Up to 6 marks	
	For a reasonable conclusion on Boltzman's performance compared to General Machines – Up to 3 marks	
	Total for part (c) – Up to 16 marks	16
(c)	For each relevant difficulty of implementing JIT – 1 mark Additional marks awarded for relating the difficulty to Boltzman	
	Total for part (d) – Up to 7 marks	7

BPP LEARNING MEDIA

Marks

(d) For each relevant point relating to the suitability of the balanced scorecard as a performance measurement system at Boltzman – 1 mark

(For answers structured around the four perspectives of the scorecard, no more than 2 marks are to be allocated to a single perspective.)

Total for part (d) – Up to 9 marks	9
Professional marks – for style and structure of report – Up to 4 marks	4
Total =	**50**

Report

To: Board of Boltzman
From: Consultant
Date: [today's date]
Subject: Performance management initiatives

Introduction

This report looks at a number of performance management issues at Boltzman, in particular the way Boltzman measures and manages its performance in relation to its key stakeholders, and whether the aspects of performance being measured are ones which are important to the stakeholders. We then also benchmark Boltzman's performance against General Machines, and look at the problems which Boltzman could face in its move towards JIT manufacturing. We finish by assessing the suitability of the balanced scorecard as a potential performance measurement system for the company.

(a) **Stakeholder management**

The management approaches which are appropriate for different stakeholder groups depend on the **power** the groups have to influence strategic decisions at Boltzman and their **interest** in doing so.

Shareholders – Shareholders have high power but have little interest in the strategic decisions being taken by Boltzman – provided those decisions lead to satisfactory financial results. As such, they should be kept satisfied, and this can be done by ensuring that their financial targets are met.

Employees – Employees overall have little power, and only moderate interest; therefore the most appropriate way of managing them is to keep them informed of strategic decisions.

However, the sub-group of key employees who work in product development have high power because Boltzman cannot afford for them to leave. As such, these key employees need to be kept satisfied, for example by continuing to provide them with training and opportunities to develop their skills through working with new technologies.

Customers – Boltzman's customers appear to be its key stakeholder group, and they also appear to have a relatively high degree of bargaining power over it. The fact that Boltzman cannot afford to lose one of its major customers means that any strategic decisions need to be acceptable to them.

Given that some of the parts are specifically designed for each customer, it would also seem appropriate to the key customers to be involved in product development, to ensure that the products meet their requirements. This level of co-operation should also help to strengthen the relationship between Boltzman and its customers.

Suppliers – Their low power and relatively low level of interest mean that Boltzman's suppliers should require minimal effort.

The suppliers have low bargaining power in relation to Boltzman, which means that the company should be in a strong position to negotiate a favourable price for the goods it buys from them, and to ensure that the quality of them is maintained.

However, if Boltzman introduces JIT manufacturing it will need good relationships with its suppliers (as we will discuss in part (c) of this report), so this could increase the power of its suppliers.

Appropriateness of performance measures

Boltzman's performance measures should focus on the aspects of its performance which are important to its key stakeholders – which, in this case, are its customers and its shareholders.

Customers – None of the suggested performance measures relate to the interests of Boltzman's customers, which is a major drawback. For example, it would be useful to have some measures looking at customer satisfaction, in terms of both quality and value for money.

Shareholders – The shareholders are interested in financial returns, and four out of the five suggested measures (return on capital employed (ROCE), EVA™, revenue growth and net profit margin) relate to financial performance. This focus on financial performance is consistent with the shareholders' position as important stakeholders. Moreover, the use of EVA™ suggests that Boltzman is specifically aware of the need to maximise shareholder wealth, rather than simply to generate short-term profits.

Employees – The suggested measure – average pay per employee – makes no distinction between the key group of skilled employees and the other employees, which limits its usefulness. It would be more useful for Boltzman to compare the average of its product development staff (key staff) against a suitable industry benchmark, because retaining these staff is likely to be critical for the company's competitive success.

Suppliers – Given the relatively low power of Boltzman's suppliers, it is appropriate that none of the suggested measures relate to them. However, this will have to change if JIT is introduced – and, for example, the reliability of supplier deliveries becomes critical to Boltzman's internal processes.

(b) **Benchmarking**

Additional measures – The two additional indicators used in the benchmarking exercise have been chosen to provide some measures of Boltzman's performance in relation to its customers. As we have previously identified, customers are key stakeholders, but none of the performance measures previously suggested are customer focused. Therefore, including these additional indicators marks an improvement in the measures used.

Product development should help to maintain innovation in the business, which in turn should help to support ongoing growth. The number of customers who recognise Boltzman as a top tier supplier provides some insight into its bargaining power with its customers, and it gives some indication of the customers' perception of the quality of Boltzman's products.

Benchmarking results

	Boltzman	*General Machines*
Return on capital employed (see Working)	15.5%	9.2%
EVA™ (see Working)	\$97m	\$(1,165)m
Revenue growth (20X3–20X4)	6.4%	1.0%
Average pay per employee	\$54,618	\$52,299
Net profit margin	8.2%	3.3%
Additional indicators:		
Product development cost (percentage of revenue)	11.2%	10.2%
Top tier supplier status (out of 20)	13	14

Performance analysis

Financial performance – Boltzman appears to be performing better than General Machines in relation to all the financial indicators (ROCE, EVA™, and net profit margin).

Boltzman also appears to have better growth prospects than General Machines, and this may in part be a consequence of the greater attention it pays to product development.

Currently, General Machines is larger than Boltzman and has top tier status with marginally more large customers, but if Boltzman's growth rate (relative to General Machines) continues it may soon become larger than General Machines, and achieve top tier supplier status with more customers.

Benchmarking method

Competitive benchmarking – The benchmarking exercise is an example of competitive benchmarking, since Boltzman's performance has been compared against its main competitor, General Machines. This type of benchmarking can be useful for identifying areas where Boltzman needs to improve its performance to catch up with General Machines. However, it will not identify how Boltzman can gain any competitive advantage from it.

Also, it is unlikely that a competitor will share any detailed performance information with Boltzman, so the only aspects of performance which can be benchmarked are high level strategic ones, where the relative information is already publicly available (as is the case with the financial data currently being benchmarked). As a result, however, this kind of benchmarking will not provide Boltzman with any insights into how to improve its processes.

Functional benchmarking – As well as comparing its performance against direct competitors, it may also be useful for Boltzman to monitor its performance against 'best in class' performers from other business sectors. Since Boltzman is not competing with these companies, they may be willing to share operational data with it in a way that General Machines would not be. As such, Boltzman could identify ways of improving its processes and capabilities which in turn should help to improve its overall financial performance.

Functional benchmarking could be particularly useful in relation to Boltzman's quality initiatives, since it could compare its performance with other companies which are recognised for the quality of their products, and then hopefully find ways to improve the quality of its products, and to support its aim of becoming the highest quality supplier in the marketplace.

(c) **JIT manufacturing**

As the Head of Aerospace has suggested in this email, the move to JIT manufacturing could have a significant impact on Boltzman's supply chain – both upstream (with suppliers), and downstream (with customers).

Forecasting demand – Under a JIT system, Boltzman will manufacture parts in response to customer demand, rather than holding any significant volumes of parts as inventory. However, to do this effectively, Boltzman will need to be able to forecast customer demand accurately and plan its manufacturing activities accordingly. This demand planning will require close links between Boltzman and its customers.

Suppliers – As well as not holding stocks of finished parts, Boltzman will not hold any significant stocks of components under a JIT system. Therefore, Boltzman will be reliant on its suppliers to deliver orders on time, and without any defects, in order for the manufacturing process to run smoothly. Boltzman currently uses a large number of suppliers, and so it will need to review whether they are all sufficiently reliable to operate under a JIT system. Boltzman may find it more practical to reduce the number of suppliers it deals with, and to partner with a smaller number of suppliers whose reliability can be guaranteed (both in terms of the quality of the parts they supply and in terms of delivering on time).

Disruption to the supply chain – However, reducing the number of suppliers it uses and not holding any inventory makes Boltzman more vulnerable to any disruption in its upstream supply chain. One way of reducing the risk of disruption is to use local suppliers wherever possible. However, this would reduce the choice of suppliers available to Boltzman and also increases the suppliers' bargaining power over the company.

Factory design and factory processes – Introducing JIT will also have implications for the operational processes within Boltzman. For example, JIT organises production lines around the product or component being manufactured, rather than the type of work being done. Depending on how Boltzman's production lines are currently structured, they may need to be restructured to fit with the JIT approach.

Similarly, JIT requires staff to be multi-skilled and flexible. If Boltzman's operational staff currently have narrowly defined jobs, it is likely they will need to be retrained so that they have the variety of skills required to implement JIT successfully. However, this could cause problems in itself if the staff are resistant to changes in their working patterns.

(d) **Balanced scorecard**

As we have identified in part (a) of this report, Boltzman's key stakeholders are its customers and its shareholders. However, none of the performance measures currently suggested relate to the interests of Boltzman's customers.

Customer perspective – The customer perspective of the balanced scorecard highlights the importance that successfully meeting customers' requirements will have on Boltzman's financial performance. Therefore, introducing the scorecard will reinforce the need for measures looking at customer satisfaction, which emerged from Initiative 1 (on stakeholder influence).

Financial perspective – The measures currently suggested concentrate mainly on financial aspects of performance. Again, as we noted in part (a), financial performance measures are important, especially given Boltzman's mission to maximise shareholder value.

The financial perspective of the balanced scorecard should ensure that financial indicators remain important performance measures at Boltzman.

However, the scorecard also highlights the importance that non-financial aspects of performance have in sustaining the company's financial performance. In particular, the scorecard suggests that a company's financial performance will be shaped by how well it meets its customers' needs, the quality of its internal business processes, and the degree of innovation and learning within it.

Innovation and learning – The innovation and learning perspective of the scorecard is again important for Boltzman considering the company's reputation for innovation, and for the pursuit of engineering excellence identified in its mission. If Boltzman doesn't maintain its innovativeness this could affect its competitive position which, in turn, could damage its performance in relation to the customer and financial perspectives of the scorecard.

Business processes – Boltzman's strategic aim to be the highest quality supplier in the marketplace suggests that it already needs efficient and effective business processes in order for it to achieve the levels of quality it wants to. However, the focus on business processes will become increasingly important as the company introduces lean production methods. As such, having some performance indicators focusing on process quality – as suggested by the business process perspective of the scorecard – would be suitable for Boltzman.

Shareholder concerns – Apart from their concerns about managerial autonomy, it is not clear what the shareholders' other concerns are, and therefore whether introducing the balanced scorecard will do anything to address them. Nonetheless, as the financial perspective of the scorecard addresses the question of how a company looks to its shareholders, by introducing the scorecard the board can demonstrate that it has recognised the importance of the shareholders and their concerns.

However, it is not clear how introducing the scorecard, by itself, will reduce the levels of autonomy managers will have. The shareholders' criticism in this respect appears to be about management styles and culture within Boltzman. Nonetheless, the 'balanced' nature of the scorecard means that managerial performance will be assessed under all four headings. Therefore, if the areas of performance against which managers' performance is measured are properly aligned to Boltzman's critical success factors (and, in turn, to its strategic aims and mission) this should reduce the scope for dysfunctional decision making, even if the managers still retain autonomy for their decisions.

Conclusion

Shareholders are a key stakeholder group, so the suggestion that Boltzman is not listening to shareholders' concerns needs to be addressed. The 'financial' perspective of the balanced scorecard reinforces the importance of measuring how well Boltzman is performing for its shareholders. However, the scorecard also highlights the importance of non-financial aspects of performance. Stakeholder analysis highlights that Boltzman's customers are a key stakeholder group, so the addition of customer-orientated indicators into the company's performance measures would be particularly beneficial.

The benchmarking exercise against General Machines indicates that Boltzman is currently performing well, relative to General Machines. However, it would also be useful to carry out a functional benchmarking exercise to compare some key operating processes against best in class performers.

BPP LEARNING MEDIA

Appendix

Tutorial note. ROCE figures are based on year opening capital employed figures, because this is also the starting point for working out capital employed in EVA™. However, it would have been acceptable to use closing capital employed figures when calculating ROCE (although not EVA™).

Treatment of development costs – ACCA's suggested solution for this question assumed that the development costs had been capitalised, rather than charged to profit and loss. As such they have not been added back to profit when calculating EVA™. Again, however, marks were given if an adjustment was made for product development costs.

Working: Calculation of ROCE and EVA™

	Boltzman	*General Machines*
	$m	$m
Return on capital employed		
Profit before interest and tax	2,907	1,882
Capital employed:		
Equity	8,984	9,744
Non-current liabilities	9,801	10,629
	18,785	20,373
ROCE	**15.5%**	**9.2%**
EVA™		
Profit before interest and tax	2,907	1,882
Less: Tax charge	(663)	(718)
Tax benefit of interest (28% of financing costs)	(81)	(88)
NOPAT	**2,163**	**1,076**
Capital employed	18,785	20,373
WACC: 11%		
EVA™: NOPAT – (Capital employed × 11%)	**97**	**(1,165)**

56 Merkland Sportswear

Text references. SWOT analysis is discussed in Chapter 1 of the BPP Study Text. The performance hierarchy linking strategic objectives and performance metrics is discussed in Chapter 2. Expected values are discussed in Chapter 5, and the value chain is covered in Chapter 4a.

Top tips.

Part (i). There are two distinct parts to this requirement: assess the current metrics; and then make suggestions for improving them. As the marking guide illustrates, the marks available were distributed roughly equally between the two parts, so to score well you needed to give due weight to both parts of the requirement.

The first part of the requirement asks you to 'assess' the existing metrics. A useful way to approach this requirement might be to ask yourself what the characteristics of effective performance metrics are, and then to consider how well MS's metrics demonstrate these characteristics. Importantly, performance metrics enable management to identify how well an organisation is performing against its critical success factors (CSFs), and how well it is achieving its strategy. In turn, this means that the aspects of performance which are being measured should be ones which are linked to key elements of an organisation's strategy.

Therefore, before you can assess MS's performance metrics, you also need to identify its strategy. The third paragraph in the question scenario – which identifies MS's aims and then its broad strategy for achieving them – is crucial here. In effect, your assessment of the metrics should be an assessment of whether or not they will enable MS's management to determine if the company is achieving its aims and strategy.

Having assessed the current metrics, you are then asked to make suggestions for improvements. However, crucially, you must do so within the constraints outlined by the CEO – ie that the existing performance headings (financial, design and brand) are retained, and that there are no more than three financial metrics, and no more than two for each of 'design' and 'brand'. The post-exam review comments (see below) indicated many candidates in the real exam failed to adhere to these constraints.

Also, note that the requirement specifically asks you to use the SWOT analysis as the basis for your suggestions. Therefore a useful approach to this part of the requirement would be to ask if the current performance metrics will allow management to assess how the issues identified in the SWOT are affecting MS's performance. If factors in the SWOT are not being covered by the performance metrics, then these can provide the basis for your suggested improvements. However, remember, your suggestions must be within the constraints outlined by the CEO.

Examining team's comments for part (i). Although part (i) was often answered reasonably well, there were still a number of weaknesses in candidates' answers. A 'significant minority' of candidates chose to assess MS's performance, rather than assessing the performance metrics.

Also, candidates need to remember that, when making suggestions, justifying the suggestion is crucial. Candidates will not score enough marks to pass the requirement by listing alternative performance metrics – to score the marks available candidates must explain why the metrics they are proposing would be beneficial to MS.

Most worryingly, however, the majority of candidates ignored the instructions from the CEO to limit the number of metrics suggested. Many answers contained long lists of new metrics, which was not what was asked for at all.

Part (ii). The requirement asks you to assess the qualitative and quantitative impact of a change of outsourcing partners for footwear manufacture. The qualitative issues (around the ethical implications of using child labour) should have been relatively easy to identify from the scenario.

The information needed to calculate the quantitative impact is provided in Appendix 3, and the comment 'It would be helpful to know how many units we would need to sell in order to cover these increased costs' should have been a clear instruction that a breakeven calculation was required here.

As the marking guide indicates, four out of the eight marks available for this requirement related to the breakeven calculation. However, when this question was examined, the post-exam report suggested that a number of candidates appeared unable to perform the calculations, and the examining team reported that this was very worrying at Strategic Professional level (which is the level of the APM exam).

Part (iii). You should have been able to score some relatively easy marks in the expected value calculation here – using the information you are given in Appendix 4 of the scenario. However, note that the requirement doesn't only ask you to calculate the operating profit, but you are also asked to evaluate expected value method as a method of decision making under risk.

Part (iv). Here again there are two parts to the requirement: (i) evaluate the impact of the new factory on the figures in the dashboard (ie the results) and (ii) evaluate the impact of the new factory on the choice of metrics in the dashboard.

To identify the relevant issues here, it is crucial to think about the new factory in the context of MS's current business model. Currently, MS outsources all of its manufacturing. However, once the new factory is set up, MS will have its own manufacturing operation. This is particularly significant when thinking about the impact the factory will have on the metrics needed to assess performance.

The examining team's comments for this part of the question are also helpful here:

Examining team's comments. Many candidates attempted to recalculate the dashboard metrics but ignored the fact that the new factory was bringing in-house an existing process and so the change in operating profit was the difference between the new factory's profit and that which was made from existing outsourced sales. However, even if no calculations were attempted a number of candidates earned enough marks to pass this requirement by simply going through the metrics and discussing how the new factory affected them and what changes should be made now that MS has a manufacturing operation – something which it did not have prior to this change.

Part (v). Note that the requirement here does not ask you to describe the value chain, or to explain the implications of the value chain for performance management in general terms, but specifically to 'Explain the implications of using the value chain for performance management at MS'. Linking your answer to the scenario was important to score well here.

A useful way of approaching this requirement could be to think how MS generates value through the different activities in its value chain, and then to consider what implications this has for the choice of performance measures or the way performance is measured at MS.

Report format. Finally, note that you were asked to write a report, and remember that there are four 'professional marks' available for the quality of your report. In this respect, markers are looking for suitable report headings, a brief introduction, and a logical structure to your report – signposted by the use of headings. They are also looking for your report to be written in a clear, concise style.

Marking scheme

		Marks
(i)	For identifying MS's aims and broad strategies – up to 2 marks For evaluating how well the metrics support each aim and strategy: Growth – 1 mark Shareholder wealth – up to 2 marks Innovation – up to 3 marks Marketing – up to 3 marks	
	For other comments/suggestions linked to SWOT analysis: Comments about supply chain management – up to 2 marks Comments about social media and IT expertise – up to 3 marks Comments about brand ambassadors – up to 3 marks	
	For adhering to the constraint on the number of metrics on the dashboard – 1 mark	
	Total for part (i) – up to 16 marks	16
(ii)	For calculations: Increased cost of sales – 1 mark Lost operating profit – 1 mark New contribution per unit – 1 mark Required sales – 1 mark	
	Comments (on qualitative and quantitative issues) – up to 4 marks	
	Total for part (ii) – up to 8 marks	8
(iii)	For calculations: Variable costs – 1 mark Revenue – 1 mark Profit – 1 mark Expected profit – 1 mark	
	For comments (on expected value method) – up to 2 marks	
	Total for part (iii) – up to 6 marks	6
(iv)	For calculations: Operating profit under third-party manufacturing – 1 mark Loss of operating profit – 1 mark New capital employed – 1 mark New ROCE – 1 mark No change to other metrics – 1 mark	
	For comments (about the impact of the new factory on the values in the dashboard, and/or on the choice of measures in the dashboard) – up to 2 marks	
	Total for part (iv) – up to 10 marks	10

		Marks
(v)	For relevant points about the implications of the value chain on performance management at MS – 1 mark per point	
	Total for part (v) – up to 6 marks	6
	Professional marks – for style and structure of report – up to 4 marks	4
		Total = 50

Report

To: Board of MS
From: Consultant
Date: [today's date]
Subject: Performance management at Merkland Sportswear (MS)

Introduction

This report looks at a number of performance management issues at MS, particularly in relation to the range of performance measures included in the dashboard. We begin by evaluating the existing measures used, before looking at the way the company's response to the child labour scandal in the sportswear manufacturing industry could affect its performance and its performance measurement system.

We finish by looking at how value chain analysis could influence performance management at MS.

(i) **Evaluation of current metrics**

MS's overall commercial aims are to grow as a business and to maximise shareholder wealth.

As these aims are essentially financial, it seems appropriate for the dashboard to include three financial measures, but only up to one each for 'design' and 'brand'.

Financial performance measures

Growth – Comparing the revenue figures to prior years can give an indication of the growth being achieved by the business. Including percentage change figure (for 20X5 compared to 20X4) on the dashboard also highlights the amount of growth achieved year on year. Similarly, the operating figures show whether this growth is profitable for MS.

However, because the dashboard doesn't give any revenue figures for the sportswear market as a whole, we cannot gauge how fast it is growing relative to its competitors, and whether its market share is growing or not.

Shareholder wealth – Return on capital employed (ROCE) shows how profitably MS is using its assets and, as such, could provide some indication of how well MS is generating wealth for its shareholders. However, ROCE is ultimately not a good metric in this respect.

One of ROCE's weaknesses is that it could encourage strategic decisions designed to increase short-term profit, potentially at the expense of investment for the future. More fundamentally, though, ROCE is a profit-based measure, and shareholder wealth would be better assessed through a **value-based measure**, which provides some insight into MS's ability to generate future cash flows. In this respect, MS should consider using **economic value added** (EVA™) as a metric instead of ROCE.

Non-financial performance

MS's broad strategy also identifies the need to create innovative products and to have an effective marketing operation – the best in Ceeland.

The current dashboard headings ('Design' and 'Brand') reflect the importance of these elements of performance. However, there are still some potential problems with the metrics used in each heading.

Design awards won – The design awards acknowledge the look and technology in a finished product; they do not directly measure the level of innovation in MS. (For example, the number of new features added to our products, or the number of new products developed would provide a more direct measure for innovation.)

BPP LEARNING MEDIA

MS's strategy also identifies that its products should help reduce the risk of injury and enhance sporting performance by their customers. The current dashboard does not measure how effectively the products are doing this. However, it could be difficult to provide metrics which cover all of these areas, given the constraints on the number of performance indicators to be included in the dashboard. As such, MS will have to decide whether reducing the risk of injury or enhancing sporting performance is likely to be the more critical success factor for its products.

Brand awareness – The level of brand awareness is likely to be influenced by the effectiveness of MS's marketing operations. The fact that brand awareness is increasing might suggest that MS's marketing operations have been effective. However, without any comparison showing brand awareness for rival brands it is difficult to tell how effective they are, and therefore whether MS has 'the best marketing operation in Ceeland'.

In this respect, market share might be a more appropriate measure – not least because it also links back to MS's aim to grow as a business.

Moreover, just because people can identify MS's logo or name one of its products does not mean they have a positive impression of the company or any desire to buy its products. By contrast, market share statistics can provide a measure of how well MS is identifying and satisfying customer requirements, and how effectively its marketing activities are influencing their purchasing decisions.

Potential improvements

Although the SWOT analysis suggests that supply chain management is a CSF for MS, the CEO's insistence that no new headings be added to the dashboard means that performance in this area cannot be reported directly.

However, MS's ability to manage its supply chain effectively will, indirectly, affect its revenue and operating profit margins. As such, it may be preferable to replace the absolute operating profit figures in the dashboard with percentage margin figures.

The following improvements could also be made to the non-financial performance metrics:

Design – We have already suggested that the number of new features added to our products might be a better performance measure than design awards won. The SWOT analysis suggests that, rather than just looking at new features, we could monitor innovation in relation to the number of new products introduced.

Brand – We have already suggested that market share would be a better metric than brand awareness.

However, the SWOT analysis also suggests that social media is going to become an increasingly important aspect of marketing activities – although MS's weak IT expertise may limit its ability to take advantage of this.

Linked to the overall performance metric of market share, MS could also monitor the number of followers it has on social media (eg on Twitter, or the number of 'likes' it has on Facebook) as an indicator of how effectively it is using these marketing channels.

Brand ambassadors – Despite the growth of social media, brand ambassadors still play an important role in promoting MS's brand, and the SWOT analysis highlights this by acknowledging the loss of a key brand ambassador as a strategic weakness. As such, it could be useful to include a metric for 'Number of ambassadors' under the 'brand' heading on the dashboard. However, as we have already suggested metrics for market share and social media followers – and can only have two in total for 'brand' – the board will have to decide whether including a metric for the number of ambassadors is more important than either of these.

(ii) **Impact of Response 1**

Qualitative impact

Although there is not currently any evidence that MS's suppliers are using illegal labour, the fact that MS does not appear to have any assurance over the labour practices used by its suppliers (and is having to review them now) means there is a risk that this could be the case.

This means that the review proposed under Response 1 should be carried out as soon as possible. If MS does find that the appropriate employment terms and conditions have been breached (and, in turn, MS's own ethical code has been breached) it should be transparent and own up to these failings. However, at the same time, MS should also explain the actions it has taken (through either Response 1 or 2) to redress the problems and to prevent them from recurring. Taking action in this way should help to restrict the level of negative stakeholder reaction to any findings.

In particular, MS will have to manage the reactions of customers and the regulator if it finds evidence of any unethical practices in its supply chain.

Customers – Such findings will damage MS's reputation for ethical sourcing, and there is a danger that customers could boycott MS's products, threatening revenue and profit growth.

Regulator – The regulator will review MS's sourcing policies (as it did with Nush), and is likely to punish MS in some way for using suppliers who have acted illegally.

Employees – Any such breach would mean that MS has failed to follow the requirements of its own ethics code (to source goods responsibly) and this could damage employees' trust in the company as a responsible employer.

Assurance procedures – More generally, the review required by Response 1 also suggests that MS could benefit from regular assurance processes over its supply chain – to ensure that its suppliers comply with relevant employment legislation on an ongoing basis. Although the constraints on the performance headings in MS's existing performance dashboard mean there isn't scope to monitor performance there, it could perhaps be monitored at departmental level within the Procurement Department.

Quantitative impact

Impact on shareholders – The increased manufacturing costs, coupled with increased compliance and marketing costs, mean that MS's operating profit will fall by $5.5 million if the number of shoes MS sells remains the same. MS will need to increase sales by 106,000 pairs of shoes to make good this shortfall.

However, since the problem of child labour appears to be a common problem among suppliers to sports footwear companies, if MS is able to demonstrate that it has responded rapidly and decisively to any potential problems in its supply chain, this action could help to differentiate it from its competitors, and in doing so could help generate these extra sales.

Annual cost:

		$m
Increase in cost of shoes purchased	$2.1 × 2 million pairs	4.2
Supplier audits		0.5
Marketing cost		0.8
Total (per year)		**5.5**

Contribution per unit	$
Price	75.0
Direct cost ($21 + $2.1)	(23.1)
	51.9

Number of units required to cover lost operating profit: **105,973**

BPP LEARNING MEDIA

(iii) Expected operating profit of the new factory

	Bad	*Medium*	*Good*	
Unit manufactured ('000)	1,800	2,000	2,200	
Revenue ($'000)	135,000	150,000	165,000	
Variable costs ($'000)	37,800	44,000	50,600	
Fixed costs	2,500	2,500	2,500	
	94,700	103,500	111,900	
Probability	0.3	0.6	0.1	
Expected operating profit ($'000)	28,410	62,100	11,190	**101,700**

The expected operating profit from the new factory (before interest and tax) is $101.7 million.

In practice, however, this is not the level of operating profit which the factory will generate in any of the three economic scenarios. Instead, the actual profit (depending on which scenario applies) will be either: $94.7 million, $103.5 million or $111.9 million.

This highlights the underlying problem of expected value calculations: they only make sense if a scenario is played out a number of times, and therefore the expected value (as an average of the individual results achieved) is a meaningful figure. However, in this case, the decision to bring all of MS's footwear in-house is a one-off event, and therefore an average figure has little relevance in the decision making.

Moreover, the expected value is dependent on the probabilities assigned to each scenario. It is not clear how these have been determined, but it inevitably involves some degree of subjectivity.

(iv) Impact of the new factory on the dashboard

Financial metrics (20X5)

	Existing factory	*New factory*	*Change (%)*
Revenue ($m)	273	273	–
Operating profit ($m) (see Working 1)	71	66	–7.0%
ROCE (see Working 2)	41.7%	30.4%	–27.1%

The new factory will not affect the number of design awards won or brand awareness levels.

Impact on financial performance

Operating profit – The decline in operating profit indicates that manufacturing all of its footwear in-house will lead to an increase in MS's costs of approximately $5 million per year.

Although the variable cost of manufacturing footwear in-house ($21–$23 per unit) is expected to be similar to that of buying footwear from an external supplier ($21 per unit), there will also be additional fixed costs associated with the new factory.

The increase in fixed costs will also lead to an increase in MS's **operational gearing**.

Non-current assets – As MS is primarily a product development and marketing operation – with no manufacturing operations of its own – it will have a relatively low level of fixed capital (buildings, equipment etc). As a result, it also has a relatively high ROCE.

However, establishing the factory will increase capital employed (as well as reducing operating profit), which explains the significant reduction in ROCE.

However, although establishing the factory (and taking full control of operations) may have a negative impact on ROCE in the short term, it could benefit MS in the longer term – for example, by helping it to avoid lost sales due to damaged reputation, or to avoid costs such as fines imposed by the regulator.

Impact on choice of metrics

Quality – If MS starts manufacturing footwear itself, then quality control will become an important aspect of performance management. Currently, product quality is not measured directly in the dashboard, but it would seem sensible to add an extra heading to reflect this new dimension – manufacturing – which has been added to MS's activities. (Alternatively, the 'design' heading could be expanded to allow additional metrics to be associated with it. But it would seem preferable to keep 'design' and 'manufacturing' as distinct activities.)

However, we must remember that MS has no experience of manufacturing. As such, it may be sensible to wait until the company has gained some operational knowledge of the factory operations before introducing a detailed metric for this area – for example, to avoid setting performance targets which are not realistic.

Gearing – The factory will cost $36 million to build and equip, as well as increasing working capital by $11 million. It is not clear how this additional capital will be funded, but if it involves debt then this will increase the company's financial gearing, and therefore the level of financial risk. There is not currently any measure of such risk on the dashboard, but again it may be necessary to add one.

Workings

1	*Impact of new factory on Operating Profit*	
	Average selling price ($)	$75
	Cost of shoes ($)	$21
	Operating profit per shoe	$54
	Operating profit on 2 million shoes bought/sold	$108m
	Operating profit from the new factory (per board's estimate given in the question scenario)	$103m
	Reduction in operating profit	$5m
2	*Impact of new factory on ROCE*	
	Current capital employed (where operating profit (PBIT) is $71m and ROCE is 41.7%)	170.3
	Additional capital employed: $36m + $11m	47
	New capital employed	217.3
	Revised ROCE: ($66m $217.3m)	30.4%

(v) **Value chain**

A value chain provides an overview of the different activities within an organisation which combine to create value for customers. By identifying the activities which create value, the organisation can then focus on improving its performance in those areas – with the result that it also improves its performance overall.

Equally, however, the value chain can help an organisation to identify which aspects of performance are most important to measure – that is, those which relate to the key value-adding activities. In this respect, we might expect the metrics included in MS's dashboard to provide the board with information about how well the company is performing in these key activities. However, the current dashboard provides very little information about MS's performance in these activities.

Marketing and sales – To a degree, the dashboard heading for 'brand' could relate to the 'marketing and sales' activities in the value chain; but, as we have already suggested, simply monitoring brand awareness can only provide limited insight into the effectiveness of MS's marketing and sales activities.

Technology – In this respect, the linkage between technology (as a supporting activity) and marketing (as a primary activity) could also become increasingly important with the growth of social media as a marketing channel.

Logistics and operations – MS's current business model (with outsourced manufacturing and third-party retailers) means that a number of the primary activities (inbound/outbound logistics; operations; sales) are performed by third parties. Currently, MS does not appear to monitor the performance of its supply chain partners, but this is perhaps something it should consider doing, since these partners are responsible for generating a significant proportion of the value in MS's products.

Procurement – Although procurement is normally classified as a supporting activity on the value chain, MS's business model means that effective procurement (coupled with effective supply chain management, particularly with its upstream manufacturers) is likely to be crucial to the company's commercial success.

Moreover, the importance of outsourced manufacturers means that MS's performance management should not focus solely on its internal value chain, but also its value network (value system) more generally. (The Nush scandal provides an important reminder of this.)

Here again, the value chain also highlights the important supporting role that technology is likely to play – for example, in ensuring that the quantities of goods produced by different third-party suppliers responds effectively to the requirements of MS's third-party retailers (for example, to avoid either over- or under-production of different product lines).

Product design – Technology could also be important at MS in relation to creating innovative products; either through the way technology is used in the design process, or the way that technological developments make new materials available for use in MS's products.

'Design' has already been identified as one of the three performance headings in the dashboard, but technology development is likely to be a key supporting activity in relation to product design.

Although we have already suggested this point (in part (iv) of this report) value chain analysis reiterates the idea that MS may need to include a wider range of metrics in its dashboard – to provide management with performance information about the range of activities which are critical in sustaining the company's commercial success.

57 Dargeboard Services

Text references. The performance hierarchy linking mission statements and performance indicators is discussed in Chapter 2 of the BPP Study Text. Reward schemes are discussed in Chapter 11. The building block model is covered in Chapter 12.

Top tips.

Part (i). A mission statement identifies an organisation's key purpose. By doing so, it can help to identify – at a high level – the aspects of performance which are important for an organisation, and therefore those aspects according to which its performance needs to be measured.

This question looks at this link between mission and performance measures, and specifically – as identified in the fourth paragraph of the scenario – whether the current set of KPIs measure the achievement of DS's mission.

The fourth paragraph of the scenario also provides a useful pointer for how to structure your answer when it says 'by showing how each [KPI] links to all or part of the mission'. In other words, a sensible approach would be to use each KPI as a sub-heading, and then evaluate the extent to which it links to the mission, and therefore monitoring it will help DS's management assess whether the company is achieving its mission. Note the verb is 'evaluate', so you need to consider both the strengths of the KPIs (where they are clearly linked to the mission) as well as their weaknesses (where they are not linked to the mission).

Are all the elements of the mission (given in the second paragraph of the scenario) covered by the current KPIs?

Importantly, though, note the instruction in the fourth paragraph of the scenario, that the CEO 'does not want suggestions of new indicators.' Therefore, if you identify limitation or problems with the current measures, you need to highlight these, but you shouldn't then suggest alternative measures which could replace them, because there would be no marks available for doing so.

Examining team's comments for part (i). This part of the question required a common task (in a performance management exam) of identifying the mission from the scenario. Candidates were good at repeating the mission from the question, but few appeared to appreciate the structure of the mission, and how certain goals were subsidiary to an overall aim. However, most scored reasonably well, as they linked the indicators given to the parts of the mission.

Part (ii). As with part (i), the fourth paragraph of the scenario identifies that your approach to part (ii) should also be to work through each of the indicators in turn, assessing the assumptions and definitions used in calculating them. So here again, a sensible approach would again be to use each indicator as a sub-heading in your answers.

The fourth paragraph of the scenario provides some key context for your assessment. There has been a suggestion that DS is producing biased results, designed to mislead the markets, and in turn to boost the share price and the value of senior management's shares. As such, a key part of your answer needs to be an assessment of whether the indicators are being manipulated to make DS's performance appear better than it is, in the way the press report is suggesting.

Note the number of marks available for this part of the question. There are 12 marks available, and there are 6 KPIs to assess. This should be a clue that, to score well in this part of the question, you can't just say there are problems with the assumptions or definitions; you need to go on and explain why this is the case, particularly, in relation to them making the results misleading.

Examining team's comments for part (ii). This part of the question required a detailed consideration of how performance measures are put together. However, candidates' responses tended to be very limited, with many candidates only scoring a single mark per indicator because they failed to develop their answers sufficiently. For example, it was often clear that a candidate had correctly identified that there was a problem with the calculation of a particular indicator, but very few candidates then attempted to quantity the impact of this problem.

Part (iii). A key issue when answering this part of the question is that you need to evaluate the dashboard in the specific context of DS, rather than evaluating performance reports in general terms.

For example, DS's mission says the company aims to provide 'world-class services' but does the information in the dashboard provide any indication about how well DS is performing against its competitors, or against best-in-class service providers?

Similarly, we know DS offers a range of different activities to its clients (cleaning, security, etc), but how does the report provide any indication of how each of the different areas is performing?

Once again, note the verb is 'evaluate', so you should try to give a balanced assessment of the dashboard – highlighting areas where it helps managers assess performance effectively, as well as its potential problems or limitations.

Part (iv). The key words in the requirement are 'as required by the CEO.' You are not asked for a general description of the building block model, or to explain how the block model works overall. Instead, you need to explain what is meant by rewards and determinants, and how the dimensions link to standards and targets. These are the specific issues which the CEO has asked you to explain, in the final paragraph of the case study scenario; and therefore these are the only issues which you should focus on in your answer.

Examining team's comments for part (iv). Responses to this question were generally poor, as many candidates ignored the detailed requirement of the CEO and provided a generic answer that irrelevantly described the whole model. The requirement stated 'Explain... As required by the CEO' which was intended as an indicator for candidates to look at what the CEO said in the scenario.

Part (v). The sequence of requirements (iv) and (v) and the context described in the final paragraph of the scenario should help provide you with some pointers for how to assess the two reward schemes.

The CEO is considering the Building Block model as a way of improving performance measurement at DS. So a good way of assessing the schemes could be to assess how well they display the characteristics of effective standards or rewards (as identified in the Building Block model).

For example, the Building Block model identifies that effective standards should be fair and achievable; and, in order for performance measure systems to operate successfully, rewards should be clear, motivating and controllable. How well do the two proposed schemes illustrate these characteristics?

The examining team's comments confirm that this was the expected approach here:

Examining team's comments for part (v). This part of the question was generally well answered, with many candidates using the Building Block model concepts to good effect by illustrating how the two reward schemes demonstrated the ideal features from the model.

Report format. Finally, note that you were asked to write a report, and remember that there are four 'professional marks' available for the quality of your report. As is the case in all report questions, markers are looking for suitable report headings, a brief introduction, a logical structure to the report – signposted by the use of headings – and a clear, concise style.

Marking scheme

		Marks
(i)	For breaking down the mission statement and identifying the key elements of DS's mission – Up to 2 marks	
	For evaluating the links between the KPIs and the mission statement – 1 mark per relevant point	
	Total for part (i) – Up to 8 marks	8
(ii)	Up to 3 marks for relevant comments on each indicator: Operating profit margin Secured revenue Management retention Order book Organic revenue growth ROCE	
	Total for part (ii) – Up to 12 marks	12
(iii)	1 mark per relevant point about DS's performance dashboard	
	Total for part (iii) – Up to 8 marks	8
(iv)	For explanation of results and determinants – 1 mark per relevant point – Up to 2 marks For explanation of standards and targets, and key characteristics (ownership; achievable targets; fair): – 1 mark per relevant point – Up to 4 marks	
	Total for part (iv) – Up to 6 marks	6
(v)	Up to 2 marks for general discussion of assessment or reward schemes For assessment of Scheme 1; 1 mark per relevant point – Up to 6 marks For assessment of Scheme 2; 1 mark per relevant point – Up to 6 marks	
	Total for part (v) – Up to 12 marks	12
	Professional marks – for style and structure of report – Up to 4 marks	4
	Total =	**50**

Report

To: Board of DS
From: Accountant
Date: [today's date]
Subject: Strategic performance reporting and reward systems at DS

Introduction

This report assesses the coherence of the choice of key performance indicators (KPIs) with the mission of DS, followed by the assumptions used to calculate them. Other aspects of the presentation of the dashboard report are then evaluated. Finally, an overview of the operation of the building block model and an assessment of two proposed reward schemes are provided.

(i) **Linking the mission to the current KPIs**

The mission statement can be broken into several parts. The principal aim is maintainable, profitable growth, and this is supported by three further goals: developing the best talent; providing world-class services; and being efficient.

The KPIs are linked to elements of this statement as follows:

- **Operating profit margin** shows that the organisation is profitable and also as a margin, it indicates efficiency in cost control.
- **Secured revenue** indicates the amount of revenue which is contracted and so has greater likelihood of being earned. Contracts give an indication of maintainability here only in the short term, however.
- **Management retention** links to the need for best talent though it does not measure developing that talent.
- **Order book** shows the maintainability into the future of the business though it does not show the average length of the contracts.
- **Organic revenue growth** shows historic growth and may indicate what the management are capable of achieving in the future.
- **ROCE** demonstrates the efficiency of profit-generation from the capital base of DS.

None of the measures are external (looking at the competitive environment) and so it is not possible to indicate if DS has 'world-class services'.

(ii) **Assumptions underlying the current KPI calculations**

Every KPI will involve some assumptions in its calculations. The aim of this section is to highlight how each indicator could be manipulated to show a better picture so that the business can avoid this in the future and the subsequent bad image portrayed in the investing community.

Operating profit margin is a standard performance measure and the only area which can be questioned is the categorisation of costs below this line; for example, the movement of operating costs into 'exceptional costs' below this line in order to artificially inflate this indicator. If the $55m reorganisation cost was included in overall operating profit, which was $91m (= 5.9% of $1,542m), then the business would show an operating margin of 2.3%. The catering business would show a loss of $39m.

Secured revenue represents long-term recurring revenue streams. A good picture will show a high percentage of secured revenue but will be below 100% so that management can indicate that budget targets are being exceeded. It is worrying that the budget is completed well after the year start as this may indicate such manipulation. If the original budgeted revenue figure is used then the secured revenue for 20X6 was 82%.

Management retention only includes retention of employees on full-time contracts which at 65% of all managers excludes a material number. Poor treatment (and thus retention) of part-time managers is therefore ignored. This may be a particular issue for managers with young children who often take advantage of such contracts.

Order book is a total 'value' figure, but is this the cash or present value figure? By choosing cash value of the contract, this will give a much larger figure than the discounted present value, especially where some revenues will not be received for 10 years.

Organic revenue growth is calculated by using the total revenue figure as reported in the accounts. The main purpose of stating organic is that it is growth from within the organisation as it stands and so acquisitions should be ignored. The current figure would fall from 7.2% overall to a less impressive 3.9%.

ROCE. Capital employed is being calculated using the statement of financial position figures which may exclude many intangible assets. As such it may overemphasise the tangible capital base which is not as important in a service business such as DS. The focus on this measure can lead to sub-optimal decisions.

(iii) **Evaluation of the strategic performance dashboard**

The current information used by the board is both financial and non-financial allowing different elements of the mission to be measured. However, none of the measures are external, looking at the competitive environment, and so it is not possible to indicate if DS has 'world-class services'. Also, the measures do not focus on shareholder concerns, although the mission statement indicates that they are the principal stakeholders. Other measures beyond ROCE might have been expected given that priority, such as EPS or dividend per share. No breakdown of ROCE is provided for each business unit, this may be due to the lack of availability of capital employed figures for the units but it does seem an odd inconsistency since ROCE is the best KPI provided for shareholder use.

No revenue figures are given and as most figures are ratios it is not possible to gauge the absolute scale of the business. It is particularly surprising that an absolute profit measure is not included on the dashboard given the importance of profitable growth to shareholders.

Generally, there is a lack of external figures to allow benchmarking or the assessment of the competitive position of DS.

The breakdown of results into business sectors will help to judge the performance of the managers of those units but they may not be comparable; for example, comparing building services and security, it seems that building services is growing more rapidly but with weaker margins. Also, it may be that the employment market is different between each sector and so no comparison of management retention figures is sensible. Again, it may be helpful to provide either an external benchmark through industry averages or an internal one through a historic trend for these sector specific indicators.

The report does have good qualities as it is brief and clearly presented. The use of ratios makes for easy understanding.

(iv) **The Building Block model**

The model takes the important step of distinguishing within the dimensions of performance between what is the desired outcome (results) and what are the drivers of those results (determinants). It then highlights the need to measure both of these within the performance reporting systems of an organisation.

The standards are the target level for the specific measures chosen for each dimension appropriate to an employee's performance. Employees must take ownership, so they need to be persuaded to accept the target and be motivated by the targets. Targets must be achievable and so challenge the employee without being viewed as impossible to achieve and therefore demotivating. For example, they must take account of external market conditions beyond the control of the employee, but this can be managed by benchmarking against an industry average. Targets must be fair; for example, different businesses within DS must be measured against their respective sector (catering, security, etc).

(v) **Assessment of the proposed reward schemes**

As the board is already considering using the Building Block model, it is appropriate to outline the main criteria in the model for reward schemes.

Rewards must be:

- Clear, that is, understood by the managers;
- Motivating, that is, of value to the employee; and
- Controllable, that is, related to their area of responsibility.

Scheme 1

The scheme has the benefit of continuing with the successful policy of offering an equity share in DS. It continues to utilise the knowledge of the line manager in performing the appraisal. It attempts to address a problem of the current scheme – that the breadth of the categories gives the line manager scope to continue to show favouritism to specific employees. The fact that the line manager's own bonus will be affected by how well they perform the appraisals should help to reduce the risk of favouritism, and improve the quality of the appraisal process. The fact that the new scheme also sets an expectation for the distribution of bonuses should bring greater transparency to the process. For example, if 50% of a manager's staff receive no bonus (rather than the expected 20%) this could indicate the manager is being too harsh in their assessment of their staff. Having an expectation of the distribution of bonus shares could also mean that forecasting staff costs will be simpler.

However, this scheme does not address the problem that the appraisal categories are vague and do not reflect the KPIs of DS. It also could create a problem, as line managers will give bonuses according to the stated expectation – for example, even where all staff are, in absolute terms, performing brilliantly, only 20% will get the maximum. Also, there is no mention of the scale of the scheme bonuses as there is for Scheme 2, where the maximum bonus available is stated as 50% of basic salary.

Scheme 2

Scheme 2 loses a key benefit of the current scheme in not rewarding in shares; however, cash is an acceptable alternative. Cash may well be a preferred option for the managers as it offers a certain value to them. This form of benefit also reduces the desire to manipulate share prices. It sets standards based on the KPIs and so should lead to greater focus by each employee on the goals of DS. Involvement of both strategic and line management in this process should lead to a better set of measures being used.

It is not clear, however, why five targets are being chosen. This seems an arbitrary figure and it may be more sensible to suggest a range from three to six (the number of strategic KPIs) to be decided by the managers in consultation. The size of the maximum reward seems likely to motivate but the equal weighting for each heading may not be effective. It requires that, say, operating profit margin has the same importance as management retention.

Mock exams

ACCA Strategic Professional – Options

Advanced Performance Management (APM)

Mock Examination 1 (ACCA September/December 2016 exam)

Question Paper		
Time allowed: 3 hours and 15 minutes		
This paper is divided into two sections:		
Section A	This ONE question is compulsory MUST be attempted	
Section B	BOTH questions are compulsory and MUST be attempted	

DO NOT OPEN THIS PAPER UNTIL YOU ARE READY TO START UNDER EXAMINATION CONDITIONS

SECTION A – This ONE question is compulsory and MUST be attempted

Question 1

Company information and objectives

Monza Pharma (Monza) is a developer and manufacturer of medical drugs, based in Beeland but selling its products all over the world. As a listed company, the overall objective of the company is to maximise the return to shareholders and it has used return on capital employed (ROCE) as its performance measure for this objective. There has often been comment at board meetings that it is good to have one easily understood measure for consideration.

The company has three divisions:

- The Drug Development Division develops new drug compounds, taking these through the regulatory systems of different countries until they are approved for sale;
- The Manufacturing Division then makes these compounds; and
- The Sales Division then sells them.

Balanced scorecard

Monza's share price has underperformed compared to the market and the health sector in the last two years. The Chief Executive Officer (CEO) has identified that its current performance measures are too narrow and is implementing a balanced scorecard (BSC) approach to address this problem. The current performance measures are:

- ROCE
- Average cost to develop a new drug
- Revenue growth

The CEO engaged a well-known consulting firm which recommended the use of a BSC. The consultants began by agreeing with the board of Monza that the objective for the organisation's medium-term strategy was as follows:

- Create shareholder value by:
  - Innovating in drug development
  - Efficiency in drug manufacturing
  - Success in selling their products

The consulting firm has presented an interim report with the following proposed performance measures:

• Financial:	ROCE
• Customer:	Revenue growth
• Internal business process:	Average cost to develop a new drug
• Learning and growth:	Training days provided for employees each year

The CEO and the Lead Consultant have had a disagreement about the quality and cost of this work and as a result the consultants have been dismissed. The CEO has commented that the proposed measures lack insight into the business and do not appear to tackle issues at strategic, tactical and operational levels.

The CEO has decided to take this work in-house and has asked you as the Performance Management Expert in the Finance Department to assist him by writing a report to the board to cover a number of areas.

Problems of using the scorecard

Following the disagreement with the consultants, the CEO is worried that the consultants may not have been clear about the problems of using the BSC in their rush to persuade Monza to use their services.

Choice of performance measures

Second, the CEO wants you to evaluate the choice of performance measures currently used by Monza and those proposed by the consulting firm.

ROCE calculations

Third, there has been a debate at board level about how ROCE should be calculated. The Marketing Director stated that she was not sure what profit figure (of which at least four were available) should be used and why, especially given the large variation in results which this gives. She also wondered what the effect would be of using equity rather than all capital to calculate a return on investment. Some basic data has been provided in Appendix 1 to assist you in quantifying and evaluating these possibilities.

Total quality management

In addition to these concerns, the board is considering introducing a total quality management approach within Monza. Obviously, quality of output is critical in such a heavily regulated industry where the products can be a matter of life and death. There has been discussion about testing this idea within the Manufacturing Division. The CEO wants to understand, first, the costs associated with quality issues within that division. To aid your analysis, he has supplied some detailed information in Appendix 2. The board requires an outline evaluation from you of how a total quality management (TQM) approach would fit within the Manufacturing Division.

New information system

Finally, the Drug Development Divisional Managers have been lobbying for a new information system which will assist their Research Chemists in identifying new drug compounds for testing. The new system will need to be capable of performing calculations and simulations which require high computational power and memory but will also need to have access to external data sources so that these scientists can keep up with developments in the field and identify new opportunities. The CEO is worried about the cost of such a new system and wants to know how it would fit within the existing lean management approach within that division.

Required

Write a report to the board of Monza to:

(i) Assess the problems of using a balanced scorecard at Monza **(8 marks)**

(ii) Evaluate the choice of the current performance measures and the consulting firm's proposed performance measures for Monza **(12 marks)**

(iii) Evaluate the effect of choosing different profit and capital measurements for different measures of return on investment and recommend a suitable approach for Monza **(11 marks)**

(iv) Analyse the current quality costs in the Manufacturing Division and then briefly discuss how implementation of TQM would affect the division **(10 marks)**

(v) Briefly advise on how the Drug Development Division can aim to make the new information system 'lean' **(5 marks)**

Professional marks will be awarded for the format, style and structure of the discussion of your answer. **(4 marks)**

(Total = 50 marks)

BPP LEARNING MEDIA

Appendix 1

Financial data for Monza for the most recent accounting period

	$m
Revenue	8,001
Costs	2,460
Gross profit	5,541
Other costs	3,248
Restructuring costs	482
Operating profit	1,811
Finance costs	266
Profit before tax	1,545
Tax	419
Profit after tax	1,126
Capital structure from the statement of financial position	
Shareholders' equity	1,161
Long-term debt	8,739

Note. Restructuring costs relate to a major project which completed during the period.

Appendix 2

Cost information for the Manufacturing Division for the most recent accounting period

(1) Batches rejected at factory valued at $17m which have a scrap value of $4m.

(2) Training of factory staff which cost $8m.

(3) Regulatory fines costing $5m (due to drug compounds being outside the specified range of mix of chemical ingredients).

(4) Discounts given following customer complaints due to late delivery costing $22m.

(5) Factory product testing department cost $12m.

(6) Cost of raw materials was $1,008m.

SECTION B – BOTH questions are compulsory and MUST be attempted

Question 2

Framiltone is a food manufacturer based in Ceeland whose objective is to maximise shareholder wealth. Framiltone has two divisions: Dairy Division and Luxury Division. Framiltone began manufacturing dairy foods 20 years ago and Dairy Division, representing 60% of total revenue, is still the larger of Framiltone's two divisions.

Dairy Division

This division manufactures cheeses and milk-based desserts. The market in Ceeland for these products is saturated, with little opportunity for growth. Dairy Division has, however, agreed profitable fixed price agreements to supply all the major supermarket chains in Ceeland for the next three years. The division has also agreed long-term fixed volume and price contracts with suppliers of milk, which is by far the most significant raw material used by the division.

In contrast to Luxury Division, Dairy Division does not operate its own fleet of delivery vehicles, but instead subcontracts this to a third-party distribution company. The terms of the contract provide that the distribution company can pass on some increases in fuel costs to Framiltone. These increases are capped at 0.5% annually and are agreed prior to the finalisation of each year's budget.

Production volumes have shown less than 0.5% growth over the last five years. Dairy Division managers have invested in a modern production plant and its production is known to be the most efficient and consistent in the industry.

Luxury Division

This division was set up two years ago to provide an opportunity for growth which is absent from the dairy foods sector. Luxury Division produces high quality foods using unusual, rare and expensive ingredients, many of which are imported from neighbouring Veeland. The product range changes frequently according to consumer tastes and the availability and price of ingredients. All Luxury Division's products are distributed using its own fleet of delivery vehicles.

Since the company began, Framiltone has used a traditional incremental budgeting process. Annual budgets for each division are set by the company's head office after some consultation with divisional managers, who currently have little experience of setting their own budgets. Performance of each division, and of divisional managers, is appraised against these budgets. For many years, Framiltone managed to achieve the budgets set, but last year managers at Luxury Division complained that they were unable to achieve their budget due to factors beyond their control. A wet growing season in Veeland had reduced the harvest of key ingredients in Luxury's products, significantly increasing their cost. As a result, revenue and gross margins fell sharply and the division failed to achieve its operating profit target for the year.

Framiltone has just appointed a new CEO at the end of Q1 of the current year. He has called you as a Performance Management Expert for your advice.

'In my last job in the retail fashion industry, we used rolling budgets, where the annual budget was updated to reflect the results of every quarter's trading. That gives a more realistic target, providing a better basis on which to appraise divisional performance. Do you think we should use a similar system for all divisions at Framiltone?' he asked.

You have obtained the current year budget for Luxury Division and the division's Q1 actual trading results (Appendix 1) and notes outlining expectations of divisional key costs and revenues for the rest of the year (Appendix 2).

Appendix 1

Luxury Division current year budget

	Q1	*Q2*	*Q3*	*Q4*	*Total*	*Q1 actual*
	C$'000	C$'000	C$'000	C$'000	C$'000	C$'000
Revenue	10,000	12,000	11,000	7,000	40,000	10,400
Cost of sales	(6,100)	(7,120)	(6,460)	(4,720)	(24,400)	(6,240)
Gross profit	3,900	4,880	4,540	2,280	15,600	4,160
Distribution costs	(600)	(720)	(660)	(420)	(2,400)	(624)
Administration costs	(2,300)	(2,300)	(2,300)	(2,300)	(9,200)	(2,296)
Operating profit	1,000	1,860	1,580	(440)	4,000	1,240

Appendix 2

Expected key costs and revenues for remainder of the current year

(1) Sales volumes are expected to be 2% higher each quarter than forecast in the current budget.

(2) Average selling price per unit is expected to increase by 1.5% from the beginning of Q3.

(3) The exchange rate between the Ceeland Dollar (C$) and the Veeland Dollar (V$) is predicted to change at the beginning of Q2 to C$1.00 buys V$1.50. For several years up to the end of Q1, C$1.00 has been equivalent to V$1.40 and this exchange rate has been used when producing the current year budget. Food produced in the Luxury Division is despatched immediately upon production and Framiltone holds minimal inventory. The cost of ingredients imported from Veeland represents 50% of the division's cost of sales and suppliers invoice goods in V$.

(4) The rate of tax levied by the Ceeland Government on the cost of fuel which Luxury uses to power its fleet of delivery vehicles is due to increase from 60%, which it has been for many years, to 63% at the beginning of Q3. 70% of the division's distribution costs are represented by the cost of fuel for delivery vehicles.

(5) The CEO has initiated a programme of overhead cost reductions and savings of 2.5% from the budgeted administration costs are expected from the beginning of Q2. Q3 administration costs are expected to be a further 2.5% lower than in Q2, with a further 2.5% saving in Q4 over the Q3 costs.

Required

(a) Using the data in the appendices, recalculate the current year budget to the end of the current year and briefly comment on the overall impact of this on the expected operating profit for the year. **(12 marks)**

(b) Evaluate whether a move from traditional incremental budgeting to a system of rolling budgets would be appropriate for Dairy and Luxury Divisions. **(13 marks)**

(Total = 25 marks)

Question 3

Alflonnso is a large producer of industrial chemicals, with divisions in 25 countries. The Agrochemicals Division produces a chemical pesticide, known internally as 'ALF', to control pests in a crop which is of worldwide significance, economically and for food production. Pesticides such as ALF only remain effective for a limited time, after which pests become resistant to them and a replacement product needs to be found. A scientific study has shown that the current variant, ALF6, is becoming ineffective in controlling pests, and in some places it has accumulated in the soil to levels which may significantly reduce crop yields in the future if it is continued to be used. The Agrochemicals Division is evaluating three new products to find one replacement for ALF6.

ALF7

ALF7 is produced by a small chemical modification to the existing product and requires little research and development (R&D) resources to develop it. As it is closely related to the current variant, it is only expected to remain effective, and in use, for three years. It is unclear whether ALF7 will accumulate in the soil in the same way as ALF6 does.

Red

Red is a new type of pesticide which will incur large amounts of R&D expenditure to develop a commercial version. In addition, the Agrochemicals Division will have to fund a long-term scientific study into the effect of Red on the environment at a cost of $4m for each of the 15 years that the product will be in use, and for 5 years afterwards.

Production of Red generates large amounts of toxic by-products which must be treated in the division's waste treatment facility. The production plant used to produce Red must also be decommissioned for cleaning, at an estimated cost of $45m, at the end of the life of the product.

Green

Green is a form of a naturally occurring chemical, thought to be safe and not to accumulate in the environment. It is expected to remain in use for eight years. Production of Green requires relatively large amounts of energy. Significant R&D expenditure is also needed to produce an effective version, as Green remains active in the environment for only a short time. Because of this, Green is unsuitable for use in climates where crop production is already difficult.

The Global Food Production Organisation (GFPO) is a non-governmental organisation which funds new ways to increase global crop production, especially in regions where food for human consumption is already scarce. The GFPO has agreed to make a significant contribution to the R&D costs of producing a replacement for ALF6, but will be unwilling to contribute to the R&D costs for Green because it cannot be used in every region. Similarly, a number of governments, in countries where Alflonnso has licences to operate its other chemical businesses, have warned the company of the potential public disapproval should the Agrochemical Division choose to replace ALF6 with a product unsuitable for use in areas where food production is scarce.

The newly appointed Chief Financial Officer (CFO) for the Agrochemicals Division has asked you as a Performance Management Consultant for your advice. 'One of our analysts in the Agrochemicals Division,' she said, 'has produced a single period statement of profit or loss (Appendix 1) to show the profitability of the three new products we are considering as replacements for ALF6.'

'I think the analyst's calculations are too simplistic,' she continued. 'The costs of the waste treatment are apportioned based on the expected revenue of the new products. This is consistent with Alflonnso's traditional group accounting policy, but I don't think this gives an accurate costing for the new products. Also, I watched a presentation recently about the use of life cycle costing and also how environmental management accounting (EMA) can help reduce costs in the categories of conventional, contingent and reputation costs, and as a result improve performance.'

Appendix 1

Single period statement of profit or loss for the replacement products for ALF6[1]

	ALF7	*Red*	*Green*
Revenue per litre ($)	8.00	13.00	11.00
Quantity sold and produced (million litres)	100	85	75
	$m	$m	$m
Revenue	800	1,105	825
Direct material, labour and energy	(524)	(724)	(565)
Factory overheads	(80)	(122)	(74)
Environmental study	–	(4)	–
Waste treatment of toxic by-products[2]	(54)	(63)	(71)
Net profit[3]	142	192	115
Average profit per litre ($)	1.42	2.26	1.53

Notes to the statement of profit or loss

1 All figures exclude the contribution from the GFPO towards the R&D costs of the new product.

2 Waste treatment is an overhead cost incurred in the division's waste treatment facility. Currently, costs of waste treatment are apportioned to products according to expected revenue. The total annual cost of the waste treatment facility, which processes a total of 55 million litres of waste each year, is $300m. Any waste treatment capacity not used by any of the three new products can be used to treat waste created during the manufacture of other products in the division. One litre of waste by-product is produced for every 12.5 litres of ALF7 produced, for every 2.5 litres of Red produced, and for every 100 litres of Green.

3 R&D costs are incurred in the division's R&D facility. In accordance with the group's accounting policy, R&D expenditure is not currently apportioned to individual products. The annual cost of the R&D facility is $60m and has a total of 30,400 R&D hours available, of which 800 hours would be required to develop ALF7, 8,500 hours to develop Red, and 4,000 hours to develop Green.

Required

(a) (i) Explain how activity-based costing may help the Agrochemicals Division in assessing the profitability of the three new products. **(5 marks)**

(ii) Using activity-based costing, and excluding the value of the grant from the GFPO, calculate the total waste treatment costs and R&D costs of the three new products. **(3 marks)**

(b) Using your answers from part (a) (ii), calculate the average net profit per litre of each of the three alternative new products over their expected life cycles and comment on the results. **(9 marks)**

(c) Advise how EMA may help improve the performance of the Agrochemicals Division. **(8 marks)**

(Total = 25 marks)

Answers

DO NOT TURN THIS PAGE UNTIL YOU HAVE COMPLETED THE MOCK EXAM

Plan of attack

What's the worst thing you could be doing right now if this were the actual exam? Panicking, and getting yourself in a right old state? Yawning, because you're exhausted from too much late-night, last-minute revision? Wondering how to celebrate the end of the exam in 3 hours and 15 minutes' time?

Well, they're all pretty bad. But what you should be doing is spending the first few minutes of the exam looking through the questions in detail, working out what topics they relate to, and the order in which to attempt them. So turn back to the exam and let's sort out a **plan of attack**.

First steps first

In our view, the Section A question is often the best place to start, since it accounts for 50% of the marks available in the exam. This means you cannot score enough marks to pass the exam without answering the Section A question.

However, make sure you look through the **whole** exam paper carefully before starting to answer any questions.

In the first five minutes of the exam, look through the case study scenarios and the question requirements and work out what topics the questions relate to. We suggest you then spend approximately the next five to ten minutes analysing the requirements of the Section A question and identifying the key issues in the scenario. Planning your answer is very important; don't just start writing your answer as soon as you open the exam paper.

If you are worried about the paper, it is likely that you believe the Section A question will be daunting. In this case you may prefer to do one, or both, of your Section B questions before tackling it. However, don't fall into the trap of spending too long on the Section B (25-mark) questions even if they seem easier. Remember the Section A question accounts for 50% of the total marks for the exam, so it is crucial to your chances of passing this exam.

It is dangerous to be over-confident, but if you're not too nervous about the exam, we suggest you should start with the Section A question. You know you've got to answer it at some stage, so you might as well get it over and done with straight away.

Make sure **you address every requirement and sub-requirement in the questions**, and also make sure you apply your answer directly to the scenario.

Remember that the basis of the APM exam is **analysis and application**, not simply knowledge recall or being able to calculate performance measures. You are being tested on your ability to apply your knowledge to a business scenario, to analyse and address the specific issues identified in that scenario.

The questions themselves

Question 1 – The scenario focuses on a company which develops and manufactures medical drugs. The company's overall objective is to maximise the return to its shareholders, but its share price has underperformed, compared to the market, for the last two years. As a result the company is looking to revise its performance measures, and is implementing a balanced scorecard in an effort to widen the range of measures it monitors. The scenario then discusses some of the measures which have been proposed for use in the scorecard.

The first part of the question looks at the problems in using the scorecard. Although the balanced scorecard is one of the most popular performance measurement systems, there are still problems associated with using it – and these are what you need to focus on here.

Part (ii) asks for an evaluation of the company's current performance measures, as well as those proposed by a firm of consultants. A key issue here is to consider how well the measures are linked to the company's overall objective – to maximise the value it generates for its shareholders.

Part (iii) then looks at the different metrics the company could use to measure return on investment, and asks you to recommend a suitable approach. However, less than half the marks in this question were for calculating ROCE and return on equity, so it is important you also discuss the measures and then recommend an appropriate one.

Part (iv) looks at the costs of quality in the manufacturing division, and how implementing TQM would affect the division's performance. Categorising the costs into the four costs of quality (prevention, appraisal, internal failure and external failure) would have been a useful structure for this analysis. In turn, the amount of 'failure' costs also highlights the potential impact that TQM – with its focus on 'zero defects' – could have on the division's performance.

The final part of the question looks at the characteristics of lean information systems.

Question 2 – The scenario focuses on a food manufacturing company with two divisions – one operating in a stable market, the other in a much more dynamic environment. The company currently has an incremental budgeting process, but there is a suggestion that it should introduce rolling budgets.

Part (a) asks for a recalculation of the budget for one of the divisions, on a rolling basis. The calculations require a careful restatement for changes in sales volume, price, costs and the exchange rate.

Part (b) then asks whether the move from incremental budgeting to rolling budgets would be appropriate for the two divisions. One of the key issues to identify here is whether the differences between the divisions mean they also need different approaches to budgeting. Rolling budgets tend to be appropriate in uncertain conditions, but would seem to be less appropriate for a division operating in a stable market.

Question 3 – The scenario for this question is quite long, and focuses on an industrial chemical company that is evaluating which of three potential new products it should choose to replace a pesticide that is becoming obsolete.

Part (a) (i) requires an explanation of how activity-based costing (ABC) could help to assess the profitability of the three new products. (Overhead costs are currently either apportioned to products on the basis of revenue, or else not at all.) Part (a) (ii) then requires a calculation of costs for the new products, using ABC.

In part (b), you need to use the figures calculated in (a) (ii) in order to calculate the profitability of the three products over their expected life cycles, and then comment on the results. Appendix 1 in the scenario shows the profitability of each of the three products for a single period, using the company's current method of overhead apportionment; so a key point to consider is how the relative profitability of each product in your calculations differs from that in Appendix 1.

Part (c) looks at how environmental management accounting can help to improve performance. The calculations and discussion from part (b) could have given some useful clues here to supplement your textbook knowledge.

No matter how many times we remind you...

Always, always **allocate your time** according to the marks for the question in total and for the individual parts.

And always read the requirements carefully and **follow the requirements exactly**. Requirement (ii) of Question 1, for example, requires you to evaluate the current performance measures **and** the measures proposed by the consulting firm, so you need to do both of these things, not one or the other.

Also, it is vital that you apply your knowledge to the scenario. If you end up discussing theories and models in general terms without applying them to the scenario you will score very few marks for this. If your answer contains irrelevant or unnecessary material, you will not be scoring marks efficiently, and you will put yourself under increased **time pressure**.

If you ran short of time on this exam, or struggled to interpret the questions, have another look at the guidance on 'Passing the APM exam' in the front pages of this Kit.

All finished with quarter of an hour still to go?

Your time allocation must have been faulty. However, make the most of any time you have left at the end of the exam. Go back to **any parts of questions that you didn't finish** because you ran out of time. Always write something rather than nothing if you possibly can, and try not to leave questions unanswered.

If you write nothing then, by definition, you cannot score any marks. Even if you write a couple of points in answer to a requirement, you could earn some marks for these – which ultimately could be the difference between passing or failing the exam.

Question 1

Text references. The balanced scorecard (BSC) is discussed in Chapter 12 of the BPP Study Text. The importance of the link between performance measures and objectives is discussed in Chapter 2. Financial performance measures (including ROCE) are discussed in Chapter 7. Costs of quality, and TQM, are discussed in Chapter 10. Lean information systems are discussed in Chapter 6a.

Top tips.

Part (i). The BSC is one of the key performance measurement frameworks covered in the APM syllabus, so you should have a good understanding of it. However, the question requirement here doesn't ask for you to describe the scorecard, or to explain how Monza could use the scorecard. The requirement asks specifically about the problems of using a scorecard at Monza. In other words, you need to think what the potential problems an organisation could face with using the scorecard, and then assess if these are likely to apply at Monza.

For example, one of the major problems with using the scorecard relate to choosing the measures to use – agreeing how many measures are required, and what the appropriate measures might be. Could this be a problem at Monza? The first paragraph of the scenario tells us that the board members frequently comment that 'it is good to have one easily understood measure for consideration' – but this would no longer be the case if the scorecard is introduced.

Part (ii) requires you to evaluate two different sets of measures:

- The **current** performance measures (ROCE, average cost to develop a new drug, and revenue growth)
- The **proposed** measures presented by the consulting firm (ROCE, revenue growth, average cost to develop a new drug, training days provided)

As such, it is important that you address both sets of measures – but hopefully you noticed how similar the two sets of measures actually are in the scenario. So, are the measures the consultants have suggested really the most appropriate to use for the scorecard perspectives, or have the consultants simply rolled forward Monza's existing measures as far as possible?

One of the key issues when evaluating performance measures is the extent to which they enable managers to assess how an organisation is performing against its objectives. The opening paragraph of the scenario identifies that Monza's overall objective is to maximise its return to shareholders. Later on, the scenario also identifies that Monza aims to create shareholder value through innovation in drug development, efficiency in drug manufacturing, and success in selling its products. So the question is: how effectively do the performance measures enable Monza to assess how well it is achieving these aims?

Note that the question verb is 'evaluate' so if there are some positive aspects about the choice of measures you should include these in your answer as well as highlighting any problems or limitations with them.

Part (iii). In order to 'evaluate the effect' of using the different measurements, you first need to calculate the returns using the different figures possible (as provided in Appendix 1).

At face value, Appendix 1 identifies four profit figures: gross profit, operating profit, profit before tax and profit after tax. However, the figures for the most recent accounting period also include restructuring costs of $482m. So, an additional consideration is the impact this could have on ROCE. Should the profit figures be adjusted to exclude these 'one-off' costs?

The Marketing Director's reference to 'using equity rather than all capital' should also have been a clue to calculate return on equity (ROE) as well as ROCE.

Remember, however, that the requirement asks you to 'evaluate the effect' of using the different measures, not simply to calculate different measures. So you also need to consider what each of the measures shows. Think about the differences in the figures used to calculate the measures: for example, ROCE (operating profit/total capital employed) compared to ROE (profit after tax/equity capital).

Comparing the measures in this way is also necessary in order to 'recommend a suitable approach for Monza' – which is the third element of the requirement. In order to make a sensible recommendation, you first need to consider the usefulness of the different measures Monza could potentially use (and then recommend the one which is most useful).

As the marking guide indicates, only 4 (out of 11) marks in this requirement are available for calculating ROCE and ROE (with a further 1 mark for calculating gearing). Therefore, in order to pass the requirement, it is essential to make some relevant comments about the different metrics.

Here again, it is also important to think about Monza's underlying objective (to maximise its returns to shareholders). Which of the two measures (ROCE or ROE) is more suitable – and why?

Part (iv). A useful starting point here would have been to categorise the information given in Appendix 2 into the different 'costs of quality' (prevention, appraisal, internal failure and external failure) and then to comment on the relative size of the costs in each category.

Even if you couldn't remember the individual 'costs of quality', you should still have been able to distinguish between 'costs' incurred in trying to prevent failure, as opposed to the costs incurred as a result of failure (or problems occurring).

The figures in Appendix 2 themselves should have given you a clue about the balance between prevention and failure, with the costs incurred on batches rejected and customer complaints being clearly the largest figures mentioned (thereby also suggesting that quality problems are having a significant adverse effect on the division's financial performance).

In this context, it should have been clear that the division's current approach to quality is substantially different to a TQM approach – where the focus is on preventing defects, and the ultimate goal is to achieve zero defects. Recognising this contrast should then help you answer the second part of the requirement: how implementing TQM would affect the division (and the way its staff think about quality).

Part (v). Although the requirement asks how the division can make its new information system 'lean', a sensible approach to this requirement will be to consider what the characteristics of a lean system are. In effect, the way the division can make its system lean is by ensuring that it has these characteristics.

(Note, however, that the requirement is about making an information system 'lean'; not, for example, making the drug manufacturing process 'lean'.)

Overall. Remember that you have been asked to write a report, so make sure the style and structure of your answer, as well as its tone, is appropriate for a report.

Examining team's comments.

Part (i) asked for an assessment of the problems of using the balanced scorecard. In questions like this, candidates should focus on the theoretical areas where they believe the problems lie, and then to illustrate these by reference to the entity in the scenario. Unfortunately, what many candidates do is address the question by discussing another performance measurement system. Making a suggestion as to an alternative may be worth merit, but it does not address the fundamental question asked. It is very important that candidates should know about the challenges arising from different management and control techniques, as well as the potential benefits from using them.

Part (ii) asked for an evaluation of the current measurements and alternatives which had been suggested. Most candidates addressed the question asked, but they must appreciate the need to ensure that suggestions are justified and supported. For example, many suggested that 'more non-financial indicators are needed'. However, such comments are not worth merit unless they are supported by reference to points such as achievement of some of the company's specific objectives. When making comments like this, candidates should ask themselves: why is that relevant? Or, how/why would it benefit the company?

Part (iii) was answered very poorly, as candidates did not demonstrate the technical knowledge that is expected at this level with regard to the composition of the measures of performance. At APM, candidates have to be able to interpret and discuss the results that measures are producing. Too many candidates described the measurements rather than evaluating their impact or usefulness. Candidates need to consider why some measures may be more appropriate than others. For example, which costs might one measure include that another doesn't? And why might this be significant in terms of performance measurement and management?

In **part (iv)**, some basic technical knowledge was lacking in the analysis of costs. However, the part of the question relating to the implementation of a new technique was generally well answered as candidates focused on specific areas around implementation and tried to relate these to the entity in the scenario.

Part (v) was generally answered poorly. Most answers mentioned and explained either lean systems only or the department's production methods only, but the question required that both be considered together to assess the effect that one had on the other.

Marking scheme

		Marks
(i)	Problems with using the BSC Up to 2 marks per relevant point, specifically related to using the scorecard at Monza Maximum for part (i) – up to 8 marks	8
(ii)	Evaluating choice of current and proposed performance measures Evaluating current measures – 1 mark per relevant point, up to 6 marks Evaluating proposed measures – 1 mark per relevant point, up to 9 marks Maximum for part (ii) – up to 12 marks	12
(iii)	Variation in calculating return on investment For calculating appropriate ROCE figures (including ROCE adjusted for restructuring costs) – up to 3 marks ROE calculation – 1 mark Gearing – 1 mark Maximum for calculations – up to 5 marks For discussion of ROCE – 1 mark per point, up to 5 marks For discussion of ROE – 1 mark per point, up to 3 marks For justified recommendation of a suitable measure – 1 mark Maximum for part (iii) – up to 15 marks	11
(iv)	Quality costs and TQM in the Manufacturing Division Discussion of categories of quality cost – up to 2 marks Calculation/identification of quality costs – up to 3 marks Discussion of results – up to 3 marks Discussing how implementing TQM would affect the division – up to 5 marks Maximum for part (iv) – up to 10 marks	10
(v)	New information system Aims of lean approach – up to 2 marks Ways of achieving a lean system – up to 5 marks Maximum for part (v) – up to 10 marks	5
	Professional marks – up to 4 marks	4
	Total =	**50**

Report

To:	The board of Monza
From:	Performance management expert
Date:	[today's date]
Subject:	**Performance measurement and management issues at Monza**

Introduction

This report addresses the problems of using the BSC within Monza. The current and proposed performance measures are evaluated and the main current measure is discussed in detail. Quality costs and the new quality programme at the Manufacturing Division are analysed. Finally, the lean philosophy is applied to the new information system for the Drug Development Division.

(i) **Problems with using the BSC**

The BSC provides no aggregate or single summary measure of performance (in the way that cash flow is used in a value-based approach, or in the way that ROCE is currently used at Monza). Also, there is no simple, direct link between the BSC measures and shareholder value, the main objective of Monza.

The measures in the scorecard can conflict; for example, cost controls (financial perspective) can obstruct the investment needed in order to speed up manufacturing processes (internal business perspective). Overall, the measures should seek to align with the fundamental need to create shareholder value.

It can be difficult to select measures. In particular, there is the danger of losing sight of key information in a plethora of indicators. This may be an issue for Monza as it has only had three indicators in the past and this will now increase significantly – a potential of twelve, if there is one for each level of management (strategic, tactical, operational) for each of the four perspectives of the BSC.

There must be management commitment to the change to the scorecard. In particular, there must not be a return to a focus on the financial measures which have been used in the past at Monza. Management should acquire the expertise for understanding non-financial measures through training.

There are potentially significant costs in collecting the additional information which will be needed for the new performance measures. Many of the measures will be non-financial and so new information systems will be required to collect and record the data.

(ii) **Choice of current and proposed performance measures**

Current measures

The current measures are all historic, financial ones and so the BSC approach will bring a longer-term view by using non-financial measures which consider those factors which might drive future growth, for example, those in the learning and growth perspective.

The current measures do not directly link to shareholder value which appears to be the overall aim of the company. A measure such as economic value added would do this more effectively.

The three measures do give a broad view of financial performance, though. ROCE is a widely used measure which it should be possible to benchmark against competitors.

As far as the divisions are concerned, there is a measure of success in selling through revenue growth, though this may be due to not only the Sales Division but also the drugs brought to market by the Development Division.

Average cost to develop a new drug is a financial measure of the Development Division's performance but this does not measure its aim of innovation in development. Indeed, this measure may conflict with that aim, as cost control of development may hinder innovative thinking. It would appear more appropriate to have a cost control measure associated with manufacturing, as its goal is to be more efficient. The performance of the Manufacturing Division is only measured indirectly through its effect on the financial performance of the company as a whole.

Consultants' proposed measures

The suggested measures do not seem to deviate much from the existing measures, though there may be an advantage in this as the new system would use existing information systems and known measures in that case. However, this advantage is secondary to the need to find measures which will drive useful performance in the four perspectives.

The proposed measures from the consultants' interim report mostly fit within the standard four perspectives of the BSC, although revenue growth is more appropriate as a measure from the financial perspective. Customer perspective measures should focus on the strategies which will achieve success in the eyes of the customers rather than just measuring the results of those strategies. Examples of this would be measuring the efficacy of the drugs which are developed by Monza or the reputation of Monza's medicines among the medical community.

Taking the others in turn, ROCE does not seem to be directly linked to shareholder value as, for example, economic value added or net present value would be. ROCE considers the performance over the whole capital base while the shareholders will be more directly concerned with returns on their equity investment. As a profit-based measure, ROCE may also be failing to target cash generation which is ultimately driving dividend payments and value creation for shareholders.

As already indicated, cost control in business processes is important but other measures of success such as time to market for the development of new products and quality initiatives should also be considered.

The fourth perspective (learning) is particularly relevant to a high-technology firm such as Monza. There will be considerable competitive advantage in having a highly skilled workforce. However, the measure proposed is imprecise as it values all training days, whether for knowledge workers or unskilled labourers, as equally valuable. Measures of the number of innovations within each division may be appropriate as these will be qualitatively different (new compounds developed, manufacturing quality improvements and sales techniques/initiatives developed).

Overall, the initial proposed set of measures does appear limited and does not address the overall aim of Monza or the problem of the narrowness of the existing set of measures.

(iii) **Variations in calculating return on capital**

	ROCE	**Return on equity**
Using:		
Operating profit (W1)	18%	
Operating profit before restructuring (W2)	23%	
Profit after tax (W3)		97%

Tutorial notes

Workings for calculations

1	Operating profit ($m):	1,811
	Capital employed ($m):	1,161 + 8,739 = 9,900
	ROCE:	1,811/9,900 = 18.3%
2	Operating profit ($m):	1,811
	Add back restructuring ($m):	482
	Operating profit before restructuring ($m):	2,293
	Capital employed ($m):	9,900
	ROCE:	2,293/9,900 = 23.2%
3	Profit after tax ($m):	1,126
	Shareholders' equity ($m):	1,161
	Return on equity:	1,126/1,161 = 97.0%

ROCE is normally calculated by dividing operating profit by capital employed (debt and equity). The calculations above illustrate the possibilities of using the different return (profit) and capital figures available.

The ROCE figure should not use gross profit, as this ignores the operating costs not directly attached to sales, and at Monza these will include significant overheads from the Drug Development and Manufacturing Divisions which are relevant to overall performance. The return figure should match with the capital used to generate that return. As ROCE is calculated based on the return on total capital, it should not include financing costs, and so profit before and after tax are not consistent with this view.

The one area that could be discussed is whether to include the one-off costs of restructuring in performance. It would probably be best to disclose both figures to the company's stakeholders and to identify how any competitor would perform such a calculation for benchmarking.

A suitable approach for Monza

ROE may be a more suitable measure given Monza's focus on shareholder (not debt provider) performance.

In this case, the relevant return figure is the profit after tax as this is the return available to shareholders after the debt providers have been paid. The figure here (97%) is very large. This is due partly to the fact that the capital figures used in these calculations are from the financial statements and are not market values. (Market values of equity and debt would give a more accurate measure of performance both for ROCE and ROE.)

Another reason why the ROE is large compared to ROCE is that Monza is highly geared (88%). ROE, therefore, demonstrates the benefit of the chosen capital structure of Monza.

Overall, therefore, ROE is a better measure than ROCE as it fits with the prioritisation of shareholders as opposed to all capital providers.

Tutorial note. Although we have recommended ROE, using ROE could have the effect of encouraging the continued heavy use of debt finance. (If a company's gearing ratio becomes too high, this can be a problem, not a benefit.)

By contrast, ROCE does not reward the excessive use of debt finance, so you could have added this point as a word of caution alongside the recommendation.

(iv) **Quality costs and TQM in the Manufacturing Division**

Quality costs are usually broken into four categories:

- Prevention costs, which relate to avoiding producing defective items in the first place;
- Appraisal costs, which relate to ensuring that the products produced meet an acceptable standard;
- Costs of internal failure, which relate to products that fail appraisal and how these are handled; and
- Costs of external failure, which relate to products that fail the standard but are still shipped to customers.

At Monza, for the most recent period, the following quality costs have been identified:

Prevention costs: $8m (training)

Appraisal costs: $12m (product testing)

Costs of internal failure: $13m (batches rejected)

Costs of external failure: $27m = $5m (fines) + $22m (discounts for late delivery)

Total raw material costs might hide relevant quality costs if the company is buying higher quality material to prevent problems of quality; however, this cannot be quantified in this scenario.

It can be seen that there were $40m of failure costs (internal and external) in the period but only $8m was spent on prevention (training). A 10% improvement in the failures could generate $4m in cost savings. In the light of this, the budget for improvements to production which prevent such failures could be significantly expanded. The analysis of quality costs should help to emphasise the importance of prevention by showing its financial value and this could be an important argument in favour of a TQM approach.

Impact of TQM on Manufacturing Division

TQM focuses on the customer perspective and the need for each part of the organisation to avoid defects in the chain of production.

Prevention is the key to improvement and so management should focus on avoiding defects through training and improved process design rather than appraisal. All employees must accept personal responsibility for their work and act to remove defects from production. Quality certification programmes are often instituted in order to encourage the focus on 'zero defects'. Quality circles may be formed as small, autonomous groups aimed at devising solutions to quality problems.

(v) **Making the new information system 'lean'**

Lean systems aim to get the right thing to the right place at the right time, first time. They aim to reduce waste while being flexible. The need for flexibility will be important for the Drug Development Division as it is constantly working in a changing environment.

The information in the system should be organised so that it can be retrieved with minimum difficulty – for example, if scientists need to access the results of past simulations.

The information will also have to be accurate so that time is not wasted in making errors.

The information should be presented clearly and, in particular, should not be excessive given the needs of the users. For example, if there are calculations and simulations which are obsolete or no longer required, these should be removed from the system.

The information should be able to be exchanged easily. This will be important in a collaborative environment such as a research group in the Development Division.

Tutorial note. The 5Ss – structurise, systemise, sanitise, standardise, and self-discipline – could also be used here as a framework for your answer.

Question 2

Text reference. Different approaches to budgeting (including rolling budgets and incremental budgets) are discussed in Chapter 3 of the BPP Study Text.

Top tips.

Part (a). Although we often tell you that the majority of the marks in APM relate to analysis and evaluation, calculations are still an important part of performance management – and therefore you should still expect there to be some calculations in the exam.

10 out of the 12 marks in part (a) of this question relate to calculation, and if you worked carefully through the information provided in Appendix 2 you should be able to score a good number of these.

However, it is important not to rush the calculations, and to think about the points carefully. For example, the increase in sales volume (point 1) will affect not only revenue but also cost of sales and distribution costs.

Similarly, point 2 tells you that the selling price increases from the beginning of Q3, so it only affects Q3 and Q4 (not Q2). However, don't forget the volume increase (from point 1) when calculating the impact of the price increase.

It is very important to lay out your workings carefully to give yourself the best chance of picking up these points. The calculations themselves aren't difficult, but it is very easy to drop marks by making careless mistakes or not thinking through the implications of the points in Appendix 2 carefully. (For example, will the movement in exchange rate increase Framiltone's costs or reduce them?)

Finally, note that as well as recalculating the budget you are asked to comment briefly on the impact this has on the division's expected operating profit.

Part (b). A sensible way to approach this question will be to think about the benefits and drawbacks of both approaches to budgeting, and the situations where each is likely to be most appropriate.

You should have identified from the scenario that the two divisions are very different: the Dairy Division is well established, operating in a saturated market (with little opportunity for growth), and much of its business is governed by long-term contracts. By contrast, the Luxury Division is a new business, focusing on growth, and with rapidly changing product ranges.

These contrasts between the two divisions should have helped you to think about which approach to budgeting might be more appropriate for each. (The key point here – and a fundamental point you should have been aware of – is that an incremental approach is likely to be appropriate in stable conditions (Dairy), whereas rolling budgets are likely to be more appropriate in dynamic conditions (Luxury).)

Examining team's comments.

Part (a) was attempted well by many candidates, and the layout of the answers were generally excellent. Although some of the calculations were tricky, candidates who read the requirement carefully should have had few problems here. However, the examining team was disappointed to see how many candidates could not adjust forecasts by a set percentage, or struggled to compensate for a change in an exchange rate. Candidates must also ensure that all relevant workings are shown. In a number of cases, incorrect answers were presented without supporting calculations, and therefore potential marks for using the correct method (even if the final answer was incorrect) were lost.

Part (b) was generally well answered, and it was pleasing to see many candidates adopting a sensible structure to their answer – explaining the budget systems (incremental; rolling), discussing their advantages and disadvantages for both divisions, and then making a suitable recommendation. Identifying a clear structure for their answers in this way helps candidates ensure that all areas of the requirement are covered.

Marking scheme

		Marks
(a)	Calculations: Use of Q1 actual figures as starting point – 1 mark Revenue: Sales volume increase – 1 mark Sales price change from Q3 onwards – 1 mark Cost of sales: Sales volume increase – 1 mark Exchange rate percentage – 1 mark Application of exchange rate change – 1 mark Distribution costs: Sales volume increase – 1 mark Fuel tax percentage – 1 mark Application of fuel tax charge – 1 mark Administration savings – 1 mark Comments on calculations (impact on operating profit) – up to 2 marks Total for part (a): up to 12 marks	12
(b)	Use of incremental budgeting in the divisions – up to 8 marks Use of rolling budgeting in the divisions – up to 8 marks Total for part (b): up to 13 marks	13
	Total =	**25**

(a) Recalculate the budget for Luxury Division to the end of the current year

	Q1 (Actual)	*Q2*	*Q3*	*Q4*	*Total*
	C$'000	C$'000	C$'000	C$'000	C$'000
Revenue (W1)	10,400	12,240	11,388	7,247	41,275
Cost of sales (W2)	(6,240)	(7,020)	(6,370)	(4,654)	(24,284)
Gross profit	4,160	5,220	5,018	2,593	16,991
Distribution costs (W3)	(624)	(734)	(682)	(434)	(2,474)
Administration costs (W4)	(2,296)	(2,243)	(2,186)	(2,132)	(8,857)
Operating profit	1,240	2,243	2,150	27	5,660

Recalculating Luxury Division's budget for the year to reflect current conditions gives a more realistic target for the division managers. For the coming year, the effect of this is very significant and represents a much more challenging target for managers as it increases the expected total annual operating profit by 42% (5,660/4,000) over the original budget.

Workings

1 *Revenue*

	Q1 (Actual)	*Q2*	*Q3*	*Q4*	*Total*
	C$'000	C$'000	C$'000	C$'000	C$'000
Original budget	10,400.0	12,000.0	11,000.0	7,000.0	40,400.0
2% sales volume		240.0	220.0	140.0	600.0
1.5% sales price			168.3	107.1	275.4
Total	10,400.0	12,240.0	11,388.3	7,247.1	41,275.4

2 *Cost of sales*

	Q1 (Actual)	*Q2*	*Q3*	*Q4*	*Total*
	C$'000	C$'000	C$'000	C$'000	C$'000
Original budget	6,240.0	7,120.0	6,460.0	4,720.0	24,540.0
2% sales volume		142.4	129.2	94.4	366.0
6.67% exchange rate*		(242.2)	(219.7)	(160.6)	(622.5)
Total	6,240.0	7,020.2	6,369.5	4,653.8	24,283.5

*6.67% = 1 – (1.4/1.5), applied to 50% of COS.

3 *Distribution costs*

	Q1 (Actual)	*Q2*	*Q3*	*Q4*	*Total*
	C$'000	C$'000	C$'000	C$'000	C$'000
Original budget	624.0	720.0	660.0	420.0	2,424.0
2% sales volume		14.4	13.2	8.4	36.0
1.31% fuel tax increase*			8.8	5.6	14.4
Total	624.0	734.4	682.0	434.0	2,474.4

*1.31% = 70% × (3/160)

4 *Administration costs*

	Q1 (Actual)	*Q2*	*Q3*	*Q4*	*Total*
	C$'000	C$'000	C$'000	C$'000	C$'000
Original budget	2,296.0	2,300.0	2,300.0	2,300.0	9,196.0
2.5% compound savings		(57.5)	(113.6)	(168.3)	(339.4)
Total	2,296.0	2,242.5	2,186.4	2,131.7	8,856.6

Workings for savings in administration costs

Q2 2,300.0 × 2.5% = 57.5

Q3 57.5 + (2,242.5 × 2.5%) = 113.6

Q4 113.6 + (2,186.40 × 2.5%) = 168.3

(b) **Incremental budgeting**

This is the type of budgeting which Framiltone currently uses. The starting point of incremental budgeting is usually the previous year's actual performance or budget. This is then updated for any known changes in costs, or for inflation. The budget would normally remain unchanged for the remainder of the year.

Incremental budgeting is suitable for use in organisations which are stable and not undergoing significant changes. This is the case for Dairy Division, which operates in a saturated market and has little opportunity to grow.

Production volumes in Dairy Division have only increased by 0.5% over a full 5 years, so it is a very stable business. Dairy Division has stability of both revenues and costs. It has long-term fixed cost and volume supply agreements with its supermarket customers. It also has similar fixed contracts with its suppliers of milk, the most significant raw material ingredient used in its products.

Though the third-party distribution company is able to pass on some increases in fuel costs to Dairy Division, these are capped at only 0.5% per year. This is significantly less than the tax increases which will increase Luxury Division's fuel costs after the start of Q3. It appears that Dairy Division has relatively little exposure to rising fuel prices.

Furthermore, these increases are agreed prior to the setting of the current year budget, so there is no need to update these costs on an ongoing basis throughout the year.

As the dairy foods market is saturated and stable, there is little opportunity for the division to incur discretionary costs such as research and development of new products.

Incremental budgeting is only suitable for business where costs are already well controlled. This is because a big disadvantage of incremental budgeting is that it perpetuates inefficient activities by often simply building inflation into previous year results or budgets. It appears that Dairy Division, having been in existence for a relatively long time, does have good cost control as it has a modern production plant and is recognised as having the most efficient production processes in the industry.

Incremental budgeting may, however, build in budget slack. Managers may spend up to their budgeted amounts in one year, so that their budget is not cut the next, which may affect their appraisal and reward in the future. It is unclear whether this is occurring at Dairy Division, though for many years (while Dairy Division was the only division at Framiltone) the budgets set following consultation with divisional managers have just been achieved. This may be consistent with the stability of the division, but could also indicate that budgets were not set at a challenging enough level, even though Dairy Division had the best performance of the two divisions last year.

It is not therefore advisable that rolling budgets are introduced in Dairy Division, as the current incremental process appears satisfactory. This is especially so since divisional managers have little experience of setting their own budgets, and the time and cost of using rolling budgets would exceed the value of them to the division.

Rolling budgets

Rolling budgets are continually updated to reflect current conditions and are usually extended by budgeting for an additional period after the current period, for example, a quarter, has elapsed. That way, the budget always reflects the most up to date trading conditions and best estimates of future costs and revenues, usually for the next four quarters.

Rolling budgets are suitable for businesses which change rapidly or where it is difficult to estimate future revenues and costs.

Luxury Division was only set up two years ago, and is therefore a relatively new business. It also operates in quite a different sector of the industry to that in which Dairy Division operates and where Framiltone has most experience. There is likely to be considerable uncertainty as to future costs and revenues as Framiltone has little direct experience on which to base its forecasts.

Whereas Dairy Division operates in a saturated and stable market, Luxury Division uses rare ingredients which are subject to variations in availability and cost, for example, as a result of poor harvests. There is no indication that Luxury Division has fixed price and volume contracts with its customers or suppliers and is therefore likely to suffer from instability of supply as well as demand resulting from changes in consumer tastes.

The frequent changes in the product range are also likely to make forecasting for a year ahead difficult. The fact that a large proportion of ingredients are imported from Veeland makes costs susceptible to changes in the C$:V$ exchange rates which can quickly make an annual budget out of date, though managers may use methods such as forward contracts to reduce these movements. If managers are appraised on a budget which is out of date or unrealistic, they are likely to give up trying to achieve the budget, which will negatively affect the performance of Framiltone.

Rolling budgets will provide a more accurate basis on which to appraise managers at Luxury Division as they incorporate the best known estimates of future costs and revenues. It can be seen by the recalculation following Q1 results that Luxury Division's revised budgeted operating profit for the year has increased significantly by 42% (5,660/4,000), most of which is due to exchange rate changes. Where costs and revenues are likely to change during the period, rolling budgets give a much more realistic basis on which to appraise divisional performance and appraise and reward divisional managers. Budgets are likely to be achievable, which will motivate managers to try to achieve them.

Though the regular updating of the budget required in rolling budgeting is costly, time consuming and possibly a distraction for divisional managers, it does seem that rolling budgets are more suitable for Luxury Division than the current incremental approach particularly as, being realistic and achievable, they will increase managers' motivation to achieve the budget and so improve the performance of the business.

Question 3

Text reference. You should already be familiar with activity-based costing from your earlier studies (in *Performance Management*), but it is revisited, in the context of activity-based management, in Chapter 12 of the BPP Study Text. EMA is discussed in Chapter 4b.

Top tips.

Part (a) (i). A useful starting point here would be to think what activity-based costing (ABC) is, and how it differs from traditional overhead allocation. Then think about the way Alflonnso currently allocates overheads to products – ie on the basis of revenue (for waste treatment overheads) or not at all (for R&D costs). How does this compare to the way overheads would be allocated using ABC? Which is likely to provide a more accurate indication of the profitability of the different products?

The calculations you need to do in part (a) (ii) highlight the importance of waste treatment overheads and R&D costs on product profitability. So, in effect, the requirements for (a) (ii) could have acted as a pointer towards some of the key issues to consider in (a) (i) – which highlights the importance of exam technique in terms of reading all the requirements for a question before starting to answer it.

Part (a) (ii). The calculations themselves should be relatively straightforward. However, note that the overheads are not allocated only to these three products. For example, the $300m of waste treatment costs relates to the total of 55 million litres, not just to the quantities of waste by-product generated by ALF7, Red and Green.

Part (b). The figures shown in Appendix 1 should have provided some context for this requirement. Appendix 1 suggests that Red is the most profitable of the three products. However, will this still be the case using ABC, and considering the products' entire life cycles?

The calculations themselves for this question are not difficult, but there are a number of elements to them, so it is important to follow a structured approach:

- Appendix 1 shows profits for a single period, and the waste treatment costs calculated in (a) (ii) are also for a single period (year). So, first you need to calculate a revised annual profit for each product.
- Next you need to multiply the revised annual profit by the product's life cycle, to find life cycle profit.
- The life cycle profit then has to be adjusted for any pre-production or post-production costs (for example, decommissioning costs).
- Finally, the total life cycle cost has to be divided by the number of litres produced over the product's life cycle to identify the average profit per litre over the life cycle.

Once you have done the calculations, don't forget you also need to comment on the results. How does the relative profitability of each of the products compare to that in Appendix 1, and what are the main reasons for any differences?

Part (c). In the scenario, the CFO talks about a presentation she watched which showed how EMA can help to reduce three categories of cost – conventional, contingent and reputation – and improve performance as a result.

As such, a sensible approach would be to use each of these categories as headings in your answer, and to consider how EMA could affect them. For example, how might EMA affect decision making, which in turn could affect the division's performance in relation to each of the categories?

The scenario highlights some potential reputation issues quite clearly – for example, about Green's unsuitability for use in climates where crop production is already difficult. The sequence of the requirements in the question should also help you here. For example, one of the main life cycle costs in your calculations in part (b) should have been decommissioning costs, which would be a good illustration of contingent costs.

The scenario might seem to give you less information about 'conventional costs' – but might this be revealing in itself? In traditional accounting systems, environmental costs are not apportioned to products, and are simply included as general overheads. If managers don't have any information about these costs, how can they manage them? How could EMA help managers in this respect (and consequently, how could it improve the performance of the division)?

Examining team's comments.

Part (a) (i) was generally poorly done, as candidates did not answer the question set. Most candidates gave definitions or descriptions of activity-based costing, but – while these were technically correct in almost every case – they did not address the specific issue of how ABC could help the Agrochemicals Division assess the profitability of its products. It is vital that candidates recognise that only around 25% of the marks in APM will be awarded to definitions and rote learned knowledge. By contrast, in this requirement, candidates could have obtained full marks without giving a definition at all, and purely applying their knowledge to the scenario.

In **part (b)**, many candidates showed a fundamental lack of technical competence by failing to distinguish between costs that occurred on an annual basis and those that related to the product's overall life.

Candidates must also appreciate that if they are asked to comment on the results, then what is required is more than simply saying 'this figure is larger than that one' – which can be seen from the figures themselves. Instead, in a question like this, the commentary should consider the implications of the figures: will they change a decision? Does the use of one technique fundamentally change the cost or product, and what are the implications of this?

In **part (c),** as in part (a) (i), the majority of the marks available were for applying EMA to the practices of the Agrochemicals Division. Would practice change? How? What might be involved? However, a number of candidates' answers' largely only defined and/or explained EMA, without considering its potential benefits to the division. Unfortunately, answers based on theory alone can only score around 25% of the marks available, meaning they fall well short of the number of marks required to pass.

Marking scheme

		Marks
(a)(i)	Generic explanation of purpose of ABC – 1 mark	
	Application to scenario – 1 mark per point	
	Total for part (a) (i): up to 5 marks	5
(a)(ii)	Waste treatment costs – 2 marks	
	R&D costs – 1 mark	
	Total for part (a) (ii): up to 3 marks	3
(b)	Revenue, direct costs, overheads (given in scenario) – 1 mark Waste treatment costs – 1 mark Total net profit over life cycle (before other life cycle costs) – 1 mark Scientific study – 1 mark Decommissioning cost – 1 mark R&D costs – 1 mark Total litres – 1 mark Average profit per litre over life cycle – 1 mark	
	Comments on calculations – up to 3 marks	
	Total for part (b): up to 9 marks	9
(c)	Description of EMA – up to 2 marks	
	Impact of EMA on each cost category: conventional, contingent, reputation – up to 3 marks per category	
	Total for part (c): up to 8 marks	8
	Total =	**25**

(a) (i) **ABC**

ABC allocates costs to products based on the activities which actually drive the cost. This helps to allocate the costs more accurately.

At Alflonnso, the group accounting policy is to allocate waste treatment overhead costs on the basis of revenue, which is arbitrary and does not reflect the cost drivers (for example, the amount of waste created by each product). From the analyst's calculations, R&D costs do not seem to be allocated to specific product costs at all. This may be appropriate elsewhere in the group, where different products may consume similar levels of overheads, but the three new products being evaluated consume quite different amounts of R&D and waste treatment overheads.

It is therefore inappropriate to charge these costs to the products on the basis of revenue. Charging these costs on the basis of the activities which drive them – which are research hours and volume of waste by-products, for R&D costs and waste treatment costs respectively – will give a more accurate costing. This will provide a better basis on which to evaluate the new products and set appropriate prices.

(ii) **Calculation of waste treatment cost**

	ALF7	*Red*	*Green*
Quantity of waste by-product (m litres)	8.0	34.0	0.75
[m litres produced/no. of m litres to make 1 litre of waste]	[100/12.5]	[85/2.5]	[75/100]
Allocated total $300m according to quantity of waste as proportion of total 55m litres:			
Annual waste treatment allocated ($m):	43.6	185.5	4.1
	[8 × 300/55]	[34 × 300/55]	[0.75 × 300/55]

R&D cost

	ALF7	*Red*	*Green*
Allocated total $60m according to required hours of research as proportion of total 30,400 hours:			
R&D treatment allocated ($m):	1.6	16.8	7.9
	[800 × 60/30,400]	[8,500 × 60/30,400]	[4,000 × 60/30,400]

(b) **Average unit cost of each product over total life cycle**

$m	*ALF7*	*Red*	*Green*
Revenue (given)	800.0	1,105.0	825.0
Direct material, labour and energy (given)	(524.0)	(724.0)	(565.0)
Factory overheads (given)	(80.0)	(122.0)	(74.0)
Waste treatment (from part (a) (ii))	(43.6)	(185.5)	(4.1)
Total annual net profit	152.4	73.5	181.9
Life cycle duration (years)	3	15	8
Total net profit over life cycle (before other life cycle costs)	457.2	1,102.5	1,455.2
Scientific study ($4m × 20 years)	–	(80.0)	–
Decommissioning cost	–	(45.0)	–
R&D cost (from part (a) (ii))	(1.6)	(16.8)	(7.9)
Total net profit over life cycle	455.6	960.7	1,447.3
No. of litres produced over the life cycle (m)	300	1,275	600
Average profit per litre over life cycle	$1.52	$0.75	$2.41

From the analyst's calculations in Appendix 1, Red has the highest profitability per litre of the three products at $2.26, but this only covers a single period. As such, it does not consider costs which occur before production commences or after it ceases. When the costs of the products over their entire life cycles are taken into account, Red has the lowest average unit profit, the highest being Green at $2.41. This change

BPP LEARNING MEDIA

has occurred as the R&D costs, the cost of the study which will span 20 years and the decommissioning costs have now been recognised. Knowing the costs over the entire life cycle of a product will help the Agrochemicals Division to better evaluate its investment decisions, determine appropriate prices and generate an acceptable margin.

(c) **EMA**

EMA involves the production of non-financial and financial information to support internal environmental management processes. This could involve measuring the physical movements of inputs to a production process, such as materials and energy, and outputs such as waste.

The Agrochemicals Division could also record financial data on costs and savings related to the environment. It appears that, in common with most other businesses, these costs are not currently identified by Alflonnso's accounting system and they lie hidden within overheads.

Managers have no incentive to reduce these environment-related costs as they are not even aware of them, or the costs of poor environmental practices. EMA allows an organisation to identify environment-related costs and take steps to control them. Such costs are often categorised into conventional costs, contingent costs and reputation costs.

Conventional costs

These costs include the cost of energy and raw materials, and may remain hidden within overheads. The energy costs of the three new products in the analyst's income statement are simply combined with raw material and direct labour costs. This does not, for example, highlight the relatively high energy cost to produce Green. Being unaware of this cost, managers are unable to take steps to redesign the specification or production process for the product in order to reduce the cost.

Contingent costs

These are costs which are incurred in the future, for example, the decommissioning costs of the plant used to manufacture Red. This cost is significant at an estimated $45m, but occurs 15 years in the future and so the estimation is unlikely to be accurate.

Identification of these contingent costs will at least allow the Agrochemicals Division to more accurately estimate the cost of each of the three new products. Also, by identifying these costs at an early stage, this may allow managers to redesign the specification or production process for the product in order to reduce the cost and help prevent managers from focusing only on short-term performance.

Reputation costs

Reputation costs are incurred where an organisation acts in a way which may cause harm to the environment, and include sales lost as a result of loss of reputation. These costs are hard to quantify. For example, the accumulation of the existing product, ALF6, in the soil is said to have a potential effect on crop yields which may lead to future claims from users of the product or to loss of sales due to its potential harm to the environment.

Similarly, Alflonnso's failure, by producing Green, to improve crop yields in countries where food production is already scarce is likely to arouse disapproval by public and governments in the 25 countries where it operates. This again may result in lost sales or refusal by governments to grant licences for Alflonnso to operate.

Making managers aware of these reputation costs should focus their attention on the need to manage the risks of them occurring.

ACCA Strategic Professional – Options

Advanced Performance Management

Mock Examination 2 (ACCA Specimen exam)

Question Paper		
Time allowed: 3 hours and 15 minutes		
This paper is divided into two sections:		
Section A	This ONE question is compulsory and MUST be attempted	
Section B	BOTH questions are compulsory and MUST be attempted	

DO NOT OPEN THIS PAPER UNTIL YOU ARE READY TO START UNDER EXAMINATION CONDITIONS

SECTION A – This question is compulsory and must be attempted

Question 1

Company information and mission

Iron Chicken (IC) is a multinational business which manufactures commercial building control systems. Building control systems include heating and air-conditioning systems, lighting controls, power and water monitoring and security systems (eg keypad access, alarms and CCTV). IC's manufacturing takes place at a number of factory sites where some products have a long product life and are simple and mass-produced while other products are complex and have a short product life due to changing technologies.

IC's mission statement is 'to create value for shareholders through control products which improve productivity, save energy and increase comfort and safety'.

A new Chief Executive Officer (CEO) has been appointed to address a decline in IC's share price in the last three years. This CEO has identified that the business has grown through acquisition and as a result she stated, 'senior management have focused on making corporate deals and not making control systems'. The CEO has declared that the business must focus on optimising its value generation rather than just getting larger through acquisitions. She has developed an improvement programme for IC.

You are a Performance Management Expert within IC, and the CEO has tasked you with aiding her on four aspects of her improvement programme:

Economic value added (EVA™)

She wants your views on the use of economic value added (EVA™) as the key performance metric at IC. You have been supplied with the current EVA™ calculation (Appendix 1) but there is some doubt about whether the junior management accountant who has done this work was sufficiently trained in the method.

Therefore, the CEO requires you to evaluate its accuracy and the assumptions which form part of the calculation and advise her on your results, providing calculations as needed.

Critical success factors (CSFs) and key performance indicators (KPIs)

The CEO believes that the poor performance of the company can be addressed by ensuring that the mission statement flows down into the performance management of the business. To that end, the following critical success factors (CSFs) and the associated key performance indicators (KPIs) have been identified.

CSF	Associated current KPI
1. Greater staff productivity	Units produced per labour hour
2. Reduction of wastage in production	Power consumed per unit produced
3. Greater innovation of products	Number of new products launched

The CEO wants you to briefly explain a weakness of the current KPI assocaited with each CSF and then provide a justified alternative KPI.

Improvement projects

In order to improve performance, the CEO plans to implement initiatives associated with 'lean' manufacturing.

Specifically, there are three projects which have been suggested, and the CEO needs your advice on these:

(1) Move to just-in-time (JIT) manufacturing
(2) Use Kaizen costing
(3) Examine the costs of quality in achieving a 'zero defects' approach to manufacturing

The CEO has stated that she needs you to explain what the three improvement projects are, how they will help to meet the CSFs at IC, and also how they will impact the existing three KPIs.

New information system

The CEO is concerned about the implications of the improvement projects for IC's information systems as she feels that the systems are not currently suitable for the plan that she has. The current information systems of the company are based around the functional departments of the business such as manufacturing, marketing, finance and logistics. Each department has developed its own system, although all feed into the finance system which is the main one used for strategic decision making. In order that the department systems can all feed through to the current finance system, these current systems only handle quantitative data. The company is considering the implementation of a new information system. This new system will introduce networking technology in order to bring together all of the departmental systems into a new, single, corporate database.

Required

Write a report to the CEO of Iron Chicken to:

(i) Evaluate the EVA™ calculation and the assumptions in Appendix 1 as required by the CEO **(15 marks)**

(ii) Respond to the CEO's request for work on the KPIs, ensuring each of the three critical success factors are addressed **(6 marks)**

(iii) Assess the three improvement projects as required by the CEO **(15 marks)**

(iv) Assess the impact of the proposed new information system on the three improvement projects **(10 marks)**

Professional marks will be awarded for the format, style and structure of the discussion of your answer. **(4 marks)**

(Total = 50 marks)

Appendix 1

Economic value added	*Year ended 30 June 20X5*	
	$m	*Note*
Operating profit	551.4	
Add back: Non-cash expenses	15.1	
Marketing capitalised	23.1	5
Less: Tax	134.8	6
Lost tax relief on interest	24.5	7
Net operating profit after tax (NOPAT)	430.3	
Capital employed		
From the statement of financial position	2,401.0	10
Marketing spend capitalised	23.1	5
Adjusted capital employed	2,424.1	

WACC = $(1/2 \times 16\%) + (1/2 \times 6.8\%) = 11.4\%$

EVA™ = NOPAT – (WACC × capital employed) = 154

Assumptions and notes

1	Debt/Equity	100.0%
2	Cost of equity	16.0%
3	Tax rate	30.0%
4	Cost of debt (pre-tax)	6.8%

5 There has been $23.1m spent on marketing each year for the last two years in order to build the brand of IC long term.

6 Tax paid in the year was $130m while the tax charged per the accounts was $134.8m.

7 Interest charged in the period was $81.6m.
Lost tax relief on this interest was 30% × $81.6m.

8 The only research and development spending identified in the last 5 years was $10m expensed during this year on a new product.

The product has not been launched yet.

9 Capital employed during the period (from the statement of financial position):

	$m
Opening	2,282.0
Change in period	119.0
Closing	2,401.0

SECTION B – BOTH questions are compulsory and MUST be attempted

Question 2

Company and industry background

Culam Mining (Culam) is a mineral ore mining business in the country of Teeland. It owns and operates four mines. A mine takes on average two years to develop before it can produce ore and the revenue from the mine is split (25:75) between selling the ore under fixed price contracts over five years and selling on the spot market. The bulk of the business's production is exported. A mine has an average working life of about 20 years before all the profitable ore is extracted. It then takes a year to decommission the site and return the land to a useable form for agriculture or other developments.

Recent events

One of Culam's foreign competitors surprised the market by becoming insolvent as a result of paying too much to acquire a competitor when the selling price of its minerals dipped as the world economy went into recession. As a result, the Chief Executive Officer (CEO) wanted to know if this was likely to happen to Culam. She had read about the Altman Z-score as a way of predicting corporate failure and had a business analyst prepare a report calculating the Z-score for Culam. The report is summarised in Appendix 1.

The analyst had done what was asked and calculated the score but had not explained what it meant or what action should be taken as a result. Therefore, the CEO has turned to you to help her to make sense of this work and for advice about how to use the information and how Culam should proceed into the future.

Required

(a) Evaluate both the result of the analyst's calculations and the appropriateness of these two models for Culam. **(10 marks)**

(b) Explain the potential effects of a mine's life cycle on Culam's Z-score and the company's probability of failure. **(7 marks)**

Note. You should ignore its effect on the Q-score.

(c) Give four detailed recommendations to reduce the probability of failure of Culam, providing suitable justifications for your advice. **(8 marks)**

(Total = 25 marks)

BPP LEARNING MEDIA

Appendix 1

Analyst's report (extract)

The Altman Z-score model is:

$Z = 1.2X_1 + 1.4X_2 + 3.3X_3 + 0.6X_4 + X_5$

Another quantitative model (Q-score model) has been produced by academics working at Teeland's main university based on recent data from listed companies on the small Teeland Stock Exchange. It is:

$Q = 1.4X_1 + 3.3X_3 + 0.5X_4 + 1.1X_5 + 1.7X_6$

Where for both models:

X_1 is working capital/total assets
X_2 is retained earnings reserve/total assets
X_3 is profit before interest and tax/total assets
X_4 is market value of equity/total long-term debt (MVe/total long-term debt)
X_5 is revenue/total assets
X_6 is current assets/current liabilities

Using the most recent figures from Culam's financial statements (year ending September 20X4), Culam's Altman Z-score is 3.5 and its score from the other model (Q) is 3.1.

For both models, a score of more than 3 (for Z or Q) is considered safe and at below 1.8, the company is at risk of failure in the next 2 years.

Question 3

Company information and mission

Stokeness Engineering's (Stokeness) mission is to provide world-leading, reduced-emission, fuel-efficient power products for the motor industry in order to optimise shareholder returns.

Stokeness has existed for only five years and is owned by its management and venture capitalists (VCs). The management were all engineers who had been working on the basic research associated with new fuel technologies and saw the opportunity to commercialise their expertise. Stokeness is highly regarded in the industry for its advanced, efficient fuel cell designs. As a result, the VCs were eager to invest in Stokeness and have assisted by placing experienced managers into the business to aid the original engineering team.

New product development

Stokeness is developing hydrogen fuel cells for use in powering large motor vehicles such as buses and trucks. They will replace standard petrol/diesel engines. The fuel cells have a clear advantage over these older technologies in having lower carbon dioxide (a greenhouse gas) emissions. The governments of many developed countries are keen to see cuts in such emissions and are supportive of a variety of possible technological solutions to this issue (such as fuel cells, electrical batteries and compressed natural gas).

External business environment

It takes five to ten years to develop a viable product for sale in this motor market. There are a number of companies developing fuel cells but Stokeness is believed to have a two-year lead over them and to be only three years away from commercial launch.

Alternate power technologies, like the hydrogen fuel cells, would be fitted by the major international vehicle manufacturers into their vehicles for sale to their customers. The vehicle manufacturers will need to form a close partnership with any engine producer in order to make their technologies compatible, and this has already begun to happen, with two of the major manufacturers signing deals with other engine makers recently.

A major problem that needs to be overcome with any of these new technologies is that there must be an infrastructure accessible to the end users for refuelling their vehicles (as the petrol station chains do for petrol engine vehicles at present).

Governments have indicated their desire to support the development of such technologies to address environmental issues and to try to establish new, high-value industries in their jurisdiction. They may do this through tax breaks and investment to support the development of the refuelling infrastructure.

Production of Stokeness's fuel cells uses a special membrane that requires rare and expensive elements. Also, it has partnered with two other engineering firms to subcontract the production of certain components in the fuel cell. Stokeness has had to share much of its fuel cell design with these firms in order to overcome certain engineering difficulties.

Also, there are a number of start-up companies developing the other technologies mentioned above, as well as large, existing diesel and petrol engine manufacturers who are constantly reducing the emissions from their existing engines.

The VCs have stressed the need to analyse competition and competitive advantage in order to understand how to make the business profitable in the long term. The Chief Executive Officer (CEO) of Stokeness wants to understand the external business environment and its effect on performance management.

Required

(a) Using Porter's five forces model, assess the impact of the external business environment on the performance management of Stokeness and give a justified recommendation of one new performance measure for each of the five force areas at Stokeness. **(16 marks)**

(b) Discuss how the problems of defining the market in measuring a market share apply for Stokeness. **(4 marks)**

(c) Assess the risk appetite of the venture capitalists and discuss how this might impact on performance measurement at Stokeness. **(5 marks)**

(Total = 25 marks)

Answers

DO NOT TURN THIS PAGE UNTIL YOU HAVE COMPLETED THE MOCK EXAM

Plan of attack

What's the worst thing you could be doing right now if this were the actual exam questions? Trying to find a pen which works? Panicking, and generally getting yourself flustered? Yawning, because you're exhausted from too much late-night, last-minute revision? Wondering how to celebrate the end of the exam in 3 hours and 15 minutes' time?

Well, they're all pretty bad. But what you should be doing is spending the first few minutes of the exam looking through the questions in detail, working out what topic areas they relate to, and the order in which you intend to answer them. So turn back to the exam and let's sort out a **plan of attack**.

First steps first

As we suggested with Mock Exam 1, in our view, the Section A question is usually the best place to start, but you may prefer to start by doing your best Section B question first. However, if you do decide to start with a 25 mark Section B question, make sure that you finish your answer in no more than 49 minutes (25 marks × 1.95 minutes per mark). Remember, the Section A question makes up 50% of the marks for the exam so you need to allow yourself enough time to answer it.

Make sure you look through the **whole** exam paper carefully before diving in to answer any questions.

In the first five minutes of the exam, look through the case study scenarios and the question requirements and work out which topics the questions relate to. We suggest you then spend approximately the next five to ten minutes analysing the requirements of the Section A question and identifying the key issues in the scenario, and how they relate to those requirements. Remember, planning your answer is very important; don't just start writing your answer as soon as you open the exam paper.

If you are worried about the exam, it is likely that you believe the Section A question will be daunting. In this case you may prefer to do one, or both, of the Section B questions before tackling it. However, don't fall into the trap of spending too long on the Section B (25-mark) questions even if they are easier than the Section A one. Remember the Section A question accounts for 50% of the total marks for the exam, so it is vital to your chances of passing this exam.

It is dangerous to be over-confident, but if you're not too nervous about the exam, we suggest you should start with the Section A question. You know you've got to answer it at some stage, so you might as well get it over and done with straight away.

Make sure you **address every requirement and sub-requirement in the questions**, and also make sure you apply your answer directly to the scenarios.

Remember that **analysis and application** are key elements in the APM exam: you are being tested on your ability to apply your knowledge to a business scenario, to analyse and address the specific issues identified in that scenario.

The questions themselves

Question 1 – The underlying context behind this question is that a new CEO has recently been appointed at an organisation with a view to improving its performance. The scenario then describes the main aspects of the CEO's improvement programme.

The first part of the question focuses on Economic Value Added (EVA™) and the adjustments which need to be made to accounting figures when calculating EVA™. Although there are some marks for calculations, the key verb here is 'evaluate' so it is important you get a balance between the numerical and narrative elements of this requirement.

Part (ii) focuses on the organisation's KPIs, and requires you to identify and explain the weaknesses of the current KPIs before recommending alternatives which overcome those weaknesses.

Part (iii) then looks at three specific initiatives the CEO wants to introduce as part of a move to 'lean' manufacturing at the organisation: JIT; Kaizen costing; and zero defects (TQM). The requirement (linked back the CEO's request in the scenario) asks for an explanation of what the initiatives are, but then looks more specifically at how they will help the organisation achieve its CSFs, and what impact they could have on its KPIs.

Part (iv) then looks at the link between the 'lean' initiatives and the organisation's information systems. The scenario explains that the organisation is thinking about implementing a new information system, and, in effect, the requirement asks how the new information could help to support the three 'lean' initiatives.

Question 2 looks at quantitative methods for predicting corporate failure, but in the context of a mining business rather than a manufacturing business. In part (a) you need to assess the risk of failure based on the calculations provided in the scenario, although the bigger issue is whether the models being used are actually appropriate for the mining company. After all, if the models are not appropriate, then the values generated by the calculation may not be a reliable indicator of the company's risk of failure.

Part (b) looks at the relationships between life cycle and the risk of failure. However, rather than using a generic product or industry lifecycle, in this case we are looking specifically at the life cycle of a mine. Finally, part (c) looks at possible ways to reduce the probability of failure in the company. Although some of these ways relate to the balance of the company's product portfolio, others also relate to wider business issues – such as managing the risks it faces in terms of fluctuating foreign exchange rates or commodity prices.

Question 3 looks at the impact the external business environment can have on performance management in an organisation.

The requirement for part (a) makes specific reference to Porter's five forces model as a framework for assessing the competitive environment and the potential impact this could have on an organisation's performance. However, the requirement also asks you to recommend a performance measure for each of the five force areas – reminding you that the focus of this question is about 'performance management' not simply environmental analysis (ie evaluating the strength of the different competitive forces).

Part (b) looks at the problems of defining the market a company is competing in – and the related issue that the market needs to be defined, before market share can be measured.

The final part of the question looks at how the risk appetite of the company's owners (venture capitalists) could influence the areas of performance which are most important to them, and therefore which will need to be measured.

Don't forget...

You **must allocate your time** according to the marks for the question in total, and for the individual parts of the questions.

And you must also **follow the requirements exactly**.

It is vital that you apply your knowledge to the scenario, in order to answer the question set. If you discuss theories and models in general terms, without applying them to the scenario, you will score very few marks for this. If your answer contains irrelevant material, you will not be scoring marks efficiently, and you will put yourself under increased **time pressure**.

If you ran short of time on this exam, or struggled to interpret the question requirements, have another look at the guidance about 'Passing the APM exam' in the front pages of this Kit.

All finished and quarter of an hour to go?

Your time allocation must have been faulty. However, make the most of any time you have left at the end of the exam. Go back to **any parts of questions that you didn't finish** because you ran out of time. Always write something rather than nothing if you possibly can, and try not to leave questions unanswered.

If you write nothing then, by definition, you cannot score any marks. Even if you only write a couple of points in answer to a requirement, you could earn some marks for these – and this could ultimately make the difference between you passing or failing the exam.

Question 1

Text references. EVA™ – including the adjustments to accounting profit required to calculate it – are discussed in Chapter 7 of the BPP Study Text. CSFs and KPIs are discussed in Chapter 2. Lean systems and enterprise resource planning systems (ERPSs) are discussed in Chapter 6a. Just-in-time, Kaizen costing, and costs of quality are discussed in Chapter 10.

Top tips.

Part (i). The fact that the scenario mentions that there are doubts about the Junior Management Accountant's ability to calculate EVA™) should have alerted you to the likelihood that some of the figures in the calculation are wrong. However, this doesn't mean that all of the figures are necessarily wrong.

As such, a sensible approach to this question would be to work through the calculation methodically (line by line) identifying whether each of the current figures is correct or not. Where a figure is incorrect, you then need to adjust the calculation accordingly. In addition – applying your knowledge of the adjustments to operating profit required when calculating net operating profit after tax (NOPAT) – you need to consider if there are any figures which have been (incorrectly) omitted completely.

However, note that the requirement asks you to 'evaluate the accuracy...' and to 'advise the CEO on your results ...' as well as providing updated calculations. As the marking guide indicates, a maximum of 8 out of the 15 marks for this requirement are available for calculations, so the written element of this answer is equally important as the calculations.

And remember that you are advising the CEO. So, as well as commenting on individual items in the calculation, it would be appropriate to consider the implications of the adjustments as a whole – for example, do they mean IC is performing better or worse than first suggested by the Junior Management Accountant's figures?

Part (ii). The wording of the CEO's underlying requirement – to explain 'a weakness' and to provide 'a justified alternative' – means that there are a number of possible answers to it. You may have recommended different alternatives to the ones suggested in the solution below, but provided they are relevant (ie they help to measure performance against the CSF) and you have justified your recommendation you would earn the marks available. Nonetheless, to score the marks it is vital that you recommend a KPI (ie something that could be measured), not an alternative CSF.

Importantly, you should not spend too long on this part of the question, as there are only six marks available for it. Given that there are three CSFs, this means there are only two marks for each CSF: one for explaining a weakness of the current KPI associated with it, and one for providing a justified alternative KPI. The instruction in the question to 'briefly explain' is important – you shouldn't waste time giving a detailed explanation, particularly as there is only one mark available per weakness.

Part (iii). The short paragraph in the scenario above the three projects – with its reference to 'lean' manufacturing – provides some useful context for this requirement. In effect, the three projects are ways of (hopefully) making IC's manufacturing 'leaner'.

As the three projects are clearly identified separately, a useful way of tackling the requirement would be to address each project in turn. Then for each project you need to do three things:

- Explain what the project is (ie what are, respectively, just-in-time manufacturing, Kaizen costing, and costs of quality/total quality manufacturing ('zero defects'))
- Explain how the project will help to achieve IC's CSFs (again the reference to 'lean' in the introductory paragraph here could provide a useful pointer here, since eliminating waste (CSF number 2) is one of the key aims of 'lean')
- Explain what impact the project will have on the KPIs (**Note.** Your focus here should be on the levels of performance as measured by the indicators; not on the choice of indicators.)

Note that for the second of the three parts you need to explain 'how' the project will help, whereas in the third you have to explain 'what' the impact will be. The distinction is important, because in some cases – eg in relation to the number of products launched – the projects may not affect the KPI. Make sure you state this, though; saying that the project will not have an impact is a valid answer, and so would earn you a mark.

Part (iv). This final paragraph of the scenario describes the new information system. In essence, the new system is an enterprise resource planning system (ERPS) so, in effect, the question is asking how an ERPS would help the three projects.

This requirement is quite challenging, but, of the three projects, the benefits can perhaps most easily be seen in relation to JIT. For example, in a demand–pull system, with no inventory, sharing information between different departments is likely to be crucial in avoiding stock-outs.

More generally, note that the scenario says that IC's current systems can only handle quantitative data. So, also think about the nature of the information required by the projects. For example, in order to reduce the level of defects, IC will presumably need to know what is causing those defects. But can a system which only handles quantitative data provide that information?

Overall. Remember that you have been asked to write a report, so make sure the style and structure of your answer, as well as its tone, is appropriate for a report.

Examining team's comments. Part (i) asked candidates to 'evaluate the accuracy' of an EVA™ calculation that had been provided. Many candidates spent time discussing the advantages and disadvantages of using EVA™ (such as it being closely related to cash flow) but this was not asked for in the requirement. Although a brief explanation of a model/technique may add some value to an answer, it does not warrant a lengthy discussion – unless this has been specifically asked for.

This type of question – which requires an evaluation of whether or not something is accurate – also requires candidates to do more than simply state whether it is right or wrong. Candidates need to state what is inaccurate, explain what the correct treatment should be, and explain why this is the case.

Worryingly, some students incorrectly interpreted a debt:equity ratio of 100% as meaning that the company was financed entirely by debt, and there was no equity. This is a fundamental error, and one which the marking team was surprised to see at this level.

Part (ii) was generally well answered, but answers to **part (iii)** were mixed. Many candidates were limited by the fact that they appear to have little knowledge of Kaizen costing and costs of quality.

Part (iv) required an assessment of the impact a new information system would have on the three improvement projects. Many candidates reiterated the features of the new system that were given in the scenario, but provided little in the way of 'an assessment' of the impact this would have on the projects.

For a question like this – requiring an assessment of the information system on the projects – a good answer will identify what the information requirements of each project are and whether or not the new system will meet those requirements. For example, the implementation of initiatives such as just-in-time manufacturing is heavily reliant on an appropriate information system allowing for co-ordination of deliveries and manufacturing schedules in order to meet customer demands.

Marking scheme

		Marks
(i)	For calculation of corrected EVA™: 1 mark for identifying correct treatment of each of the following and adjusting as necessary:	
	Non-cash expenses Marketing expenses Research and development Tax paid Capital employed – opening figure WACC Economic value added Maximum for calculation: 7 marks 1 mark per relevant point evaluating the assumptions and advising on the corrections – up to 10 marks	
	Total for part (i) – up to 15 marks	15

		Marks
(ii)	KPIs for CSFs – up to 2 marks for each CSF (1 mark for the weakness of the current KPI; 1 mark for the justified alternative) Total for part (ii) – up to 6 marks	6
(iii)	Quality improvement projects Definitions and descriptions of the projects – up to 2 marks Analysis of the impact of the projects on IC's CSFs and KPIs – up to 6 marks per project Maximum for part (iii) – up to 15 marks	15
(iv)	New unified database Definition and general points – up to 3 marks Interaction with each project – up to 3 marks each Other comments (eg quantitative vs qualitative information) – up to 3 marks Maximum for part (iv) – up to 10 marks	10
	Professional marks – up to 4 marks	4
	Total =	50

Report

To Board of Iron Chicken (IC)
From: Performance Management Expert
Date: [today's date]
Subject: Performance management issues at IC

Introduction

This report evaluates the accuracy and assumptions used in the calculation of EVA™. It then suggests new KPIs for the current CSFs at IC. Finally it considers the impact of three quality improvement projects on these CSFs and a proposed new information system.

(i) **EVA™**

Although some elements of it have been performed correctly, there are a number of errors in the existing calculation of EVA™. The correct treatments are described below, and then the corrected EVA™ is calculated.

Non-cash expenses are correctly added back to profit as such costs are treated as unacceptable accounting adjustments on a cash-based view.

Marketing activities for long-term benefit are also correctly added back as they generate future value for the business. The prior year marketing expenditure is also added into capital employed.

Research and development (R&D) expenditure should be added back to profit in the same way that the long-term marketing spending is. (**Note.** There was no R&D expenditure in the prior year.)

The **tax cost** in the calculation should be the amount paid, adjusted for lost tax on interest, not the adjusted amount of tax charged in the accounts.

The **WACC** is incorrectly calculated as it should be based on the post-tax cost of debt.

The **capital employed** figure should be based on the figure at the start of the year (opening capital employed), not the end of the year.

Economic value added	*Year ended 30 June 20X5*
	$m
Operating profit	551.4
Add back: Non-cash expenses	15.1
Marketing capitalised	23.1
Research and development	10.0
Less: Tax	130.0
Lost tax relief on interest	24.5
NOPAT	**445.1**
Capital employed	
At 20X5 year start	2,282.0
Marketing spend capitalised from YE 30 June 20X4	23.1
Adjusted capital employed at 20X5 year start	**2,305.1**

WACC = (1/2 × 16%) + (1/2 × 6.8% × (1 – 30%)) = 10.38%

EVA™ = NOPAT – (WACC × Capital employed) = **$206m**

The recalculated EVA™ has increased from $154m to $206m which still indicates a positive position for the company as it adds to shareholder wealth.

In addition to the corrections above, the following assumptions in the calculation require comment:

(1) There is an implicit assumption that accounting depreciation (included in operating profit) is equivalent to economic depreciation (which should be used for EVA™ calculations). This is questionable generally, although there is no information to allow a more accurate calculation. Also, there is additional marketing spending which will probably have a limited economic life in building the brand. No estimation of this life and the resulting additional economic depreciation has been attempted in the above calculation.

(2) It has been assumed that no amortisation needs to be charged on the R&D costs since the product has not yet launched. This is in line with the accounting treatment of such items.

(ii) **KPIs for the CSFs**

Greater staff productivity

The current measure of units produced per labour hour does not reflect the skill and effort which goes into producing different units. The products of IC range from complex to simple and so revenue per employee would better reflect the different skill levels involved in production.

Reduction of wastage

The weakness of the existing measure is that it only looks at one cost area of production (power consumption). Inventory (stock) obsolescence will measure the wastage due to technological change which is present in the complex products produced by IC.

Greater innovation of products

Measuring the number of new products launched doesn't reflect the extent to which IC's innovations can become a sustainable source of value for its shareholders. The number of patents filed will reflect greater innovation at IC, but patents also legally protect groups of products. This will represent a stronger measure of innovation than new products launched, since the patent gives legal exclusivity.

BPP LEARNING MEDIA

Tutorial note. There are many possible acceptable answers to this question. For example, alternatives you could have suggested are:

Greater staff productivity. Actual staff hours as a percentage of standard hours for actual production as this would measure staff efficiency in producing a wide range of products.

Reduction of wastage. Input/output analysis of material which looks at the percentage of material purchased which goes into the final product.

Greater innovation of products. Percentage of income earned from products which did not exist last year. This will measure the ability of IC to develop successful products. (The existing measure would record unsuccessful products as innovation.)

(iii) **Lean manufacturing projects**

The three projects link together as improvements to the quality of the manufacturing process at IC. There are common elements to these projects in the elimination of waste and empowerment of employees which will occur in the long term. In the short term, there may be increased costs due to these disruptive changes.

Just-in-time (JIT) manufacturing

JIT seeks to produce on a pull basis to meet the customers' demands, rather than to produce products for inventory, which then acts as a buffer between production levels and demand. The main impact of JIT is the reduction of inventory which is held. The main enablers for such a system are a need for close links to customers and suppliers in order to predict demand and to quickly supply that demand.

In terms of IC's CSFs, this project will improve productivity as production lines must be made more flexible to meet changes in demand, although it should be noted that there could be a negative impact as constant changes in production lines will require more time to be spent setting up new production runs. It will also help to reduce wastage through losses in inventory as there will be less inventory. It also pushes some of the responsibility for improved quality of components (and reduced wastage) on to suppliers. However, it does not directly impact on product innovation.

The project will not necessarily immediately change any of the existing KPIs as it is about producing the right products at the right time, not necessarily producing more products for any given input, and it does not impact directly on new product launches.

Use Kaizen costing

Kaizen costing aims to reduce current costs of production through continuous improvement. Each period, goals for lower costs are set and then performance monitored against these using variances. At the end of the period, a new lower cost goal is set for the next period. The process also often uses target costing to set the initial planned cost of a product thus incorporating the idea of only producing what the customer values. The purpose is to build into the control of the production process the idea of continuous improvement.

This project has the explicit aim of reducing waste and improving productivity and so is directly linked to the first two CSFs. As a result, it will have an impact on the KPIs which are related to productivity and resource consumption. The project will also require the empowerment of staff to make improvement decisions within their quality circles (teams) and so it may give scope for more innovative thinking. However, this thinking is not aimed at producing new products but at improving the production process, so new product innovation may only be affected indirectly.

Costs of quality and a 'zero defects' approach to manufacturing

Costs of quality can be broken down into four parts:

(1) Prevention costs which occur before or during production and aim to prevent the production of defective products;

(2) Appraisal costs which occur after production and aim to check that products meet quality standards;

(3) Internal failure costs which occur when products are identified as defective before delivery to the customer and so are scrapped or reworked; and

(4) External failure costs which occur when defective products are delivered to the customer.

The 'zero defects' approach is also known as 'total quality management' (TQM). The TQM philosophy is that it is better to spend money on prevention, which involves challenging all aspects of the production process in order to improve and so avoid failure costs.

This project will affect the CSFs relating to improved productivity and waste by reducing defective products, provided that staff time is not adversely affected by aiming for perfection in production. In terms of the KPIs, it may lead to increased time in production but reduced wastage. It will not have a direct impact on power consumption. Again, this project is unlikely to affect the number of new products launched as it focuses on the production process, not product development.

(iv) **New information system**

The move to a single database for the organisation will integrate the subsystems from different functions (such as production and sales). It will require existing systems to be networked and compatible or else be replaced. It will affect overall decision making by improving the visibility of each function's operations to the others and to the strategic decision makers. This shift is often achieved by using an ERPS and a strategic enterprise management system.

The unified database will be critical in achieving the goal of JIT manufacturing as close links between production scheduling and demand forecasts will be required in order to match production runs with demand forecasts/orders. Also, the production schedules will need links to inventory levels in warehousing so that inventory is run down before new production is initiated. As closer communication with suppliers and customers will also be required, some change to existing information systems will be necessary in any case. It may be worthwhile to consider including electronic data interchange (EDI) in the specifications of the new system.

In using Kaizen costing, cross-functional communication will be important. The design team will need to communicate with the production team so that the design is more easily streamlined for production. The financial systems will need to be frequently updated for information from the quality circles as improvements are made. This will affect the Kaizen cost targets which need to be continually monitored and new targets set regularly. Quality circles often involve groups from across the business and so a common information system will facilitate communications amongst them.

The introduction of TQM will require clearer reporting of quality costs to assist in the ongoing motivation of staff, which is often a problem in TQM. Informing the quality teams of the impact that increased prevention costs are having on lowering failure costs will be important in maintaining the push to zero defects. The quality improvements and changes to production processes will need to be communicated across IC's different sites which the new database can facilitate.

The nature of the data used in the current system is quantitative but with the new projects there will be a need to communicate qualitative information, for example, relating to the nature of defects or the new production processes put in place. This will require a fundamental change to existing systems which again motivates the change to a new database.

Question 2

Text reference. Corporate failure, and quantitative methods for predicting corporate failure, are discussed in Chapter 14 of the BPP Study Text.

Top tips.

Part (a). It is vital that you recognise that there are two parts to this requirement: (i) first you are asked to evaluate the results of the analyst's calculations; then (ii) you are asked to evaluate the appropriateness of the two models (Z-score and Q-score) for Culam.

The first part should be relatively simple (Culam's score is above the 'safety level' in both models), but there is also relatively little to say in the first part of the requirement. Therefore, the majority of the marks actually relate to the second part of the requirement.

Although the models suggest Culam can be considered safe, how reliable are they actually likely to be? For example, how closely does Culam – a mining company based in Teeland – resemble any of the companies Altman studied when he developed the Z-score model? Similarly, the scenario tells us that the Q-score model has been developed by studying the companies on the 'small Teeland stock exchange'. What is the significance of Teeland's stock exchange being small?

Part (b). A useful way to approach this part of the requirement could be to think about the different characteristics of a mine's life cycle. The opening paragraph of the scenario identifies that a mine has three distinct stages in its life cycle: development; production; then decommissioning.

What will the financial characteristics of each of these stages be? And how will these different characteristics affect the Z-score?

Part (c). The requirement here asks you to give **four detailed** recommendations, and to justify how they will help reduce the probability of failure. The reference to 'detailed recommendations' should have been a clue that basic suggestions such as 'increase revenues' or 'reduce costs' were not going to be sufficient to earn the marks available here.

The scenario should also have given you some pointers here. The first paragraph tells you that Culam's revenue is split 25:75 between fixed price contracts and sales on the spot market, and that most of the production is exported. Neither of these points was relevant to parts (a) or (b) of the question, suggesting they were relevant here. Do these circumstances present any risks to Culam? What could it do to reduce those risks?

Marking scheme

		Marks
(a)	For general interpretation of the calculations – 1 mark	
	For general description of how a quantitative model works – 1 mark per relevant point – up to a maximum of 4 marks	
	For relevant comments on the problems with the models, in relation to their use at Culam – up to a maximum of 9 marks	
	Total for part (a): up to 10 marks	10
(b)	For general issues around life cycles and the probability of failure – up to 2 marks	
	Description of a mine's life cycle (development – production – decommissioning) – 1 mark	
	For explaining the impact of the life cycle on Culam's Z-score – up to 6 marks	
	Total for part (b): up to 7 marks	7

Marks

(c) Up to 2 marks for each valid recommendation – 1 mark for the improvement being recommended and 1 mark for the justification – up to 8 marks

Possible recommendations include, but are not limited to:
Increasing size of the business – portfolio effect
Learn from the mistakes of others – avoid big project failures
Use of fixed price contracts to avoid volatile commodity prices
Use of foreign exchange hedging to avoid revenue volatility

Total for part (c): up to 8 marks — 8

Total = 25

(a) **Results of the calculations**

In both calculations, Culam's score is greater than the score at which it is considered safe. Therefore, the models suggest that the company is not at risk of failing in the next two years. However, the models are only valid for a single point in time, and do not indicate whether Culam's financial condition is improving or deteriorating.

Moreover, Culam should not place too much confidence in these results because there are a number of factors which reduce how appropriate the models are for assessing its risk of failing.

Z-score

Quantitative models use financial ratios to predict the likelihood of business failure and bankruptcy. Altman's research (from which the Z-score was devised) looked at a range of variables in relation to companies which failed and which didn't fail. From this, he identified that the five key indicators of the likely failure – or not – of a company were: liquidity; profitability; efficiency; leverage; and solvency. These characteristics are represented, in turn, by the five ratios used to calculate a company's Z-score.

The Z-score model enables analysts to identify companies which share the characteristics of ones which have previously failed, and are therefore at risk of failing themselves.

However, there are a number of factors which affect the reliability of the Z-score model, and three of these could significantly reduce its appropriateness for Culam.

Industry characteristics – The model will be most relevant for companies in similar industries and of similar size to the ones which Altman analysed in his initial research. Altman's data was primarily collected from the manufacturing sector, whereas Culam is a mining company. As such, it may not be appropriate to use the model without some modification to reflect the different financial characteristics of the mining companies compared to manufacturing companies – for example, their capital intensiveness.

Geographical location – The companies Altman studied were US companies, whereas Culam is based in Teeland. Apart from the fact it only has a small stock exchange, we do not know anything about the economy in Teeland, and therefore how similar or dissimilar it is to the US. However, if, for example, Culam is a developing country, this would reduce the relevance of comparisons based on the US.

Historical context – Altman's research was conducted in the late 1960s, and so the data used in his model is about 50 years old now. The global economy has changed significantly during that time, so it is debatable how relevant the original data is, generally, for companies today.

Q-score

Reliability of model – The Q-score model appears to overcome some of the limitations of the Z-score model – because it is based on recent data, and it relates to local (Teeland) companies rather than US ones.

However, Teeland's stock exchange is only small, which will reduce the sample size from which the academics developed their model. Perhaps more importantly, it is not clear how many companies in Teeland have failed recently; but if this number is small, this means the academics have derived their model from very limited data.

Industry characteristics – It is also not clear what the mix of companies listed on Teeland's stock exchange is like. For example, if the majority of the companies listed on the stock exchange are manufacturing or service companies, then their financial characteristics may not be comparable with Culam's.

Therefore, neither the Z-score nor the Q-score are likely to provide a reliable indicator of Culam's risk of failing. Moreover, given the nature of Culam's business model, its survival could also depend on world commodity prices and foreign exchange rates. However, both models focus only on its internal financial characteristics, rather than looking at any external environmental factors.

(b) **Impact of mine's life cycle on Z-score**

In total, a mine has a 'life' of 23 years: 2 for its initial development, 20 in production, and 1 for decommissioning.

Development phase – In the first two years, no revenue or profits will be generated, and the mine will require a large amount of capital investment. This investment, coupled with the underlying asset value of the mine and its ore, means that Culam's total assets will be increasing during this period.

X1, X2, X3 and X5 in the Z-score all use 'total assets' as their denominator, meaning that the Z-score will fall during this period, given the absence of any revenue or profit from the mine.

The weightings in the model mean that X3 (PBIT/total assets) has the greatest impact on the overall score; therefore the fact that the mine is not generating any profit during this period could lead to quite a significant reduction in Culam's Z-score.

Production phase – In this phase, the mine will be earning revenues, and hopefully will be profitable.

However, the asset value of the mine will begin to fall, as reserves of the ore begin to be extracted, and as the capital investment begins to be depreciated. Therefore, we would expect the Z-score to be higher during this period.

Decommissioning phase – In this final phase, there will be no revenues, although the value of Culam's assets will also be falling. As such, we could again expect a relatively low Z-score in this phase, although probably not as low as during the initial development phase (because the value of total assets will be lower now).

Life cycle and probability of failure

Since Culam only owns four mines, the phase in which any one mine has reached in its life cycle could have a significant impact on the company's overall Z-score. For example, if two mines are being developed at the same time, then this is likely to lead to a significant reduction in the Z-score.

Although Culam will need to develop new mines to sustain its business as its existing mines reach the end of their lives, the capital investment required during the development phase will make significant demands on its financial resources. As such, the extent of the financial resources which Culam can call on over the life of the mines could be crucial in dictating its survival.

(c) **Recommendations for reducing the probability of failure**

Increase number of mines – As Culam currently only has four mines, the performance of any single mine will have a significant impact on the company's overall results. For example, if one of the mines proves much less profitable than had been expected, this could potentially threaten the future of the whole group.

If Culam increases the number of mines it owns, this will reduce its dependence on any single mine.

Effective due diligence – However, the recent demise of its competitor highlights that Culam must be careful not to pay too high a price for any new mines it acquires. As such, undertaking suitable due diligence and carrying out detailed risk analysis in advance of acquiring a new mine (or any other significant capital investment) should help reduce the probability of failure.

Securing long-term contracts – Currently, Culam sells 75% of its output on the spot market, and only 25% under long-term fixed price contracts. This mix makes Culam's revenues and cash inflows vulnerable to fluctuations in the commodity prices. However, if Culam increased the proportion of its output it sold under long-term contract this would provide greater certainty over its future revenues.

Hedging – Another way in which Culam could look to reduce risk is by using hedging techniques to reduce the volatility of its revenues and cash flows. As Culam currently sells 75% of its ore on the spot market it could benefit from hedging against a fall in the market prices of its ores.

In addition, the bulk of Culam's production is exported. Assuming that many of Culam's customers will be large industrial companies, it is likely that they will want to use their own currency for buying the ores rather than local currency of Teeland. Therefore, Culam could be vulnerable to fluctuations in foreign exchange risks, since its revenues will be earned in foreign currencies while its costs will be denominated in the local currency of Teeland.

As such, hedging against foreign exchange rate risk could also help to reduce the risk of failure.

BPP LEARNING MEDIA

Question 3

Text reference. Porter's five forces model is discussed in Chapters 1 and 5 of the BPP Study Text.

Top tips.

Part (a). Although this part of the question should offer some relatively easy marks (for analysing the impact the different forces could have on Stokeness), it is important that you realise that the requirement isn't only about the impact of the five forces. You also have to recommend a performance measure for each of the five forces.

This second element of the requirement (recommending new performance measures) requires careful thought. The performance measures need to measure the strength or impact of each of the **five forces** themselves, not primarily different aspects of Stokeness's own performance. So, for example, what would be a suitable measure to indicate the threat of new entrants?

Also, in relation to the first part of the requirement, note that you are asked about the impact of the five forces on **performance management** at Stokeness, not, for example, how the five forces could be used to assess the attractiveness of the industry. In other words, you should be thinking about how Stokeness could use an understanding of the five forces to improve its performance or develop its strategy, rather than simply identifying that a particular force is strong or weak.

Part (b). A key question here is: 'Who are Stokeness's competitors?' Is it competing against all engine manufacturers (including manufacturers of petrol/diesel engines)? Is it competing against suppliers of all the alternative technologies? Or is it only competing against other fuel cell manufacturers?

These questions should highlight the problem Stokeness faces when measuring a market share: unless it has identified its market, how can it measure its share of that market?

Part (c). Even though this part of the question is only worth five marks, in effect there are still two different elements to it: the VCs' risk appetite, and key issues in performance measurement at Stokeness.

Stokeness appears to be a technology start-up company, which suggests the VCs were prepared to accept a relatively high degree of risk by investing in it. Equally, they will expect returns from the company in the future. However, currently, Stokeness is still three years away from a commercial launch. So, for the moment, the key aspects of its performance relate to this pre-launch phase; for example, has Stokeness got sufficient cash to sustain it until it can begin to sell its products? If Stokeness runs out of money before it launches its fuel cells, then there is little chance of it generating any returns for the VCs in future.

Examining team's comments. Part (a) was generally well done, with candidates making good use of the information in the scenario to give useful performance management advice to Stokeness. However, many candidates appeared not to read the second part of the requirement fully: this asked for a **justified** recommendation of **one new** performance measure for each of the five forces. Instead, they simply produced a list of performance measures for each area, often also including market share, meaning that they failed, in three different ways, to answer the question.

Part (b) was poorly answered. Many candidates chose to answer the question 'How do you measure market share' thereby completely missing the point of the question actually set. However, better candidates realised that the definition of market (and hence its size) depended on whether you were talking about hydrogen fuel cells, alternative energy power technologies, or any sort of power unit (including existing petrol/diesel engines).

Similarly, in part (c), many candidates wasted time listing the different possible risk appetites, despite these not being required by the question set. Candidates are reminded that it is vital to read the requirement carefully, and to answer the question asked – not an alternative question of their own creation.

Marking scheme

		Marks
(a)	For each of Porter's five forces: Up to 4 marks for performance management implications of the force, and justifying a suitable performance measure Total: up to 16 marks	16
(b)	For each valid point made about the problems of defining Stokeness's markets – 1 mark per point Total: up to 4 marks	4
(c)	For assessing the risk appetite of the VCs – 1 mark per valid point; up to 2 marks For assessing the VCs' impact on performance measurement at Stokeness – 1 mark per valid point; up to 3 marks Total: up to 5 marks	5
		Total = 25

(a) **Threat of new entrants**

Barriers to entry – The threat of new entrants into the fuel cell market will be determined by the extent of the barriers to entry into the market. The barriers to entry appear to be high, given the technical skills and the length of time required to develop a viable product.

These barriers to entry will be strengthened further by the need to develop a relationship with the vehicle manufacturers who will be the customers for the fuel cells. Even if a potential new entrant develops a viable product, they will not be able to establish themselves in the market unless they can attract any buyers for their product.

Performance measure: Patented revenue – One of the ways in which technology firms can create a barrier to entry into their markets is by registering patents over new products or technologies. In this respect, Stokeness needs to ensure that it obtains patents for new cell designs or technology processes which could provide it with competitive advantage.

A suitable performance measure to use here would be the percentage of revenue which is generated from patented protects. This will indicate the degree to which Stokeness's patents will act as a barrier to entry.

Other performance measures:

Customer loyalty – If vehicle manufacturers (customers) are committed to using Stokeness's cells on a long-term basis, this will make it harder for new entrants to join the market.

To this end, it would be useful to measure customer loyalty by looking at the number (and value) of the long-term contracts Stokeness has to supply fuel cells to vehicle manufacturers.

Ratio of fixed cost to total cost – This gives an indication of the capital required to develop and produce fuel cell products, and therefore the level of amount of capital a potential new entrant would need to be able to enter the market. If large amounts of capital are required, this could make it harder for new entrants to join the market.

Threat of substitutes

Alternative fuel sources – The existing petrol/diesel engines remain a substitute for Stokeness's products, especially as their manufacturers are reducing the level of carbon dioxide emissions from these engines. Equally, electrical batteries and compressed natural gas products could also be substitutes for the fuel cells.

The petrol/diesel engines still have a number of strengths in the market; in particular, they are the only fuel source for which there is an infrastructure in place which enables end users to refuel their vehicles easily.

Performance measure: Output – The level of threat from substitute products could be measured by analysing the power output of different types of power supply compared to the level of emissions they produce and the cost of producing the power.

The cost of creating different engine types and the price of the fuels required to run them are likely to be very significant in determining the extent to which different types of engine are considered viable by vehicle manufacturers.

Bargaining power of suppliers

Component elements – The membrane which is used to produce the fuel cells requires rare and expensive elements. As a result, the **suppliers' bargaining power is high**. Stokeness's ability to produce the fuel cells will depend on the price and availability of the elements required for the membrane.

In particular, if the supply of these elements is controlled by a small number of suppliers they will be in a particularly strong position to dictate the price of the elements.

Subcontractors – The engineering firms to which Stokeness has subcontracted the production of certain components for the fuel cell also have a high bargaining power because of the knowledge they have gained of Stokeness's products. In this respect, it is important that there is a non-disclosure agreement in place to protect any commercially sensitive details of the products.

The size of the two engineering firms relative to Stokeness is not clear from the scenario, but it is possible that one of them may also consider some kind of forward vertical integration if they feel that Stokeness's products are going to be commercially successful.

Performance measure: Switching cost – The power of the suppliers could be measured by estimating the cost involved in switching to an alternative supplier. This cost could include any penalty fees payable to the existing suppliers, as well as the opportunity cost of lost sales arising as a result of delays incurred in switching supplier. These delays could be quite significant, given the specialist nature of Stokeness's product, which any new suppliers would have to understand, and tailor their processes to, before production could re-commence.

Other performance measures:

Proportion of cost – An alternative measure of the suppliers' bargaining power could be taken as the price of the suppliers' components in relation to the cost of the fuel cell as a whole. Such a measure can give an indication of the importance of the components to the overall fuel cell.

Number of suppliers – It could also be useful to monitor the number of suppliers, because this will indicate the level of competition in that market. If the number of potential suppliers available to Stokeness increases, this could reduce their bargaining power.

Bargaining power of customers

Large manufacturers – Stokeness's customers are manufacturers of large vehicles, such as buses and trucks. It is likely there will only be relatively few of these companies, but they will be quite large, giving them significant bargaining power. Crucially, the manufacturers have a choice of what fuel source to use (for example, fuel cells or standard petrol/diesel engines), and before they agree to use Stokeness's cells they will need to be sure that the cells are compatible with the existing technologies used in the vehicles.

Switching costs – However, once customers have committed to using a particular type of power source, the cost of switching to an alternative source is likely to be high. This may reduce the bargaining power of customers, but only once Stokeness has secured them as customers. In this respect, the fact that Stokeness has a two-year lead over the other companies developing fuel cells could be a significant advantage to it, if it can secure some significant contracts before the competitors have developed their cells.

Given the relative size of Stokeness compared to the manufacturing companies, and the potential importance of the fuel cells in the engine production process, one of the manufacturers might try to acquire Stokeness.

However, this might prove to be an attractive option for the venture capitalists, depending on the price offered.

Performance measure: Discounts requested – The level of discount which customers request would provide Stokeness with an indicator of how strong the customers perceive their bargaining power to be. If the customers feel that Stokeness's fuel cells will provide them with a significant competitive advantage, then they will be less likely to press hard for a discount.

Other performance measures:

Switching costs – The costs which a manufacturer would incur to switch from one power source to another could also be used as an indicator of the strength of the bargaining power of customers. The higher these costs are, the less likely a customer will want to switch power source, thereby reducing their bargaining power. Although Stokeness is unlikely to be able to calculate this figure exactly, it should nonetheless be able to make an estimate of it.

Number of alternative suppliers – The number of alternative suppliers which customers could choose from could also affect the customers' bargaining power.

Competitive rivalry

Development advantage – As Stokeness has a two-year lead over the other companies developing fuel cells, the level of existing competition from these companies currently seems low. If Stokeness patents any key technologies it develops, this should help sustain its competitive advantage over its direct competitors.

Moreover, if Stokeness is able to secure contracts with some of the vehicle manufacturers before the other companies have developed their products, this will make it harder for the competitors to break into the market. In turn, this could help reduce the level of competitive rivalry in the industry in the future.

Performance measure: Launch date – Once Stokeness and then the competitors have launched their products, it will be possible to measure the strength of competitive rivalry by analysing market share. Until that point, however, there isn't a 'market' to analyse. Instead, the time until the commercial launch date of a viable fuel cell is a key performance measure. Although it may be difficult to obtain exact information about competitors' expected launch dates, Stokeness should try to monitor these alongside its own.

This measure highlights the importance of avoiding any overruns in the development process, and in delivering a commercially viable product as soon as possible, thereby maintaining Stokeness's competitive advantage over the other companies which are also developing fuel cells.

Other performance measures:

Partnership agreements – An alternative measure could be the number of partnership agreements signed, with vehicle manufacturers, or the projected revenues – or volumes – under such agreements.

(b) **Market definition**

The problem of defining the market is a particular issue for Stokeness because there could be some significant variations in the extent of that market.

Overall large vehicle market – In the broadest terms, Stokeness makes power supplies for large commercial vehicles such as buses and trucks. Therefore, its market share could be seen as the number of commercial vehicles powered by Stokeness's fuel cells as a proportion of the total number of commercial vehicles.

However, such a broad definition would include vehicles powered by standard petrol/diesel engines in the overall market, many of which were produced before Stokeness was even formed. If Stokeness wants to measure its share of the entire market on a more comparable basis, it may be preferable to focus on new vehicles only – that is, the proportion of the new vehicles manufactured each year which are powered by Stokeness cells.

Fuel cells – At the other extreme, Stokeness could define its market purely as the market for fuel cells, and therefore measure its performance against other fuel cell makers.

Alternative engine technologies – In between these two extremes, Stokeness might consider itself to be competing in the market for alternative engine technologies (for example, electrical batteries, compressed natural gas).

Because these three markets are so different in size, Stokeness will need to define which one it sees as most important to measure its performance in, so that it can set appropriate market share targets.

(c) **Technology start-up** – Stokeness seems to be a technology start-up company, which suggests that it is a risky company for external investors to invest in. Equally, however, it offers the prospect for high returns if its fuel cell technologies prove successful. Therefore, it appears that the VCs are risk seeking by investing in Stokeness.

However, it appears that the VCs have tried to moderate the level of risk to some degree by placing commercially experienced managers into the business to assist the engineers who founded it. Moreover, because the VCs now have some of their own employees on the management team, this will give them a high degree of influence at Stokeness.

Medium/long-term returns – Given that Stokeness is still three years away from the commercial launch of its cells, the VCs will not begin to see any returns from their investment until the medium to long term. However, the VCs could use net present value calculations, based on projected returns, as a performance measure in this respect.

Cash flow and cash control – In the shorter term, it is vital that Stokeness does not run out of cash while it is still developing its product (and hence not yet generating any revenue from it). Consequently, monitoring actual expenditure against budget and cash outflows will be key performance measures, to ensure that spending is kept under control.

Development targets – Stokeness needs to measure key non-financial aspects of performance as well as financial ones. Crucially, the point at which Stokeness can start selling a commercially viable product and therefore start acquiring customers will have a significant impact on its cash flow and NPV calculations. If the launch of the product falls behind schedule, this will increase the risk of the company running out of cash.

Therefore, it will be important for Stokeness to measure operational progress against key milestones: for example, completing successful test runs of the product.

Customer acquisition – Equally it will be important for Stokeness to sign contracts with customers, in order to secure revenue. Therefore, performance measures showing the number of definite customers signed up and the number of potential leads would also be useful.

ACCA Strategic Professional – Options

Advanced Performance Management

Mock Examination 3

(Including questions from ACCA September/December 2017 exam)

Question Paper	
Time allowed: 3 hours and 15 minutes	
This paper is divided into two sections:	
Section A	This ONE question is compulsory and MUST be attempted
Section B	BOTH questions are compulsory and MUST be attempted

DO NOT OPEN THIS PAPER UNTIL YOU ARE READY TO START UNDER EXAMINATION CONDITIONS

SECTION A – This question is compulsory and must be attempted

Question 1

Company information and objectives

Thyme Engine Products (Thyme) manufactures jet aircraft engines for the commercial aircraft market. This is a worldwide business although Thyme's production and development are all based in the country of Beeland. Thyme is a listed company and its stated overall objective is to be 'a world-class jet engine manufacturer trusted by our customers to deliver excellent products'. Its promise to its shareholders is that it will maximise their returns. The strategy to achieve this is to use world-class engineering to design engines and high quality production and customer service in order to drive profitable growth.

Thyme's share price has recently suffered as a result of the failure of a new engine design which led to large cash losses and a difficulty in obtaining new financing. There has also been a bribery scandal involving a senior manager and one of its key customers. As a result, a new chief executive officer (CEO) has been employed and she has begun a major review of systems at Thyme.

Performance reporting – dashboard

The first area which the CEO wants to examine is the information given to the board for strategic decision-making in both the planning and controlling of the business. The government of Beeland has been encouraging information sharing between businesses and has recently sponsored awards for management accounting. The winner of the engineering sector has produced a sample dashboard template (with dummy figures) for an annual review and this is given in Appendix 1. The CEO realised that the winner had a very similar overall objective and strategies to Thyme and wants to know what it is about this dashboard that helped it win the award. She does not want a new dashboard for Thyme at this stage but there may be some useful, specific comments to make about the contents of the dashboard given Thyme's recent problems.

Integrated reporting

The CEO has also recently been reading about integrated reporting and in the light of this review of the dashboard, the CEO has also asked for your views on how integrated reporting might have an impact on the type of information prepared by the company's management accountants.

Total quality management

As high quality engineering products lie at the heart of Thyme's competitive advantage, there has been a total quality management (TQM) approach to the management of all resources and relationships throughout the business. Thyme currently has a project under consideration to develop a new simple jet engine which would compete in the crowded market for small corporate jets. In order to compete in this market, it is believed that a target costing approach to this new engine would be beneficial. The CEO wants you to calculate the target cost gap for the new engine using the data in Appendix 2. Next, she wants to know how the use of target costing would fit within the existing TQM approach for this new engine.

Quality costs

The new engine project has further raised the profile of quality as a broad issue at Thyme and the CEO wants your advice on the costs associated with quality. She needs to know the cost of each of the four categories of quality costs. She has gathered data in Appendix 3 for this exercise. She is happy that she has identified that prevention costs are complete but is worried that some of the possible costs for the other three categories are missing and needs suggestions of cost areas to be examined to identify these missing items. Finally, she needs advice on the relative importance to Thyme of each of the four categories.

Required

Write a report to the CEO of Thyme to:

(i) Evaluate why the dashboard in Appendix 1 was award winning, as requested by the CEO **(15 marks)**

(ii) Explain broadly the role of the management accountant in providing information for integrated reporting **(6 marks)**

(iii) Calculate the target cost gap for the new engine (using the data in Appendix 2) and assess how the use of this target cost will fit within the TQM approach **(12 marks)**

(iv) Categorise and calculate the costs of quality (given in Appendix 3). Suggest cost areas to be examined as required by the CEO, and evaluate the relative importance of each category to Thyme **(13 marks)**

Professional marks will be awarded for the format, style and structure of the discussion of your answer. **(4 marks)**

(Total = 50 marks)

Appendix 1

Award winning performance dashboard

Report for the year to June 20X7

	20X5	*20X6*	*20X7*	*Budget variance 20X7*	*Growth 20X6 to 20X7*	*Budget 20X8*
Financial						
Revenue ($m)	10,652	11,213	11,500	234F	2.6%	11,776
Operating profit margin	16.2%	16.8%	17.2%	0.2 percentage points F	0.4 percentage points	17.2%
EVA™	746	774	815	48F	5.3%	803
Total shareholder return	6.5%	6.8%	11.1%	4.5 percentage points F	4.3 percentage points	7.5%
Design						
Class leading products in:						
Fuel efficiency	3	3	3	0		3
Noise levels	2	2	3	1F		3
Chemical emissions	1	2	3	1F		3
Manufacturing						
Percentage of orders right first time	92.0%	92.4%	93.7%	0.7 percentage points F		93.0%
Delivery						
Deliveries on time	88.0%	89.9%	88.2%	0.2 percentage points F		88.0%
Market share						
(as percentage of market leader)	33.0%	35.2%	38.1%	1.1 percentage points F		39.0%

Commentary:

The revenue growth of the business remains strong above the average growth for the sector of 1.5%.

EVA™ is positive and growing indicating increased shareholder wealth.

Healthy and continuing growth in market share reflects an increased number of class-leading products and improvements in 'right on time' service to customers.

There have been no major new business risks arising during the period while market volume growth continues as expected.

Appendix 2

New jet engine

		$'000/engine
Competitor price		2,500
Raw materials		200
Subcomponents bought in		600
Skilled labour		625
General labour		125
Production overheads		275
Planned profit margin	15%	

Notes

1 Design and development has cost $120m and the engine is expected to sell approximately 1,200 units over its lifetime.

2 Sales and marketing costs are expected to be approximately 20% of the selling price.

3 The planned selling price is expected to match the competitor's price with the brand reputation of Thyme providing the competitive edge.

Appendix 3

Quality costs identified in current year

	$m
Repairs and replacements under customer warranties	223
Customer relationship management – complaint handling	56
Performance testing of final assembly	110
Performance testing of subcomponents from suppliers	28
Costs of re-inspection after repairs arising from final assembly testing	95
Training in quality control	11
Maintenance of inspection equipment	36

Notes

1 The company spent $92m in the year buying higher quality raw materials to use in manufacture.
2 The company's revenue was $11,500m in the current year.

Section B – BOTH questions are compulsory and MUST be attempted

Question 2

Company background and mission

Cod Electrical Motors (Cod) manufactures electrical motors for some of the 24 different European domestic appliance manufacturers. Their motors are used in appliances such as washing machines and refrigerators. Cod has been in business for over 50 years and has obtained a reputation for producing reliable, low cost motors.

Cod has recently rewritten its mission statement, which now reads:

'Cod Electrical Motors is committed to providing competitively priced, high quality products, with service exceeding customer expectations. We will add value to our business relationships by investing in product development and highly trained personnel.'

Performance information

The board has recognised that its existing key performance indicators (KPIs) do not capture the features of the corporate mission. It is worried that the staff see the mission statement as a public relations exercise rather than the communication of Cod's vision.

The monthly board papers contain a simple performance summary which is used as the key performance measurement system at that level. However, several of the board members have asked that the information provided in the board papers should be revised to provide a more coherent set of performance measures.

Example of board papers for November 20X1:

Cod Electrical Motors

Key performance indicators for November 20X1

	This month	*YTD*	*Comparative*
Profit ($m)	2.1	25.6	1.9
Free cash flow ($m)	3.4	17.6	1.6
Return on capital employed (%)	12.4	11.7	11.8

Notes

1 The year end is 31 December.
2 The comparative figure is for the same month in the previous year.
3 ROCE is an annualised figure.
4 YTD means year to date.

There are additional performance indicators not available to the board that line management use for a more detailed picture of Cod's performance. These are shown in Appendix 1.

Required

(a) With reference to Cod's mission statement and its existing KPIs, discuss why it is important for KPIs to reinforce the features of an organisation's mission. **(6 marks)**

(b) Explain how the performance pyramid (Lynch and Cross) can help Cod's board to reach its goal of a coherent set of performance measures. **(6 marks)**

(c) Evaluate the current system using the performance pyramid and apply the performance pyramid to Cod in order to suggest additional KPIs and a set of operational performance measures for Cod. **(13 marks)**

(Total = 25 marks)

Appendix 1

Additional performance information:

	Note	20X1	20X0
	1		
Activity			
No. of orders		2,560	2,449
No. of deliveries		1,588	1,660
Staff			
No. of staff (FTE basis)	2	1,229	1,226
No. of staff training days		2,286	1,762
No. of vacant posts	3	11	17
Customers			
No. of orders with a complaint	4		
Late delivery		26	25
Product quality		39	31
Customer service		21	24
Other		52	43
Preferential supplier status	5	14	12
Production			
New products			
Begun in year to date		2	1
In development at month end		4	3
Launched in year to date		1	1
Quality			
Internal failure costs ($'000)		3,480	2,766
External failure costs ($'000)		872	693

Notes

1 Figures are year to date with comparatives from the previous year quoted on the same basis.
2 FTE = Full-time equivalent staff numbers.
3 Post is considered vacant if unfilled for more than four months.
4 Complaints are logged and classified into the four categories given when received.
5 Number of customers where Cod holds preferred supplier status.

Question 3

Organisational background

Tosemary and Rhyme Hospital (TRH) is a small hospital for the treatment of patients with only minor injuries. Patients arriving at TRH with more serious injuries are referred to a larger hospital nearby. Those with minor injuries are admitted into TRH and wait to be seen by a doctor. After treatment, most patients leave the hospital and need not return. If their treatment has failed, however, they are re-admitted for additional treatment.

Patients do not have to pay for treatment at TRH, which is a not-for-profit, public sector hospital. It is funded entirely by the government from taxation and a fixed level of funding is received from the government each year. It is up to TRH to allocate its funding to different areas, such as doctors' salaries, medicines and all other costs required to run a hospital.

Objectives

TRH's objectives are:

- To give prompt access to high quality medical treatment for patients
- To provide value for money for the taxpayer, as measured by the '3Es' framework of economy, efficiency and effectiveness
- To contribute to medical science by developing innovative ways to deliver treatment to patients

Concerns about performance measurement systems

It has been suggested to TRH that the hospital has inadequate performance measurement systems in place to assess whether it is achieving its objectives, and that insufficient attention is given to the importance of non-financial performance indicators. You have been asked for your advice, and have met with some of the doctors to get their opinions.

One senior doctor has told you, 'I think TRH always delivers value for money. We've always achieved our total financial budgets. Doctors here work much longer hours than colleagues in other hospitals, often without being paid for working overtime. There is not enough government funding to recruit more doctors. At busy times, we've started referring more patients arriving at TRH to the larger hospital nearby. This has helped reduce average waiting times. Patients arriving at TRH are now seen by a doctor within 3 hours 50 minutes rather than 4 hours as was previously the case. So, we're already doing all we can. I don't know how much time we spend developing innovative ways to deliver treatment to patients though, as most of the performance data we doctors receive relates to financial targets.'

Recent performance data for TRH and national average information has been provided in Appendix 1. This is indicative of the data which the doctors at TRH receive.

Required

(a) Explain why non-financial performance indicators are particularly important to measure the performance of not-for-profit organisations such as TRH. **(5 marks)**

(b) Justify one performance measure for each of the components of the value for money framework used at TRH and, using the measure, evaluate whether TRH is delivering value for money. **(10 marks)**

(c) Evaluate the extent to which the management style at TRH can be said to be budget constrained and advise on the implications of this approach for managing TRH's performance. **(10 marks)**

(Total = 25 marks)

Appendix 1

Data for the year ended 31 August 20X7

	TRH	*National average*[1]
Number of doctors	25	24
Total doctors' salaries including overtime	\$3.75m	\$4.20m
Total doctors' salaries budget including overtime	\$3.75m	\$3.20m
Number of patients treated	24,375	20,000
Average staff satisfaction rating[2]	9%	89%
Number of patients re-admitted	1,830	300

Notes

1 National average for other public sector minor injuries hospitals.

2 Staff satisfaction rating was obtained by conducting a survey of all 25 doctors. A survey score of 100% represents 'totally satisfied', and a score of 0% represents totally unsatisfied.

Answers

DO NOT TURN THIS PAGE UNTIL YOU HAVE COMPLETED THE MOCK EXAM

Plan of attack

What's the worst thing you could be doing when you enter the exam hall if this were the actual exam? Trying to find a pen which works? Panicking, and worrying you haven't done enough preparation? Wondering how to celebrate the end of the exam in about three and a quarter hours' time?

Well, they're all pretty bad. But what you should be doing is spending the first few minutes of the exam looking through the questions in detail, working out what topic areas they relate to, and the order in which you intend to answer them. So turn back to the paper and let's sort out a **plan of attack**.

First steps first

As we have already suggested in Mock Exams 1 and 2, in our view, the Section A question is usually the best place to start, but you may prefer to start by doing your best Section B question first. If you decide to start with a 25 mark Section B question first, though, make sure that you do not spend too long on it, so that you don't subsequently have sufficient time to answer the Section A question properly. Remember, the Section A question accounts for 50% of the marks for the exam so you need to allow yourself enough time to answer it. You cannot pass the exam without answering it!

Make sure you look through the **whole** exam paper carefully before diving in to answer any questions.

In the first five minutes of the exam, look through the question requirements and work out which they relate to. We suggest you then spend approximately the next five to ten minutes analysing the requirements of the Section A question, and identifying the key issues in the scenario, and how they relate to those requirements. Remember, planning and preparing your answer is very important; don't just start writing your answer as soon as you open the exam paper.

If you are worried about the exam, it is likely that you believe the Section A question will be daunting. In this case, you may prefer to do one, or both, of the Section B questions before tackling it. However, don't fall into the trap of spending too long on the Section B (25-mark) questions even if they seem easier than the Section A one. Remember the Section A question accounts for 50% of the total marks for the exam, so it is crucial to your chances of passing this exam.

It is dangerous to be over-confident, but if you're not too nervous about the exam, we suggest you should start with the Section A question. You know you've got to answer it at some stage, so you might as well get it over and done with straight away.

Make sure **you address every requirement and sub-requirement in the question**, and also make sure you apply your answer directly to the scenario.

As we have said before, remember that **analysis and application** are key elements in the APM exam: you are being tested on your ability to apply your knowledge to a business scenario, in order to analyse and address the specific issues identified in that scenario.

The questions themselves

Question 1 features a company that has recently experienced a number of problems, and as a result a new CEO has been appointed. She has begun a review of the company's systems, and the scenario describe some of the areas the CEO has been looking at in her review.

The first part of the question focuses on performance reports, and the information they provide to their users. An example of an 'award winning' dashboard is given in Appendix 1, and you are asked to evaluate why it was award winning. Although the verb here is 'evaluate', the context of the requirement means you need to focus on the good features of the dashboard.

Part (ii) focuses on integrated reporting, and how the information required for an integrated report might differ from that required for a 'traditional' annual report.

In Part (iii), you are told that the company is looking to develop a new product, and believes that using a target costing approach would be beneficial in order to ensure the new product is competitive. There are two elements to the question: first you need to calculate the target cost gap for the product, and then you need to assess whether the use of target costing will fit with the company's total quality management (TQM) approach to managing its resources.

Part (iv) continues the theme of 'quality' in relation to the 'costs of quality': ie costs of prevention; appraisal; internal failure and external failure. Within the overall requirement, you are asked to do a number of different things: 'categorise and calculate'.... 'suggest'.... and 'evaluate', so it is important you address all of the different elements in your answer.

Question 2 explores the importance of linkages and hierarchy in performance management.

Part (a) looks at the relationship between an organisation's mission and its KPIs. The company's mission and its KPIs are both given in the scenario, but as the scenario acknowledges: the board has recognised that the KPIs do not capture the features of the mission. In effect, this requirement is looking at the potential implications of this disconnect between the KPIs and the mission.

Parts (b) and (c) then look linkages and performance metrics in the context of the 'performance pyramid.' In part (b) you need to think about the key characteristics of the pyramid as a performance measurement system, and how these could improve the performance information being provided to the board (for example, by providing information about the range of different objectives identified in the pyramid).

Identifying the range of objectives in the pyramid is also relevant for part (c), where you are asked to use the pyramid to evaluate the company's current performance measurement system. (For example, if the company used the pyramid, would the information the board receive be superior to the information they currently receive?)

However, as well as evaluating the current system, you also need to suggest additional KPIs and a set of operational performance measures the company could use. The additional performance information, given in Appendix 1, should help you identify some suitable KPIs and performance measures.

Question 3 looks at performance management in not-for-profit organisations; specifically, in the context of a public sector hospital.

The scenario notes that there has been a suggestion that the hospital pays insufficient attention to non-financial performance indicators, in relation to assess whether it is achieving its objectives. Part (a) asks why non-financial performance indicators are particularly important in measuring the performance of not-for-profit organisations, such as the hospital.

Part (b) looks at 'value for money' (3Es) as a framework for measuring performance in not-for-profit organisation. First, you need to identify a suitable performance measure for each of the Es, and explain ('justify') why it is suitable. Then you need to calculate the hospital's performance for each measure, and use the figures you have calculated to evaluate whether the hospital is delivering value for money (compared to the national average – which you also need to calculate for the measures in question).

The final part of the question looks at the management style in the hospital, and the impact that the management style could have on performance management in the hospital. The penultimate paragraph of the scenario provides you with some valuable clues, which you should use to support your answer. As with many APM questions, there is more than one verb in the requirement ('Evaluate'.....and 'advise') so make sure you read the requirement carefully and answer both parts of it.

Don't forget...

You must **allocate your time** according to the marks for the question in total, and for the individual parts of the questions.

And you must also **follow the question requirements exactly**.

It is vital that you apply your knowledge to the scenario, in order to answer the question set. If you discuss theories and models in general terms, without applying them to the scenario, you will score very few marks for this. If your answer contains irrelevant material, you will not be scoring marks efficiently, and you will put yourself under increased **time pressure**.

If you ran short of time on this exam, or struggled to interpret the question requirements, have another look at the guidance about 'Passing the APM exam' in the front pages of this Kit.

All finished and quarter of an hour to go?

Your time allocation must have been faulty. However, make the most of any time you have left at the end of the exam. Go back to **any parts of questions that you didn't finish** because you ran out of time. Always write something rather than nothing if you possibly can, and try not to leave questions unanswered.

If you write nothing, then, by definition, you cannot score any marks. Even if you write a couple of points in answer to a requirement, you could earn some marks for these – and they could ultimately mean the difference between you passing and failing the exam.

Forget about it!

Don't worry if you found the paper difficult. It is more than likely that other students did too. However, once you've finished the exam you cannot change your answers so don't spend time worrying about them. Instead, you should start thinking about your next exam and preparing for that. Or, if this is your last exam, forget about it for now.

Question 1

Text references. Performance reports are discussed in Chapter 6b of the BPP Study Text, as is the role of the management accounting in providing information for integrated reporting. Target costing, total quality management (TQM) and costs of quality are all discussed in Chapter 10.

Top tips.

Part (i). There is a technical article on ACCA's website (and mentioned in the BPP Study Text) about 'Reports for Performance Management' which highlights four basis criteria which can be used to evaluate an organisation's performance reports:

- **Purpose** – What is the purpose of the report? Does the report provide information which is relevant to the organisation's performance against its mission or objectives?
- **Audience** – Who is the report produced for? Is it appropriate for its audience and their requirements?
- **Information** – What information is needed – financial and non-financial; quantitative and qualitative? Does the report provide the information which is needed to fulfil its purpose and satisfy its audience?
- **Layout** – Does the report make it clear for readers to identify the most important information?

Although you didn't have to use these criteria to answer the requirement, they could have given you a useful framework for answering this question. For example, does the report provide information which is relevant to its objectives and strategies (which are 'very similar' to Thyme's, as described in the first paragraph of the scenario)? Also, Thyme's board need information for 'planning and controlling', so does the report provide information which support both of those aspects of performance management?

Note, however, that the question doesn't simply ask you to evaluate the dashboard, but rather to evaluate why it was 'award winning'. Whereas an evaluation of the dashboard would require you to look at its advantages and disadvantages, your focus here should be primarily on its advantages (which have made it award winning).

Note also, that the requirement refers back to the CEO's request in the scenario. At the end of the third paragraph, you are told that 'there may be some useful, specific comments to make about the contents of the dashboard given Thyme's recent problems.' Remember, the dashboard in Appendix 1 is for the award-winning company (not Thyme) so the question here is whether Thyme should include some additional measures on its dashboard in relation to the specific issues it has faced.

Part (ii). Although the requirement doesn't make any mention to the CEO's request (unlike requirement (i)) referring back to the context of the scenario could be very useful here as well. The fourth paragraph of the scenario tells you that the CEO wants to know 'how integrated reporting might have an impact on the type of information prepared by the company's management accountants.'

As such, a sensible way to approach this question will be to think how the information required for integrated reporting differs from that used in traditional annual reporting – for example, in relation to the 'six capitals'. The management accountant's role will be to provide the information – but, as different information is required what impact might this have on the accountant? For example, will changes be required to the information systems to enable different aspects of performance to be measured?

Part (iii). There are two elements to this requirement ('calculate...' and 'assess...') and it is vital that you address both of them in your answer.

The requirement is worth 12 marks in total, but the marking guide shows it would be possible to score up to 6 marks for calculations. These should have been relatively easy marks.

However, once you've done the calculations don't just ignore them. Although the requirement doesn't specifically ask you to comment on the cost gap, it would be helpful to think what the implications of it are – in the context of the TQM approach at Thyme. For example, there is currently a cost gap, but this is a new product. As Thyme gains experience in producing it, might its costs per unit come down?

At the same time, think about the key features of the TQM approach – one of which is continuous improvement. How does this link to the idea of closing a cost gap?

Part (iv). Although at first glance there might appear to be a single requirement here, there are actually four different elements, so it is vital that you read the requirement carefully in order to identify these different elements:

- Categorise the quality costs
- Calculate the costs in each category
- Suggest cost areas to be examined
- Evaluate the relative importance of each cost category

The first element here is essentially a test of knowledge. What are the four categories of quality cost? (The final paragraph of the scenario identifies one of these for you – prevention costs – which should help jog your memory as to what the other three categories are.)

The second element should also be relatively straightforward: identifying which category the costs in Appendix 3 relate to, and then calculating the total for that category. Don't overlook the 'Notes' though: the cost of buying higher quality raw materials is also a quality cost, even though it is not included in the list of quality costs identified in the current year.

The third element refers you back to the CEO's requirement in the scenario. In the last paragraph you are told: '[the CEO] is happy that prevention costs are complete, but is worried some costs for the other three categories are missing, and needs suggestion of cost areas to be examined to identify these missing items.' One approach here could be to think about the costs which have already been identified in each category, and then think if there are any costs which might be associated with these, but which have not yet been identified. For example, although costs of re-inspection after repairs arising from final assembly testing are included, the costs of those repairs themselves don't appear to be.

When considering the final element of the requirement – the relative importance of each cost category – remember the context of the scenario. Thyme adopts a TQM approach, and one of the key aims of TQM is to get things right first time. Which of the costs of quality is likely to be most important in helping to get things right first time?

Overall. Remember that you have been asked to write a report, so make sure the style and structure of your answer, as well as its tone, is appropriate for a report.

Examining team's comments

Part (i). Similar questions to this have been examined in previous exam and, as such, candidates tended to score relatively well here. However, a significant number of candidates provided very superficial answers; for example, stating that 'there is not a lot of detail in the report'. This could be an advantage or a disadvantage, depending on the users of the report, so it is essential to explain why something is good or bad. Also, this particular question required candidates to focus on the elements of the report that were particularly good, so parts of answers that discussed negative aspects scored very few marks.

Part (ii). This question explored the role of the management accountant in providing information for integrated reporting, so it was essential for candidates to relate their answers to integrated reporting. Many candidates did not seem familiar with this type of report, and so discussed – in general terms – changes to the role of the management accountant in recent years. The examining team would like to remind candidates that technical articles are made available on the ACCA website to assist candidates in their studies, and candidates should read these articles. Several of the topics examined in recent exam sittings, including integrated reporting, have been discussed in technical articles.

Part (iii). The calculations in this section were performed well by most candidates. However, we would remind candidates to present calculations in a logical order to allow the marking team to award marks for method even if the final answer is incorrect. Good candidates also went on to discuss the results well.

Part (iv). Many candidates performed well on the calculations although some were not able to categorise the costs correctly. Also, candidates should pay close attention to all the verbs within a requirement. This part of the question specifically asked for four things (categories, calculate, suggest and evaluate) and candidates' performance would be improved if their answers addressed each of these separately.

Marking scheme

		Marks
(i)	1 mark per relevant feature of the dashboard which helps to make it award-winning, with additional marks (1 mark per relevant point) for illustrating and these features. Relevant features (and supporting illustrations) include, but are not limited to: Achievement of the strategies of the business • Breaking down the strategy, and linking to measures in the dashboard Balanced view • Financial and non-financial; different perspectives; results and determinants; internal and external views Planning and control • Short and long-term views; forward focus for planning; trends/budgets for control Presentation • Brevity; narrative points; link to other strategic issues; eg risks Specific issues at Thyme not measured in the sample template – up to 3 marks Total for part (i) – up to 15 marks	15
(ii)	Description of Integrated Reporting – up to 3 marks Impact on management accountant – up to 6 marks Total for part (ii) – up to 6 marks	6
(iii)	Calculations: 1 mark for each of the following: Target cost 2,125 Production costs 1,825 Design and development 100 Sales and marketing 500 Target cost gap 300 (12% of current cost) Current profit margin $0.075m (or 3%) Discussion of cost savings – 1 mark Definition of target costing – 1 mark Definition of TQM – up to 2 marks Fit between target costing approach and TQM – up to 6 marks Maximum for part (iii) – up to 12 marks	12
(iv)	Definition of quality costs – up to 2 marks Calculations: 1 mark for cost in each category (either absolute value or % of revenue) Prevention $139m 1.21% Appraisal $138m 1.20% Costs of internal failure $95m 0.83% Costs of external failure $279m 2.43% Total $651m 5.66% Discussion of results – up to 2 marks Identification of other quality costs which appear to be omitted – up to 6 marks Relative importance of categories of quality costs – up to 4 marks Maximum for part (iv) – up to 13 marks	13
	Professional marks – up to 4 marks	4
	Total =	**50**

BPP LEARNING MEDIA

Report

To: CEO of Thyme
From: Accountant
Date: [today's date]
Subject: Reporting performance and quality issues at Thyme

Introduction

This report analyses the positive features of the award winning dashboard identifying some areas which specifically apply to Thyme. Next, the role of the management accountant in providing information for integrated reporting is explained. Then, the target cost gap for the new engine is calculated and an evaluation is provided of the use of this target cost within the TQM approach. Finally, issues associated with the costs of quality at Thyme are addressed.

(i) **Positive features of the award winning dashboard**

The following are features of the dashboard which will have impressed the assessors' minds when making the award. They are placed in a priority order of most important first, and then there are a few specific comments about the possible use of such a template at Thyme.

Achievement of the objectives and strategies of the business

The critical measure of whether the dashboard is fit for its purpose is whether it answers the question: has the business achieved its key objectives?

The dashboard measures all of the key objectives of the business growth of the firm:

(1) Shareholder wealth and returns through EVA™ and TSR; and
(2) Growth through revenue and market share growth.

It also measures the strategies used to achieve these results:

(1) World-class engineering to design engines through the class leading design specifications;
(2) High quality production through fault rates in manufacturing and delivery; and
(3) Customer service through those same fault rates and market share (an indirect indicator).

Balanced view

The report presents a balanced view of the business's performance. It deals with various perspectives (shareholders (TSR), customers (market share), internal business (fault rates) and innovation (design position)) which are used in the balanced scorecard approach. This is also achieved using both internal and external data (fault rates and average sector growth). It presents both the results and the determinants of those results by giving financial and non-financial indicators. For example, revenue growth will be driven by the customers' view of product and service, so design and manufacturing quality measures are important. Short- and longer-term measures are given such as profit margin and economic value added.

Planning and control

The dashboard should allow the board to perform both its vital functions in planning and controlling the business. The forecasts for next year (budgets) are given and also, as noted above, there are non-financial determinants of performance such as design and customer service which will drive the future short-term competitive position of the business.

The control activities of the board are served by providing historic trends and also current budget variances. The major headings are provided for under the financial headings with activity measured by revenue, profit by the margin and shareholder wealth by economic value added.

Presentation

The dashboard is kept brief as the board will have an opportunity prior to the board meeting to use it to identify issues requiring further analysis at the meeting. There is a short narrative commentary which deals with the major commercial points arising from the dashboard and also, gives further external market data as context for the figures (eg. average sector growth). It is also worth noting that the narrative picks up on strategic issues of risk and opportunity which can be more difficult to capture in numerical form. Hence, the commentary appears appropriate to assist in an annual review of the business.

Specific issues at Thyme

There are certain issues particular to Thyme which may be added to the example dashboard, though if these are deemed short term, then they may not necessarily appear on this main dashboard view. The example dashboard does not show measures of cash flow performance (such as free cash flow generated) nor gearing ratio, although both of these measures would be important for future fund raising. There are no measures associated with governance and ethics which in the light of the bribery scandal may have a higher priority at Thyme. Ethical training costs may give a measure of this area.

(ii) **Integrated reporting**

There is no standard format for integrated reporting. However, there are changes in focus of the company's reporting which will require the input of the management accountants of that business. Integrated reporting has a focus on opportunities and risk, how resources are allocated and performance both recent historic and expected in the future. There are six capitals involved in value creation including traditional tangible and financial assets but also including human, intellectual, environmental and social assets.

For the management accountant, these newer forms of capital will require information systems capable of capturing and processing such non-financial measures. The forward-looking nature of such reporting will require more information of a forecast nature (with the accompanying requirement to understand their estimating assumptions). The more strategic view which integrated reporting intends to give also requires reporting on factors which drive long-term performance.

A key part of the integrated report is linking performance to strategic goals and the ability to create value. This will require a less structured and more contingent approach to reporting. In other words, pro-forma reporting must be better tailored to the specific business's situation. However, it is considered a key requirement of such reporting that it is concise and so the management accountant must help to ensure that only the key information is reported.

It can be seen that the dashboard discussed in the above section of this report achieves many of these requirements.

(iii) **New jet engine: target costing and TQM**

	$'000
Target cost	2,125 (to give 15% profit margin on a price of $2,500k)
Production costs	1,825
Design and development	100
Sales and marketing	500
Current cost	2,425
Target cost gap	300 (12% of current cost)

The target cost for the new engine is $2.125m and the current estimated cost is $2.425m. Therefore, there is a need to cut costs by 12% to achieve the target profit margin. It is common for the initial costs to be higher than the target cost and for cost savings to be achieved as the product reaches maturity in its lifecycle. However, it should be noted that, even at this higher initial cost, the engine will be still making a small profit per unit (of $0.075m; giving a 3% margin).

Target costing involves setting a selling price based on what will be competitive in the market then deducting a target profit margin to obtain the target cost. An estimate is made of the cost of the engine based on the current design specification. The gap between this cost and the target cost is the target cost gap and opportunities to bridge this gap are sought by amending the product design or cutting costs in production.

Total quality management (TQM) is a management approach which seeks to have no defects in resource or relationship management. It aims to have a culture of continuous improvement in the organisation.

In this new engine project, the TQM philosophy will fit well with the need to cut a relatively small amount of costs (12%) in order to meet the target. The production team will experience a learning curve associated with such a new product, and will make small but frequent improvements as they do so, which should help the required cost savings to be achieved.

Given the size of the cost gap, it does not seem that a major redesign of the engine is required.

(iv) **Quality costs**

There are four categories of quality costs:

- **Prevention costs** are costs to prevent the production of engines which fail to meet specifications;
- **Appraisal costs** are costs incurred in inspecting products to ensure that they meet specifications;
- **Costs of internal failure** are costs associated with making good products which are identified as sub-standard before delivery to the customer; and
- **Costs of external failure** are costs associated with making good products which are identified as sub-standard after delivery to the customer.

Working: Costs of quality by category

	$m
Prevention	139 (= training, 11 + higher quality materials, 92 + maintenance, 36)
Appraisal	138 (= performance testing: 110 + 28)
Costs of internal failure	95 (= re-inspection)
Costs of external failure	279 (= repairs and replacements, 223 + complaint handling, 56)
Total	651

Tutorial note. The marking guide for this question indicates that if candidates showed the costs in each category as a % of total revenue, rather than $m figures, they also earned the marks available.

Comments on results

The total quality costs are 5.7% of revenue which seems surprisingly low for an organisation which recognises this as a key competitive advantage; notable is the large size of the external failure costs of 2.4%.

Possible other relevant costs

Overall, there are likely to be administrative costs associated with many of these categories and some attribution of overhead should be undertaken beyond the customer complaint handling mentioned.

Appraisal costs include performance testing of final assembly and performance testing of subcomponents from suppliers. There may also be costs associated with inspection of raw materials inward since these make a difference to quality (shown by the higher purchase costs).

Internal failure costs include costs of re-inspection after repairs after final assembly testing. There must also be costs associated with repairing faulty goods identified at final testing and possibly also scrapping failed products. It is possible that there is idle time costs due to work held up by internal identification of faulty products.

External failure costs include customer complaint handling and replacements under warranties. There is also the cost of damage done to Thyme's brand by such problems although many customers will accept that these are inevitable and provided they are infrequent and covered by warranty, they need not be important.

New products such as the new jet engine will likely generate additional failure costs while production methods are optimised.

Relative importance of categories

Given the high cost of external failure and the importance of reputation for Thyme, the most important category is prevention.

It would be appropriate for Thyme with a TQM approach to be spending heavily in this area. This will still need to be combined with warranty spending in order to protect the reputation of Thyme when problems do occur. As prevention succeeds, so the importance of the other categories will decline. It is worrying that external failure costs are more than twice internal failure costs, which suggests that final testing is not identifying a significant number of the faults in production.

Question 2

Text reference. The performance hierarchy (linking mission, objectives, and KPIs) is discussed in Chapter 2 of the BPP Study Text. The performance pyramid is covered in Chapter 12.

Top tips.

Part (a). The board's concerns (identified in the fourth paragraph of the scenario) should provide you with some context for this requirement. In effect, the board is highlighting that because the KPIs are not integrated with the mission statement, the mission has become seen as little more than a public relations exercise.

Crucially, though, the key part to this requirement is the relationship between the KPIs and the mission statement, so you should not spend a long time discussing the characteristics of mission statements or KPIs in isolation.

Equally, you are asked to make reference to Cod's mission statement, so make sure you do. Again, this should help you identify some of the reasons for the board's concern – because the mission identifies a number of aspects of performance, none of which are then measured by the KPIs.

In effect, **part (b)** then asks you to explain how the performance pyramid can help to address some of the weaknesses in Cod's KPIs which you should have identified when answering part (a): for example, the absence of any non-financial measures alongside the financial ones, and the need to create an integrated hierarchy of performance measures throughout the organisation.

Although you need to link your answer to the scenario, this question is essentially about the benefits of the performance pyramid as a performance measurement system.

It is important that you read the requirement to **part (c)** very carefully because there are three sub-requirements within it: (i) use the performance pyramid to evaluate Cod's current performance management system; (ii) apply the performance pyramid to suggest additional KPIs, and (iii) apply the performance pyramid to suggest a set of operational performance measures for Cod.

For part (ii) you need to think about how Cod's existing additional performance information could be used to monitor customer satisfaction, flexibility and productivity (the business unit level criteria in the pyramid). Then for part (iii) you need to think about how the information could be used to monitor quality, delivery, process time and waste (the operational criteria in the pyramid).

Remember, however, that the focus of this question (in parts (b) and (c)) is on evaluating the performance **systems** at Cod, not on evaluating Cod's performance as an organisation.

Marking scheme

		Marks
(a)	For describing mission and KPIs – ½ mark each	
	For discussing the importance of the linkages between KPIs and mission statement (with suitable references to Cod) – 1 mark for each relevant point, up to a maximum of 5 marks	
	Maximum for part (a): up to 6 marks	6
(b)	Diagram illustrating the performance pyramid – Up to 2 marks	
	For explanation of how the pyramid can help Cod reach its goal of a coherent set of performance measures – 1 mark for each relevant point, up to a maximum of 4	
	Maximum for part (b): up to 6 marks	6

		Marks
(c)	Describe performance drivers (customer satisfaction; flexibility; productivity) – ½ mark per point, up to 1½	
	Assessment of current system – up to 2 marks	
	New KPIs suggested – 1 mark per KPI, up to a maximum of 4 marks	
	Operational measures suggested – 1 mark per measure, up to a maximum of 6 marks	
	(**Note.** To score all 6 marks available, all **four** areas of the operational level of the pyramid must be addressed.)	
	Maximum for part (c): up to 13 marks	13
	Total =	**25**

(a) An organisation's mission statement reflects its underlying purposes. By doing so, the mission statement can also help to identify the aspects of performance which the organisation considers to be important in helping it to achieve its corporate vision, and therefore which need to be measured and managed.

Cod's mission statement identifies a number of areas which are important for its competitive success: competitive pricing, high quality, excellent customer service, product development (innovation) and staff training.

However, while the mission statement identifies areas which are important, the way they are presented is too high level and open-ended for the board to be able to measure Cod's actual performance against them. Therefore, the mission statement needs to be translated into more specific objectives and targets against which performance can be measured.

As their name suggests, KPIs should focus on factors which are central to a company's success or failure. Critically, however, Cod's current KPIs focus solely on financial performance, meaning there is no obvious alignment between them and the key aspects of performance identified in the mission statement. For example, despite the mission statement identifying quality, customer service and product development as important to Cod, none of the KPIs reflect this. Consequently, at a strategic level, Cod is not measuring how well it is performing in any of the areas which the mission has suggested are important.

In turn, this lack of integration between the KPIs and the mission statement might also explain why the employees view the mission statement as being merely a public relations exercise. Since none of the elements of the mission statement are measured – via the KPIs – this could lead to a perception amongst the staff that these elements are not actually very important after all. Equally, the perception could be that the only elements of performance which management are really interested in are the financial measures (profit, cash flow and return on capital employed (ROCE)).

The importance of KPIs being aligned to the mission statement is also reinforced by the adage 'What gets measured, gets done'. If the aspects of performance in the mission statement are those which are important for Cod then, in order to ensure that employees focus on them, then those aspects of performance also need to be reflected in the KPIs and related performance targets.

(b) Lynch and Cross's performance pyramid stems from an acknowledgement that traditional performance measures based on financial indicators such as profitability, cash flow and ROCE do not address the driving forces that guide an organisation's ability to achieve its strategic objectives. This appears to be the problem with Cod's current performance measures.

Range of objectives – By contrast, instead of focusing purely on financial objectives, the pyramid focuses on a range of objectives for both **external effectiveness** (eg customer satisfaction) and **internal efficiency** (eg flexibility and productivity).

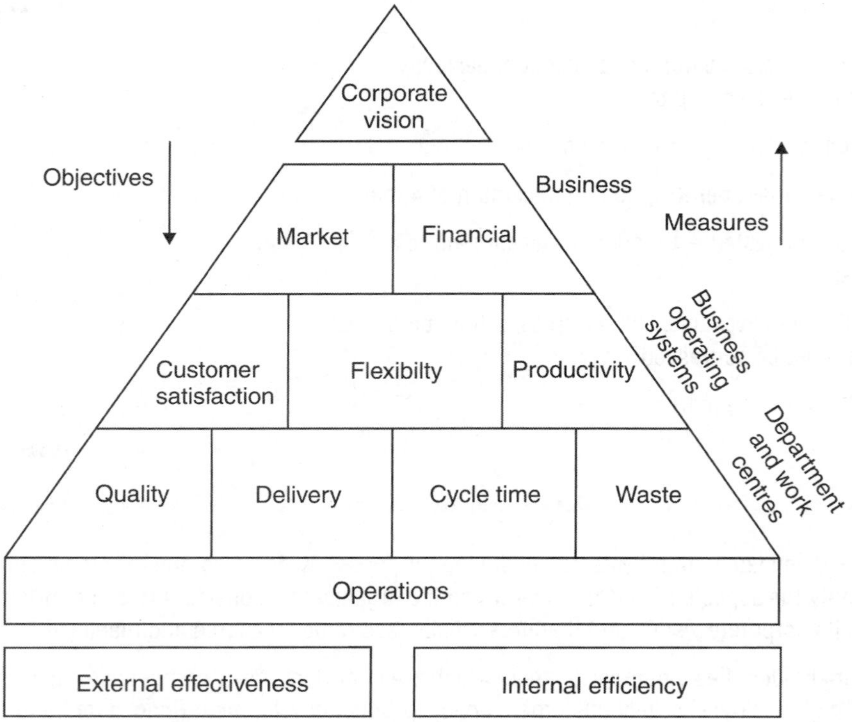

Performance hierarchy – The pyramid also highlights the way that different levels in an organisation support each other and relate to each other. This will allow Cod to develop a coherent set of objectives which are derived from the overall corporate vision.

The nine dimensions of the pyramid link strategic objectives (market satisfaction, financial measures) to operational objectives (quality, delivery, cycle – or process – time, and waste) through the themes of external effectiveness and internal efficiency.

Linkages and support – In order for Cod to develop a coherent set of performance measures it is important the objectives and measures at each level of the organisation (strategic, tactical and operational) support each other. The performance pyramid highlights the importance of these linkages between the different levels of the organisation, and the overall link between Cod's vision and mission and its day to day operations.

Appreciating these linkages will help Cod devise a coherent set of performance measures. For example, increasing quality should increase customer satisfaction, and in turn increase Cod's market share.

(c) **Customer satisfaction, flexibility and productivity** – The performance pyramid suggests that the strategies developed to achieve an organisation's financial and market objective should focus on three key driving forces: customer satisfaction, flexibility and productivity.

Currently, Cod's KPIs do not address any of these three areas, although the performance information already available means that Cod could develop non-financial KPIs for each of the three areas (see below).

It could be argued that some of these non-financial measures are more appropriate to the tactical and operational levels of the management hierarchy rather than the strategic (board) level. However, the existing performance information does not appear to be linked to the current KPIs, which suggests the board is right to be concerned about the current KPI system.

Additional KPIs

Customer satisfaction

Complaints – Customer satisfaction levels could be measured by the percentage of orders with complaints against them.

	20X1	*20X0*
Orders with a complaint	138	123
Number of orders	2,560	2,449
% with complaint	5.4%	5.0%

Preferred supplier status – The number of customers who have awarded a preferred supplier status could also be seen as an indicator of customer satisfaction.

	20X1	*20X0*
Preferential supplier status	14	12
Number of customers	24	24
% preferred status	58.3%	50.0%

Flexibility

Products launched – The number of new products launched in a year can be seen as an indicator of innovation.

Productivity

Quality costs – Failure costs (internal + external) can act as an indicator of inefficient production. Failure costs have increased from $3.46 million in 20X0 to $4.35 million in 20X1.

Operational performance measures

The operational performance measures suggested by the pyramid will relate to the four areas of quality, delivery, process time and waste.

Quality

Failure costs – Cod's additional performance information already shows **failure costs** and these could be used as a measure for quality. However, they would be improved as measures if actual costs were compared to budgeted costs.

Customer complaint numbers could also be used as a measure for quality, in particular those relating to product quality. However, there could be problems with using the information as it stands because there is no indication about the seriousness of the complaint or the consequences of it (for example, discounts or refunds offered).

Equally, the number of complaints being classified as 'Other' is also a concern. These need to be broken down into further subcategories to help identify the causes of the complaint more accurately, and therefore identify which aspects of operational performance need improving.

Delivery

Customer complaint numbers – It is important for Cod to become (and remain) a preferred supplier for as many manufacturers as possible. Customer satisfaction is vital to achieving this, so again customer complaint numbers will be important here. If complaints relating to product quality are used as a measure of quality, then complaints relating to late delivery and customer service can be used as measures of delivery.

Staff measures – The number of **training days** and the number of **vacant posts** could also be used as measures relating to delivery. An increase in the number of training days should help improve quality and delivery, while posts remaining vacant are likely to have a detrimental impact on them. However, Cod's current performance information on training days could be improved by comparing them to benchmarking, for example, to see how they compare to competitor organisations.

Cycle time (or Process time)

The performance information which Cod currently collects does not appear to be useful for measuring process time. It is possible that the number of **new products** being developed in a year could give an indication of the time to market. However, the performance measure would be improved if Cod specifically measured the **time to market** for each new product developed, and possibly then also compared this to an industry benchmark.

Waste

The current performance information does not appear to be useful for measuring waste in production. Variance analysis (comparing actual performance to budget) of **idle time** for employees and **materials usage** would be instructive measures here.

Question 3

Text reference. Issues surrounding performance measurement in not-for-profit organisations are discussed in Chapter 9a of the BPP Study Text. Management styles are discussed in Chapter 11.

Top tips.

Part (a). A useful starting point for this requirement might be to think about the objectives of not-for-profit organisations, and how these differ from the objectives of commercial organisations. Then think how the nature of these objectives will influence the aspects of performance which are important to measure.

A key point to remember in relation to performance management in any organisation is that performance indicators should measure how well an organisation is performing against its objectives. The scenario clearly states TRH's objectives – eg to give prompt access to high quality medical treatment for patients. The key aspects of this objective (promptness; high quality) are non-financial; so what implications does this have for the type of performance indicator which are important for TRH to measure?

Part (b). The second of TRH's objectives tells you the three elements of the value for money framework - economy, efficiency and effectiveness – and you should use these to structure your answer.

For each of the three Es you need to do two things: (i) select – and **justify** – an appropriate performance measure, using the data provided in Appendix 1; (ii) compare TRH's performance for that measure against the national average, in order to **evaluate** whether TRH is delivering value for money.

Note, however, that for the first element you aren't simply asked to identify a performance measure, but to justify it. To score well here you need to explain how the measure you have selected will help TRH assess the economy, efficiency or effectiveness of its performance as appropriate.

For the second element, you need to calculate the relevant performance indicators for TRH, and for the national average. However, remember the verb here is 'evaluate', and not just 'calculate'. So, for example, if TRH's performance for a given metric is worse than the national average, what does this suggest about how well TRH is delivering value for money?

Part (c). The model underlying this requirement was Hopwood's management styles – budget -constrained; profit-conscious and non-accounting, and, the question you need to ask yourself is: what are the characteristics of a budget constrained style?

Even if you couldn't remember much about the model, the penultimate paragraph of the scenario gave you some clues which you might have been able to use. For example, there is a focus on achieving financial budgets; and most of the performance data relates to financial targets.

In effect, these are of the key characteristics of budget-constrained management – and identifying this should have helped you realise that the management style at TRH is budget-constrained.

Note, however, that the question doesn't only ask about the style, but also asks to advice on the implications of this for managing TRH's performance. Again, the penultimate paragraph of the scenario could be very useful here. For example, if doctors at TRH have to work longer hours than their colleagues, often without being paid overtime, what could the consequences of this be – in terms of quality of medical treatment, or in terms of staff retention?

As we noted in relation to part (a), it is important that an organisation's performance management systems enable it to measure how well it is performing against its objectives. This point is also relevant here: if TRH's managers are focusing primarily on short-term financial performance, what implications could this have on TRH's ability to achieve its objectives?

Marking scheme

		Marks
(a)	Importance of non-financial performance indicators – 1 mark per relevant point	
	Maximum for part (a): up to 5 marks	5
(b)	Definition of value for money (3 Es) – 1 mark	
	For each 'E' (economy, efficiency, effectiveness):	
	Selecting, and justifying, an appropriate performance measure, and using this to evaluate whether TRH is delivering value for money – up to 4 marks each	
	Maximum for part (b): up to 10 marks	10
(c)	Evaluating the extent to which TRH's management style is budget constrained – 1 mark per relevant point	
	Advising on the implications of a budget-constrained approach at TRH – 1 mark per relevant point	
	Up to a maximum for part (c) of 10 marks	10
	Total =	25

(a) **Lack of profit-making objective**

Not-for-profit organisations do not, by definition, have profit as an overriding motive. Patients are not charged for receiving treatment, so TRH does not have a revenue stream. It may also be difficult to define a cost unit as this could be cost per patient arriving at hospital or cost per patient successfully treated.

Not-for-profit public sector organisations, such as TRH, have strict constraints on the amount of funding they receive, such as a fixed amount of funding received entirely from the government. They cannot obtain funding from elsewhere, so financial measures cannot be ignored completely. TRH must exist within its financial means, and the use of budgets to control costs is critical.

TRH provides an essential public service. Political, legal and social influences would prevent it from closing down a service just because it became more expensive or uneconomic to provide it. For all of these reasons, financial objectives are less relevant than for most commercial organisations, and its objectives are mainly non-financial in nature.

Not-for-profit organisations also undergo more public scrutiny and have multiple stakeholders, so non-financial indicators will be necessary to manage expectations. For example, patients are stakeholders who will have relatively little interest in how TRH exists within its financial constraints. They will have much more interest in non-financial performance, such as how quickly and successfully they are treated.

Multiple objectives

Not-for-profit organisations have multiple objectives, and it may be unclear which are the most important. Except for some aspects of giving value for money to the taxpayer, TRH's objectives are all non-financial.

The outputs or benefits of the services provided are non-financial in nature, for example, giving prompt and high-quality treatment to patients. Therefore non-financial performance indicators are required to measure performance.

(b) Value for money in public sector organisations can be measured using the 'three Es': economy, efficiency and effectiveness.

Economy

Economy means obtaining resources at the lowest cost. Doctors' salaries will be a significant expense for TRH, and salary per doctor is a suitable measure of economy. Doctors at TRH have an average salary of $150,000 ($3.75m/25), compared to the national average of $175,000 ($4.20m/24).

The relatively lower salaries of doctors may be due to differences in levels of experience or that they work unpaid overtime. It may also be one of the reasons why the staff satisfaction is so much lower at 9% compared to the national level of 89%.

Efficiency

Efficiency relates to obtaining the greatest possible outputs from the resources available. Treating patients is a key objective of TRH, and the number of doctors is an important resource. The number of patients treated per year by each doctor is a good measure of efficiency. In TRH, each doctor treats an average of 975 (24,375/25) patients per year, 17% more (975 vs 833) than the national average 833 (20,000/24). This may be because they work longer hours than their colleagues in other hospitals.

Effectiveness

Effectiveness means how well TRH achieves its objectives. TRH has multiple objectives, one of which is to provide high quality medical treatment for patients. Where patients are re-admitted to TRH because their treatment had failed, this represents a failure to provide high-quality medical care, so the rate of re-admission of patients is a measure of effectiveness. The rate of re-admission at TRH is 7.5% (1,830/24,375), much higher than the national average of 1.5% (300/20,000). TRH seems to have performed relatively very poorly in this respect.

Summary

Overall, the results from the measurement of the 3Es are consistent with the doctor's comments that they are working without being paid overtime and treating more patients than their colleagues in other hospitals. TRH appears to deliver better economy and efficiency than the national average. This seems to be reducing performance, however, in respect of providing high-quality medical treatment for patients, where TRH is less effective than the national average.

(c) **Extent to which the management style is budget constrained**

A budget-constrained management style emphasises the need to achieve short-term performance measures, for example, the annual financial budgets.

The doctor said that TRH has always achieved its total financial budgets, and this is supported by the fact that the doctors' salaries for the year to 31 August 20X7 equalled the budget set for the period. Though it is unclear what NFPIs are measured at TRH as a whole, doctors receive only a limited set of financial and non-financial performance data. The discussion about this data, however, is mainly related to financial targets. This implies greater emphasis is given to performance against financial targets, rather than non-financial ones.

All of this suggests that TRH has a budget-constrained management style. An advantage of this is that it ensures TRH operates with the financial constraints of the fixed amount of funding received from the government.

Implications of a budget-constrained approach at TRH

This management style encourages short-termism, by encouraging doctors to work long hours without being paid overtime, or not making funding available to recruit new doctors to alleviate the situation. An implication of this is that TRH may reduce its performance against its objectives, and this is already seen by the relatively high rates of re-admission as an indicator of a reduced quality of medical treatment. Job-related tension is a consequence of a budget-constrained management style, and the low staff satisfaction score could have resulted from this.

This management style encourages manipulation of results, or the way they are measured, to show better performance. At busy times, more patients are referred to the nearby larger hospital. There is apparently no medical need for this, which is inconsistent with the objective to deliver high-quality treatment. It appears to be a way to distort waiting times to demonstrate improved performance in treating patients promptly. From patients' perspective, though, this will mean they are treated less promptly than if treated at TRH.

Being unable to recruit new doctors reduces TRH's flexibility in reducing waiting times at busy periods, as the steps already taken seem to have had minimal effect. This management style does not encourage innovation, probably because doctors have insufficient time for this. Though this may have long-term benefits, it seems to be taken as less important than the other key objectives, to provide prompt, high-quality treatment.

BPP LEARNING MEDIA

Review Form – Advanced Performance Management (02/18)

Name: ______________________ **Address:** ______________________

____

____

How have you used this Kit?
(Tick one box only)

☐ On its own (book only)
☐ On a BPP in-centre course ______________
☐ On a BPP online course
☐ On a course with another college
☐ Other ______________

Why did you decide to purchase this Kit?
(Tick one box only)

☐ Have used the complementary Study text
☐ Have used other BPP products in the past
☐ Recommendation by friend/colleague
☐ Recommendation by a lecturer at college
☐ Saw advertising
☐ Other ______________

During the past six months do you recall seeing/receiving any of the following?
(Tick as many boxes as are relevant)

☐ Our advertisement in *Student Accountant*
☐ Our advertisement in *Pass*
☐ Our advertisement in *PQ*
☐ Our brochure with a letter through the post
☐ Our website www.bpp.com

Which (if any) aspects of our advertising do you find useful?
(Tick as many boxes as are relevant)

☐ Prices and publication dates of new editions
☐ Information on product content
☐ Facility to order books
☐ None of the above

Which BPP products have you used?

Study Text	☐	*Passcards*	☐	*Other*	☐
Practice & Revision Kit	☑	*i-Pass*	☐		

Your ratings, comments and suggestions would be appreciated on the following areas.

	Very useful	*Useful*	*Not useful*
Passing APM	☐	☐	☐
Questions	☐	☐	☐
Top Tips etc in answers	☐	☐	☐
Content and structure of answers	☐	☐	☐
Mock exam answers	☐	☐	☐

Overall opinion of this Practice & Revision Kit *Excellent* ☐ *Good* ☐ *Adequate* ☐ *Poor* ☐

Do you intend to continue using BPP products? *Yes* ☐ *No* ☐

The BPP author of this edition can be emailed at: accaqueries@bpp.com

Review Form (continued)

TELL US WHAT YOU THINK

Please note any further comments and suggestions/errors below.